A Teacher's Guide to Adapted Physical Education
Fourth Edition

D1603916

A Teacher's Guide to Adapted Physical Education

Including Students with Disabilities in Sports and Recreation

Fourth Edition

by

Martin E. Block, Ph.D.
University of Virginia
Charlottesville

with invited contributors

·P·A·U·L·H·
BROOKES
PUBLISHING Co.®

Baltimore • London • Sydney

Paul H. Brookes Publishing Co.
Post Office Box 10624
Baltimore, Maryland 21285–0624

www.brookespublishing.com

Typeset by Absolute Service, Inc., Baltimore, Maryland.
Manufactured in the United States of America by
Sheridan Books, Chelsea, Michigan.

Cover images are ©istockphoto/Willard/ponsulak/bmcent1/jarenwicklund/poco_bw/DenKuvaiev/kiki_
jimenez.

Library of Congress Cataloging-in-Publication Data
The Library of Congress has cataloged the print edition as follows:

Block, Martin E., 1958-
  A teacher's guide to adapted physical education: including students with disabilities in sports and
recreation, fourth edition / Martin E. Block. — Fourth edition.
     pages   cm
  Summary: "Thoroughly updated and expanded to be primary text for adapted physical
education (APE) courses, this textbook is the authoritative guide for making physical
education inclusion work. Inclusion expert Martin Block and a team of highly respected
contributors provide current foundational information on laws and standards, as well as
vital practical information on planning and implementing instruction, behavioral support
strategies, considerations for a wide range of activities and environments and various
settings including community recreation programs, multicultural considerations, and
more. The book is filled with concrete, easy-to-implement, low-cost adaptations; examples
that model problems and solutions; a helpful resource list; and guidance on key issues
like safety, behavior problems, group games, and social acceptance. The cutting-edge
information makes this an ideal text for coursework, and several photocopiable forms
make it a helpful companion for inservice physical educators planning their classes. NEW
TO THIS EDITION: 9 new chapters detail disability-specific information, expanding
the textbook application to APE courses—More photos and illustrations throughout the
book—Alignment to key elements from the NASPE standards for general PE and the
Adapted Physical Education Standards (APENS) for APE—Features for textbook use, such
as chapter objectives and more case studies—For instructors, PowerPoint slides and sample
syllabi for using the text in Inclusion in PE or APE classes"—Provided by publisher.
  Includes bibliographical references and index.
  ISBN 978-1-59857-669-6 (paperback)—ISBN 978-1-59857-776-1 (pdf ebook)—ISBN 978-1-59857-773-0
(epub ebook)
  1. Physical education for people with disabilities.   2. Mainstreaming in education.   I. Title.

GV445.B56 2016
371.9'04486—dc23   2015006836

British Library Cataloguing in Publication data are available from the British Library.

2020   2019   2018   2017   2016

10   9   8   7   6   5   4   3   2   1

Contents

About the Author

Martin E. Block, Ph.D., is a professor with the Department of Kinesiology in the Curry School of Education at the University of Virginia. Dr. Block has been the director of the master's program in adapted physical education at the University of Virginia since 1993. During that time, he has supervised and graduated more than 120 master's students. Prior to returning to college to earn his Ph.D., Dr. Block served as an adapted physical education specialist in Virginia and Maryland, working with children with severe disabilities and learning and behavior problems. Dr. Block has been a consultant to Special Olympics, Inc., helping to create the Motor Activities Training Program, a sports program for athletes with severe disabilities. He has authored or coauthored 5 books, 20 chapters in books, and more than 75 peer-reviewed articles and has conducted more than 100 international and national presentations on various topics in adapted physical education. Dr. Block is the president of the International Federation of Adapted Physical Activity (2015–2019) and has served as president of the National Consortium for Physical Education and Recreation for Individuals with Disabilities and as chair of the Adapted Physical Activity Council within the American Alliance for Health, Physical Education, Recreation, and Dance. He also was named the Virginia College Professor of the Year in 2004 by the Virginia Association of Health, Physical Education, Recreation, and Dance.

About the Downloadable Materials

Purchasers of this book may download, print, and/or photocopy Figures 3.2, 18.1–3, 19.2–4, 20.2, 20.6, and the Appendix for Chapter 5 for educational use. These materials are included with the print book and are also available at **www.brookespublishing.com/block/materials.**

Also, for instructors, PowerPoints are available to help you teach a course using *A Teacher's Guide to Adapted Physical Education, Fourth Edition.* Please visit **www.brookespublishing.com/block** to access customizable PowerPoint presentations for every chapter.

About the Contributors

Jason C. Bishop, Ph.D., CAPE, is an assistant professor with a joint appointment with the College of Physical Activity and Sport Sciences and the Davis College of Agriculture, Natural Resources and Design at West Virginia University in the area of adapted physical activity and health disparities. Dr. Bishop's research interests include the motor development of children with attention-deficit/hyperactivity disorder and increasing physical activity participation of people with disabilities.

Ron Davis, Ph.D., is a professor in the kinesiology department in the area of adapted physical education at Texas Woman's University. His research interests focus on performance and training for athletes/individuals with disabilities.

Alicia Dixon-Ibarra, Ph.D., MPH, is a postdoctoral scholar with the College of Public Health and Human Sciences at Oregon State University. Her research focuses on improving the health behaviors of individuals with a disability, including developing and implementing physical activity health promotion programs for people with disabilities and utilizing her epidemiology degree to analyze national surveillance system data to describe the health status of people with disabilities.

Simon Driver, Ph.D., is director of rehabilitation research at Baylor Institute for Rehabilitation in Dallas, Texas. Dr. Driver's research focuses on improving the health behaviors of individuals with a disability.

Steven Elliott, Ph.D., is an associate professor and the associate director in the School of Health and Applied Human Sciences at University of North Carolina, Wilmington (UNCW). The recipient of the 2012 Chancellor's Teaching Excellence Award at UNCW, his research agenda has two major foci: issues surrounding the inclusion of children with special needs into regular physical education classes and the application of instructional strategies, models, and theories to enhance student learning and assessment.

M. Kathleen Ellis, Ph.D., is a professor of kinesiology at West Chester University of Pennsylvania. Dr. Ellis is the director of the Deaf studies program, focusing on deafness-specific areas of research, including the impact of deafness and cochlear implants on physical activity and fitness.

John Foley, Ph.D., is a professor in the Department of Physical Education at the State University of New York (SUNY) at Cortland and director of the SUNY Cortland Physical Activity Laboratory. Over the past 25 years, he has worked extensively with individuals with disabilities in various sports, recreation, and fitness environments. He is an active member of the SUNY Cortland Institute for Disability Studies and focuses his research on ways to increase physical activity and reduce the sedentary behaviors of individuals with disabilities. His work has been published in peer-reviewed journals in the fields of public health, exercise science, and adapted physical activity.

Sean Healy, Ph.D., is an assistant professor of adapted physical education/pedagogy, Department of Kinesiology and Recreation Administration, Humboldt State University, Arcata, California. His research focuses on physical education for children with autism and online education programming.

Hester Henderson, Ph.D., is an associate professor with the Department of Exercise and Sport Sciences at the University of Utah. Her research interests are in the area of behavior management and individuals with disabilities as well as measuring motor skill performance and fitness of individuals with disabilities and determining the effectiveness of interventions to improve motor skills and fitness.

Mel Horton, Ed.D., CAPE, is Assistant Dean of Assessment & School/Community Partnerships at Central Connecticut State University in New Britain, Connecticut. Her research focuses on general and adapted physical education teacher education.

Aija Klavina, Ph.D., is a professor with the Latvian Academy of Sport Education in the areas of adapted physical activity and physiotherapy. Her research focuses on exploring the collaboration and directed learning strategies (e.g., peer tutoring) to improve interaction behaviors between students with and without disabilities in inclusive physical education.

Luke E. Kelly, Ph.D., CAPE, is the Virgil S. Ward Professor of Education in the Department of Kinesiology at the University of Virginia. Dr. Kelly's research focuses on developing functional physical education curricula, based on the achievement-based curriculum model, to accommodate the needs of all students and on developing functional physical and motor skill assessments and training physical educators to competently use these instruments.

Barry Lavay, Ph.D., is a professor in the kinesiology department and the adapted physical education coordinator at California State University, Long Beach. Dr. Lavay's scholarship interests are in the area of physical education pedagogy for children with disabilities and more specifically applied behavior analysis and effective instructional practices.

Lauren J. Lieberman, Ph.D., is the Distinguished Service Professor with the Department of Kinesiology, Sport Studies, and Physical Education at the State University of New York, College at Brockport. She teaches in the area of adapted physical education. She is the founder and director of Camp Abilities, a sports camp for children with visual impairments, and conducts her research in the areas of inclusion in physical education and physical activity for children with sensory impairments.

Cathy MacDonald, Ph.D., is an assistant professor in the Department of Physical Education at the State University of New York at Cortland. Dr. MacDonald's research has addressed evidence-based practices in physical education and the promotion of self-determination for individuals with a disability.

Cathy McKay, Ed.D., CAPE, is on the faculty in the Department of Kinesiology at James Madison University, Harrisonburg, Virginia. Dr. McKay's research focuses on Paralympic Sport education, relational leadership and values-based leadership, and changing attitudes and perceptions toward inclusion through contact.

Thomas E. Moran, Ph.D., CAPE, is an associate professor of the physical health education teacher education program within the Department of Kinesiology at James Madison University in Harrisonburg, Virginia. He is founder and project director of Overcoming Barriers and executive director of Empowerment3—Center for Physical Activity & Wellness for Underserved Youth.

Iva Obrusnikova, Ph.D., is an associate professor with the Department of Behavioral Health and Nutrition at the University of Delaware. She is the director and founder of the Delaware Center on Health and Disability. Her research focuses on exploring different instructional strategies to promote physical activity and the inclusion of children with developmental disabilities in general physical activity settings.

Ana Palla-Kane, Ph.D., is a faculty member in the Department of Kinesiology at the University of Maryland. She works in the area of adapted physical activity and in the development of strategies that increase the accessibility of adapted physical activity programs for individuals with disabilities. She has studied the impact of diversity in the delivery of quality physical education and physical education teachers' perceptions and attitudes toward teaching students with disabilities. She is interested in studying pregnancy in women with disabilities, especially aspects of prenatal care related to accessibility and participation in physical activity prior to and during pregnancy.

Marla Runyan is a teacher of students with visual impairments at Perkins School for the Blind in Watertown, Massachusetts. She is one of only a handful of athletes who has competed in both the Olympics and Paralympics. She won multiple gold medals at the Paralympics, and she was a two-time Olympian, finishing eighth in the 1,500-meter in the 2000 Sydney Olympics, making Marla the first legally blind athlete to compete in the Olympics.

Amanda Stanec, Ph.D., is founder and owner of Move Live Learn. Amanda's research focuses on social justices issues in sports and physical activity. In her work, Amanda takes a comprehensive approach to supporting physical and health literacy for all.

Katie Stanton-Nichols, Ph.D., is an associate professor and director of the Motor Activity and Ability Fitness Clinics with the Department of Kinesiology at Indiana University–Purdue University Indianapolis (IUPUI). She also is a senior scholar at IUPUI's Center of Service and Learning. Her research focuses on understanding the physical activity needs of families who have children with disabilities and on the assessment and evaluation of service learning in adapted physical activity programming and behavioral intervention for children with disabilities.

Andrea Taliaferro, Ph.D., CAPE, is an assistant professor in the College of Physical Activity and Sport Sciences, Department of Coaching and Teaching Studies, at West Virginia University. Dr. Taliaferro's research interests include physical education teacher preparation and the self-efficacy to work with students with disabilities as well as community-based recreational opportunities for individuals with disabilities.

Acknowledgments

I would like to thank several people for their support and assistance in the development and completion of this book. First, I would like to thank my family—my wife, Vickie, and my two daughters, Samantha and Jessica. It is such a source of pride for my wife and me to see our two beautiful daughters growing up to be accomplished young women.

I would like to give a special thanks to all my coauthors. For the first time, this book has disability-specific chapters, and I was thrilled to get some of the leaders in physical education for children with specific disabilities to write these chapters. Also, it is wonderful to get Luke E. Kelly to write the program planning/assessment chapter (Chapter 4), Ron Davis to coauthor the Game and Sports Modification (Chapter 7), Barry Lavay and Hester Henderson to coauthor the behavior chapter (Chapter 19), Andrea Taliaferro and Thomas E. Moran to coauthor the community recreation chapter (Chapter 20), Aija Klavina and Cathy McKay to coauthor the social facilitation chapter (Chapter 17), and Cathy MacDonald and John Foley to author the collaboration chapter. It also has been nice to continue to have Steven Elliott and Amanda Stanec, Iva Obrusnikova, and Mel Horton and Ana Palla-Kane update their excellent chapters. It is particularly gratifying that many of the coauthors of this book are my former doctoral students who are emerging into the next generation of leaders in pedagogy and adapted physical education.

I would like to thank the staff at Paul H. Brookes Publishing Co. for guiding me through the process of completing this book. In particular, Steve Plocher and Rebecca Lazo were wonderful advocates in helping get the book accepted by Brookes. Steve did a great job of editing early versions of each chapter and gently keeping me on track to meet deadlines. Thank you all for your time and effort.

I would like to thank all my master's degree students who provided physical education to students with disabilities during their internships while attending the University of Virginia. Observing you teach children with disabilities led to many of the suggestions provided in this book. Although you may have thought I was teaching you when I came to supervise you, in many cases, you were teaching me by demonstrating unique teaching techniques, motivating lesson plans, and how to get along with others in the school. I am so pleased that most of you continue to teach general or adapted physical education in public schools across the United States.

Finally, thanks to all the children with and without disabilities, physical education teachers, special education teachers, therapists, and parents whom I have interacted with over the past several years. I have learned so much from these interactions, and you have truly been my best teachers. I look forward to more interactions and conversations in the future.

Previous editions of my book were dedicated to my mother, who for many years worked with children who were blind. She passed away in 1992, but I still think of her and am inspired by her every day. This edition of my book is dedicated to my father, who recently celebrated his 99th birthday. His continued love of learning, his wonderful sense of humor, and his unconditional support for me throughout my life have in large part made me the person I am today.

SECTION I

Foundations

CHAPTER 1

What Is Physical Education?

Steven Elliott, Amanda Stanec, and Martin E. Block

OBJECTIVES

1. Describe the standards and characteristics of quality physical education

2. Understand how quality physical education supports individuals' physical literacy development

3. Recognize the benefits of quality physical education

4. Learn the legal definition, components, and objectives of physical education

5. Understand developmentally appropriate programming in physical education

6. Name and describe curriculum models in physical education

7. Become familiar with the status of physical education in the United States

8. Define and describe adapted physical education

9. Identify individuals qualified to provide adapted physical education services

Stephen is a happy-go-lucky 10-year-old fifth grader who loves life and enjoys attending Maya Angelou Elementary School. School is a little more challenging for Stephen because he has a severe visual impairment, but with the help of his orientation and mobility specialist, and occasional help from peers and teachers, he has learned to navigate the school independently with his cane. He participates in general physical education twice a week with Mrs. Deacon, a general physical education teacher; there is no adapted physical education specialist in this school district.

Stephen and his classmates love Mrs. Deacon's class for a number of reasons. First, they always know ahead of time what they will be doing because Mrs. Deacon has a physical education page on the school web site where she posts a list of units or themes as well as an outline of how each day's activities fit into the theme. Some themes focus on learning one specific skill, such as the overhand throw or jumping rope, whereas other themes revolve around learning multiple skills and concepts related to a specific topic such as dancing, gymnastics, physical fitness, or a modified sport. Each theme lasts 2–4 weeks depending on the number of skills within the theme and the skill level of the students. Several themes are revisited two and even three times during the year, such as physical fitness, which is a districtwide priority, and themes with skills that are difficult to master (e.g., overhand throw). Students are also encouraged to practice skills at home. This thematic approach allows Mrs. Deacon to help her students focus on, improve, and eventually master specific skills within a theme regardless of their individual ability level.

Second, Mrs. Deacon communicates to her students specific areas in which each child needs to improve—that is, rather than holding all students to the same standard in each skill or concept, Mrs. Deacon gives each child individual goals based on his or her ability. For example, in an overhand throw unit, some students practice their follow-through, some focus on fully extending their arm back, and others work toward mastery/competence in all the components of the overhand throw in an authentic environment (i.e., applying distance and accuracy strategies in a modified small-sided game setting). Stephen has not mastered the trunk action of turning his body sideways to the target and then toward the target when throwing, and he does not have the most skillful arm action pattern needed to get the most power from his throw. During throwing practice, he is given feedback on these patterns from peers who have already mastered the overhand throw.

Third, Mrs. Deacon provides a lot of choices of activities and equipment during practice and games. For example, in her introductory volleyball skill unit for fifth graders, students can choose how to serve (e.g., underhand or overhand), the type of ball, and the distance, and they can practice serving into a suspended parachute, over a large refrigerator box, into a curtain on the stage, or against the wall. This gives each student a chance to be successful and challenged at her or his own level.

Fourth, Mrs. Deacon always finds a way to make sure all her students are active and engaged in fun activities. Students have their own pieces of equipment (unless involved in partner or group work), and the gymnasium is set up so that there is more than enough space for everyone to move at the same time in a safe manner. Also, Mrs. Deacon plays games that reinforce a particular skill theme. Very rarely does she play traditional sports following regulation rules, which often result in students standing around and getting fewer turns. She also does not play elimination games in which students have to sit out for extended periods of time. Instead, students play tag games while practicing dribbling, keep-away games to reinforce passing and trapping, and a small-sided modified version of basketball in which successful passing, moving to space, and communication are the assessment criteria—not how many successful baskets a player makes. To increase moderate to vigorous physical activity, all the students wear a pedometer to record the amount of steps they take in each class and set individual and class goals to increase their motivation.

Fifth, Mrs. Deacon uses a variety of teaching strategies, such as cooperative learning, reciprocal teaching (i.e., peer tutoring), child-designed activities (i.e., student centered), task sheets (i.e., support

motivation), and guided discovery (i.e., prompting). For example, during a fitness-themed unit, Mrs. Deacon has students do cooperative push-ups. Students are placed into groups of four and told to determine how many push-ups they could do, with proper form, as a team. Each group earned a total score, and cooperative teams worked to set goals related to their previous day's performance. The goals ranged from individual members maintaining their personal best score while demonstrating mastery to improving the group's overall score.

What type of physical education program do you envision? Is it similar to Mrs. Deacon's: a carefully planned, comprehensive program that is aligned to national and state standards and designed to meet each student's needs? Do you make an effort to teach your students skills and concepts and support them making connections from their experiences in physical education to their experiences outside of school? Do your students receive lots of practice opportunities in activities in which they can be successful, regardless of individual ability levels?

Before you can provide an appropriate program for students with disabilities who are included in your general physical education class, you must develop a quality general physical education program. The purpose of this chapter is to review the basics of quality physical education. This chapter also provides information about the legal basis for students with disabilities accessing physical education services as outlined in the Individuals with Disabilities Education Act (IDEA) and the 2004 reauthorization of this act—the Individuals with Disabilities Education Improvement Act (IDEA) of 2004 (PL 108-446). Finally, a discussion of developmentally appropriate practices in physical education and a definition of adapted physical education are provided.

WHAT IS QUALITY PHYSICAL EDUCATION?

A careful examination of Mrs. Deacon's program reveals that she has structured her curriculum and teaching practices around the national standards for physical education. The national standards for physical education were originally provided by the National Association for Sport and Physical Education (NASPE, 1995b, 2004) and updated in the third edition by the Society of Health and Physical Educators (SHAPE, 2014).

The movement toward national physical education standards started in 1986, when NASPE first attempted to answer the question "What should physically educated students know and be able to do?" This culminated in the creation of a definition of a physically educated person that included five major focus areas. In the 1990s, this definition was applied to selected grade levels through 20 outcome statements with sample benchmarks and published in the NASPE (1992) report *Outcomes of Quality Physical Education Programs*. According to the report, a physically educated student is one who

1. HAS learned the skills necessary to perform a variety of physical activities

2. DOES participate regularly in physical activity

3. IS physically fit

4. KNOWS the implications of and the benefits from involvement in physical activities

5. VALUES physical activity and its contributions to a healthful lifestyle (NASPE, 1992, p. 3)

This was followed by the release of the landmark report *Moving into the Future: National Standards for Physical Education* (NASPE, 1995b), which included assessment guidelines designed to complement the 1992 outcome statements and benchmarks. A second edition of *Moving into the Future: National Standards for Physical Education* was released in 2004 and included learning objectives in the psychomotor, cognitive, and affective domains of learning. Finally, in 2014, the newly named Society of Health and Physical Educators (SHAPE), formerly known as the American Alliance for Health, Physical Education, Recreation, and Dance (AAHPERD), released the third edition of the national standards and grade-level outcomes for K–12 physical education. The new national standards clearly identify what students should know and be able to do as a result of a quality physical education program and provide a tool for physical educators to use in planning curricula, designing units and lessons, and assessing and tracking student progress across grade levels. As of 2014, the five national content standards are as follows (SHAPE, 2014):

- *Standard 1:* The physically literate individual demonstrates competency in a variety of motor skills and movement patterns.

- *Standard 2:* The physically literate individual applies knowledge of concepts, principles, strategies, and tactics related to movement and performance.

- *Standard 3:* The physically literate individual demonstrates the knowledge and skills to achieve and maintain a health-enhancing level of physical activity and fitness.

- *Standard 4:* The physically literate individual exhibits responsible personal and social behavior that respects self and others.

- *Standard 5:* The physically literate individual recognizes the value of physical activity for health, enjoyment, challenge, self-expression, and/or social interaction (National Standards for K–12 Physical Education used with permission from SHAPE America – Society of Health and Physical Educators. © 2013, SHAPE America – Society of Health and Physical Educators, 1900 Association Drive, Reston, VA 20191, www.shapeamerica.org. All rights reserved.).

The third edition of the national standards has three key changes from the previous editions. First, the writing team included the term *physical literacy* in the goal of physical education. As the new NASPE standards culminate to suggest, physical literacy is a concept that influences the whole person. A physically literate person is someone who develops competence and confidence to participate in a wide variety of physically active environments (Physical and Health Education Canada, 2014). In addition, physically literate individuals are motivated to apply physical activity behaviors in order to benefit themselves, others, and the environment. Although physical education is not the only system in which physical literacy should be fostered in students, physical literacy should be the intent of physical education curriculum and subsequent programs. Physical literacy is also a concept that is important to individuals throughout a lifespan. Quality physical education programs should prepare students to live as physically literate people throughout their lives.

Physical literacy aligns with recommended pedagogical practice in physical education as it is individualized. This enables individuals with disabilities, and those without disabilities who have different skill levels and experiences, to progress at a rate that is developmentally appropriate and meets their individual needs. Thus, differentiated instruction and modifications (e.g., equipment, rules, tasks) are necessary in quality physical education programs that intend to foster students' physical literacy. For example, Stephen and some of his classmates were still working on mastering the overhand throw, whereas most peers in his class were applying an already mastered overhand throw to sports skills such as softball and volleyball. In addition, students were encouraged to use different equipment when practicing skills to enhance their success and confidence, and various task challenges such as trying to hit targets of different sizes from different distances ensured all students would be successful yet challenged at their unique skill level.

Assessing physical literacy is always similar to formative assessment in that it tells the assessor where the student is on particular components of her or his journey in physical literacy. This information can help students set goals related to their physical literacy, and the act of goal setting will support them throughout their lives.

Second, the third edition of the national standards combined two previous standards (Standards 3 and 4) into one standard (Standard 3) that emphasizes how physical educators help students gain the knowledge and skills needed for achieving and maintaining health-related fitness and participating in lifelong physical activity.

The third key change in the latest edition of the national standards is the inclusion of grade-level outcomes. The grade-level outcomes are organized by standard (S1, S2, S3, S4, or S5), level (E = elementary, M = middle, and H = high school), outcome number (which do not reflect any particular priority), and grade level. For example, S2.E1.3 refers to Standard 2, Elementary outcome 1, Grade 3, which states that students should be able to "recognize the concept of open spaces in a movement concept" (SHAPE, 2014, p. 32).

According to SHAPE, the overall goal of physical education is to "develop physically literate individuals who have the knowledge, skills and confidence to enjoy a lifetime of healthful physical activity" (2014, p. 11). Mrs. Deacon and other effective physical educators are meeting this goal by employing various teaching strategies to promote student learning in physical education, including the following:

- Providing all students with the opportunity to learn by ensuring that all students are kept physically active at an appropriate level for more than 50% of the class time

- Teaching meaningful content aligned with state/national standards for physical education

- Delivering appropriate instruction and providing students with a variety of activities that can be individualized to each student's ability level

There are multiple textbooks, book chapters, and articles that have described how to design quality physical education programs. Pangrazi (2007) identified and described eight components of a quality physical education program:

1. A quality physical education program is organized around content standards that offer direction and continuity to instruction and evaluation.

2. A quality program is centered on the developmental urges, characteristics, and interests of students.

3. Quality physical education makes physical activity and motor skill development the core of the program.

4. Physical education programs teach management skills and self-discipline.

5. Quality programs emphasize the inclusion of all students.

6. In a quality physical education setting, instruction is focused on the process of learning skills rather than on the product or outcome of the skill performance.

7. A quality physical education program teaches lifetime activities that students can use to promote their health and personal wellness.

8. Quality physical education teaches cooperation and responsibility and helps students develop sensitivity to diversity and gender issues.

Benefits of Quality Physical Education

Quality physical education plays a key role in developing physically literate individuals, along with families, sports, community/recreation programs, and early childhood centers. In turn, a physically literate person is someone who is physically active enough for health benefits. These individuals derive benefits as noted by the Centers for Disease Control and Prevention (CDC, 2014b) including 1) building and maintaining healthy bones and muscles; 2) reducing the risk of developing obesity and chronic diseases such as diabetes, cardiovascular disease, and colon cancer; and 3) reducing feelings of depression and anxiety and promoting psychological well-being. In addition to health (mental, physical, social) benefits, research highlights positive associations between physical activity (at moderate to vigorous intensities) and academic performance, including improvement in academic achievement and grades, academic behavior and time on task, and factors that influence academic achievement, such as concentration and attentiveness in class (CDC, 2014b; Ratey & Hagerman, 2008; Tremblay, Inman, & Willms, 2000).

Other benefits of quality physical education programs include the development of a variety of motor skills and abilities related to lifetime leisure skills; improved understanding of the importance of maintaining a healthy lifestyle throughout life; improved understanding and appreciation of the human body and how it can move; improved knowledge of rules, strategies, and behaviors of particular games and sports; and improved self-confidence and self-worth as they relate to physical education and recreation activities (Graham, Holt-Hale, & Parker, 2013; NASPE, 2004; Sherrill, 2004). Quality physical education prepares students to be physically and mentally active, fit, and healthy for a lifetime. Numerous studies that have been published in highly respected academic journals that describe the many benefits students receive from a quality physical education program. For a more thorough description of the benefits of a physical education program, we refer you to a summary of the research on the association between school-based physical activity, including physical education, and academic performance produced by the CDC (2010c) and an article entitled "Top 10 Reasons for Quality Physical Education" by Le Masurier and Corbin (2006).

Benefits of physical education are just as important for students with disabilities, and physical activity may bring additional benefits (e.g., decrease symptoms of disability) to students with disabilities. Most individuals with disabilities have limited recreation skills, which greatly restrict their abilities to participate in community activities and interact with peers who do not have disabilities. Extra free time coupled with limited recreation skills often leads to a sedentary lifestyle, which in turn can lead to health and social problems (Block, Taliaferro, & Moran, 2013). Quality physical education programs can help students with disabilities acquire critical lifetime leisure skills, including an

appreciation for continued participation in active recreational pursuits.

Legal Definition of Physical Education

The amount of physical education that a child without special needs receives varies among states, school districts, and sometimes schools within the same school district. There are no federal laws that mandate that physical education should be taught in public schools to students without disabilities (Siedentop, 2004). Typically, minimal standards for physical education requirements are set at the state level (NASPE & American Heart Association, 2012), with each school district given the opportunity to interpret the state standards for their schools. State and school districts, however, are responsible for providing physical education to students with special needs.

Physical education services, specially designed if necessary, must be made available to *every* child with a disability receiving a free appropriate public education (Winnick, 2011, pp. 3–20). Physical education has been required since the enactment of the Education for All Handicapped Children Act of 1975 (PL 94-142). It has remained an essential part of special education services through its many reauthorizations (see Table 1.1 for a brief chronology).

Table 1.1.   Chronology of the Individuals with Disabilities Education Act (IDEA)

Act/year	Description
Education for All Handicapped Children Act (EHC) of 1975 (PL 94-142)	Landmark legislation that provided free appropriate public education, including physical education, for all eligible children ages 3–21. EHC was reauthorized by PL 101-476 and PL 105-17.
Education of the Handicapped Act (EHA) Amendments of 1983 (PL 98-189)	Increased funding and provided *incentives* for states to develop and implement an early intervention system to serve children with disabilities from birth to age 5. States were not mandated to provide services to children birth to age 3 at this point.
EHA Amendments of 1986 (PL 99-457)	*Required* states to provide services to eligible preschoolers ages 3–5 years or lose some federal funding. Part H of PL 99-457 (now referred to as Part C of IDEA) commissioned funds to states to develop and implement a comprehensive, multi-disciplinary, interagency program of early intervention services for infants and toddlers with disabilities (birth to age 3) and their families.
Individuals with Disabilities Education Act (IDEA) of 1990 (PL 101-476)	All references to *handicapped* are replaced with the term *disability.* Major changes include new definitions of attention-deficit/hyperactivity disorder and traumatic brain injury and the creation of an eligibility category for autism. Emphasized the least restrictive environment (LRE), with a focus on training general education personnel and the use of assistive technology. Added the term *transition services,* which emphasized a coordinated effort to help students ages 16 and older (14 years and older for students with severe disabilities) acquire the skills needed to move from school to postschool activities, including social services, recreation, therapy, and rehabilitation counseling.
IDEA Amendments of 1997 (PL 105-17)	Greater focus on parental rights and participation in the planning process, on LRE, and on justification of placement in settings other than general education; required general educators to participate in all IEP meetings
Individuals with Disabilities Education Improvement Act (IDEA) of 2004 (PL 108-446)	Aligned with the No Child Left Behind Act of 2001 (PL 107-110), reinforcing the need for highly qualified special education teachers and the inclusion of children with disabilities in statewide assessment

In fact, physical education is the only curriculum area that lawmakers placed in the definition of special education:

> (25) The term *special education* means specially designed instruction, at no cost to parents, to meet unique needs of a child with a disability including—
>
> > (A) instruction conducted in the classroom, in the home, in hospitals and institutions, and in other settings; and
> >
> > (B) instruction in *physical education* [emphasis added]. (IDEA 2004, 20 U.S.C. §§ 1400 *et seq.*)

Unfortunately, many parents, professionals, and administrators are unfamiliar with the physical education requirements in the law, and students with disabilities continue to be excluded from physical education or receive inappropriate physical education services (Blinde & McCallister, 1998; Coates & Vickerman, 2010; Fitzgerald & Stride, 2012; Goodwin & Watkinson, 2000). This is exactly what lawmakers feared would happen when they placed the following comments into the rules and regulations of the original law:

> Special education as set forth in the Committee bill includes instruction in physical education, which is provided as a matter of course to all non-handicapped students enrolled in public elementary and secondary schools. The Committee is concerned that although these services are available to and required of all students in our school systems, they are often viewed as a luxury for handicapped students. . . . The Committee. . . specifically included physical education in the definition of special education to make clear that the Committee expects such services, specially designed where necessary, to be provided as an integral part of the education program of every handicapped child. (Federal Register, 1977, p. 42489)

The regulations for IDEA and its reauthorizations define physical education services as follows:

> (a) *General.* Physical education services, specifically designed if necessary, must be made available to every child with a disability receiving FAPE. (Assistance to States for the Education of Children with Disabilities, 2006, § 300.307[a])

This statement reinforces the notion that all students with disabilities must receive some form of physical education. Many school districts have placed physical education on their individualized education program (IEP) forms (essentially a place to check general or adapted physical education) to make it clear that each child must receive some form of physical education services. IDEA regulations state,

> (b) *Regular physical education.* Each child with a disability must be afforded the opportunity to participate in the regular physical education program available to typically-developing students unless:
>
> > (1) the child is enrolled full time in a separate facility; or
> >
> > (2) the child needs specially designed physical education, as prescribed in the child's individualized education program. (Assistance to States for the Education of Children with Disabilities, 2006, § 300.307[b])

This statement suggests that many students with disabilities can receive a safe, successful, and meaningful physical education experience in general and do not need any special goals or objectives on their IEP (Bateman, 2012). However, some students might need some modifications to the curriculum, equipment, and/or instruction to be successful in general physical education. These subtle modifications might include an interpreter for a child who is deaf, a beep ball for a child who is blind, a peer tutor for a child with an intellectual disability to help clarify tasks and/or to facilitate social interaction, or a teacher assistant for a child who has autism to help identify when the child is being triggered in order to help intervene and avoid an episode caused by the trigger. These individually determined accommodations need to be noted on the child's IEP (Bateman, 2012; Block & Burke, 1999):[1]

> (c) *Special physical education.* If specially designed physical education is prescribed in a child's individualized education program, the public agency responsible for the education of that child shall provide the services directly, or make arrangements for it to be provided through other public or private programs. (Assistance to States for the Education of Children with Disabilities, 2006, § 300.307[c])

If assessments determine that a child with a disability needs special physical education, then individual goals and objectives for physical education should be created by the child's IEP team and placed in the child's IEP (Bateman, 2012; Block &

---

[1]In this book, the terms *accommodations* and *modifications* are used interchangeably.

Burke, 1999). For example, a 10-year-old boy with cerebral palsy needs to learn how to walk using a special gait trainer. Because this is a unique goal for this child (i.e., does not match what other 10-year-olds are doing in physical education), this goal and incremental short-term objectives should be written into his IEP. It is important to note that qualifying for special physical education and having IEP objectives for physical education does not necessarily mean that the child will be pulled out into a separate adapted physical education program. Many students with disabilities can work on their unique IEP goals and objectives within the general physical education setting. For example, this boy can practice walking in his gait trainer while the other students are running laps during warm-up, playing tagging and fleeing games, or playing games that require running, such as basketball and soccer. He might need a peer or an assistant for safety, but he should be able to work on his unique goals while having an opportunity to interact with peers without disabilities:

> (d) *Education in separate facilities.* The public agency responsible for the education of a handicapped child who is enrolled in a separate facility shall insure that the child receives appropriate physical education services in compliance with paragraphs (a) and (c) of this section. (IDEA 2004, 20 U.S.C. §§ 1400 *et seq.*)

This means that a child with a disability who is educated in a separate facility such as a school for the deaf must still receive physical education services, specially designed if necessary (Bateman, 2012). Clearly, lawmakers define physical education as an important, *direct service* that should be a part of every student's educational program.

All students should receive physical education services, whereas only those students who need extra support to benefit require related services (including physical, occupational, or recreation therapy). Related services *cannot* be considered a substitute for the physical education requirement, nor can recess, unstructured free time, or training in sedentary recreation activities (e.g., board games, card games; Block & Burke, 1999; Winnick, 2011, pp. 3–20).

Components of Physical Education

Although it is clear that physical education should be viewed as an important part of a student's overall education program, what exactly did the lawmakers

mean by *physical education?* Physical education is further defined in PL 94-142 and IDEA and its amendments as

> the development of physical and motor fitness, fundamental motor skills and patterns, and skills in aquatics, dance, and individual and group games and sports (including intramural and lifetime sports). The term includes special physical education, adapted physical education, movement education, and motor development. (IDEA 2004, 20 U.S.C. §§ 1400 *et seq.*)

The following sections provide a detailed examination of each component contained within this definition.

Physical and Motor Fitness

Physical and motor fitness refers to development of both health- and skill-related fitness. Health-related fitness focuses on factors pertaining to a healthy lifestyle and the prevention of disease related to a sedentary lifestyle (Graham et al., 2013; Pangrazi, 2007). Pangrazi (2007) and Lacy (2010) provided the following definitions of the specific components of health-related fitness:

- *Cardiovascular endurance (aerobic endurance):* The ability of the heart, blood vessels, and the respiratory system to deliver oxygen efficiently over an extended period of time. Moving (e.g., riding a bike, walking, jogging) without stopping for extended periods of time retains or increases cardiovascular efficiency.

- *Body composition:* The division of total body weight into two components: fat weight and lean weight. It is essentially a measure of the amount of body fat a person carries. A fit person has a relatively low percentage of body fat. Performing aerobic and strength activities as well as following a reasonable diet will help retain or decrease the percentage of body fat.

- *Flexibility:* The ability to move the musculature (i.e., muscles, tendons, and ligaments) through their full range of motion. Flexibility is joint specific, so it must be measured and stretched at several joints. Stretching activities help musculature retain or increase elasticity.

- *Muscular strength:* The ability of muscles to exert force (e.g., to lift heavy objects). Lifting weights or other objects that are heavier than what one lifts in day-to-day activities increases muscular strength.

- *Muscular endurance:* The ability of muscles to exert force over an extended period of time.

Lifting weight or heavy objects repeatedly retains or increases muscular endurance.

Skill-related fitness refers to specific fitness components associated with successful performance in specific motor activities and sports (Graham et al., 2013; Pangrazi, 2007). Lacy (2010) and Pangrazi (2007) provided the following definitions of the specific components of skill-related fitness:

- *Agility:* The ability to rapidly and accurately change the position of the body in space. Quickly changing positions in wrestling, performing a dance with a large group in a small space, or avoiding a tackler in football are examples of agility.

- *Balance:* The maintenance of equilibrium while stationary (static balance) or moving (dynamic balance). Performing a headstand or maintaining balance while swinging a golf club are examples of static balance. Walking a balance beam successfully, running in a football game, or descending a steep single track on a mountain bike without falling are examples of dynamic balance.

- *Coordination:* The ability to simultaneously perform multiple motor tasks smoothly and accurately. Hitting a tennis ball, using a smooth throwing pattern when pitching a ball, dribbling a soccer ball, or playing sledge hockey are examples of athletic skills that require coordination.

- *Power:* The ability to transfer energy explosively into force. Examples of skills that require power include the standing long jump, the shot put, and kicking a soccer ball.

- *Speed:* The ability to perform a movement in a short period of time. A batter running to first base or a wheelchair basketball player maneuvering his or her chair while dribbling a ball quickly down the court are examples of activities that require speed.

- *Reaction time:* The difference between the stimulation (i.e., seeing, hearing, feeling something) and the response (i.e., moving) to the stimulation. A sprinter's response to the starting gun, a racquetball player's reaction to a hard-hit ball, or a skateboarder's response to an obstacle that quickly appears are examples of activities that require short reaction time.

Fundamental Motor Skills and Patterns

Fundamental motor skills and patterns refer to the development of basic motor skills that form the foundation for more advanced, specific movements used in individual and team sports and activities (Gabbard, 2011; Gallahue, Ozmun, & Goodaway, 2012; Graham et al., 2013; Pangrazi, 2007). Each fundamental motor skill has a distinct pattern or structure that defines the movement. Fundamental movement patterns are usually divided into locomotor and manipulative patterns. Locomotor patterns are movements used by individuals to travel from one place to another; manipulative patterns are used to propel balls away from the body or receive balls. Table 1.2 provides more detailed descriptions of the most common fundamental locomotor and manipulative patterns as described by Graham et al. (2013) and Gallahue et al. (2012).

Aquatics

Aquatics refers to activities conducted in the water, including swimming, which involves moving independently in the water using various strokes and water exercises that work on the development of health-related fitness (Lepore, 2011; Lepore, Gayle, & Stevens, 2007).

Rhythm and Dance

Rhythm and dance refer to the ability to repeat an action or movement with regularity and in time to a particular pattern (Kassing & Jay, 2003). Rhythm involves three major components: tempo (speed), pattern (even or uneven beats), and accent (emphasis; Kassing & Jay, 2003). Dance is a combination of movement and rhythm in which movement qualities, movement components, and rhythmic movements are purposefully integrated into a progression with a beginning, middle, and end (Boswell, 2011). Dance can include anything from basic rhythmic activities and action songs for young students to traditional dances (e.g., ballroom, folk, square), aerobic dances, and modern dances (creative dance) for older students and adults (Boswell, 2011; Graham et al., 2013).

Individual Sports and Pursuits

Individual sports and pursuits include culturally popular activities that involve one player or teams of no more than two players. Popular individual sports and pursuits in the United States are listed in Table 1.3. Activities within each sport can include working on skills, playing lead-up games (simpler or modified forms of traditional sports that help students acquire game skills and concepts), playing recreational games, or playing competitive games. In addition, many of these sports are considered lifetime leisure activities because they can be played across the lifespan.

Table 1.2. Description of fundamental locomotor and manipulative patterns

Walking	Standing upright with eyes forward, swing one leg forward while swinging the opposite arm forward. Then swing the other leg forward and the other arm forward.
Running	Standing upright with eyes forward, bend arms at elbow. Push off and swing one leg forward while swinging opposite arm forward. Then swing the other leg forward and the other arm forward.
Jumping	Stand upright with eyes forward and feet shoulder width apart. Bend legs at knee and bring both arms behind body. Simultaneously, lean forward, swing arm forward, and forcefully straighten out legs.
Galloping	Standing upright with eyes forward, start with one leg forward of the other. Slide the back leg toward the front leg, and then step forward with the front leg. Pump arms either together or alternating.
Hopping	Stand upright with one leg bent so that the foot is off the ground. Bend the support leg at the knee while bringing both arms back behind the body. Simultaneously, lean forward, swing arms forward, and forcefully straighten out support leg.
Skipping	Alternate hopping on one foot, then stepping onto the other foot, and then hopping with that foot. Hop-step on one foot, followed by a hop-step on the opposite foot.

Description of fundamental manipulative patterns	
Throwing	Propelling a small ball away from the body using one hand. Skillful throwing is initiated by a forward step with opposite leg, followed by hip and trunk rotation, and concluded with a whipping arm action.
Catching	Receiving and controlling a ball that is tossed or kicked to student. Skillful catching is noted by extending arms to meet the ball, retracting hands upon contact with the ball, and using hands to catch the ball rather than trapping the ball against body.
Striking (bat)	Propelling a ball away from body by hitting ball with a long-handled implement. Skillful, two-handed striking consists of stepping forward, followed by quick hip, trunk, and arm rotation; swinging horizontally; and whipping arms forward in a forceful follow-through.
Striking (racket)	Propelling ball away from body by hitting ball with a racket. Skillful, one-handed striking consists of stepping forward, followed by quick hip, trunk, and arm rotation; swinging horizontally; and whipping arm forward in a forceful follow-through.
Kicking	Propelling ball away from body by using foot to impart force on ball. Skillful kicking consists of planting support leg next to ball, bringing leg back by flexing knee, forcefully swinging leg forward to contact ball, and then continuing to swing leg forward in forceful follow-through.
Punting	Propelling ball away from body using foot to impart force on ball. Punting is different from kicking in that the ball is held and then dropped by the punter, and the ball is punted before it touches the ground.

Note. Locomotor patterns can also include pushing a manual wheelchair or controlling an electric wheelchair.

Team Sports

Team sports include culturally popular sports that involve three or more players per side. Popular team sports in the United States are listed in Table 1.4. As is the case with individual sports, activities in each team sport can include working on skills, playing lead-up or modified games, playing recreational games, or playing competitive games. It is interesting to note that some team sports (e.g., football) are not considered lifetime leisure activities because most individuals do not participate in these activities after middle age. Team sports such as volleyball and softball are played by older adults and could be considered lifetime leisure activities.

Objectives of Physical Education

The purpose of a quality physical education program is to support physical literacy development so

Table 1.3. Popular individual sports and pursuits

Archery	Martial arts
Badminton	Racquetball
Bocce	Roller skating
Bowling	Scuba diving
Cycling	Shooting
Croquet	Skiing
Fencing	Snowshoeing
Darts	Swimming
Golf	Table tennis
Gymnastics	Tennis
Hiking	Track and field
Horseback riding	Water skiing
Kayaking	Weight training
	Yoga

Table 1.4. Popular team sports

Basketball	Rugby
Baseball	Soccer
Field hockey	Softball
Floor hockey	Team handball
Football	Ultimate Frisbee
Lacrosse	Volleyball

that individuals choose to be physically active for a lifetime. The *Healthy People 2020* report released by the U.S. Department of Health and Human Services (2010a) clearly states objectives for health and physical education. The overall goal of *Healthy People 2020* is to identify the most significant preventable threats to health and to establish national goals to reduce these threats. The following objectives identify how physical education in public schools can help in this effort:

1. Increase the proportion of the nation's public and private schools that require daily physical education.

2. Increase the proportion of adolescents who participate in daily school physical education. (U.S. Department of Health and Human Services, 2010a)

The components of physical education help define the types of activities that should be included in a comprehensive physical education program. However, presenting activities without purpose or focus is not effective physical education. Quality physical education programs use these activities to promote more global physical education objectives that facilitate psychomotor (motor and fitness performance), cognitive (intellectual skills), and affective development (feelings, opinions, attitudes, beliefs, values, interests, and desires) (Sherrill, 2004).

DEVELOPMENTALLY APPROPRIATE PROGRAMMING IN PHYSICAL EDUCATION

The NASPE has provided leadership and professional guidance to the field of physical education for many years. In addition to the national content standards in physical education, NASPE has also produced guidelines for appropriate instructional practices at each of the three levels (elementary, middle, and high school). These appropriate practices, first produced in 1992, were revised in 2014 (third edition) and represent expert consensus opinion about important appropriate and inappropriate practices observed frequently in K–12 school physical education. These documents organize teacher practices into five separate sections: learning environment, instructional strategies, curriculum, assessment, and professionalism.

The appropriate instructional practice guidelines have proved to be an excellent resource for parents, school administrators, and teachers who are responsible for providing physical education and are

Table 1.5. Sample components from the appropriate practices for elementary physical education document

Component	Forming groups/partners
Appropriate practice	Groups/partners are formed in a way that preserves the dignity and self-respect of every child. For example, a teacher privately forms groups or teams by using knowledge of children's skills abilities in ways that will facilitate learning. Groups or teams may also be formed by grouping clothing colors, birthdays, and favorite activities.
Inappropriate practice	Groups or teams are formed by student "captains" publicly selecting one child at a time, exposing the less-skilled students to peer ridicule or embarrassment. Groups or teams are formed by pitting boys against girls, emphasizing gender differences rather than cooperation.

From SHAPE America. (2004). *Appropriate practices for elementary school physical education,* a position statement of the National Association for Sport and Physical Education, developed by the Middle and Secondary School Physical Education Council (MASSPEC). Reston, VA: Council on Physical Education for Children (COPEC). Used with permission from SHAPE America—Society of Health and Physical Educators, 1900 Association Drive, Reston, VA 20191, www.shapeamerica.org.

available in booklet form or in a side-by-side comparison grid (available at http://www.shapeamerica.org/standards/guidelines/upload/Appropriate-Instructional-Practices-Grid.pdf). Sample components from the appropriate practices for elementary physical education document (see Table 1.5) and the appropriate practices for high school physical education document (see Table 1.6) are presented.

Physical education is composed of several different components designed to promote certain global objectives (i.e., to be physically literate), and it is important that all students receive training in all components if these objectives are to be achieved. Yet, should young students learn how to either play team sports or participate in intricate dances? Should older students and young adults participate solely in simple rhythm activities or activities that promote fundamental motor skill development? The answer is no. Students should be exposed to all physical education components, but these should be presented across the lifespan of the student. The term *developmentally appropriate* refers to presenting activities that are geared to a student's developmental status, previous movement experiences, fitness and skill level, body size, and age (Council on Physical Education for Children [COPEC], 1992). Developmentally appropriate practices suggest that programming as well as instruction should be different for preschool-age students, compared with that for elementary-age students or for secondary-age students.

Table 1.6. Sample components from the appropriate practices for high school physical education document

Component	Warm-up activities
Appropriate practice	Teachers design warm-up activities that are instructionally sound. They use warm-up activities to reinforce/practice skills from previous lessons as well as to lead into the day's lesson. Warm-up activities are safe, appropriate exercises that accommodate different fitness levels and produce perspiration as a sign of internal body heat. Stretching occurs after an appropriate general warm-up activity. Teachers consider warm-up in relation to the total lesson and ensure that students understand why and how to warm up appropriately.
Inappropriate practice	Teachers have students warm up on their own, possibly without supervision. A single warm-up routine is used regardless of the lesson, ignores individual fitness levels, and/or is potentially unsafe. Mass exercise sessions are conducted without instructional focus. Stretching occurs without general warm-up.

From SHAPE America. (2004). *Appropriate practices for high school physical education, a position statement of the National Association for Sport and Physical Education,* developed by the Middle and Secondary School Physical Education Council (MASSPEC). Reston, VA: Council on Physical Education for Children. Used with permission from SHAPE America—Society of Health and Physical Educators, 1900 Association Drive, Reston, VA 20191, www.shapeamerica.org.

Wessel and Kelly (1986) outlined major content areas for general physical education activities broken down by grade level (see Table 1.7). Note that younger students are learning activities that promote development of motor skills and movement competencies, whereas older students are learning to apply these skills and competencies to culturally popular sports and lifetime leisure/fitness activities.

Most physical educators understand what is appropriate for younger students and what is appropriate for older students. However, this understanding is often lost when it comes to students with disabilities. Often, physical educators present activities based on a student's supposed *mental* rather than *chronological age.* Unfortunately, such an approach may result in students with disabilities graduating from school with a smattering of developmental skills but with no real ability to participate in lifetime leisure activities. It is critical that students with disabilities, including students with severe disabilities, be exposed to chronological age–appropriate activities that will lead to the development of functional skills that they can use when they graduate from school (see Block, 1992, and Krebs & Block, 1992, for in-depth discussions of helping students acquire lifetime leisure skills).

CURRICULAR MODELS IN PHYSICAL EDUCATION

Effective physical educators have adopted the NASPE national standards to create standards-based curriculum plans that follow a distinct instructional and/or curriculum model. There are several types of instructional and curriculum models that have been adopted by school districts and individual schools. Each of these models has a main theme that indicates the content emphasis and major learning outcomes designed for that model (Metzler, 2011). Specific instructional and curriculum models that are popular in physical education include the personalized system for instruction, cooperative learning, peer teaching, teaching games for understanding, teaching personal and social responsibility, movement education, health-related physical education, the academic inclusion model, and the skill theme approach (Metzler, 2011). One of the more popular contemporary curriculum models has been the sport education model. This model acknowledges that sport is the content of physical education at the secondary level and provides students with an authentic sport experience within physical education classes.

There is a movement in many school districts to implement a curriculum commonly referred to as the "new physical education," which involves creating more engaging and developmentally appropriate programs for students. There is no room in the new physical education for games such as dodge ball, red rover, and relay races, all of which have been placed into the physical education hall of shame, or other games characterized by elimination of participants, low activity time, lack of a meaningful learning objective, lack of content progression, safety issues, or an overemphasis on fun rather than skill acquisition (Hastie & Martin, 2006; Williams, 1992, 1994, 1996). The new physical education stresses the importance of lifetime fitness in addition to modified versions of team sports, and curricula typically involve instruction about heart rate zones, problem solving, and cooperation. Many schools that have implemented the new physical education have taken advantage of grant opportunities such as the Carol M. White Physical Education for Progress Grant to buy equipment such as pedometers, heart rate monitors, climbing walls, inline skates, dance pads, and exercise bikes with video game consoles (McCollum, Elliott, Burke, Civalier, & Pruitt, 2005).

The past 10 years also has witnessed the introduction of new curricular models such as the Physical Best curriculum from SHAPE and the

Table 1.7. Major content areas for general physical education by grade level

Lower elementary school (K–3rd grade)	Upper elementary/middle school (4th–7th grade)		High school (8th–12th grade)
Locomotor patterns	**Locomotor patterns for sports**		**Locomotor sports**
• Run • Skip • Jump • Slide • Gallop • Leap • Hop • Climb	• Locomotor patterns used in sports • Combine two or more locomotor patterns • Locomotor patterns used in dance • Locomotor patterns used in leisure activities		• Track events • Special sports applications
Manipulative patterns	**Manipulative patterns for sports**		**Ball sports**
• Throw • Catch • Kick • Strike	• Throw • Catch • Kick • Strike	• Volley • Dribble • Punt	• Basketball, soccer, softball, volleyball, bowling, golf, tennis, racquetball, etc.
Body management	**Body management for sports**		**Body management for sports**
• Body awareness • Body control • Space awareness • Effort concepts	• Gymnastics • Body management skills applied to sports		• Body management skills applied to sports
Health and fitness	**Health and fitness**		**Health and fitness**
• Endurance • Strength • Flexibility to perform locomotor and manipulative skills	• Cardiorespiratory endurance • Muscular strength and endurance • Flexibility		• Personal conditioning • Lifetime leisure exercises • Introduction to body composition concepts
Rhythms and dance	**Dance**		**Dance**
• Moving to a beat • Expressing self through movement • Singing games • Applying effort concepts	• Folk • Modern • Interpretive • Aerobic		• Folk • Modern • Interpretive • Aerobic and social
Low organized games	**Lead-up games to sports**		**Modified and regulation sports**
• Relays and tag games • Games with partners • Games with a small group	• Lead-up games to team sports		• Modified sport activities • Regulation sports

From Wessel, J.A., & Kelly, L. (1986). *Achievement-based curriculum development in physical education.* Philadelphia, PA: Lea & Febiger; reprinted by permission.

SPARK curriculum. These two curricula are inclusive in nature and provide activities with suggestions on how to make modifications for students at different skill levels. Critics of packaged physical education programs argue that they may not be culturally responsive, relevant, or best meet the needs of the students at the local level.

The Physical Best program is a comprehensive health-related program that promotes inclusion through educating all students regardless of athletic talent, physical and mental abilities, or disabilities (SPARK Physical Education Curriculum, n.d., para. 1). The Physical Best curriculum is linked to the FITNESSGRAM assessment program and provides ready-to-use plans that are aligned with the national

standards. This curriculum has become increasingly popular with physical educators as it teaches cognitive knowledge through physical activity.

SPARK is an evidence-based organization dedicated to developing, delivering, and researching the effectiveness of its physical education and physical activity programs, resource development, and professional development offerings to increase the number of healthy school communities. The SPARK program was designed to be an inclusive, active, and fun curriculum and has been proven to work with both physical education specialists and classroom teachers (Dowda, Sallis, McKenzie, Rosengard, & Kohl, 2005). "SPARK curricula are designed to be practical and effective tools for all physical education/activity providers and are presented in three-ring binders for fast access to materials" (SPARK, n.d., para. 2). The lesson plans include simple directions, important teaching cues, assessments, and activity modifications for students at different skills levels. Programs such as SPARK can support quality physical education lessons, but physical education specialists should always consider their students, instructional time, and the whole child while developing their individual physical education programs.

Status of Physical Education

Quality physical education is an essential element in the formative growth of school-age students, and many organizations and government agencies have released guidelines for how much physical activity and physical education students should receive. Among other critical elements of a quality physical education program, NASPE recommends that schools provide 150 minutes per week of instructional physical education for elementary school students and 225 minutes per week for middle and high school students throughout the school year (SHAPE, 2014).

The prevalence of physical education is inconsistent throughout the country, as recommended physical education instructional time differs among grade levels and states. The 2012 survey of physical education coordinators in all 50 states and the District of Columbia revealed the following information (NASPE & American Heart Association, 2012):

- The majority of states (74.5%) mandate physical education for Grades K–12, but most do not mandate specific amounts of time, and more than half allow exemptions, waivers, and/or substitutions.
- Physical education is mandated in elementary schools in 84.3% of states.
- Physical education is mandated in middle schools in 80.4% of states.
- Physical education is mandated in high schools in 86.3% of states.
- At the elementary school level, only 31.4% of states specify a minimum "minutes per week" or "minutes per day" that students must participate in physical education. Only three states (New Jersey, Louisiana, and Florida) require the nationally recommended 150 minutes per week.

Another of NASPE's critical elements of a quality physical education program states that physical education should be delivered by certified/licensed physical education teachers. The 2012 Shape of the Nation (NASPE & American Heart Association, 2012) reported that the majority of states require that physical education teachers have some sort of licensure or certification. Of the states that reported data in the Shape of the Nation survey, licensure was required at the elementary level in 78.4% of the states, at the middle school level in 82.4% of the states, and at the high school level in 90.2% of the states.

WHAT IS ADAPTED PHYSICAL EDUCATION?

As noted previously, the legislators who created PL 94-142 believed that students with disabilities could benefit from physical education and that physical education services, modified when necessary, should be a part of all students' educational programs. Although legislators realized that many students with disabilities could participate in general physical education without the need for modifications to the general program, they also realized that some students with disabilities would have difficulty safely and successfully participating in and benefiting from general physical education without modifications or support. Thus, various adaptations would be necessary for these students to truly benefit from physical education. When students with disabilities need extra support to benefit from general physical education or when these students need a special physical education program, they qualify for "specially designed physical education," or adapted physical education (Auxter, Pyfer, Zittel, & Roth, 2010; Winnick, 2011, pp. 3–20).

Definition of Adapted Physical Education

Adapted physical education is a subdiscipline of physical education with an emphasis on physical education for students with disabilities. The term adapted physical education generally refers to school-based programs for students ages 3–21; the more global term adapted physical activity refers to programs across the lifespan, including post-school programs (Sherrill, 2004). Because this book focuses on school-age students, the term adapted physical education is used throughout.

Various definitions of adapted physical education have been developed over the past 20 years (e.g., Auxter et al., 2010; Sherrill, 2004; Winnick, 2011, pp. 3–20). However, the following definition by Dunn and Leitschuh seems to be most appropriate: "Adapted physical education programs are those that have the same objectives as the regular physical education program, but in which adjustments are made in the regular offerings to meet the needs and abilities of exceptional students" (2010, p. 5). Note that both general and adapted physical education share the same objectives. In addition, the components of physical education as defined in IDEA 2004 should be included in a comprehensive adapted physical education program. The major difference between general and adapted physical education is that in the latter, "adjustments" or adaptations are made to the regular offerings to ensure safe, successful, and beneficial participation (Dunn & Leitschuh, 2010; Sherrill, 2004). Simple adaptations such as asking a peer to provide assistance, modifying the equipment and rules of games, or providing alternative activities under the guidance of a trained adapted physical education specialist do little to disrupt the learning environment and create a productive and enjoyable physical education experience for all students.

Many adaptations can be implemented within the general physical education setting. For example, a high school–age student who has spina bifida can work on special stretching exercises during general physical education while her peers perform their warm-up activities. Similarly, this student can work on individual goals such as pushing her wheelchair forward and developing the ability to play wheelchair basketball while her peers practice their running and regular basketball skills. This student may require special equipment such as a wheelchair, a lower basket, and a smaller, lighter ball, as well as extra assistance in the form of a peer tutor, volunteer, or paraprofessional. However, she can easily be accommodated in the general program and still receive an appropriate, individualized physical education program designed to meet her unique needs.

Objectives of adapted and general physical education are the same, and how objectives are prioritized vary from individual to individual in both. Therefore, although individualization is one of the hallmarks of adapted physical education programs, the wide range of skill level in general physical education classes requires careful planning for students without disabilities as well. However, meeting specific objectives with students with disabilities is crucial. For example, maintenance of low levels of health-related physical fitness might be a priority for a student with muscular dystrophy or cystic fibrosis but not for a physically fit student without disabilities. Because activities that promote physical fitness, motor skill development, and social development are offered to some extent or another in general physical education, it is relatively easy to accommodate students with disabilities who have these goals as priorities.

Finally, it is important to note that adapted physical education should not be viewed as a place a child goes or as a person who provides these special services. Rather, adapted physical education is a service that can be provided in a variety of settings (including general physical education) and by a variety of qualified people (including, in many states, a general physical education specialist). Thus, a child with a disability could receive adapted physical education services (individual goals and objectives for physical education) within a general physical education setting provided by a general physical education teacher. Decisions regarding what services will be provided, where they will be provided, and who will provide them vary from state to state but generally are left up to each child's IEP team.

Who Is Qualified to Provide Physical Education Services?

Legislators wanted to make sure that only "qualified" individuals would provide physical education services to students with disabilities. However, legislators felt strongly that determining who was qualified to provide services to students with disabilities (including physical education services) should be left up to each state: "Qualified means that a person has met State educational agency approved or recognized certification, licensing, registration, or other comparable requirements which apply to the area in which he or she is providing special education or related services" (Federal Register, 1977, p. 42479). This has not changed with any of the reauthorizations of IDEA. Legislators intended for states to establish requirements for physical education specialists who work with students who have disabilities (Kelly, 1991; National Consortium for Physical Education and Recreation for Individuals with Disabilities [NCPERID], 2006). States that do not require any special training/licensure often certify many professionals as qualified to provide physical education services to students with disabilities. In many states, these professionals include general physical education teachers, special education teachers, and general classroom teachers. Unfortunately, many of these qualified professionals do not have any training, knowledge, or experience to provide physical education to students with disabilities (Block & Obrusnikova, 2007; Combs, Elliott, & Whipple, 2010; Doulkeridou et al., 2011; Hersman & Hodge, 2010).

Since the mid-1990s, a national examination known as the Adapted Physical Education National Standards (APENS, 2014a; NCPERID, 2006) examination has been offered. Individuals who have a baccalaureate degree in physical education, a minimum of 200 hours of practicum experiences in adapted physical education, satisfactory completion of a minimum of 9 credits in adapted physical education coursework and 3 credits of coursework from a related field (e.g., special education, speech therapy, occupational therapy, physical therapy, recreation, psychology) as documented with official college/university transcripts (up to 3 credits of adapted physical education coursework can be awarded with documented years of experience teaching adapted physical education), and a valid teaching license can sit for the exam. Those who pass the exam become Certified Adapted Physical Educators (CAPE; APENS, 2014b). It is hoped that more professionals will become CAPEs and that more states will recognize the need to hire more CAPEs to provide physical education to students with disabilities. There are no requirements for local school districts to hire CAPEs (NCPERID, 2006).

A 2010 position paper from the American Association for Physical Activity and Recreation (AAPAR) and the NCPERID also provided criteria for "highly qualified" personnel who teach adapted physical education to students with disabilities. Specifically, they identified the following minimum requirements for all adapted physical education professionals who would be considered "highly qualified" (AAPAR & NCPERID, 2010):

- *Requirement 1:* Bachelor's degree in physical education teacher education and state licensure to teach physical education

- *Requirement 2:* Twelve semester hours specifically addressing the educational needs of students with disabilities, with a minimum of nine semester hours specific to adapted physical education

- *Requirement 3:* Minimum of 150 hours practicum experience

- *Requirement 4:* Professional preparation programs must be based on standards for adapted physical education.

SUMMARY

Physical education consists of a diverse program of activities, including motor skills, physical fitness, and individual and team sports. These activities should be presented in such a way that they facilitate the achievement of global physical education objectives, including motor skill competency, social and cognitive development, and healthy self-concept. How much time and emphasis a particular student spends working on a particular component (as well as how these skills are presented) varies based on several factors such as a student's age, abilities, and interests.

Physical education is considered a direct service in IDEA and its amendments, which means that all students, including students with disabilities, are required to receive physical education. In addition, specialized physical education services, which can be provided in inclusive or separate settings, should be provided to any child with disabilities who requires them. Physical education plays a key role in developing physically literate citizens.

CHAPTER 2

What Is Inclusion?

Martin E. Block and Iva Obrusnikova

OBJECTIVES

1. Describe the evolution of inclusion, including the early years, special schools, mainstreaming, and the regular education initiative

2. Understand least restrictive environment and the continuum of placements as defined by the Individuals with Disabilities Education Improvement Act

3. Define inclusion

4. Describe the rationale for inclusion as well as the benefits of inclusion

5. Describe key aspects of No Child Left Behind as they relate to placement decisions and "highly qualified teachers"

6. Describe federal activity, most notably the U.S. Government Accountability Office's report *Creating Equal Opportunities for Children and Youth with Disabilities to Participate in Physical Education and Extracurricular Athletics* and the U.S. Department of Education's response

7. Describe specific philosophies that support inclusion

8. Summarize research on inclusion in physical education

Jeremy has been a proud member of Rocky Crest Elementary School since kindergarten. As a rising fifth grader, he is one of the elite students at school—the oldest and biggest group (and if you ask Jeremy, the smartest group, too!) that will be moving on to middle school next year. But Jeremy is not worried about sixth grade. He is excited about starting his last year at Rocky Crest. Outsiders might find Jeremy's attitude somewhat surprising, given that Jeremy has Down syndrome. He clearly is smaller than all his peers, has very little speech, wears glasses and hearing aids, and does academic work on par more with kindergartners and first graders rather than fifth graders. His latest evaluation found that his IQ is in the range of 40–50, and the school district has given him the special education label of moderate intellectual disability.

Although some might argue that Jeremy would be better served in a special education class for children with intellectual disabilities, Jeremy has been in general education classes (including general physical education) since kindergarten. Not only has he been enrolled in general education classes but also his peers and his teachers have always treated Jeremy as a true member of the class, and he has been making excellent progress toward his individualized education program (IEP) goals and objectives. This often requires informal meetings with all the students in the class, the classroom teacher, and the special education teacher. But once everyone learned about Jeremy, his abilities and interests, his unique needs, and how important it is to make Jeremy truly a member of the class, the students and the teachers did a wonderful job of accepting Jeremy. The special education teacher also explained to Jeremy's general education teachers and to his classmates that Jeremy usually needs to work on different skills from other students but that Jeremy could work on these different skills in the general education environment with support from his peers and from his special education teacher. For example, when Jeremy was in fourth grade, his classmates worked on fractions and decimals. During this time, Jeremy worked on reading the price tags on clothing and food labels and simple addition using pretend dollar bills. A peer sitting next to him often helped Jeremy, checking his work and guiding him to the next activity in his packet.

Physical education was a fun time for Jeremy when he was in kindergarten and in first and second grade. However, starting in third grade, physical education became a little more of a struggle for Jeremy. He was clearly falling further behind his peers. Jeremy could see how much better his peers were than he was in physical fitness, ball skills, and games. This started to frustrate Jeremy, and he began to act out or just sit in the corner. Fortunately, Mrs. Hobbs (his general physical educator) had worked with Jeremy since he was a kindergartner. She knew that she also had the support of the special education teacher and a traveling adapted physical education specialist who came to work with Jeremy one-to-one on locomotor patterns and ball skills. Adaptations to help Jeremy were not that difficult to create and implement, and before long Jeremy was back to his old self, doing the best he could with that ear-to-ear smile.

First, Mrs. Hobbs talked to Jeremy about his abilities and all the things he could do. For example, Jeremy was really good at kicking balls and performing log rolls. She also reminded Jeremy that every year, he had the best score on the sit-and-reach test of flexibility. That made Jeremy smile. She then reminded Jeremy that physical education at Rocky Crest was a time for everyone to improve. It did not matter how good you were; it only mattered how hard you tried and whether you achieved the goals you created for yourself for each skill.

Jeremy soon began to participate again. During the mile run, Jeremy knew that his goal was to walk the long straight part and run the shorter straight part of the track that Mrs. Hobbs had laid out around the soccer field. Jeremy knew that if he could just do this run–walk–run–walk that Mrs. Hobbs would be proud of him. It also helped that Jeremy's peers would encourage him every time they ran past him. During a throwing unit, Jeremy knew that he could stand closer to the target. In fact, Mrs. Hobbs encouraged all the students to choose a

distance and a target that allowed them to throw using the correct overhand pattern. Jeremy was surprised to see some of his classmates standing at the same distance that he did and aiming at the same target. And as with the encouragement during the mile run, it was fun to have Jeremy's classmates remind him of the correct throwing pattern and then tell him he was doing a good job. Jeremy liked trying to say the words "side-orientation" and "step with opposite foot." And when the class played tagging and fleeing games for warm-ups, Jeremy was as successful as his peers at avoiding being tagged and tagging. Jeremy was pretty sure he remembered his classmates being faster, but he was surprised at his own speed and ability to catch his friends. (It was nice that his classmates helped Jeremy by running a little slower when he was "it.")

Although this scenario may seem too good to be true, such programs are being implemented in many schools. When done right, inclusion demonstrates that students with disabilities can receive an appropriate and challenging education within the general physical education setting (Block & Obrusnikova, 2007). But what exactly does *inclusion* mean? This chapter reviews the concepts of the least restrictive environment (LRE), mainstreaming, the regular (general) education initiative, and inclusion. Included is a rationale for inclusion programs as well as a review of research that has demonstrated the potential success of inclusive physical education programs.

EVOLUTION OF INCLUSION

The Early Years: Limited Access to Education

Inclusion has grown out of a long history of how individuals with disabilities are viewed. The biggest hurdle for children with disabilities in the first part of the 20th century was simply to receive any special education. Children with mild disabilities were placed in general education classes without any special support. As long as they kept up with the other students in the class and did not cause any problems, the teacher and their classmates accepted them. There were no special services and no trained specialists to help the child with disabilities or the general education teacher (Lewis & Doorlag, 1991). If the child was falling behind, causing problems, or was perceived as having disabilities that were too severe for the child to benefit from education, then the child was simply sent home and excluded from the public schools (Beirne-Smith, Patton,

& Hill, 2015; Karagiannis, Stainback, & Stainback, 1996; Sigmon, 1983). As noted by Sigmon, "Almost all children who were wheelchair-bound, not toilet trained, or considered uneducable were excluded because of the problems that schooling would entail" (1983, p. 3). The one exception was special schools for children who were deaf or blind.

Special Schools/Special Classes

From 1950 to the early 1970s, educating children with disabilities was done primarily in special schools. Initially, parents who were frustrated with the lack of special education for their children with disabilities within the public schools founded many of these special schools on their own. Many of these schools were in the basements of churches, with parents serving as teachers. These parents also formed groups such as the Association for Retarded Citizens (now known as The Arc) to advocate for more educational opportunities for their children (Beirne-Smith et al., 2015; Karagiannis et al., 1996). This advocacy as well as a new awareness of the needs and capabilities of children with disabilities led to the public schools developing special schools or special classes for children with disabilities. For example, the New York City Board of Education established hundreds of schools for children who were "disturbed" and "maladjusted" (Kauffman, 1993). In other communities, one school within a district was dedicated to all children with a particular type of disability. If there were several special classes, then a wing or annex of the school housed these special classes.

Special schools and classes were developed based on the reasoning that children with disabilities needed a highly structured, very intense, and unique teaching environment conducted by a trained specialist (Lewis & Doorlag, 1991). It was also understood that children with disabilities were not wanted in general schools or classrooms, and their removal would inevitably benefit children without disabilities (Chaves, 1977). Even when special classes were housed in general school buildings, rarely did students with disabilities (or, for that matter, the staff who served these students) become true members of the school. And children with more severe disabilities were still excluded from education in many states (Stainback, Stainback, & Bunch, 1989).

The most popular model for educating children with disabilities was special schools that had special education teachers and therapists with special training and who used special materials, equipment, and teaching methodologies. Although such special training was certainly warranted, the end result was a rather elaborate dual system of education with general education on the one hand and special education on the other (Stainback et al., 1989). Programs for children with specific types of disabilities became so specialized that different day and residential facilities were created for children with learning disabilities, hearing impairments, visual impairments, intellectual disabilities, emotional disturbance, and physical disabilities. (Many of these special schools are still in existence today.)

While the special school/special class model proliferated in the 1960s and early 1970s, many were beginning to find fault with the system. Reports to Congress in the early 1970s suggested that labeling and separating children with disabilities from their peers without disabilities led to stigma, ridicule, and poor self-image (Lewis & Doorlag, 1991; Osgood, 2007; Turnbull, 1990).

Second, there was a concern that many children with disabilities were placed in special programs without first determining whether the student could benefit from general education placement (a practice that continues today despite the LRE mandate; Brown, 1994; Causton & Theoharis, 2014; Stainback et al., 1989). There was no effort to determine if individually prescribed curricular and instructional adaptations could occur within the general setting (Block, 1994; Snell & Drake, 1994; Snell & Eichner, 1989). Furthermore, it was becoming clear that many children with disabilities were able to participate at least in some of the activities of the general class, and almost all could benefit from contact with their typically developing peers (Lewis & Doorlag, 1991; Osgood, 2007).

Third, following the *Brown v. Board of Education* (1954) ruling, there was evidence suggesting that separate but equal self-contained classrooms tended to be unequal (Karagiannis et al., 1996; Stainback et al., 1989; Taylor, 1988). Special class placement in the 1960s and early 1970s often meant having the "worst" teacher, the most inferior facilities, and limited educational materials (Lewis & Doorlag, 1991). Stories about being placed in a small room in the basement of the school next to the boiler or having untrained teachers were not uncommon at the time. In addition, children with disabilities who were in special classes in general schools were inexplicably excluded from assemblies and other schoolwide activities (Lewis & Doorlag, 1991).

Fourth, there was growing concern over the "terminal aspects of special education" (Turnbull,

1990, p. 150). At the time (and still evident today), children with disabilities were placed in separate special education programs; many of these children would spend the rest of their education in these separate programs (Taylor, 1988). Tracking students with disabilities into special classes without any opportunity to move out of these classes was common (Karagiannis et al., 1996).

In addition to the problems associated with special schools and special classes, there was a growing awareness of civil rights. The *Brown v. Board of Education* decision as well as the Civil Rights Act of 1964 (PL 88-352) led to examination of the practice of separating children with disabilities from the mainstream of public education (Beirne-Smith et al., 2015; Osgood, 2007; Stainback et al., 1989). There was also increasing advocacy for children with disabilities to learn in a more normalized school environment with their peers without disabilities (Karagiannis et al., 1996; Nirje, 1969; Wolfensberger, 1972). And lawsuits in Pennsylvania (*Pennsylvania Association for Retarded Children v. Commonwealth of Pennsylvania*, 1971) and the District of Columbia (*Mills v. Board of Education of District of Columbia*, 1972) established the rights of children with disabilities within these jurisdictions to a free appropriate public education.

Federal Intervention: Individuals with Disabilities Education Act and Least Restrictive Environment

Out of this dissatisfaction with special education and a realization that children with disabilities could benefit from more interactions with children without disabilities, the federal government enacted the Education for All Handicapped Children Act in 1975 (PL 94-142). Now known as the Individuals with Disabilities Education Act (IDEA), this landmark legislation guaranteed the rights of individuals with disabilities to a free appropriate public education. Included in this legislation was a provision designed to ensure that children with disabilities would have greater opportunities to be placed in general education programs and to interact with peers without disabilities. Termed the *least restrictive environment* in IDEA, the provision directs public agencies to provide the following:

(1) To the maximum extent appropriate, children with disabilities, including children in public or private institutions or other care facilities, are educated with children who are not disabled; and

(2) That special classes, separate schooling, or other removal of children with disabilities from the regular

educational environment occurs only when the nature or severity of the disability is such that education in regular classes with the use of supplementary aids and services cannot be achieved satisfactorily. (20 U.S.C. § 1412[5][B])

This passage suggests that the LRE for students with disabilities was, whenever possible, the same environment in which students without disabilities received their education. Clearly, lawmakers advocated placing students with disabilities in general schools and general classrooms (including general physical education) whenever possible (Aufsesser, 1991; Osgood, 2007; Taylor, 1988). This passage also suggested that *appropriate* placement of students with disabilities into general settings may necessitate the use of supplementary aids, support, and services. Without such support, the student may fail in the general setting. In other words, it might not be the setting that is inappropriate but rather the support that is given to a student within that setting (Block & Krebs, 1992). The LRE provision is still contained in the most recent reauthorization, IDEA 2004 (PL 108-446).

Although segregated placement was not prohibited under the law, school districts were required to clearly demonstrate that a child with a disability placed in a separate setting could not be satisfactorily educated within the general setting, even with supplementary aids and services (Arnold & Dodge, 1994; Hollis & Gallegos, 1993; Lipton, 1994; Maloney, 1994; Osborne, 1996). Lawmakers wanted to prevent the unnecessary placement of children with disabilities in separate programs while ensuring that students with and without disabilities were educated together whenever possible. The practice of simply placing students in separate programs based on a label or preplacement evaluation was considered a violation of the intent of the act (Bateman & Chard, 1995; Lipton, 1994; Maloney, 1994; Osborne, 1996).

However, placement options other than the general education classroom for children with disabilities were still required under the law. Lawmakers made this clear when they added a statement regarding a "continuum of alternative placements":

(a) Each public agency shall ensure that a continuum of alternative placements is available to meet the needs of children with disabilities for special education and related services.

(b) The continuum. . .must—

(1) Include the alternative placements listed in the definition of special education (instruction in regular classes, special classes, special

schools, home instruction, and instruction in hospitals and institutions); and

(2) Make provisions for supplementary services (such as resource room or itinerant instruction) to be provided in conjunction with regular class placement. (IDEA 2004, 20 U.S.C. §§ 1400 *et seq.*)

An example of a continuum of placement options for physical education can be found in Table 2.1. Note that, by strict definition of the law, school districts should offer these or similar options for physical education placement because not all children with disabilities within a district can be accommodated within only one or two of these options. For example, a child with cerebral palsy who is hospitalized could not receive physical education within the general setting.

Although the continuum of placement provision is important and continues to be a part of IDEA, it should be read within context. Data presented to Congress in the 1970s showed that more than half of the students with disabilities in the United States were in educational programs that were deemed inappropriate for their needs, and an estimated 1 million children with disabilities were excluded entirely from the public school system. Prior to 1975, many children with disabilities resided at home, in residential facilities, or in hospitals. The few day programs that were available for students with disabilities usually were separate from public school buildings (e.g., in churches or rented office spaces). In most cases, these residential facilities, hospitals, and day programs did not provide any systematic educational programs (Brown, 1994; Stainback et al., 1989). Rather, these children were more or less "warehoused"; their basic needs were taken care of but not their educational and social needs. As noted by Turnbull (1990), the dual system of education prior to 1975 had a variety of effects, one of which was the denial of educational opportunities for children with disabilities.

In light of the exclusion of educational opportunities, lawmakers made a clear statement that regardless of where a child with a disability resides or the level of severity of disability, he or she still must receive education commensurate with individual abilities and needs. Thus, even children who were not in traditional school programs were guaranteed free appropriate public education under the law (Turnbull, 1990). It was never the intent of lawmakers to have these separate placements become an option for placing students with disabilities unless such placements were determined "least restrictive" for the child with a disability. Lawmakers appeared to favor having students with disabilities educated alongside peers without disabilities whenever appropriate. It seems unlikely that they meant for the continuum statement to serve as a justification for placement in these separate settings (Taylor, 1988; Turnbull, 1990).

In summary, Congress created the educational setting and LRE statements in the federal laws as a reaction to inappropriate special education practices at the time. These statements showed Congress's strong preference that children with and without disabilities should be educated together to the maximum extent possible. In addition, LRE brought attention to the notion that most children with disabilities could receive an appropriate education within the general setting if given supplementary services and aids. A continuum was presented to ensure that students already placed in these more restrictive environments would receive appropriate educational programs. Finally, the law clearly noted that all placement decisions needed to be made on an individual basis.

Mainstreaming

Administrators and educators in 1975 were faced with the dilemma of implementing the provisions and mandates of PL 94-142. It was clear that lawmakers wanted as many children with disabilities as appropriate to be educated alongside children without disabilities. But how to provide special education within the general setting was

Table 2.1. Sample of continuum of placement options for physical education

- Full-time general physical education (GPE), no support needed
- Full-time GPE, accommodations needed (e.g., interpreter, adapted equipment, special instructions)
- Adapted physical education (APE) provided within the GPE setting (child has unique goals and objectives and needs special accommodations, but accommodations can be carried out within the GPE setting)
- APE provided within GPE setting, direct support from APE specialist (APE specialist comes into GPE to help child work on his or her unique goals and objectives and with special accommodations)
- APE provided part time within GPE and part time in a special APE class
- APE provided full time in special APE class in general school building
- APE provided full time in special APE class in special school
- APE provided full time in special APE class, either at home, in a hospital, or in a treatment facility

never really made clear. Slowly, students with disabilities were moved from special schools to special classes within general schools, and more efforts were made to integrate children with disabilities into general education classes and general school activities when it was deemed appropriate. However, determining when to place children with disabilities into general education programs and how to support these children within special programs was confusing to many professionals. In an effort to provide some direction as to how to implement the law, the Council for Exceptional Children (CEC, 1975) coined the term *mainstreaming* to describe the process of placing students with disabilities in general education classes with appropriate support services as determined by the student's IEP. CEC suggested that mainstreaming entail the following:

- Providing the most appropriate education for each student in the least restrictive setting

- Placing students based on assessed educational needs rather than clinical labels

- Providing support services to general educators so they may effectively serve children with disabilities in the general setting

- Uniting general and special education to help students with disabilities have equal educational opportunities

Likewise, CEC noted that mainstreaming did not entail the following:

- Wholesale return of all exceptional children to general classes

- Permitting children with special needs to remain in general classes without the support services they needed

- Ignoring the need of some children for a more specialized program that could be provided in the general education program

Despite this definition, mainstreaming became associated with unsuccessful dumping of students with disabilities into general education classes without support (DePaepe, 1984; Grosse, 1991; Lavay & DePaepe, 1987). In contrast to what CEC suggested, children with disabilities who were mainstreamed into general education classes (including general physical education classes) were asked to follow the same curricular content, use the same materials and instruction, and follow the same pace as the other students in the class. Not surprising, many children with disabilities failed in such settings. The term *mainstreaming* has been so misused that it is rarely used today in special education literature.

Regular Education Initiative

Despite the setback with mainstreaming, more and more children with disabilities were receiving some or all of their education in general education settings. In addition, research in the 1970s and 1980s began to show that special class placements were rather ineffective in educating students with disabilities (e.g., Madden & Slavin, 1983; Schnorr, 1990; Semmel, Gottlieb, & Robinson, 1979; Wang & Baker, 1986). For example, Wang, Reynolds, and Walberg (1987) suggested that traditional "pull-out" programs were limited for a variety of reasons, including that the system for classifying students with disabilities was not educationally sound, that there was virtually no evidence to suggest that students with disabilities were making any educational gains simply based on special education placement, and that special class placement promoted isolation and stigmatization.

In 1986, Madeleine Will (then assistant secretary for the Office of Special Education and Rehabilitative Services, U.S. Department of Education) called for a regular education initiative (REI). In her article "Educating Students with Learning Problems: A Shared Responsibility," Will (1986) argued that the dual system of separate special and general education was not effective for students with mild disabilities. Will suggested several changes to the dual system, all of which were designed to appropriately serve students with disabilities in general education. She proposed increased instructional time, empowerment of principals to control all programs and resources at the building level, provision of support systems for general education teachers, and the use of new approaches such as curriculum-based assessment, cooperative learning, and personalized curricula (Will, 1986). Proponents of REI encouraged the scaling back of traditional special education classrooms in favor of a new merger between special and general education.

Some advocates noted that students with severe disabilities could learn important life skills in the general setting without interfering with the program for students without disabilities (Snell, 1988; Snell & Eichner, 1989; Stainback & Stainback, 1990; Taylor, 1988). In addition, heterogeneous grouping actually enriched all students (Stainback & Stainback, 1990). Although REI was initially argued from a philosophical/moral point of view, research began to support including students with severe disabilities in general education (e.g., Chadsey-Rusch, 1990; Condon, York, Heal, & Fortschneider, 1986; Peck, Donaldson, & Pezzoli, 1990; York, Vandercook, MacDonald, Heise-Neff, & Caughey, 1992).

WHAT IS INCLUSION?

Inclusion is an outgrowth of the regular education initiative of the 1980s and is used to describe the philosophy of merging special and general education (Lipsky & Gartner, 1987; O'Brien, Forest, Snow, & Hasburg, 1989; Stainback et al., 1989; Taylor, 1988). The term reflects a philosophy in which all children, regardless of abilities or disabilities, are educated within the same environment, an environment where each child's individual needs are met (Causton & Theoharis, 2014; Downing, 2002; Karagiannis et al., 1996). The philosophy of inclusion is perhaps best summed up by the following statement: "Although some children, especially those with severe and multiple disabilities, may have unique ways of learning, separating them from others who learn in a different way is unnecessary and could prevent them from achieving their full potential" (Downing, 2002, p. xii). It is also important to note that an inclusion philosophy goes beyond simply physically placing a child in a general education classroom (Block, 1999; Bricker, 1995; Brown et al., 1989; Downing, 2002; Ferguson, 1995; Snell, 1991; Stainback & Stainback, 1990). As noted by Stainback and Stainback, "An inclusive school is a place where everyone belongs, is accepted, supports, and is supported by peers and other members of the school community in the course of having his/her educational needs met" (1990, p. 3).

Embedded within this definition was the understanding that children with disabilities would receive an individually determined, appropriate program with supplementary services and supports to meet their unique needs (Block, 1994; Stainback & Stainback, 1990, 1991). However, these services would be provided to the child with a disability within the general education environment (Downing, 2002). In terms of physical education services, this meant that individually determined goals, objectives, and accommodations would be provided within the general physical education setting by an adapted physical education specialist, trained general physical education specialist, trained teacher assistant, or trained peer tutor (Block, 1999). This notion of bringing services to the general education setting provided continual opportunities for the child with disabilities to interact with, learn from, and form friendships with peers while ensuring that the child received an appropriate, individualized program (Downing, 1996; Stainback & Stainback, 1990, 1991).

Another critical tenet of the inclusion philosophy was that children with disabilities were the responsibility of both general and special education staff (Downing, 2002; Giangreco & Doyle, 2007; Givner & Haager, 1995; Sailor, Gee, & Karasoff, 1993; Stainback & Stainback, 1990). Unlike traditional self-contained programs in which the special education teacher (with the support of related services personnel) was solely responsible for a child's education, in inclusive programs, it was the responsibility of all the school staff to make sure that each child's educational program was carried out appropriately (Downing, 1996; Sailor et al., 1993; Stainback & Stainback, 1990, 1991). However, it was unreasonable to expect the resources, knowledge base, and personnel available in general education to serve the needs of children both with and without disabilities (Stainback & Stainback, 1991). Yet, it also was becoming clear that special education resources and personnel could not serve all the needs of children with disabilities. The inclusion philosophy suggested that only through the merger of resources, knowledge, and talents of general and special education could both children with and without disabilities receive a comprehensive, appropriate education (Lipsky & Gartner, 1998; Sailor et al., 1993; Stainback & Stainback, 1991). Continual support and training for the general education teacher was certainly required to make such a merged system work. In addition, the use of various coteaching arrangements (i.e., the general and special education teacher dividing and sharing class instruction) might be an effective way to facilitate inclusive programs (Lipsky & Gartner, 1998). For example, Block and Zeman (1996) noted the effectiveness of having the adapted physical education specialist work with students with and without disabilities and coteach various aspects of the general physical education lesson. Coteaching arrangements also have been advocated by Grenier (2011), Lipsky and Gartner (1998), and Sherrill (2004).

Providing services within general education did not necessarily mean that all services for a particular child would always take place within the general education setting (Block, 1994; Brown et al., 1991; Lipsky & Gartner, 1998; Sailor et al., 1993). For limited periods of time during the school day, a child with a disability (as well as any other child in the class) could receive specialized instruction using

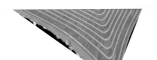

specialized equipment in specialized environments outside the general education classroom. For example, a high school student with severe intellectual disabilities may need extra time in the locker room with the support of a teacher assistant getting dressed to go back to class. This student may leave general physical education 10 minutes early so he can work on these functional dressing skills. However, this student is still perceived as a member of the general physical education class (Block, 1994; Lipsky & Gartner, 1998).

Historic Rationale for Inclusion

Students with disabilities have traditionally been viewed as fundamentally different from students without disabilities. At the time inclusion was first being proposed, several authors argued that a dual system of education is not necessary to provide appropriate educational services to students (e.g., Rainforth, York, & MacDonald, 1992; Snell & Eichner, 1989; Stainback & Stainback, 1991; Will, 1986). For example, Stainback et al. (1989) outlined a rationale for one educational system for all students that included the following key points:

- *Instructional needs of all students vary from individual to individual:* A student with disabilities should be viewed as just another student whose instructional needs should be individualized to optimize learning. Individualization can be implemented in an inclusive setting just as easily as in a segregated setting. For example, most physical education classes are composed of students with varying motor abilities, physical fitness, and knowledge of the rules and strategies of games. Good physical educators present activities in such a way that individual students' needs are accommodated. A student with disabilities is just another student who requires activities to be individualized to accommodate his or her unique abilities.

- *A dual system is inefficient because there is inevitably competition and duplication of services:* The majority of activities presented in general physical education programs are the exact same activities that are presented in specialized adapted physical education programs. For example, most elementary-age students in general physical education work on the development of fundamental motor patterns, perceptual motor skills, physical fitness, and simple rhythms and games. These same activities are appropriate for elementary-age students

with disabilities. Similarly, high school students work on individual and team sports, including lifetime leisure sports and physical fitness. Again, adapted physical education programs designed for high school students with disabilities work on the exact same activities. With a dual system, two professionals are teaching the same activities at the same time. A more logical and cost-effective model would be to include students with disabilities into the general program with modifications as needed to ensure their success.

- *Dual systems foster inappropriate attitudes:* Students with disabilities, especially students who spend most of their time separated from their peers without disabilities, are viewed as different by general education teachers and peers (e.g., Voeltz, 1980, 1982). Teachers assume that educational programs that take place in special education must be extraordinary—that is, special education staff often are viewed as exceptional people who have different skills and abilities from general education staff and who use different equipment and materials with their students. Similarly, students with disabilities often are viewed as more different from than similar to students without disabilities when, in fact, the opposite is true. They probably enjoy watching the same television shows and listening to the same music, cheer for the same sports teams, enjoy the same recreational activities, and hate cleaning their rooms and doing their homework. Unfortunately, teachers and peers who are not exposed to students with disabilities may view them as people who should be pitied, teased, or feared. By combining students with and without disabilities, teachers learn that teaching students with disabilities is not that different from teaching typical students. Similarly, peers without disabilities quickly learn that students with disabilities are more similar than different (Forest & Lusthaus, 1989; Stainback et al., 1989).

Benefits of Inclusion

In addition to the rationale for merging general and special education, there are benefits available in inclusion programs that are not available in segregated settings. Downing (2002), Snell and Eichner (1989), and Stainback and Stainback (199? 990) outlined several benefits of including s   ith disabilities into general educati   ee Tables 2.2 and 2.3).

Table 2.2. Benefits of inclusion for students with disabilities

- Opportunity to learn social skills in integrated, more natural environments with natural cues and consequences; no need to generalize to integrated environments later in life
- More stimulating, motivating environment (e.g., hallways, the cafeteria, the recess yard, the bus loading area); dress, conversations, and social exchanges are characteristic of their age and location
- Opportunity to learn appropriate social skills (e.g., refrain from stigmatizing behavior, use appropriate greetings, wear age-appropriate clothes)
- Availability of age-appropriate role models without disabilities
- Participation in a variety of school activities suited to chronological age and neighborhood (e.g., assemblies, music, art, athletic events)
- Potential for new friendships with peers without disabilities
- Includes parents, special education teachers, and other special education staff into general schools, giving them new experiences and relationships and, thus, less isolation

Sources: Downing (2002); Snell and Eichner (1989); Stainback and Stainback (1985, 1990).

FEDERAL LAWS AFFECTING INCLUSION IN PHYSICAL EDUCATION

In 2001, Congress amended the Elementary and Secondary Education Act of 1965 (PL 89-10) as the No Child Left Behind Act (NCLB). NCLB is essentially a national extension of the standards-based education reform movement based on the Improving America's Schools Act of 1994 (PL 103-382). The major focus of NCLB is "to ensure that all children have a fair, equal, and significant opportunity to obtain a high-quality education and reach, at a minimum, proficiency on challenging State academic achievement standards and State academic assessments" (20 U.S.C. §§ 6301 *et seq.*). It encourages states and school districts to keep up with

Table 2.3. Benefits of inclusion for staff members and students without disabilities

- Special education teachers (as well as adapted physical educators) tend to have higher expectations for students with disabilities in inclusive environments than for those in self-contained environments.
- Special education teachers learn what is appropriate for children without disabilities.
- With guidance from adults, students' attitudes toward students with disabilities improve.
- With guidance from adults, students without disabilities learn to appreciate individual differences.
- Students without disabilities gain perspective. For example, having acne or getting a C on a test seems less devastating when the person next to you is working as hard as he or she can to keep his or her head up and eyes focused.
- Everyone learns to face individuals with disabilities with greater personal knowledge and optimism and less prejudice.

Sources: Downing (2002); Snell and Eichner (1989); Stainback and Stainback (1985, 1990).

standards-based reforms. Two key aspects of the law include new requirements designed to close the achievement gap that exists among students who are economically disadvantaged, are from racial or ethnic minority groups, have disabilities, or have limited English proficiency and to give assurances that there is a highly qualified teacher in each classroom for each subject being taught (Wright, Wright, & Heath, 2004). The act covers all states, school districts, and schools that accept federal Title I grants. (Title I grants provide funding for remedial education programs for poor and disadvantaged children in public and even some private schools [Wright et al., 2004].)

One important concept in NCLB is the provision for "highly qualified teachers." Too often teachers without specific training in their subject area were teaching in the public schools. For example, a teacher without certification in mathematics might be asked to teach an introductory geometry class. Obviously, this teacher—regardless of his or her best intentions—could not teach geometry as well as someone with a strong foundation in mathematics. This is particularly problematic for students in lower income school districts who are more likely than their peers in wealthier districts to have teachers who were not "highly qualified" in the subject matter they are teaching (Wright & Wright, n.d.). As directly stated in the law, physical educators should be trained in all aspects of health and physical education in order to be considered highly qualified. It is important to note that IDEA 2004 also requires school districts to hire special education teachers who are "highly qualified." This new provision has been somewhat controversial for special education teachers who teach multiple content areas. For example, some special education teachers may teach all content areas (mathematics, language arts, science, and social studies). Should these teachers be certified in all of these content areas? Also, although not specifically mentioned in IDEA 2004, a physical education teacher who works with students with disabilities should have training in adapted physical education in order to become highly qualified.

An important concept within the law is the concept of *adequate yearly progress* (AYP). Schools are expected to make AYP toward meeting state standards in reading, mathematics, and science and to measure this progress for each student in order to receive federal funds (Paige, 2003). For example, in Virginia, the AYP for 2005 was that 65% of all students throughout the state pass the reading test (i.e., read at grade level). The AYP calculations permit a school and school district to incorporate a percentage adjustment for children with disabilities who are receiving services under IDEA 2004 and have an IEP. This way, the school will not be adversely affected as the result of providing educational services to children with disabilities (Wright et al., 2004). In most cases, the percentage of student scores that can be exempt from AYP is 1% of the overall school-age population (representing those students with the most severe disabilities). However, this means that the scores of most students with disabilities in the school district will be counted toward AYP. The law recognizes that most students have disabilities that are not related to their cognitive ability and allow them to keep up with their peers academically and take standardized assessments successfully. For example, a student with a visual impairment might need a version of the test in braille. These students with disabilities may require modifications or accommodations in order to take the general assessment; however, they must perform just like other students in their class.

As noted by Wright and Wright (2004),

> Since a large number of students with disabilities would have to fail in order for this failure to have an impact on the district's AYP status, and since a great many students with disabilities can succeed on standardized tests, a finding of "needs improvement" achieves the primary goal of this law—it shines a light on those groups of students for whom the American dream of a quality public school education has not always been a reality. If we allow this light to dim—by exempting the scores of more students from AYP—students with disabilities will recede back into the shadowy backrooms they inhabited for all those years before laws were passed to protect their civil rights.

Federal Activity and Inclusive Physical Education

As noted earlier, IDEA specifically recognizes physical education as a direct service that should be afforded to all students with disabilities. In addition, the LRE mandate specifies students with disabilities should participate in general physical education whenever possible. However, based on concerns from national advocacy organizations and prompted by the U.S. Congress, the U.S. Government Accountability Office (GAO) was asked in 2010 to examine 1) what is known about the physical education opportunities available at schools and how the schools provide them, 2) what is known about the extracurricular athletic opportunities available at schools and how the schools provide

them, and 3) how the U.S. Department of Education assists states and schools in these areas. GAO analyzed federal survey data; reviewed relevant federal laws and regulations; and interviewed state, district, and school officials in selected states, as well as parents and disability association officials. Specific to physical education, the GAO report found most students with disabilities are included in general physical education classes. For many children with disabilities, physical education is the one general education class they regularly take. To facilitate their participation, teachers may make accommodations for some students, such as providing additional modeling or repetition. Unfortunately, whether any accommodations are provided is left up to the individual physical education teacher and his or her knowledge and skills in making accommodations. Furthermore, specific documentation on accommodations might not be specified in a child's IEP. In addition, many state, district, and school officials interviewed for the study cited limited teacher preparation and budget constraints as key challenges to appropriately serving students with disabilities in general physical education. For example, many suggested general physical education teachers needed more training opportunities on working specifically with students with disabilities, yet resources for training were not always available. The report also found the U.S. Department of Education had provided little information or guidance on physical education for students with disabilities (GAO, 2010).

A key recommendation of the GAO report was for the Secretary of Education to facilitate information sharing among states and schools on ways to provide opportunities in physical education and extracurricular athletics to students with disabilities. This recommendation resulted in *Creating Equal Opportunities for Children and Youth with Disabilities to Participate in Physical Education and Extracurricular Athletics*, a report written by the U.S. Department of Education (2011). Perhaps the most important point made in this report was the reaffirmation of the physical education requirement for all students with disabilities specified in IDEA as well as the recognition of the importance of physical education for the lifelong health of all students with disabilities. The 20-page report also contains a summary of suggestions to increase physical education and extracurricular athletic opportunities for students with disabilities, including accessibility, equipment, personnel preparation, teaching styles, management of behavior, program options, curriculum, and assessment strategies.

For example, treadmills were suggested for students with ambulation difficulties in an effort to provide an even, predictable walking surface. In addition, Wii, Xbox, PlayStation, or other entertainment systems should be used to simulate participation in sports that some students with disabilities cannot do in the traditional way. Finally, the report also encouraged states and school districts to provide training opportunities for general physical education teachers on how to adapt physical education classes for students with disabilities. Both the GAO report and the response from the U.S. Department of Education provide support for the importance of physical education and extracurricular sport opportunities for students with disabilities. Yet, both reports clearly identify a persistent lack of teacher training and preparation as key barriers to successful inclusion of physical education for students with disabilities.

SPECIFIC STRATEGIES THAT SUPPORT INCLUSION

Inclusion should not be confused with early attempts at mainstreaming. Mainstreaming tended to place students with disabilities into general education without support. In addition, students often were expected to follow the general curriculum. In contrast, inclusion suggests each student's unique educational needs be met through adaptations to the curriculum and with the provision of supports. The following, adapted from Stainback and Stainback (1990), outlines key strategies regarding inclusion.

Adapt the Curriculum

One of the greatest misconceptions of inclusion is that all students must somehow fit into the existing curriculum. In many cases, the curriculum used in the general class is not appropriate for students with disabilities. In such cases, the curriculum must somehow be adapted to meet the unique educational objectives and learning needs of the student. For example, an elementary student with cerebral palsy may have difficulty performing activities in a typical tumbling/gymnastics unit. This student could work on balance skills, rolls, and movement concepts, but he or she will work on these skills differently. This child might, for example, work on simple sitting balance while his or her peers work on more complex sitting balances such as a v-sit. While other students work on forward and backward rolls, this student might work on independently rolling from the stomach to the back and then getting to a standing position. Note how all students work on the same basic physical education educational objective (movement control) and learn together within the same general physical education activities (tumbling unit), but some students are evaluated using different curriculum objectives.

In some cases, the curriculum may not seem to match the needs of a particular student at all. In such cases, different parts of the curriculum might be presented at different times for different students. For example, a middle school student who is blind may not need to work on lacrosse, an activity found in many physical education curricula in the mid-Atlantic and northeast United States. This student might be given opportunities to feel the equipment and learn the rules of lacrosse, but during most of the lacrosse unit, this student may work on the softball/beep baseball skills of throwing, striking with a bat, and retrieving beep balls. Still, the basic skills of lacrosse are catching with a lacrosse stick, tossing with a lacrosse stick, and advancing the ball by tossing or running. Softball is part of the middle school curriculum and also includes skills of catching (with hands), tossing (throwing), and advancing the ball (striking). Thus, this student works on similar educational objectives (catching, tossing, and advancing a ball) but in a way that is more beneficial to him or her. In addition, this student can work on these skills within the general physical education class. (See Chapters 5, 6, and 7 for more information on adaptations.)

Integrate Personnel and Resources

Another misconception of inclusion is that students with disabilities will be dumped into general programs without support. As noted, the inclusion philosophy directs that students be supported in general education classes. Supports include specialized equipment; special instruction; and personnel such as volunteers, teacher assistants, and education specialists—many of the same supports that would have been given to a student in a segregated program. Students might have special equipment such as walkers, gait trainers, mats, or bolsters that should be brought to general physical education.

Utilize Natural Proportions

One of the reasons early attempts at mainstreaming in physical education often failed was that entire special education classes (up to 10 students) were placed in one general physical education class.

Such a situation was doomed because no physical educator could adequately meet the needs of all these students plus those of a class full of children without disabilities. Inclusion philosophy suggests that students with disabilities be placed following the principle of *natural proportions*, meaning that the normal distribution of individuals with and without disabilities be maintained when placing students in general classes. Data suggest that perhaps 10%–15% of the school-age population has some type of disability, with more who have high-incidence disabilities such as learning disabilities, emotional disabilities, and intellectual disabilities and fewer who have low-incidence disabilities such as cerebral palsy, hearing impairments, and visual impairments. Such numbers translate to two or three students with disabilities (usually mild disabilities) in each class. Such a situation is much more manageable for the general physical educator.

RESEARCH ON INCLUSION IN PHYSICAL EDUCATION

There have been several significant studies from 2005 to 2014 examining issues and questions surrounding inclusion in general physical education. These studies have continued to shed some light onto the realities of inclusion in general physical education. The following provides a brief review of these studies. This review is organized into four themes: 1) support, 2) attitudes of students without disabilities, 3) lack of training and negative attitudes of general physical education teachers, and 4) social isolation of students with disabilities.

Beliefs and Experiences of Students with Disabilities

Regular involvement in physical activity by children and youth is beneficial for the development of children's motor skills, fitness, social competence, and friendships (Pellegrini & Smith, 1998). There is accumulating evidence that children with disabilities do not engage in sufficient amounts of physical activity due to negative social, psychological, and emotional outcomes associated with poor motor competence (e.g., Causgrove & Watkinson, 2002; Pan, 2008). General physical education creates a unique environment that provides many opportunities for physical activity, communication, and quality interpersonal interactions (Tannehill, MacPhail, Halbert, & Murphy, 2013). While the potential for physical activity and social interactions is there, the perceived meanings and consequences of the common practices in general physical education can also make inclusion of children with disabilities in general physical education challenging.

A number of research studies published in the last decade explored inclusion in general physical education from the perspective of students with disabilities (Asbjørnslett & Hemmingsson, 2008; Bredahl, 2013; Fitzgerald, 2005; Herold & Dandolo, 2009; Spencer-Cavaliere & Watkinson, 2010). While these studies reported many benefits of being included in general physical education, they also reported negative experiences expressed by the students with disabilities. The three themes of negative experiences that emerged from the studies are feeling different, lacking competence, and not having friends.

The first theme that emerged from interviews with children and youth with disabilities was the notion of "feeling different" (Bredahl, 2013; Fitzgerald, 2005; Fitzgerald & Stride, 2012; Herold & Dandolo, 2009; Spencer-Cavaliere & Watkinson, 2010). These feelings manifested themselves through 1) the type of activities in which the students were involved (e.g., playing bocce instead of soccer, individual activities instead of class activities), 2) the locations in which the activities were taken place (e.g., away from the class or in a separate room), 3) the types of social roles or activity positions given by the teacher (e.g., spectator, goalie, score keeper), 4) the exemptions and preferential treatment given by the teacher (e.g., waiving the requirement of going outside in the cold weather), 5) the interruptions of and dependency on a personal assistant, and 6) the students' own sense of physicality. "Normalized practices" that are often prevalent in general physical education (Tannehill et al., 2013) promote the type of physicality that is difficult to obtain for most students with disabilities (Fitzgerald, 2005). It promotes specific bodily ideals that are associated with masculinity and mesomorphic body type (Tinning & Glasby, 2002). If a student's physique, behavior, abilities, or skills do not match the norm or are not compatible with the styles, manners, and routines of the setting, the student will most likely struggle to be accepted and feel treated differently by the peers and even the teacher. Some most commonly stated examples of peer reactions to these differences were name calling, staring, and being asked questions about the disability. This may lead to students with disabilities feeling insecure and excluded in general physical education (Asbjørnslett & Hemmingsson, 2008; Fitzgerald, 2005; Spencer-Cavaliere & Watkinson, 2010).

The second most common theme that emerged from the interviews was characterized by the students' perceptions of lack of competence (Asbjørnslett & Hemmingsson, 2008; Bredahl, 2013; Fitzgerald, 2005; Fitzgerald & Stride, 2012; Spencer-Cavaliere & Watkinson, 2010). General physical education provides many opportunities for making one's abilities, skills, and behaviors clearly visible (Tannehill et al., 2013). The interviews revealed that if students with a disability had difficulties executing a task or controlling movements or behaviors due to their disability, they were subjected to their peers noticing the challenges, which caused them to feel embarrassed, incompetent, and inadequate. Such feelings were even more prevalent when peers without disabilities were frustrated with the challenges the students with disabilities faced (e.g., they would get angry when the student did not catch a ball; Bredahl, 2013). While it is expected of general physical education teachers to provide modifications and accommodations to avoid such situations and better meet the needs of their students with disabilities, the qualitative studies (Asbjørnslett & Hemmingsson, 2008; Bredahl, 2013; Fitzgerald, 2005) revealed that not all teachers always listened to their students. The students complained during the interviews that their teachers were either not willing or lacked the knowledge to adjust the demands of the general physical education curriculum to the students' needs. Most students associated the unrealistic demands and the lack of adequate accommodation with their experiences of failing and embarrassment (Bredahl, 2013). Being pushed beyond their individual physical limitations was particularly noted among students with less visible or less comprehensive disabilities such as being partially sighted or having a minor degree of cerebral palsy (Asbjørnslett & Hemmingsson, 2008; Bredahl, 2013). This suggests the importance of assessment in general physical education to appropriately meet the needs of students with disabilities.

The final theme that emerged from the interviews was "not having friends" (Asbjørnslett & Hemmingsson, 2008; Seymour, Reid, & Bloom, 2009; Spencer-Cavaliere & Watkinson, 2010). This theme is closely related to the other two previous themes. The significance of others appears to be an overarching theme of inclusion research from the perspectives of children with disabilities (Janney & Snell, 2006). The findings revealed that friends were more likely to extend invitations to play; offer encouragement; and help the students feel accepted, important, valuable, and included. In contrast, not having friends was associated with feeling excluded, feeling left out, getting teased or laughed at, and having limited engagement in activities. The potency of friendships has the potential to compensate for the student's lack of perceived and actual competence (Spencer-Cavaliere & Watkinson, 2010).

To promote more desirable learning experiences in general physical education for young individuals with disabilities and ultimately increase their levels of physical activity, general physical education teachers need to do a better job of assessing and learning about their students' needs and seek further education or training on how the general physical education curriculum can be adequately adapted so that inclusion of students with disabilities in general physical education is more successful. Using a more natural type of support (e.g., peer tutors rather than paraeducators) may also be necessary to promote social inclusion and friendships (e.g., Klavina & Block, 2008). The shift in the student's perceived competence coupled with the teacher creating an environment that promotes individual progress rather than normative standards, cooperation rather than competition, and friendships or positive social relationships may help students with disabilities demonstrate more adaptive and less maladaptive behaviors (e.g., being off task) in general physical education (Causgrove & Dunn, 2006).

Beliefs and Experiences of Students without Disabilities

A number of research studies have suggested that beliefs of students without disabilities also play a critical role in fostering feelings of acceptance, respect, and perceived competence in students with a disability (e.g., André, Deneuve, & Louvet, 2011; Asbjørnslett & Hemmingsson, 2008; Kalymon, Gettinger, & Hanley-Maxwell, 2010; Obrusnikova, Block, & Dillon, 2010; Obrusnikova, Dillon, Block, & Davis, 2012; Seymour et al., 2009; Spencer-Cavaliere & Watkinson, 2010; Verderber, Rizzo, & Sherrill, 2003). In particular, researchers have found that a majority of middle school–age students without disabilities tend to have positive beliefs toward playing with a peer with a disability in their general physical education classes, which seems to lead to stronger intentions to play with this peer (Obrusnikova & Dillon, 2012; Obrusnikova et al., 2011; Obrusnikova et al., 2012; Verderber et al., 2003). However, there are still students with less favorable beliefs, who may have weaker intentions to play with a peer with a disability in general physical education and contribute to social exclusion.

Evidence exists that various attributes can affect beliefs and consequently intentions of students without disabilities to play with a peer with a disability in general physical education. The most frequently cited attributes of the student without a disability associated with favorable beliefs are being a girl (Obrusnikova & Dillon, 2012; Obrusnikova et al., 2011; Obrusnikova et al., 2012; Verderber et al., 2003) and having strong social responsibility and task-involved goals (Obrusnikova & Dillon, 2012). Students with stronger social responsibility goals (i.e., students with secure, positive relationships with their teachers and peers) have been reported to be less hostile and withdrawn, to engage in more prosocial and less maladaptive behaviors, and, possibly, to be more likely to play with a student with a disability in general physical education (Obrusnikova & Dillon, 2012). Furthermore, students without disabilities with stronger task-involved goals (i.e., students who focus on skill development, demonstration of competence, task mastery, and self-referenced performance) were found to have positive beliefs, whereas students with stronger ego-involved goals (i.e., students who focus on the demonstration or proving of competence, self-worth, and norm-referenced performance) were found to have less positive beliefs to play with a peer with a disability in general physical education (Obrusnikova & Dillon, 2012). One of the explanations for this association is that students with higher task-involved goals may be more focused on being an active participant in all aspects of the learning process compared with those who are more focused on demonstrating competence and outperforming others.

Interviews and self-reports with students without disabilities revealed the following attributes of students with disabilities that were associated with less favorable beliefs or experiences by students without disabilities: 1) having different interests and lower level of competence (André et al., 2013; Kalymon et al., 2010; Obrusnikova et al., 2010; Seymour et al., 2009), 2) not spending time interacting with students without disabilities during and outside of the school (Kalymon et al., 2010; Seymour et al., 2009), 3) having a lower social status among peers (Kalymon et al., 2010; Obrusnikova et al., 2010), 4) being given differential treatment by adults (Kalymon et al., 2010), and 5) being assisted by an adult (Kalymon et al., 2010).

In summary, studies shed light on the mechanisms underlying the effects of certain student and contextual variables on beliefs and intentions of students without disabilities to socially interact with students with disabilities in general physical education. In order to influence those beliefs, certain learning environments or conditions need to be fostered in general physical education. For example, by creating a task-involved motivational climate (e.g., rewarding task mastery and individual improvement), general physical education teachers can emphasize a task orientation for their students and, as such, provide a better learning environment for the inclusion of children with disabilities in general physical education (Chen, 2001). It is also important to foster students' awareness of the affective benefits of interacting with a peer with a disability in general physical education, including the development of a sense of connection, relatedness, and belonging to the class (Kalymon et al., 2010; Obrusnikova et al., 2012; Spencer-Cavaliere & Watkinson, 2010). Furthermore, the teacher needs to provide students without disabilities with knowledge about and positive learning experiences with their peers with a disability in general physical education. This will help them understand the peer's personality, interests, abilities, and limitations and increase their control and confidence in their ability to interact with the peer in general physical education (Kalymon et al., 2010; Obrusnikova et al., 2011; Obrusnikova et al., 2012; Spencer-Cavaliere & Watkinson, 2010). Providing a diversified curriculum that includes cooperative learning experiences, such as adventure education lessons, where communication and teamwork are the focus of the lesson rather than physical performance, may also influence student beliefs and intentions (André et al., 2013; Obrusnikova & Dillon, 2012).

General Physical Educators' Beliefs About Inclusion and Teaching Students with Disabilities

Research conducted with students with disabilities revealed that general physical education teachers are critical to the success of inclusion in general physical education. General physical education teachers waver in their beliefs to work with individuals with disabilities in their general physical education classes based on a number of teacher-related and student-related variables (Ammah & Hodge, 2006). Among the teacher-related variables associated with more favorable beliefs were being a female (Fejgin Talmor, & Erlich, 2005; Meegan & MacPhail, 2006), having adequate academic preparation (Obrusnikova, 2008; Özer et al., 2013; Tripp & Rizzo, 2006), having positive clinical experiences (Obrusnikova, 2008; Özer et al., 2013; Tripp & Rizzo, 2006), receiving information about the student's label or disability (Grenier, 2011; Tripp & Rizzo, 2006), and having a higher level of perceived competence to work with students with disabilities (Obrusnikova, 2008; Özer et al., 2013; Tripp & Rizzo, 2006).

The most common student-related variables associated with favorable beliefs were the type and the degree of a student disability. Research indicates that general physical education teachers hold less favorable beliefs to teach students with severe disabilities or those who exhibit inattentiveness, hyperactivity, or have emotional-behavioral disorders (Ammah & Hodge, 2006; Hersman & Hodge, 2010; Hodge et al., 2009; Obrusnikova, 2008; Sato, Hodge, Murata, & Maeda, 2007). The difficulties that the teachers experience in accommodating a wide range of abilities and managing student behaviors during general physical education instruction seem to adversely affect their self-confidence and perceived behavioral control (Hersman & Hodge, 2010; Hodge et al., 2009; Sato & Hodge, 2009). This ultimately contributes to their negative feelings about inclusion in general. Still, there are teachers who like to take on the challenge of having students with severe disabilities in their classes because they get motivated to educate themselves on how to modify instruction and activities to meet their student's needs in general physical education (Grenier, 2006; Hersman & Hodge, 2010; Hodge et al., 2009).

Most studies reported that patience coupled with more and better quality professional training, positive clinical experiences, and adequate support and teaching conditions are critical in facilitating a teacher's sense of behavioral control associated with teaching efficacy (Hersman & Hodge, 2010; Sato & Hodge, 2009). However, consistent with prior research on inclusion (e.g., LaMaster, Gall, Kinchin, & Siedentop, 1998), general physical education teachers still do not perceive their professional preparation, clinical experiences, support, and teaching conditions as being adequate (Fejgin et al., 2005; Hersman & Hodge, 2010; Jerlinder, Danermark, & Gill, 2010; Sato & Hodge, 2009; Vickerman & Coates, 2009). For example, general physical education teachers in Fejgin et al. (2005) complained that they do not receive support and professional help from the other members of the instructional team such as school counselors, special education teachers, and adapted physical education teachers. This situation is problematic because in many studies on inclusion, teachers express the need for collaboration and professional help when planning instruction (Fejgin et al., 2005; Grenier, 2011). In other studies (e.g., Ammah & Hodge, 2006;

Hersman & Hodge, 2010; Hodge et al., 2009; Sato & Hodge, 2009), teachers were concerned about the lack of parental involvement or administrative support and various contextual issues (e.g., lack of adequate equipment, limited instructional space, large or overcrowded classes), particularly when working with students with emotional and behavioral disorders (Fejgin et al., 2005). The contextual issues were perceived to negatively affect the teaching methods the teachers select, the pace of the lessons, classroom safety, students' level of motivation to participate in activities, and the type of social interaction between students with and without disabilities (Fejgin et al., 2005; Hersman & Hodge, 2010; Suomi, Collier, & Brown, 2003). If the means provided to teachers are not sufficient in order to fulfill the demands, inclusion will not be effective and teachers will not always be in favor of having students with disabilities in their classes (Fejgin et al., 2005; Sato & Hodge, 2009; Vickerman & Coates, 2009).

Again, the findings in this section support the belief that general physical education teachers, although trying, are a bit apprehensive and nervous about including students with disabilities in their program. While no one is asking general physical education teachers to be perfect, the research suggests a few steps to follow if we want to ensure better quality physical education for students with disabilities. First, both teacher training programs and schools must strive to provide high-quality learning experiences to ensure that their graduates feel competent in teaching students with a wide range of disabilities in their classes (Ammah & Hodge, 2006; Elliot, 2008; Tripp & Rizzo, 2006). Rather than adding more specialized coursework in adapted physical education, universities should consider restructuring their physical education program and infuse information about teaching students with disabilities in other pedagogy-based courses (Tripp & Rizzo, 2006). Teaching about the different labels from a medical or categorical perspective in adapted physical education courses should be replaced with a noncategorical approach by teaching about the child's educational needs and the strategies that can be used to effectively address those needs (Grenier, 2011; Tripp & Rizzo, 2006). Classroom experiences should also be supplemented with opportunities to explore and experiment with a variety of teaching behaviors during clinical experiences involving students with a wide range of abilities (Ammah & Hodge, 2006; Tripp & Rizzo, 2006). Second, school districts should engage practicing general physical education teachers in effective professional development initiatives that will focus on programming for children and youth with different abilities (Akuffo & Hodge, 2008; Hodge & Akuffo, 2007). Third, characteristics of the work environment are also important. Teachers are more likely to be receptive to inclusion if they 1) have support from the administration, parents, and direct or indirect services providers; 2) are given smaller classes or larger spaces, and 3) have adapted equipment and assistive devices available to them (Fejgin et al., 2005; Sato & Hodge, 2009; Vickerman & Coates, 2009).

SUMMARY

In summary, there continues to be a growing shift from segregated special education programs to a merger between general and special education. As always, the bottom line in any educational program for students with disabilities is to provide quality programming designed to meet each student's individual needs. With proper preparation and support, quality programming can take place in inclusive settings. Benefits to participants both with and without disabilities provide an additional incentive to integrate students into general programs whenever possible.

CHAPTER 3

A Team Approach to Inclusion in Physical Education

Martin. E. Block, Cathy MacDonald, and John Foley

OBJECTIVES

1. Define collaboration and collaborative team

2. Define and differentiate among shared information, shared decision making, and shared implementation

3. Define and describe the physical education integration team

4. Define the various collaborative team members

5. Describe strategies for positive communication, including listening skills

Emily's mother, Mrs. Jones, introduced herself to Mr. Spencer, the special education teacher at Columbia Elementary School. Mrs. Jones was a pleasant woman who clearly loved her daughter and cared about her welfare. Not surprisingly, she also seemed to know a lot about Emily's condition. Emily was starting kindergarten at Columbia, but she was not like any kindergartner the staff and students had ever seen. Emily was born 6 weeks prematurely and weighed only 2 pounds and 1 ounce at birth. She was in the neonatal intensive care unit of the local children's hospital for 4 months before she was able to go home. Emily has spastic quadriplegic cerebral palsy and uses a wheelchair. Her disability affects all four of her limbs and causes her muscles to be tight and stiff. She has little intelligible speech

other than yes-and-no responses and a few single words. She uses an iPad with touchscreen technology to communicate simple needs and choices to her teachers and friends at school as well as at home. Emily is fed through a gastronomy tube, although she can eat some mashed foods by mouth in small amounts. Clearly, Emily's school attendance requires a tremendous amount of support.

Mrs. Jones called a meeting with all school personnel, including the speech teacher, physical and occupational therapists, and kindergarten teacher who would be working with Emily in the upcoming year. Mrs. Peters, the physical education teacher at Columbia, attended this meeting and was overwhelmed when she heard about Emily. How could Emily participate safely in general physical education? How could Mrs. Peters work with Emily while supervising and working with all the other students in her class? What accommodations would be necessary to accommodate all of Emily's physical and health issues? Clearly, Mrs. Peters would need information and support from Emily's parents as well as a variety of special education professionals who have more experience and knowledge about children like Emily. But to which specialists should Mrs. Peters turn for help? How would this help be provided? Mrs. Peters knew she needed help, but she did not even know where to start.

A variety of professionals are routinely involved in the development and implementation of a student's individualized education program (IEP), especially for children with more severe disabilities

(Orelove, Sobsey, & Silberman, 2004). Although some school districts may not employ all the professionals described in the case study, all school districts should have access to these professionals at least on a consultative basis. Together, all those who work with a student with a disability, including the general physical educator(s), are members of the student's *collaborative team* (Rainforth & York-Barr, 1997). These professionals can be invaluable resources to general and adapted physical educators who are attempting to include students with disabilities into general physical education. The purpose of this chapter is to define a collaborative team and explain the key professionals who are members of this team. Specific references to how team members can facilitate inclusion into physical education are provided. In addition, the importance of communication in collaborative teaming is discussed.

COLLABORATIVE TEAM

IEPs are considered to be more effective and comprehensive when based on a team approach, and in turn the IEP process has been considered as a tool for collaboration and communication (Clark, 2000). All students receiving special education services are required to have an IEP, which specifies in writing all aspects of their educational program and is meant to ensure services are individualized as needed to provide every student with a disability a free appropriate public education in the least restrictive environment (Bateman & Herr, 2003). Many professionals are involved in the development and implementation of a student's IEP. In fact, the Individuals with Disabilities Education Improvement Act (IDEA) of 2004 mandates that a student's IEP be developed by a team that includes the student (when appropriate), his or her parents, teachers, therapists, and a representative from the local education agency. Although IEP teams are designed to encourage teamwork and interaction among team members, some team members may choose to work in isolation from other professionals providing therapy or services that they consider unrelated to general education (Craig, Haggart, & Hull, 1999). In noncollaborative models, children may be pulled out of class for therapy or for adapted physical education a few times per week. Unfortunately, a pull-out model does not allow the specialist to learn about the general education environment and makes it difficult for specialists to share their knowledge about how to support the child (Craig et al., 1999). To illustrate, an adapted physical education specialist might be helping a child who uses a wheelchair to hit a baseball off a tee and throw a baseball with the goal of having the child play little league baseball. However, what if she does not share this information with the general physical education teacher, parents, or other professionals who work with this child? The adapted physical education specialist may not have realized that the student has been playing on junior-level wheelchair basketball and tennis teams for the past year, and his parents and physical education teacher have been working with him to improve on these basic skills. This isolationist approach results in inappropriate programming and limits the carryover and generalization of important skills.

Fortunately, most professionals are interested in working cooperatively and collaboratively with other professionals during the development and implementation of a student's IEP. Martin (2005) noted that collaboration is working together toward a common objective. Sharing expertise and resources among many professionals provides greater problem-solving abilities and enables all individuals involved in the student's educational program to utilize recommended teaching practices (Craig et al., 1999; Orelove et al., 2004; Rainforth & York-Barr, 1997). Collaborative teams meet regularly to continually interact, plan, and modify a student's educational program. For instance, a collaborative team that meets twice per month is stumped on how to help a preschool student with autism who does not verbally communicate with parents, friends, and teachers. In one of the meetings, the speech therapist shares with team members how she uses a picture board to help this student communicate. At future meetings, the team discusses whether the new picture board program should be continued, changed, or dropped.

Ideally, the IEP team works together in a decision-making partnership, with results emerging from participation and agreement among team members. The decision-making process should be based on three elements: 1) shared information, 2) shared decision making, and c) shared implementation (Martin, 2005). Shared information refers to each individual's unique contribution to an understanding of the child's needs. For example, the special education teacher may contribute knowledge of the student via classroom observations, whereas the parents will be able to describe experiences at home, including relationships with siblings. Shared decision making supports the idea that "two heads are better than one" and increases the probability of wise decision making. Finally, shared implementation suggests that if all team members participate and believe in the process, they are more likely to support its implementation. For example, if the general physical educator assists the behavioral therapist in developing a behavior plan, he or she is more likely to use it regularly in physical education. Together, the three elements contribute to the best possible plan for the student.

It should be noted that the formation of a collaborative team usually is not required by administrators. Thus, a team approach will only work if team members have a strong commitment to work together and to share information and ideas. Auxter, Pyfer, Zittel, and Roth (2010) noted that the collaborative models are a foreign concept to most general physical educators, who are used to working independently. Such an autonomous approach may work for children without disabilities, but it will not work for children with disabilities. Fortunately, most general physical educators quickly realize they need the expertise of others to safely and successfully develop and implement individualized physical education programs for students with disabilities.

Collaborative Team Defined

Rainforth, York, and MacDonald (1992) coined the term *collaborative teamwork* to refer to the interaction and sharing of information and responsibilities among team members. As King-Sears, Janney, and Snell elaborated, "Collaborative teaming is two or more people working together toward a common goal. Working together can mean setting goals, identifying problems, assessing students' needs and skills, exchanging information, brainstorming, problem-solving, making plans, and implementing and evaluating plans" (2015, p. 6). Rainforth and her colleagues noted that the concept was developed as a hybrid of the transdisciplinary model and the integrated therapy model. In the transdisciplinary model, parents and professionals share information and techniques. Professional boundaries are removed so that each team member is committed to promoting the student's overall functional independence and participation in age-appropriate activities and routines (Craig et al., 1999). For example, the physical therapist shares information on positioning, while the speech therapist shows how to work on language development. In the integrated therapy model, therapy is conducted within functional contexts (Craig et al., 1999). Taken together, the collaborative model focuses on team members sharing information and working together to provide students with disabilities necessary educational and therapeutic services within functional activities (Craig et al., 1999). Thus, a paraprofessional who has learned how to perform range-of-motion activities might perform these activities during warm-ups in general physical education, and the student remains with the group while the program is performed. Thus, specialists (including the adapted physical educator) spend more time in general education (including general physical education) settings rather than pulling children out in isolated settings. Characteristics of collaborative teamwork as outlined by Rainforth and York-Barr (1997) can be found in Table 3.1. It is important to note how equal participation, shared responsibility, interdependence, and the utilization of functional settings are critical aspects of collaborative teamwork.

The collaborative model allows team members to integrate their programs into a student's daily life routines (Craig et al., 1999). In addition, team members are encouraged to work together to help students in various settings. For example, a speech teacher along with a student's parents may accompany a student to a local gym to work on that student's communication skills. Parents and family members are particularly important as they can practice physical education skills at home or take their child to local recreation facilities to follow up on community-based recreation training (Horton, Wilson, & Gagnon, 2003; Kozub, 2001).

Table 3.1.   Characteristics of collaborative teamwork

1. Equal participation in the collaborative teamwork process by family members and the educational service providers on the educational team
2. Equal participation by all disciplines determined to be necessary for students to achieve their individualized educational goals
3. Consensus decision making about priority educational goals and objectives related to all areas of student functioning at school, at home, and in the community
4. Consensus decision making about the type and amount of support required from related services personnel
5. Attention to motor, communication, and other embedded skills and needs throughout the educational program and in direct relevance to accomplishing priority educational goals
6. Infusion of knowledge and skills from different disciplines into the design of educational methods and interventions
7. Role release to enable team members who are involved most directly and frequently with students to develop the confidence and competence necessary to facilitate active learning and effective participation in the educational program
8. Collaborative problem solving and shared responsibility for students learning across all aspects of the educational program

From Rainforth, B., & York-Barr, J. (1997). *Collaborative teams for students with severe disabilities: Integrating therapy and educational services* (2nd ed., p. 23). Baltimore, MD: Paul H. Brookes Publishing Co.; reprinted by permission.

Meeting with the Physical Education Integration Team

The physical education integration team (PEIT) is the subcommittee of the IEP team most concerned with physical education. The PEIT is organized and run by a team leader (usually the adapted and/or general physical educator). This team solicits information from key members, documents decisions that were made during the meeting, and keeps all team members informed of pertinent information. Although it may be difficult to get all team members together for ongoing team meetings, it is imperative that all key team members, particularly the general physical educator, attend at least one preplanning meeting before the student with disabilities is included in the general physical education class.

It is important during PEIT meetings that team members introduce themselves and offer their assistance to the general physical educator. Most general physical educators are not part of the special education loop and might not be familiar with the roles of various specialists. One way of introducing team members is to utilize the concept of *role release* (Woodruff & McGonigel, 1988). Role release is a systematic way for team members to share ideas about their discipline and begin to work collaboratively to develop and implement the best possible program for a student with disabilities. Team members basically train one another to use their expertise from their various disciplines (Craig et al., 1999; King-Sears et al., 2015). Role release in introductory meetings should include the following: *role extension*, in which all team members begin to acquire knowledge about each other's disciplines (e.g., team members describe their role in the educational program of the student); *role enrichment*, in which team members begin to share information about basic practices (e.g., team members share their recommended teaching practices related to a particular student); and *role expansion*, in which team members exchange recommended teaching practices across disciplines (e.g., team members explain how other team members can utilize these recommended teaching practices in their setting). By the end of the first meeting, the general physical educator should feel that he or she has real resources to go to in order to answer specific questions about the student's physical education program. In addition, the general physical educator should have a greater understanding of the student's overall educational program (not just physical education) and how he or she can assist other team members in meeting other educational goals. Role release in future meetings should include *role exchange*, in which team members begin to implement teaching techniques from other disciplines, and *role support*, in which team members back each other up as they assume the roles of other disciplines.

A great deal of information should be presented at this initial meeting so that team members can make informed decisions regarding the development of the student's individualized physical education program and strategies for inclusion. Various team members will be able to provide different aspects of the information. For example, vision teachers can provide information about a student's visual abilities, physical therapists can provide information about a student's motor abilities and physical fitness, the general physical educator can provide information about the general physical education curriculum and class format, and the student and his or her parents can provide information about a student's likes and dislikes. Key information and the team members most likely to provide this information are presented in Figure 3.1.

Although future team meetings are important and should be planned, some members may not be able to attend meetings regularly. In such cases, the team leader should share information from team members with the team. For example, if the general physical educator cannot attend a meeting, he or she can provide information to the team leader regarding how well the student is doing, what modifications and teaching approaches have been effective or ineffective, and what the next physical education unit will include. Similarly, the student's physical therapist can provide information regarding any physical changes in the student that may affect his or her physical education program. Although formal team meetings provide the best means for discussing the student's program, team members must feel comfortable communicating with each other whenever the need arises.

COLLABORATIVE TEAM MEMBERS

A variety of professionals can be involved in the collaborative team. While each team member has specific responsibilities, the collaborative model suggests that each member assist other professionals in carrying out their responsibilities. In addition, the collaborative approach prevents holes in services or needless duplication of services for a particular student. The following describes the specific responsibilities of collaborative team members as well as how they can assist both general and adapted physical educators in successfully including students with disabilities in general physical education. Note that the key when determining which

	P/S	SE	MD	PT	OT	VT	ST	PY	PE	APE
Information regarding the student										
Information on specific disability of the student with emphasis on how this disability will affect abilities in general physical education	X	X	X	X	X	X	X		X	
Medical and health information regarding the student, particularly as related to contraindicated activities	X	X	X	X						
Behaviors of student, including what behaviors to expect, what generally causes behavior outbursts, and what behavior program is in place for the student	X	X						X		
Communication abilities of student, including how the student communicates, how well the student understands verbal directions, and how to best communicate with the student	X	X					X			
Special equipment (if any) the student uses and whether this equipment will be brought into general physical education	X			X	X	X				X
Personal hygiene skills of student, including locker room skills, ability to dress and undress, and ability to take a shower and perform personal grooming skills	X	X		X	X					
Motor skills, including general information regarding physical fitness, fundamental motor skills, and perceptual motor abilities	X		X	X					X	
Specific information regarding recreation activities available in the student's community or neighborhood	X								X	X
Interests of student and student's parents, particularly as the student reaches high school and begins to develop interests in particular lifetime leisure skills and possibly sports	X									
Special sports opportunities such as Special Olympics	X			X					X	X
Specific goals developed for student that are not directly related to physical education but that can be worked on in the physical education setting	X	X	X	X	X	X	X	X	X	X
Activities that take place in general physical education										
Length of a typical physical education class and how the period is broken down (e.g., 10 minutes for locker room, 25 minutes for activity)									X	
The daily routine that usually takes place in general physical education									X	
The typical teaching style (movement education, direct teaching, highly structured)									X	
The minimal skills needed in the locker room									X	

Figure 3.1.   Which team members to seek for specific information. (*Key:* P/S, parent and/or student; SE, special education teacher; MD, physician; PT, physical therapist; OT, occupational therapist; VT, vision therapist; ST, speech therapist; PY, psychologist; PE, general physical educator; APE, adapted physical educator.)

professional is involved in a particular student's IEP is "whether a professional's services and skills are deemed necessary for a student to benefit from his or her IEP" (Orelove et al., 2004, p. 3). For example, a collaborative team for a child who does not have a visual impairment would not include a vision specialist. However, this does not mean that team members cannot ask this professional for advice. The general physical educator might want some general information on how to make the physical education environment more visually stimulating and visually safe for children who have trouble with activities that require tracking balls, such as volleyball and basketball.

Adapted Physical Education Professionals

Many school districts in the United States require physical education for children with disabilities to be administered by a qualified adapted physical education professional who meets state requirements and competencies (Kelly, 1991; National Consortium for Physical Education and Recreation for Individuals with Disabilities [NCPERID], 2006). A highly qualified adapted physical education teacher must be a physical education teacher first, with strong content knowledge and the ability to apply it to students with disabilities. The teacher should also have additional knowledge related to disability such as assessment, IEPs, special education law, and behavior management. Highly qualified individuals obtain their training from a graduate program based on state or national standards—with 12 hours specifically addressing the needs of students with disabilities and with at least 9 of these hours specific to adapted physical education—and acquire 150 hours of practical experience (American Association for Physical Activity and Recreation [AAPAR] & NCPERID, 2010; Lytle, Lavay, & Rizzo, 2010). One way for school districts to ensure they are getting a qualified adapted physical education professional is to hire a certified adapted physical educator (CAPE). CAPEs are licensed physical education specialists who have documented practical experience and training in adapted physical education and who have successfully passed the Adapted Physical Education National Standards (APENS) exam (NCPERID, 2006).

The major role of adapted physical education professionals is to create a specialized program and adaptations and assist in the identification and remediation of physical education–related problems of students who have disabilities (NCPERID, 2006; Sherrill, 2004). Specific services provided by adapted physical education professionals include assessment, program planning, writing individualized physical education programs, participating in IEP meetings, directly implementing rehabilitative programs for students with disabilities, consulting with general physical educators and parents, fitness and leisure sports for individuals with disabilities, and advocating for children with disabilities in physical education and sports (McCubbin, Jansma, & Houston-Wilson, 1993; Sherrill, 2004).

While most adapted physical education professionals work directly with students with disabilities, many are increasingly working as consultants (Block & Conatser, 1999; Kudláček, Ješina, Štěrbová, & Sherrill, 2008; NCPERID, 2006). In this role, the adapted physical education professional helps others (usually the general physical educator and parents) work more successfully with children with disabilities.

The adapted physical education professional can assist the general physical educator in including students with disabilities into general physical education in a variety of ways. First, the adapted physical education professional can take all the information provided by the other team members, including specific information about the student's physical and motor skills, and present it to the general physical educator in a way that is meaningful and practical. Second, the adapted physical education professional can provide specific information to the general physical educator about modifying physical education activities to safely and successfully include the student with disabilities. This can be accomplished through meetings, coteaching, or providing written modifications to lesson plans (Akuffo & Hodge, 2008; Block & Conatser, 1999; Grenier, 2011). Because the adapted physical education professional knows more about how specific types of disabilities affect physical education, he or she is a vital member of the team.

Fewer than 20 states have any special requirements for adapted physical education professionals other than a general physical education teaching license. Thus, many school districts employ adapted physical education professionals who do not have any specialized training, experience, or knowledge regarding children with disabilities (Winnick, 2011). Many smaller school districts do not have anyone on staff designated as an adapted physical education professional.

General Physical Education Professional

General physical education professionals are specifically trained and licensed to teach physical education, traditionally to children without disabilities.

Changing legislation and roles now require these professionals to work with all children in their schools, including children with disabilities (Winnick, 2011). Many will enjoy their new role and acclimate quickly to working with children who have disabilities, whereas others will be more resistant to change. In either case, general physical education professionals should be included and welcomed to the collaborative team. General physical education professionals have a great deal of knowledge about all components of physical education (i.e., physical fitness, fundamental motor skills, individual and team sports and games). In addition, they have direct information on the behaviors and attitudes of children in their physical education classes. Perhaps of greatest importance, the general physical educator knows which units to teach and when to teach them, which teaching approach to use, what equipment is available, how many students are in each class, and the pace and dynamics of each class (Council for Exceptional Children [CEC], 1999).

It is important to remember that most general physical education professionals have had very little training or experience in working with students who have disabilities and thus might be a little apprehensive about how to include a student with disabilities into their general program (U.S. Government Accountability Office, 2010; Hodge & Akuffo, 2007; Obrusnikova, 2008). Most general physical education specialists have had only one survey course in adapted physical education during their formal training and may have very little practical experience working with children who have disabilities (Piletic & Davis, 2010). It is the responsibility of all team members to make general physical education specialists feel as comfortable as possible with inclusion. It is the responsibility of the general physical education teacher to have an open mind about inclusion, provide opportunities for interaction between students with and without disabilities, and serve as a role model to students without disabilities by respecting the students' individual differences.

According to IDEA 2004, a general educator must be included on the IEP team if the student is or may be taking part in any general education (including general physical education). This does not necessarily mean that the general physical education specialist must attend every IEP meeting for every child in his or her building who has a disability. However, this does mean the special education teacher should invite the general physical education specialist to IEP meetings and seek his or her input on physical education programming for children with disabilities.

Special Education Teacher

The special education teacher is the primary advocate and program planner for the student with disabilities (CEC, n.d.; Stainback & Stainback, 1985). His or her role is to develop and assist in the implementation the student's IEP, including the initiation and organization of inclusive activities. In addition, the special education teacher coordinates all supports and related services a student needs (Stainback & Stainback, 1985). The special education teacher typically knows more about the student than any other team member, with the exception of the student's parents, including the student's developmental history, health and medical background, behaviors and behavior plans, communication and cognitive skills, self-help skills, learning style, successful teaching techniques, and likes and dislikes (CEC, n.d.). In addition, as coordinator of all the student's services, the special educator can quickly communicate information to other team members. The special education teacher can also assist in the training of peer tutors and paraprofessionals.

Building Principal

The building principal is responsible for everything that takes place in his or her school, including physical education programs and programs for students with disabilities. Thus, although not directly involved in program planning or implementation, the building principal has a vested interest in the success of the inclusive physical education program. Principals who support inclusive physical education can have a direct impact on the attitudes of general physical education staff. In addition, principals can help team members gain important resources such as extra support, special equipment, and gym time. Finally, the principal can act as a go-between to other administrators such as directors of physical education or special education at a school-system level.

School Nurse

More students with special health care needs are entering public schools (Kline, Silver, & Russell, 2001), making the school nurse an invaluable resource to the team regarding health and medical information, daily care, and emergency planning. School health professionals (mainly nurses) are primarily responsible for diagnosing and treating minor injuries and illnesses, handling medical emergencies and contacting other emergency personnel, and monitoring and administering prescription medications. In some schools, nurses are also responsible for specific health care procedures such as suctioning a student's tracheostomy (i.e., hole in throat used for breathing), conducting postural drainage for students with cystic fibrosis, administering clean intermittent catheterization for students who do not have bladder control, and tube feeding students who cannot receive adequate nutrition through oral feeding. Because the school nurse has direct access to the student's parents and physicians, he or she can act as a link between a student's parents and physicians and the school. For example, if a question arises as to the effects of vigorous exercise on a seizure disorder, the school nurse can contact the student's parents and physicians to get an immediate answer. The school nurse should act as a consultant to the team, and team members should feel free to contact the nurse if they have any questions regarding a particular student's health or medical state (Porter, Branowicki, & Palfrey, 2014).

Physical Therapist

According to IDEA 2004, physical therapy vaguely means "services provided by a qualified physical therapist" (Individuals with Disabilities Education Improvement Act [IDEA] of 2004, 20 U.S.C. §§ 1400 *et seq.*). According to the American Physical Therapy Association, "The physical therapist provides services aimed at preventing the onset and/or slowing the progression of conditions resulting from injury, disease, or other causes" (2014). In school settings, physical therapists specialize in gross motor development (movements that involve large muscles of the body), utilizing various techniques to relieve pain and discomfort, prevent deformity and further disability, restore or maintain functioning, and improve strength and motor skill performance (Hanft & Place, 1996; Sherrill, 2004). Physical therapists also work on activities of daily living (ADLs; e.g., getting around the school building, dressing, sitting properly) and addressing architectural barriers. Techniques include therapeutic exercise, developmental therapy, and assistive devices such as gait trainers, walkers, braces, canes, crutches, and wheelchairs. The type of therapy will depend on the goals that have been set by the IEP team (Hanft & Place, 1996; Sherrill, 2004). In most states, physical therapists must have a written referral from the child's physician (usually an orthopedic surgeon) before they can provide therapy to children with disabilities. However, with the doctorate in physical therapy (DPT), school districts have the option of hiring a physical therapist who can provide services without a doctor's prescription. The physician is supposed to provide a diagnosis, goals to be

accomplished, and instructions regarding precautions and contraindications, but this often does not happen.

The physical therapist knows a lot about the student's physical condition and should be included in decisions regarding activities or positions, selection of motor skills for training, positioning and limb use for optimum functioning, and modifications to equipment and rules of the game. For example, for a third-grade student who is learning to walk with a walker in a general physical education class, the physical therapist can provide information regarding what warm-up activities are appropriate or inappropriate; how to modify appropriate warm-up activities and what alternative warm-ups could be used at other times; how far and how fast the student should be expected to walk; the student's aerobic capacity, strength, and flexibility; and suggestions for modifications to activities in general physical education.

Occupational Therapist

According to IDEA, occupational therapists utilize various techniques to improve, develop, and/or restore functions impaired or lost through illness, injury, or deprivation; improve ability to perform tasks for independent functioning when functions are impaired or lost; and prevent, through early intervention, initial or further impairment or loss of function (IDEA of 2004, 20 U.S.C. §§ 1400 *et seq.*). According to the American Occupational Therapy Association (2015), "Occupational therapy is skilled treatment that helps individuals achieve independence in all facets of their lives. It gives people the 'skills for the job of living' necessary for independent and satisfying lives." In schools, occupational therapists focus on helping students with disabilities perform ADLs as independently as possible. Another major focus of school-based occupational therapy is the presentation of sensorimotor integration activities designed to assist children with disabilities to fully utilize and integrate vestibular information (i.e., information from the inner ear that tells a person where the head is in relation to gravity), tactile information (sense of touch and feedback from touch sensors on the skin), and visual information (Hanft & Place, 1996). The occupational therapist can be an important resource on the team regarding a student's abilities (and possible adaptations) in self-help and personal hygiene skills needed in the locker room prior to and after a physical education class; fine motor skills, fundamental manipulative skills, and sport-specific manipulative skills;

and skills related to sensory integration such as static and dynamic balance, tactile awareness, and proprioception.

Recreation Therapists

According to IDEA, the primary responsibilities of recreation therapists include assessment of leisure function, therapeutic recreation services, recreation programs in schools and community agencies, and leisure education (IDEA of 2004, 20 U.S.C. §§ 1400 *et seq.*). According to the American Therapeutic Recreation Association (ATRA, 2015), "a recreational therapist utilizes a wide range of activities and techniques to improve the physical, cognitive, emotional, social, and leisure needs of their clients." Recreational therapists assist clients to develop skills, knowledge, and behaviors for daily living and community involvement. The therapist works with the client and his or her family to incorporate specific interests and community resources into therapy to achieve optimal outcomes that transfer to real life situations.

Basically, recreation services are used to improve functional abilities, enhance well-being and facilitate independence, teach or enhance recreation skills and attitudes that can be used throughout life, and promote health and growth through leisure and recreation experiences (Etzel-Wise & Mears, 2004). Recreation therapy includes an array of programs, such as music, art, dance, drama, horticulture, camping, and sports and fitness. Recreation therapy utilizes a child's existing skills and interests and facilitates new skills for daily living and leisure functioning (ATRA, 2015). Recreation therapy is provided by trained and licensed recreation therapists who, like physical therapists, must have physician's referral before they can provide therapy to children with disabilities. For this reason, recreation therapists are more common in children's hospitals and rehabilitation centers than in public schools.

Recreation therapists can provide the team with information regarding recreation/leisure assessment, availability of community recreation facilities, and suggestions for adaptations in performing recreation/leisure programs. This information can be particularly important to physical educators who are assisting the student with disabilities make the transition from a school-based physical education program to a postschool recreation program. Recreation therapists also often have a good understanding of how well the child is dealing emotionally with his or her disability.

Speech Therapist

The primary role of the speech therapist is defined in IDEA as follows:

> Identification of children with speech or language disorders, diagnosis and appraisal of specific speech or language disorders, referral for medical or other professional attention necessary for the rehabilitation of speech or language disorders, provision of speech and language services for the rehabilitation or prevention of communicative disorders, counselling and guidance for parents, children, and teachers regarding speech or language disorders. (IDEA of 2004, 20 U.S.C. §§ 1400 *et seq.*)

Speech therapists can assist team members in understanding a student's receptive and expressive language abilities and how best to communicate with certain students. For example, some students might understand verbal cues and simple demonstrations, whereas other students might need sign language or physical assistance. Students with disabilities communicate via speech, sign language, communication boards, and electronic devices such as Canon Communicators or speech synthesizers. Knowing how to best present information to students as well as understanding how a student might express his or her desires is extremely important for successful inclusion in physical education.

Audiologist

Audiologists are trained professionals who work with students with hearing impairments. The major role of the audiologist is to determine a student's hearing loss and abilities and recommend special augmentative hearing devices such as hearing aids. In addition, audiologists often consult with speech therapists to determine a particular student's potential for speech and language development (American Speech-Language-Hearing Association, 2015). An audiologist can assist the general physical educator by explaining a student's hearing loss and specifying his or her residual hearing abilities. In collaboration with the speech therapist, the audiologist can recommend ways to communicate with a student who has a hearing impairment. For example, an audiologist might suggest that a student who has a severe hearing loss be provided with verbal directions repeated by a peer or have demonstrations to supplement verbal commands. In addition, the audiologist can explain safety precautions for this student such as avoiding contact to the ear while he or she is wearing his hearing aids or taking the aids out when swimming.

Vision Specialists

Vision specialists (also called vision teachers) are certified professionals trained in meeting the educational needs of children with visual impairments (Brasher & Holbrook, 1996; Brown & Beamish, 2012). Vision teachers' major goal is to help students with visual impairments become as functional and independent as possible. Specifically, for students with low vision, goals include learning orientation and mobility skills necessary to move about in various environments and learning adapted techniques for classwork such as reading large print, using felt-tip markers, using a magnifying glass, and using computers. For students who have very limited vision or who are blind, goals include orientation and mobility skills such as using a cane and a sighted guide and learning adapted techniques for classwork such as using braille and computers. Vision teachers also encourage movement and introduce toys that are visually or tactually interesting, stimulate the use of all senses, teach prereading skills such as tracking and finger positioning, teach braille reading, and help with daily living skills such as eating and dressing (Brasher & Holbrook, 1996; Brown & Beamish, 2012).

Vision teachers work very closely with other professionals and serve as some children's primary teacher. They can be invaluable to adapted and general physical educators. For example, a vision teacher can show how to make a student with a visual impairment feel more comfortable in the gym environment, how to appropriately interact with the student, and how to assist the student. Vision teachers can also provide ideas for adapted equipment, safety precautions, and rule modifications such as guide ropes for running, beeper balls for softball, and tandem bike riding. Many vision teachers have easy access to adapted equipment such as beeper balls and balls with bells, and many teachers are knowledgeable about special sports programs designed for individuals with visual impairments such as the United States Association of Blind Athletes (USABA).

Orientation and Mobility Specialist

Orientation and mobility (O&M) specialists (also called O&M teachers or travel instructors) are certified teachers who have specialized training in teaching children and adults with visual impairments how to travel safely and efficiently in a variety of environments (Brasher & Holbrook, 1996). Initially, O&M specialists work with children on general space awareness, body image, and directionality (e.g., over, under, left, and right). As the child progresses, O&M training moves to more specific travel skills, including traveling within a room and between rooms. Depending on the child's visual and cognitive abilities and age, the O&M specialist might have the child use a sighted guide, a cane, or a dog (Academy for Certification of Vision Rehabilitation and Education Professionals, 2005). O&M specialists can be an invaluable aid by teaching the child to independently move from the classroom to the gym and orienting the child to the locker room, pool area, gymnasium, and any other physical education environments. Finally, the O&M specialist can help identify dangerous places in the gym, show how to help a child with a vision impairment move more safely in the gym, and give ideas for adapting equipment and rules.

Paraprofessionals

Paraprofessionals (also known as paraeducators, educational aides, instructional assistants, teaching assistants, education support professionals, and individualized learning assistants) are hired to assist teachers, including general physical educators, in implementing a student's IEP. Paraprofessionals work under the supervision of a teacher or other professional who is responsible for the overall management of the class, creation and implementation of the IEP, and assessment of the student's progress (Doyle, 2008). In inclusive programs, the paraprofessional is often the person who has the most one-to-one contact with the student with a disability.

Paraprofessionals vary greatly in their background and training, from certified special education teachers to individuals with virtually no prior experience with students who have disabilities. In addition, paraprofessionals are utilized differently by different teachers. Some paraprofessionals are only responsible for noninstructional responsibilities such as clerical work (e.g., making copies, lunch count, attendance); monitoring students in the hallway, at lunch, or on the playground; setting up the classroom for the teacher; or providing specific personal care such as dressing, feeding, and repositioning (Doyle, 2008). Others have more instructional responsibilities such as observing, recording, and charting a student's behavior and academic progress; assisting in full classroom instruction; assisting with individualized instruction; tutoring small groups of students; implementing and reinforcing teacher-developed lessons; contributing ideas and suggestions regarding a child or group of children; and participating in team meetings (Doyle, 2008).

Regardless of the exact role of paraprofessionals, their close contact to the student with a disability enables them to provide unique insight to the needs and interests of the student. Thus, paraprofessionals can provide valuable information to the team regarding the student's behaviors at certain times during the day, communication skills, likes and dislikes, preferred positions, and effective adaptations and activities. In many programs, the paraprofessional accompanies the student to physical education (Horton, 2001; Lieberman, 2007). It is important to note that paraprofessionals *are not* responsible for the initial design and development of instructional procedures for students with disabilities in physical education, assessment, or decision making (Doyle, 2008). While paraprofessionals can be included in the process, the general physical educator should be responsible for developing lesson plans and training the paraprofessional to implement these plans. In addition, the general physical education teacher must be prepared to provide the paraprofessional with some directions regarding the plan for the day, what peers should be encouraged to work on with the child with a disability, what modifications and adapted equipment to anticipate for certain activities, what activities might be inappropriate, and how to help the child work on specific skills and be part of the group (Horton, 2001; Lieberman, 2007).

Assistive Technology Service Personnel

Assistive technology professionals support students with disabilities in selecting, acquiring, or using technology. The Assistive Technology Act Amendments of 2004 (PL 108-364) defined assistive technology as "any item, piece of equipment, or product system, whether acquired commercially, modified, or customized, that is used to increase, maintain, or improve functional capabilities of individuals with disabilities."

Examples of assistive technology include computers, manual and power wheelchairs, augmented communication devices, and hearing aids. Given that technology is more accessible than ever, more students with disabilities are benefiting in schools. For instance, some children with autism spectrum disorders communicate more frequently when using iPads as opposed to printed pictures (Flores et al., 2012).

Parents

Parents and caregivers are often overlooked resources in the education of their children with disabilities even though by law they should be an integral part in the development of IEPs (Kozub, 2001). In fact, the IDEA Amendments of 1997 strengthened the role of the parent by noting that parents' concerns, as well as the information they provide about their child, must be considered when developing and reviewing the IEP. In addition, IDEA 2004 requires one or both parents of a student with a disability to be present at each IEP meeting or at least be given the chance to participate.

But more than a legal mandate, parental participation on the collaborative team is critical for developing an appropriate IEP. Parents know more practical information about their child than any professional. In addition, parents often have developed successful management and training techniques that can be useful in the classroom and in physical education. Parents have reported feeling alienated by the educational terms often used and pressured to go along with the placement and goals the school staff had predetermined. In addition, parents have reported feeling that school staff have failed to understand their perspectives and even exhibit a lack of respect regarding the contributions they have made (Childre &Chambers, 2005; Spann, Kohler, & Soenksen, 2003). Simple strategies such as ensuring the IEP meeting is held in a comfortable, homelike place, providing the parents with a chance to prepare for the meeting, and avoiding the use of jargon may help parents speak up (Furney & Salembier, 2000). Parents should be encouraged to share their goals and expectations for their child as well as their personal recreation interests so that the physical educator can gear the adapted physical education program to meet the unique needs of the family (Kozub, 2001). It is much easier to get support from home when parents are included in the decision-making process. For example, if a family enjoys playing tennis and going hiking during their weekend leisure time, then it would make sense to target these skills for their middle school student with a disability. These skills will likely be practiced at home and, when mastered, can help the individual participate more successfully at home and school. Figure 3.2 provides a simple form that can be sent home to parents to get their input regarding the family's recreational hobbies and what physical education goals they would like to target for the child. This information can then be shared with the collaborative team during the IEP meeting.

Parent Physical Education Interest Form

Student's name: _____

Person filling out this form: _____

Date: _____ Student's age: _____

1. What do you do as a family for recreation (e.g., play tennis, go for walks, go swimming)?

   _____

   _____

   _____

   _____

2. What activities do you see other children in your neighborhood doing that you think your child would enjoy (e.g., bike riding, soccer, tee ball, rollerblading)?

   _____

   _____

   _____

   _____

3. What community-based recreation sport program does your child participate in or would you like to see your child participate in (e.g., tee ball, soccer, any Special Olympics or other special sport program)?

   _____

   _____

   _____

   _____

4. Do you have any fitness concerns for your child that you would like to be addressed in physical education (e.g., upper body strength, flexibility, endurance, body weight)?

   _____

   _____

   _____

   _____

5. What other specific things would you like your child to work on during physical education (i.e., what would be your dream physical education program)?

   _____

   _____

   _____

   _____

Figure 3.2. Parent physical education interest form.

Student with a Disability

The student with a disability should be included on the team whenever possible (Price, Wolensky, & Mulligan, 2002). According to IDEA 2004, children ages 16 and older are required to be invited to IEP meetings when postsecondary goals or transition services are being discussed (although students of any age can be invited to participate), and decisions must be based on their interests and preferences. Yet research on student participation in IEP meetings suggests that when they do attend, they might play a passive rather than active role (Mason, Field, & Sawilowsky, 2004). A student who is included in the process of developing his or her educational program is more likely to be committed and motivated to work on specific program goals (MacDonald & Block, 2005). In fact, students who are actively involved are more likely to reach their goals, improve their academic skills, develop self-advocacy and communication skills, graduate from high school, and obtain better jobs (Thomas & Wehman, 2010; Wehmeyer, Abery, Mithaug, & Stancliffe, 2003). After all, the team is really in place to discuss the student's present and future (CEC, 1999). Also, participation is the first step in helping children learn to be their own best advocate (Pennell, 2001).

Levels and kinds of participation will vary from student to student depending on their age and ability to communicate and participate in the meeting. For example, an elementary-age student with spina bifida might attend a PEIT meeting to discuss alternative ways he or she might participate in warm-up activities when the class is working on locomotor patterns. Similarly, a high school–age student who is blind might choose a cardiovascular training program (e.g., aerobic dance, stair climber, stationary bike, walking the track) that meets his or her interests. Students who are given choices tend to be more motivated learners. In addition, having the child present at team meetings helps the team focus on the child's needs rather than their own schedules and problems.

If a student with a disability is going to attend a collaborative team meeting, then someone should talk to the student ahead of time about who will be attending the meeting, what will be discussed, questions he or she may be asked by team members, and what information he or she can share with the team (CEC, 1999). Also, team members should be careful to use terminology that the student understands. For nonverbal students, interests and abilities can be shared with the group via videotapes or portfolios.

COMMUNICATION: THE KEY TO COLLABORATIVE TEAMING

The way in which team members communicate with each other is often more important than what they are communicating. Being able to express ideas, articulate requests clearly and in a nonthreatening way, elicit information from others, and listen to how others feel are critical to successful collaborative teaming (Hanft & Place, 1996; King-Sears et al., 2015; Kurpius & Rozecki, 1993; Martin, 2005; Sherrill, 2004). Unfortunately, communication is such a difficult process that misunderstanding and miscommunication frequently occur (Heron & Harris, 1993).

Reaching a Consensus

With so many voices involved in team meetings, it is sometimes difficult to reach a consensus. In fact, each team member is usually invested in his or her position and argues strongly for what he or she believes. The discussion sometimes becomes an ugly exchange of demands rather than a cooperative problem-solving venture. Martin (2005) suggests using principled negotiation in IEP meetings, a strategy developed by Roger Fisher and William Ury of Harvard University. It consists of four elements: 1) people, 2) interests, 3) opinions, and 4) criteria. The first element, *people*, considers who individuals are and what they bring to the table in terms of attitudes, feelings, and past experiences. For example, the special educator may want to help the student by implementing new technology but feels conflicted due to lack of energy, time, and support. By understanding where this teacher is coming from, team members are more likely to understand why implementing new technology may take more time and require providing the teacher more support. *Interests* refer to the goals people are trying to achieve and their underlying interests in moving toward a particular outcome. For example, a parent may want his or her child to stay in regular physical education full time despite the child's disruptive behavior because he or she fears the child will feel "different" or that pulling the child out will damage the child's self-esteem. Being aware of why the parent wants his or her child in general physical education can help the team understand his or her feelings and generate solutions for preserving the child's self-esteem. For example, a team might consider educational programming, staffing, professional development, or additional training, technology, and community resources. Finally, the *criteria* define the basis upon which decisions are made from the possibilities put forth by the team. All members should have a mutual understanding of how they will make decisions. Typically, criteria will be based on legal requirements, test results, observations, and expert recommendations.

Strategies for Communication

Because so much of collaboration revolves around communication, it is critical for team members to understand how to establish and maintain effective communication (King-Sears et al., 2015; Martin, 2005; Munk & Dempsey, 2010). Heron and Harris (1993) suggested that to establish open channels to communication, team members must first gain acceptance from each other and work to minimize resistance and manage conflict.

Gaining Acceptance

Gaining acceptance and establishing rapport among team members is extremely important (Hanft & Place, 1996; Pedron & Evans, 1990). Collaborative teaming is much easier if positive relationships are established from the beginning (see Table 3.2). Hanft and Place (1996) noted that all collaboration should start with the explicit goal of establishing positive relationships among team members through effective interpersonal and communication skills. Important aspects of gaining acceptance include genuineness (conveying sincerity), positive regard (treating others with respect), empathy (understanding the other's perspective), and congruence (establishing a common ground to converse and share thoughts and feelings honestly; Heron & Harris, 1993; Kurpius & Rozecki, 1993).

Minimizing Resistance

Related to gaining acceptance is anticipating and dealing with resistance. Establishing trust and a genuineness to the interests of other team members and the

Table 3.2.　Strategies to create positive relationships

1. Honor each member's style of interaction.
2. Acknowledge caseloads or class size and the demands that accompany this workload.
3. Honor each member's teaching and management style.
4. Invite others to visit your program.
5. Bring snacks to share.
6. Write frequent thank-you notes.
7. Invite families of other professionals to participate in special events, such as open houses or other activities.

Reprinted, with permission, from S.L. Kasser and R. Lyttle, 2005, Inclusive physical activity: A lifetime of opportunities (Champaign, IL: Human Kinetics), 68.

student is perhaps the best way to overcome resistance (Gutkin & Curtis, 1982; King-Sears et al., 2015; Kurpius & Rozecki, 1993; Martin, 2005). Margolis and McCabe (1988) provided the following suggestions for creating trust: Provide complete and unhurried attention, keep your word, listen to understand rather than to challenge, respond to requests for assistance in a timely manner, use easily understood language (i.e., avoid jargon), share expertise without dominating the discussion, and use active listening techniques (discussed later in this chapter).

Managing Conflict

Conflicts will arise regardless of best efforts in interpersonal and communication skills. The majority of typical communications that occur during collaborative teaming are negotiations and conflict resolution (Causton & Theoharis, 2014; Hanft & Place, 1996; Munk & Dempsey, 2010). Conflict can arise for many reasons and can affect the teaming process both favorably and unfavorably. Heron and Harris (1993) suggested the following five strategies for dealing with conflict:

1. Withdraw if neither the goal nor the relationship is important (e.g., the general physical education teacher is not going to change, and the student with disabilities is reasonably accommodated).

2. Force the issue and use all your energy to accomplish the task if it is important but the relationship is not (e.g., student is in danger or the program is completely unacceptable and your relationship with a team member is short term).

3. Smooth things over if you want to be liked and accepted and if the relationship is more important than the task (e.g., a student with disabilities is being reasonably accommodated, you want to maintain a good relationship with the adapted physical educator, and you know he or she will be getting more of your students in the future).

4. Compromise if the task and the relationship are important but time is limited (e.g., develop reasonable accommodations for a student with spina bifida to participate in a basketball unit that starts next week, knowing that with more time, you might suggest other accommodations).

5. Confront the situation if the task and the relationship are equally important (e.g., take time to really problem-solve how a child's unique goals and objectives can be embedded in the general physical education curriculum).

Note that confrontation is viewed as a problem-solving technique to resolve conflicts between team members (Causton & Theoharis, 2014; Heron & Harris, 1993; Munk & Dempsey, 2010). As long as confrontation avoids emotional reactions such as hostility or anger, then it is a positive way for both parties to agree upon a course of action. If a team member becomes angry, Margolis and Fiorelli (1987) suggested the following: Maintain composure, listen carefully and empathetically, encourage the team member to identify and share the reasons for his or her anger and fully release the anger, resist attempts to invalidate the information that has been shared, note areas of agreement, move slowly from problem perception to problem definition, and help the team member maintain self-respect. The goal is to defuse the situation, maintain a relationship with the team member, and return to solving the problem at hand. Team members need to realize that each team member has different experiences than they do, and understanding and valuing these differences is critical for successful communication.

Listening Skills

Table 3.3 provides a list developed by West, Idol, and Cannon (1989) of the critical interpersonal and communication skills needed for effective collaboration. Of these, listening behaviors, including nonverbal listening skills, have been

Table 3.3. Interpersonal and communication skills needed for consultation

Interpersonal	Communication
Caring	Listening
Respectful	Acknowledging
Empathetic	Paraphrasing
Congruent	Reflecting
Open	Clarifying
Positive self-concept	Elaborating
Enthusiastic attitude	Summarizing
Willingness to learn from others	Grasp overt meaning
Calm	Grasp covert meaning
Stress free	Interpret nonverbal communication
Risk-taker	Interview effectively
Flexible	Provide feedback
Resilient	Brainstorming
Manage conflict and confrontation	Nonjudgmental responding
Manage time	Develop action plan

From West, J.F., Idol, L., & Cannon, G.S. (1989). Collaboration in the schools: *An inservice and preservice curriculum for teachers, support staff, and administrators.* Austin, TX: PRO-ED; reprinted by permission.

reported to be the most critical skills (Gutkin & Curtis, 1982; King-Sears et al., 2015; Kurpius & Rozecki, 1993; Martin, 2005). Communication involves more than just presenting information and asking questions. In fact, one of the most important communication skills in collaborative teaming is being a good listener (Covey, 1989; King-Sears et al., 2015). If a team member cannot first fully understand other team members and their unique situations, then it will be impossible to be able to discuss an appropriate solution.

Although most team members understand the need to be a good listener, many team members forget to listen. Covey (1989) suggested that listening with the intent to fully understand often is threatening or unnatural because trying to fully understand someone else's perspective may cause you to change your perspective or value system. In addition, team members may not be good listeners because of the natural tendency to first be understood. Many people's first reaction to another person talking is to listen with the intent to speak. For example, many team members might listen not so much to truly understand another's concerns but rather to wait for the first opportunity to give an opinion or solution. If team members are waiting to speak, then they are not fully listening. Kurpius and Rozecki (1993) suggested some other common barriers to listening, including a tendency to judge or evaluate a team member's statements, inattention or apathy, asking too many questions prematurely, feeling the need to define and solve the problem quickly, and pursuing one's own agenda regardless of the team member's needs. Unfortunately, a team member instinctively recognizes half-hearted attempts at listening, and this creates feelings of mistrust.

Collaborative teaming is more than simply one team member giving advice to another team member. Advising does not consider the other team member's preference. This is often the case when one team member tries to fix another team member's problem by telling him or her what to do (Hanft & Place, 1996). In contrast, true collaborative teaming incorporates all team members' perspectives. Solutions are reached as a team, thus empowering and elevating each team member in the decision-making process. As each team member takes ownership of the decision-making process, his or her self-esteem is enhanced as the solution becomes resolved, and the team member becomes aware of his or her own resources and establishes an increased sense of confidence (King-Sears et al., 2015; Martin, 2005).

To be a better listener, Kurpius and Rozecki (1993); Seaman, DePauw, Morton, and Omoto (2007); and Sherrill (2004) suggested the following two responses: clarification (questioning) and reflection. *Clarification* refers to asking questions in such a way as to help the team member focus more clearly on the situation. It also is a way to get the team member to talk about and elaborate on specific problems. Questions are used to gain more information about a particular issue and to clarify or confirm the information that is presented (Kasser & Lytle, 2005). Questioning has to be done delicately as to not threaten the team member, causing him or her to become defensive. Kasser and Lytle (2005) and Snell and Janney (2005) noted that open-ended questions rather than yes/no questions encourage team members to clarify their points of view. For example, a question such as "Can you give us some examples of what you meant when you said that including this student in general physical education is not working right now?" encourages the general physical education teacher to clarify his or her statements.

Reflection refers to team members listening to each other and then trying to rephrase the information. Reflective listening "assures the speaker that his or her message is heard and is viewed as important" (Sherrill, 2004, p. 75). For example, a general physical educator talks about problems he or she is having with two students with behavior problems who are "driving me crazy." After listening for several minutes and helping the general physical educator clarify key points, team members help the general physical educator reflect by saying "Sounds like you are really frustrated that these two boys were placed in your class without your prior knowledge and without any support from the special education staff." Note how reflection not only is rephrasing what a team member said but also includes that team member's feelings and emotions. Reflecting on a team member's feelings helps the team member feel valued, encourages the team member to continue discussing the issue, and ultimately focuses energies toward identifying and resolving the targeted problem (Gutkin & Curtis, 1982; Sherrill, 2004).

Listening requires more than picking up key words. When a team member talks, other team members need to pay close attention to body language, emotions, and tone (Gutkin & Curtis, 1982). For example, a general physical educator says, "I'm really all right with my situation." This phrase can be said and expressed in numerous ways with completely different meanings. Therefore, team members need to listen with their ears, eyes, and heart and then respond clearly, specifically, and contextually from within that team member's frame of reference. If complete attention is given to that team member, then other team members will be able to better understand the full message. Team members also need to convey through their body language their true interest in listening and understanding the other team members. Nonverbal communication can be just as important as verbal communication (Johnston & Wayda, 1994). Miscommunication often results from nonverbal factors such as facial expressions, vocal intonations, body postures and movement, and use of space. While usually unintentional, a team member's nonverbal behaviors can convey lack of interest or concern, lack of genuineness, and/or a general sense of uncomfortableness with other team members (Heron & Harris, 1993).

The importance of communication in collaborative teaming cannot be overstated. Effective communication allows for a free flow of information among the team members. Ineffective communication leads to misunderstandings and conflicts. Team members' ability to be open, listen with the intent to understand, and reduce conflict will inspire openness and trust and increase the overall effectiveness of collaborative teaming.

SUMMARY

Many individuals are involved in the education of students with disabilities. While each may have unique goals and objectives for the student, they all want to see the student reach his or her potential. The best way to provide services to students with disabilities is for all these individuals to work collaboratively by sharing information and working together. Such a team approach allows a variety of professionals to provide input and assist in making important decisions regarding the student's program. In addition, each professional has information that can help other professionals do their job better.

General physical educators often feel isolated and uninformed about students' abilities and disabilities. In many cases, students with disabilities are placed without any team planning into general physical education programs on the first day of school. A team approach provides the general physical educator with a wealth of resources that can help him or her develop and implement an individualized program as well as answer specific questions as they arise. Specialists can provide the general physical educator with important information that will help him or her provide the best physical education program to students with disabilities. The key to successful collaborative teaming is communication. All team members must learn how to be good listeners and work together to solve problems rather than simply giving advice to the general physical educator.

SECTION II

Inclusive Practices and Planning

CHAPTER 4

Program Planning and Assessment

Martin E. Block and Luke E. Kelly

OBJECTIVES

1. Understand how general physical education and adapted physical education curricula are created

2. Understand and be able to explain the relationship between general physical education and adapted physical education curricula

3. Understand why and how assessment is used to guide all planning and instructional decisions in physical education

4. Understand and be able to apply the six curriculum planning and assessment processes needed to address the physical education needs of students with disabilities

5. Understand how the physical education curriculum and assessment are used to guide decisions regarding placement, support, and inclusion of students with disabilities in physical education

6. Understand and be able to apply the five components of the achievement-based curriculum model to teaching physical education to students with disabilities

---

Mark has spina bifida and can independently ambulate with his crutches. He has been included in general physical education for the past 4 years. Next year, he will be starting fourth grade. At his individualized education program (IEP) meeting,

the physical education teacher recommends that he continue to be included in general physical education. Mark's parents question whether general physical education is the most appropriate placement for Mark. They state that Mark has always liked physical education. They also acknowledge that the physical education teacher has made numerous accommodations for Mark over the years to include him in various physical education activities. Their concern is that Mark is beginning to complain about going to physical education and not being able to keep up and do the same activities as the other students. Mark states that "the other kids are getting better and faster at everything, and I am getting worse." The physical education teacher explains that due to his disability, Mark cannot move as quickly as the other students and requires more rest breaks than his peers. He acknowledges that Mark's skill level is lower than the other students but explains that should be expected given his disability. He states that what is most important is that Mark is with his peers and is always trying his best. He is a model to the other students for the effort he makes in physical education activities when they are so hard for him to do and he knows the other students are better than he is. The physical education teacher states that Mark is an inspiration to the other students and that he frequently recognizes Mark for his outstanding effort. He recommends that Mark stay in general physical education, and he promises to be more attentive to Mark's concerns about his performance impairments and to help him deal with this issue. The parents thank the physical education teacher and agree to sign off on the IEP and Mark's placement in general physical education for the next year.

Reflect for a moment on this scenario. What were the issues and what information was used to guide the decisions that were made? Whose needs were being addressed? If Mark stays in general physical education, will his physical education needs be addressed and will he, upon graduation from high school, likely have the necessary physical and motor skills he needs to live a full, active, and healthy life?

PHYSICAL EDUCATION CURRICULA

The term *curriculum* is commonly used to describe what is taught and learned in school. So what is a physical education curriculum? A physical education curriculum is typically a written document that delineates what content is to be taught, when the content should be taught and learned, and what skills or competencies the students will exit with when they complete the curriculum. Figure 4.1 shows a diagram that illustrates a typical physical education curriculum. In this example, students learn and master body management and fundamental motor skills in the elementary grades, lead-up games and team sports in the middle school grades, and lifetime sports skills in high school with an emphasis on health-related fitness being infused throughout the program.

What is not always clear is the philosophy behind how the curriculum content is selected. One way is to take a bottom-up approach, where as much content as possible is included in each category shown in Figure 4.1 (i.e., body management, fundamental motor skills, combination skills, team sports, and lifetime sports). The goal here is to err on the side of being inclusive and to expose students to as many possibilities as possible. The downside of the bottom-up curriculum approach is that these curricula typically include more content than there are resources to implement them in physical education. Collectively, resources include factors such as the amount of time allocated for physical education instruction, class size, class composition, facilities, equipment, and teacher competency. As a result, many students in bottom-up curricula do not master the foundational skills in the elementary grades and then lack the prerequisite skills to learn the more advanced skills in the team and lifetime sport activities in the secondary grades. The end result is that they can leave high school without having mastered any lifetime sports or physical activities. An alternative method for selecting the curriculum content is to use a top-down approach. In this approach, the content included in the physical education curriculum is determined in advance by determining what goals or lifetime sports and activities the students should master by the time they finish the program. The goals are then task analyzed to identify the specific

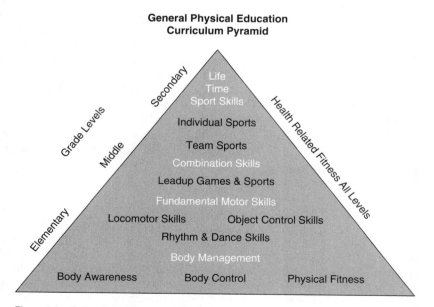

Figure 4.1. Delineation of the general physical education content. (From Kelly, L.E. [2011]. *Designing and implementing effective adapted physical education programs.* Urbana, IL: Sagamore; reprinted by permission.)

body management, fundamental motor skills, combination skills, sports, and physical activities that must be learned to achieve these goals. The major difference between the top-down and bottom-up approaches is that in the top-down approach the number of goals and objectives are adjusted according to the resources available in the school.

Using the Achievement-Based Curriculum Model

A physical education curriculum is the first of five elements needed to design and implement an effective physical education program. The five required elements or processes are program planning, assessing, implementation planning, teaching, and evaluation, as shown in the achievement-based curriculum (ABC) model in Figure 4.2 (Kelly & Melograno, 2015). While each component is depicted in the figure as a discrete entity, they are all dependent on each other. You need a program plan (note in this chapter the terms *program plan* and *curriculum* are used interchangeably) to know what content to assess, you cannot plan a lesson until you assess the students and know what they need to learn on the objectives to be taught, you cannot teach until you plan the lesson, and you cannot evaluate until data are collected related to how much progress the students have made, how effective the instruction was, or the degree to which the program plan has been achieved.

The ABC program planning process is designed to develop accountable top-down physical education curricula that lead to the achievement of clearly defined functional program goals (Kelly & Melograno, 2015). In addition, the process accounts for the following: local constraints such as amount of instructional time, class size, facilities, and teacher competency; the unique learning needs of the students; and ensuring the content in the program is mastered. It is important to note that the ABC process does not dictate what content should be included in any program or how the content is to be taught. These decisions are made by the teachers who design and implement the curriculum.

Assessment is the second component of the ABC model and is the key to its implementation. Assessment is a prerequisite for all decisions. In program planning, you need to know the students' present levels of performance, their strengths and weaknesses, and their potential future work and living settings. The first step in designing instruction once an ABC program plan is developed is assessing. You cannot plan a lesson to teach a skill until you know what focal points of the skill the students currently can and cannot perform. When you are teaching, you cannot provide students with feedback on what they are doing wrong or determine how effective your instructional activities are unless you continuously assess. Finally, you cannot evaluate student progress, teacher effectiveness, or program effectiveness unless you have at least pre- and postinstruction assessment measures.

So what is assessment? It is a dynamic process that precedes and informs all decisions made in physical education. These decisions can range from determining who should receive adapted physical education, where the best placement for a student

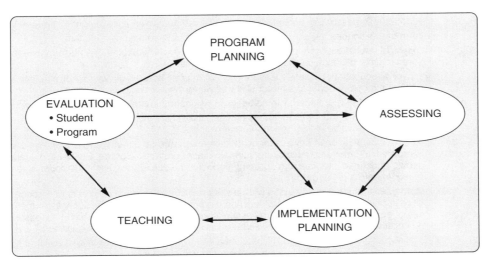

Figure 4.2. Achievement-based curriculum model. (Reprinted by permission of Waveland Press, Inc. from Kelly-Melograno DEVELOPING THE PHYSICAL EDUCATION CURRICULUM: AN ACHIEVEMENT-BASED APPROACH Long Grove, IL: Waveland Press, Inc., © [2004 Reissued 2015] All rights reserved.)

is, or how the number of practice trials a student performs in class can be increased? Assessment allows teachers to get an accurate picture of what a student can do physically and motorally at that point in time so that informed program planning and instructional decisions can be made. As used in this chapter, *assessment* is an umbrella term that describes the process used by teachers to make informed decisions. To avoid any confusion, common terms used related to assessment in physical education are defined in Table 4.1 (Horvat, Block, & Kelly, 2007).

In general, assessment instruments in physical education can be divided into two broad categories: norm-referenced instruments (NRIs) and criterion-referenced instruments (CRIs). Both categories have strengths and weaknesses that must be considered

when selecting an assessment instrument to make an informed decision.

NRIs have standardized administrative procedures that describe the conditions under which the test must be administered. These procedures are very descriptive and must be followed exactly if the normative data provided with the test are to be used. For example, most NRIs provide a script for what must be said to the person being tested for each item and how each item is to be scored. To enhance the accuracy of the scoring, most NRIs focus on measuring the products of performance that are easier to accurately and reliably judge such as the number of repetitions, distance, or time. The major advantage of NRIs is that they provide normative standards (e.g., percentiles, age equivalents) that describe how a relatively large sample of students

Table 4.1. Assessment terminology

Term	Description[a]
Administrative feasibility	A term used to describe the preparation required to administer a test and that accounts for factors such as the amount of training required to learn how to administer the test, the cost of the training and testing materials, the number of participants that can be tested at one time, and the time needed to administer the test
Assessments	A term used interchangeably along with *instruments* and *tests* to describe various instruments used in physical education. Assessments describe the procedures (e.g., instructions, testing environment setup, equipment, scoring) used to collect information on the behaviors being assessed. Instruments tend to be collections of test items that measure different fitness and motor skill abilities.
Evaluation	A term frequently used interchangeably with *assessment*. In physical education, evaluation commonly refers to the process of comparing and interpreting assessment scores (e.g., pre- and posttest measures).
Formative evaluation	In physical education, formative evaluation focuses on the process or how motor skills are performed in terms of which focal points are performed correctly or incorrectly. Formative evaluation is an ongoing process designed to shape performance over time.
Instruments	A term used interchangeably along with *assessments* and *tests* to describe various assessment instruments used in physical education. Instruments describe the procedures (e.g., instructions, testing environment setup, equipment, scoring) used to collect information on the behaviors being assessed. Instruments tend to be collections of test items that measure different fitness and motor skill abilities.
Items	A term used to describe a single fitness or motor skill item in an assessment instrument
Measurement	A term that describes the actual data that are collected in an assessment item
Product measures	In physical education, product measures collect data on the outcome of a performance, such as measures of time, distance, or the number of repetitions.
Process measures	In physical education, process measures collect data on how a skill was performed, such as whether each of the components of a motor skill was performed correctly or incorrectly.
Psychometrics	Refers to the statics provided with an assessment instrument to document its validity and reliability
Reliability	A value between 0 and 1 that indicates how consistently the test measures what it purports to measure. The closer the value is to 1, the more reliable the test.
Summative evaluation	The form of evaluation in physical education where performance and progress across multiple measures is reported in one summative score such as a letter or numeric grade. Summative evaluation typically occurs at defined intervals (e.g., grading periods) and applies established standards (e.g., requirements to earn a given grade).
Tests	A term used interchangeably along with *assessments* and *instruments* to describe various assessments used in physical education. Tests describe the procedures (e.g., instructions, testing environment setup, equipment, scoring) used to collect information on the behaviors being assessed. Tests tend to be collections of test items that measure different fitness and motor skill abilities.
Validity	A statistical value between 0 and 1 that indicates how accurately a test measures what it purports to measure. The closer the value is to 1, the more valid the test is.

[a]Definitions derived from Horvat et al. (2007).

with defined characteristics (e.g., age, gender) performed on the test. These norms can be used to interpret a student's test performance in comparison with this sample. NRIs are particularly valuable when discrepancy decisions need to be made. For example, for a student to qualify and receive a special education label, at least two NRIs must be used, and the results must show a discrepancy of at least two standard deviations below the performance level demonstrated by students in the normative group.

CRIs in physical education tend to focus more on evaluating the process or how skills are performed as opposed to the products produced by the performance. For example, a CRI on throwing would look at how the components (i.e., side orientation, arm extension, arm position, weight transfer) were performed instead of measuring how far the ball was thrown or how many times it hit a target. The student's performance is scored by judging the student's observed performance with the performance criteria used to define the skill components. Credit is given for the number of components performed correctly on two out of three trials. Figure 4.3 shows a sample CRI for throwing from Everyone Can! (Kelly, Wessel, Dummer, & Sampson, 2010). Note that skill Level 1 focuses on the how the skill is performed. Once a student demonstrates mastery of the first skill level, then the focus is on meeting criteria for distance and accuracy in skill Levels 2 and 3. While CRIs have standardized instructions, they are typically more flexible that NRIs. The goal in most CRIs is to get an accurate assessment of the student's performance. If after a verbal request and a demonstration, a student does not attempt to throw, it would be permissible to either repeat the request and demonstration or communicate the request by another means such as showing a picture or a short video. Another advantage of CRIs is that they can be easily modified to meet the unique needs of students with disabilities. For example, the components of the skill can be modified to describe how the skill is performed from a wheelchair or the focal points of a skill can be broken down into even smaller components so that instruction and progress can be adjusted for students with more severe disabilities. For example, the side orientation focal point for the overhand throw in Figure 4.3 could be broken down into six smaller focal points: 1) stand with the nondominant side toward the target, 2) stand with feet shoulder width apart, 3) stand with weight evenly distributed on both feet, 4) keep eyes on target, and 5) hold ball in dominant hand at waist level. The Test of Gross Motor Development

(Ulrich, in press) is an example of a CRI that also provides age-equivalent standards that can be used to interpret student performance on six locomotor and seven object control skills.

The greatest disadvantage of CRIs is that they typically require more training to develop the teachers' skills of observing and accurately judging whether the skill components are performed correctly. Most motor skills require only a few seconds to perform but require that several components be observed. To be functional and not exhaust the students being assessed, a physical educator should be able to observe a student performing any skill within three trials and accurately evaluate which components were performed correctly two out of three times.

The greatest advantage of CRIs is that the results typically reveal what the student is doing wrong on the skill being assessed and therefore are directly applicable to designing the instruction. For example, if a student when throwing demonstrates correct side orientation and the "T" position for arm extension but does not throw overhand (i.e., throwing hand does not pass over the shoulder), then the teacher knows that is the component to focus on next during instruction. By comparison, if an NRI was used and the results indicated the student threw a ball 65 feet and was in the 47th percentile, how do these results help the teacher determine what to teach?

The third component of the ABC model is implementation planning, also commonly referred to as lesson planning. This component focuses on how to develop assessment-based lessons that maximize student achievement by ensuring a high number of practice trials; frequent, immediate, and instructionally relevant feedback; and high on-task time. Teaching is the fourth component of the ABC model and focuses on organizing and managing the instructional environment so that the lesson plan is implemented as intended and students learn the content that is taught. Evaluation is the last component and focuses on how ongoing assessment data can be used to evaluate student progress, teacher effectiveness, and the overall program.

While the integration of all five components is required to conduct an effective physical education program, program planning and assessment are essential for the success of this model. In simple terms, the plan indicates what content should be taught and when, and assessment identifies specifically what to focus on during instruction and how the instruction should be delivered. This chapter is designed to focus on these two critical processes

EVERYONE CAN

Assessment Item: OVERHAND THROW

Equipment and Space Requirements:

- Use a tennis ball (2.5-inch [6.3 cm] diameter) for skill level 1. Use a softball (12-inch circumference, official weight) with a no-sting surface for skill level 2 and skill level 3.
- Use a 4-foot square vertical target placed 2 feet off the ground (target markings may be taped to a wall).
- Throw in an outdoor field or large gymnasium at least 70 feet (21.3 m) in length (10-foot [3 m] staging area plus 60-foot [18 m] throwing distance).

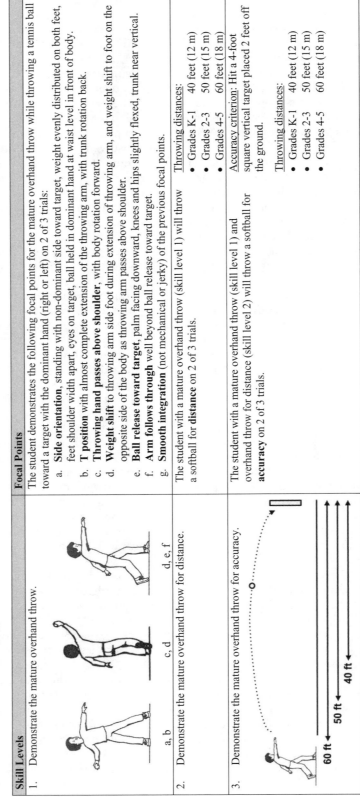

Skill Levels	Focal Points
1. Demonstrate the mature overhand throw. a, b c, d d, e, f	The student demonstrates the following focal points for the mature overhand throw while throwing a tennis ball toward a target with the dominant hand (right or left) on 2 of 3 trials: a. **Side orientation,** standing with non-dominant side toward target, weight evenly distributed on both feet, feet shoulder width apart, eyes on target, ball held in dominant hand at waist level in front of body. b. **T position** with almost complete extension of the throwing arm, with trunk rotation back. c. **Throwing hand passes above shoulder,** with body rotation forward. d. **Weight shift** to throwing arm side foot during extension of throwing arm, and weight shift to foot on the opposite side of the body as throwing arm passes above shoulder. e. **Ball release toward target,** palm facing downward, knees and hips slightly flexed, trunk near vertical. f. **Arm follows through** well beyond ball release toward target. g. **Smooth integration** (not mechanical or jerky) of the previous focal points.
2. Demonstrate the mature overhand throw for distance.	The student with a mature overhand throw (skill level 1) will throw a softball for **distance** on 2 of 3 trials.	Throwing distances: • Grades K-1 40 feet (12 m) • Grades 2-3 50 feet (15 m) • Grades 4-5 60 feet (18 m)
3. Demonstrate the mature overhand throw for accuracy.	The student with a mature overhand throw (skill level 1) and overhand throw for distance (skill level 2) will throw a softball for **accuracy** on 2 of 3 trials.	Accuracy criterion: Hit a 4-foot square vertical target placed 2 feet off the ground. Throwing distances: • Grades K-1 40 feet (12 m) • Grades 2-3 50 feet (15 m) • Grades 4-5 60 feet (18 m)

Reference Data: A baseline distance of 60 feet is used in fast pitch softball.

Figure 4.3.   Everyone Can! assessment item for the overhand throw. (Reprinted, with permission, from Kelly, L.E., Wessel, J.A., Dummer, G.M., & Sampson, T., 2010, *Everyone can! Skill development and assessment in elementary physical education online resource.* [Champaign, IL: Human Kinetics].)

that are essential for providing appropriate physical education services to students with disabilities. To illustrate the role and interaction between curriculum planning and assessment, the chapter has been organized around six questions physical educators must be able to answer for each student they serve that has a disability. These questions are outlined in Table 4.2 along with the recommended processes and decisions physical educators need to make to answer them. Each of the questions is then examine in detail in the remainder of the chapter.

WHO QUALIFIES FOR ADAPTED PHYSICAL EDUCATION SERVICES?

All students with disabilities are required to receive physical education services, although not all will automatically qualify for adapted physical education services (Block & Burke, 1999). Therefore, the first programmatic question to be addressed is who qualifies for adapted physical education services. As mandated in the Individuals with Disabilities Education Act (IDEA) of 1990 (PL 101-476) and its amendments, the student's IEP team should decide whether he or she qualifies for adapted physical

education. Furthermore, decisions should not be based on a label, what services other students in the district receive, or what services are currently available.

If a student qualifies for special education, they are assigned a special education label such as "student with autism," "student with an intellectual disability," or "student with a learning disability." Once a student has qualified to receive special education services, the next question is which special education services the student requires. In some school districts, students qualify automatically for adapted physical education services simply because they have a particular diagnosis. In some school districts, students with learning disabilities often do not get adapted physical education services because it is assumed that they do not have any special motor or fitness needs. However, students who use wheelchairs usually qualify for adapted physical education because it is assumed that the goals for these students are completely different from their peers without disabilities. Such practices are in direct violation of the law, which specifically mandates that all students with disabilities be evaluated to determine if they require special physical

Table 4.2   Curriculum planning and assessment decision process for adapted physical education

Question	Process	Decisions
1. Who qualifies for adapted physical education services?	Needs assessment (NA) to determine present level of performance (PLOP)	Compare and interpret the NA results related to general physical education curriculum and district eligibility criteria for adapted physical education.
2. What functional physical education goals does the student need to achieve to live an active and healthy life?	Use an ecological approach and evaluate the NA data and input from multiple sources to determine fitness and lifetime physical activity goals for the student.	Create an achievement-based adapted physical education curriculum for the student. The scope and sequence of this curriculum will indicate what content will be taught, when it is targeted to be mastered, and what goals will be achieved by the end of high school.
3. What physical education content should be included on the student's IEP?	Identify the objectives targeted to be achieved this year in the ABC-APE curriculum.	State in the IEP the goals and objectives from the achievement-based adapted physical education curriculum to be achieved, who should teach them, how they should be taught, how they will be evaluated, and how much time will be devoted to physical education.
4. What is the least restrictive physical education setting for this student?	Compare student's PLOP and achievement-based adapted physical education goals and objectives for the year with the general physical education curriculum and the continuum of placement options available.	To the maximum extent possible, place the student in the least restrictive environment where he or she can achieve the achievement-based adapted physical education goals for the year along the continuum from adapted physical education to general physical education. Students can have different placements throughout the year based on their learning needs and the general physical education curriculum content.
5. How is daily physical education instruction planned and implemented?	Review assessment data on objectives targeted for instruction and identify the next focal points to be mastered.	Determine what the student must learn on each skill focal point and then determine how to teach this content given the student's learning attributes.
6. How is student IEP and achievement-based adapted physical education curriculum progress evaluated?	Collect continuous assessment data on the objectives in the achievement-based adapted physical education curriculum/IEP.	Review the evaluation data annually to evaluate and revise the IEP. Every 3 years, review the evaluation data to confirm eligibility and make any needed revisions to the achievement-based adapted physical education curriculum.

education services (Bateman & Herr, 2003; IDEA 1997; Osborne, 1996; Wright & Wright, n.d.). More important, no one has taken the time to assess each student's strengths and weaknesses before determining who qualifies for adapted physical education. Although many students with learning disabilities do in fact have motor and learning impairments that justify specialized physical education, many students who use wheelchairs can do quite well in general physical education without any special support.

NRIs, or standardized tests, are commonly used to determine if a student qualifies for adapted physical education. An NRI is a test in which a student's score is compared with the scores of others on the same test—that is, the score is compared with a set of norms (Horvat et al., 2007; Kelly & Melograno, 2015). Norms are established by testing a representative sample from a particular population. For example, for a test to be valid for children 2–6 years of age, a large sample of children ages 2–6 should be tested to develop norms. These norms can then be analyzed and organized to describe scores that correspond to a certain percentage of the population. To illustrate, a particular score on a test might represent a point where 75% of the norm sample scored below that particular score (75th percentile). School systems can then establish minimal cutoff scores that correspond to who does or does not qualify for adapted physical education. Such an approach is by far the most widely used approach in adapted physical education (Ulrich, 1985). Many states even have set criteria based on standardized test results for determining who qualifies for adapted physical education services. Sherrill (2004) noted that students in Alabama and Georgia who score below the 30th percentile on standardized tests of motor performance qualify for adapted physical education services. Sherrill suggests that students who consistently score below the 50th percentile should qualify for special physical education services.

For example, the Bruininks-Oseretsky Test (BOT) of Motor Proficiency, the standardized test most often administered by adapted physical education specialists (Ulrich, 1985), is often used to determine which students qualify for adapted physical education (see Figure 4.2). The BOT is a valid NRI designed to measure specific motor abilities of children 4 ½–14 ½ years of age. Areas evaluated include running speed and agility, balance, bilateral coordination, response speed, strength, upper limb coordination, visual-motor coordination, and upper limb speed and dexterity. A school system might decide that a student with a total score below the 30th percentile qualifies for adapted physical education.

Although the BOT is reported to be valid and reliable, it is important to question whether the information obtained from this type of test is relevant to the needs of individual children. What information do data collected from the BOT give the team that would help them determine if a student needs adapted physical education services? Will a student who performs at the 20th percentile have difficulty in general physical education activities? Will a student who does poorly on subtest items such as response speed or bilateral coordination do poorly with activities in general physical education without extensive support? Does the BOT reliably predict how well a second-grade student will do in a unit that focuses on locomotor patterns or how well a middle school student will do in a softball unit?

Similarly, why does performance at or below the 20th percentile on the Physical Best Fitness Test qualify a student for adapted physical education services? Physical Best measures health-related physical fitness for students ages 5–18 years. Areas evaluated include cardiovascular endurance (1-mile run), percentage of body fat (skinfold), muscular strength (sit-ups and pull-ups), and flexibility (sit and reach). Does a student's poor performance on any or all of these items predict how well that student will do in general physical education? Will limited abdominal strength as measured by sit-ups help determine if a high school student will be unsuccessful or need modifications to popular lifetime leisure activities such as softball, tennis, or golf? It should be clear that the BOT, Physical Best, and similar tests are not related to what really takes place in general physical education. Yet, these types of tests are frequently used to make decisions regarding who qualifies for adapted physical education services.

Needs Assessment

Given the limitations of the discussed methods for making accurate eligibility decisions, it is highly recommended that an adapted physical education needs assessment (NA) based on the school's general physical education curriculum be used (Kelly, 2011). This method is preferred because the data collected and the comparisons made are directly related to the content taught in the general physical education program. The only prerequisites for using the NA method are that the school's general physical education curriculum must be clearly defined and that it actually be followed by the general physical education teachers implementing the program. An NA instrument can be created by simply collecting and organizing into an instrument the assessment items that already exist in the general physical education curriculum.

An NA instrument is created by identifying the content in the general physical education curriculum that is targeted to be mastered at each grade level. The NA instrument can cover a wide range of grades, but since most students requiring specially designed instruction are identified early, the instruments typically focus on the elementary grades or in many cases just the first few elementary grades. Once the range of grades is determined, the next step is to review the general physical education curriculum scope and sequence chart and identify which objectives students are targeted to master at the end of each of these grades. The CRIs for these objectives are then collected from the general physical education curriculum and organized in a notebook. These test items should be organized in the curriculum categories (e.g., body awareness, locomotor, physical fitness) and listed developmentally within each category from the easiest to the most difficult. The order is very important. When students are assessed we want the assessment to be a positive experience. For this to happen, we need to ensure they experience more success than failure. With the NA this done by administering the items in each category developmentally from the easiest to the hardest and stopping after a student fails two items in a row in any category. After all the

Needs Assessment Summary

Student name: Kason Kamide   **Date:** April 1, 2015   **Assessor:** Simon Driver

Goal/grade	K					1						2						Goal %
Body awareness	#	M	A	C	E		#	M	A	C	E		#	M	A	C	E	Mastery
Parts (5)	5	y	A	A	A	Planes (5)	5	y	A	A	A	Personal space (6)	6	y	A	A	A	100%
Actions (6)	6	y	A	A	A	Directions in space (6)	6	y	A	A	A								
Gen space (6)	6	y	A	A	A														
Locomotor																		00.0%
Run (5)	3	n	A	B	B	Hop (6)	2	n	B	B	C	Skip (6)	2	n	B	B	C	
Gallop (6)	3	n	A	B	C	Slide (6)	2	n	B	B	C								
Object control																		60.0%
Underhand roll (5)	5	y	A	A	A	Kick stationary (6)	6	y	A	A	A	Kick moving (5)	3	n	B	B	B	
Underhand throw (5)	5	y	A	A	A							Catch (5)	2	n	B	B	C	
Body control																		16.7%
Log roll (4)	4	y	A	A	A	Shoulder roll (5)	0	n	B	B	C	Backward roll (5)	0	n	B	B	C	
						Forward roll (5)	0	n	B	B	C	2 Point Balances (4)	1	n	B	B	C	
						Bal. beam walk (5)	1	n	B	B	C								
Rhythm dance																		80.0%
Even beat	4	y	A	A	A	Accent beat (4)	4	y	B	B	B	Polka (6)	2	n	B	C	C	
Uneven beat(4)	4	y	A	A	A	Com. movement (5)	5	y	B	B	B								
Social																		100%
Follow instruction (5)	5	y	A	A	A	Work habits (6)	6	y	A	A	A								
Fitness																		25.0%
												Partial curl-ups (4)	2	n	B	B	C	
												Stretching (5)	5	y	A	A	A	
												Warm-up (6)	3	n	B	B	A	
												Card. resp. exertion (6)	3	n	B	B	C	
Grade % Mastery	9/11 = 81.8%					6/11 = 54.5%						2/11 = 18.2%						
Overall % Mastery	9/11 = 81.8%					15/22 = 68.2%						17/33 = 51.5%						51.5%

(*Key*: Goal/grade, the name of the objective with the total number of focal points in (); #, the number of focal points the student successful demonstrated two out of three times; M, y/n is reported to indicate if mastery of all the focal points was demonstrated; A, a rating of the student's level of attention during the assessment: ratings: A, above average; B, average; C, below average; C, a rating of the student's apparent comprehension of what skill should be performed: ratings: A, above average; B, average; C, below average; E, a rating of the effort the student exhibited performing this item: ratings: A, above average; B, average; C, below average).

Figure 4.4. Sample needs assessment summary report.

assessment items are administered, the data collected are organized in an NA summary form (see Figure 4.4).

The goal of an NA is to get an accurate measurement of which general physical education objectives the student being evaluated has and has not mastered. To obtain accurate data, you must elicit the student's best performance and effort. This can be a challenging task with students with disabilities because many know they are not good at motor skills and that they cannot perform them as demonstrated. The following four recommendations increase the likelihood that valid data will be collected (for more detail on how to create and administer an NA instrument, see Kelly, 2011):

1. Practice and learn how to administer the CRIs on your NA instrument so you can assess them in three trials or fewer. If a student cannot do any of the focal points on the first two trials or if he or she does them all correctly on the first two trials, then there is no need for a third trial. If you have to observe a student several times to assess each objective, two negative things can potentially happen. First, the student will become fatigued, which can negatively affect the student's performance on later objectives in the assessment. Second, the student might begin to think he or she is doing something wrong when you keep asking to do the skill again, which can also affect the student's performance.

2. Get to know the student informally before the formal assessment. You can visit with the student in the classroom or maybe at lunch and just talk with him or her for a while. Once you have established a rapport with the student, you can let him or her know you will be coming back to visit in a few days and play some games.

3. Create a safe and distraction-free environment to administer your assessment. Make sure the student cannot be observed by others, remove any unnecessary equipment, and make sure the student looks relaxed and comfortable before you start the assessment. When in doubt, ask if the student is comfortable.

4. Make the assessment fun. Remember your goal is to measure their best performance. To do this, you want to maximize their success, minimize the amount of failure, and administer the assessment as quickly as possible. Within each category of objectives on the NA, always start with the easiest one and work your way through the items developmentally. If a student fails two items in a row in a category, do not assess the remaining objectives in that category. The logic

here is that if the objectives are in developmental order and the student has just failed two, he or she will likely not be successful in performing any of the remaining items. After every time a student clearly fails an item—that is, it's clear to you that the student is aware that he or she could not perform the skill—have the student do a simple skill you know he or she can perform. A good technique is to make the assessment a game called "Show and Do." You and the student take turns demonstrating movements and then try to copy each other's movements. Since you want the student to experience success, I usually start with a few simple and silly tasks that aren't on the test. I also pretend to have difficulty occasionally performing some of the skills they demonstrate, particularly after the student has just failed two items. Then I say something such as, "These movements are getting hard. Let's try some different types of movements."

When the NA is completed, add the results recorded on the individual CRI score sheets to the NA summary form (see Figure 4.4). These results represent the student's present level of performance (PLOP). Take a moment to review the needs assessment summary. Note that next to the name of each objective there is a number in parentheses. This number indicates the total number of focal points for that objective that must be demonstrated to achieve mastery. Five values are recorded for each objective assessed in the NA. The values in the # column equal the actual number of focal points the student successfully demonstrated during the assessment of that objective. The y or n in the column labeled M indicates whether the student demonstrated mastery (i.e., the # value = the value in () to the right of the objective name). The A, C, and E columns stand for attention, comprehension, and effort. These behaviors are rated for each objective assessed using a 3-point scale: A = above average, B = average, C = below average. Percentages are calculated on the bottom of the form and in the far right column. At the bottom of each grade column, two percentages are calculated: grade mastery and overall mastery. The grade mastery is calculated by dividing the number of objectives the student demonstrated mastery of at that grade level by the total number of objectives targeted to be mastered at that grade level. For example, for the kindergarten objectives Kason demonstrated mastery of 9 of the 11 objectives targeted for that year, so his grade mastery for first grade was 81.1%. At the bottom of each grade column is the overall mastery. This value is calculated by dividing the cumulative number of objectives mastered by the end of any given grade level by the total number of objectives that should have been mastered by the end of that grade level. For example, at the end of second grade, Kason has demonstrated mastery of 15 of the total of 22 objectives for an overall mastery of 68.2%. Finally, at the bottom of the far right column, it can be seen that of the 33 objectives that should have been mastered by the end of second grade, Kason has only mastered 17 of these for an overall mastery level of 51.5%.

When using the NA method to determine eligibility, the school district must set the eligibility criteria or cutoff level—the deficit required to receive adapted physical education services. A common cutoff score for the NA method is 60%. The logic here is if a student at the lower elementary grades is already 40% or more behind on mastering the basic physical and motor skills, which are the building blocks for more advanced skills, that student is going to require some curricula modifications and specialized instruction. In Kason's case, it can be seen that he is falling further behind the other students each year: 18.2% behind at the end of kindergarten, 31.8% behind at the end of first grade, and 48.5% behind at the end of second grade. The NA results should also be reviewed by the IEP team in terms of the student's behavior during the assessment as well as where the student's greatest strengths and weaknesses are across the physical education content categories. During the NA, in addition to recording the student's assessment performance on each objective, the assessor would also rate and record their attention, comprehension, and effort (ACE) behaviors. These ratings are recorded on the score sheet. These behavior ratings provide valuable information when interpreting the student's performance and making placement decisions. Reviewing Kason's ACE behaviors, it can be seen that overall he appeared to attend well during the assessment, understood what skill he was being asked to perform, and generally gave a good effort. However, when the skill was difficult for him and overall when the skills became more difficult, his effort started to decline. Analysis of the student's performance across the different physical education content categories also provides valuable information for the next important decision—what functional physical education goals does this student need to achieve to live an active and healthy life?

It is important to understand why using an NA based on the general physical education curriculum is critical for this decision. The general physical education curriculum is designed around the learning needs, long-term goals, and attributes of students without disabilities and the time they need to learn a series of physical and motor objectives each year that culminate in them achieving a number of goals in fitness, team sports, lifetime sports, and physical activity when they finish high school. The number of goals (e.g., ability to play functional games such as tennis, golf, volleyball) to be achieved in general physical education as well as the number of objectives (i.e., the individual skills needed to play a functional game of tennis) to be achieved for each goal are based on a number of school factors such as the amount of time allocated for physical education instruction, class sizes, equipment, and facilities.

When evaluating whether a student with a disability requires adapted physical education or general physical education, there are two key factors to consider:

1. Can the student with the disability realistically learn and master the objectives and goals in the general physical education curriculum within the parameters of the curriculum (e.g., time available for instruction, class size)?

2. Are the goals and objectives in the general physical education curriculum appropriate for the student with the disability? That is, is there a high probability that the student will be able to master the general physical education goals and then use them later in life to maintain their health, physical activity, and fitness?

For many students with disabilities, the answer to one or both of these questions may be no. For example, Jerry has an intellectual disability and potentially could learn the objectives in the general physical education curriculum, but there would not be enough time available in the general physical education curriculum for him to learn all the content. That is because Jerry is likely to enter the general physical education curriculum 2–3 years behind the skill level of his peers and then will learn skills at a slower rate in general physical education due to his disability. That is not because he is not trying hard or cannot learn the skills but rather his lower intellectual functioning slows down the learning process. Since the students in the general physical education curriculum advance through the objectives at a typical developmental rate, Jerry will fall further and further behind each year and eventually will not have the prerequisite skills to successfully participate in the general physical education curriculum. If left in the general physical education curriculum, he will likely graduate without achieving any of the general physical education goals, which means he will not have any functional lifetime fitness or physical activity skills to help him maintain his health, fitness, and activity levels as an adult.

For students with other types of disabilities, the general physical education curriculum goals may not be appropriate. For example, Alisa has moderate to severe spastic cerebral palsy in her legs and mild spastic cerebral palsy in her arms. She uses a wheelchair as her primary means of locomotion. Due to the nature of her disability, she is significantly developmentally delayed in the motor domain and learns motor skills very slowly. Given the constraints of her condition, she needs a physical education curriculum where the goals are tailored to her movement strengths and learning rate. This might mean she leaves school after 12 years of physical education with functional skills in bowling, sit volleyball, bocce, wheelchair ping pong, and her own cardiorespiratory and exercise routine that she can perform independently at a local health club.

The reality here is that many students with disabilities usually enter the general physical education curriculum developmentally behind and then learn physical and motor skills at a slower rate due to their various disabilities. If the magnitude of these delays, as identified on the adapted physical education NA, meets the school's eligibility criteria, then these students will qualify for adapted physical education services.

What functional physical education goals do the students need to achieve to live and active and healthy life?

Physical Education Goals and Individualized Education Programs

Once it has been determined that a student requires adapted physical education services, the next step is to determine which specific goals the student needs to achieve in physical education so that he or she can develop and maintain physical and motor skills and live an active and healthy life after graduation. Unfortunately, in many schools this step is confused with creating the IEP goals and objectives for the student. The problem with creating the IEP goals at this time is that the IEP requires the goals be set for only 1 year. Instead of evaluating and determining the physical education goals that need to be included in a student's overall physical education program in order to address the student's long-term needs and then analyzing these goals to determine the appropriate IEP goals for any given year, the focus is often on what the student can do that is already being taught in the general physical education program that year? Unfortunately, a series of 1-year IEPs developed using this approach does not culminate in the student developing competency in any functional goals that can be used to maintain health and fitness after graduation.

Trying to develop the IEP too soon is further complicated by the traditional assessment data used to determine students' eligibility for adapted physical education. Since many schools use traditional NRIs that only produce discrepancy scores, they do not have performance data that can be used to develop long-term goals for students. Usually, information taken from the classification assessment is used to develop the student's IEP. This makes the assessment tools used for classification critical. Unfortunately, in the traditional approach, the use of standardized tests forces practitioners to follow a developmental, or "bottom-up," approach. In the bottom-up approach, impairments at the lower end of the developmental continuum become the focus of a student's physical education program without regard to how these skills affect the acquisition of real-life skills (Brown et al., 1979; Kelly, 2011; Kelly & Melograno, 2015; Kelly et al., 2010). In practice, IEP goals and objectives become items a student fails on developmental tests or tests of motor abilities. For example, a student who does poorly on upper limb speed and dexterity (e.g., sorting cards quickly) might have as a goal on his IEP to improve upper limb response speed with specific activities such as repeatedly touching nose with index fingers, touching thumb to fingertips, or pivoting the thumb and index fingers. Similarly, a student who cannot stand on tiptoes for 5 seconds with eyes open or stand on one foot with hands on hip for 5 seconds (items on the Peabody Developmental Motor Scales) would have an IEP goal to improve static balance and a short-term instructional objective of standing on tiptoes and balancing on one foot. While upper limb response speed and static balance may be problematic for this student, is working on these nonfunctional skills in isolation appropriate? How do these goals relate to skills the student will need to be successful in current and future physical education and recreation environments? Again, although the long-term goals may be appropriate, the short-term instructional objectives are nonfunctional and bear no relation to the skills a student needs to be successful in general physical education.

What should occur after students qualify for adapted physical education services is their NA results are compared with the general physical education curriculum to determine the percentage for their overall mastery of the general physical education curriculum content and the nature of their impairments. The magnitude of their impairments should be examined in relation to the various content categories (e.g., body awareness, locomotor skills, object control skills) as well as their attention, comprehension, and effort behavior during the assessment. This information is then used to determine if their adapted physical education curriculum will be a modified version of the general physical education curriculum or if the magnitude of their needs warrants creating a unique achievement-based adapted physical education curriculum for them. The critical point here is that the question being addressed is which physical and motor skills this student needs to learn and master in physical education so that he or she can live an active and healthy life after graduating rather than "Can we find something this student can do in the general physical education curriculum?"

Using Response to Intervention

Chapter 9 presents an alternative approach for determining whether a student has a learning disability. This approach, known as *response to intervention* (RTI), focuses on how a student responds to ever-increasing levels of instruction. Stephens, Silliman-French, Kinnison, and French (2010) suggest using RTI for determining who qualifies for adapted physical education.

Tier 1

Within Tier 1, all students in each physical education class receive high-quality instruction, and all students are informally screened in basic motor skills such as throwing, catching, running, and jumping. General movement concepts such as being able to change speeds and directions and space awareness (i.e., moving around the gym space safely) are also included in the screening. This initial observation/screening can be quite easy to conduct. For example, a physical educator can have students play a game in which they are constrained to perform locomotor patterns and demonstrate basic patterns, movement concepts, and space awareness. The physical educator observes students during the first few weeks of school and identifies any students who seem to be struggling with these basic movements. Similarly, the first few weeks of school could include stations where students demonstrate object control skills such as overhand throwing, kicking, catching, and striking. Again, the physical educator could move from station to station during these first few weeks of school, observing and taking note of students

who are struggling to demonstrate the most skillful pattern (or at least a pattern that is appropriate for their age). Tier 1 can last 3–5 weeks.

Tier 2

Students identified as being "at risk" during Tier 1 receive supplemental instruction in small groups in areas where they demonstrate motor impairments. For example, several first and second graders are identified as stepping with the same-side foot when throwing rather than with their opposite foot. As part of Tier 2 procedures, these students are given extra instruction and practice opportunities in performing the overhand throw. When setting up skill stations, students who are demonstrating the most skillful throwing pattern are grouped together, and the physical educator makes it a point to go to that station to provide extra instruction and feedback to the student. Similarly, the physical educator can go to those students who struggle with locomotor patterns and give them extra feedback and instruction on how to perform these patterns correctly. Tier 2 lasts 4–6 weeks, with students showing significant progress in motor skill performance removed from the "need to be monitored" list. Students not showing adequate progress are moved to Tier 3.

Tier 3

Within Tier 3, students who are not making adequate progress in general physical education in Tier 2 are provided with more intensive and targeted instruction matched to their motor impairments and rates of progress. Again, interventions are provided by the physical educator in small-group settings. Support to the physical educator on how to intervene could be provided by the school district adapted physical education specialist (when available), a special education teacher who knows the student well (e.g., teacher can provide ideas for motivating and communicating with the student, such as using picture schedules and other visual supports for a student with autism), or in some cases by an occupational or physical therapist who can provide some insight on why the student might be struggling with demonstrating a skill and how to help the student practice and master the skill. In addition, the general physical educator could search online and through books on how to help students who are struggling to develop motor skills. For example, PE Central (http://www.pecentral.com) has a nice array of resources to help physical educators teach motor skills, and Everyone Can! (Kelly, 2011) has motor skills broken into teachable components along with specific activities to help students master these components. A longer period of time—say, 6–8 weeks—is recommended for instruction in Tier 3. Students who continue to show too little progress at this level of intervention are then considered for more intensive interventions as part of Tier 4.

Tier 4

Within Tier 4, students receive individualized, intensive interventions that target the students' motor and related skill impairments that are preventing skilled performance. Either the general physical educator or adapted physical education specialist provides intervention. As noted earlier, many school districts do not employ adapted physical education specialists, so this level of intervention will be provided by the general physical educator with support of the special education teacher, therapists, and the student's teacher assistant. For example, a student with autism who was not making adequate progress will receive one-to-one instruction. The general physical educator uses the same visual supports noted in Tier 3. However, with one-to-one instruction and support of the teacher assistant, the student is able to stay on task longer and get more practice trials with specific feedback. If the student begins to make progress at this level with one-to-one support after 6 weeks or so of intense instruction, then continued one-to-one instruction with the general physical educator, along with gradual reintegration into a small group, is warranted. However, if the student still does not make adequate progress toward targeted goals even with this intense instruction, then the student is referred for a comprehensive evaluation and considered for eligibility for adapted physical education services under IDEA.

Some Things to Consider with Response to Intervention and Physical Education

For RTI to work, there are several assumptions that must be met. First, the physical education program must be a skill-based program in which the focus is on teaching students how to perform locomotor and object control skills (or sports skills at the middle and high school levels). This model would be more difficult to implement if the general physical education program focused more on a game-play approach in which students are exposed to a variety of skills and activities but are not taught skills to mastery. Similarly, this model would not work if

the physical education program focused on physical fitness and just getting the students to be active for 30 minutes. Second, the general physical educator has to have the competence and confidence to 1) identify students who are displaying performance deficits, 2) analyze motor skills qualitatively and identify which components a student is not performing correctly, and 3) provide appropriate activities to remediate missing components. For example, a physical educator would have to be able to identify the students who are not performing throwing and catching skills at a skillful level, identify specifically which components of the throw and catch individual students are not performing, and finally create and implement activities to help these students master the missing components. This becomes even more challenging when the physical educator has two or three classes in the gym as the same time with upward of 75 students in one class. Third, Tiers 3 and 4 will only work if the physical educator is given time to work with students in small groups and one to one.

DETERMINING WHAT TO TEACH: IDENTIFYING FUNCTIONAL GOALS

Once a student qualifies for adapted physical education services, the NA results are reviewed by an ecological team composed of the IEP committee with input from local agencies that provide physical activity, fitness, recreation, and sporting programs in the community. The goal of this group is to consider this student's future employment and living arrangement upon graduation to determine what physical education goals would have the greatest benefit for maintaining the student's health and fitness and enhancing his or her ability to participate and interact with other members of the community. Based on the input from the ecological team, the physical educator then creates an adapted physical education curriculum for the student following the ABC planning process (Kelly, 2011). Table 4.3 shows some of the common factors the ecological team considers when developing physical education curriculum goals for students with disabilities.

Before reviewing the ABC planning steps, it is important to understand why we are creating a unique adapted physical education curriculum for each student with a disability and why this level of planning is necessary. Figure 4.5 illustrates the relationship between the general physical education and adapted physical education curricula. Note that for many students with mild disabilities, their

Table 4.3.   Factors to consider when prioritizing goals and objectives and their applications to physical education

Factor	Application to physical education
What are the student's physical and motor strengths and weaknesses as well as current and future physical activity needs?	Consider how these fit with the general physical education goals and community play/recreation activities.
How much time do you have to teach skills, and how much instruction will the student need to master skills?	Younger students can be exposed to a greater variety of skills, whereas older students should focus on skills needed to participate in specific lifetime leisure activities.
What are the student's interests?	What recreational/sport activities does the student prefer?
What are the parents' interests?	What recreational/sport activities do the student's parents prefer?
What are peers' interests?	What activities do peers play on the playground, in the neighborhood, and in community recreation?
What recreation facilities are available in the community?	Prioritize activities that will be available to the student in his or her community.
What equipment/transportation is available?	Consider any special equipment needs (e.g., bowling ramp, flotation devices) the student might have.
What support is available?	Think about who can assist the student in physical education and recreation. Are specially trained professionals needed to work with the student (e.g., vision therapist)?

adapted physical education curriculum falls within the general physical education curriculum—that is, they work on the same goals and objectives as the students without disabilities. The major difference is they work on achieving fewer overall curriculum goals and/or fewer objectives within each goal. This reduction in content is necessary because most of them start the general physical education curriculum with delays and learn at slower rates. Ideally, these delays would be addressed by proportionally increasing the amount of instructional time students with disabilities received in physical education, but unfortunately, this is not possible

in most schools. Therefore, if physical education instructional time is held constant for all students, students with disabilities will master fewer goals and/or objectives in their curricula. It is also important to note in Figure 4.5 that the following can occur as the severity of disability increases: The amount of shared content with general physical education decreases, the amount of content that can be included in the adapted physical education curriculum further decreases, and in many cases the functional level of mastery at the end of the adapted physical education curriculum may be lower than the general physical education curriculum. For example, it may require several years or 10 times as much instruction and practice time for a student with severe spastic cerebral palsy and an intellectual disability to learn to bowl independently. It is therefore imperative that the goals and objectives that students with disabilities do work on in physical education are achieved and have the greatest carryover benefits for their future employment, living, health, fitness, and PA opportunities.

The ABC planning steps are illustrated in Table 4.4 with the intent of highlighting some of the key issues involved in developing adapted physical education curricula. To illustrate the planning process, a sample adapted physical education curriculum plan is presented for a student named Beth who has Down syndrome. More detailed information on how to design and implement achievement-based adapted physical education curricula is provided in the references at the end of the book (Kelly, 2011; Kelly & Melograno, 2015; Kelly et al., 2010).

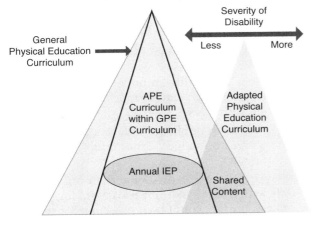

Figure 4.5.   Relationship between the general physical education and adapted physical education curricula. (From Kelly, L.E. [2011]. *Designing and implementing effective adapted physical education programs.* Urbana, IL: Sagamore; reprinted by permission.)

Table 4.4.　ABC planning steps

1. Define curriculum goals and rationales.
2. Identify and rank objectives by goal.
3. Determine the emphasis each goal should receive in the curriculum.
4. Calculate the amount of time available.
5. Calculate average objective mastery time.
6. Determine how much content can fit in the curriculum.
7. Sequence the goals and objectives developmentally.

Step 1: Define the Student's Curriculum Goals

This step is performed by the adapted physical education teacher with significant input from the ecological team (e.g., student's parents and other members of the IEP committee). The purpose of this step is to determine what functional physical activity skills the student will be able to perform at the end of the physical education curriculum. Given that most students that qualify for adapted physical education services have significant motor delays and learn motor skills at a slower rate, most adapted physical education curricula have fewer goals than the general physical education curriculum. Table 4.5 shows sample curriculum goals for three physical education curricula: a general physical education curriculum, an adapted physical education curriculum for a student with a mild disability, and an adapted physical education curriculum for a student with a more severe disability. Brief phrases are used to describe the goals in the table. Each goal would be written as a functional statement and supported by at least three rationale statements justifying the value of the goal for the target audience. The curriculum goals in Table 4.5 parallel the pyramid shown in Figure 4.1. Note that the adapted physical education goals for the student with the mild disability parallel the general physical education goals. The only difference is that the student with the mild disability is only expected to master six of the general physical education nine goals. However, the student with the more severe disability is expected to master only four goals, and these goals have been tailored to address the student's unique physical education needs. For the purposes of illustrating the planning process, we are going to define a curriculum for Beth, a student with Down syndrome who is just starting kindergarten. After discussing Beth's NA results with her parents as well as the parents' short- and long-term interests for Beth, the following three physical education goals were developed along with their supporting rationales.

Table 4.5.　Sample curriculum goals for three different physical education curricula

General physical education	Adapted physical education	Adapted physical education
	Mild disability	Severe disability
1. Soccer		
2. Volleyball	1. Sit volleyball	1. Volleyball
3. Basketball	2. Wheelchair basketball	
4. Softball		
5. Tennis	3. Wheelchair tennis	2. Tennis
6. Golf	4. Golf	3. Bowling
7. Rock Climbing		
8. Fitness	5. Fitness	4. Fitness
9. Social/respect[a]	6. Social/respect	

[a]For the adapted physical education curriculum for the student with a severe disability, the social and respect objectives will be integrated into the other four curriculum goals.

Goal 1: Beth will be able to play a functional game of tennis.
　Rationale:

1. Tennis is a lifetime sport that can be played throughout the lifespan.
2. Tennis can be used to maintain health and fitness.
3. Tennis requires minimal equipment, and there are many public tennis courts near where Beth lives.

Goal 2: Beth will be able to play a functional game of volleyball.
　Rationale:

1. Volleyball is a game played by Beth's family, and the family also wants Beth to eventually participate in Special Olympics volleyball.
2. Volleyball can be used to maintain health and fitness.
3. Volleyball requires minimal equipment, and there are many public volleyball courts near where Beth lives.

Goal 3. Beth will be able to independently perform a fitness routine at a local fitness club.
　Rationale:

1. Physical fitness is very important for individuals with Down syndrome because many become obese and/or exhibit poor muscular strength.
2. Beth's parents belong to a local fitness club.
3. Beth will need to learn how to use the equipment in the fitness club before she can begin to independently use it at the club.

Step 2: Delineate the Objectives for Each Curriculum Goal

Once the curriculum goals are determined, the second step in the ABC planning process is to determine what knowledge and skills students must master to functionally perform and achieve each curriculum goal. Table 4.6 shows a sequence of learning objectives that Beth must master to learn and achieve her three curriculum goals. This list of objectives includes both the prerequisite skills (e.g., body parts and running) taught during the elementary school years and the basic sports skills (e.g., forehand and backhand tennis strokes) typically taught in the middle and high school grades. The objectives in the lists are usually grouped in logical categories (e.g., locomotor skills, object control skills, fitness), listed developmentally within each category, and ranked from 1 (the most important) to the least essential or optional objectives (e.g., top-spin serve). Organizing the objectives in this manner facilitates determining how many and which objectives can ultimately be included in the final curriculum. At this point, it is important to highlight two important principles of the ABC model. First, all objectives included in the final curriculum are expected to be taught and mastered by the students. Second, all objectives in the curriculum must be measureable—this means there is an assessment item for each skill that defines what students must do to demonstrate mastery. Figure 4.3 shows a sample assessment item for the overhand throw. Note that the overhand throw has been divided into three skill levels. The first skill level focuses on the key focal points that define how the skill is performed. Once the first skill level is mastered, the students then focus on the products of the skill (e.g., distance and accuracy) that are needed for various games and sports.

Step 3: Determine the Emphasis Each Goal Should Receive in the Curriculum

How much emphasis should each goal receive in the curriculum? This step in the ABC planning process is designed to ensure that each goal receives the appropriate amount of emphasis developmentally within the curriculum so that all the objectives identified for each goal can be achieved within the total time for the curriculum. During this step, the teacher distributes the instructional time available (out of 100%) each year across each of the curriculum goals. Because many goals share the same prerequisite basic skills (e.g.,

body management, locomotor skills), time must be allocated for these skills in the lower grades for each goal. Table 4.7 shows a sample goal emphasis chart for Beth's curriculum. Note that although time for most goals is distributed across many years in the curriculum, some goals receive more and less emphasis at different grades or program levels. The difference in emphasis can be the result of a number of factors such as the number of objectives that must be achieved to perform the goal, the difficulty of the objectives, the time needed for students to master them, or practical issues such as what grade levels have access to certain facilities. A review of Table 4.7 shows that Beth's adapted physical education teacher put more emphasis on the sports skills goals equally across the curriculum compared with the fitness goal. For the fitness goal, she started with a lower emphasis at the elementary level, gradually increasing the emphasis as Beth progressed through middle school and high school. The logic behind this strategy was probably to develop Beth's motor skills first so that she could then use these skills to work on her fitness.

Step 4: Calculate the Amount of Time Available

How much instructional time is available for Beth's adapted physical education curriculum? The purpose of this step is to determine how much time is available for physical education across all the years in the curriculum. The actual amount of time mandated for physical education instruction can vary greatly between states and even between school divisions within the same state. Many states, for example, only require students to take physical education for 1 or 2 years during high school. It is important to note that if students qualify for adapted physical education and they have not achieved all the goals in the adapted physical education curriculum, they can and should receive physical education during all their high school years.

Table 4.8 shows two charts. The first chart shows the annual amount of time available for physical education by the number of days of instruction per week. The second chart shows the actual calculation of the amount of instructional time available for Beth's physical education curriculum. A review of these charts reveals two important factors. First, not much time is allocated for physical education in most schools. For example, many elementary-age students only receive a total of 30 hours of instruction in physical education each year (Kelly & Melograno, 2015). The second factor is that a lot of instructional time is lost in physical education

Table 4.6. Sample curriculum goals and objectives for Beth's adapted physical education curriculum

Goals	Tennis		Volleyball		Fitness	
Content areas	Objective	Rank	Objective	Rank	Objective	Rank
Body awareness	Body parts	1	Body parts		Body parts	
	Body actions		Body actions	1	Body actions	
	General space	.	General space		General space	1
	Personal space	2	Personal space		Personal space	
Locomotor	Run forward		Run forward		Run forward	2
	Run backward	3	Run backward			
	Lateral movement		Lateral movement	2		
	Changing direction	4	Changing direction			
	Vertical jump	16				
Object control	Catch		Catch	3		
	Underhand toss	5	Underhand toss			
			Underhand strike	4		
	Overhand throw	6	Overhand throw			
	Forehand strike	7				
	Backhand strike	8				
	Overhead strike		Overhead strike	5		
Fitness	Aerobic endurance		Aerobic endurance		Aerobic endurance	3
	Arm and shoulder strength		Arm and shoulder strength		Arm and shoulder strength	4
	Leg strength		Leg strength		Leg strength	5
	Arm and shoulder flexibility		Arm and shoulder flexibility		Arm and shoulder flexibility	6
	Leg and trunk flexibility		Leg and trunk flexibility		Leg and trunk flexibility	7
Social/cognitive	Rules of tennis	9				
			Rules volleyball	6		
	Tennis strategy	10				
			Volleyball strategy	7		
	Tennis etiquette	14				
			Volleyball etiquette	13		
	Tennis honor system	21				
			Volleyball honor system	15		
	Doubles play	15				
			Team play	8		
Advanced skills	Forehand strike with racket	11				
	Backhand strike with racket	12				
	Overhead serve with racket	13				
	Forehand slice with racket	17				
	Backhand slice with racket	18				
	Volley with racket	20				
	Top spin serve with racket	19				
			Volleyball set	11		
			Volleyball bump	9		
			Underhand serve	10		
			Overhead serve	12		
			Spike	14		

Note. Since each objective only needs to be mastered once, objectives that apply to multiple goals (e.g., body parts or run forward) are only listed and ranked once. The shaded cells indicate where the duplicate objectives have been removed.

Table 4.7. Sample curriculum goal emphasis worksheet (%)

Goal[a]	Elementary	Middle	High school	Average
Tennis	45	35	43	41
Volleyball	45	40	29	38
Fitness	10	20	33	21
Total	100	100	100	100

[a]The body awareness, locomotor, object control, and social/cognitive objectives needed to learn and master each goal must be considered when estimating the percentage for the goal emphasis for each program level.

in many schools. For example, 10% of the available instructional time is typically removed in the ABC process to account for lost instructional time due to teacher absences, lost instructional days due to school closings for weather events, and lost instructional time when the gym is reallocated to other events (e.g., voting on election day, assemblies). What is most important in this step is that an accurate estimate is determined. When in doubt, you want to underestimate the amount of actual instructional time available. If you overestimate the time available, you will try to include more content in the curriculum. If you then find that there is actually less time available, that means you will not have enough time to teach the content that must be mastered for the students to achieve their curriculum goals. If you underestimate, you should have enough time to teach mastery of all the content in the curriculum. If it turns out you master all the objectives for a given goal in less time, you can always add more advanced objectives.

Step 5: Calculate the Average Objective Mastery Time

How much time will Beth need to learn the objectives in her adapted physical education curriculum? This is one of the unique steps in the ABC planning process. In this step, physical education teachers need to determine how long it takes them to teach the various objectives in the curriculum. These estimates are then used to determine the average mastery time for the physical education curriculum. In a general physical education curriculum, these estimates are made by all the physical education teachers that implement the curriculum. For adapted physical education curricula, these estimates are typically made by the adapted physical education teacher. Table 4.9 shows Beth's adapted physical education teacher's estimates. Because different objectives (e.g., body parts versus catching) require different amounts of time, teachers are asked to rate sample objectives in several content areas (see Table 4.6 for the content areas in Beth's curriculum). The first column in the table shows the six categories used to organize the objectives for Beth's three curriculum goals. For each category, a typical (i.e., not the easiest and not the hardest for the student to learn) objective for that category is identified. Then the adapted physical education teacher estimates how many minutes it would take her to teach Beth to mastery for that sample objective. It is important to emphasize that this is the total amount of time she feels is needed to ensure that Beth will master the objective. For many students with disabilities, they only practice their motor skills when they are in physical education, and this must be accounted for in the mastery

Table 4.8. Worksheet for calculating instructional time

Chart A: Annual time available in physical education by number of days per week					
Days of physical education per week	1	2	3	4	5
Total instructional days available per year	36	72	108	144	180
Minutes per class	30	30	30	30	30
Total time scheduled per year in minutes	1,080	2,160	3,240	4,320	5,400
Uncontrolled lost instructional time	108	216	324	432	540
Available instructional time per year in hours	16.2	32.4	48.6	64.6	81.0

Chart B: Calculation of instructional time for Beth's adapted physical education curriculum							
Level	Grades	Weeks per year	Minutes per class	Classes per week	Total minutes	Minus 10% lost time	Hours per year	Total hours available
Elementary	6	36	30	2	12,960	11,664	32.4	194.4
Middle	3	27	45	3	10,935	9,841.5	54.7	164.0
High school	2	18	90	3	9,720	8,748	72.9	145.8
Total	11					30,253		504.2

time estimates. It is important to note that these estimates are specific to Beth and that another student with a disability working on the same objectives might require different time estimates.

Step 6: Determine How Much Content Can Fit in the Curriculum

How much content can be included in Beth's adapted physical education curriculum? With the values calculated in curriculum planning Steps 3–5, the total amount of content or number of objectives that can be included in the curriculum can now be calculated as shown in Table 4.10. First, the total number of objectives that can be included in the curriculum is calculated by dividing the total time available for physical education instruction in the curriculum in Step 4 (i.e., 504.2 hours) by the objective mastery time calculated in Step 5 (i.e., 14.8 hours). The result is 34 objectives (504.2 / 14.8 = 34). Once the total number of objectives that can be worked on in a curriculum is determined, the next step is to determine how many objectives can be worked on for each curriculum goal. This is done by multiplying the percentage for the goal emphasis values calculated for each goal in Step 3 by the total number of curriculum objectives in the program (i.e., 34). The calculations of these values for Beth are shown in Table 4.10. The number of objectives that can be worked on for each goal is shown in the far right column of the table (e.g., 14 for tennis, 13 for volleyball, 7 for fitness). Once teachers know how many objectives can be worked on for each goal, they go back to the ranked lists of objectives for each goal created in Step 2 and take the top-ranked objectives. For example, for tennis, they would take the objectives ranked 1–14.

To determine how much content can be included in Beth's curriculum, we first need to divide the total amount of time available for her curriculum (i.e., 504.2 hours) by the average mastery time for the curriculum (i.e., 14.8 hours). This calculation (504.2 / 14.8 = 34) reveals that a total of 34 objectives can be included in Beth's adapted physical education curriculum. To determine how many of these objectives can be worked on for each goal, the percentage for each goal emphasis is multiplied by the total number of objectives in the curriculum as shown in Table 4.10.

Step 7: Sequence the Goals and Objectives Developmentally

What is the scope and sequence of content for Beth's curriculum? Now that you know what content needs to be included in the curriculum, the last step is to sequence this content across the grades in the curriculum. This is referred to as creating the curriculum scope and sequence chart. The end result of this process is shown in Table 4.11. Looking at Table 4.11, it can be seen that all the objectives identified in Step 6 for each of Beth's goals are included in the curriculum and are listed down the left side. These objectives are no longer listed by goals but have been reorganized in logical skill categories (e.g., locomotor skills, object control skills, advanced skills) and then listed developmentally within these categories. Organizing the objectives in this manner distributes them across the years in curriculum in terms of when they need to be taught so that all curriculum goal objectives are achieved by the end.

Achievement-Based Curriculum Planning Summary

It is important to review a few key concepts regarding the ABC planning process. First, the ABC planning process is a decision-making process.

Table 4.9. Calculating average objective mastery time for the curriculum

Content category	Sample objective	Average teacher time Estimates (a)	Total no. of objectives in this content area (b)	Weighted estimate Column (a) × (b)
Body awareness	General space	830	4	3,320
Locomotor	Run backward	900	5	4,500
Object control	Catch	960	7	6,720
Fitness	Aerobic endurance	840	5	4,200
Social/cognitive	Volleyball rules	800	10	8,000
Advanced skills	Backhand strike	960	12	11,520
Total			43	38,260

Note. The average time needed to master an objective in the curriculum is then calculated by dividing the total amount of time needed for all objectives (i.e., 38,260 minutes, or 637.6 hours) by the total number of possible objectives (i.e., 43, which is the sum of all the objectives in the goal delineations). This calculation (637.6 / 43 = 14.8) reveals that on average, 14.8 hours (or 890 minutes) are needed to teach a typical objective in this curriculum for Beth.

Table 4.10. Calculating how much content can be included in the curriculum

Goals	Goal emphasis (%)	Total no. of objectives	No. of objectives per goal[a]
Tennis	41.0	34	14
Volleyball	38.0	34	13
Fitness	21.0	34	7
Total	100	34	34

[a]These values have been rounded up or down to the closest whole number.

From Kelly, L.E. (2011). *Designing and implementing effective adapted physical education programs.* Urbana, IL: Sagamore; adapted by permission.

The ABC model does not dictate the goals, the content to be included in the curriculum, or how it is to be taught. These decisions are made by the physical educators, parents, students, and IEP members that make up the ecological team creating the student's physical education curriculum. Second, one of the major differences between achievement-based curricula and traditional curricula is the amount of content included in achievement-based curricula. This is because achievement-based curricula are designed around the unique needs of the student, the actual resources available for physical education

Table 4.11. Scope and sequence of Beth's adapted physical education curriculum

Goal area	Objective	K	1	2	3	4	5	6	7	8	9	10
Body awareness	Body parts	**	R									
	Body actions	—	**	R								
	General space	—	**	R								
	Personal space	**	R									
Locomotor	Run forward	—	**									
	Run backward		—	**								
	Lateral movement		—	—	**							
	Changing direction											
Object control	Catch	—	—	**								
	Underhand toss	**										
	Underhand strike	—	—	**								
	Overhand throw		—	—	**							
	Forehand strike			—	—	**						
	Backhand strike			—	—		**					
	Overhead strike				—	—		**				
Fitness	Aerobic endurance						—	—	—	—	**	R
	Arm and shoulder strength				—	—	—	**				
	Leg strength					—	—	—	**		R	
	Arm and shoulder flexibility		—	—	—	**						
	Leg and trunk flexibility	—	—	—	**		R		R		R	
Social/cognitive	Rules of tennis				—	—	**	R	R			
	Tennis strategy								—	—	—	**
	Tennis etiquette									—	—	**
	Rules volleyball				—	—	**	R	R	R		
	Volleyball strategy							—	—	**	R	
	Volleyball etiquette							—	—	**	R	
	Team play				—	—	—	—	**	R	R	
Advanced skills	Forehand strike with racket						—	—	—	—	**	
	Backhand strike with racket								—	—	—	**
	Overhead serve with racket						—	—	**			
	Volleyball set					—	—	**				
	Volleyball bump		—	—	—	**						
	Underhand serve				—	—	**					
	Overhead serve						—	—	—	**		

Key: **, mastery expected by the end of this grade; —, objective is introduced or worked on during this grade; R, objective is reviewed or time is allocated for maintenance.

instruction (e.g., time, class sizes, equipment, facilities, teacher competency), and the most accurate time estimates needed for mastery of the objectives. These are critical factors because the achievement-based adapted physical education curriculum is designed not only to simply expose students to the physical education content and give them an opportunity to learn it but rather to ensure that students have the appropriate instruction and time to master all the content so that their long-term curriculum goals are achieved. Finally, achievement-based physical education curricula are designed to promote accountability. The curriculum scope and sequence chart provides a framework so that students, teachers, parents, and administrators can continuously evaluate progress and determine if the curriculum is meeting its intended goals. When problems are encountered, they can be identified early, analyzed, and then solutions can be implemented to minimize any negative impact on the curriculum and ensure its success.

What Content Is Included on the Student's Individualized Education Program?

The development of the student's IEP is an important process because the IEP will guide the student's specific activities for the next year (Bateman & Herr, 2003; Wright & Wright, n.d.). What content goes in the IEP is a straightforward process when the student has an achievement-based adapted physical education curriculum. Once an achievement-based adapted physical education curriculum has been created, it provides the foundation for the physical education component of the IEP. Reviewing Beth's achievement-based adapted physical education curriculum scope and sequence chart in Table 4.11, it shows when instruction should begin and when mastery is expected for all objectives across all the years/grades in the curriculum. Because the IEP is designed to focus on just 1 year of a student's physical education curriculum, the content for the IEP can be taken directly from the scope and sequence chart. For example, when Beth enters the sixth grade, she is expected to master three objectives that year: the overhead strike, arm and shoulder strength, and the rules of tennis. In addition, she will begin/continue working on eight other objectives: aerobic endurance, leg strength, volleyball strategy, team play, forehand stroke with racket, backhand stroke with racket, volleyball set, and volleyball overhead serve. These objectives become her IEP goals and the focal points of these

skills (e.g., preparation position, arm extension, weight transfer) become the short-term objectives in the IEP. At the start of each year, the students should be assessed on these objectives to determine their entry levels (i.e., PLOP), and these assessment results are then used to guide instruction. At the end of the year, prior to their next IEP meeting, they are reassessed to monitor and document their progress. The IEP should also address who will provide the instruction and any accommodations or supports the student may need during instruction.

What Is the Least Restrictive Physical Education Setting for This Student?

Once it has been determined that a student qualifies for adapted physical education services and has an IEP, the next decision is to determine where the students will receive physical education services. IDEA 2004 mandates that placement decisions be based on the concept of the least restrictive environment (LRE). Students with disabilities must be educated with their peers without disabilities, and separate programming should only occur when education in the general setting cannot be satisfactorily achieved with the use of supplementary aids and services (Bateman & Herr, 2003; Block, 1996). Therefore, assessment data should be used to first determine how much support a student with a disability needs to be successful in general physical education. Only after it has been clearly and objectively found that a student with a disability cannot be successfully placed in general physical education can that student be placed in an alternative physical education setting (Block & Krebs, 1992; Sherrill, 2004).

In theory, information obtained from assessment data should be used to determine how much support a child needs to be successful in general physical education or, if the child cannot be successful in general physical education with support, what alternative placement would be appropriate for the student. In reality, placement decisions tend to be an either/or decision process: general physical education with no support or separate physical education (Jansma & Decker, 1990). In addition, decisions tend to focus on placement options rather than on the provision of support to help the child be successful in general physical education (Block & Krebs, 1992). Again, there tends to be a domino effect: The use of a standardized assessment tool determines classification, which influences IEP goals, which in turn influence placement. The use of standardized tests to develop IEP goals usually results in goals and objectives that bear no resemblance to activities that take place in general physical education. Furthermore, these types of assessment data do not help the team determine whether the child will be successful in general physical education or what types of supports are needed for the child to be successful in general physical education. For example, it is difficult for general physical educators to see how working on upper limb speed and dexterity (IEP goals based on results of standardized assessments) are related to lessons on locomotor patterns and body awareness. Thus, the teacher concludes that the student should be placed in a separate adapted physical education class. The use of assessment data that are not related to the child's current and future environments often leads to inappropriate placement decisions.

Placement decisions can be greatly facilitated by using the achievement-based adapted physical education curricula developed for students with disabilities. The ABC planning process ensures that the adapted physical education goals are appropriate and that the amount of content included in the adapted physical education curricula is achievable given the local constraints (i.e., resources, amount of instructional time available). The ABC plans also developmentally sequence the content and organize the content in an easy-to-read scope and sequence chart. The challenge is to find a setting where students can maximize achievement of their physical education goals and objectives and still be included in general physical education curriculum. Because the goal is to include all students to the maximum degree possible in general physical education, placement decisions should begin there and then work down the continuum of placement options as needed until the appropriate balance is obtained.

The adapted physical education scope and sequence charts can be compared with the general physical education curriculum to identify common objectives or related objectives that can be worked on together. Figure 4.6 shows a comparison of a K–5 elementary general physical education curriculum (represented by the large pyramid) and a K–5 adapted physical education curriculum (represented by the small pyramid within the large pyramid). Although the general physical education curriculum has 10 more objectives than the adapted physical education curriculum, all 16 objective of the adapted physical education curriculum are included in the general physical education objectives. This means that the adapted physical education student included in the general curriculum can work

on the 16 objectives in the adapted curriculum and that he or she has approximately 40% more time to master these objectives each year. As another example, a student with wheelchair mobility objectives could work on these during the same general physical education class activities only substituting his wheelchair skills for the general physical education locomotor objectives being practiced by the general physical education students. In reality, the majority of students with mild and moderate disabilities will most likely have achievement-based adapted physical education plans that are narrower pyramids within the general physical education curriculum. These students should, in most cases, be able to work on their objectives independently within the general physical education or require only minor accommodations. The important point to emphasize is that every placement decision must be individualized and based on the unique needs of the student and the unique characteristics of the target placement.

It is important to understand that placements should be viewed as fluid and do not have to be fixed at a given point on the continuum for an entire year. In many cases, it may be appropriate to include some students with disabilities in a general physical education during units in which their learning objectives are comparable with the objectives being taught in general physical education and then also have instruction in a separate adapted physical education setting during other units in which their objectives are not compatible.

How Is Daily Physical Education Instruction Planned and Implemented?

The last and perhaps most relevant aspect of assessment is how to help students acquire the targeted goals and objectives on their IEPs. Unfortunately, decisions at this level traditionally have been based on standardized test results, which focus on general motor abilities, developmental levels, and physical fitness. These tests frequently produce summative scores, product scores, or normative values. IEP goals based on these scores focus on the outcomes of performance such as the following:

- The student will be able to throw a regulation softball 100 feet.
- The student will improve his eye–hand coordination from the 30th percentile to the 40th percentile by the end of the third grade.
- The student will be able to run a mile under 12 minutes by the end of this year.

Pyramid and Scope & Sequence Comparison

GPE Scope & Sequence

Goal Area	Objective	Grades					
		K	1	2	3	4	5
Body Awareness	Body Parts		**				
	Body Actions	--	**				
	Personal space	--	--	**			
Personal/ Social	Follow Instructions	**	R	R	R	R	R
	Work Habits	--	**	R	R	R	R
Locomotor	Run	**					
	Gallop		**				
	Hop	--	--	**			
	Slide		--	--	**		
	Slip			--	--	**	
Rhythm & Dance	Even Beat	**					
	Uneven Beat		**				
	Accented Beat		--	**			
Physical Fitness	Partial Curl-ups			--	**	R	R
	V-Sit Reach			--	**	R	R
	Push-ups				--	**	R
	Endurance Run		--	--	--	--	**
	Underhand Roll						**
Object Control	Underhand Throw	**					
	Body Mass Index	--	**				
	Catch	--	--	**			
	Kick Stationary Ball		--	--	**		
	Two-arm Sidearm Strike			--	--	**	
	Hand Dribble			--	--	**	
	Overhand Throw			--	--	--	**
	Set Shot				--	--	**

APE Scope & Sequence

Goal Area	Objective	Grades					
		K	1	2	3	4	5
Body Awareness	Body Parts	**	R				
	Body Actions	--	**	R			
	Personal space	--	--	**	R		
Personal/ Social	Follow Instructions	**	R	R	R	R	R
	Work Habits	--	--	--	**	R	R
Locomotor	Run	**					
	Hop	--	--	**			
	Jump			--	--	**	
Physical Fitness	Partial Curl-ups				--	--	**
	V-Sit Reach			--	**	R	R
Object Control	Underhand Roll	--	**				
	Underhand Throw		--	**			
	Catch	--	--	--	**		
	Kick Stationary Ball			--	--	**	
	Overhand Throw			--	--	--	**

Figure 4.6. Comparison of the general physical education and adapted physical education scope and sequence content. (From Kelly, L.E. [2011]. *Designing and implementing effective adapted physical education programs.* Urbana, IL: Sagamore; reprinted by permission.)

Unfortunately, these tests and the IEP goals created based on them usually provide no information on how to adapt instruction to help a student acquire critical physical education skills and be successful in general physical education. For example, it is not clear in any of the sample goals listed what the student is doing wrong in his or her performance that is producing the poor score. Why is the student unable to throw a ball 100 feet? Is it that he has an immature throwing pattern, that he doesn't understand what it means to throw a ball 100 feet, or that he has a mature throwing pattern but needs to work on his strength? A poorly motivated student may need a different type of instruction from a student who actually has low fitness or poor motor control. Similarly, how do you cue a student who has trouble with upper limb activities? Do you give him extra practice on upper limb skills, or do you need to modify instruction? Perhaps the skill needs to be broken down into smaller steps, or the student needs physical assistance, or perhaps the student needs adapted equipment. Unfortunately, information from standardized assessment tools does not provide information regarding instruction. Thus teachers are forced to make instructional decisions based on what they think is best for a particular student.

In the ABC model, the first step would be to examine the achievement-based adapted physical education plan and identify what content is scheduled to be taught next. The student's IEP could also be consulted because it would include the same content as the adapted physical education curriculum. The next step would be to assess the student using CRIs to determine which focal points of the skills the student can already perform and which ones still need to be worked on. Refer back to Figure 4.3, which shows CRI for the overhand throw. Note that the performance of the skill is divided into three skill levels. The first skill level focuses on how to perform the skill and delineates the criteria, commonly referred to as focal points or skill components, that are required to correctly perform the skill. The second and third skill levels focus on the products of the skill. For the overhand throw, the products are usually accuracy and distance. The focal points for most motor skills are listed in the order in which they are performed. The student is typically given a verbal request and a demonstration and then given three trials to perform the skill. The student's performance is recorded on a score sheet (see Figure 4.7). Credit for having a focal point

is awarded if the student demonstrates it correctly on at least two out of three trials. Performance on each of the focal points is evaluated using three simple symbols: O = student did not demonstrate the focal point; / = student understands the focal point and is starting to perform it, but it still needs work; and X = student correctly demonstrates the component on at least two out of three attempts.

Figure 4.8 shows a typical preassessment score sheet for a student on one objective: the catch. Examining the score sheet, it can be seen that this student has mastered one focal point, as indicated by the X under column a (i.e., stand in path), but still needs work on the remaining four focal points. The / on the second focal point on the score sheet indicates that the student's performance on this focal point is emerging, and therefore this would be the logical focal point to focus on next. The teacher would mark this focal point with a colored pencil (shown by little dots) to indicate that this is the student's initial learning expectation. Next, the teacher would look at the remaining focal points that still need to be mastered and determine how many of

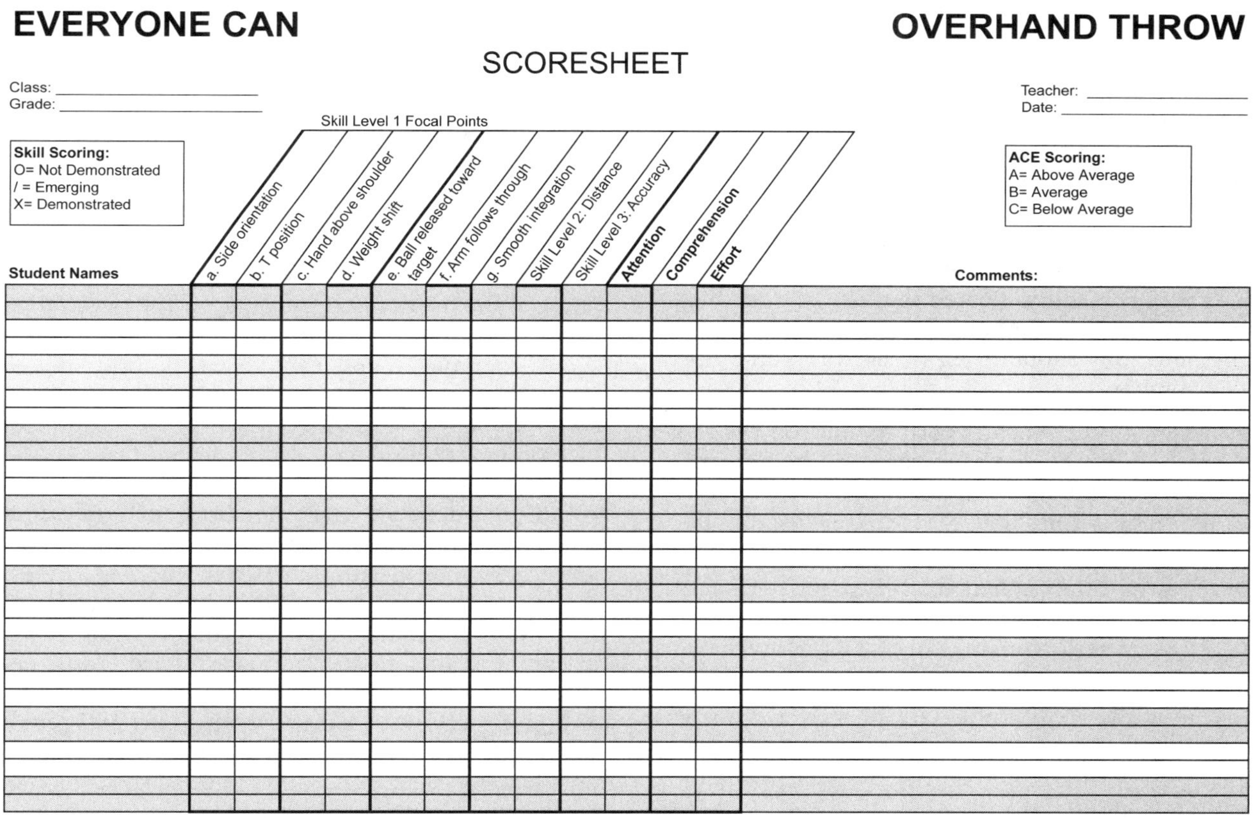

Figure 4.7. Everyone Can! score sheet for the overhand throw. (Reprinted, with permission, from L.E. Kelly, J.A. Wessel, G.M. Dummer, and T. Sampson, 2010, *Everyone can! Skill development and assessment in elementary physical education online resource.* [Champaign, IL: Human Kinetics].)

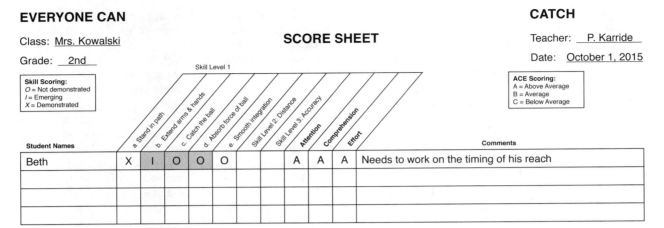

Figure 4.8. Sample Everyone Can! score sheet for the catch. (Adapted, with permission, from L.E. Kelly, J.A. Wessel, G.M. Dummer, and T. Sampson, 2010, *Everyone can! Skill development and assessment in elementary physical education online resource.* [Champaign, IL: Human Kinetics].)

these should be mastered this year. Those focal points would then be marked with a different color (shown as shaded gray) to indicate that these are the student's target learning expectation. In Beth's case, the teacher has marked focal points c and d as Beth's target learning expectations on this objective for this year.

Once you know which focal point needs to be worked on, you can begin determining how to organize and plan your instruction. This planning must consider where the student will receive this instruction and who will provide it. If the instruction is provided outside of the adapted physical education setting or by a teacher who is not an adapted physical educator, then how this information will be communicated to those responsible for the instruction must also be planned. The following questions should then be used to guide lesson development:

- How will the correct performance on the target focal point be communicated to the student so that the student understands what he or she is doing wrong and what needs to be done to correct it?

- How will the student actually practice this component and how many practice trials will the student need to change his or her performance?

- How will the student know when he or she is doing the focal point right or wrong? Who will provide this feedback and how frequently will it be provided?

- What should the student do when he or she thinks the component has been mastered or if the student feels like he or she still just can't do it?

- How will the teacher know if the student is learning and making sufficient progress?

One of the advantages of using the Everyone Can! (Kelly et al., 2010) assessment items and scores sheets, as shown in Figures 4.3 and 4.7, is that they are complemented by an extensive set of instructional resources. For each of the 70 objectives included in Everyone Can!, teachers are provided assessment items, score sheets, and assessing activities. In addition, for each focal point of each objective, teachers are also provided with large-group instructional activities, task cards, games, and posters highlighting the key components of the various focal points. Figures 4.9–4.12 show examples of these materials for the "T position" focal point of the overhand throw. One of the advantages of these materials is that they come as Microsoft Word documents and can be easily printed and given to aids, peer tutors, parents, and students, when appropriate, to guide them as the various focal points are worked on.

The takeaway is that the major difference between instruction (i.e., combination of implementation planning and teaching) in the ABC model and traditional instruction is that the ABC model is based on assessment and data. Unfortunately, in many physical education and adapted physical education programs, instruction is provided on the objectives targeted for instruction, but no assessments are performed. In some cases, some incidental learning occurs, but in most cases, no learning occurs because the instruction is not specific enough to change the students' existing behavior. This is particularly true for students with disabilities. When assessment-based instruction is used, it will

EVERYONE CAN

Teaching Instructional Activities: OVERHAND THROW

Teaching the Overhand Throw:

- When the emphasis is on a specific focal point, students should be practicing the focal point as an integrated part of the overhand throw.
- Use instructional cues that "paint a picture" or that describe the feel of the desired action. Make certain that students understand the instructional cues.
- Communicate the focus of instruction through demonstrations, station task cards, posters, or multiple methods.
- Design instruction so students receive feedback from the teacher, other students, and self-assessment.
- Use a variety of games and activities that emphasize the focal points.

Reminders:

- Maximize participation. Provide all students with many opportunities to practice. Have enough equipment for all students. Students cannot practice if they do not participate in the activity.
- Avoid elimination games.
- Minimize competition. When the emphasis shifts from playing to winning many students will regress back to their former immature movement patterns.

Skill Level 1 Focal Points	Organization/Materials	Activities/Games	Cues	Feedback
a. **Side orientation**, standing with non-dominant side toward target, weight evenly distributed on both feet, feet shoulder width apart, eyes on target, ball held in dominant hand at waist level in front of body.	Organization: Throwing stations: Throwing relays: Materials: • Motivating targets. • Tape to mark throwing lines. • Footprints to mark side orientation. • Several tennis balls for each student.	Activities: Demonstrate side orientation and then have the class perform the following activities: *Throwing stations*: Create several stations with one or more students at a station. Use footprints to mark side orientation. Students throw toward targets on/near the gym walls. When all students finish throwing, students shag the balls and repeat the task. *Throwing relays*: Create several stations with 3-4 students at a station. The student at the front of the line throws the ball, then takes a position at the back of the line. Other students provide feedback. Repeat the relay. <u>Small group games</u>: Ball Wall Bounce, Balloon Blast, Boundary Ball, Circle Ball, Get to 5, Go and Grab, Hot Potato, Name Ball, Net Fielding, Pin-Point Accuracy, Sponge Ball Fight, Target Practice, Throw and Block, X Ball. <u>Large group games</u>: Boundary Ball, Clean Out The Backyard, Leader Class, Sponge Ball Fight.	Say: Stand sideways Look at the target	Teacher: Physically assist students having trouble so that they know what the correct side orientation position feels like. Give positive feedback when students demonstrate the correct side orientation position. Students: Partners should give each other feedback on their side orientation position. Give positive feedback when other students demonstrate the correct side orientation position.

Figure 4.9. Sample Everyone Can! instructional activity. (Reprinted, with permission, from L.E. Kelly, J.A. Wessel, G.M. Dummer, and T. Sampson, 2010, *Everyone can! Skill development and assessment in elementary physical education online resource.* [Champaign, IL: Human Kinetics].)

EVERYONE CAN

Station Task Card: OVERHAND THROW
T Position

Using Stations for Teaching:

- Teachers create as many stations in the physical activity area as needed.
- Each station should focus on only one focal point of the skill being taught.
- The number of students assigned to each station should permit maximum practice of the skill. In most cases, groups of 4 to 6 students work best.
- Assign students to work at stations where they can focus on skill components they need to learn (e.g., focal points performed unsuccessfully during assessment).
- Students can work independently at a station using a student task card, or the station can be supervised by the teacher, a teacher assistant, a volunteer, or a peer tutor.

Skill Level 1 Focal Points	Organization/Materials	Activities/Games	Cues	Feedback
b. **T position** with almost complete extension of the throwing arm, with trunk rotation back. **Non-throwing hand points toward target** **Hand reaches back with ball** **Weight on foot on same side as throwing arm**	**Organization:** *Activity #1:* Target distance should be 15-20 feet (4.5-6 m) from thrower. Target height should be approximately equal to thrower's height. *Activity #2:* Students sit or stand facing the teacher. **Materials:** • Tape or jump ropes to mark throwing line. • A paper target and tape to hang the target on the wall for each pair of students. • Several yarn balls or sponge balls for each pair of students (tennis ball or baseball size). • A container with balls placed at waist height behind the student.	**Activities:** Demonstrate the T position with almost complete extension of the throwing arm, with trunk rotation back. Then have students perform the following activities. 1. Tape a paper target to the wall. One student: (a) moves into the T position with the non-throwing hand pointing at the target, throwing hand reaching back with the ball, and weight on the throwing-side foot; and (b) throws the ball overhand at the target. The partner gives feedback about the T position. Students switch roles after several attempts. Repeat the activity until both partners execute the focal point correctly at least three times. 2. Place balls in a container behind students at waist level and have them reach back to grab a ball as they prepare to throw. Students say "T," "for Take and Throw." **Small group games:** Ball Wall Bounce, Balloon Blast, Boundary Ball, Circle Ball, Get to 5, Go and Grab, Hot Potato, Name Ball, Net Fielding, Pin-Point Accuracy, Sponge Ball Fight, Target Practice, Throw and Block, X Ball.	**Say:** Stand sideways to the target. Make a T with your body. Reach back with the ball. Use the other arm to point to the target. Put your weight on the throwing side leg.	**Teacher:** Review the correct T position and make sure students understand what to do at the stations. **Students:** Give positive feedback when other students demonstrate correct position when throwing. Help other students' correct errors in their T position by providing feedback and physical assistance if needed. Call the teacher if your group is having trouble at this station.

Figure 4.10. Sample Everyone Can! task card. (Reprinted, with permission, from L.E. Kelly, J.A. Wessel, G.M. Dummer, and T. Sampson, 2010, *Everyone can! Skill development and assessment in elementary physical education online resource.* [Champaign, IL: Human Kinetics].)

EVERYONE CAN

Game: CLEAN OUT THE BACKYARD

Object of the Game: To throw an assortment of balls over a net, and to return balls as they are thrown over

Assessment Items:
Overhand throw
Underhand throw
Underhand roll

Play Groupings and Grades:
Group Size: Large
Grade Levels: K-5

Physical Activity Rating:
[x] Easy (can sing)
[x] Moderate (can talk)
[ ] Vigorous (cannot talk)

Organization and Materials

Organization: Play this game in a space the size of a basketball court or smaller, either indoors or outdoors. Bisect the playing area with a volleyball net. Use existing lines, cones, or other markers as boundaries. Students are scattered on each side of the net.

Net

Materials:
• Volleyball net and poles
• One or more small lightweight balls for each student in the game

Directions and Teaching Alternatives

Directions: Divide the class into two teams of equal numbers, with one team on each side of the net. Scatter an assortment of small balls and objects (Nerf balls, yarn balls, tennis balls, bean bags, etc.) on the floor on each side of the net. When the teacher gives a starting signal, every student picks up a ball and throws it to the other side of the net, then continues to pick-up and throw additional balls. The object of the game is for one team to have a clean back yard (no balls on their side of the net). The teacher should specify overhand or underhand throw (balls thrown over the net) or underhand roll (balls rolled under the net). Emphasize throwing or rolling fast and hard.

Teaching Alternatives:
• Continue play for a set duration of time.
• Periodically stop the game and give directions to emphasize a different focal point for the overhand throw, underhand throw, or underhand roll.
• Change the height of the net to accommodate students' skill levels and heights.
• Add a restraining line and ask that students throw from behind the line so that they must throw harder and farther.

Figure 4.11. Sample Everyone Can! game card. (Reprinted, with permission, from L.E. Kelly, J.A. Wessel, G.M. Dummer, and T. Sampson, 2010, *Everyone can! Skill development and assessment in elementary physical education online resource.* [Champaign, IL: Human Kinetics].)

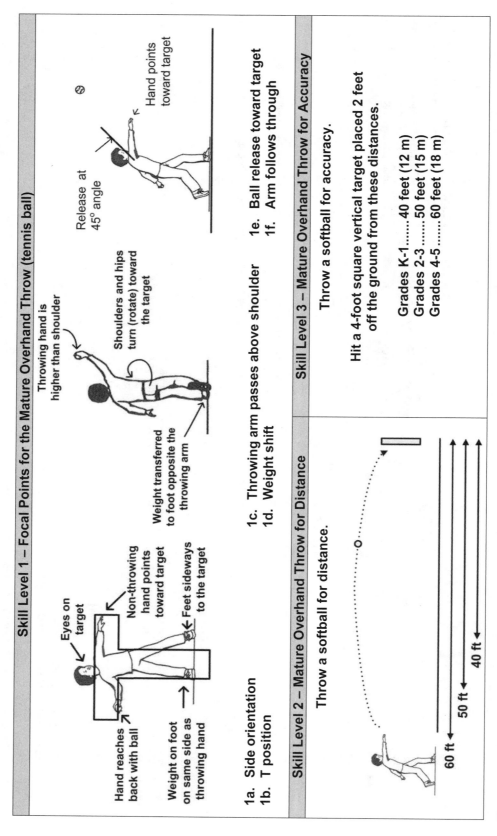

Figure 4.12. Sample Everyone Can! posters for the overhand throw. (Reprinted, with permission, from L.E. Kelly, J.A. Wessel, G.M. Dummer, and T. Sampson, 2010, *Everyone can! Skill development and assessment in elementary physical education online resource.* [Champaign, IL: Human Kinetics].)

be clear to both the teacher and the students when the instruction is working, when it is not, and when changes need to be made.

How Are Student Learning, Individualized Education Program Achievement, and Adapted Physical Education Curriculum Progress Evaluated?

Ongoing evaluation is critical to determining if the students are making progress toward achieving their IEP and achievement-based adapted physical education goals and for guiding daily instruction. If a student is not making adequate progress, then ongoing evaluation can quickly discover the problem. If ongoing evaluations are not conducted at all or conducted only at the end of a unit or year, then a student could waste all that instructional time and not make any improvement on his or her target objectives (Kelly & Melograno, 2015). What is even worse is that when students do not make any progress on specific skills, they tend to avoid those skills and the activities that they are used in because they have had no success. This further reduces their learning opportunities and the number of potential practice trials.

For evaluation to be meaningful, it must be based on assessment data and address three areas: student progress, teacher effectiveness, and program progress. Typically very little evaluation is performed in physical education, particularly if the students are fully included in general physical education. Even when students receive adapted physical education, evaluation is delimited to students' progress on their IEPs and is frequently based solely on informal observations and teacher perceptions. This problem is further complicated by using NRIs, which are not instructionally relevant, as the primary form of assessment. Teachers that use NRIs soon learn that the value of the information provided by these tests does not justify the time and effort needed to implement them and thus frequently stop assessing. It should be clear that physical education teachers must use CRIs to adequately teach all students and especially students with disabilities. Hopefully, a persuasive argument has been presented in this chapter for the value of CRIs and to encourage teachers to use them.

One of the greatest benefits of using the ABC model is that the built-in assessment process captures all the assessment data needed to evaluate student progress, teacher effectiveness, and program progress. These data are captured on the CRI score sheets used for each objective. Figure 4.13 shows a score sheet with pre- and postassessment data for a self-contained adapted physical education class of students working on the catch. Take a moment and look at Tamika's performance. On the initial assessment, she could perform the first two focal points. Catching the ball with her fingers was set as her initial learning expectation because that performance was emerging. Focal points d and e were identified as her target learning objectives for the year. The postassessment at the end of the year shows that she can now correctly perform 4 of the 5 focal points for skill Level 1 as indicated by the Xs over the / and O. Her performance is summarized on the right-hand side of the form. The first column (A) shows her entry level of 2 focal points. The second column (B) shows the total number of focal she was expected to be able to demonstrate at the end of the year (i.e., 5), which is the sum of the entry score plus her target (2 + 3). The third column (C) shows her exit score at the end of the year was 4. The fourth column (D) contains an "N," indicating that she did not meet her target learning expectation of 5 focal points. The fifth column (E) also contains an "N," indicating she has not mastered this objective yet. The last column (F) contains the value 80, indicating she has currently mastered 80% of this objective.

Table 4.12 shows an example of an individual student progress report for Beth. This report is computer generated and summarizes the same categories of evaluation data shown in Figure 4.13 only for all the objectives that Beth worked on in her adapted physical education program over the course of a year in sixth grade. The only difference in the data reported in the computer-generated report is that the Y/N column for whether mastery was demonstrated has been omitted because this can be interpreted by the mastery percentage in the last column. An individual report like this can be used at the annual IEP meeting to report the progress the student made on the IEP objectives. It can also be used in conjunction with the student's achievement-based adapted physical education plan to set the goals and objectives for next year's IEP. From the data in the current report (see Table 4.12), it can be seen that Beth will need to continue working on the overhand strike objective, which should have been mastered this year. Additional objectives would then be added to her IEP for next year from the objectives listed on her curriculum scope and sequence chart that are targeted to be mastered in that year.

EVERYONE CAN

SCORESHEET

CATCH

Class: Mrs. Ghooly
Grade: 4th

Teacher: Mr. Andrews
Date: October 24, 2010

Skill Scoring:
O = Not demonstrated
I = Emerging
X = Demonstrated

ACE Scoring:
A = Above Average
B = Average
C = Below Average

Skill Level 1

Students Names	a. Stand in path	b. Extend arms & hands	c. Catch the ball	d. Absorb force of ball	e. Smooth integration	Skill Level 2: Distance	Skill Level 3: Accuracy	Attention	Comprehension	Effort	Comments	A	B	C	D	E	F
Tom	X	X	O	I	O			A	A	A	Trapping ball with palms	2	5	5	Y	Y	100
Beth	O	X	O	O	O			B	B	B	Is not ready to catch - no prep position	1	3	3	Y	N	60
Mark	I	O	O	O	O			C	B	C	Appeared very distracted	0	3	2	N	N	40
Lori	O	O	O	O	O			B	B	C	Is definitely afraid of the ball	0	2	3	Y	N	60
Kevin	X	X	X	O	O			A	A	A	Good	4	6	6	Y	Y	100
Tamika	X	X	I	O	O			A	A	A	Has the idea of using just her fingers, just needs more practice	2	5	4	N	N	80
Jamil	X	X	X	I	O			B	B	B	Almost has retraction	3	5	5	Y	Y	100
Sue	X	O	O	O	O			A	B	B	Is trapping the ball againts the chest	2	4	5	Y	Y	100
Jeff	O	O	O	O				C	C	C	Looks away when ball approaches	0	2	2	Y	N	40
Ismail	X	X	X	O				A	A	A	Good	4	6	6	Y	Y	100
										Average =		1.6	4.1	4.1	80	50	78

Evaluation Values

Figure 4.13. Catch score sheet with pre- and postassessment data. (Adapted, with permission, from L.E. Kelly, J.A. Wessel, G.M. Dummer, and T. Sampson, 2010, *Everyone can! Skill development and assessment in elementary physical education online resource.* [Champaign, IL: Human Kinetics].)

(*Key:* A, entry # of focal points; B, target + entry # of focal points; C, exit # of focal points; D, Y/N whether exit # > or = to target expectation; E, Y/N whether the objective has been mastered; F, % mastery; exit # / total # focal points.)

Table 4.12.   Sample individual progress report

Monticello Middle School

Student Progress Report

Student: Beth Holmstrup

Teacher: Garth Britton

Grade Level: 6th grade

Date: June 10, 2014

Objectives to be mastered	Entry	Target	Exit	Target met	Mastery (%)
Overhead strike (8)	6	8	7	N	87
Arm and shoulder strength (7)	6	7	7	Y	100
Rules of tennis (90)	78	90	92	Y	100
Achievement				66%	95.6
Objectives still being worked on					
Aerobic endurance (6)	2	3	3	Y	50
Leg strength (6)	4	5	5	Y	83
Forehand strike with racket (7)	2	3	3	Y	43
Backhand strike with racket (7)	1	2	1	N	14
Volleyball set (7)	5	6	7	Y	100
Volleyball overhead serve (7)	2	3	4	Y	57
Team plan (90)	70	80	85	Y	94
Volleyball strategy (90)	20	40	45	Y	50
Achievement				87.5%	61.4

In addition to evaluating how much progress students make toward achieving their IEP and yearly adapted physical education curriculum goals, it is important to also evaluate the effectiveness of the instruction provided by the teacher. This is a formative method of evaluation with the goal of identifying areas in which improvements are warranted. Again, this form of evaluation can be done using the pre- and postassessment data recorded on the students' objective score sheets. For example, look back at the score sheet in Figure 4.13. It is important to notice that averages are computed at the bottom of each of the six columns on the right side of the form. Just reading this line, it can be seen that the class started with an average mastery of 1.6 focal points on this objective, and the teacher's expectation was that she could increase their performance to 4.1 focal points. Column C's average of 4.1 indicates that overall the class made the gain she wanted, but the 80% overall target achievement in column D indicates that two of the students missed their target goals by one focal point. Finally, the average for the last column indicates that only 78% of the students mastered this objective this year. Although 78% looks pretty good, in the ABC model 100% of the students have to master their objectives. Closer examination of the data in column F reveals that five of the students

still need to master this skill and two of the students are only at 40% mastery. Given these results, the teacher needs to examine how she can improve her teaching of this objective. She might also have to consider either starting to work on this objective sooner in the curriculum or potentially moving the mastery grade up by one grade. The important point is that the teacher can see from this analysis that she has a problem and begin to make changes to rectify it before the students fall too far behind. In the absence of this information, this teacher could conclude that all the students made some improvement and that everything is going fine.

How Are Students' Progress on Their Individualized Education Programs and Achievement-Based Adapted Physical Education Evaluated?

The last evaluation area in the ABC model is program achievement. The focus here is on evaluating the degree to which students are achieving the overall goals in their achievement-based adapted physical education curriculum. Table 4.13 shows a simple cumulative program evaluation form that was created by simply modifying the content in

Table 4.13.　Sample cumulative program evaluation report

River School Physical Education
Cumulative Progress Report

Student: Beth　　　　　**Date:** October 1, 2015　　　　　**PE Teacher:** Jason Bishop

Summary: By the end of this year (fourth grade), Beth should have mastered a total of 15 program objectives. She has demonstrated mastery of 16 objectives for a current mastery rate of 106%.

Goal area	Objective	Grade										
		K	1	2	3	4	5	6	7	8	9	10
Body awareness	Body parts	** 100	R									
	Body actions	— 60	** 100	R								
	General space	— 60	** 100	R								
	Personal SPACE	** 100	R									
Locomotor	Run forward	— 80	** 100									
	Run backward		— 60	** 100								
	Lateral movement		— 20	— 60	** 90	100						
Object control	Catch	— 20	— 40	** 80	100							
	Underhand toss	** 100										
	Underhand strike	— 50	90	** 100								
	Overhand throw		— 40	80	** 100							
	Forehand strike			— 50	70	** 100						
	Backhand strike			— 30	60	80	**					
	Overhead strike				— 20	50	—	**				
Fitness	Aerobic endurance						—	—	—	—	**	R
	Arm and shoulder strength				— 30	40	—	**				
	Leg strength					— 20	—	—	**		R	
	Arm and shoulder flexibility		— 60	80	90	** 100						
	Leg and trunk flexibility	— 40	60	80	** 100		R		R		R	
Social/cognitive	Rules of tennis				— 20	—	—	**	R	R		
	Tennis strategy								—	—	—	**
	Tennis etiquette										—	**
	Rules volleyball				— 40	—	**	R	R	R		
	Volleyball strategy							—	—	**	R	
	Volleyball etiquette								—	**	R	
	Team play				— 10	—	—	—	**	R	R	

(continued)

Table 4.13. Sample cumulative program evaluation report *(continued)*

Goal area	Objective	Grade										
		K	1	2	3	4	5	6	7	8	9	10
Advanced skills	Forehand strike with racket						—	—	—	—	**	
	Backhand strike with racket						—	—	—	—	**	
	Overhead serve with racket								—	—	—	**
	Volleyball set					—	—	—	**			
	Volleyball bump		—	—	—	**						
			30	50	80	100						
	Underhand serve			—	—	—	**					
				80	100	100						
	Overhead serve							—	—	—	**	
Yearly % mastery		3/3	3/3	2/3	3/4	3/3						
		100	100	67	75	100						
Cumulative % mastery		3/3	6/6	8/9	11/12	15/15						
		100	100	89	92	100						

Note. The numeric values reported in the table indicate the student's percent mastery of that objective at the end of that grade.

Key: **, mastery expected by the end of this grade; —, objective is introduced or worked on during this grade; R, objective is reviewed or time is allocated for maintenance.

the student's scope and sequence chart. Examining Table 4.13, it can be seen that percentages have been added to each cell where instructional time was allocated to work on each objective. The expectation is that at the grade level where the ** indicate the objective should be mastered, the percentage should equal 100. Minor deviations of 10%–15% around a few objectives in any given year are not uncommon, and these can usually be adjusted for in the next year. However, when there are major discrepancies in mastering individual objectives (i.e., deviations of 30% or greater for the year in which they should have been mastered), the teacher should evaluate whether it is appropriate to move the mastery expectation to a higher grade. If there are major discrepancies on multiple objectives related to a specific goal, the teacher should evaluate whether there is enough time remaining in the program to address these discrepancies or whether the time related to this goal should be reallocated to other goals.

It is highly recommended that the adapted physical education teacher review the student's cumulative program evaluation report with the parents each year at their IEP meetings. It is important to highlight the student's cumulative percentage for mastery to date as well as objectives that were targeted for mastery but not mastered during the current year. In Table 4.13, looking at the last row at the bottom of table in the fourth-grade column (seventh column in from the left), it can be seen that Beth has mastered all 15 of the objectives targeted in her program for 100% mastery. In fact, Beth actually mastered one additional objective early that was targeted for achievement in fifth grade,

so her actual mastery was 106%. When looking at Beth's cumulative mastery over the first 4 years of her program, it can be seen that in second grade she only mastered two of the three objectives targeted for that year. In third grade she mastered the objective that was carried forward from second grade and then only two of the three objectives targeted for mastery in third grade. The yearly mastery for third grade was adjusted to indicate the additional objective and that she only mastered 75%, or three out of four, of the objectives targeted for that year. Then in fourth grade, she caught up and achieved all the objectives targeted for mastery that year plus one (underhand serve) that was not scheduled to be mastered until the end of fifth grade.

One of the advantages of having both an achievement-based adapted physical education curriculum and the IEP is that the built-in evaluation procedures in the ABC model can be used to evaluate progress on the IEP annual goals and objectives as well as the students' overall progress on their achievement-based adapted physical education curriculum. A progress report such as the one in Table 4.12 would also be accompanied by instructions that explain in more detail the definitions of the objectives, how they are measured, and what the values in the various columns represent. Looking at Table 4.12, the left-hand column of the report lists in two sections the objectives that Beth was targeted to either master or continue working on during the sixth grade. These are the same objectives listed in her achievement-based adapted physical education scope and sequence chart for sixth grade, which would also be listed as the long- and short-term goals and objectives in her IEP for sixth grade. Let's examine how Beth did on the overhead strike objective. The number 8 in parentheses indicates that this objective has eight focal points. Beth's entry score indicates that at the beginning of the year, she could correctly perform six of these focal points. Beth's teacher set a target learning expectation at the beginning of this year that Beth would be able to perform all eight focal points for this objective by the end of the year. The value of 7 in the exit column indicates that at the end of the year, Beth could correctly perform only seven of the eight components, which was one less than what her teacher had set as the target. As a result, there is an "N" in the target met column indicating that Beth did not meet her target learning expectation on this objective. The final column reports Beth's overall mastery on this skill, which is 87%. This value is calculated by dividing the exit number (7) by the mastery number (8). At the bottom of each section of the report, two achievement percentages are calculated. The first indicates the percentage of target learning expectations that were achieved. For the three objectives Beth was expected to master by the end of sixth grade, she met her teacher's target expectations for two of the three objectives, resulting in a 66% achievement rate. In overall mastery terms, she had an average mastery rate of 95.6% (i.e., the sum of her percentages for mastery [287] divided by 3). The same procedures were applied to the other objectives she worked on this year. The major difference being she was not expected to master these objectives but instead to show meaningful progress as indicated by achieving the teacher's target expectations. Overall, Beth's report shows she is making excellent progress on achieving the objectives in her achievement-based adapted physical education curriculum as scheduled. Next year in seventh grade, she will need to master the last focal point in the overhand strike. Fortunately, she should have time because she has already mastered the volleyball set, which was not targeted to be achieved until the end of seventh grade.

APPLYING WHAT YOU HAVE LEARNED

Let's review the case study at the beginning of this chapter and apply the adapted physical education decisions that have been discussed. It can be seen how asking and addressing a systematic set of questions can improve both the quality of the decisions made and the quality of the services provided to students with disabilities in physical education.

Question 1: Does Mark qualify for adapted physical education services? How was he assessed?

What is his present level of performance? Does he meet the school district's eligibility criteria? In the opening scenario, none of these questions were asked or answered based on assessment information. It can be assumed that Mark was considered eligible solely because he had a physical disability.

Question 2: What functional physical education goals does Mark need to achieve to live an active and healthy life? In the case study, Mark's long-term physical and motor needs were not considered. The first decision made was a placement decision—that is, could he be accommodated in general physical education in kindergarten? This decision was then continued each year for the next 3 years. Based on the scenario, it can be seen that although Mark initially liked general physical education, he has slowly fallen further and further behind his peers and is now starting to dislike physical education. Unfortunately, there was no discussion of Mark's PLOP or of his long-term needs. Had Mark been adequately assessed, an achievement-based adapted physical education curriculum could have been developed when he started kindergarten that focused on his physical education needs using a wheelchair, which would have freed up his arms for motor skills and given him greater mobility. It is highly likely that this achievement-based adapted physical education curriculum could have been implemented in the general physical education curriculum. The major potential differences would have been that Mark would work on 1–2 fewer goals or maybe fewer objectives in some of the remaining goals. In general physical education, Mark would be working on parallel objectives that would allow him to participate in the general physical education class, and that would have had greater carryover value for his use later in life. For example, students in the general physical education curriculum would typically be required to master eight locomotor skills (run, hop, gallop, slide, skip, leap horizontal jump, and vertical jump) during their elementary years. Mark's achievement-based adapted physical education curriculum would substitute six wheelchair mobility skills (moving forward, backward, turning, wheelies, curb hopping, and 360-degree wheelie turns) for his locomotor skills. It should be noted that this adjustment results in him working on 25% fewer locomotor objectives (i.e., six compared with eight), which in turn provides him 25% more time to master his six mobility objectives.

Question 3: What physical education content should be included in Mark's IEP? Because Mark was fully included in general physical education, no physical education content was required to be included in his IEP. Because there were no physical education objectives in the IEP, no data were collected and reported at each subsequent IEP meeting. As a result, Mark fell further and further behind in his motor skills, and this lack of progress was not noticed for 4 years until Mark started to complain. Even then, it was ignored at his next IEP meeting. Had Mark been appropriately assessed and had an achievement-based adapted physical education curriculum been created, he would have been required to have physical education goals and objectives in his IEP. The IEP would identify the objectives targeted to be mastered each year in his achievement-based adapted physical education curriculum, and data would need to be provided at each subsequent IEP meeting to show how he was progressing.

Question 4: What is the least restrictive physical education setting for Mark? In the case study, Mark was automatically placed in general physical education because the general physical education teacher was willing to accept him and make accommodations. Unfortunately, this placement decision was not made based on an assessment of Mark's physical and motor needs. If Mark had been appropriately assessed and an achievement-based adapted physical education curriculum created to address his physical education needs, it is highly likely that general physical education would still have been the LRE for him to have been placed. The major difference would be that he would now be working on objectives designed to meet his needs (i.e., his achievement-based adapted physical education curriculum) in general physical education and not just being accommodated while he tried to do the general physical education objectives. Using the example outline of locomotor skills in Question 2, Mark would now be in general physical education working on his mobility skills while the other students worked on their locomotor skills. It is also highly likely that Mark would be able to work on his mobility skills with little to no modifications using the same activities the general physical education class was performing.

Question 5: How is daily physical education instruction planned and implemented? In the case study, the focus of daily instruction for Mark in general physical education was on how to include him in the general physical education activities while still focusing on the general physical education objectives. Now that Mark has an achievement-based adapted physical education curriculum, the focus is on which focal points he needs to learn based on the objectives in his curriculum. Initially, the general physical education teacher may require some assistance from an adapted physical education teacher to learn how to integrate Mark's objectives

into the general physical education activities. However, over time the general physical education teacher would learn to make these adjustments independently.

Question 6: How is a student's IEP and achievement-based adapted physical education curriculum progress evaluated? Again, in the case study, no evaluation takes place other than the perceptions of the physical education teacher and the parents because there are no physical education objectives in the IEP. Had Mark been appropriately assessed and placed, continuous assessment and evaluation data would have been collected throughout the year on the objectives in the IEP. Each year at the IEP meeting, his performance data would be reviewed both in terms of the progress on that year's objectives and on the overall progress on the achievement-based adapted physical education curriculum.

SUMMARY

The goal of this chapter was to introduce you to the essential programming decisions physical educators must be able to make to appropriately address the physical education needs of students with disabilities. Six critical questions were presented to guide you through how to make a series of assessment-based decisions from determining who qualifies for adapted physical education services to how to determine what you should be teaching each day. The ABC model was presented as a systematic method for integrating and addressing these questions.

It should now be clear that every school must have established procedures and eligibility criteria for determining who qualifies for adapted physical education services. These procedures should involve assessing students' present level of performance on the scope and sequence of the content in the general physical education curriculum and then analyzing these data to determine if they meet the school district's eligibility criteria for adapted physical education services. When students qualify for adapted physical education services, this means that their current PLOP indicated that there was a significant discrepancy between their performance levels and the performance levels of the students in the general physical education curriculum. Given that the amount of time available for physical education instruction is very limited and usually held constant for all students, it is improbable that students with disabilities who are already significantly behind based on the PLOP will be able to learn the general physical education content at a rate necessary to master and achieve the general physical education goals. As a result, students with disabilities that require adapted physical education services need to have their own physical education curricula that are designed based on their PLOP, learning rates, and their long-term physical and motor needs. Once achievement-based adapted physical education curricula are developed for students with disabilities, their curriculum scope and sequence charts can be used to develop the physical education portions of the IEP and to guide placement decisions. For most students with mild and moderate disabilities, there will be significant overlap between the goals and objectives in their adapted physical education curricula and the general physical education curriculum. The major differences will be that they will likely have fewer goals and/or fewer objectives within similar goals. To the maximum degree possible, the goal should be to include students with disabilities in general physical education so that they can work on their goals and objectives with their peers. For students with more severe disabilities, there will likely be greater differences between their physical education goals and the general physical education goals, but there should still be many opportunities where they can be included in general physical education to work on their own goals and objectives.

Given the limited time available for physical education in the overall school curriculum, the time that is available for physical education must be used judiciously. Instruction in physical education must be assessment based and focused on mastering a series of objectives that lead to the achievement of functional goals that allow students to develop and maintain their health, fitness, and activity levels as adults. This is particularly true for students with disabilities that tend to have greater health, physical activity, and fitness needs. As a physical educator, it is your responsibility to ensure that all your students with disabilities have the requisite physical and motor skills needed to maintain their health and fitness, enhance their employability, and maximize their ability to participate and interact with other members of the community throughout their lifespans.

CHAPTER 5

Instructional Modifications

Martin E. Block, Aija Klavina, and Ron Davis

OBJECTIVES

1. Define instructional modifications and use the four-point method to determine if a modification is appropriate

2. Define, describe differences, and provide examples of differentiated instruction and universal design for learning

3. Define and describe examples of the following instructional modifications: teaching style, class format, peer tutoring, cooperative learning, instructional cues, and visual supports

There was no doubt that DJ could be a challenge. Everyone at Henry Elementary School knew about DJ. In fact, several neighbors and even a local convenience store near Henry Elementary knew about DJ. DJ has autism, and ever since he started at Henry, he has been a ball of energy. Despite having a teacher assistant assigned to him, several times DJ has managed to escape school grounds and run through the neighborhood and into the convenience store. Now as a third grader, DJ is only slightly more on task than he was when he was a kindergartner.

Ms. Bowers recently graduated from college, and she is eager to start her first job taking over for the school's physical education teacher, who is out for a year on maternity leave. During the week of in-services, she met with DJ's special education teacher and teacher assistant, and she did not seem to be too rattled by what she heard. Ms. Bowers worked with some children with Asperger syndrome when she did her student teaching, and she was able to handle those children without any problem. But Ms. Bowers was soon to find out that those children were nothing like DJ!

Ms. Bowers met DJ along with the third-grade class at 9:15 on a sunny, warm Monday morning. It did not take long for DJ to show his true colors. While Ms. Bowers was talking to the class about her rules for the gymnasium, DJ was rocking and making odd sounds. Then while the students were sitting and listening to Ms. Bowers talk about all the things they were going to do that year, DJ stood up and ran around the room, touching all the pictures that Ms. Bowers so carefully put up the previous week. When Ms. Bowers asked DJ to return to the group, DJ decided he had enough and ran out the rear exit door onto the playground. Both DJ's teacher assistant and Ms. Bowers quickly ran after DJ and caught him on a swing.

DJ certainly was not like the children Ms. Bowers worked with during her student teaching. How was she going to communicate with DJ? How was she going to help him understand what he was supposed to do when he was in physical education? How was she going to get him to stop and start? (She used the word freeze during her student teaching, but she was pretty sure that was not going to work with DJ.) Was DJ going to be able to handle large-group activities, or would DJ do better with a partner and small-group activities? Could DJ handle the guided discovery model of teaching that Ms. Bowers became so fond of during her student teaching, or would he need more direct instruction? Ms. Bowers recalled something she heard in her undergraduate adapted physical education class about picture schedules, but would that work with DJ?

Students with disabilities often can be safely and successfully included in general physical education without drastically changing the program or causing undue hardship for the general physical education teacher. However, the general physical educator (with support from the collaborative team) must be prepared to make modifications to how the class is organized, how information is presented, and how support personnel are utilized. The first step in accommodating students with disabilities in general physical education is determining how you will organize your class and present information. Once you understand how you will teach, then you can make modifications to accommodate students with disabilities. Instructional modifications can make a tremendous difference between success and failure for students with special needs, and most modifications are relatively easy to implement. For example, students with visual impairments would not understand what to do in physical education if you used only demonstrations. The simple addition of verbal cues would allow these students to be successful.

The purpose of this chapter is to introduce a variety of instructional modifications to accommodate students with disabilities in general physical education. These instructional modifications (adapted in part from Eichstaedt & Lavay, 1992; Seaman, DePauw, Morton, & Omoto, 2007; and Sherrill, 2004) illustrate how subtle changes in how you organize your class and present information can better accommodate students with disabilities (see Table 5.1). The goal of these modifications is to allow all students, including students with disabilities, to participate in a general physical education setting that is safe and challenging and affords opportunities for success. Which techniques you choose to implement will depend on the particular needs of the student with disabilities, the age group you are working with, the skills you are focusing on, the makeup of your class, the availability of equipment and facilities, the availability of support personnel, and your preferences. Although specific examples are provided, it is important that you focus on the general process of how to make modifications. If you understand the general process of creating and implementing appropriate

Table 5.1.　Instructional modifications that can facilitate inclusion

Class organization
• Teaching style
• Class format

Information presentation
• Verbal cues
• Demonstrations
• Level of methodology
• How students communicate with you
• Starting and stopping signals
• Time of day
• Duration
• Order of learning
• Size and nature of group
• Instructional setting
• Eliminating distractors
• Providing structure
• Level of difficulty
• Level of motivation

instructional modifications, then you can apply this process to a variety of situations.

Support personnel and especially peers can be very helpful when developing and implementing any modification. Chapter 3 reviews members of the collaborative team who can offer support, and Chapter 4 explains how team members can help determine which types of modifications are most appropriate for particular students. Peers and support staff also can assist the general physical educator in implementing specific modifications. Support staff can include classmates, older peer tutors, volunteers, teacher assistants, or specialists. All the instructional modifications outlined in the following section (as well as the curricular modifications outlined in Chapters 6 and 7) can be more effectively implemented if support personnel are in the gymnasium to assist the general physical educator. Even having a parent volunteer or the school custodian for a few minutes to provide individual assistance to a student with disabilities can make a tremendous difference. For example, imagine a student who is learning how to walk with a walker. During a warm-up in which students are practicing galloping, skipping, and hopping, this student moves among his peers practicing walking with his walker with assistance from a peer or parent volunteer to prevent him from falling.

MODELS RELATED TO MODIFICATIONS

Before talking about specific instructional modifications, it is important to review two of the more popular models for accommodating the needs of diverse learners: differentiated instruction (DA) and universal design for learning (UDL). These models are broad, class- or schoolwide approaches that focus on not only students with disabilities but also all students in the school, taking into account the wide variability in skills, experiences, and learning styles of students within the student body at large (Janney & Snell, 2013). These models are applicable to the present chapter as well as Chapter 6 (curricular modifications) and Chapter 7 (game modifications). It is important to note that using these models across the entire student body makes it easier to make modifications for students with disabilities. For example, a physical educator may feel intimidated by the prospects of accommodating an elementary-age child with a visual impairment in a throwing and catching unit. How can a child with limited vision be able to successfully throw and catch? However, using differentiated instruction, this physical educator thinks of all the students as individuals with unique strengths and weaknesses and who all need some level of accommodation. There are balls of different sizes for throwing and catching, there are different starting distances for throwing and catching, and there are targets of different sizes. Finally, children are encouraged to set individual goals depending on their abilities, such as trying to hit a small target 1 out of 5 tries or a large target from 10 feet away 4 out of 5 times. With all these accommodations designed to make sure all the children in the class are successful and challenged at their own levels, the physical educator realizes it is not such a big stretch to accommodate the child with a visual impairment. For this child, a medium-size Nerf ball is used for catching and tossing with a peer, and the peer stands only 3–4 feet away from the child. Interestingly, there are other children in the class who are more comfortable standing close to their partner when catching, and there are other children in the class who prefer the softer Nerf ball.

Differentiated Instruction

Differentiating instruction is a proactive approach that involves giving all students in the class different options in how they are presented information and how they demonstrate understanding and knowledge of concepts and content (Tomlinson, 2001). Differentiated instruction takes into account individual student readiness, interests, and learning styles when planning instruction (Gregory & Chapman, 2013; Huebner, 2010; Janney & Snell, 2013). Tomlinson (2001) makes a good point noting that differentiated instruction is not individualized

instruction. Individualized instruction involves doing something different for each individual child, and this can be untenable in a typical classroom of 20–30 children let alone a physical education setting that may have double or triple that number of students. Rather, differentiated instruction offers several options for learning, and it does not assume that each individual child would need a separate, unique adaptation. Recall the earlier example in which the student with a visual impairment was in a throwing and catching unit. Rather than creating a unique accommodation for this student, the teacher proactively created a number of ways to experience, practice, and measure success in throwing and catching for all students. This student has the opportunity to be successfully included in the unit not by having unique, individual accommodations but by taking advantage of the planned differentiated options offered to all children in the class.

Tomlinson (2001) and Janney and Snell (2013) point out that differentiated instruction provides multiple choices to three specific areas related to instruction and learning: content, process, and product.

Content is what the student is expected to learn. Different levels of content can be offered to the students. For example, in a ninth-grade physical education class starting a soccer unit, basic skills, concepts, and rules are presented to the least skilled and least physically fit children who have no experience (and probably no interest) in soccer. This level of content may be perfect for including a student with a severe intellectual disability or a student with cerebral palsy who uses canes for ambulation. It also would be easy to recruit peers from this less skilled group to help students with disabilities. The level of content would be different for students in the class who are more athletic and physically fit but who have not had much experience with soccer. These students would be expected to master basic skills and be introduced to more advanced skills. In addition, more advanced concepts would be presented as well. Finally, advanced concepts and strategies would be offered to those students who play soccer for the high school team or in their community who have much more previous knowledge, experience, and skills in soccer compared with other students, including those with more mild disabilities who may play soccer in their community.

Process is how students make sense of concepts and content presented. This includes providing differentiation in instructional strategies, materials used, conditions in which the student is expected to learn, and activities presented. In physical education, instructional strategies might include a verbal presentation of how to do the overhand throw along with a demonstration. In addition, the teacher has copied pictures of the components of the overhand throw from the third edition of the Test of Gross Motor Development (Ulrich, in press) and posts them at each throwing station. Finally, the teacher takes a video of a student in the class demonstrating all the components of the overhand throw, which can be used for students who need extra reminders on how to perform a skillful throw or who learn best by seeing a video model. In this way, there are four modes of instruction available to all students (verbal, demonstration, picture, and video). A child with autism who needs visual supports could easily be accommodated within this class using the pictures and video models, whereas a child with a visual impairment would take advantage of the verbal presentation of the components, and a child with a hearing impairment would take advantage of the demonstration and visuals. Again, note how the accommodations are proactive and not designed for any particular student; yet by differentiating, all students—including those with disabilities—are accommodated.

Product refers to how students demonstrate what they have learned. For example, in the throwing unit, three types of product measurement are used: 1) demonstrating improvement in mastery of the components of a skillful throw, 2) demonstrating improved distance in throwing, and 3) demonstrating improved accuracy when throwing. By nature, individual student learning styles and needs are taken into account in this case. Since the teacher focuses on improvement, all children regardless of their starting point will have a chance to show improvement, from the child who shows improvement by mastering one component of the overhand throw, to another child who was close to mastery and shows improvement by mastering that last component, and finally to other students who already mastered all the components who are showing improvement through increased distance and accuracy. See Ellis, Lieberman, and LeRoux (2009) for additional examples of differentiated instruction applied to an inclusive physical education setting.

Universal Design for Learning

Universal design is based on the philosophy that the physical environment and the activities engaged within the environment should be used by all individuals without adaptations or specially designed equipment (Janney & Snell, 2013; Opitz & Block, 2006). Examples of universal design can be found in our local communities, such as door handles that are levers and not door knobs, which would require a person to reach, grab, and turn the handle instead of simply pushing the handle down to open the door. In most metropolitan areas, you encounter universal design each time you cross a busy street corner and use a curb cut. Curb cuts provide a ramped entry allowing you to easily step into the street whether walking or using a wheelchair, cart, or stroller. Many airports have moving sidewalks to shuttle travelers from one terminal to another. Each entry and exit point of these sidewalks is designed with visual and auditory cues to alert travelers that they are about to engage or leave the moving surface. Some moving sidewalks go a step further and include flashing lights that change colors as you move from entry to exit. These examples provide engagement for all travelers within the environment, not just those using wheelchairs, service animals, or auditory devices.

The use of UDL instruction in physical education must be planned in detail to reach all students (Lieberman & Houston-Wilson, 2009). The difference between the use of UDL instruction and making adaptations for specific populations is in the planning; you must focus your instruction on the needs of all students, not just those from a single disability group (e.g., orthopedic, visual, cognitive). For example, when teaching a unit on softball using UDL instruction, what would be a single piece of equipment that could be used to 1) maintain the integrity of the game, 2) include all students, and 3) address movement concerns? To answer this question, the teacher must be able to identify all the components of the game from the following perspectives: contextual (e.g., getting runners out or running to the correct base in the correct order), skills (e.g., hitting a pitched ball), and student learning (e.g., how many outs in an inning? what is foul territory?). This is not the same planning process when deciding how to "adapt" the game of softball for a person who is visually impaired; that approach focuses on one disability population, whereas UDL considers all students. The use of UDL for instruction is a challenging approach, but fortunately there are guiding principles.

Principles of Universal Design for Learning

There are nine principles supporting UDL for instruction (McGuire, Scott, & Shaw, 2006) that could be applied to physical education and used to address the educational needs of students with disabilities. Table 5.2 provides suggested examples of how UDL can be used to address instruction and learning for all students. General or adapted physical educators

Table 5.2.   Principles of universal design with application to physical education

Principle	Definition	Application to physical education
1. Equitable use	Instruction is designed to be useful to and accessible by people with diverse abilities and should provide the same means of use for all students whenever possible.	Use color-coded signs to direct movement around the play space (red = stop; green = go) coupled with auditory cues.
2. Flexibility in use	Instruction is designed to accommodate a wide range of individual abilities and should provide choice in the methods of use.	Post pictures on exercise equipment demonstrating appropriate use of the machine or show short You-Tube videos; support with physical cues as needed. Allow students to select level of difficulty for engaging with equipment but ensure safety procedures are being followed.
3. Simple and intuitive	Instruction is designed to be straightforward; unnecessary complexity should be eliminated.	Use iPad videos to demonstrate desired movement (e.g., throwing); support with auditory (one word) and physical cues as needed.
4. Perceptible information	Instruction is communicated effectively regardless of students' sensory abilities.	Use stations for activity (fundamental skills or exercise), combined with Principle 2, and provide pictures, videos, or tactile input from peer partners.
5. Tolerance for error	Instruction anticipates variation in individual student learning pace and prerequisites.	Provide students choices for distance, object, and movement to complete the task (e.g., throwing at target, striking a ball) that become developmentally more challenging as they progress.
6. Low physical effort	Instruction is designed to minimize non-essential physical effort in order to allow maximum attention to learning.	[a]This principle may not apply to physical effort required in a course (in this case, physical education).
7. Size and space for approach and use	Instruction is designed with consideration for appropriate size and space for approach, reach, manipulations, and use regardless of the student's body size, posture, mobility, and communication needs.	Consider placement of equipment; entry and exit pathways; and areas needed for students using wheelchairs, guide canes, scooters and be sure to address high-volume use of boom boxes, iPads, or videos.
8. A community of learners	The instructional environment promotes interaction and communication among students and between students and teacher.	Color code sections of your workspace to promote certain activities (blue: group discussions; green: sharing stories; yellow: creative ideas) and then allow all students to engage with these areas on their own.
9. Instructional climate	Instruction is designed to be welcoming and inclusive.	Consider using more assistive technology (e.g., iPads, tablets, use of program apps) for instruction. Encourage students to teach peers, make their own instructional videos, or role-play a sports scenario.

From Scott, S.S., McGuire, J.M., & Shaw, S.F. (2001). *Principles of universal design for instruction.* Storrs, CT: University of Connecticut, Center on Postsecondary Education and Disability; adapted by permission.

planning to teach with UDL principles should make sure they use an intentional instructional approach (i.e., proactively thinking of the needs of all learners) to ensure all students receive a meaningful experience (Higbee, 2008).

SELECTING APPROPRIATE MODIFICATIONS

Not all instructional modifications are necessarily good. For example, perhaps you consider slowing down your speech when talking to the entire class to accommodate a child who has trouble with understanding verbal directions. Although such an accommodation will help this one student, it would also highlight his differences. Furthermore, such an accommodation would waste the time of

peers without disabilities, who before long would come to resent having this student with a disability in their class. Before implementing an instructional modification, it is important to determine whether a particular modification might have a negative effect on the student with disabilities, peers without disabilities, or the teacher. If the modification has a negative effect on any or all these individuals, then it probably is not the most appropriate modification. Lieberman and Houston-Wilson (2009) created a checklist to help determine the appropriateness of modifications (see Table 5.3). In addition, the following four criteria should be used whenever considering a particular modification:

1. *Does the change allow the student with disabilities to participate successfully yet still be challenged?* Finding the balance between

Table 5.3. Adaptation checklist

- Is the adaptation safe?
- Does the modification maintain the concept of the game?
- Was the child included in the adaptation, and does he or she embrace the concept?
- Is the game still age-appropriate?
- Is the child still included successfully?
- Is the adaptation holding the child back and not affording a challenge?
- Does the adaptation still allow the child with a disability to work on either class goals or IEP goals?
- Does the adaptation alienate the child from the rest of the class?
- Other?

Reprinted, with permission, from L.J. Lieberman and C. Houston-Wilson, 2002, *Strategies for inclusion: A handbook for physical educators* (Champaign, IL: Human Kinetics), 63.

success and challenge can be very difficult, but it is critical for children with disabilities. Not providing necessary accommodations can cause the child with disabilities to be confused or to fail, but providing too much support makes the activity too easy for the child. For example, a child who is blind might simply need to have a peer help him or her find a throwing station, find the bucket of balls, and then face the correct direction. This student can then do the activity independently. There is no need for the teacher, teacher assistant, or peer to provide additional physical assistance to this student.

2. *Does the modification make the setting unsafe for the student with a disability or for peers?* Safety should always be a top priority when determining accommodations. Often, simple instructional accommodations can make the setting safer for all students. For example, an impulsive student often gets distracted by extraneous equipment such as mats stored to the side of the gym. He has been known to leave the group, climb on the mats, and then jump down before the teacher even knows he is gone. To accommodate this child (and others who have been distracted by the stack of mats), the teacher has stored the mats behind a curtain on a corner of the stage that is connected to the gym. Now this student is not distracted by the mats.

3. *Does the change affect peers without disabilities?* As noted, some accommodations can affect the entire class and should be used cautiously.

4. *Does the change cause an undue burden on the general physical education teacher?* One of the greatest concerns of general physical educators is that accommodations are going to be too difficult to implement. Yet many modifications can be very simple to implement. For example, a student with an intellectual disability might not be able to understand the teacher's verbal cue to stop. One simple solution might be to have peers near the student give him or her an extra cue or a hand signal. This simple accommodation allows the student to be successful without causing an undue hardship on the physical education teacher.

CLASS ORGANIZATION ACCOMMODATIONS

Teaching Style

Teaching style refers to the learning environment, the general routine, and how the lesson is presented to the class. Mosston and Ashworth (2002) described several different teaching styles commonly used by physical educators (see Table 5.4). They suggested these various teaching styles could be arranged across a spectrum that reflected decisions made by the teacher and by the student. On one side of the spectrum, teachers make all or most of the decisions for students regarding what to do, when to do it, how to do it, how long to do it, with whom (if anyone) to do it, and with what equipment to do it. These styles are referred to as *reproductive styles* because students are supposed to reproduce or replicate a particular movement pattern. For example, students learning how to shoot a basketball are given a basketball and asked to follow the step-by-step directions given by the teachers. The goal is for students to copy the teacher's pattern as accurately as possible (see Figure 5.1). The major advantage of these types of styles is that students know exactly what they are supposed to do, and teachers are more apt to have control over the class. The major disadvantage of these styles is that students are more passive rather than active learners (i.e., they are told what they are supposed to learn rather than discovering what is important to learn), and students are less likely to be creative and discover unique and different ways to solve movement problems.

On the other end of the spectrum, students make most or all the decisions. Teaching styles on this side of the spectrum are referred to as *productive styles* because students are supposed to produce or discover the most appropriate movement pattern to solve a particular movement pattern (see Figure 5.2). In some cases, there is no absolute right or wrong movement pattern, and students learn through discovery which pattern fits best

Table 5.4. Mosston and Ashworth's teaching styles

Reproductive styles	
Command	To learn to do the task accurately and within a short period of time, following all decisions made by the teacher. Invokes an immediate response to a stimulus. Performance is accurate and immediate. A previous model is replicated.
Practice/task	This style offers the learner time to work individually and privately and provides the teacher with time to offer the learner individual and private feedback. The essence: Time is provided for the learner to do a task individually and privately, and time is available for the teacher to give feedback to all learners, individually and privately.
Reciprocal	In this style, learners work with a partner and offer feedback to the partner, based on criteria prepared by the teacher. The essence: Learners work in a partner relationship, receive immediate feedback, follow criteria for performance designed by the teacher, and develop feedback and socialization skills.
Self-check	The purposes of this style are to learn to do a task and to check one's own work. The essence: Learners do the task individually and privately and provide feedback for themselves by using criteria developed by the teacher.
Inclusion/invitation	The purposes of this style are to learn to select a level of a task one can perform and to offer a challenge to check one's own work. The essence: The same task is designed for different degrees of difficulty. Learners decide their entry point into the task and when to move to another level.
Productive styles	
Guided discovery	The purpose of this style is to discover a concept by answering a sequence of questions presented by the teacher. The essence: The teacher, by asking a specific sequence of questions, systematically leads the learner to discover a predetermined target previously unknown to the learner.
Convergent discovery	Here, learners discover the solution to a problem and learn to clarify an issue and arrive at a conclusion by employing logical procedures, reasoning, and critical thinking. The essence: Teachers present the question. The intrinsic structure of the task (question) requires a single correct answer. Learners engage in reasoning (and other cognitive operations) and seek to discover the single correct answer/solution.
Divergent discovery	The purpose of this style is to engage in producing (discovering) multiple responses to a single question. The essence: Learners are engaged in producing divergent responses to a single question. The intrinsic structure of the task (question) provides possible multiple responses. The multiple responses are assessed by the possible-feasible-desirable procedures, or by the verification "rules" of the given discipline.
Learner's individual designed program	The purpose of this style is to design, develop, and perform a series of tasks organized into a personal program with consultation with the teacher. The essence: The learner designs, develops, and performs a series of tasks organized into a personal program. The learner selects the topic, identifies the questions, collects data, discovers answers, and organizes the information. The teacher selects the general subject matter area.

Source: Mosston and Ashworth (2002).

with which particular situation. For example, a teacher might want her students to discover which throwing pattern is the best for bowling, for playing catch with a water balloon, and for throwing a basketball and softball. Obviously, each situation requires a unique movement pattern. Students who learn by actively experimenting and discovering for themselves the most appropriate patterns tend to be more invested in their learning and retain what they have learned longer.

Some objectives in physical education can be achieved more effectively with certain styles. For example, accurate replication of a precise movement pattern such as learning how to grip and swing a golf club might best be taught through various reproductive styles. In contrast, creating different types of pyramids in a gymnastics unit or developing a repertoire of locomotor patterns and movement concepts might best be taught through various productive styles. In addition, some students will respond better to certain teaching styles. For example, children who need more structure and direction, such as students with attention-deficit/hyperactivity disorder, autism, or an intellectual disability, do better in reproductive learning styles such as command or reciprocal styles. Students with unique movement abilities but typical intelligence, such as children with cerebral palsy or muscular dystrophy, may learn to compensate by discovering for themselves the best way to move. It is important to recognize the importance of the objectives of the activity and how each student learns. Then

We are going to learn how to shoot a basketball today. Everyone has a basketball.

1. Okay, I want you to hold the basketball in your dominant hand (the one you use to write with).

2. Okay, now pretend that you are a waitress holding a tray of food and hold the ball with your palm facing upward. You want the ball to be even with and slightly to the side of your face. In this position, I also want you to make sure your elbow (the arm holding ball) is pointing toward your target.

3. Okay, now place your other hand gently to the side of the ball. This hand is used to keep the ball aiming straight and not falling out of your other hand.

4. Let's quickly check hand positions; your dominant hand is behind the ball with your elbow facing your target, and your nondominant hand is to the side of the ball.

5. Okay, stand so that you are facing your target (stomach facing target) with your feet about shoulder-width apart.

6. Now we are going to bend our knees slightly, maybe 3 or 4 inches.

7. This is going to be tricky: Straighten your knees and your arms at the same time to shoot your basketball. If you time this correctly, you will be able to shoot the ball from pretty far away.

8. One more important thing: When you finish shooting, your shooting arm should be straight, with your hand pointing toward the target. Try and let the ball roll off your fingertips by snapping your wrist like you are reaching into a cookie jar. Hold this position for a few seconds like a statue so you can really feel the correct follow-through.

9. Okay, get your ball and find a place near a wall on the gym to practice shooting. I want you to focus on the correct form of the skill like we just practiced. You are going to shoot the ball 10 times. This is not a race; I want you to practice the correct form.

10. Each time you prepare to shoot, say the following cue words to yourself:
    a. Waitress
    b. Elbow
    c. Bend
    d. Jump
    e. Cookie

Figure 5.1. Scripts for the reproduction style of teaching: elementary school basketball shooting.

We are going to try lots of different ways to move. There is no right or wrong way; I want to see you be really creative when you move. Okay, here we go:

1. Show me how you can travel using any locomotor pattern you want; be sure to use different pathways (straight, curvy, or zigzag).

2. Now pick a different way to travel and try different levels—high, medium, or low.

3. Now pick a different way to travel and this time try different speeds—fast, medium, or slow.

4. Now pick a different way to travel and this time you can be really loose and floppy or you can be really stiff and straight.

5. Now pick a different way to travel, and this time move really loudly or really softly with your feet.

6. Okay, now pick your favorite way to travel and this time, pick a pathway and a speed.

7. Okay, now pick your second favorite way to travel, using a different level and different force.

Middle/High School Soccer Unit

There are several different ways to dribble around your opponent in soccer, including a stop and go, faking to the left or right, and a double fake. There are many other ways. For the next several minutes I want you to choose a partner and try different ways of dribbling around your partner. There is no right or wrong way; the goal is to find a few different ways that work best for you. Be creative.

Figure 5.2. Script for the production style of teaching: lower elementary school locomotor patterns and movement concepts.

and only then can the teacher choose the most appropriate teaching style.

With inclusive physical education classes, it may be necessary to provide different teaching styles for different students in the same class. Teachers can still employ the general principles of one particular teaching style to help a particular student while using another style for the majority of the class. For example, in the context of a command style used to teach the overhand throwing pattern, a teacher could allow a student who has cerebral palsy to explore different throwing patterns (guided discovery) that meet his or her unique needs. Similarly, a teacher presenting body awareness concepts in a divergent (productive) style could give very specific information on what to do, how to do it, when to do it, and where to do it using a command (reproductive) style for a student with an intellectual disability. Again, the key is deciding on objectives for the class as well as individual students, how the class learns best as well as how individual students learn best, and which teaching style will be most effective.

Class Format

Class format refers to how members of the class are organized. Seaman et al. (2007) outlined seven class formats commonly used in physical education settings:

1. *One-to-one instruction:* one teacher or assistant for every student

2. *Small group:* 3–10 students working together with a teacher or assistant

3. *Large group:* entire class participating together as one group

4. *Mixed group:* using various class formats within one class period

5. *Peer teaching or tutoring:* using classmates or students without disabilities from other classes for teaching and assisting students with disabilities

6. *Teaching stations:* several areas in which smaller subsets of the class rotate through to practice skills

7. *Self-paced independent work:* each student works on individual goals at his or her own pace following directions on task cards or with guidance from the teacher or assistant

In addition, *cooperative learning* is a class format that can facilitate inclusion in physical education. The following briefly reviews selected class formats and how they can be used in inclusive physical education settings. Again, no class format is necessarily wrong or right. It is just important that the goals of your lesson match the learning needs of your class. You want to find the best class format to help your students (including the student with a disability) achieve your goals for the lesson.

Peer Tutoring

Peer tutoring involves students helping students. Because it can be difficult for a general physical education teacher to work individually with children with disabilities, peers without disabilities can be trained and then assigned to provide extra instruction and support. In addition, peer tutoring creates a setting in which the student with a disability receives one-to-one instruction and increased practice and reinforcement (Lieberman & Houston-Wilson, 2009). Peer tutoring has been recognized as an effective inclusion strategy for many decades and widely used in inclusive classroom settings (Ernst & Byra, 1998). Regarding physical education, peer tutoring programs have been successfully applied to students with mild and moderate disabilities (e.g., DePaepe, 1985; Houston-Wilson, Dunn, van der Mars, & McCubbin, 1997; Lieberman, Dunn, van der Mars, & McCubbin, 2000; Lieberman, Newcomer, McCubbin, & Dalrymple, 1997; Webster, 1987) and also to students with severe and multiple disabilities (Klavina & Block, 2008). Peer tutoring is a type of collaborative learning in which students support each other rather than relying only on assistant teacher or paraprofessional assistance. *Collaborative learning* is an umbrella term for the educational approach of interactive learning effort by students or students and teachers together. The development of social skills is the key to high-quality group learning. This approach provides significant peer effects with benefits to all students but particularly for students with disabilities. Peers provide more natural supports, increase social interactions and communication skills, and maintain or enhance students' academic engagement.

There are different types of peer tutoring the teacher can use: one-to-one peer tutoring, classwide peer tutoring, and small-group tutoring.

One-to-one peer tutoring using classmates within the class provides a situation in which the child with a disability receives instructions, increased practice, increased reinforcement, and continuous feedback on progress by the tutor on a one-to-one basis (Delquadri, Greenwood, Whorton, Carta, & Hall, 1986). In this case, a classmate without disabilities is the tutor and a student with disabilities is the tutee. However, a single peer tutor does not need to be paired with the student for the entire class session; several students (tutors) can be trained to work with a student with disabilities and take turns assisting him or her to reduce fatigue and boredom in peer tutors. Also, this instructional practice provides an opportunity for more social interactions for a student with disabilities with different classmates. Having classmates in the same class provide extra instruction and support is the most cost-effective method and the easiest to set up. The tutors are already in class and available, and classmates know each other and are familiar with the routine of that class. Note that students with mild disabilities (e.g., autism, learning disabilities, emotional and behavioral disabilities, and hearing impairments) also can learn tutoring skills and be involved in the dyadic, reciprocal relationships. Also, research shows that the responsibility of peer tutoring improves the academic performance of students who have problems paying attention, problems learning, and who are considered "at risk" by their parents and teachers of failing in school (Kalkowski, 2001). To avoid labeling or the perception of students without disabilities that peers with disabilities are only ones who need help, all students can be involved in peer support. For example, a teacher might encourage students to be a good friend and to see if somebody needs help, extra instruction, or feedback during physical education. When all students from the class are involved in peer-mediated support, this is called classwide peer tutoring.

Classwide peer tutoring (CWPT) was developed by special education professionals in early 1980s for two reasons: 1) to support the inclusion of students with diverse abilities within the general education setting and 2) to increase at-risk students' involvement in learning (Kamps et al., 2008). Typically in CWPT, all students work together in tutor–tutee pairs. The tutor demonstrates the skill and provides feedback to the tutee or assists in accomplishing the task. Students change roles during the session according the teachers' instructions. In this case, only the student without disability provides tutoring. However, if the student's disability is mild or moderate, then roles of tutee and tutor can be changed. Ayvazo (2010), Johnson and Ward (2001), and Ward and Ayvazo (2006) presented successful CWPT in teaching striking and catching skills of students with autism spectrum disorder. Similarly, Klavina, Jerlinder, Kristen, Hammar, and Soulie (2014) implemented a type of CWPT approach across three elementary school classes in Sweden involving 42 students, including 4 students with moderate and mild disabilities. All students,

including those with disabilities, were taught how to be a good friend, how to collaborate, and how to do activities together. The teachers' reports after the study indicated that students gained knowledge on coactivity and learned positive peer perception that, overall, benefited their self-esteem and improved the class climate. Also, students stated that they gained positive experiences by learning how to implement knowledge of providing assistance from training to practice. Students noted they became a better friend and made a great effort to interact with and compliment peers with disabilities.

Small-group tutoring (four to six students per group) in an inclusive class consists of general education students with and without disabilities. The groups can be arranged by skill, for example, one group practices basketball drills, another works on catching skills, and so forth. Children without disabilities are matched with children with impairments. It is recommended that the general physical education teacher selects children for each group so there is good skill balance among students. For students with a disability, the small-group peer collaboration arrangement also increases their social interactions with classmates and helps them feel a sense of belonging to the group or of being part of the team. Small-group peer tutoring is recommended when including a student with severe and/or multiple disabilities. Klavina and Block (2008) indicated that peer tutoring intervention promoted physical and social affiliation of the student with severe and/or multiple disabilities with a group of classmates, including trained tutors as well as other classmates who did not serve as tutors. In addition, peer tutors feel more confident and more comfortable when being in a group rather than one-to-one with a peer who might have multiple health and/or behavioral issues.

In *cross-age peer tutoring*, the tutor is older than the tutee. However, studies in physical education using peer tutors from other classes or age groups have indicated that these tutors needed extra time to get adjusted to the new class setting and to adjust to their roles (Lieberman et al., 2000). Student pairings may include a variety of combinations such as elementary students with high school students or older students with disabilities with younger students with disabilities (Miller & Miller, 1995). Tutors become models of appropriate skill performance, encourage social interaction, and facilitate academic success of a tutee (Barbetta, Miller, Peters, Heron, & Cochran, 1991; Gaustad, 1993; Miller & Miller, 1995). Cross-age tutoring can enhance the self-esteem of tutors who provide individualized instruction to tutees and can also result in friendly relationships outside the class and an improved school atmosphere for the tutor (Kalkowski, 2001). Some schools allow peer tutoring to count toward required community service. Other schools have peer tutoring classes in which students register for credit, go through training, and meet regularly to discuss tutoring. One advantage is that older peers often are more reliable and focused than same-age classmates, and older peers often can handle more responsibility. In addition, some students with disabilities behave better with an older peer rather than a classmate. However, it may be difficult to free up older students from their academic classes to come and help in physical education (see Houston-Wilson, Lieberman, Horton, & Kasser, 1997, for more information on cross-age peer tutors).

Regardless of the model used, training peer tutors is critical for success (Lieberman & Houston-Wilson, 2009). Training can be formal such as a partner club (Eichstaedt & Lavay, 1992; Sutherland, 1999) or informal and part of the general physical education class. Training can take several days or can be conducted in two or three general physical education class sessions. There are several stages to implement a peer tutoring training program:

Selection of Peer Tutors To select peer tutors, the general physical education teacher can simply ask for volunteer students who are willing to participate in peer tutoring. Also, the teacher might look for students who already show supportive behavior toward a peer with disabilities, such as pushing a peer in a wheelchair during warm-up, being willing to be a partner, or including him or her in the team. Then teachers might select peer tutors thought to be most appropriate based on their caring nature and ability to follow the requirements of the peer tutoring program (Klavina & Block, 2008). Peer buddy programs or peer support training courses provided by the school might also be helpful sources for identifying prospective tutors. The ideal situation would be selecting multiple peer tutors from the same group or class who are familiar with the student with a disability. The physical education teacher might create a schedule so peer tutors know which days they are tutoring.

Training Many authors who have written about peer tutor training have indicated specific components as part of their training program such as the following: disability awareness concepts; use of person-first language; and instructional strategies on how to use cues, how to provide prompts and feedback, and how to provide physical assistance to the student with disabilities (Block, 1995a, 1999;

Greenwood & Todd, 1988; Houston-Wilson, 1997; Lieberman et al. 2000; Lieberman et al., 1997; Sherrill, Heikinaro-Johansson, & Slininger, 1994). For example, Klavina and Block (2008) developed the Peer Tutor Training Manual for elementary-age children, which includes the five TIP-TAP (tips for teaching, assisting, and practicing) steps for peer tutoring: 1) instruction, 2) demonstration, 3) physical assistance, 4) feedback, and 5) error correction (see Appendix 5A at the end of this chapter for more on TIP-TAP). Tutors should have at least three training sessions of 20–30 minutes before they begin tutoring. During the first session, students and a teacher discuss disability awareness and person-first language. In addition, the rules and roles of being a peer tutor should be covered (e.g., being friendly, talking softly, providing praises). In the second and third sessions, students are assigned to work in pairs or small groups to practice the rules and roles of peer tutors (e.g., TIP-TAP steps). Figure 5.3 provides an example of a peer tutoring worksheet for catching that can be used during the training as well as later with a student with a disability. The student with disabilities might join the practical sessions and be paired with students without disabilities during activity trials. It is recommended that selected activities match the general physical education unit for the school so that training sessions are similar to what the tutors would experience in the general physical education class setting. The teacher might use the Peer Tutor Training Evaluation forms (see Appendix 5B) to see if students have sufficiently learned the tutoring steps. It is also important for the teacher to praise and acknowledge participation of students with and without disabilities in training. The teacher can be vitally important in helping maintain peers' confidence and enjoyment, especially when tutoring a student with severe and/ or multiple disabilities (Cole, 1988; Logan et al., 1998). In addition, immediate and ongoing feedback should be provided to individual peer tutors during or after physical education sessions to correct interaction behaviors and improve the ways they provide teaching instructions during peer tutoring.

Implementation of Peer Tutoring A major advantage of implementing peer tutoring is that it allows students with disabilities to achieve the social and academic benefits afforded by their peers without disabilities (Cullinan, Sabornie, & Crossland, 1992; Sherrill et al., 1994). However, the real challenge for a general physical education teacher is to determine and modify goals and objectives for the student with disabilities in such a way that accommodations do not limit the experience for peers

Worksheet for Catching

Name: _____ Date: _____

Equipment: soft ball

1. Tell your friend that you will catch the ball five times.

2. Watch your friend do the catching task steps described below.

Step number	Description of step	Picture
1	Hands in front of the body	
2	Elbows bent	
3	Extend arms in front to catch ball	
4	Catch the ball with hands only	
5	Elbows flexed, bring the ball to the chest	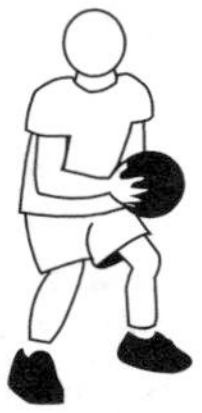

Notes:

_____

_____

Figure 5.3.　Example of peer tutor worksheet for catching. (From Klavina, A. [2007]. *The effect of peer tutoring on interaction behaviors in inclusive physical education* [Unpublished doctoral dissertation]. University of Virginia, VA; reprinted by permission.)

without disabilities. For example, how can peer tutors provide assistance to the student with severe cerebral palsy during general physical education, including multiple skill stations? First, the teacher needs to explain to peer tutors the appropriate modifications for the student with cerebral palsy at each skills station and provide teaching instructions in handout form (see Figure 5.4). Illustrations of targeted skills combined with simplified description of cues, prompts, skill analyses, and the types of assistance are particularly effective (e.g., "Stand in front of a student and physically assist to lift up arms by holding around wrists."). Table 5.5 provides an example of a peer tutoring instruction handout form.

Teaching Stations

Task teaching (also called station learning or learning centers) is a simple and popular way to organize inclusive general physical education classes (Block, Oberweiser, & Bain, 1995; Graham, Holt-Hale, & Parker, 2013). The teacher sets up three or

Peer Tutoring Task Sheet

Student: _____ Peer tutor: _____

Student's goals:

_____

_____

_____

Directions for the peer tutor: Circle the type of prompt, reinforcement, or method of communication used with the tutee. Then watch the tutee perform the skill while you focus on and comment on one component of the skill. Give the tutee a plus (+) if he or she performs the component correctly and a minus (–) if he or she does not perform the skill component correctly. After five trials, switch roles with the tutee so that you are the tutee and your partner is the tutor.

Types of prompts	Types of reinforcers	Communication
Natural	"Good job"	Talking
Verbal	High five	Show how
Gestures	Pat on the back	Pictures
Demonstration	Shooting baskets	
Partial physical	Token	
Physical assistance	Food	

Components of skill	
Dominant hand above nondominant hand	_____
Side orientation	_____
Weight transfer	_____
Follow-through	_____

Figure 5.4. Peer tutoring task sheet for teaching striking the stationary baseball ball. (From Klavina, A. [2007]. *The effect of peer tutoring on interaction behaviors in inclusive physical education* [Unpublished doctoral dissertation]. University of Virginia, VA; reprinted by permission.)

Table 5.5. Peer tutor instruction handout

Skill Station: Push-ups

Modifications for student with cerebral palsy: Lifting arms up.

Task analyses

1. Look at a peer tutor with head in a straight-up position.
2. Lift both arms while keeping head straight and eyes focused on peer tutor.
3. Keep arms up for 5 seconds as if giving a high-five.

Teaching instruction: Stand in front of your peer.

Verbal cue: "We are going to lift our arms up like we are giving a high-five." Demonstrate the task.

Verbal prompt: "Look at me."

If necessary, provide gestural prompt by pointing at the student.

Praise: "Good looking."

Verbal cue: "Lift your arms up."

Verbal prompt: "Reach my arms." Hold your arms up.

If necessary, provide physical assistance by holding peer's arms around wrists.

Praise: Say something like, "Good reaching!" or "High-five!," or just smile.

From Klavina, A. (2007). *The effect of peer tutoring on interaction behaviors in inclusive physical education* (Unpublished doctoral dissertation). University of Virginia, VA; reprinted by permission.

more places around the gym with various activities. Children are assigned to a station and rotate to a different station when they have completed certain activities or when the teacher signals the group to move to a new station. For example, a teacher might set up hierarchical or progressive stations in which students are placed according to level of skill. As they progress in skill level or master some aspect of a skill, they move to a new station. Alternately, a teacher might simply assign groups of five to seven students to a station. After 3–5 minutes, the teacher signals students to rotate to the next station.

Stations can be independent, unrelated activities (e.g., jumping rope, throwing and catching, sit-ups/push-ups, tumbling) or can revolve around a theme (e.g., throwing at targets, throwing to a partner, throwing into a curtain, throwing over a net). In either case, there should be multiple challenges at each station to accommodate the varying abilities of children in the class. For example, the teacher might set up a kicking station in which students stand at different distances from the target, use balls of different sizes, and have targets of different sizes to hit. This way, each child who comes to the station is challenged at his or her own level and has the opportunity to be successful. In addition, the teacher might have a list of different ways to perform the skill to make it more challenging (e.g., at the kicking station: use your opposite leg, try to kick a moving ball, or try to chip the ball into the air). Again, this allows the more skilled

students to work at the same station as the less skilled students.

Because stations accommodate children of different abilities, they are ideal for including children with disabilities. For example, a 12-year-old girl with severe cerebral palsy is in a swimming class at her middle school. Some students in the class swim year-round, others can swim but need work on stroke refinement, and still others are learning basic strokes. In order to accommodate the range of abilities in this class, the physical education teacher has set up different stations for students in the class to work on the following skills: butterfly/breaststroke, backstroke, freestyle, and diving. The physical education teacher directly supervises the diving station while she watches the other stations from afar. A lifeguard also watches the swimmers. The student with cerebral palsy has a teacher assistant helping her. Students were previously tested on the various strokes and know what components of each stroke on which to focus. The teacher divides the class, sending seven students to each station. At the station is a list of activities including swimming a distance in a given period of time, swimming a particular distance using a particular stroke, and swimming using a kickboard focusing on one or two aspects of the stroke (see Figure 5.5). Each student knows to work independently on his or her own tasks, but students also are encouraged to help each other improve their strokes. For example, while resting after doing the butterfly for 25 meters in less than 2 minutes, a student watches and gives feedback to another student who is trying to gather enough courage to put his face in the water during the breaststroke. At the same station, the child with cerebral palsy is learning how to lie on her stomach and lift her head out of the water to clear an airway. A teacher assistant helps her do this task while a peer provides encouragement as he rests after his swim.

Cooperative Learning

Another class format option is *cooperative learning* in which students work together to accomplish shared goals. Group goals can only be accomplished if individual students in the group work together (Grineski, 1996; Johnson & Johnson, 1999; Luvmour & Luvmour, 2013; Orlick, 2006). In cooperative learning, students are instructed to learn the assigned information and to make sure that all members of the group master the information (at their level). For example, each child in the group must perform a set number of push-ups for the team to reach its shared goal of 180 push-ups. One girl who is very strong and who is trying to break the school

Breaststroke/Butterfly Station

Practice your personal challenge based on your pretest results (which are posted in the gym). When you have mastered a particular challenge, move to the next challenge. Help and encourage peers.

Challenges

_____ Lie on stomach and lift head out of water. Repeat several times.

_____ Hold onto gutter and perform correct leg movements for breaststroke 20 times.

_____ Hold onto kickboard and perform correct leg movements for breaststroke 20 times.

_____ Place kickboard under stomach, and practice correct arm movements for breaststroke 20 times.

_____ Place kickboard under stomach, and practice correct breathing pattern for breaststroke 20 times.

_____ Place kickboard under stomach, and practice correct arm and breathing pattern for breaststroke 20 times.

_____ Without kickboard, do complete breaststroke for five strokes.

_____ Do complete breaststroke for 10 strokes.

_____ Do breaststroke for length of pool.

_____ Do breaststroke for length of pool as fast as you can. Record your time: ____________________. Rest and repeat.

_____ Students on swim team: Do complete butterfly for length of pool as fast as you can. Record your time: ________________. Rest and repeat.

Figure 5.5. Breaststroke/butterfly station.

record is trying to do 100 push-ups. Another child in the group usually can do 35 push-ups, two other children in the group are trying to do 20 pushups, and a child with an intellectual disability is trying to do 5 push-ups. In order for the team to be successful, each person must meet his or her individual goal. Members of the team encourage each other to reach these goals that, in turn, help the team reach their shared goals.

Often, individuals in the group are given specific jobs or tasks that contribute to goal attainment. Cooperative learning encourages students to work together, help each other, and constantly evaluate each member's progress toward individual and group goals. For example, in a gymnastics unit, a team of four members must balance so that a total of two feet, two hands, two elbows, and two knees touch the ground. The team, which includes a child who is blind and has poor balance, together decides the best way to solve the challenge. After much discussion and experimentation, the team comes up with the following solution: The child who is blind stands on two feet and holds the ankles of another student who is standing on her hands (she needs the support or she will fall). Another student gets on his elbows and knees (feet up) while a fourth student sits on his back. The student sitting on his back helps balance the person standing on his hands. The only way this team could be successful was for everyone to work together.

For cooperative learning to be effective, students must perceive that they are positively linked to other students in their group and that each member can and must contribute to the success of the group. In addition, each member of the group must understand his or her role in the group (Grineski, 1996). Less skilled students, including students with disabilities, could be perceived to be the weak link in the group if all members believe that they must each perform the same task. However, if the group understands that each member has a unique task that maximizes his or her skills and contributes to the group goal, then the method will be effective. For example, a group of third graders is working on the skill of striking. The teacher divides the class into small groups of three to four students. The cooperative task for each group is to hit 50 paper and yarn balls across the gym with each member hitting each ball only once and with each student working on one key aspect of a skillful striking pattern. Because no student can hit the ball across the gym by himself or herself, only through group cooperation can the ball get across the gym. In Group A, a skilled student begins the process by hitting a pitched ball as far as possible (pitched by one of the group members). This student is working on timing and hitting the ball up into the air. A less skilled group member then walks to where the ball lands, picks up the ball, places it on a batting tee, then hits the ball forward as far as possible. This student is working on shifting weight and stepping, and the skilled student provides feedback to the less skilled student. Finally, the tee is moved to where the ball landed and is placed on the tee for a student who is blind. This student is working on hitting the ball off the tee with his hand using proper preparatory position, stepping, and using a level swing. Both the skilled and nonskilled students help position the student and provide him with feedback. The process is repeated until the group hits 50 balls. The group must work together to accomplish its goal, and each student must contribute in his or her own way. In addition, it benefits the group if each member improves his or her skill level. If a group member uses better form, then the ball will be hit farther and, in turn, help the team accomplish its goal (Luvmour & Luvmour, 2013; Orlick, 2006; Rohnke, 2010).

Using Multiple Formats

The best format for any situation will vary based on numbers, attitudes, and types of students with and without disabilities; type and flexibility of the facility; and availability of resources. In most situations, a combination of the class formats is most effective. For example, a student with severe disabilities can be included in a high school physical education class during a basketball unit in which the teacher utilizes a combination of peer tutors, stations, self-paced learning, and large-group instruction. Students begin the class by following the teacher through various warm-up activities (*large group*). The student with severe disabilities is assisted in these warm-up activities by his physical therapist who works on specific stretching and strengthening activities. Following warm-ups, students rotate through several basketball *stations* at their own pace, working on tasks geared to their ability level. Students choose which station to go to, but they can only stay at one station for 10 minutes and no more than seven students can be at any one station at one time. All students have a task card with a hierarchy of tasks that they move through at their own pace. In order to move to the next level on a hierarchy, the student must have another student confirm that he or she can perform the skill in four of five trials (*stations/self-paced learning*). Peers who chose the same station as the child with disabilities are cued by the teacher to help this child as needed (*peer tutoring*).

The culminating activity for the day is a game of basketball. Skilled students go with a class leader and play regulation games of five-on-five basketball, learning set plays and strategies (*small group*). Less skilled students, including the student with severe disabilities, go with the general physical education teacher who organizes a modified game. In today's version of the game, the defense must play a passive zone defense (i.e., cannot steal the ball unless it is passed directly to them). In addition, every player on the offensive team must touch the ball one time before a player can shoot, and students can get points for hitting the backboard (1 point), rim (2 points), or making a basket (3 points). Students who cannot reach a 10-foot basket can shoot at an 8-foot target on the wall, and the student with severe disabilities can score by pushing the ball off his lap tray into a box on the floor with assistance from a peer.

ACCOMMODATIONS IN HOW INFORMATION IS PRESENTED

Verbal Instructions

Verbal instructions refer to the length and complexity of commands or verbal challenges used to convey information to the class. Students with autism or intellectual disabilities who cannot understand complex commands or students with hearing impairments who cannot hear verbal commands may need to have instruction delivery modified. Seaman et al. (2007) suggested the following ways in which instructions can be modified for students who have difficulty understanding verbal language: Simplify words used, use single-meaning words (e.g., run to the base versus go to the base), give only one command at a time, ask the student to repeat the command before performing it, say the command and then demonstrate the task, or physically assist the student.

Although these modifications might be helpful for a student with a language disorder, such modifications might not be needed for the majority of students in the class. These modifications can still be implemented without changing the way instruction is delivered to the rest of the students. For example, a teacher might give complex verbal directions including information about abstract strategies and team concepts to the class. When the teacher is finished instructing the class, a peer could repeat key directions to the student with an intellectual disability. The peer can demonstrate some strategies and concepts, whereas abstract concepts can be translated into more concrete examples or skipped altogether. Similarly, a peer can demonstrate and mimic directions to a student with a hearing impairment after the teacher presents verbal directions to the class.

Demonstrations

Demonstrations can vary in who gives demonstrations, how many are given, how often they are given, and the best location for a demonstration. Modifications to demonstrations could be as simple as having students with poor vision stand close to the teacher. For students with intellectual disabilities, the teacher might need to highlight key aspects of the demonstration or have a peer repeat the demonstration several times. For example, the teacher could demonstrate the starting preparatory position, backswing, trunk rotation, and follow-through for the overhand throw to the class. For a student with an intellectual disability just learning to throw, the teacher (or peer) might repeat the demonstration, focusing on just one aspect (e.g., stepping with opposite foot) so that this student knows what component he should focus on.

Visual Supports

Many people with autism are thought to be visual learners. Temple Grandin, a person with autism who is now a successful college professor and author of several books, explained how she was a visual learner:

> I think in pictures. Words are like a second language to me. . .when somebody speaks to me, his words are instantly translated into pictures. . .One of the most profound mysteries of autism has been the remarkable ability of most autistic people to excel at visual spatial skills while performing so poorly at verbal skills. (Grandin, 2006, p. 1)

To accommodate these visual strengths, many have suggested the use of visual supports for students with autism (e.g., Bernard-Opitz & Häußler, 2011; Bondy & Frost, 2011; Cohen & Sloan, 2008). *Visual supports* refer to any kind of visual prompt that helps a student understand and interact with his or her world (Bondy & Frost, 2011; Savner & Myles, 2000), and the use of visual supports to accommodate children with autism in physical education has been recommended in several papers (Block & Taliaferro, 2014; Blubaugh & Kohlmann, 2006; Fittipaldi-Wert & Mowling, 2009; Green & Sandt, 2013; Groft-Jones & Block, 2006; Silla & Burba,

2008). One study showed that visual supports significantly improved scores on the Test of Gross Motor Development (TGMD-2) in children with autism compared with just a verbal cue or demonstration (Breslin & Rudisill, 2011). Visual supports help students understand and follow rules, know what is happening in their day, understand how to complete an assignment and when an assignment is complete, make a transition from one activity to another, and make choices about what they want. Visual support also allows the student to become more independent (Bondy & Frost, 2011; Savner & Myles, 2000). There are many different kinds of visual supports that can be used in physical education.

Visual Schedules

Visual schedules set out a plan for the entire day, for part of the day, or for a particular class (e.g., for physical education). The amount of time as well as the number of activities placed on a schedule varies from student to student. For example, one child might have a daily picture schedule that includes pictures of people and places he will go during the day. Pictures include his classroom teacher and her classroom, the music teacher and her room, the physical education teacher and the gymnasium, the cafeteria worker and the cafeteria, the playground, the occupational therapist and the therapy room, and the bus driver and the bus. By having visual cues to remind the child of all the activities during the day, he will be less likely to get confused and upset during transitions. New activities such as field trips or assemblies can easily be added to the child's picture schedule each morning.

Picture schedules also can be used for a particular class period such as physical education (see Figure 5.6). For example, a student with autism is given a new physical education schedule each day. Before class, the general physical educator places select pictures on a special clipboard. The pictures show the child doing various activities in the order in which these activities will be presented during physical education that day. Every time an activity is completed, the student is prompted to point to the next picture on the schedule. This type of schedule helps this child understand the physical education activities of the day.

For younger students, it is best that pictures are used to represent the activities, although for older students, written words may be sufficient. In addition, to increase independence for an older student, a smaller pocket schedule can be created that the student can refer to during the physical education class. *First-then* boards are a simple version of a schedule.

Figure 5.6. Sample picture schedule for physical education. Once activities have been completed, they would be moved to the "Finish" column.

As the name suggests, they present only two activities: an activity to be done first and an activity to be done afterward. First-then boards are beneficial for two reasons. First, they present the child with clear expectations of the activities he or she will do. Second, they take advantage of the Premack principle (presenting a desired activity after a less desired one) so the student will be motivated to complete the first activity. Place a picture of the activity the child needs to complete under "first," and place a picture of the rewarding or preferred activity under "then."

When might you use a schedule in physical education?

- When a student exhibits significant disorganization
- When a student is a strong visual learner
- When a student fails to complete tasks in a timely manner
- When a student requires structured activities
- When a student is defiant or oppositional
- When a student exhibits frustration or anger while making a transition between activities

For example, when Damien first entered physical education, he was regularly frustrated by the many transitions between activities that occurred. This resulted in Damien becoming agitated, loud, and disruptive to the other students. Due to his difficulty in making a transition between activities, Damien spent much of physical education sitting on the sideline, not participating in the class's activities. When a schedule was introduced (Figure 5.7), physical education drastically improved for Damien. He was now prepared for the transitions that would occur in the physical education class and was therefore less anxious and frustrated.

Information Sharers

Many children with disabilities cannot answer the question, "What did you do in school today?" Information sharers help these children communicate with parents and siblings. Information sharers also

Figure 5.7. Sample visual schedule for physical education.

prompt verbal students to answer and elaborate on questions about the day. For example, when a student returns from physical education class, the classroom teacher asks, "What did you do in physical education today?" The student has a picture of a ball, which prompts him or her to say, "Played volleyball." Information sharers also can be used for safety purposes. For example, a child could have a picture of his body and could point to where he is hurt.

Checklists/Organizers

Checklists and organizers break skills into manageable steps so that the student can complete them. Many students can complete the beginning or end of a task or perhaps one or two steps in the middle of a task. Checklists and organizers promote independence by prompting the student to remember and then execute the various steps needed to complete a task. For example, a checklist in physical education might have pictures of the 10 stretching and strengthening activities that all students are expected to do upon arrival into the gym. Checklists also can be used to help middle and high school students become more independent in the locker room by visually reminding them exactly what to do.

Visual Behavioral Supports

Visual behavioral supports remind the student of behavior expectations. Visual behavioral support systems usually include the expected behaviors, such as how to act in physical education, along with reinforcement. For example, Jessica has trouble sitting and keeping her voice down when the teacher takes roll at the beginning of her middle school physical education class. After Jessica dresses out and sits in her squad, she looks at her visual behavioral support (a file card she brings with her to physical education). The card has a small picture of Jessica sitting nicely in her squad. It also has a picture of a person with their mouth closed. A smiley face reminds Jessica that if she sits quietly in her squad during roll call, she will earn a star. Jessica has learned that if she receives five stars during physical education, she can help the general physical educator put the equipment away (a favorite activity of Jessica's). Again, this visual behavior prompt allows Jessica to be more independent in general physical education and more responsible for her own behavior.

Countdown Strips and Visual Timers

Visual supports can also be very useful for keeping students on task and help them know when a task is finished. Many students, particularly those with autism and attention-deficit/hyperactivity disorder, will be more inclined to stay on task if the activity has a clear, observable end point. To achieve this, you may use a number of visual supports. A countdown strip is a visual support that allows the students to count down how many times they must complete an activity. This could be a simple visual such as a strip of paper with the numbers 0 to 10. Each time an activity is completed (e.g., each time the student practices the overhand throw), the student moves a clothes peg to the next number until the student reaches 0. An alternative strategy may to stand up 10 cones. Each time the student completes the activity, he or she knocks down a cone. All the cones knocked down signify the task is complete. A visual will serve the same purpose when you would like a student to keep participating in an activity for a certain length of time. A kitchen egg timer may be used for this purpose, or, if the student uses a tablet, various timer apps exist also.

Level of Methodology

Sometimes, it is important to decide whether you need a completely different way to communicate and instruct particular students. *Levels of methodology* refer to the various methods a teacher can use to present information and communicate with a student. Some students will respond quite well to verbal cues given to the class, whereas other students may need extra verbal cues, demonstrations, visual cues, or even physical assistance to understand directions and perform skills correctly.

One consideration when instructing students is the level of cues presented, or the prompt hierarchy (Janney & Snell, 2016). Prompts are cues given to students. Instructional prompts range from nonintrusive prompts such as a student following natural cues in the environment (e.g., student sees peers stand up and run around the gym and the student quickly stands up and runs with peers) to intrusive prompts such as physical assistance (e.g., physically helping student hold a bat and then strike a ball off a tee; see Figure 5.8). Each type of prompt can be further broken down into levels. For example, physical assistance can vary, from physical assistance in which the student passively allows the teacher to help him to physical assistance in which the student actively tries to perform movement. Ideally, students will follow natural prompts in the environment, but many students with disabilities will need extra prompts to understand directions and

Responds to natural cues in environment
Responds to verbal cues
Responds to pointing and gestures
Uses picture cards
Requires demonstration
Requires physical prompting

Figure 5.8. Least to most intrusive level of prompts.

instruction. Students with severe intellectual disabilities or autism often benefit from a multisensory approach in which several types of prompts are provided (e.g., verbal cue, then demonstration, then physical assistance).

Speech therapists or special education teachers can help physical educators decide which level of prompt is needed for a student to understand directions and instruction. However, most physical educators will quickly discover on their own how best to prompt students.

If it is clear that a student will not be able to respond to a verbal cue or demonstration, then the physical educator or tutor should start with physical prompts or assistance so that the student will not fail the task or be confused (Janney & Snell, 2016). For example, if you know one of your students with cerebral palsy needs physical assistance to toss a ball, it makes no sense to first give him or her a verbal cue, then point, then gesture, then demonstrate, then touch, and finally physically assist the student. Time is wasted, and the student experiences failure for five of six cues. Because the ultimate goal is to have students follow natural cues whenever possible, however, an attempt should be made to systematically fade extra prompts during the course of the program. For example, students with intellectual disabilities can learn to focus on natural cues in the locker room at their local gym for locating an empty locker and walking to the weight room independently.

How Students Communicate

Another consideration when instructing students with disabilities is to determine *how they will communicate* with you and each other. Many students with disabilities will be able to respond using clear, concise speech. Some students will speak in one- or two-word sentences, other students may communicate with gestures or signs, others may communicate by pointing to pictures, and still others may use sophisticated computer-assisted speech synthesizers or keyboards. Regardless of how a student communicates, it is important that you understand each student's mode of communication. Not being able to communicate can be frustrating for the student and can sometimes lead to behavioral outbursts.

Starting and Stopping Signals

It is also important to find the best way to give *starting and stopping commands* to students who do not respond to traditional signals. Students with hearing impairments may need hand signals, and students with autism or severe intellectual disabilities may need physical assistance to stop. Accommodating a student who needs different starting and stopping signals does not mean the general physical educator has to change what he or she has used successfully for years. The general physical educator can use one cue for the entire class and also provide hand signals or physical assistance to students who need extra cues. For example, the teacher could use a whistle to indicate when to stop and start for fouls and throw-ins in a soccer game during a high school physical education class. When students hear the whistle, they know to locate the student with a hearing impairment and raise their hand (indicating to stop or start).

Time

Time of day or season that a child is going to be included is another important consideration. Some students who receive medication (e.g., children with attention-deficit/hyperactivity disorder) might be placed in a general physical education class that meets in the afternoon, after they have taken their medicine. Students who tire might be better served in a morning general physical education class. Changing the time a student goes to physical education can be tricky, so whenever possible, such modifications should be decided before the school year begins.

Duration

Duration refers to how much time a student will be engaged in an activity. Duration can include number of weeks for a particular unit, number of physical education periods per week, how long the student will participate each period, or how long the student will be engaged in each activity during the period. For example, a student with an intellectual disability might need 6 weeks to reach his goals, whereas his peers without disabilities need only 3 weeks. A student with an attention-deficit disorder can tolerate a station or activity for 1 minute, whereas his peers are expected to stay at a station for up to 5 minutes. A student with an intellectual disability might need to stay at that station for 10 minutes. The key is to be flexible in allowing some students with disabilities to come to physical education more often than most other students in the school or allowing some students to participate in only some of the activities during general physical education.

Duration also refers to how long a student will stay in a game situation. A student with asthma or a heart condition might play the game for 2 minutes and then rest on the sideline for 2 minutes. Although many programs are locked into daily schedules, adjustments can usually be made to accommodate students with special needs. For example, a student with an intellectual disability has a goal of learning the skills needed to play softball. The softball unit in general physical education lasts 3 weeks, during which time this student has not acquired the targeted softball skills. While the class moves to volleyball, this student can continue to work on softball skills with a peer who already has good volleyball skills (does not need extra practice in volleyball), with another student who also needs extra work on softball, with a cross-age peer tutor, with a teacher assistant, or with a volunteer. The student can still do warm-ups with the general class.

Order of Learning

Order of learning refers to the sequence in which various aspects of a particular skill are presented. Most teachers teach skills such as the sidearm strike in tennis by teaching the whole task in order from first to last components (e.g., preparatory position, step, swing, follow-through). A student with a learning disability, however, might need to focus on one aspect of the movement at a time: first learning to step and swing, then learning the preparatory position, and finally learning the follow-through. Other students might benefit from even smaller skill steps. The teacher can present the whole task to the majority of the class and then change the order of learning or break down the skill more slowly (or have a peer do this) for a student with a learning disability.

Size and Nature of Group

Size and nature of the group refer to how many students will be at a station or in a game as well as the makeup of the group. Students who have trouble working in large groups can be placed in smaller groups during station work. Students with an intellectual disability who are slower and less skilled than their peers can be placed on a team that has more players than their opponent's team. Similarly, the teacher can select teams so that each team has an equal number of skilled, average, and unskilled players. Players of similar ability can then be paired up against each other in the game (e.g., guarding each other in a game of soccer or basketball). The teacher should select teams so that students with lower abilities (or disabilities) are not always picked last. Also, skilled students should be encouraged to use appropriate sportsmanship during the selection process (see Chapter 7 for more detail on modifying games).

Instructional Setting

Instructional setting refers to where the class is conducted, including indoors or outdoors, temperature, lighting, floor surface, boundaries, and markings on walls. Most teachers cannot make major changes to their instructional setting to accommodate students with special needs, but there are some simple modifications that can make a setting more accommodating. For example, cones or brightly colored tape can be used to accentuate boundaries. Carpet squares or small tumbling mats can cushion falls. Carpet squares, poly spots, or Hula-Hoops can be used to mark a student's personal space. Partitions can be used to block off parts of the gym for students who are easily distracted.

Eliminate Distractions

It is important to reduce or eliminate *extraneous noises, people, or objects* so that the student can focus on instruction. Many students are easily distracted and have difficulty focusing on important instructional cues. For example, balloons and cones set up in the environment for a later activity might be extremely distracting for a student with an intellectual disability or attention-deficit/hyperactivity disorder. To help students focus, position them so that they are facing away from distractions. Also, avoid setting up equipment until it is ready to be used. Store equipment in a barrel, box, or bag or cover it with a tarp until it is needed. In many elementary schools, gymnasia double as the cafeteria, and teachers and students walk through the gym/cafeteria in the morning to give the lunch count to cafeteria workers. Students with attention-deficit/hyperactivity disorder can be placed in a physical education class later in the day when no one walks through. Similarly, some gyms have stages where

music or drama classes are conducted. Schedules should be established so that no other classes are in session. Finally, teachers can help students focus on the task at hand by providing extra cues and reinforcement and by making instruction more enticing. For example, using music during warm-ups can drown out the sound of noisy distractions in the environment. When the music is turned off and the environment is relatively quiet, the teacher can then give directions. Whistling and loud clapping are other ways to return a student's focus to the teacher.

PROVIDE STRUCTURE OR ROUTINE

All children learn best and are most cooperative when they know the class routine and what is expected of them. Although most students can handle occasional changes to *class structure or routines*, change can lead to confusion, withdrawal, misbehavior, and even self-abuse in some children with disabilities. It is important that the class structure remains as constant as possible for students who do not do well with change. Even if you do not have a routine for most students, it is important to establish set routines for the students with disabilities. Even if most students do different warm-ups every day, establishing a set warm-up routine for a student with autism will make it less likely that he or she is confused or upset (see Figure 5.9).

---

1. Do 10 toe-touches.

2. Lie on back, bend knees, fold arms in front of chest, and do 10 sit-ups.

3. Roll over on stomach, put hands to either side of face, bend knees, cross left foot over right foot, and do 10 modified push-ups.

4. Roll over and sit on bottom, bring bottoms of feet together so that they touch, hold onto ankles, try to push knees toward ground, and hold for 10 seconds.

5. Stay in sitting position, stretch both legs in front, and keeping legs together and legs straight. Start with hands on knees and slowly crawl hands down toward ankles. Stop when you feel a good stretch and hold for 10 seconds.

6. Stand up, place hands on hips, keep body straight, and turn from side to side 10 times.

7. Stand up, gently roll head in a circle so that you are looking down at your toes, then to the side, then up to the ceiling, then to the other side, and then back down to the ground again. Do this 5 times.

Figure 5.9. Sample checklist for a child with high-functioning autism during warm-up.

LEVEL OF DIFFICULTY OR COMPLEXITY

Complexity refers to the difficulty level of skills, formations, game rules, and game strategies. Again, a teacher can vary the level of difficulty for particular students without changing the difficulty level for the rest of the students. For example, a team might play a complex zone defense in basketball, but all a student with intellectual disabilities needs to know is to stand on a poly spot and keep her hands up. Similarly, most students can work on stepping, rotating their body, and lagging their arm in the overhand throw, whereas a student just learning how to throw can work on simply getting her arm into an overhand position while throwing. Specific examples of how to modify skills and group activities are presented in Chapter 8.

LEVELS OF MOTIVATION

Level of motivation refers to how much and the types of reinforcement particular students need to be motivated to participate in physical education activities. Many students without disabilities are intrinsically motivated to participate in physical education. Students who know that they have difficulty in physical education might need more encouragement, such as verbal praise, extra privileges, free play, tokens, or even tangible reinforcers such as food. For example, a student with a severe emotional disturbance can be reinforced for staying engaged in a physical fitness activity for 10 minutes by allowing the student to do an activity he really likes for a few minutes after the fitness activity.

SUMMARY

Students with disabilities often have difficulty understanding what to do in general physical education classes. Yet simple modifications to how the class is organized and how information is presented can make a tremendous difference in the success of these students. Many of the instructional modifications outlined in this chapter can help children without disabilities, too, who will respond to accommodations in class formats. Similarly, providing a variety of cues and stopping and starting signals and eliminating distractions will help all students understand what is expected of them in general physical education.

As outlined in this chapter, most instructional accommodations can be implemented without affecting the program for children without disabilities. However, remember that any changes that are made to accommodate a student with a disability should be viewed cautiously and should meet the four criteria.

Peer Tutor Training Manual 2014

Peer Tutor Training Manual

What is a tutor? A tutor is similar to a teacher. It is someone who is good at something or knows something and can help others learn also.

How are you different?

There are things that make us similar to everybody else in the class. What are some of these things?

_____

_____

What makes you different from everybody else in the class? What are some of these things? _____

_____

_____

There are many things that are fun for us that we are really good at doing.

One of things *I'm really good* at is _____

There are also some things that are difficult for me to learn. Some of my classmates are good at these things, and I wish I were too.

One thing that *is hard for me* is _____.

When I can't do that well, I feel _____.
I get upset about some things when I'm with my friends.

One thing that makes me feel upset is _____.

I notice that my friends act differently when they are upset. Some of them cry and want to be alone and others want to be around friends.

When I'm upset, I usually _____.

When I feel different, I hope that my friends will

- Treat me nicely
- Be patient
- Be my friend
- Not laugh at me
- Help me feel better
- Tell me what to do
- Show me how to do

RULES AND ROLES OF PEER TUTOR

- Smiling and being friendly
- Talking softly
- Asking your friend questions like "How are you?" or "Can I help you?"
- Saying things like "Very good!," "I like the way you are listening," "Nice job," and "Wow, you are doing great!"
- Never saying or doing things to make your friend to feel bad
- Working together
- Asking for teacher help if you are confused or if there are problems

TAP (TEACHING, ASSISTING, PRACTICING) STEPS FOR PEER TUTORS

Step 1: Say what you are going to do

"Mary, we are going to roll a ball."
"Kristin, this is your turn to roll the ball."
"Next, we will play bowling."
"Jim, show me how you play bowling."
Give some of examples of your own.

Step 2: Tell what to do to get the task done correctly

"Mary, keep your arms in front to catch a ball."
"Jimmy, swing the bat all the way back."
"Kristin, try to push the ball harder."
"John, go straight."
Give some of examples of your own.

Step 3: Demonstrate (show) how to do the task

You should make sure that your friend watches you when you demonstrate the activity.
"Jimmy, lift your arms up like this."
"Kelly, watch me swing a bat."
"Mary, hold the ball like this."
"Kristin, you should move your arms like this when running."
Give and demonstrate some examples of your own.

Step 4: Help your peer to do the activity

Physical assistance is used to help your friend if it is difficult for him or her to do the activity. Always ask first, "Can I help you?" or "I'm going to help you. Is it okay?"
For example, you may hold your friend's arm to help him or her to go or run straight. Usually the teacher will tell and show you what to do.

From Klavina, A. (2007). *The effect of peer tutoring on interaction behaviors in inclusive physical education* (Unpublished doctoral dissertation). University of Virginia, VA; reprinted by permission.
In *A Teacher's Guide to Adapted Physical Education: Including Students with Disabilities in Sports and Recreation, Fourth Edition*, by Martin E. Block.

Step 5: Give praise or correct a mistake
General praise
"Good job!"
"Great!"
"Awesome!"

Specific praise
"Good bending knees with your jump."
"I like how you lift your arm when you throw the ball."
"I like the way you are looking at the target."

Error correction
"Good try, but you did not lift your arm."
"You pushed the ball, but you did not follow it with your eyes."
"Great running, but you should run to the yellow cone first."

Repeat the five TAP steps of peer tutoring:

1. _____

2. _____

3. _____

4. _____

5. _____

What can you do if your peer does not behave nicely?

When this happens, you should say, *"It is time to work. If you want to participate in this activity together with me, you need to* _____ *(describe the task)."* If your friend continues to behave inappropriately, you should *ask the teacher for help*.

Tips for TAP (teaching, assisting, practicing): "TIP-TAP"

1. Tell what you will do

"We are going to play bowling!"

2. Do activity together

3. If correct, praise

"Good job!"
"Very good!"
"You are doing great!"

4. If not, say what to do to accomplish the task correctly

Demonstrate

Correct mistakes

Help

"You should push the ball harder."
"Push the ball like this."
"Good try, but you did not extend your arms."

5. If you have a problem, ask for teacher help

(page 4 of 4)

Peer Tutor Training Evaluation

Peer Tutor Training Evaluation

Name: _____ Date: _____

Please mark the correct answer with an X

1. What is the first step in peer tutoring instructions?
   ____ Cue
   ____ Direct verbal prompt
   ____ Model

2. When you say to the student "Good job!" or "You did great!" it is called
   ____ Specific praise
   ____ General praise
   ____ Verbal feedback

3. When the student does not respond correctly to verbal prompt, then you
   ____ Provide physical assistance
   ____ Model
   ____ Ask teacher for help

4. What is the highest or most intrusive level of prompt in prompting hierarchy?
   ____ Full physical prompt
   ____ Physical guidance
   ____ Gesture

5. Mark each of the following statements as either antecedent (A), behavior (B), or consequence (C):
   ____ Johnny is given a ball and asked to throw it in the basket.
   ____ Johnny drops the ball and runs away from the activity place.
   ____ Johnny is taken to time-out for 1 minute.

6. Which of the following statements is positive and specific?
   ____ Good bending knees with your jump.
   ____ Good try, but you did not lift your arm.
   ____ I like the way you are looking at the target.

Curricular Modifications

Martin. E. Block

OBJECTIVES

1. Define curriculum modifications and use the four-point method to determine if a modification is appropriate

2. Describe the differences between multilevel curricular selection, curricular overlapping, and alternative programming

3. Describe and apply the following two models to modifications: developmental task analysis and ecological task analysis/constraints

4. Demonstrate an ability to apply modifications to physical education activities based on functions such as strength, endurance, speed, balance, and coordination/accuracy

5. Demonstrate an ability to apply modifications to physical education activities based on specific characteristics of disabilities, including physical disabilities, intellectual disabilities/autism, hearing impairments, visual impairments, and behavior disorders

Charmaine is a 7-year-old girl who loves physical education, but she and her elementary physical education teacher, Mr. Harper, know that physical education can be a real challenge for Charmaine. Charmaine has spastic, diplegic cerebral palsy (stiff in all four limbs but more in her legs than her arms). She comes to general physical education in a walker that she uses fairly competently. She does not have any cognitive impairments, so she understands exactly what she is supposed to do, but her body is not able to respond. Specifically, Charmaine has trouble in games and activities that require speed (tagging games), accuracy and coordination (catching and throwing activities and jumping rope), and strength (throwing a ball across the gym, kicking a ball hard, shooting a ball up into a basket). In other words, Charmaine has challenges with pretty much every general physical education activity. Mr. Harper really wants to help Charmaine, but he is stumped. Kindergarten and first-grade physical education activities were fairly easy to modify, but the kids in second grade are bigger, faster, and more skilled. Mr. Harper worries that Charmaine will not be successful without major modifications to the activities and games in general physical education; he also worries that these major modifications are going to "water down" the program for his students without disabilities. What can Mr. Harper do?

Nick is a ninth grader at Middlebrooke High School. He enjoys listening to his favorite college teams—the University of Maryland football and basketball teams—on the radio. He also attends as many games as he can, with his dad providing play-by-play and Nick reacting intently to the sounds of the crowd. Nick relies on his listening skills because he is blind. Nick lost his sight gradually due to an optic nerve disease and now is almost totally blind. Nick loves sports, but he needs a lot of modifications to be successful when participating in sports in physical education. High school will be a real challenge for Nick and his physical education teachers. Clearly, activities that use balls (e.g., soccer, volleyball, basketball, football) are going to be the greatest challenge for Nick. Are there ways that Nick's physical education teachers can modify these activities so that Nick can participate in skill work and lead-up games? What types of modifications would work for someone like Nick?

Curricular modifications refer to any adaptation made to the general education curriculum in order to prevent a mismatch between a student's skill level and the lesson content and to promote student success in learning targeted individualized education program (IEP) objectives and appropriate skills (Block & Vogler, 1994; Giangreco & Putnam, 1991). Curricular modifications might include changes to equipment and changes to the rules of games.

As with instructional modifications, some modifications will only affect the student with a disability (e.g., lowering a basket, making a target larger), whereas other modifications may affect the entire class (e.g., having all students do a simpler locomotor pattern during warm-ups). Changes that affect the group should be implemented cautiously to avoid negatively affecting the program for students without disabilities. However, as with instructional modifications, some changes that affect the entire class can be positive. For example, the differentiated instruction and universal design principles presented in Chapter 5 suggest giving all students choices in the equipment they use and offering multiple activities. Using such universal approaches allows the physical educator to not only accommodate the student with a disability but also help less skilled students be more successful while still challenging more skilled students.

The purpose of this chapter is to introduce a variety of curricular modifications that can be used to accommodate students with disabilities in general physical education. These modifications have been organized as follows: 1) a general model for making curricular modifications for all students following differentiated instruction and universal design, and 2) specific curricular modifications for students with functional impairments. Modifications for children with specific types of disabilities (e.g., a child with a visual impairment) can be found at the end of each disability-specific chapter. The goal of all these modifications is to allow all students to participate in a general physical education program that is safe and challenging and affords opportunities for success. Which techniques

you choose depends on the particular needs of the student with disabilities, the age group of your students, the skills you are focusing on, the makeup of your class, availability of equipment and facilities, availability of support personnel, and your preference. Although specific examples are provided, it is important that you focus on the general process of how to modify your physical education programs. If you can understand the general process of creating and implementing appropriate modifications, then you can apply this process to a variety of situations.

DETERMINING WHETHER A CURRICULAR MODIFICATION IS APPROPRIATE

Not all modifications are necessarily appropriate for a particular child with a disability in a particular situation. One simple way to determine which modification to use is to ask what effect that modification will have on the student with disabilities, peers, and the general physical educator. If the modification has a negative effect on any or all these individuals, then it probably is not the most appropriate modification. The following four criteria as well as the adaptation checklist in Table 5.3 in Chapter 5 should be used whenever considering a curricular modification. If the modification does not meet these standards, then alternative modifications should be considered.

1. *Does the change allow the student with disabilities to participate successfully yet still be challenged?* For example, a student with intellectual disabilities might not be able to kick a regulation soccer ball back and forth with a partner. A simple modification might allow the student and his partner to kick a large playground ball or volleyball trainer back and forth. Such a modification allows the student to be successful yet challenges him at his level.

2. *Does the modification make the setting unsafe for the student with a disability or for peers?* For example, you want to include a student who uses a wheelchair at a soccer dribbling station, but you are worried other children will bump into this child. One solution is to mark off an area with cones for the child who uses a wheelchair. You also should remind peers at the beginning of the class and several times during the class to be careful around the student.

3. *Does the change affect peers without disabilities?* Making all targets larger and making all students stand closer to the targets is

unnecessary and unfair for all students. Similarly, making all children walk during warm-ups to accommodate a child who uses a walker does not make sense. Rather, make accommodations that only affect the student with disabilities. Even better, follow differentiated instruction principles by providing different targets and different distances and then allowing the student to choose the target and distance that challenges her.

4. *Does the change cause an undue burden on the general physical education teacher?* For example, a general physical educator wants to include a student who has cerebral palsy and is learning how to walk with a walker in warm-up activities that include performing locomotor patterns to music. Because this student needs help to walk with his walker, the general physical educator feels that it is her duty to assist this student during warm-ups. This affects her ability to attend to and instruct the other students. A better modification might be assisting this student for part of warm-ups and then letting him creep on hands and knees (still his most functional way of moving). Or, if walking with the walker is a critical goal for this student, older peer tutors, a teacher assistant, a volunteer, or the physical therapist can come into physical education (at least during warm-ups) to assist this student.

GENERAL CATEGORIES OF CURRICULAR MODIFICATIONS

Although specific modifications vary from student to student, generally speaking three distinct categories of curricular modifications may be necessary: *multilevel curricular selection, curricular overlapping,* and *alternative programming* (Block & Vogler, 1994; Giangreco & Doyle, 2000; Giangreco & Putnam, 1991).

Multilevel Curricular Selection

Multilevel curricular selection is designed for children with mild disabilities who can follow the general education curriculum with only slight accommodations. In other words, the general education curriculum is appropriate, but the level at which the curriculum is presented may be above the child's ability level. This level of modification is similar to differentiated instruction. For example, a child with Asperger syndrome is in a general physical education throwing and catching unit in fourth grade. Throwing and catching are

appropriate activities for this child, but he cannot throw and catch as well as his peers. To accommodate his needs, the teacher allows him to stand closer to targets when throwing, throw at a larger target, stand closer to peers when catching, and use a lighter, larger ball when catching. In fact, by utilizing differentiated instruction, this teacher offers all children the opportunity to choose how close they stand to the target, which size target to throw to, and which balls to catch. Each child works on the same curricular content but at a level that accommodates his or her individual abilities.

Curricular Overlapping

The general education curriculum may be inappropriate for children with more severe disabilities. In such cases, the student should work on his or her unique physical education IEP objectives. But rather than working on these objectives away from his or her peers, these objectives can be embedded or overlapped within the general physical education curriculum. Such a model is known as *curricular overlapping.* For example, a fourth-grade child with severe cerebral palsy is learning how to walk with a walker. The general and adapted physical education teachers note that learning to use a walker is not included on the general physical education curriculum. However, within a chasing and fleeing unit, this student can work on walking while other students work on chasing and fleeing. The student gets to participate with peers in the activities, but her focus is on her unique objectives. Figure 6.1 provides other examples of how a child's unique IEP objectives are overlapped within the general physical education curriculum.

Alternative Activities

Some children's unique IEP objectives cannot be safely and/or meaningfully overlapped within the general physical education curriculum. In such cases, the child with disabilities needs to work on his or her unique IEP objectives separately. For example, a high school student with severe intellectual disabilities and severe cerebral palsy might get hurt in a regulation or modified game of volleyball, plus these activities do not match his or her IEP objectives for physical education. In order to make this student's alternative activities inclusive, peers without disabilities can rotate away from the game to participate in the alternative activity. This allows the child with disabilities to work on his unique objectives while affording opportunities to interact with peers without disabilities.

Student: Emilio   **Grade:** Fourth grade

Age: 10 years   **Unit:** Introduction to soccer skills

Activities in GPE soccer unit	Emilio's IEP objective for physical education				
	Walk with walker	Throw overhand	Catch	Sidearm strike	Upper-body
Move from class to gym	X				
Warm-ups	X				X
Chipping station				X¹	
Passing/trapping station		X²	X²		
Shooting station		X³			
Dribbling station	X⁴				
Lead-up game	X				
Move from gym to class	X				

Key:

X¹ Emilio uses a bat to hit soccer balls placed on a cone to practice his striking goals.

X² Emilio bends over to pick up balls that are passed to him by a partner; he then throws the ball back to his partner, who has to trap it.

X³ Emilio throws smaller playground balls into the goal rather than trying to kick the ball into the goal.

X⁴ Emilio kicks and then walks after the soccer ball, with a focus on walking with his walker in a cluttered area.

Figure 6.1.   Individualized education program (IEP) objectives overlapped within general physical education (GPE) activities.

GENERAL MODELS FOR MAKING CURRICULAR MODIFICATIONS

Rather than specific guidelines for specific students, the model outlined here provides a process that general physical educators and other team members can use to accommodate students with disabilities in general physical education. Again, once you understand the process of manipulating the equipment and the task, you can accommodate any student who enters your program. The following provides general guidelines for making curricular accommodations for students with a wide range of disabilities.

Developmental Task Analysis

A variety of task and environmental factors can influence motor performance. The teacher can modify many of these factors to differentiate instruction, thereby making the activity easier or more challenging for particular students. Herkowitz's (1978) *developmental task analysis* is designed to

systematically identify task and environmental factors that influence movement patterns. The model includes two components: 1) general task analysis (GTA), and 2) specific task analysis (STA). GTA involves outlining all task and environmental factors that influence movements of children in general categories (e.g., striking, catching, jumping). These factors are then listed hierarchically in terms of levels of difficulty from simple to complex. Figure 6.2 provides an example of a GTA for striking. Note how this grid provides the general physical educator with information on how various task factors influence specific movements. The general physical educator could then use this information to modify these factors and differentiate instruction to make a movement or activity simpler or more complex for all students in the class.

Once the teacher has a general understanding of how task and environmental factors affect movement, an STA can be developed that examines in greater detail how select factors influence a specific

Factors	Size of object to be struck	Weight of object to be struck	Speed of object to be struck	Predictability of trajectory of object to be struck	Length of striking implement	Side of body to which object is travelling	Anticipatory locomotor spatial adjustments
Simple	Large	Light	None Slow	No movement	None	Favored side	No adjustment
↓	Medium	Moderate	Moderate	Down incline	Short	Nonfavored side	Minimal adjustment
Complex	Small	Heavy	Fast	In air	Long	Midline	Maximal adjustment

Figure 6.2.   General task analysis (GTA) for striking. (From Herkowitz, J. [1978]. Developmental task analysis: The design of movement experiences and evaluation of motor development status. In M. Ridenour [Ed.], *Motor development: Issues and applications* [p. 141]. Princeton, NJ: Princeton Book; adapted by permission.)

movement. STAs are developed by creating activities that utilize two to four factors from the GTA. Like the GTA, these factors are then broken down into levels of difficulty and listed hierarchically from simple to complex. In the STA, however, levels of difficulty refer to specific factors. Figure 6.3 provides an example of an STA for striking. Note how more specific, observable information is provided in this STA. The teacher can quickly evaluate how specific levels of difficulty in various factors influence movement performance in various children. The goal is to get the student to perform the task under the most complex circumstances, in this case using a 36-inch plastic bat to strike a tennis ball. STAs also can be used to help less skilled students and students with disabilities become more successful in a particular task. For example, a student who has limited strength could use an 18-inch wooden dowel rather than a 36-inch plastic bat to strike, or a student who has difficulty contacting a tennis ball can hit a 9-inch beach ball rather than a tennis ball. Limitations such as strength and visual-motor coordination can mask a student's ability to perform a task using a more skillful pattern. By

simply altering task and environmental demands, these students might be able to demonstrate more skillful patterns. Teachers also can use STAs to evaluate a student's present level of performance (i.e., circumstances under which a student can perform a given task) as well as progress the student is making (see Herkowitz, 1978, for examples of STA evaluation grids).

Ecological Task Analysis/Constraints Model

Davis and Burton (1991) developed a type of task analysis that extends Herkowitz's (1978) developmental task analysis. They noted that Herkowitz's model has two major flaws: 1) It did not consider the goal of the given task and 2) it did not consider the attributes of the mover. The goal of the task can have a tremendous influence on the movement pattern a mover displays. For example, a mover might throw using what appears to be a very inefficient movement pattern (e.g., not stepping or stepping with the same-side foot, not extending his arm in backswing, having very little follow-through), but if

Levels	Size of ball	Factors influencing student performance	
		Length of striking implement	Predictability of trajectory of ball
Simple	S1 12-inch ball	L1 Hand	P1 Rolled along ground
	S2 9-inch ball	L2 Ping-Pong paddle	P2 Bounced along ground
↓	S3 4-inch ball	L3 18-inch dowel rod	P3 Aerial ball
Complex	S4 Tennis ball	L4 36-inch plastic bat	

Figure 6.3.   Specific task analysis for striking. (From Herkowitz, J. [1978]. Developmental task analysis: The design of movement experiences and evaluation of motor development status. In M. Ridenour [Ed.], *Motor development: Issues and applications* [p. 143]. Princeton, NJ: Princeton Book; adapted by permission.)

the goal of the task was to throw a dart at a dartboard from 10 feet away, this movement pattern might be very appropriate. Also, movers with different capabilities and physical characteristics respond quite differently to changes in task factors. For example, the size of a mover's hand and his or her own innate balance abilities will affect how much ball size and balance requirements affect performance (Block & Provis, 1992).

In an effort to correct these flaws, Davis and Burton (1991) proposed the *ecological task analysis model* (ETA), which utilizes the constraints model originally outlined by Newell (1986) and expanded in several publications (Davids, Button, & Bennett, 2008; Haywood & Getchell, 2014; Haywood, Roberton, & Getchell, 2012; Newell & Jordan, 2007; Pope, Liu, Breslin, & Getchell, 2012). The constraints model is highlighted by the interaction of three specific types of constraints: organismic, environmental, and task constraints. Constraints associated with the individual are known as *organismic constraints* and include factors such as the person's height, strength, weight, balance, or eye–hand coordination. Although attempts should be made to remediate organismic constraints when possible, such constraints can be difficult to change quickly (e.g., how long would it take to increase a student's balance or a child's speed). Therefore, when using the constraint model for teaching motor skills, organismic constraints are accounted for and accommodated as opposed to manipulated. For example, a child who is challenged by eye–hand coordination issues (perhaps due to a visual impairment) could use slower moving objects for catching, such as scarves. Similarly, a child who is challenged by speed due to cerebral palsy or muscular dystrophy would be given safe places to go to during tagging and fleeing games.

Environmental constraints are factors related to the child's environment such as gravity, light within the space, temperature, or barriers in the space. Many environmental constraints cannot be altered. For example, it would not be possible to change the temperature or lighting outside. However, in some cases environmental factors can be adjusted to help the child be more successful in movement activities. Lighting can be enhanced inside, and bright colored cones can be used to highlight boundaries for a child with a visual impairment or a child with autism.

Task constraints are anything having to do with the task itself. Unlike organismic and environmental constraints, task constraints often can be manipulated to make tasks more challenging for skilled children and easier for less skilled children.

Newell (1986) divided task constraints into three categories: 1) the goal of the task without any specific rules on how to perform the task (e.g., getting a ball into an elevated basket or using your feet to get a ball into a goal), 2) rules specifying a specific response or way to perform a skill (e.g., doing a cartwheel or somersault has to be performed a specific way), and 3) implements that constrain a movement pattern (e.g., having to strike a ball with a golf club, tennis racquet, or baseball bat).

Given this background on the constraints model, Davis and Burton (1991) outlined three of the major tenets of ETA:

1. Actions are the result of the complex relationship among the task goal, the performer, and the environment. ETA includes a description of the task goal and the performer as critical factors in movement outcome. For example, a 6-year-old child with autism is displaying what seems to be an immature running pattern. She does not swing her arms forcefully to aid in the run, her back trailing leg does not bend to 90 degrees, and she barely has a flight phase. It could be concluded that this child displays gross motor delays. However, a more careful analysis considers the goal of the task as well as the environment. This girl was running slowly in a small space to retrieve a ball. She was constrained by the small space (environmental constraint) as well as the goal of the task (simply retrieve a ball on the floor without any need for speed). If this same girl were asked to run outside in a larger space (different environmental constraint) with the goal of trying to tag a friend (different goal), then her pattern may suddenly appear to be more advanced.

2. Tasks should be categorized by function and intention rather than movement pattern or mechanism of performance. The same function can be achieved through very different movement patterns. While a particular pattern might be most efficient for a group of movers who have similar abilities and physical characteristics, other movers with different abilities and characteristics might find a different movement pattern more efficient. This is particularly true for students with disabilities, who often have unique abilities and characteristics. Rather than describing a movement pattern such as skipping or throwing, ETA utilizes a functional task category that describes the general intent of the movement. Skipping thus becomes one form of the function *locomotion* (to move from one place to another), and throwing becomes

one form of the function *propulsion* (to propel a stationary or moving object or person). Within each functional task category are criteria for performance. For example, under locomotion, criteria include to move with efficiency, precision, accuracy, speed, and/or distance. Each mover might use a different pattern to accomplish a given function and criteria. One child with cerebral palsy might use a walker, another might use crutches, and yet another might push a wheelchair, yet all are trying to meet the goal of moving as quickly as possible across the gym.

3. Invariant features of a task and variations within a task may be defined in terms of essential and nonessential variables, respectively. Essential variables describe the invariant characteristics of the movement (i.e., the underlying patterns that organize and define a movement). Relative timing between the two lower limbs in walking or galloping is an example of an essential variable. For practical purposes, broader descriptors of patterns of coordination, such as arm action in throwing, also can be viewed as essential variables. Nonessential variables refer to dimensions or control parameters that, when scaled up or down, may cause the mover to change to a new, qualitatively different pattern of coordination (i.e., a new essential variable). These control variables can include physical dimensions of the mover, such as limb length or weight, body proportions, or postural control, or they can refer to task factors such as ball size, weight of the striking implement, or size of the target. For example, throwing a ball at a wall from 5 feet away would result in the student displaying a pattern of coordination (essential variable) that is characterized by no stepping, no preparatory backswing, and no trunk rotation. As the student moves away from the wall (scale up nonessential variable of distance to throw), his throwing pattern will stay intact up to a critical distance. At that critical distance (given that the student has the underlying ability to display a different throwing pattern), the student's pattern will abruptly change to a qualitatively different throwing pattern, stepping with opposition, trunk rotation, and preparatory backswing.

According to Davis and Burton (1991), using the ETA, a teacher can more accurately determine under which set of conditions the student is able to achieve the task, the set of conditions that elicit the most efficient and effective pattern (i.e., optimal performance), and the dimension values at which the student chooses to use a different skill to perform a task (e.g., changes from galloping to running). ETA appears to be a viable approach to understanding how a student prefers to move and how changes in task variables affect movement. (For more practical application of the ETA model, refer to Davis et al. [2008], Getchell and Gagen [2006], and Haywood and Getchell [2014].)

ACCOMMODATIONS FOR STUDENTS WITH SPECIFIC FUNCTIONAL IMPAIRMENTS OR SPECIFIC DISABILITIES

Some physical educators feel more comfortable with specific suggestions on how to accommodate students with distinct impairments or disabilities. This section presents modifications designed to accommodate students with specific impairments or disabilities. Although it is difficult to generalize modifications across categories, the specific modifications reviewed in this chapter should give general physical educators and other team members ideas on how to modify activities. Still, it is important to focus on the functional strengths and weaknesses of particular students rather than their diagnostic labels. For example, functionally, students with cerebral palsy can be quite different. Some may have trouble with coordination, whereas others might have trouble with strength. As you read this section on specific disabilities, try to think of students' specific functional impairments. As always, utilize team members to provide more specific information regarding particular students.

In many cases, these modifications can be utilized as part of a differentiated instruction model as opposed to a specific modification for a child with a disability. For example, rather than having a lower basket and smaller ball just for a child with a disability to accommodate limitations in strength, have baskets of various heights and balls of various sizes available for all children in the class to choose to match their unique levels of strength and coordination. No doubt there will be other children in the class besides the child with a disability who would be more successful and thus more motivated to try harder and to use proper basketball shooting technique if a lower basket and smaller ball were made available.

Include the student with a disability whenever possible when deciding how to adapt an activity in general physical education. Lieberman and Houston-Wilson (2009) noted that many students with disabilities are happy to have activities modified to help them become more successful in general physical education. These students also know which modifications have worked and which have not worked in previous general physical education and recreation settings (MacDonald & Block, 2005). However, Lieberman and Houston-Wilson pointed out that some students with disabilities prefer fitting in rather than being successful, and these students may not want any modifications. It is important to honor a student's wishes regarding modifications to general physical education activities.

Finally, consider the "five Ss" of equipment adaptations outlined by Healy (2013) when differentiating instruction or when accommodating one child with a unique limitation:

1. *Surface:* Alter the texture of the surface of equipment. For example, taping string around a ball can enhance the grip and feel of the ball, which may help children with autism or visual impairments to utilize proprioceptive skills. The addition of color to the surface will also help children with visual impairments see the equipment more clearly and to cue children with intellectual disabilities and autism on where to grip a piece of equipment.

2. *Speed:* Slowing down the speed of some equipment can help many children with coordination problems. Balls can be adapted so that they are slower moving for easier catching, kicking, or striking. For example, using a deflated ball or soccer ball wrapped in a trash bag when dribbling in soccer slows the ball down, and using a balloon or small beach ball slows the ball down when teaching catching.

3. *Size:* All equipment can be adapted in size to allow the user to be more successful. Racquets can be shortened and lightened (e.g., using a racquetball racquet rather than a tennis racquet), and balls can be smaller and lighter (e.g., using Nerf basketball to replace a regulation basketball or a volleyball trainer instead of a regulation volleyball). Ideally, a variety of balls and targets of different sizes can be offered to all students to differentiate instruction. Similarly, the size of nets, basketball rings, bowling pins, goals, Hula-Hoops, poly spots, skipping ropes, and other equipment should also be adapted to suit the child.

4. *Sound:* The addition of sound to sports equipment is important to children with visual impairments. Sound can be added to balls, targets, cones, and other equipment. This can be achieved relatively easily by fastening security beepers or bells to equipment using Velcro or tape.

5. *Support:* Adding extra support when teaching ball skills makes activities less dynamic and increases the child's chance of success. For example, placing a ball on a tee or suspending a ball from the net of a basketball hoop will help children practice striking with a bat or racquet. For children with balance difficulties, provide a chair they can lean on or have them stand near a wall for balance.

Accommodations for Students with Specific Functional Impairments

Functional impairments, such as challenges with strength or endurance can often be remediated so that the student can perform the skill at a higher level. *Structural impairments,* however, such as extreme short stature (dwarfism), visual impairments, or a physical disability cannot be remediated. In these situations, modifications to activities can allow the student to perform the skill more successfully. The following sections (adapted from Arbogast & Lavay, 1986; Herkowitz, 1978; Sherrill, 2004) outline general factors that can be manipulated to accommodate students with specific impairments (see Table 6.1). Again, many of these accommodations can be made for the entire class, thereby following the principles of differentiated instruction.

Specific Adaptations for Students with Impairments in Strength, Power, and Endurance

Lower the Target   Students who do not have the strength to get an object to a target can have the target lowered. For example, a student who cannot reach a 10-foot basket in basketball can shoot at a 6- or 8-foot basket. Similarly, a student who cannot hit a ball over a regulation volleyball or badminton net can have the net lowered. By lowering the target, students will have a greater opportunity for success that in turn will encourage them to continue practicing the skill. Targets set at reasonable heights also facilitate desired movement patterns. For example, students who cannot reach a 10-foot basket with a basketball using a "typical" shooting pattern often resort to different, less effective shooting patterns (e.g., sidearm hurl, underhand, tossed backward over their head).

Reduce the Distance   Many physical education activities require students to throw, pass, serve, or shoot a ball or run a certain distance. These distances, although necessary when playing intramural or interscholastic games, can be altered

Table 6.1. Adaptations for students with functional impairments

---

Students with impairments in strength, power, and endurance

- Lower targets.
- Reduce distance/playing field.
- Reduce weight and/or size of striking implements, balls, or projectile.
- Allow student to sit or lie down while playing.
- Use deflated balls or suspended balls.
- Decrease activity time/increase rest time.
- Reduce speed of game/increase distance for peers without disabilities.

Students with limited balance

- Lower center of gravity.
- Keep as much of body in contact with the surface as possible.
- Widen base of support.
- Increase width of beams to be walked.
- Extend arms for balance.
- Use carpeted rather than slick surfaces.
- Teach students how to fall.
- Provide a bar to assist with stability.
- Teach student to use eyes optimally.
- Determine whether balance problems are related to health problems.

Students with problems of coordination and accuracy

- For catching and striking activities, use larger, lighter, softer balls.
- Decrease distance ball is thrown and reduce speed.
- For throwing activities, use smaller balls.
- In striking and kicking, use stationary ball before trying a moving ball.
- Increase the surface of the striking implement.
- Use backstop.
- Increase size of target.
- In bowling-type games, use lighter, less stable pins.
- Optimize safety.

Sources: Arbogast and Lavay (1986); Herkowitz (1978); Sherrill (2004).

when teaching skills or playing lead-up or recreational games in physical education. Distances can be reduced so students with disabilities can be successful. For example, a student could push his or her wheelchair to a first base that is half the distance of the general first base to accommodate his limited speed. Such accommodations do not give either team any advantage yet allow the student with disabilities an opportunity to be successful. For games that require running up and down an entire floor or field (e.g., basketball or soccer), games can be played using the width of the field rather than the length or half-court games can be played. Another modification that would not affect the entire class is allowing a particular student to play in just half the field (e.g., just play defense or offense), or place the

student in a position that requires less movement (e.g., playing defensive back in soccer rather than midfielder or playing lineman in football rather than wide receiver).

Shorten/Lighten Racquets Students with limited arm or grip strength or those who have smaller-than-typical hand size may have difficulty holding large/heavy striking implements or balls. For example, a regulation tennis racquet might be too long and heavy for a student with muscular dystrophy. Allowing this student to use a racquetball or badminton racket or a tennis racket with the handle cut off would allow this student more success. Some students might need to simply be encouraged to choke up on the racket. Similarly, a student with small hands might have difficulty gripping a softball with one hand and resort to throwing the softball with two hands. Balloons, beach balls, or Nerf balls can be a good substitute for balls that are too heavy or too intimidating for a student.

Allow Student to Sit or Lie Down While Playing Activities played while lying or sitting demand less fitness than games played while standing or moving. Students with limited strength and endurance can be allowed to sit down when the ball is at the other end of the playing field or while playing in the outfield. These students also can be allowed to sit while practicing some skills. For example, a student with a heart condition who tires easily can warm up with the class by performing every other locomotor pattern the class performs. The student can be allowed to sit down when he is not performing a locomotor pattern.

Use Deflated Balls or Suspended Balls By their nature, balls tend to roll when put in motion. Although most young children enjoy chasing balls, students who fatigue easily may use up all their energy and miss out on important practice trials. Balls that are deflated or paper balls (e.g., crumpled up piece of paper wrapped with a few pieces of masking tape) do not roll away. Also, balls suspended from a basket or ceiling or balls tied to a student's wheelchair are easy to retrieve.

Decrease Activity Time/Increase Rest Time Games and practice sessions can be shortened for students who fatigue easily. Students can be allowed to play for 5 minutes and then rest for 5 minutes, or all students play for 3 minutes and then rotate to an activity that requires less endurance. For example, a game of sideline basketball could be played in which three players from each team play for 3 minutes while the other players on each team stand on opposite sidelines prepared to assist their teammates. Another possibility is to allow free substitutions in a game. For example, a student with asthma can come out of a soccer game every 2 or 3 minutes.

Reduce Speed of Game/Increase Distance for Peers without Disabilities Many games move quickly, leaving slower players and players with limited endurance behind. Modifications can be made so that races and games are fairer for students with limits in speed and endurance. For example, slower students in a relay race need only go up and back one time, whereas more skilled students go up and back two times. Similarly, a special zone in soccer can be marked off for a student who has limited speed. When the ball goes into the zone, this student is the only one who can kick the ball.

Specific Adaptations for Students with Limited Balance

Lower Center of Gravity Allow students to perform activities while sitting down or on hands and knees. Also, encourage students to bend knees while moving, stopping, and standing. For example, a student should be encouraged to land with his or her feet apart when jumping down from a box. When performing locomotor patterns, students should be encouraged to perform animal walks that lower the center of gravity (e.g., crawling, creeping, bear walking) or to move with knees bent when performing locomotor patterns such as running and jumping.

Keep as Much of Body in Contact with the Surface as Possible Allow students to walk or run flatfooted rather than on tiptoes, or allow students to perform balance activities on three or four body parts rather than on one or two body parts. For example, allow a student to jump on two feet while his classmates hop on one foot.

Widen Base of Support Encourage students to stand with feet farther apart to provide more stability—for example, while preparing to catch a ball. Similarly, allow students to walk or run with feet apart until they develop more postural control.

Increase Width of Beams Students should be allowed to walk on the floor or on wider beams until they develop more postural control. For example, a balance station could have 2-inch × 4-inch, 2-inch × 6-inch, 2-inch × 8-inch, and 2-inch × 10-inch beams. In addition, a hierarchy of challenges can be set up, beginning with walking with one foot on and one foot off the beam, using a shuffle step across the beam, and walking across the beam holding on to the wall or a peer's hand.

Extend Arms for Balance Encourage students to hold their arms out to the side when performing balance activities. For example, have a student hold arms out to the side while walking on a beam or when learning how to walk, run, jump, or hop.

Use Carpeted Rather than Slick Surfaces When possible, provide surfaces that increase friction. For example, learning how to roller skate on a tumbling mat or carpeted surface is easier than learning how to skate on a gym floor. Similarly, it is easier to perform various locomotor patterns on a carpeted surface as opposed to a slick surface. Finally, encourage students to wear rubber-soled footwear rather than shoes with slick bottoms.

Teach Students How to Fall Students who have problems with postural control will fall often. Teach these students how to fall safely by practicing how to fall on mats. For example, a simple game like "Ring around the Rosy" requires all students to fall, affording them practice in falling forward, backward, and sideward. See an excellent paper by Molinar and Doprotka (2014) on teaching children with disabilities how to fall safely.

Provide a Bar to Assist with Stability During activities that require balance, such as walking across a balance beam or kicking, allow student to hold on to a wall, bar, chair, or table for extra stability. Allowing students to use balance aids may enable them to exhibit more advanced motor patterns. The balance aid can be gradually faded away as the skill becomes more engrained.

Teach Students to Use Eyes Optimally Vision plays a critical role in postural control. Teach students how to use their vision to facilitate balance. For example, students can be taught to focus their vision on a stationary object on a wall while walking a beam or while performing standing balance activities.

Determine Whether Balance Problems Are Related to Health Problems Balance problems may be related to health problems such as inner ear infections. Talk to the student's special education teacher, parent, or physician to determine whether there are any health problems that might negatively affect balance. In addition, find out if the student is taking any medications that might affect balance. Balance difficulties due to health problems or medications might be acute in nature, in which case you might want to have the student avoid activities that require balance. If the problem is more chronic, then you should implement some of the earlier modifications described.

Specific Adaptations for Students with Problems of Coordination and Accuracy

Use Large, Light, Soft Balls   Large balls are easier to catch and strike than smaller balls. However, large balls may promote an immature catching pattern (scooping into body rather than using hands). If a student is unsuccessful or frightened of small, hard balls (e.g., softball), then the use of a large Nerf ball, balloon, or punch ball is appropriate. Gradually introduce a small ball to elicit a more skillful pattern. In addition, balls tossed directly to a student are easier to catch than balls tossed to a student's side, whereas balls tossed to a student's side are easier to strike than balls tossed directly at student.

Decrease Distance Ball Is Thrown and Reduce   Reduce the distance that balls are thrown for students who have difficulty tracking balls. For example, one student might be allowed to hit a ball pitched from 10 feet away in a game of softball, whereas other students are expected to hit a ball pitched from 20 feet. Similarly, a ball can be tossed slowly for some students, faster for others, and still faster for more skilled students. Ideally, you will vary distance and speed so that each student is challenged at his or her level yet has an opportunity to succeed.

Throw Small Balls   Allow students who have trouble gripping to use smaller balls or yarn balls, Koosh balls, paper balls, or bean bags. Have a variety of balls available.

Strike or Kick Stationary Balls   Allow students to first kick a stationary ball or strike a ball on a tee. Suspended balls that move at slower speeds and at a known trajectory are also easier than moving balls. Again, allow the student to be successful and demonstrate a skillful pattern with adaptations and then gradually fade away the adaptations as the student gains confidence and skill.

Increase the Surface of the Striking Implement   Allow students to use lighter bats with a larger striking surface or a racket with a larger striking surface. Again, have a variety of striking implements for students to choose from.

Use Backstops   Students who miss the ball often may spend most of their time retrieving the ball rather than practicing the skill. This does not promote good use of practice time, and it can become very frustrating for the student. When working on striking, kicking, or catching activities, have a backdrop, backstop, net, or rebounder available. You can also attach a string to a ball and then to a student's wheelchair for ease of recovery.

Increase Size of Target   Allow students to throw or kick to larger targets, or allow students to shoot at larger basket. In addition, give points for coming close to a target, such as hitting the rim or backboard in basketball. Less skilled students can be allowed to stand closer to the target in order to promote initial success and then gradually allow them to move back as they become more accurate.

Use Light, Unstable Pins When Bowling   In games or activities in which the goal is to knock something down, use light objects (e.g., milk cartons, aluminum cans) so that any contact with the object will result in success. In addition, use more pins and spread them out farther than normal so that tosses or kicks that would normally miss the target still result in success.

Optimize Safety   Students who have trouble with coordination are more prone to injury, especially in activities that involve moving balls. These students should be allowed to wear glasses protectors, shin guards, helmets, and face masks. When necessary, provide a peer tutor who can protect the student from errant balls.

Adaptations for Students with Specific Types of Disabilities

Chapters 8–16 of this book provide information regarding adaptations for students who have intellectual disabilities, learning disabilities, attention-deficit/hyperactivity disorder, autism spectrum disorders, behavior disorders, hearing impairments, visual impairments, physical disabilities, and other health impairments. As noted, a diagnostic label does not provide much information about a student's functional abilities. As you think of your particular students, not only consider the information and strategies in the chapters on their particular disabilities but also cross-reference the modifications presented there with modifications outlined in the previous section on functional impairments.

SUMMARY

This chapter has reviewed a variety of ways that curricular modifications can accommodate students with disabilities into general physical education. Children with mild disabilities can be included in general physical education with multilevel curricular selection in which they work on the same content as their peers but at a different level. Children with severe disabilities can be included in general physical education while working on their own IEP objectives—either overlapped within general physical education activities or presented through an alternative activity.

Each child should be viewed as an individual with unique strengths and weaknesses, and any modifications should be developed based on each child's unique needs. The goal of any modification is to allow the child to be safely, successfully, and meaningfully included in general physical education, work on his or her unique IEP objectives, and have the opportunity to interact with peers who do not have disabilities. Modifications must be made carefully and thoughtfully if they are to be effective.

CHAPTER 7

Game and Sport Modifications

Martin E. Block and Ron Davis

OBJECTIVES

1. Describe four factors used to determine whether a game modification is appropriate

2. Using Morris and Steihl's model, describe and provide examples of how to modify the basic structure of any game

3. Describe and provide an example of how to manage a game's degree of difficulty

4. Describe and provide an example of the functional approach to modifying movement experiences

5. Explain the purpose and benefits of using disability sports in physical education and provide an example of how you might implement a disability sports unit in physical education

Travis is an 11-year-old boy who is excited to be starting middle school in the fall. Travis had a very positive experience in elementary school. He particularly enjoyed his experiences in general physical education with Mrs. Carr, his general physical education teacher. Mrs. Carr always seemed to know how to present activities in a way that allowed Travis to be successful. Travis was born with a rare physical condition known as arthrogryposis. Arthrogryposis begins during fetal development and causes the child to have no muscles or extremely atrophied muscles in the arms and legs and his or her elbow and knee joints (and sometimes ankle, hip, wrist, and shoulder joints) to be frozen. In Travis's case, this condition has not affected his cognitive development. Travis uses a manual wheelchair to move around school and is pretty independent in the classroom, bathroom, and cafeteria (although he needs a little help with carrying a tray in the cafeteria and pulling up his pants in the bathroom).

As noted, Mrs. Carr did a wonderful job accommodating Travis in physical education. For locomotor patterns, Travis would use his wheelchair. For ball skills, Travis figured out his own way to throw, catch, strike, and kick. He was well liked by his peers, and they had no problem modifying games so that Travis could have as much of a chance as his peers to be successful. However, middle school general physical education may pose some problems for Travis. Most notably, the middle school program at Travis' school focuses on team sports such as basketball, soccer, and volleyball; for the most part, these games are played using regulation equipment following standard rules. Travis will not be successful in team sports played using regulation equipment following standard rules. The general physical educators are willing to accommodate Travis but are concerned that accommodations will ruin the game for the peers in the class without disabilities. They also are concerned that even with accommodations, Travis will not be able to participate safely in any team sports.

Group games and team sports are popular activities in general physical education. When used properly, group games and team sports can facilitate skill development as well as promote an understanding of rules, strategies, and concepts. Some group games also can be designed to promote sportsmanship, cooperation, and teamwork. Unfortunately, group games and team sports often promote competition and adherence to rules designed for very skilled athletes (Kasser, 1995; Morris & Stiehl, 1999). For example, it is not unusual to see upper level elementary school physical education children playing regulation basketball games in which 10-foot baskets are used and professional rules are strictly followed even though most students at this age cannot reach a 10-foot basket or follow the rules of the game. Skilled students might enjoy these games, but the majority of students quickly become frustrated and passive, unhappy participants. Many general physical educators assume that group games and team sports are beyond the skill level or cognitive ability of students with disabilities, so these students are relegated to watching from the sideline, keeping score, or keeping time. When allowed to participate in the game, they rarely have success because they cannot perform the skills as quickly or as accurately as their peers.

Fortunately, many general physical educators modify games and team sports so that all students can successfully participate. Some modifications can be relatively simple such as allowing a child to hit a ball off a tee in softball or standing closer when serving in volleyball. Other modifications might require changes for everyone, such as requiring all players to touch the ball one time before shooting in basketball. Still other modifications might change a game so much that a teacher might want to offer two or three different types of games: one volleyball game that is played with regulation rules, one in which children use a volleyball trainer and are allowed to stand closer when serving, and one with a lower net that has a cooperative rather than a competitive focus.

This chapter presents a variety of modifications to group games and team sports that can be used when including children with disabilities in general physical education. As in the previous two chapters, the first part of this chapter focuses on a general process or model for making modifications to group games or team sports. Once a physical educator understands the general process for modifying group games and the components of games that can be manipulated, then he or she can apply this process to a variety of game situations. The second part

of this chapter presents a variety of alternative ways to present group games, including adventure activities, cooperative games, and new games, and using disability sports to promote inclusion. Finally, a list of modifications to popular individual and team sports is presented with suggestions for children with physical disabilities, intellectual disabilities, and visual impairments. The specific type of game modification will vary based on each individual child's needs, the abilities and competitive nature of the class, and the purpose of the game. All children with a similar disability will not benefit from similar modifications; each child and each situation should be analyzed separately.

BASIC PRINCIPLES FOR MODIFYING GAMES AND SPORTS

Group games and team sports can facilitate skill development, promote an understanding of rules and strategies, and teach concepts such as sportsmanship and teamwork. Unfortunately, general physical educators often feel compelled to strictly follow the regulation rules of group games and team sports, which may lead to limited success and even the exclusion of lesser skilled students and students with disabilities. General physical educators should be aware of several basic principles regarding the use of group games and sports in their program.

- *Games are not sacred but kids are:* If a game is not appropriate for even a single player, it is worth examining and altering to accommodate that player. The design of a game strongly influences each student's experience. Children who always get tagged or are never given the ball are probably not benefiting from the intended purposes of the game (Morris & Stiehl, 1999).

- *Not all games are for everyone, at least not in their traditional configurations:* For example, in its current form, professional baseball might be ideal for some players. Few would argue, however, that professional rules, equipment, and expectations are appropriate for third graders. Instead, to accommodate this group, substantial alterations are necessary. There are many different ways to play games. If the purpose of your physical education program is to include everyone regardless of ability level, experience, or motivation, then a single, standard game design with strict rules might not be appropriate (Morris & Stiehl, 1999).

- *You can modify any game to include anyone:* Games can accommodate a wide spectrum of abilities, interests, needs, and resources. This will require modifications to various components of games such as the number of players, equipment, and how a player moves (see the Games Design Model section). Some modifications might be for only one child (e.g., allowing a child who moves slowly a safe area in a tag game); other modifications might involve several children (e.g., children who miss their first serve in volleyball get to take a step closer and try again). The key is thinking of alternative ways to play the game to accommodate all children (Morris & Stiehl, 1999).

- *Whenever possible, include the students with a disability when making decisions regarding adaptations to games and activities:* Some students with disabilities will know through past experiences how best to modify an activity to meet their individual needs. Other students may not want any special modifications to games, choosing instead to do the best they can following the regulation rules. In either case, the student with a disability should have a say in modifications that will affect his or her successful participation (Lieberman & Houston-Wilson, 2009; MacDonald & Block, 2005).

- *Get input from classmates without disabilities before creating and implementing modifications:* Classmates without disabilities will be more likely to embrace modifications to games and sports if they contribute to these modifications. For example, rather than telling the class about three modifications to a softball game to accommodate a student in a wheelchair, ask the group how they can modify the game so that students who cannot hit a pitched ball can still participate successfully.

- *Give the student as many choices as possible:* Usually, there is more than one way to modify a game. Choices allow the student with a disability to be more comfortable in the game. Choices also allow the student with disabilities more ownership in the modifications, which will motivate the student (Lieberman & Houston-Wilson, 2009; Stiehl, Morris, & Sinclair, 2008).

- *Participating with physical assistance is an acceptable way to participate in an activity, especially when the alternative is not participating:* Students with more severe disabilities may need physical guidance and even hand-over-hand assistance to safely and successfully participate in many games. It is easy to dismiss a student with severe, multiple disabilities from participation.

However, these students can still enjoy the excitement and camaraderie of playing a game or being a member of a team, even if participation requires a great deal of assistance.

- *On occasion, play multiple games simultaneously, with some games following regulation rules and others having modifications:* Skilled students without disabilities should be allowed to play regulation games to challenge and improve their skills. Too often, modified games are forced onto skilled students without disabilities, and these students may come to resent having a peer with a disability in their general physical education class. A good solution is to occasionally allow regulation games for the skilled students and modified games for less skilled students. For example, at the end of a high school volleyball unit, the general physical educator has the students play competitive games. However, this class of 50 students is very diverse, including some girls who play on the varsity volleyball team, some boys and girls who are very athletic, some boys and girls who are not very athletic, a child with autism, and a child with muscular dystrophy who uses an electric wheelchair. To accommodate this range of abilities, the general physical educator has set up three nets. The first net is set at regulation height for 18 students (three teams of six per team), who are very skilled at volleyball. These 18 students will play following the regulation rules of volleyball. It is not uncommon to see an overhand serve and bump, a set, and then a spike during the game, and the goal is clearly to win. The second net also is set at the regulation height for 18 students divided into three teams who understand the game of volleyball but who play at more of a recreational level. A volleyball trainer (larger, lighter volleyball) is used instead of a regulation volleyball. Underhand serving is popular in this game, and rarely does anyone spike the ball. Rules such as carrying the ball and double hits are relaxed, and students are allowed to stand closer to the net when serving. Although someone does keep score, clearly winning is less important than playing the game. The third net is set at the height of a tennis net, and 14 students (including the student with autism and the student with muscular dystrophy) are assigned to this group. Students in this court are still learning the very basics of volleyball, and most have very limited volleyball skills. A beach ball is used instead of a volleyball, and rules are very relaxed. Students keep score and the game is competitive, but the goal is to have fun.

Determining Whether a Modification Is Appropriate

Not all modifications are appropriate for a particular child with a disability in a particular situation, especially in group games in which some modifications can change the game so drastically that it is no longer fun or motivating for children without disabilities. One simple way to determine which game modification to use is to consider the effect of the modification on the student with disabilities, other classmates, and the general physical educator. If the game modification has a negative effect on any of these individuals, then it probably is not the most appropriate modification. The following four criteria should be used whenever considering a particular game modification. If the proposed game modification does not meet the standards set by these criteria, then an alternative modification should be considered:

1. *Does the game modification allow the student with disabilities to participate successfully yet still be challenged?* For example, in a softball game, a student with an intellectual disability might not be able to hit a softball pitched from the regulation mound. However, this student can hit the ball if the pitcher stands a little closer and tosses it over the plate. Such a modification allows the student to be successful but also challenges him or her. Game modifications should be designed to meet each individual child's unique needs.

2. *Does the game modification make the setting unsafe for the student with a disability or for peers?* For example, to include a student who uses a wheelchair in a game of volleyball, you say that the student must play one of the back positions so that other students are less likely to bump into the student. In addition, you place cones around the student's chair so that classmates without disabilities who get too close to the student hit the cones before the wheelchair. Finally, you remind peers at the beginning of the class and several times during the class to be careful around the student who uses a wheelchair. Peers will quickly learn to be careful, and the student can safely participate in the activity.

3. *Does the game modification negatively affect peers without disabilities?* This point is particularly important when playing group games. For example, an elementary class playing a game of tag includes a student who has autism-like behaviors and is not aware of the rules of the game. To include this student, you specify that when he is the tagger, all students must sit down and let him tag them. Obviously, students without disabilities are not thrilled with the idea of sitting down and letting another student tag them, regardless of his ability. Better modifications would be making the game space smaller, eliminating safe places, and assisting the student to tag his peers. Similarly, it might be fun for a high school class to play sit-down volleyball for a day to accommodate a student who uses a wheelchair or play beep softball to accommodate a student who is blind, but such changes implemented for an entire unit negatively affect the program for students without disabilities.

4. *Does the game modification cause an undue burden on the general physical education teacher?* For example, a ninth grader with advanced muscular dystrophy who uses an electric wheelchair is fully included in general physical education. For a unit on soccer, you could consider changing the game to accommodate this student. However, this would be difficult. Another solution is to work with this student off to the side of the field one-to-one; however, this prevents you from supervising and instructing the other students. A better solution is to have this student play a permanent throw-in position. The student moves his electric wheelchair along the sidelines of the field. When the ball goes out of bounds, a player retrieves the ball, gives it to the student in a wheelchair, and then the student in the wheelchair throws it back into play (pushing the ball off his lap). This way, the student is part of the game and works on his goals of moving his electric wheelchair and moving his arms. Furthermore, this simple modification is relatively easy for the general physical educator to implement.

GAMES DESIGN MODEL

Morris and Stiehl (1999) developed a systematic approach for analyzing and changing group games, built around three of the premises noted earlier: 1) games are not sacred, kids are; 2) games are for everyone, but not in their traditional configurations; and 3) any game can be modified to include anyone. Their approach follows three basic steps.

Understand Any Game's Basic Structure

First, key aspects of any game can be analyzed and then modified to accommodate the needs of

Table 7.1. Games Design Model: components to be manipulated

Purposes	Players	Movements	Objects	Organization	Limits
Development of motor skills	Individuals	Types	Types/uses	Types	Performance
Enhancement of self-worth	Groups	Location	Quantity	Location	Environment
Improvement of fitness	Numbers	Quality	Location	Quantity	
Enjoyment	Relationships				
Satisfaction		Quantity			
Development of cognitive skills		Sequences			

Reprinted, with permission, from G.S.D. Morris and J. Stiehl, 1999, *Changing kids' games*, 2nd ed. (Champaign, IL: Human Kinetics), 18 [or 139].

students of varying abilities. Table 7.1 outlines how Morris and Stiehl (1999) conceptualized six major aspects of games and variations that can change the nature of the game.

Purposes of games can vary from one simple focus (e.g., improving one motor skill) to expecting students to acquire a variety of skills, concepts, and behaviors. Not all students involved in a game necessarily have to work on the same goals. For example, a locomotor game played by all students in a kindergarten physical education class could have various goals for various students, including improving walking gait for a student with cerebral palsy, improving hopping skills for students with limited locomotor abilities, and improving skipping skills and general space awareness in skilled students. Similarly, goals for a game of soccer played by all students in tenth-grade physical education could include improving cardiovascular fitness for a student with Down syndrome, improving range of motion for a student with cerebral palsy, developing basic skills and understanding of the rules of the game for lower ability students, and using various strategies for skilled students.

Players involved in the game can vary in two major ways: how they are grouped and how many players are involved. Players can be grouped homogeneously by gender, size, or skill level; players can be grouped heterogeneously so that each team has an equal representation of skilled and unskilled players; or players can be randomly assigned to groups. The number of players involved in a game can vary by having more than, less than, or the same number of players than a particular game calls for. Group size can be varied so that a particular team might have more or less players than other teams. How players are selected for a particular group as well as the number of players involved in a game will have a profound effect on how successfully a student with disabilities is included. For example, a teacher needs to break down her seventh-grade physical education class into

four teams for a modified game of volleyball. The class includes a student named Bill who has muscular dystrophy, uses an electric wheelchair, and has limited strength and mobility in his upper body. The teacher decides to group the teams by skill level, with each team having skilled players, average players, and unskilled players. Bill is assigned to Team A. Teams B–D also have unskilled players, so this will not be an unfair disadvantage to Team A.

Movement refers to the types of movements involved in a particular game and how these movements are used. Types of movements include different types of locomotor, nonlocomotor, manipulative, and body awareness skills. Type of movements can be varied so that skilled and nonskilled students work on different skills during the game; a student with disabilities might work on even different skills. Other ways in which Morris and Stiehl (1999) suggested that movements could be modified include locations of movement (personal space, general space, following certain directions, levels, or pathways), quality of movement (variations in force, flow, and speed requirements), quantity of movement (several repetitions, a few repetitions), variations in relationships (moving with or without object or other players), and sequences (following a particular sequence or having no sequence). Modifications in movement are excellent ways to ensure that students with disabilities are appropriately and successfully engaged in general physical education activities.

For example, Susie is a third grader who has severe intellectual disabilities and autism-like behaviors. Susie's class is working on the ball skills of dribbling and passing a playground ball, skills that Susie does not do independently. The class consists of 40 students who have varying abilities, so the teacher has modified the movement requirements so that all students are challenged yet successful in the activity. More skilled students are working on dribbling the ball while running in and out of cones and passing by playing a game of keep-away with one person in the middle trying to steal the pass from two players who pass the ball back and forth using different passing patterns. Students who can dribble and pass but who still need practice on these skills are working on dribbling the ball while jogging forward and passing the ball back and forth with a peer from various distances depending on each student's strength. Students who are just learning how to dribble and pass are working on dribbling a ball while standing in one place and passing a ball so that it hits a large target on the wall. Finally, Susie is working on dribbling by dropping the ball and catching it before it bounces again (with assistance from different peers in her class). Susie works on passing by handing the ball to a peer upon a verbal request. During relay races at the end of class, each student uses the skills he or she has been working on—that is, some students have to dribble between cones, some students have to dribble while jogging forward, some students have to dribble the ball 10 times, and Susie has to drop and catch the ball with assistance. The basic movements are similar, but how these movements are operationalized during practice as well as during the game vary from student to student depending on each student's abilities.

Objects refer to any equipment used during practice or during a game. Objects can vary in terms of how a student moves in relation to the object (e.g., going under, over, or through hoops; catching, kicking, or throwing a ball), how the object moves a student (e.g., scooter boards, skates, tricycles), how an object is used to send other objects away (e.g., bats, hockey sticks, rackets, feet), or how objects are used to gather other objects in (e.g., gloves, hands, lacrosse sticks, milk cartons). In addition, the number and placement of objects in the environment can vary depending on the needs of each student. For example, some students might use regulation-size bats to send objects away from their body, other students might use slightly larger bats, and still other students might use a very large bat and hit a very large ball. Varying the objects will ensure that each student is working at a level that meets his or her unique needs.

Organization refers to decisions regarding the patterns, structure, and location of players. Some games might have very strict patterns to follow, such as relay races in which students are expected to line up behind each other. However, the structure can be altered in which players are allowed to move anywhere they wish in the environment. Modifications can also be made to the location of players and objects within the boundaries. For a student with limited mobility or strength, a fair accommodation

would be to have another student stand near him when it is his turn to toss a ball to them or to tag them. Similarly, how far each student has to run in a relay race could vary based on individual abilities.

Limits refer to the general rules for players. Some games might have movements that are deemed acceptable or necessary. For example, it might be necessary for a skilled student to dribble through several cones in a relay race. It might be unacceptable for skilled students to spike a volleyball unless it goes into a certain zone. Limits also refer to the physical aspects of the environment and activity. Physical aspects of the environment can vary in terms of the width of the field, size and type of equipment, and number of players in the game. Activity conditions can vary in terms of how long the game is, how long a particular student plays, scoring, or rules. For example, a skilled student might get one pitch in a softball game, a less skilled student gets three pitches, and a student with disabilities hits the ball off the tee.

Modify a Game's Basic Structure

The second level of game analysis involves applying the components outlined previously to specific games—that is, devise and modify games based on the purpose of the game, how many players will be involved, and the game's movements and objects, among others.

Modifying a game's basic structure can take two distinct forms. The components can be manipulated to make up a completely new game (see Table 7.2). For example, if students are to develop and improve kicking skills, a game could be devised in which equal teams of three players are given one large box to kick. The object of the game is to kick the box across the gym. Each player on the team must kick the box at the same time, and players cannot touch or kick another team's box. This novel game ensures that teammates work together and that each player gets many turns to practice the skill of forceful kicking.

A second way of manipulating game components is to modify traditional games. Game analysis can be used to modify traditional sports that tend to be dominated by a few skilled players so that everyone has an opportunity to participate, improve skills, and contribute. For example, basketball can be changed to focus on improving passing skills and teamwork. Six teams of five players are selected by the teacher so that each team has an equal representation of skilled and nonskilled players. Points can be scored by making baskets, but a team that passes the ball to each player before someone shoots gets

Table 7.2.   Sample modifications for a soccer game

Component	Skilled child	Typical child	Child with Down syndrome
Purposes	Use opposite foot; cross ball to far post	Improve basic skills of passing, dribbling, shooting, and playing defense	Work on fitness (moving and running)
Players	11 versus 11 or 5 versus 3 With skilled players only having three players	11 versus 11 or 7 versus 7	7 versus 7 or 5 versus 3 Put player with Down syndrome on team with more players
Movements	Practice one-to-ones to beat an opponent off the dribble; work on changing speeds	All regular movement	Allow moving slower and even walking when child gets tired
Objects	Regulation ball; smaller goals to make it more challenging	Regulation ball	Regulation ball when playing on playground; Nerf ball when playing in modified game; larger goals when playing in modified game
Organization	Regulation boundaries	Regulation boundaries or smaller field	Play "zone soccer" in which players have to stay in particular zones. Place one or two players from each team with similar abilities in zones. Put player with Down syndrome in the same zone as lesser skilled players or those who will share the ball.
Limits	Cannot dribble (has to trap and then pass ball); has to use opposite foot when shooting; cannot go past midfield when playing defense or offense	No limits	No one can steal the ball from player with DS; player with DS is allowed free pass to teammates and a free shot at goal.

double points for every basket. In addition, every time a different player makes a basket, the team gets 5 bonus points. This encourages teammates to pass the ball before shooting. In addition, some players must shoot at a 10-foot basket, whereas other players can shoot at an 8-foot basket. Manipulating game components is an easy way to ensure that the class is focused on specific goals and that maximum participation and practice is afforded to each student.

Manage a Game's Degree of Difficulty

The third level of analysis is the most important in terms of accommodating students with disabilities. This step involves analyzing each of the game components and then creating a continuum from easy to difficult that is used to make a game or skill easier or more difficult for particular students. Skilled students can be challenged by making the activity more difficult, and students with lower abilities or specific disabilities can become more successful by making the activity easier. Morris and Stiehl (1999) outlined the following strategy for identifying degree of difficulty:

1. *Identify factors that may limit a player's performance:* List the various aspects of the task that can be manipulated. External factors such as ball size, size of targets, and speed of objects should be the focus at this level. A student's personal abilities such as visual perception or strength should not be considered at this level of analysis

because these factors cannot be influenced directly by game analysis. However, personal limitations can be accommodated by making simple changes in task complexity. For example, a larger, slower moving ball can be used for kicking or striking by a student who has a visual perception problem or a visual impairment.

2. *Diagram the task complexity spectrum:* Factors identified are sequenced along a continuum from less difficult to more difficult. For example, ball speed in kicking might be listed (see Figure 7.1). All the factors related to targeted skills should be sequenced. These sequences will begin to help you understand how to modify activities to accommodate varying abilities.

3. *Begin to create tasks that vary in difficulty:* Finally, compile all the factors and sequences into a *task complexity (TC) spectrum* for a particular skill. An example of one of Morris and Stiehl's (1999) TC spectrums is presented in Figure 7.2.

Figure 7.1.   Sequence of factors for kicking.

TC	Size of support base	Center of gravity	Speed	Time
Easy	Eight body parts	Directly over and close to base of support	Slow	8 seconds
↓	Four body parts	Slightly off center and above base of support	Fast	18 seconds
Difficult	One body part	Moderately off center and far above base of support	Faster	30 seconds

Figure 7.2. Task complexity: balance factors. (Reprinted, with permission, from G.S.D. Morris and J. Stiehl, 1999, *Changing kids' games*, 2nd ed. [Champaign, IL: Human Kinetics], 18 [or 139].)

Game categories (e.g., limits, players) also can be modified to make a particular game easier or more difficult for a group of children. For example, having four teams and four separate goals in soccer would make the game more difficult; having two teams of just three players on each team would make the game easier. Similarly, having a smaller playing field would make soccer easier for players with limited endurance, but a smaller tennis court would make the game more difficult for a skilled player. The TC spectrum shows in one schematic how several factors can be manipulated to accommodate a student with disabilities, make a task slightly less difficult for a student just learning a skill, or make an activity more challenging for a skilled player.

FUNCTIONAL APPROACH FOR MODIFYING MOVEMENT EXPERIENCES

Another model for analyzing and modifying games is the functional approach for modifying movement experiences (FAMME) model (Kasser & Lytle, 2013). Similar to Morris and Stiehl's (1999) model, the FAMME model is designed to help the general physical educator systematically analyze a child's strengths and weaknesses as they relate to the skills needed in a particular game. This information is then examined to create individually determined modifications that facilitate the successful participation of a child with a disability. (Table 7.3 shows the FAMME model applied to a game of tag.) The model has the following four steps.

Table 7.3. Application of functional approach for modifying movement experiences (FAMME) model for game of tag

Underlying components of tag	Child's functional differences	Modifications
Concept understanding	Does not understand rules of tag	Peer to TA helps student move around setting and avoid being tagged. Make space smaller when student is tagger; have peer or TA help student find people to tag
Balance	Okay	None needed
Coordination	Okay	None needed
Agility/speed	Slower than peers	Peers and TA help student avoid tagger. Make space smaller when student is tagger; have peer or TA help student find people to tag
Sensory perception	Okay	None needed
Strength (legs)	Okay	None needed
Endurance	Tires after about 3 minutes	Allow student to sit out and rest for 1 minute every 3 minutes.
Flexibility	Okay	None needed
Attention	Maintains attention for only a few seconds	Peers or TA help student stay on task
Self-control	Can easily lose control and tantrum	Peers or TA calm student; if student begins to get upset, allow him to leave setting and get a drink of water

Reprinted, with permission, from S.L. Kasser and R. Lyttle, 2005, *Inclusive physical activity: A lifetime of opportunities* (Champaign, IL: Human Kinetics), 68.

Note. Targeted student is a second grader with autism who comes to general physical education with a teacher assistant (TA).

Determine Underlying Components of Skills

The first step in the model involves carefully examining the underlying requirements of a particular game or activity. These components are the basic prerequisites that any student needs to successfully participate in an activity. The first column of Table 7.3 shows the basic requirements for playing tag. Most games require some basic elements such as a certain amount of strength, flexibility, endurance, speed, and agility. For a game of tag, strength and flexibility are not as important as speed, agility, and endurance. Softball, however, requires upper body strength and eye–hand coordination but does not require much agility, speed, or endurance. Underlying components of any game will be unique depending on the specific nature of the game. In addition to physical requirements of games, students must understand the basic concept or goal of the game as well as rules that govern the game. For example, in a simple game of tag, a student needs to know the goal and the rules.

Determine Current Capabilities of the Individual

The general physical educator identifies the student's abilities and disabilities as they relate to a particular activity or game. As noted in Chapter 6, it is more important to understand a student's functional abilities and impairments rather than to simply rely on a label. Knowing that a student has cerebral palsy or an intellectual disability does not really predict how well a student will do in a volleyball game or what modifications might be necessary. Kasser and Lytle (2013) suggested focusing on the following major functional areas: strength, flexibility, balance/postural control, coordination, speed/agility, endurance, concept understanding, attention, self-responsibility/self-control, and sensory perception. When possible, match these functional characteristics to the specific requirements of an activity or game. For example, it is important to note that a student has limited endurance in a game such as tag or soccer. However, limited endurance would not be an issue in a bowling unit.

Match Modification Efforts to Capabilities

In this step, specific modifications are prescribed that help a student who has a particular functional impairment (e.g., strength) be successful in an activity or game that requires strength (e.g., serving a volleyball over the net). For example, tagging requires understanding the basic concept of tag and rules of the game. A student with autism has difficulty understanding the concept and rules of tag. Therefore, a modification is needed for this student to participate safely and successfully in tag. The suggested modification focuses on a peer or teacher assistant helping this student to move away from the tagger. When this student is the tagger, the space is reduced and a peer or teacher assistant assists this student in moving toward and tagging peers.

Evaluate Modification Effectiveness

The final step in the FAMME model is evaluating the effectiveness of the modification. Kasser and Lytle (2013) created a list of seven questions that a general physical educator can use to determine a modification's effectiveness:

1. Is the modification age appropriate?
2. Is the modification functionally appropriate?
3. Does the modification allow the participant to be as independent as possible?
4. Does the modification ensure maximum participation of the participants?
5. Does the modification avoid singling out or spotlighting high- or low-ability participants?
6. Does the modification allow for optimal challenge for everyone in the activity?
7. Is safe participation ensured for all participants once the modification is implemented?

UNIQUE GAMES AND GROUP ACTIVITIES THAT CAN FACILITATE INCLUSION

Adventure and Initiative Games

Adventure and initiative games are centered on group problem solving and by nature require the active involvement of all participants. For example, the Project Adventure (PA) program is based on the philosophy that people are usually more capable (mentally, emotionally, and physically) than they perceive themselves to be. PA games and activities give people opportunities to challenge themselves and to take risks within the supportive atmosphere of a group. Adventure means any new experience that elicits excitement. (Ellmo & Graser, 1995, p. 4)

Goals of the adventure program are as follows:

- To increase the participant's sense of personal confidence
- To increase mutual support within a group

- To develop an increased level of agility and physical coordination

- To develop an increased joy in one's physical self and in being with others

- To develop an increased familiarity and identification with the natural world

These goals are achieved through the use of noncompetitive games, group problem solving, initiatives, and rope course events to create excitement and achieve students' goals of facilitating personal learning and growth. Group initiative activities are designed to facilitate active membership and teamwork within a group that has a problem to solve. This problem-oriented approach can be used in developing decision making, team building, and leadership. In terms of including students with disabilities, group initiative activities can be used to highlight the importance of including all students in the class to achieve a team goal. The rules of the game do not permit exclusion of any participants. In fact, initiative games help team members focus on each person's strengths and how they can best contribute to the solution to the problem. Students can then apply cooperative problem-solving skills learned in initiative games to include students with disabilities into more traditional team sports (Rohnke, 2010; Rohnke & Butler, 1995).

An example of a simple initiative game is Reach for the Sky (Rohnke, 1977). The object of the game is to place a piece of tape as high as possible on a wall. Teams of as few as 3 and as many as 15–20 players work together to build a human tower to place the tape as high as possible on the wall. Groups quickly realize that heavier students should be on the bottom supporting smaller players. A student who uses a wheelchair can be a good support on the bottom of the tower, using his wheelchair as a base and having him use his arms to help hold another student in place. Smaller students, such as those with fetal alcohol syndrome, can be near the top of the tower. Thus individuals' strengths are highlighted rather than their weaknesses, and students without disabilities learn to appreciate how each person can contribute to team efforts.

Transferring this concept to traditional games, students without disabilities can focus on both a student's strengths and his or her weaknesses when modifying the game. For example, in a game of basketball, a student who uses a wheelchair can be seen as a tough obstacle to get around as a point guard positioned in a 2-1-2 defense alignment. The student with attention-deficit/hyperactivity disorder might be a chaser while playing defense, chasing the ball and harassing any player who has the ball.

In a game of football, the student who uses a wheelchair can be an offensive lineman, protecting the quarterback by moving his wheelchair so that oncoming rushers must run around him. Make sure that you talk to the group about safety, especially being aware of a student who uses a wheelchair. In addition, you might want to make special rules for the student who uses a wheelchair, limiting the range in which he or she can move so that students without disabilities have safe areas. Students will learn quickly with proper instruction.

One of the nice aspects of group initiative games is that there are no set solutions or answers. Solutions will depend on the unique characteristics of each member and how these characteristics interact with those of other group members. This fact should be pointed out to the group at the end of each initiative game or at the end of a class that included several initiative games. Group discussions are a critical part of the adventure process, and participants are encouraged to share how they solved problems during the activity. Group discussion is a good place to help focus on how each member of the team contributed to the group goal. Group discussions also can be used to guide students to think of how children with different disabilities/abilities can be included in an activity and contribute to the team (see Ellmo & Graser, 1995; Rohnke, 1977, 2010; and Rohnke & Butler, 1995, for samples of adventure games and initiative games).

Cooperative Games

Cooperative sports and games are designed to help students work together to overcome challenges rather than against one another to overcome other people. The major goal of cooperative games is to create an environment where children play together to achieve a common goal rather than against each other to see which child or small group can win. Through the cooperative game process, children learn in a fun way how to become more considerate of one another, more aware of how other people are feeling, and more willing to operate in one another's best interests (Luvmour & Luvmour, 2013; Orlick, 2006).

The major difference between traditional games and cooperative games is the focus and structure. As Orlick explained, traditional games such as King of the Mountain have one person as king, and all others are to be pushed down the mountain. Players are compelled to work against each other, and only one player can achieve the goal of the game. Thus, the game has an inherent competitive focus and structure. In contrast, a cooperative version of the same game, People of the Mountain, has a completely different focus in which the objective is to get as many people as possible to the top of the mountain, requiring children to work together. The focus of the game is inherently cooperative and encourages classmates to help and support each other. In addition, everyone is a winner in this game.

Many physical education programs present skill development through competitive activities. Although fun and motivating for skilled students who can win competitive games, students with less ability (including students with disabilities) rarely have an opportunity to win. In addition, competitive team sports force skilled players to pressure less skilled players. Mistakes are more glaring, and often, more skilled players dominate the game. Less skilled players lose confidence and self-esteem and learn how to avoid fully participating in the game. For example, after miskicking a soccer ball during a soccer game and being ridiculed by his teammates and teased by his opponents, a less skilled player avoids kicking the ball by positioning himself away from the action. An alternative to competition in physical education is cooperation. Cooperative games can be implemented at various levels.

One alternative is to play only cooperative games such as People of the Mountain in which the focus of all activities is cooperation. This approach is most appropriate for elementary children who are learning how to work together and who have not been exposed to traditional sports. A second alternative is to play within a traditional competitive structure but focus on cooperation rather than competition. For example, a game of volleyball can focus on how many different players on a team can hit the ball before it goes over the net. Such an approach is appropriate for students just learning skills who need practice in a game atmosphere without the added pressure of competition. A third alternative is to include self-paced activities that are not assessed or scored. For example, Clean Out Your Backyard is a fun throwing game for young children in which yarn balls are thrown back and forth toward each other. For older students, a basketball game can be less competitive by simply not keeping score. Finally, a fourth alternative includes goal-oriented play in some situations and lighthearted play in other situations. For example, some days, the class can work on basketball following traditional rules, and on other days, the focus can be on which team passes the ball the most before shooting and which team has the most players score.

Most traditional physical education activities, including group games and team sports, can easily become more cooperative by making just a few changes.

Cooperative Games and Sports (Orlick, 2006) and *Everyone Wins: Cooperative Games and Activities* (Luvmour & Luvmour, 2013) present several suggestions for making traditional competitive games cooperative. For example, Musical Hoops is a cooperative version of Musical Chairs. In traditional Musical Chairs, chairs are taken away and children compete against each other for a chair. The quickest children usually get to sit in the remaining chairs, whereas less skilled players, including students with disabilities, are the first to be eliminated. In Musical Hoops, when the music stops and hoops are taken away, players must share the remaining hoop. Imagine an entire class of kindergartners, including a student who is blind and another with cerebral palsy who is much slower than his peers, working together to fit into one hoop!

Another example is Alaskan Rules Baseball. One of the problems in traditional baseball is that players in the field stand around waiting for the ball to be hit to them. Even if a ball is hit to a less skilled player or a player with a disability, chances are that a more skilled player will run over and try to field the ball. What results are skilled players getting more turns, whereas less skilled players and players with disabilities get fewer practice turns and are bored. In Alaskan Rules Baseball, all players in the field must touch the ball before a player is out. The first player who gets to the ball picks it up, and all other players on the team line up behind that player. The ball is then passed (or tossed) from player to player. When the last player has the ball, he or she yells "stop," at which time the batter's turn is over. The batter gets one run for every base he or she touches.

New Games

New Games are games that allow individuals of all ages and abilities to play in an atmosphere of fun and creativity. The following are the major philosophies of New Games (Fluegelman, 1976; LeFevre, 2012):

- Individuals choose games and make changes to rules as needed so that everyone can be involved.

- Modifications can occur at any time during the game (even in the middle of the game).

- Everyone should enjoy the activities. If everyone is not having fun, then modifications are probably needed.

- Fair, fun competition is important, but winning is de-emphasized.

The original *New Games Book* (Fluegelman, 1976) and *More New Games* (Fluegelman, 1981) and

Best New Games—Updated Edition (LeFevre, 2012) have descriptions of hundreds of games that can be played by as few as two players and as many as 100 players. Games are also categorized by how active the participants are. New Games lend themselves nicely to including students with disabilities and can be a fun rainy day activity for students without disabilities. The following are two examples of New Games that can easily accommodate students with varying abilities.

People to People

Pairs of students stand in a circle facing one player who is the leader. The leader calls a name of two body parts (e.g., back to back), and the partners must touch their backs together. When everyone is touching backs, the leader then calls two more body parts (e.g., head to knee) and the partners must touch their head to their partner's knee. The game continues until the leader says "people to people" at which time everyone (including the leader) tries to find a new partner. Whoever is left without a partner is the new leader.

Amoeba Tag

Players scatter about the playing area, and one player is designated "it." Players move about the playing area while "it" tries to tag a player (every so often change the way players move such as galloping, skipping, jumping, hopping, traveling at different levels or following different pathways). When a player is tagged, he or she holds the taggers hand, and both players become "it." When another player is tagged, he or she holds hands with the two-person "it" to form a three-person "it." As new people are tagged, they join the everincreasing "it." Eventually, all but one player is "it."

TEACHING ADAPTED SPORTS TO ADDRESS INCLUSION

It is safe to say that sports such as basketball, soccer, volleyball, and tennis are taught in some manner in almost all upper elementary, middle, and high school general physical education curricula. These same sports, and more, have corollary adapted sports. So why not consider teaching adapted sports as a means of including all students in your physical education classes?

Learning about adapted sports, and how to teach it, will help teachers improve programming for all students. By expanding your general physical education curriculum to include adapted sports you will 1) improve social interactions between students with and without disabilities by creating a common ground between these two groups, 2) help all students see their classmates as more *alike* than *different*, 3) engage everyone in the athleticism within adapted sports (e.g., wheelchair basketball, sitting volleyball, or goalball for those with visual impairments), and 4) continue to improve the health and fitness of all participants. Sports is *universal* and provides a common ground for interactions among different cultures, societies, and organizations and varying levels of functional ability (Davis, 2011).

Promoting Inclusion by Implementing Traditional and Adapted Sports in General Physical Education

The reason for selecting sports as a means of inclusion in physical education is that "sport is sport." Sport is universal and it affects every fiber of our society (e.g., ethnicity, work, recreational, social, educational). Consider in 2013, when for the first time in the history of the Paralympic Games, the Winter Paralympics were broadcast live on the National Broadcasting Company (NBC). One of the more memorable competitions witnessed worldwide was the U.S. sled hockey team's gold medal game against Russia. Played by athletes with amputations or other physical impairments, the sport was presented as just that: "sports." After 5 minutes of watching this game, it is likely anyone watching was not focused on the athletes' impairments but rather the sport itself. They saw hockey the sport, not hockey by athletes with disabilities. So why not move this paradigm into the general physical education classes? Why not use adapted sports as a way to include everyone in the activities? As a general physical education teacher, including adapted sports units within your curriculum will help create a more comprehensive experience for all students. If we attempt to teach students with disabilities how to participate in traditional sports using modifications and adaptations, why can't we reverse that paradigm and ask students without disabilities to participate in adapted sports?

Whether you select to teach students with disabilities traditional sports or you choose to teach students without disabilities adapted sports, you should take a systematic approach. There are four key steps suggested by Davis (2011) that will assist you regardless of your path to inclusion.

Table 7.4. Comparison of traditional and adapted sports for curriculum consideration into general physical education classes

Traditional sport	Adapted sport
Basketball	Wheelchair basketball
Soccer	Indoor wheelchair soccer Power soccer
Volleyball	Sitting volleyball
Tennis	Wheelchair tennis

Table 7.6. Skill similarities between traditional and adapted sport

Traditional sport	Adapted sport	Skills
Basketball	Wheelchair basketball	Pass, dribble, shoot, retrieve, transition
Soccer	Indoor wheelchair soccer	Pass, dribble, shoot, block, retrieve
Volleyball	Sitting volleyball	Pass, block, serve, rotation
Tennis	Wheelchair tennis	Serve, forehand, backhand, volley

Four Key Steps to Including Adapted Sports in General Physical Education

1. Determine the sport to play and then cross-reference that sport to an adapted sport.

2. Learn about similarities and differences between traditional and adapted sports skills and rules.

3. Assess the performance of all students for the skills needed to successfully participate.

4. Implement and teach using the traditional and/or adapted sport.

Step 1: Determine the Traditional Sport and Cross-Reference with Adapted Sport

As you consider including adapted sports into your traditional sports curriculum, you must first be aware of the sports that are represented in both categories. Many of the traditional sports have an equal counterpart in adapted sports, which will help you expand and develop a more comprehensive curriculum as you move toward a more inclusive teaching environment (see Table 7.4).

There are also several adapted sports that do not have a traditional sports counterpart that would be appropriate for inclusion into your general physical education curriculum (see Table 7.5). Adapted sports supplemented into your traditional curriculum will help you deliver a more comprehensive program and develop student interaction (i.e., social) for all skill levels (Davis, 2011).

Table 7.5. Adapted sport supplements to traditional sport in general physical education

Adapted sport	Possible supplement to traditional sport
Goalball: played by blind and or visually impaired	Volleyball and basketball
Beep baseball: played by blind and or visually impaired	Softball
Slalom: wheelchair obstacle course	Track and field

Step 2: Learn About Similarities and Differences Between Traditional and Adapted Sports Skills and Rules

The next step you should consider is learning about the skill and rule similarities between selected traditional and adapted sports. Identifying similarities between the two categories of sports will help you implement an inclusive curriculum. Review Tables 7.6–7.8 and Figures 7.3–7.5 to identify similar skills and rules between traditional and adapted sports that apply to basketball, soccer, volleyball, and tennis.

Many of the adapted sports have similar rules to their traditional sports counterpart; however, the interpretation of rules often is not as similar and will require you to learn the differences. Keep in mind you have the choice of modifying rules of the sports to help address the needs of all your students. Rule modification is an acceptable way to address inclusion; remember your selected rule modifications must work for all students.

Step 3: Assess the Performance for All Students on the Skills Needed to Successfully Participate

When considering inclusion of students with and without disabilities in the same setting, assessment

Table 7.7. Sitting and traditional volleyball rule interpretations

	Rule for volleyball	Rule for sitting volleyball
Serving (underhand or overhand)	Both feet behind the serving line	Buttocks behind serving line, legs allowed on the court
Passing (overhand or underhand)	May pass using momentary jump or airborne movement	Must remain seated on the floor; no lifting of buttocks to gain an advantage
Setting	Same as Passing	Same as Passing
Blocking	Not allowed to block serve	Allowed to block serve

Table 7.8. Examples of traditional and adapted sports rules for basketball and soccer

	Rule	Traditional sports	Adapted sports
Basketball and wheelchair basketball	Traveling	One step with ball, must dribble before second step	Two consecutive touches to the handrim with ball possession; must dribble, pass, or shoot before third touch
	Lane violation	Three seconds without attempt to shoot	Four seconds without attempt to shoot
Soccer and wheelchair soccer	Throw-in	Two hands, overhead	Two hands, overhead
	Goalie-area violation	Offense or defense allowed inside	Offense or defense not allowed inside

is preeminent, as was discussed in Chapter 4. The students' interaction with the environment (authentic) is one of the first assessments that should take place. This assessment is predicated on student functional abilities and how those abilities to meet the demand of the tasks are presented in various environments. Presented here is a modification of Newell's model of the interactions among the student's skills, the environment, and the task (Newell, 1986). Rather than offer the interactions in the model identified by constraints (e.g., student age, body type, gender), this modification focuses on the complexity of the task and environment interaction and the student's functional ability using a four-quadrant model (Davis, 2011).

Davis's environmental interaction model (see Figure 7.5) is presented as a vertical axis representing the *performer's functional ability* and a horizontal axis representing the *difficulty of the task and environment*. These axes intersect to create a four-quadrant (Quad 4) model to demonstrate dynamic positive (+) or negative (–) environmental interactions. As you apply the Quad 4 model to activity selections, you should consider the potential for your students' success (+) or nonsuccess (–). Any task–environment interaction with a student's functional ability resulting in a negative experience should be changed. For example, a student with high functional ability should experience positive environment interactions, or Q1, with difficult or complex tasks. The same with a task considered simple for a lower functioning student such as Q3. Selecting a task that is simple for a high-functioning student or a difficult task for a low-functioning student could result in unsuccessful task–environment interactions and thus require adjustments. The quadrants are meant to be considered *starting* points (i.e., initial assessments between the students' functional ability and the environment/task interaction). Skill performance assessment can follow this initial task–environment assessment.

Assessing Skill Performance   Once you have assessed the task–environment interaction for the students in your class, one type of skill assessment that could be used to assess performance is a content-referenced or curriculum-embedded criteria assessment. Conducting this type of assessment for a student with a disability is the same process used with students without a disability.

When you commit to using the combination of a traditional and adapted sports curriculum, you will recognize the similarities rather than the differences. For example, the skills in traditional basketball are pass, dribble, shoot, rebound, ball movement, and ball retrieval. When you teach passing (e.g., chest pass), you might break down the teaching points in the following manner:

- Eyes on target
- Two hands on ball
- Elbows flexed in preparation
- Elbows extend at ball release
- Thumbs point downward
- Follow-through

Figure 7.3. Shooting in wheelchair and traditional basketball.

Figure 7.4. Chest pass in wheelchair and traditional basketball chest pass.

These same teaching points could be used in teaching the chest pass from the adapted sport of wheelchair basketball. By transferring these criteria to an assessment checklist and adding a quantitative measure, you can develop your assessment instrument and apply these same teaching points to skill analysis for both traditional and adapted sports (see Figure 7.6, modified from Davis, 2011). For scoring, you could place an X if the student demonstrated the criterion, a slash (/) for attempting the criterion, or a zero (0) if the student could not perform the criterion. You could design similar

assessments for the other basketball skills such as dribble, shooting, or ball movement. All students bring their own unique set of skill abilities; once you have assessed environmental interaction and skill performance, you are ready to plan your teaching by developing unit and lesson plans. In addition, you now have information that could contribute to a student's IEP (e.g., present-level statements, annual goals, and short-term objectives).

Step 4: Implement and Teach Using Traditional and/or Adapted Sport

In order to implement and teach, you need to make sure you have planned for the following: the amount of time available, number of objectives to be mastered, equipment available, types and severity of disabilities in your class, opportunities to practice new skills outside the school setting, logistical concerns, and skills needed to be successful. As previously mentioned, when delivering the lesson in class, considerations must include teaching format, teaching style, and curriculum delivery. Whether you have decided to include one student with a disability in a traditional sport unit or to teach all students with and without disabilities an adapted sport, planning is the key ingredient. Figure 7.7 is offered as a general unit planning document that can help you implement your traditional sport curriculum with modifications for students with disabilities or include an entire adapted sport in your traditional curriculum. It shows a plan for teaching an entire adapted sport unit for all students, in this case sitting volleyball. This is a 45-minute class for 3 days per week using 1) 8 minutes of warm-up, 2) 5 minutes of instruction, 3) 25 minutes of activity, and 4) 7 minutes of cool-down.

Functional ability
High

(Less successful)   (Successful)
−Q2   +Q1

Interaction

Task   Environment
(simple)   (complex)

⊕

(Successful)   (Less successful)
+Q3   −Q4

Function low

Figure 7.5. Quad 4 environmental interaction model. (Adapted, with permission, from R.W. Davis, 2011, *Teaching disability sport: A guide for physical educators*, 2nd ed. [Champaign, IL: Human Kinetics], 22.)

Chest pass	Trials 1–5					Comments
Eyes on target	X	X	X			Needed verbal cues to keep eyes on target
Two hands on ball	X	X	X	/	/	Needed verbal and PA to hold the ball correctly
Elbows flexed in preparation	/	X	X	X	/	Needed PA to hold the ball correctly in prep
Elbows extend at ball release	0	/	/	/	/	Extension limited
Thumbs point downward	0	0	0	/	/	Extension limited
Follow through	/	/	/	/	/	Need reminders to follow through

Figure 7.6.   Criterion assessment for chest pass in wheelchair basketball. (*Key:* X, accomplished; /, with assistance; 0, not accomplished; adapted, with permission, from R.W. Davis, 2011, *Teaching disability sport: A guide for physical educators*, 2nd ed. [Champaign, IL: Human Kinetics], 20.)

SPECIFIC MODIFICATIONS TO TRADITIONAL TEAM AND INDIVIDUAL SPORTS

Even when adapted sports are integrated into the general physical education curriculum, many middle and high school programs will still likely emphasize traditional individual and team sports. The disability-specific chapters provide information on specific ways to modify selected individual and team sports to meet the needs of students with disabilities. Information includes general suggestions for modifying skill work, general suggestions for modifying games, and modifications for students with specific disabilities. These modifications are not comprehensive but rather suggestions for modifying traditional individual and team sports. As you begin to learn more about the functional skills of

your students as well as how to utilize these modifications, you will quickly begin to incorporate your modifications that meet the needs of your particular students.

SUMMARY

Some accommodations may be necessary if students with disabilities are to be successfully and meaningfully included in group games and team sports. These modifications can be implemented without necessarily changing the general format of the game or forcing skilled students to play at a lower level (e.g., simply allowing the student to use a lighter racquet in tennis or slightly shortening the bases in softball). However, modifications can include specific changes to rules of games such as giving students free passes in basketball or setting up special zones in soccer. In either case, these

Monday	Tuesday	Wednesday	Thursday	Friday
Curr type: same	Curr type:	Curr type: same	Curr type:	Curr type: multilevel
Class format: large group	Class format:	Class format: large group	Class format:	Class format: large and small group
Tch style: command	Tch style:	Tch style: practice/trial	Tch style:	Tch style: reciprocal
Activity name: correct sitting position and floor movement	Activity name:	Activity name: serving	Activity name:	Activity name: serve and rally
Teaching cues: eyes on target	Prompts/cues:	Teaching cues; strike with cupped hand	Prompts/cues:	Teaching cues: push on floor to move positions
Fingertip control				
Modification: use traditional or volley lites	Modification:	Modification: Place ball on tall traffic cone for SWD as needed.	Modification:	Modification: Allow one bounce if needed to help students move on the floor.

Figure 7.7.   Unit planning document for sitting volleyball. *Key:* curr, curriculum; tch, teaching; SWD, student with disability. (Adapted, with permission, from R.W. Davis, 2011, *Teaching disability sport: A guide for physical educators*, 2nd ed. [Champaign, IL: Human Kinetics], 18.)

accommodations can be the difference between successful inclusion and frustration for students with and without disabilities.

This chapter has outlined Morris and Stiehl's (1999) Games Design Model and Kasser and Lytle's (2013) FAMME model for modifying group games and team sports as well as unique games modifications such as initiative games, adventure games, cooperative games, and New Games. In addition, information was presented on how to use adapted sports within traditional sports in your general physical education curriculum to support and highlight the strengths of students with disabilities and to teach students without disabilities about Paralympic sports. Finally, take advantage of the specific modifications to traditional individual and team sports found in the disability-specific chapters of this book. As noted in the previous two chapters, these modifications are not meant to be an exhaustive list but rather help general physical educators and other team members begin to think of simple yet innovative ways to safely and successfully include students with disabilities into group games and team sports. As noted throughout this chapter, it is important to focus on the functional abilities and impairments exhibited by each of your students.

Understanding Specific Needs

CHAPTER 8

Intellectual Disabilities

Katie Stanton-Nichols and Martin E. Block

OBJECTIVES

1. Define intellectual disability, including defining and contrasting intelligence quotient versus adaptive behavior

2. Describe causes of intellectual disability

3. Define Down syndrome and common characteristics associated with it

4. Define fragile X and common characteristics associate with it

5. Define "levels of intensity of support"

6. Describe teaching models for children with intellectual disability including levels; simplify, refine, extend, apply (SREA); and teaching style, rules/regulations, environment, and equipment (TREE)

7. Describe strategies to deal with issues related to communication, attention, and practice

8. Describe the Special Olympics and the following key aspects of the program: divisioning, Unified Sports, Motor Activities Training Program, and Young Athletes

Kasey is someone everyone just loves the minute they see her. No one is sure if it's her smile, how hard she tries, or the fact that she stands just under 5 feet tall. Kasey has Down syndrome, which among the many attributes includes an intellectual disability. Kasey cannot read above a kindergarten level, and she gets confused and a little anxious when there are lots of people around and lots of people talking. However, she is in middle school, and she is on the lowest level volleyball team (there are so many girls who want to play volleyball that they have five teams divided by skill level). Kasey loves going to practice, and you can see she really tries her best. She is really well liked by her peers and coaches (her head coach also is one of the school's physical education teachers), which is kind of amazing given that she cannot serve a ball over the net or do any of the passes unless the ball is gently tossed to her from a few feet away. But Kasey and her teammates don't seem to mind. Kasey's teammates are great with her. Kasey often doesn't fully understand what the coach is saying or what she wants the players to do, so Kasey's peers repeat directions and sometimes add extra demonstrations or assistance. Kasey also loses focus easily and sometimes just sits down to rest, but her peers are great at coaxing her back to practice. Kasey also loves to talk to her teammates, even though they have a difficult time understanding her.

Alejandro also is a middle school student with intellectual disabilities, but no one is quite sure what caused his intellectual disability. Unlike Kasey, Alejandro is very athletic and physically fit, and he can do many of the skills his peers can do in physical education. His biggest problem is his behaviors—he gets distracted and off task really easily, and unlike Kasey, gentle reminders from his peers often do not work. Sometimes, he gets really silly and just starts singing, talking loudly to peers, or even gets up and starts running, all while his physical education teacher is trying to give directions. His physical education teacher knows he is not doing these things to be disrespectful to her; he just seems to get full of himself and cannot control his impulses to do something. Alejandro's peers are pretty good about not getting too distracted by him, and they try to get him to sit down and listen. Still, when Alejandro gets going, it is difficult not to lose focus and look at him.

As a physical educator, you may have encountered students with intellectual disabilities in your classroom. There are approximately 447,000 students with intellectual disabilities receiving special education services in the United States (U.S. Department of Education, 2013). Students with intellectual disabilities are often fully included in the classroom setting, and research has demonstrated high success rates engaging students with intellectual disabilities in physical education classes. The purpose of this chapter is to present information about intellectual disabilities. The chapter begins with a definition of intellectual disabilities and common characteristics of individuals with intellectual disabilities. This will be followed by a review of teaching strategies to help students with intellectual disabilities be successful in general physical education. The chapter concludes with information about Special Olympics, a sports program designed specifically for children and adults with intellectual disabilities.

WHAT ARE INTELLECTUAL DISABILITIES?

Determining who has an intellectual disability requires diagnostic cognitive testing by qualified personnel, such as the school psychologist. Most students are diagnosed with an intellectual disability after the age of 5 but will be considered developmentally delayed or "at risk" prior to an official diagnosis. Public schools use the definition provided by the Individuals with Disabilities Education Improvement Act (IDEA) of 2004 (PL 108-446). According to IDEA 2004, intellectually disability is defined as "significantly sub-average general intellectual functioning, existing concurrently with deficits in adaptive behavior and manifested during the developmental period, that adversely affects a child's educational performance" (34 CFR § 300.8[c][6]). Intellectual disability is also defined slightly differently according to the American Association

on Intellectual and Developmental Disabilities (AAIDD; 2010). While the IDEA definition focuses on educational performance, the AAIDD definition tends to put more focus on adaptive behavior (e.g., social skills, communication skills, life skills): "Intellectual Disabilities is a disability characterized by significant limitations in both intellectual functioning and in adaptive behavior as expressed in conceptual, social, and practical adaptive skills. This disability originates before the age of 18" (AAIDD, 2010, p. 1).

The following details the two key concepts within the definition of intellectual disabilities: intellectual functioning and adaptive behavior. Recall that to qualify as a child with an intellectual disability, the child must have significant impairments in both intellectual functioning and adaptive behavior.

Intellectual functioning (intelligence) refers to general mental capability. It involves the ability to reason, plan, solve problems, think abstractly, comprehend complex ideas, learn quickly, and learn from experiences (AAIDD, 2010). An individual will have a range of intelligence depending on his or her experience, general aptitude, and desire to learn certain subjects. However, to qualify for services, students with disabilities must display "subaverage" intellectual functioning, as measured by IQ scores.

IQ scores obtained from standardized tests are used to quantify intelligence. Average IQ is 100 with a standard deviation of 15. Standard deviation (*SD*) is a statistic used to describe the degree to which an individual's score varies from the average or mean score. Two *SD*s above or below 100 (+/–30 IQ points, or 70–130) marks the range of typical intelligence. An IQ of 130 or higher (+2 *SD* above the average of 100) represents a child who would be classified as a "genius." An IQ of 70 or lower (–2 *SD* below the average of 100) would represent a child who would be classified as having an intellectual disability (Beirne-Smith, Patton, & Hill, 2015). Note that due to measurement error, a child might still be considered as having an intellectual disability with an IQ as high as 75 (AAIDD, 2010).

To understand the typical bell curve, consider how "most" individuals reason and solve problems. Most (approximately 95%) individuals function quite well through the day and are able to handle a range of complex issues encountered. However, a smaller percentage (approximately 2.5%) will fall below the mean IQ such that when attempting certain tasks, their ability to reason or conceptualize is significantly impaired. Historically, IQ was the mechanism used to classify various levels of

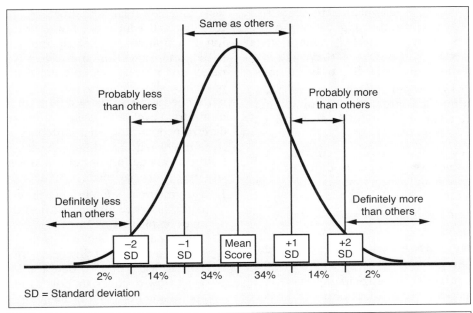

IQ	Standard deviation	Label
55–70	2–3	Mild intellectual disability
40–55	3–4	Moderate intellectual disability
25–40	4–5	Severe intellectual disability
Below 25	5+	Profound intellectual disability

Figure 8.1. Typical bell curve. (From Dunn, W. [n.d.]. *The bell curve: The normal distribution.* Retrieved from http://classes.kumc.edu/sah/resources/sensory_processing/learning_opportunities/sensory_profile/bell_curve .htm; adapted by permission.)

severity in children with intellectual disabilities (using the outdated term *mental retardation*). The following shows how IQ and *SD* were used, as illustrated in Figure 8.1:

The number (e.g., 75) is not as indicative of ability as are behavior attributes. Adaptive behavior refers to conceptual, social, and practical skills that people have learned so they can function in their everyday lives. Significant limitations in adaptive behavior affect a person's daily life and the ability to respond to a particular situation or to the environment. Similar to IQ, limitations in adaptive behavior are determined by using standardized tests that are normed on the general population, such as the Vineland Adaptive Behavior Scale. Significant limitations in adaptive behavior are defined as performance that is two *SD*s below the mean on either one of the three types of adaptive behavior (conceptual, social, or practical) or on a composite score of adaptive behavior score (AAIDD, 2010). Table 8.1 gives specific examples of adaptive behaviors.

Within the context of significant impairments in IQ and adaptive behavior, the AAIDD (2010)

Table 8.1. Adaptive behavior examples

Conceptual skills	Practical skills	Social skills
1. Using receptive and expressive language 2. Reading and writing 3. Understanding money concepts 4. Self-direction	1. Engaging in personal activities of daily living (ADL; e.g., eating, dressing, mobility, toileting) 2. Engaging in instrumental ADL (e.g., preparing meals, taking medication, using the telephone, managing money, using transportation, doing housekeeping activities) 3. Using occupational skills 4. Maintaining a safe environment	1. Interpersonal 2. Responsibility 3. Self-esteem 4. Gullibility 5. Naïveté 6. Following rules and obeying laws 7. Avoiding victimization

definition and classification manual presents five assumptions essential to the application of the definition. These assumptions help practitioners consider the larger environment as they take into account actual impairments leading to limitations:

1. Limitations in present functioning must be considered within the context of community environments typical of the individual's peers and culture.

2. Valid assessment considers cultural and linguistic diversity as well as differences in communication and sensory, motor, and behavioral factors.

3. Within an individual, limitations often exist with strengths.

4. An important purpose of describing limitations is to develop a profile of needed supports.

5. With appropriate personalized supports over a sustained period, the life functioning of the person with intellectual disabilities generally will improve.

Levels of Support

Because measurements of IQ do not provide useful information for families and educators to determine strengths and weaknesses, an appropriate educational plan, or how much support a child would need to be successful in various educational and community settings, AAIDD recommends a different model based on "levels of intensity of supports." Supports are resources and individual strategies needed by individuals with intellectual disabilities to facilitate development, education, interests, and personal well-being (AAIDD, 2010). Supports can be provided by a variety of individuals such as parents, friends, teachers, therapists, and doctors. Natural supports (i.e., those that occur naturally in a particular setting) should be used whenever possible. For example, a teenager wants to work out at a local gym. Parents and teachers can take the child to the gym and teach him how to use the equipment. However, most gyms have paid personal trainers who can help this child just as they would help anyone else who wants to learn how to use the weights and cardio equipment. Using the personal trainer would provide a more natural and "typical" type of support compared with having a parent or teacher help the child.

The supports approach evaluates the specific needs of the individual and then suggests strategies, services, and supports that will optimize individual functioning. AAIDD (2010) recommends that an individual's need for supports be analyzed in at least nine key areas including human development, teaching and education, home living, community living, employment, health and safety, behavior, social, and protection and advocacy. To illustrate, under community living, recreation facilities and programs should be examined to determine supports needed by an individual with an intellectual disability. Level of intensity of support can then be determined, noting that different recreation settings might require different levels of support. The following are definitions of the four levels of intensity of support outlined by AAIDD (2010):

1. *Intermittent:* Supports are provided on an *episodic* (as needed) basis. Intermittent supports may be of high or low intensity. For example, the teenager highlighted in the earlier example who wants to go to the local gym may need support to learn how to take the local bus to the gym, how to check in, how to access the locker room, and how to use the equipment. But once this child has mastered these tasks independently (or with natural supports from staff at the gym), then no further support is needed.

2. *Limited:* Supports occur in some dimensions regularly *for a short period of time.* Time is limited but not of an intermittent nature. This level of support may require fewer staff members and cost less than more intense levels. Continuing with the previous example, another child may need longer periods of support to master accessing and using the gym. This might mean that once a week, a parent or peer buddy goes on the bus with the child to remind him how to pay and which stop to exit at. Unlike the first child who was able to master bus riding after just a few sessions with a peer buddy, this child may need support for several weeks or months. However, like the first child, this child can utilize natural supports at the gym.

3. *Extensive:* Supports are characterized by *ongoing, regular involvement* (daily) in at least some environments (e.g., work or home) and are *not time limited.* Another child with a more significant intellectual disability might need a peer buddy with him or her on the bus and in the gym. This child most likely will never be able to be independent on a bus or utilize the personal trainers at the gym. However, with extensive support of a peer buddy or family member, this child can still take advantage of all the benefits of the gym, perhaps going more slowly and for shorter periods on a stationary bike rather than a treadmill or elliptical machine and using simple hand weights rather than machines.

4. *Pervasive:* Supports are characterized by their *constancy and high intensity.* Supports are provided in several environments and are potentially life-sustaining in nature. More staff members are needed and with more intrusive support. Children who need pervasive support would most likely not be able to access the gym like their peers. However, a peer buddy, parent, or nurse could bring this child to the gym to listen to the sounds and watch others working out.

CAUSES OF INTELLECTUAL DISABILITIES

Intellectual disability is mostly idiopathic (i.e., no known cause) in nature and may be a result of many factors, including prematurity, anoxia during the birth process, poor maternal nutrition, drug abuse during pregnancy, and/or exposure to certain environmental factors (Beirne-Smith et al., 2015; see Percy, 2007, for a detailed review of biological and environmental factors associated with intellectual disabilities). However, research (Shapiro & Batshaw, 2013) suggests mild intellectual disabilities are more likely linked with racial, social, and familial factors, whereas severe intellectual disabilities are more likely linked with biological/genetic factors.

AAIDD (2010) adopted a multifactorial approach when determining the cause of an intellectual disability. There are two key points to the multifactorial approach. First are the kinds of causal factors that contribute to intellectual disabilities, which the AAIDD divided into the following four categories: biological, social, behavioral, and educational (see Figure 8.2). The second key point when examining cause is timing of the occurrence of the casual factors. AAIDD divided timing into three periods of development: prenatal (prior to birth), perinatal (around the time of birth), and postnatal (after birth). If you link causal factors with timing, it is easy to recognize how specific factors may affect child development. For example, if a woman has poor nutrition and lack of access to prenatal care (biological and social factors, respectively), fetal development is at risk. If a child has limited caregiver interaction and decreased stimulation after birth (postnatal), the child is at risk for difficulties developing certain skills such as language.

Chromosomal Abnormalities

Chromosomal abnormalities are the leading cause of intellectual disability. Abnormalities can be inherited and are always congenital. There is a wide array of chromosomal abnormalities that cause any range of intellectual disabilities, and the two most common chromosomal abnormalities are fragile X syndrome and Down syndrome.

Fragile X Syndrome

Fragile X is a genetic (i.e., inherited) condition. It is caused by a change or mutation in the genetic information on the X chromosome (X chromosome appears to be broken or dangling; see Figure 8.3). The gene FMR1 (fragile X mental retardation 1), which we all have, is altered in a way that affects neurological development. How fragile X is passed down from parents and grandparents is very complex, but in general the longer the family history of fragile X, the more severe the condition. Because boys have only one X chromosome (boys have X and Y chromosomes), boys with fragile X will display all the characteristics associated with fragile X. Because girls have two X chromosomes, the normal X chromosome counteracts the damaged X chromosome. As a result, girls do not display the characteristics of fragile X but can be carriers. Fragile X is generally considered the most common inherited form of intellectual disability (0.05–1/1000 births) and accounts for as much as 10% of population of individuals with intellectual disabilities. Fragile X also is associated with autism and learning disabilities (Mazzocco & Holden, 2007).

Fragile X syndrome does not cause any gross, physical anomalies. However, there are certain *physical characteristics* associated with the syndrome, including large ears; long, narrow face; prominent forehead; slightly larger head (these

- *Biological factors* such as genetic (e.g., Down syndrome, fragile X) or nutritional (e.g., PKU) disorders

- *Social factors* related to social and family interactions, such as child stimulation and adult responsiveness

- *Behavioral factors* related to harmful behaviors, such as maternal substance abuse that leads to fetal alcohol syndrome (FAS)

- *Educational factors* related to the availability of family and educational supports that promote mental development and increase adaptive skills

Figure 8.2. Causal factors related to intellectual disability. (Key: PKU, phenylketonuria.)

Figure 8.3. Karyotype of fragile X syndrome.

children have slightly larger brains than typically developing children); and larger testicles. In addition, many children with fragile X will have a high palate (roof of mouth), heart murmur (mitral valve prolapse), extreme flexibility (loose connective tissue), visual problems (variety of problems), low muscle tone (but not as significant as children with Down syndrome), and motor tics (Weber, 2000).

Regarding *cognitive development*, children with fragile X will display a wide range of cognitive abilities ranging from typical IQ to learning disabilities to mild intellectual disabilities to severe intellectual disabilities and autism. Severity is believed to be determined by inherited history (i.e., number of generations through which the syndrome has been passed). Some children with fragile X have cognitive strengths beyond their IQ expectations such as memory about special subjects (e.g., cars, dogs). Sensory issues also are associated with fragile X. Some children with fragile X might be extra sensitive to touch, might not like the way certain clothes feel, and might not like being touched. Sound sensitivity and auditory processing difficulty also are associated with fragile X, and these children may not be able to process auditory cues and may be distracted by sounds in the environment. Finally, some of these children will be easily overwhelmed by visual information, confused or upset by flashing lights, or uncomfortable in settings where there is a lot of movement (Mazzocco & Holden, 2007).

Unique behaviors also are common in children with fragile X, especially those toward the autism spectrum. Poor eye contact is the most notable characteristic of fragile X, and in some cases, it is almost impossible to get a child with fragile X to look another person eye-to-eye. Other behaviors include hand flapping, stiffening the body, tantrums, difficulty relating to others, perseveration (difficulty stopping once an activity is started), hyperactivity, short attention span, anxiety, and hypervigilance (i.e., intense interest in events, such as knowing all names of children in class and who is absent). On a positive note, children with fragile X tend to be very social and friendly, and they have excellent imitation skills. They also model many behaviors they see (both positive and appropriate as well as negative and inappropriate).

Regarding *motor development*, children with fragile X tend to be stronger in fine rather than gross motor skills. Early fine and gross motor milestones may be slightly delayed, but these children tend to catch up and have relatively typical fine and gross motor skills. Children with more severe intellectual disabilities or autism tend to have greater gross motor delays. In addition, lack of opportunity due to behaviors and limited play/sport opportunities can contribute to motor delays (Weber, 2000).

Down Syndrome

Down syndrome, also known as trisomy 21, is a genetic mutation that occurs randomly and can also be related to the mother's age. Instead of 46 chromosomes (23 pairs), the child has 47 chromosomes, with the extra chromosome in the 21st pair of chromosomes (thus the name trisomy 21). The extra chromosome causes a genetic imbalance that which alters typical development, thus children with Down syndrome often share similar facial, morphologic, and intellectual attributes (Lovering & Percy, 2007).

Down syndrome comes in three genetic forms: nondisjunction, translocation, and mosaicism. The most common type is nondisjunction, which results in a triplication of the 21st chromosome (see Figure 8.4). The exact cause of the extra 21st chromosome is unknown. Down syndrome occurs in approximately 1/600–1/700 live births (about 15,000 per year), and it is the most common chromosomal abnormality that allows embryonic development (Roizen, 2013). Increasing maternal age is associated with increased incidence of Down syndrome:

- 1/1,500 at age 20
- 1/800 at age 30
- 1/100 at age 40
- 1/10 at age 50

Attributes Associated with Down Syndrome

Individuals with Down syndrome display a unique array of characteristics with the severity of these characteristics varying from child to child. The actual genetic condition, however, lends itself to similar issues across the population (Lovering & Percy, 2007; Roizen, 2013).

Low muscle tone (hypotonia)/joint laxity is seen to some extent in all children with Down syndrome. Signs and symptoms of hypotonia include atypical joint laxity, considerable muscular flexibility, and problems related to balance and strength, especially during the first year of development. Hypotonia can cause issues related to strength, coordination, and postural control.

Unique facial features are another very noticeable attribute found in all children with Down syndrome. The nasal bridge in the nose is flatter and smaller, which may affect breathing, causing children to breathe through the mouth. The eyes appear to slant and also have small fold of skin at the inner corner, called an epicanthal fold. The mouth

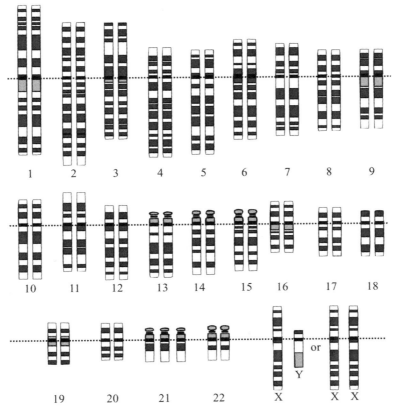

Figure 8.4. Karotype showing trisomy 21.

appears small, and the roof of mouth may be shallow. It is not uncommon to see children with their tongue out of their mouth, referred to as protruding tongue. Teeth may come in late and in unusual order and tend to be smaller than normal, and the ears may fold over and be set slightly lower on the head. Ear passages also may be small, causing conductive hearing loss. Physical growth is atypically slow and often stops early. As a result, individuals with Down syndrome tend to be short, often only reaching a maximum height of 5 feet or lower.

Sensory impairments are common in children with Down syndrome. There are many types of vision problems associated with Down syndrome such as cataracts, strabismus, and nystagmus as well as refractive errors, with nearsightedness being the most common. Many children with Down syndrome will wear glasses to accommodate nearsightedness. The most common hearing problem associated with Down syndrome is bilateral conductive hearing loss (25–50 dB), which can be accommodated with hearing aids. Children with Down syndrome also display kinesthesis problems such as having difficulty discriminating tactual input and copying movements.

Cardiac problems are also common in children with Down syndrome, and as many as 40%–50% of children with Down syndrome are born with some type of heart problem. In fact, cardiac problems are the major cause of the high mortality rate of infants and children with Down syndrome. Common cardiac defects are ventricular septal defects (i.e., defect in the wall of the septum) between the right and left ventricles. Heart conditions are usually treated early in life with surgery or medication, and once corrected, there should be no other cardiac problems or restrictions.

Atlantoaxial instability (AAI) is another characteristic of Down syndrome and one that physical educators should be keenly aware of. AAI is an increase in the laxity of the transverse ligaments between the atlas and axis (C1–C2) of the cervical vertebrae. Twelve percent to 20% of children with Down syndrome have "asymptomatic AAI," and 1%–2% have the more dangerous "symptomatic AA subluxation." Symptoms of AA subluxation include hyperreflexia (i.e., reflexes are more sensitive to stimulation), muscle weakness, and difficulty walking. Diagnostic x-rays can detect AA subluxation, and surgery can repair the subluxation. Children with AA subluxation who have not had surgery should not participate in activities that hyperflex or put pressure on the neck (e.g., tumbling, football).

Perhaps the most significant issue for children with Down syndrome are the fundamental motor delays that appear very early in life (Block, 1991). Although children with Down syndrome demonstrate extreme motor delays, they tend to follow the typical course of development. Delays are due in large part to hypotonia, joint/ligamentous laxity, and hyperreflexia.

Some of the first notable differences seen in children with Down syndrome are delays in the emergence and integration of reflexes and automatic movement patterns. These delays are present in the majority of children with Down syndrome. For example, most infants will walk between 9 and 13 months of age; however, children with Down syndrome are considered "late onset upright movers" and will often not walk independently until 24 months (Latash, 1992). Research has suggested that poor trunk stability, strength, and potentially motivation may be primary limiters to upright locomotion. Late onset of upright locomotion can significantly delay other gross and fine motor skills such as reaching, grasping, jumping, and running (Wang & Ju, 2002).

Early intervention can improve motor development in infants and reduce inevitable delays. However, as children with Down syndrome reach elementary age, they tend to fall further behind their same-age peers. Balance issues begin to play a bigger role in motor delays in elementary school, and impairments in physical fitness (including obesity) become more apparent, which can further affect motor development. As the child with Down syndrome reaches adolescence, there is usually some improvement in muscle tone, strength, and stability. This is particularly true if the child receives quality physical education and participates in community sports and recreation programs.

COMMON CHARACTERISTICS OF INTELLECTUAL DISABILITIES

Intellectual disability as a category encompasses a wide variety of attributes. As previously mentioned, the category itself includes characteristics related to intellect and behavior. Children with intellectual disabilities will most likely have delays or impairments in one or more of the following areas compared with typically developing peers: cognition, gross and fine motor skills, physical fitness, social skills, communication, and behaviors. The extent of the delays will vary based on many factors, including the severity and nature of the intellectual disability (biological factors tend to lead to great impairments),

comorbidity of sensory and/or physical impairments, health problems, availability and quality of services, and support by parents, the school, and the community (Beirne-Smith et al., 2015).

There has been a debate on whether children with intellectual disabilities are following a typical but delayed pattern of development compared with their typically developing peers (Beirne-Smith et al., 2015). Those who believe in typical but delayed development argue that children with intellectual disabilities behave similarly to those who have a similar mental age, such that a 16-year-old child with a mental age equivalent to a 5-year-old would demonstrate cognitive, social, and behavioral skills similar to a typically developing 5-year-old. Proponents of this delay model would suggest that teaching approaches should be similar to those used with typically developing children of the same mental age but with chronological age–appropriate materials.

For example, a typically developing 5-year-old most likely will not be able to read but should be able to identify letters and some words. Besides sight words, children at this age are encouraged to sound out first letters of words in order to decode the word (e.g., *d* for dog). A 16-year-old who functions like a 5-year-old would most likely not be able to read the name of the weight machine (e.g., chest press); however, he or she could be taught to identify key sight words (e.g., press) and to match the words on a workout sheet with the name on the machine. In addition, this student can be encouraged to sound out the first letters of the name on the machine in an effort to decode and read the word (e.g., *ch* for *chest*, *sh* for *shoulder*).

In contrast, others believe children with intellectual disabilities are qualitatively different from peers without intellectual disabilities in how they process information, interact with peers, and behave (Beirne-Smith et al., 2015). In this view, implications for teaching suggest unique methods of instruction to match the unique impairments and strengths of the child with intellectual disabilities. For example, using the earlier example of the 16-year-old who is going to the local gym to work out, he or she may not be able to visually process written words in the same way as children without intellectual disabilities. Helping this child understand which machine to use might require looking at a series of pictures of the various workout machines to know which machine to use next.

Cognitive Traits

Cognition requires the ability to take in, process, translate, and make meaning of information. As an individual sees, hears, or feels "information," he or she has to "make sense of" the information such that he or she can use it. Having an intellectual disability suggests that these individuals struggle to make sense of what they may see, hear, or feel or the rate at which they can process the information is delayed. The degree to which one struggles is very dependent on the individual and his or her experience.

The complexity of cognition has been studied extensively over the years. *Executive function* is a global term used to describe a set of core skills humans need to engage. Diamond and Taylor (1996) argue that executive function is a result of three different skills developed during childhood and adolescence: 1) inhibitory control, 2) working memory, and 3) cognitive flexibility. Executive function is linked to the development of the prefrontal cortex, the area of the brain that is responsible for planning complex cognitive behavior and decision making.

Inhibitory control is defined as the ability to resist the desire to do one thing and instead choose another more appropriate action. For example, a student may have a strong desire for a particular piece of equipment. Rather than simply taking the equipment from another student, he or she may ask if they can take turns using the piece of equipment. Working memory (similar to short-term memory) is the ability to use memory in a functional manner. Also referred to as "metacognition," working memory allows individuals to use their memory skills to reflect on what they are currently learning and "see connections" with prior knowledge.

Diamond (2013) argues that working memory is essential to creativity. Working memory can be seen in physical education when learning about concepts such as body awareness and spatial awareness. Working memory skills can also be seen when someone is asked to be "strategic" in a game setting. The last concept in executive function is cognitive flexibility. Cognitive flexibility is needed for problem-solving skills and helps individuals traverse through situations in which empathy and reflection may be needed.

Executive function as a skill can be used to conceptualize intellectual "disability." Certain traits are paramount in intellectual disabilities. For example, students with intellectual disabilities are similar to typically developing peers but learn much more slowly. Students with intellectual disabilities may exhibit shorter attention spans, be partially fixated on routines or sameness, struggle to understand abstract concepts, and demonstrate poor problem-solving skills. If one considers these traits within executive function, intellectual disabilities can be viewed as a lack of inhibitory control, working memory, and/or cognitive flexibility that therefore impedes one's ability to engage in learning and intentional behavior.

Motor and Physical Fitness Traits

Motor and physical fitness traits can vary greatly depending on the individual, secondary motor impairments (e.g., a child with intellectual disabilities who also has cerebral palsy), movement experiences, and the support/encouragement to be physically active by family and physical education teachers. Generally speaking, individuals with intellectual disabilities will score below their same-age peers without disabilities in motor and physical fitness measures. Children with more severe intellectual disabilities tend to have more significant impairments in most motor and fitness areas compared with those with more mild intellectual disabilities (e.g., Skowronski, Horvat, Nocera, Roswal, & Croce, 2009). Severe intellectual disabilities are more typically caused by biological factors (e.g., having a chromosomal disorder), which often result in a greater likelihood of having secondary sensory and/or physical impairments.

Significant differences between individuals with and without intellectual disabilities have been found in overall physical activity (Frey, Stanish, & Temple, 2008), running (e.g., Frey, McCubbin, Hannigan-Downs, Kasser, & Skaggs, 1999; Pitetti & Fernhall, 2004), physical activity (e.g., Faison-Hodge & Porretta, 2004; Foley, 2006), strength (e.g., Pitetti & Yarmer, 2002), body composition (e.g., Pitetti, Yarmer, & Fernhall, 2001), fundamental motor patterns (Rintala & Loovis, 2013), and balance and coordination (Lahtinen, Rintala, & Malin, 2007). For example, Anardag, Arikan, Yilmaz, and Konukman (2013) found significant differences between women with and without intellectual disabilities in body mass index, muscular endurance, maximum walking distance, peak VO2, balance, flexibility, and power. Similarly, Barnes, Howie, McDermott, and Mann (2013) found most participants with intellectual disabilities were overweight or obese and with physical activity levels below national averages. However, they also found that those who said they were more active (e.g., played basketball with friends in the evening) had a lower body mass index. It interesting to note that even athletes with intellectual disabilities (i.e., those who competed with the International Sports Federation for Persons with Intellectual Disability) showed lower cardiovascular capacity and strength compared with age-matched physical education majors, although there were no differences in other measures such as running speed, flexibility, and muscular endurance (van de Vliet et al., 2006). Deficits also are apparent in fine motor tasks. For example, Carmeli, Bar-Yossef, Ariav, Levy, and Liebermann (2008) found individuals with intellectual disabilities did not perform as well as their age-matched peers in three eye–hand coordination tests.

As stated previously, comparing same-age children with and without intellectual disabilities, one consistently finds that students with intellectual disabilities are well below their peers when it comes to cardiorespiratory ability (Barnes et al., 2013). Several theories have been posited regarding the difference. Pitetti et al. (2001) discovered that individuals with mild to moderate intellectual disabilities, including those with Down syndrome, have chronotrophic incompetence. Generally speaking, chronotrophic incompetence is the inability to reach maximum heart rate (defined as 220 beats/minute).

More important, research has found that exercise programs can improve cardiorespiratory endurance as well as other physical fitness measures (Barwick et al., 2012), even for those with more severe intellectual disabilities (Escobar, Sanders, Lawson, & Benitez, 2013). For example, combined exercise training (endurance and strength training) has significant positive effects on total cholesterol levels, aerobic capacity, muscle strength, and resting systolic blood pressure in adults with intellectual disabilities (Calders et al., 2011). Similarly, Frey et al. (1999) found trained runners with mild intellectual disabilities could achieve high levels of physical fitness that are comparable to individuals without intellectual disabilities.

Recommendations for Testing and Teaching

Several recommendations have been given regarding testing and improving cardiorespiratory endurance for individuals with intellectual disabilities. Due to the demands of cardiorespiratory testing, the following recommendations are given to ensure accurate results. When giving field-based tests, teachers should make sure the student is properly motivated and understands specific testing procedures such as "do your best" or "keep a good pace." Therefore, teachers may consider pairing these students with a typically developing peer to help keep a steady pace and provide encouragement.

When planning for activities to improve cardiorespiratory endurance, it is important to consider issues that may affect a student's desire to perform aerobic activities. Fitness is a conceptual term. Most individuals understand that being "fit"

Table 8.2. Recommended fitness programming modifications

Cardiorespiratory	Muscular strength
Standard formulas for improving aerobic endurance do not always apply.	Early sessions should focus on proper form, safety, and identifying proper machines.
Start slowly (3–5 minutes of aerobic exercise) to build confidence and tolerance.	Machines are often a better choice for safety than free weights.
Build in reinforcements for success.	Use pictures to help individuals learn how to use machines.
Music and partnerships can be reinforcing.	Teach weightlifting etiquette.
Vary training modalities (e.g., walking, stationary bike, treadmill).	Provide verbal encouragement and, when necessary, external rewards.
Treadmills and stair climbers may challenge balance; use cautiously.	

means aerobic endurance, muscular endurance, and flexibility. The desire to be fit requires commitment and perseverance. Collectively, these concepts require a high degree of executive function. To improve desire and adherence to exercise for students with intellectual disabilities, several modifications can be employed. Table 8.2 outlines generally recommended modifications for cardiorespiratory programming.

Social/Behavior Traits

It is difficult to separate social and behavioral traits in some individuals with intellectual disabilities. As stated previously, although students with intellectual disabilities will develop similarly to their typically developing peers, the rate of development, particularly social/emotional development, may be significantly delayed. Common traits observed include emotional immaturity, trouble with group activities, being overly aggressive or passive, and difficulty developing friendships with typically developing peers (the latter is not necessarily the result of intellectual disabilities but rather of social acceptance). Social development is arguably one of the more challenging issues teachers may face in the classroom. Disruptive behaviors such as acting out, inappropriate touching, or passive "I can't" gestures (e.g., refusal to move) can be difficult to manage in a classroom setting.

It could be argued that behavior is a direct result of lack of understanding and inappropriate expectations. Rather than focus on behavior as a teaching and learning issue, behavior can be best viewed from the perspective of understanding. Snell, Martin, and Orelove (1996) suggest that aberrant behavior may be a product of need rather than simple disobedience. The authors suggest that behavior communicates either social-communicative or sensory functions. These disruptive or destructive behaviors are more than a simple act of disobedience but rather the inability to understand what is required or the lack of skills to effectively participate. For example, low expectation, ignoring rather than expecting, or not teaching can easily cause behavior issues. When these types of teaching behaviors are combined with disability attributes (e.g., poor inhibitory control, and minimal selective attention), it is easy to see how behavior challenges can occur.

Meaningful Behavior Management Techniques

Behavior management is best when designed to be easy to apply by a variety of team members and measured across settings. The techniques used should work to not only decrease or eliminate unwanted behaviors but also increase desired behaviors that facilitate a positive teaching and learning environment. Chapter 19 features extensive coverage of behavior management strategies, including the following commonly used techniques:

- Premack principle
- Token economies
- Contingency contracts
- Positive behavior support

For example, a teacher may wish to decrease the number of off-task behaviors demonstrated by a student with intellectual disabilities and consequently increase the on-task time. Therefore, the chosen behavior management strategy should focus on the antecedents that trigger on- versus off-task behavior as well as consequences for off-task behavior and rewards for on-task behaviors. Generally speaking, teachers should consider the following before adopting a single inclusive technique:

- Size of class
- Teaching style (e.g., command versus exploratory)
- Frequency of student–teacher interaction
- Family involvement
- Amount of teaching time

TEACHING PHYSICAL EDUCATION TO STUDENTS WITH INTELLECTUAL DISABILITIES

Generally speaking, students with intellectual disabilities can be very successful in an inclusive physical education setting. In many situations, the teacher will not have to make modifications for students with intellectual disabilities; however, teachers must be aware that like many of their peers without disabilities, there will be activities that require minor to significant modifications to facilitate success.

In this section, we will discuss teaching alternatives to maximize learning. The modification strategies discussed are similar and can be considered a variation on the same theme. Depending on your teaching style and curriculum, you may be more drawn to one strategy but all can be equally effective. The practice of modification follows three basic principles: 1) who you are teaching, 2) what you are teaching, and 3) where you are teaching (also referred to as person, task, and environment). These basic tenets of modification hold true to almost every teaching situation and can be considered good overall teaching practices.

General Approaches

Whereas all students benefit from teaching modifications (i.e., teaching to the individual), there are certain general principles that apply to students with intellectual disabilities (Auxter, Pyfer, Zittel, & Roth, 2010). Table 8.3 summarizes these general principles, organized around a framework of who, what, and where.

Specific Instructional Modifications

Table 8.3 lists general modifications that can be easily applied in physical education environments and are generally considered good teaching practices. However, there will be times when more strategic and involved instructional modifications will have to be employed. In the following section, three specific instructional modifications will be described: level teaching; simplify, refine, extend, apply; and teaching style, rules/regulations, environment, and equipment.

Level Teaching

Level teaching takes the concept of a "game" and considers the task, person, and environment to create different levels of the game. For example, a middle school teacher is planning on a volleyball unit as part of her lead-up to a games series. After 2 weeks of practicing skills, she concludes with a week of game play. She has several students whose skills levels vary, including three students with intellectual disabilities who will need some assistance as well. To accommodate for students' varying abilities, the teacher decides to set up three volleyball courts.

Table 8.3. General modifications

Communication (who)	Practice (what)	Curriculum (who)	Environment (where)
Use shorter sentences. Shorten instructional cues. Use gestures and demonstrations to supplement verbal cues. Repeat directions and have the student repeat directions back to you. Use more demonstrations and provide physical assistance. Give more feedback after practice trials. Provide praise often and be specific. Teach age-appropriate skills.	Give extra practice trials. Teach students how to rehearse and practice. Expect students to take more time to master skills. Gear activities, equipment, and interactions to the student's chronological age rather than his or her mental age. Allow choices in *what* is to be done, *when* it is to be completed, *where* the activity will take place, and *with whom* the child participates. Activities need to be perceived as fun. Activities may need to be shortened to reduce problems with attention span. Promote active participation (e.g., multiple turns, little downtime, no elimination games).	General education curriculum may need adjustments such as reduced number of objectives to be mastered. If student is severely delayed, may need to develop an alternative physical education curriculum with different goals and objectives. Older students with intellectual disabilities need to focus on lifetime leisure activities. Activities may need to provide a greater degree of early success to encourage adherence.	Environment should be structured and visually appealing. Reduce playing area to reduce distractions. Anticipate behavior problems, and plan to structure environment to promote appropriate behaviors and deal with behavior problems.

The first court (Level 1) has the following task and environmental modifications:

- No net but rather a set of cones to designate opposing sides
- Poly spots to designate individual court placement
- Student choice of "volleyball" (e.g., beach ball, volleyball trainer)
- Student can take as many hits as needed to get the ball over the cones.
- Serve can be thrown or hit over the cones.

The second court (Level 2) refines Level 1 and increases the difficulty. This particular court has the following task and environmental modifications:

- Net is either regulation height or slightly lower.
- Spot for server
- Use of regulation volleyball or options for two different balls
- Four hits versus three
- Serve can be under- or overhand; server can also have three attempts to get ball over net.

The third court (Level 3) mimics the game of volleyball. Students can choose selected modifications (as needed) to help with game play, but the assumption is that students at this level have the skills needed to play a more traditional game. Modifications could include the following:

- Two service attempts
- Four versus three hits over the net
- Ball goes over the net regardless of type of hit

Level teaching has several advantages. Students can select their level of play (which encourages responsibility) but can also be challenged to move up a level or be asked to move "down" a level in order to maximize their skill. The inclusion of all ability levels is facilitated. Instead of working around one or two students, the teacher encourages practice to maximize skill. And finally, level teaching can be practiced as part of a student's daily activities such as station work.

Simplify, Refine, Extend, and Apply

When considering any activity, there are multiple ways it can be simplified. The concept of simplify, refine, extend, and apply (SREA) applies to any activity that is being considered. Simplify suggests bringing the task down to its most simple level. For example, throwing is simply a grasp and release skill. For each step, the teacher is adding on to the most simple step to make the task either more applicable or more like how it is typically performed. To apply this concept, the teacher must consider the following:

- What is being done (i.e., the task)?
- Who is doing the task (i.e., the person)?
- Where is the task being performed (i.e., the environment)?

The task has multiple components, such as the equipment being used, the physical elements of the task itself, and the product of the task (e.g., target, distance). Regarding the environment, distractions (e.g., noise, music, equipment, being outside

Simplify	Refine
Task/equipment:	Task/equipment:
1. Bat or noodle with hand prints for hand placement	**Keep the same as simplify but add:*
2. Tee	1. Different sized bats some with hand placement
3. Foot prints next to tee for stance	2. Choice of balls, some baseball size "like"
4. Large, light weight ball for easier contact	
Environment:	Environment:
1. Secluded area (e.g., using mats to block distractions)	1. Have two areas set up, one with little distraction, the other open to gym.
Person:	Person:
1. Use a task card for activity completion.	1. No changes but work towards more independent work
2. Utilize peer-tutoring.	
3. Earn points/rewards for on-task behavior.	
Extend	**Apply**
Task/equipment:	Task/equipment:
1. Ball hanging from string	1. Choice of bats
2. Flat bat	2. Smaller balls
3. Tee options if needed	3. Tossed or pitched ball
Environment:	Environment:
1. Open to full gym	1. None
Person:	Person:
1. Use a task card for activity completion.	1. Earn points/rewards for on-task behavior.

Figure 8.5. Two-hand sidearm strike.

versus inside) that may affect performance or the student should also be taken into consideration. In this case, we consider both the teacher and the students. The teacher may have to modify his or her teaching style. The student may need to be paired (e.g., peer tutoring) or may need specific behavioral parameters placed on his or her performance. Many modifications can be made using this model!

For example, an elementary school teacher is teaching striking skills in his class. For the next week, he is focusing on the two-hand sidearm strike. This can be a challenging skill for all students but especially those that may struggle with eye–hand coordination, tracking, and laterality, as many students with intellectual disabilities do. Utilizing the SREA model, Figure 8.5 provides some options for modification.

TREE Framework

Developed by Dr. Peter Downs (http://theinclusion club.com), TREE, which stands for teaching style, rules/regulations, environment, and equipment, is a slightly different take on the level approach and the SREA model. Dr. Downs refers to these components as common parts of the environment that can be easily adapted to any teaching space. Teaching style could include methods or how much assistance a student requires. For example, the teacher could consider giving verbal as well as physical assistance to help a student complete a task.

Rules and regulations are aspects of the activity that often define a game or sport. Games and sports often have specific rules and regulations that give structure to the activity. Basketball is basketball because of the rules and regulations applied to the sport. But these can be easily adapted in a physical education class. For example, one could argue that a person can dribble even if he or she takes more than two steps in between bouncing the ball or that a three-point shot does not have to be from a specific distance.

Equipment and environment were reviewed in earlier examples but consider other elements such as surface (e.g., grass is harder to move on than a flat surface) or lighting. Equipment can change by size, color, or texture. Dr. Downs stresses that the TREE framework can be easily applied but must always keep the integrity of the activity in mind. Dr. Downs refers to this conundrum as the "balancing act." Teachers should strive to maintain activity quality such that the activity is challenging and reinforces skill development but at the same time does not purposely exclude those who may require modifications.

SPECIAL OLYMPICS

Special Olympics is an international sports program for children and adults with intellectual disabilities. The program includes year-round training and competition in a variety of Olympic-type sports (see Tables 8.4–8.6) with competition open to athletes ages 8 and older (with no age limit). The philosophy of Special Olympics is that individuals with intellectual disabilities receive appropriate instruction and encouragement, receive consistent training, and compete among those of *equal* abilities. As a result of participating in Special Olympics, athletes will grow physically, emotionally, and socially, which ultimately will lead to success in all aspects of the individual's life. Special Olympics grew out of a summer day camp for young people with intellectual disabilities that Eunice Kennedy Shriver established in her own backyard in Maryland. The goal was to learn what these children could do in sports and other activities—and not dwell on what they could not do. Her vision and drive for justice eventually grew into the Special Olympics movement. The first International Special Olympics Summer Games were held July 19–20, 1968, at Soldier Field in Chicago, Illinois. A thousand athletes with intellectual disabilities from 26 U.S. states

and Canada competed in track and field and swimming. From those first international games, there has been a steady growth in the number of athletes worldwide who participate in Special Olympics. The latest annual census shows Special Olympics has more than 4.2 million athletes representing more than 200 countries, competing in 70,000 competitions around the world.

SPECIAL OLYMPICS POLICY FOR DOWN SYNDROME ATHLETES

- Gymnastics, high jump, equestrian, football, cycling, swimming diving are *not allowed* in case of atlantoaxial instability

Table 8.4. Special Olympics summer sports

- Aquatics
- Athletics
- Badminton
- Basketball
- Bocce
- Bowling
- Cricket[a]
- Cycling
- Equestrian
- Football
- Golf
- Gymnastics (artistic and rhythmic)
- Judo[a]
- Kayaking
- Netball[a]
- Powerlifting
- Roller skating
- Sailing
- Softball
- Table tennis
- Tennis
- Volleyball
- Team handball

Source: Special Olympics (n.d.)
[a]May be national only.

Table 8.5. Special Olympics winter sports

- Alpine skiing
- Cross-country skiing
- Figure skating
- Floorball
- Floor hockey
- Snowboarding
- Snowshoeing
- Speed skating

Source: Special Olympics (n.d.)

Table 8.6. Prohibited Special Olympics sports

Prohibited sports and events
• Athletics: javelin, discus, hammer, pole vault, triple jump
• Aquatics: platform dive
• Gymnastics: trampoline
• Cross-country skiing: biathlon, ski jumping
• All martial arts sports except judo
• Other: rugby, shooting, fencing, archery

Source: Special Olympics (n.d.)

There are some unique aspects of Special Olympics that separates it from other traditional or disability sports programs. First, athletes are never charged fees to participate in Special Olympics activities. Second, sports opportunities are available for athletes of all ability levels from elite, world-class athletes with intellectual disabilities to those with more severe intellectual disabilities and limited motor and sports skills. Third, all athletes receive some type of award for participating in the program. Fourth, there is a random draw to advance to higher level competitions. For more information on Special Olympics, see Chapter 20.

Unique Special Olympics Programs

Unified Sports is a program that combines approximately equal numbers of individuals with intellectual disabilities (athletes) and without intellectual disabilities (partners) on the same sports teams for training and competition. All participants are of similar age and ability. Unified Sports is an important program because it expands sports opportunities for athletes and partners seeking new challenges. In addition, Unified Sports dramatically increases inclusion in the community by helping to break down barriers that have historically kept people apart. At the same time, Unified Sports provides a valuable sports opportunity to individuals who are not presently involved with Special Olympics or other sports programs (Special Olympics, Connecticut, n.d.). These opportunities often lead to improved sports skills, higher self-esteem, equal status with peers, and new friendships (Special Olympics, n.d.-c, Special Olympics, Connecticut, n.d.). Unified Sports has been designed with the flexibility to be implemented within Special Olympics programs (e.g., a Unified competition at a state or national game), in the community (e.g., Unified teams playing in regular community sports programs such as recreation softball and volleyball leagues), and in schools (e.g., Unified teams from one school playing against Unified teams from another high school; Special Olympics, n.d.-c).

Motor Activities Training Program (MATP) was designed by Special Olympics for athletes with severe intellectual disabilities who are unable to participate independently in official Special Olympics sports competitions due to limitations in motor and fitness skill and/or cognitive abilities (Special Olympics, n.d.). Often, MATP participants have secondary disabilities such as cerebral palsy or sensory impairments that make competing in traditional Special Olympics sports impossible without physical assistance or adapted equipment. For example, an athlete might not have the strength or motor control to shoot a basketball to a regulation basket, kick a soccer ball with enough force to get it into the goal, or walk or run in a race without assistance. Similarly, MATP athletes have cognitive impairments that make it impossible to follow rules of the sports without support.

This is what makes MATP unique to Special Olympics and other sports organizations. In MATP, athletes are allowed to participate with physical assistance and/or adapted equipment, and rules are modified to ensure success. Although added support and modifications to equipment and rules ensure success for each MATP athlete, such unique modifications make it impossible to compare one athlete to another in competition. For example, one athlete may need to push a small basketball off his lap tray on his wheelchair and into a basket placed on the floor. Another athlete can shoot to a regulation-height basket with a playground ball if a peer tutor or teacher is there to give extra verbal and gesture cues. How can these two athletes be compared to determine who should win a basketball-shooting contest? Given this challenge, Special Olympics decided to make MATP a noncompetitive program. There are no rules that govern competitions, and there is no award system for first, second, and so forth. Instead, athletes compete against themselves to demonstrate their "personal best" in a sport skill. Each athlete is called to demonstrate a particular sport skill for which he or she has been training for 6–8 weeks, and with encouragement from fans and with whatever support and adaptations are needed, the athlete demonstrates his or her personal best. The athlete is then given a "Challenge Medal" indicating a personal best in the competition (Special Olympics, 2005).

The *Young Athletes Program* was established by Special Olympics International to provide early developmental opportunities for preschool children through guided motor activities. Children ages 2 ½ to 7 with intellectual disability typically have little access to motor activity programs, including organized play, and sports skill development. The activities presented in the program are designed to advance development of children who typically lag behind their peers without intellectual disability (Special Olympics, n.d.-e).

The Young Athletes curriculum builds on the Young Athletes core program activity guide and training video resources as well as scripted lesson plans for use over an 8-week period. For each week, there are 3 days of lesson plans for a total of 24 days. Lessons are designed in sequence to help children become acquainted with the activities and build skills through repetition. Activities include basic fitness activities, body awareness, spatial concepts, adaptive skills (e.g., following directions, imitating motor movements), basic fundamental motor skills, and balance skills.

ORGANIZATIONS

American Association for Intellectual and Developmental Disabilities
501 NW 3rd Street, Suite 200, Washington, D.C. 20001
Phone: 202-387-1968
http://aaidd.org

The Arc
1825 NW K Street, Suite 1200, Washington, D.C. 20006
Phone: 800-433-5255
http://www.thearc.org

Special Olympics
1133 NW 19th Street, Washington, D.C. 20036
Phone: 202-628-3630
Phone: 800-700-8585
http://www.specialolympics.org

International Sports Federation for Persons with Intellectual Disabilities
Sheffield, United Kingdom S25 9EQ
Phone: +44 845 600 9890
http://www.inas.org

Eunice Kennedy Shriver National Institute of Child Health and Human Development
31 Center Drive, Building 31, Room 2A32, Bethesda, MD 20892
Phone: 800-370-2943
http://www.nichd.nih.gov/health/topics/idds/Pages/default.aspx

National Association for Down Syndrome
1460 Renaissance Drive, Suite 405, Park Ridge, IL 60068
Phone: 630-325-9112
http://www.nads.org

National Fragile X Foundation
1615 Bonanza Street, Suite 202, Walnut Creek, CA 94596
Phone: 800-688-8765
http://www.fragilex.org

CHAPTER 9

Learning Disabilities

Jason Bishop and Martin E. Block

OBJECTIVES

1. Describe the characteristics of learning disabilities

2. Identify the various methods of diagnosing learning disabilities

3. Identify and describe the causes and specific types of learning disabilities

4. Describe the key factors of including students with learning disabilities in the general physical education class

---

Lexi's favorite class is physical education. This is not surprising given that Lexi is the fastest and all-around most athletic girl in her fourth-grade class. She already has won awards for local 2K fundraising races, and she is the star of her soccer, baseball, and basketball teams. In physical education, she is confident and popular, and most of her peers look up to her and want to be on her team or be her partner. This is a bit of a paradox as Lexi is the exact opposite in her fourth-grade classroom. All that confidence and popularity are replaced by anxiety and feelings of isolation. Lexi has a learning disability, and she has really struggled with reading. She was diagnosed with a learning disability in late first grade when she still had not learned to read, and with some extra support from a resource teacher,

she finally mastered the basics of reading in third grade. However, it still takes Lexi two to three times longer to read a few pages compared with her peers. And speed is not the only issue; she struggles with comprehending what she has read and often fails relatively simple review quizzes in her class. She is smart; testing confirmed that her IQ was actually above average. She knows she has a learning disability, but this confident, athletic girl is slowly losing the battle with academics and is beginning to dread going to school.

Mark, a classmate of Lexi's, also has a learning disability, but his disability is in the area of mathematics. Even simple addition and subtraction, which should be easy for fourth graders, is a challenge for Mark. However, he likes school and does well in in all other academic subjects. Similar to Lexi, Mark also goes to the resource room for help with math, and he is slowly improving. Unlike Lexi, Mark does not do well or like physical education. Mark's learning disability has led to some perceptual motor problems. Most would describe Mark as clumsy. He has kind of a funny way of running—he does not really bend his knees or have a narrow foot placement like most of his peers. He also struggles with pretty much any skill involving a ball, and this has resulted in frustration and embarrassment in lead-up basketball, volleyball, and soccer games. He has developed one good skill in physical education—the ability to cope and avoid. For example, in a three-on-three mini soccer game the other day in physical education, Mark managed to run around and look engaged in the game, but he also managed to never touch the ball. He did the same thing earlier in the year during a game of ultimate Frisbee that was the culmination of a throwing and catching unit; he ran around looking busy and active, but a closer inspection revealed he managed to never touch a Frisbee during the entire 15 minutes of the game. While Mark's strategy is working for him in terms of coping in physical education, he is systematically avoiding the practice he needs to improve his skills.

Lexi and Mark are great examples of the wide range of skills and impairments in children who have learning disabilities. Children with learning disabilities have strengths and often excel in many areas. On the other hand, these children struggle in one or more specific academic and sometimes motor areas. This is what makes having a learning disability such a challenge. The children clearly have strengths, but then there are the weaknesses. These students do not have an intellectual disability or autism, so they are clearly aware of their struggles. They also do not have any outward sign of a disability like children who have physical or sensory impairments, so family, teachers, and parents may not see the struggles faced by these children. However, learning disabilities are real. They affect the brain's ability to receive, process, store, respond to, and communicate information. Learning disabilities are actually a group of disorders, not a single disorder (National Center for Learning Disabilities [NCLD], 2014).

The purpose of the first part of this chapter is to review the definition and characteristics and the various types of learning disabilities followed by their implications for physical education.

WHAT ARE LEARNING DISABILITIES?

A learning disability is a neurological disorder that results in a person processing and making sense of information differently than those without learning disabilities. As a result, children with learning disabilities may have difficulty reading, writing, spelling, reasoning, recalling, and/or organizing information. This does not mean the child has an intellectual disability or is not as smart as his or her peers. Rather, it is just that the brain in children with learning disabilities is "wired" differently, which may require the teacher to find different ways to teach these children. A learning disability is a lifelong challenge that cannot be cured or fixed. However, with proper support and intervention, children with learning disabilities can succeed in school and go on to successful, often distinguished

careers later in life. Walt Disney, Albert Einstein, and Tom Cruise are just a few well-known, very successful people who have learning disabilities (LDOnline, 2010; Lerner & Johns, 2014; NCLD, 2014).

A key to the diagnosis of a learning disability is a distinct and unexplained gap between a person's level of expected achievement and actual performance. In other words, the child is clearly at (or above) age level in several academic areas, but in one or more specific areas, the child demonstrates significant delays. It also is important to note that learning disabilities range from mild to severe, and it is not uncommon for people to have more than one learning disability (Lerner & Johns, 2014; NCLD, 2014). Learning disabilities affect each child differently, and the specific learning disability affects each child differently at various stages of development. A first grader who is just learning to read and struggles compared with his peers is likely to be less stressed compared with a high school student who has dreams of going to college yet struggles to read and comprehend history, math, science, and English textbooks. Finally, many confuse a learning disability with attention-deficit/hyperactivity disorder (ADHD). While these two disabilities may present similar characteristics such as challenges with concentration, memory, and organizational skills, they are not the same disorder. However, reports suggest 6%–20% of children with learning disabilities also have ADHD (Cantwell & Baket, 1991; Dietz & Montague, 2006; Mayes, Calhoun, & Crowell, 2000; Scbnoes, Reid, Wagner, & Marder, 2006).

Individuals with Disabilities Education Act's Definition of a Specific Learning Disability

The Individuals with Disabilities Education Act (IDEA) has the following definition of specific learning disability:

> SLD means a disorder in one or more of the basic psychological processes involved in understanding or in using language, spoken or written, that may manifest itself in the imperfect ability to listen, think, speak, read, write, spell, or to do mathematical calculations. The term includes such conditions as perceptual disabilities, brain injury, minimal brain dysfunction, dyslexia, and developmental aphasia. The term does not include learning problems that are primarily the result of visual, hearing, or motor disabilities; of intellectual disability; of emotional disturbance; or of environmental, cultural, or economic disadvantage. (Individuals with Disabilities Education Improvement Act [IDEA] of 2004, 20 U.S.C. §§ 1400 et seq.)

Incidence of Learning Disabilities

Learning disabilities are the most common type of disability found in school-age children. More than two million children (ages 6–21) have some form of a learning disability and receive special education in school. In fact, the most prevalent disability category of students ages 6–21 served under Part B of IDEA 2004 is *specific learning disabilities,* comprising 40.7% of children receiving special education services (U.S. Department of Education, 2014b).

Diagnosing a Learning Disability

Historically, learning disabilities were diagnosed by giving a child a battery of standardized tests and looking for a discrepancy between intellectual potential and academic performance. An uneven pattern within and among areas of cognitive, affective, and motor development has always been a hallmark of the diagnosis of a learning disability (Lerner & Johns, 2014). In other words, a child might do well in reading and math but do very poorly in writing given the child's intellectual level. Intellectual, sensory, physical, and/or emotional disabilities as well as environmental disadvantage have to be excluded to receive the label of learning disability. Neurological testing can also be considered when diagnosing a learning disability. However, central nervous system dysfunction may or may not be clear in children who have learning disabilities (Lerner & Johns, 2014; NCLD, 2014).

A newer approach to diagnosing a learning disability that has been approved under IDEA 2004 is RTI. RTI is a multitiered approach to the early identification and support of students with learning and behavioral needs (Fletcher, Barth, & Stuebing, 2011; Kovaleski, van der Heyden, & Shapiro, 2013; RTI Action Network, n.d.). The RTI process begins with high-quality instruction and universal screening of all children in the general education classroom. Struggling learners are provided with interventions at increasing levels of intensity to accelerate their rate of learning. These services may be provided by a variety of personnel, including general education teachers, special educators, and specialists. Progress is closely monitored to assess both the learning rate and level of performance of individual students. Educational decisions about the intensity and duration of interventions are based on individual student response to instruction. RTI is generally described as a three-tiered model (Fuchs & Fuchs, 2001; Kovaleski et al., 2013; RTI Network, 2014):

Within *Tier 1,* all students receive high-quality instruction provided by qualified personnel to ensure any academic impairments or delays are not due to inadequate instruction. All students are screened on a periodic basis to establish an academic and behavioral baseline and to identify struggling learners who need additional support. Students identified as being "at risk" during Tier 1 receive supplemental instruction during the school day in small groups within their regular classroom. Tier 1 should last from 6 to 8 weeks, and students showing significant progress are generally returned to the regular classroom program. Students not showing adequate progress are moved to Tier 2.

Within *Tier 2,* students not making adequate progress in the regular classroom in Tier 1 are provided with more intensive, targeted instruction matched to their needs on the basis of levels of performance and rates of progress. Again, interventions are provided in small-group settings, usually by the general education teacher but with support from the special education teacher, in addition to instruction in the general curriculum. A longer period of time (8–12 weeks or so but not exceeding a grading period) may be required for this tier. Students who continue to show too little progress at this level of intervention are then considered for more intensive interventions as part of Tier 3.

Within *Tier 3,* students receive individualized, intensive interventions that target the students' skill impairments by either the general or special education teacher. Students who do not achieve the desired level of progress in response to these targeted interventions are then referred for a comprehensive evaluation and considered for eligibility for special education services under IDEA. Data collected during all three tiers are included and used to make the eligibility decision.

CAUSES OF LEARNING DISABILITIES

There are many possible factors that can lead to a dysfunction in one or more of the areas of the brain responsible for perceiving, integrating, and/or acting on information that may contribute to learning disabilities (Lerner & Johns, 2014):

- *Neurological factors:* These include known or suspected brain damage caused by such things as infection, trauma to the skull, anoxia, and fetal alcohol syndrome. In some cases, clear *hard signs* of neurological differences or damage can be found through electroencephalography, reflex tests, or other neurological tests. However, in many cases, such hard signs are not apparent. In such cases, *soft signs* (i.e., subjective results of neurological tests) may be used to diagnose a learning disability, for instance, when results of the neurological testing are not completely typical, but they are not sufficiently atypical to support conclusive diagnosis of neural damage.

- *Genetic factors:* Heredity factors have been linked to learning disabilities because there is higher incidence of learning disabilities in children whose parents and/or grandparents had them.

- *Environmental factors:* Learning disabilities by definition are not caused by economic disadvantage or cultural differences, nor are they the result of lack of educational opportunity (NCLD, 2014). However, children who experience severe stimulus deprivation or are denied timely and effective instruction during critical times in early development are at high risk for showing signs of learning disabilities.

CHARACTERISTICS AND SPECIFIC TYPES OF LEARNING DISABILITIES

The term *specific* is used to note certain types of learning disabilities. As noted earlier, a child might have only one of these specific learning disabilities or may have multiple learning disabilities. The following are the most common specific learning disabilities (NCLD, 2014):

- *Dyslexia:* Dyslexia is the name for specific learning disabilities in reading. Dyslexia is often characterized by difficulties with accurate word recognition, decoding, and spelling, all of which may result in poor reading, reading comprehension, fluency, and reading out loud. Dyslexia is a language-based processing disorder. Children with dyslexia have a neurological disorder that causes their brains to process and interpret information differently.

- *Dyscalculia:* Dyscalculia refers to a wide range of lifelong learning disabilities involving math. There is no single type of math disability. Dyscalculia can vary from person to person, and it affects people differently at different stages of life. Work-around strategies and accommodations help lessen the obstacles that dyscalculia presents.

- *Dysgraphia:* Dysgraphia is a learning disability that affects writing, which requires a complex set of motor and information processing skills. Dysgraphia makes the act of writing difficult. It can lead to problems with spelling, poor handwriting, and putting thoughts on paper. People with dysgraphia can have trouble organizing letters, numbers, and words on a line or page. This can

result partly from visual-spatial difficulties (i.e., trouble processing what the eye sees) and/or language processing difficulties (i.e., trouble processing and making sense of what the ear hears).

- *Dyspraxia:* Dyspraxia is a disorder that affects motor skill development. People with dyspraxia have trouble planning and completing fine motor tasks. This can vary from simple motor tasks such as waving goodbye to more complex tasks such as brushing teeth. It is not technically a learning disability but often coexists with other learning disabilities and conditions that affect learning.

Information Processing Disorders

Processing disorders underlie many types of learning disabilities (NCLD, 2014). There are two major types of processing disorders related to learning disabilities. *Auditory processing disorders* cause difficulty in distinguishing the difference between similar sounds, among other difficulties. Auditory processing disorders may explain why some children may have trouble with learning and performance. *Visual processing disorders* can cause difficulty in seeing the difference between two similar letters, shapes, or objects or noticing the similarities and differences between certain colors, shapes, and patterns. Visual processing disorders include dyslexia, dysgraphia, and dyspraxia.

Behavior Characteristics

There is no specific relationship between having a learning disability and specific behavior problems. Children with learning disabilities can be as socially and behaviorally appropriate as their peers without learning disabilities. However, having a learning disability and struggling academically, especially when peers seem to be picking up skills so quickly, can lead to behavior problems. For example, children with learning disabilities may have lower overall self-concept due to prolonged experiences of failure as well as lower self-esteem in specific academic or movement areas related to the learning disability. Children who are not diagnosed quickly with a learning disability and fail academically without knowing why they are struggling academically are particularly vulnerable to lower overall self-concept and specific self-esteem (Burden, 2005; Peleg, 2009). This is why early diagnosis of a learning disability is so critical. Motor difficulties and repeated failures in gross motor performance also can lead to lower self-efficacy toward physical education, recreation, and sport (Doyle & Higginson, 1984; Henderson, May, & Umney, 1989;

Shaw, Levine, & Belfer, 1982; Van Rossum & Vermeer, 1990; Willoughby, Polatajko, & Wilson, 1995).

Similarly, children with learning disabilities may develop mood and anxiety disorders due to lack of progress and perceived academic failure (Cowden, 2010; Peleg, 2009). Some children with learning disabilities who experience repeated failure may develop anxiety and rebel at home when it comes time to do homework, and others may act out in school or develop test anxiety. Negative behaviors toward academics may flow into interactions and relationships with peers, which may isolate the child with a learning disability. Limited social skills are particularly true in children who have both learning disabilities and ADHD (Wei, Yu, & Shaver, 2014). Finally, and not surprisingly, some children with learning disabilities will lose their motivation to go to school and even develop depression when they know they are likely to fail (Gallegos, Langley, & Villegas, 2012). Again, early diagnosis and strong academic and personal support for children with learning disabilities are critical to prevent these behavior problems.

Health/Medical Characteristics

There is no relationship between having a learning disability and any specific health and/or medical problem. Children with learning disabilities should be as healthy as children without learning disabilities.

Motor Characteristics

Many children with learning disabilities are athletic and quite skilled in the motor domain. Famous athletes with learning disabilities include Olympic gold medalist Bruce Jenner, basketball star Magic Johnson, football star Dexter Manley, and baseball star Pete Rose (Levinson Medical Center for Learning Disabilities, n.d.).

However, there is research, albeit somewhat older, suggesting some children with learning disabilities have significant delays in areas related to overall coordination, including eye–hand coordination, response speed, and static and dynamic balance compared with peers without learning disabilities (Beyer, 1999; Bluechardt, Wiener, & Shephard, 1995; Bruininks & Bruininks, 1977; Cermak, Ward, & Ward, 1986; Geuze & Borger, 1993; Longhurst, Coetsee, & Bressan, 2004; Pyfer & Carlson, 1972). Similarly, research examining one specific aspect of coordination found significant differences between children with and without learning disabilities. For example, Fawcett and Nicolson (1995); Getchell, McMenamin, and Whitall (2005); Rousselle and

Wolff (1991); Wolff, Michel, Ovrut, and Drake (1990); and Yap and Van der Leij (1994) found children with learning disabilities had more difficulty in consistency and coordinating two tasks at one time such as walking and clapping or balancing and listening compared with age-matched peers without learning disabilities. Woodard and Surburg (1999) found children 6–8 years of age with learning disabilities demonstrated midline crossing inhibition compared with age-matched peers without learning disabilities. Kerr and Hughes (1987) found children 6–8 years of age were 1–2 years delayed compared with age-matched peers in a reciprocal finger-tapping task. Finally, Lazarus (1994) found children 7–14 years of age with learning disabilities had greater levels of overflow (i.e., an inability to keep one arm or leg still while moving the other arm or leg) compared with same-age peers without learning disabilities. In addition to impairments in coordination, research shows many children with learning disabilities performed at a lower developmental level compared with peers without learning disabilities in fundamental motor patterns such as throwing and catching and jumping and hopping (Bradley & Drowatzky, 1997; Woodard & Surburg, 1997, 2001).

TEACHING PHYSICAL EDUCATION TO STUDENTS WITH LEARNING DISABILITIES

As noted earlier, as many as 1 in 5 children with learning disabilities will have motor impairments. These children are more likely to experience less success in physical education and as a result develop coping behaviors in an attempt to avoid physical activity (Dunn & Dunn, 2006; Thompson, Bouffard, Watkinson, & Causgrove Dunn, 1994). For example, Dunn and Dunn (2006) found children with movement difficulties in a general physical education setting spent less time successfully performing assigned activities, spent more time experiencing difficulty in the given tasks, and spent more time in off-task behaviors when compared with peers without disabilities. Special teaching strategies and other accommodations are necessary for children with learning disabilities and related motor impairments to ensure successful experiences in physical education, which in turn will lead to greater effort, motivation, and learning. The following are some suggestions for accommodating students with learning disabilities who have motor impairments.

- *Reduce class size:* Smaller class sizes allow the teacher extra time to work with children individually. This may be difficult to do when children attend general physical education with their general education class. However, when possible, children with learning disabilities and related motor impairments should have physical education with just their class of 20–30 students as opposed to a double or triple class of 50–75 students, which often happens in general physical education.

- *Use peer tutors:* Since adjusting class size can be difficult if not impossible, peer tutors are an effective model for providing the student with a learning disability individualized instruction. Peers can be trained in how to repeat key instructions, how to analyze and provide specific skill feedback, and how to modify equipment and the task so the child gets many opportunities for successful practice.

- *Offer learning strategies:* Teachers (and peer tutors) should provide appropriate learning strategies to help disorganized learners focus on a skill. Many students with learning disabilities will have trouble understanding what to do and how to organize their environment for effective practice. Providing picture cues of critical skill components, video cues and then video feedback/analysis of performance (easily done on a smartphone), and additional cues such as footprints on the floor to help a child with a learning disability understand what to do and how to do it.

- *Provide structured practice:* Many students with learning disabilities will not understand the concept of practice and using feedback. The physical educator, with help from a peer tutor, may need to carefully structure the practice setting so the child gets plenty of practice opportunities. For example, a bucket filled with yarn balls will cue the child on how many times he or she should throw to a target. In addition, the child may need to learn how to listen for and observe visual feedback on performance. For example, after each throw, the child should be taught to listen to and watch his peer tutor for specific feedback. The child can be asked, "What did I just say you did well, and what did I say you needed to work on?" to verify the child was listening and understood the feedback.

- *Address component skills:* In some cases, children with learning disabilities may do better if they are encouraged to focus on one component of a skill at a time rather than the entire skill. For example, when teaching throwing, it might help to have the child focus on stepping with the opposite foot and mastering that component

before adding the stepping motion with the upper-body throwing motion. It should be noted that for some students, teaching the part-whole method may actually have a negative effect on learning the skill, so it is important to determine which teaching method is best for each child.

- *Teach students how to use psychological techniques such as goal setting and mental preparation before practicing and performing a skill:* For example, Hodge, Murata, and Porretta (1999) found mental preparation (closing one's eyes and going through the components of the skill to be performed) significantly improved throwing patterns in elementary-age children with learning disabilities and attention deficits compared with matched participants who did not do a warm-up or did a traditional stretching warm-up.

- *Identify success for the child:* Most children, those with and without learning disabilities, will likely focus on how far they threw a ball, how many times they hit a ball, how many baskets they made, or how many times they kicked the ball into the goal. Reframe success for children with learning disabilities by focusing on qualitative components rather than the end result. For example, using correct form in shooting should be a measure of success rather than making a basket. Points could be given based on using the correct technique rather than actually making a basket.

- *Adapt equipment for success:* Larger targets and goals are easier to hit; larger balls are easier to dribble, kick, and hit; and standing closer to the target or service line (volleyball) will allow the child a great chance for success. Recall that lower self-esteem is an issue for children with learning disabilities who constantly fail, so creating opportunities for success is extremely important for these children.

- *Teach skills rather than playing games:* Also teach skills to mastery and not just exposure to enhance self-efficacy and self-concept (Revie & Larkin, 1993; Valentini & Rudisill, 2004). Many physical education programs in the middle and high school move to a team sports model. Unfortunately, the sports units are relatively short (2–3 weeks), and the focus is on playing the game and exposing students to various sports rather than teaching the skills needed to play the game. Teaching the skills needed to be successful in the game and extending units to ensure more mastery of critical skills and concepts as opposed to just exposing children to the general idea of the game is critical for all children in physical education but particularly those with learning disabilities. Children with learning disabilities and related motor impairments often will not have the skills to be successful in traditional sports without first learning how to perform specific, sports-related skills. This will inevitably lead to failure, frustration, and lack of motivation. For example, teach the forearm pass, overhead pass (setting), and underhand serve over the course of several classes to help all children master the fundamentals of volleyball. Then, once you begin to play actual volleyball games, the children will have a greater chance of being successful and enjoying the game.

- *Experiment with practice schedules:* Find out what schedule works best with each child with a learning disability. One student suggested that constant practice schedules improved learning of a simple motor task compared with random practice schedules (Heitman, Erdmann, Gurchiek, Kovaleski, & Giley, 1997). However, for some children with learning disabilities and attention-deficit/hyperactivity disorder, a more random practice setting might force the child to stay interested and focused since each trial or every few trials would seem like a new, novel activity.

- *Use a variety of senses when giving instruction to students with perceptual problems:* Some students will do better when listening to instruction, others will do better when watching a demonstration or video model, others will do better when seeing pictures of the skill broken into components, and still others may do best when physically guided into the correct pattern. They key is to experiment to determine the best way to present instruction that will lead to understanding and ultimately successful performance.

- *Review previously acquired skills before teaching more advanced skills:* Do not assume that a child has mastered a skill after a few classes. Even if the child seemed to have mastered a skill in a previous class, it makes sense to make sure the child has truly mastered the skill. In addition, practicing a skill the child has mastered will lead to success and improve confidence and self-esteem.

- *Add relaxation training to the program:* Relaxation helps keep the children calm and focused and reduces performance anxiety. One study showed relaxation training improved reaction time on a visual-choice motor test and also reduced unrelated behaviors in children with learning disabilities (Brandon, Eason, & Smith, 1986).

- *Eliminate embarrassing teaching practices that force comparison among students:* For example, stagger the start time in the mile run for the class so it becomes difficult if not impossible to see who is the slowest in the class. Make your teams rather than have peers pick teams. Avoid having two or three students pitted against each other in some form of elimination game.

- *Use cooperative teaching styles:* These increase students' social interaction and self-concept. Whenever possible, switch traditional competitive games to cooperative games. For example, see how many times the volleyball can be passed back and forth over the net rather than seeing which team can win. In a tagging game, have peers who are tagged hold hands and keep adding more peers to make a long line of taggers (addition tag) rather than having students eliminated when tagged. A study by Amael, Benoit, and Pascale (2013) found that risk-taking, cooperative activities facilitated helping behaviors and the acceptance of peers with learning disabilities.

- *Include perceptual-motor activities:* Add activities to the curriculum such as balance; body awareness; tactile, visual, or auditory stimulation; and other similar activities to remediate specific impairments in these areas. It is particularly helpful if you know the child's specific area of impairment so you can present activities to help the child improve. Activities should be as functional as possible. For example, a child with balance problems could practice walking on a balance beam, but this is a rather nonfunctional activity. A better activity would be practicing stepping when throwing a softball, performing a chest pass in basketball, or leaping in preparation for a kick in soccer. Similarly, catching balls tossed of different sizes from different angles and at different distances is a better way to work on functional eye–hand coordination as opposed to simply tracking a swinging ball. There are many perceptual motor activities that can be found online that can easily be incorporated into a learning station during physical education.

Note one cautionary item regarding perceptual-motor training and children with learning disabilities. Perceptual-motor training as a treatment for learning disabilities was popular in the 1960s and 1970s based on clinical, classroom, and anecdotal reports of success remediating specific learning problems. The basic concept behind the theory is that perceptual-motor problems cause learning problems. Unfortunately, analysis of hundreds of studies showed perceptual motor training was not an effective method for remediating specific learning disabilities (Hallahan & Cruickshank, 1973; Kavale & Mattson, 1983). Perceptual-motor training quickly fell out of favor with the learning disability community in the 1980s, leading the Council for Learning Disabilities to issue a position statement opposing "the measurement and training of perceptual and perceptual-motor functions as part of learning disability services" and calling for "a moratorium on assessment and training of perceptual and perceptual-motor functions in educational programs" (1986, p. 247).

Interestingly, perceptual-motor training has seen a resurgence in programs for children with learning disabilities, including Educational Kinesiology/ Brain Gym (Cammisa, 1994; Freeman & Dennison, 1998), which includes stretching and unique movements designed to stimulate brain function, and the Dore method (Dore, 2014), which includes balance activities, throwing and catching bean bags, and a range of stretching and coordination exercises. Both programs purport to improve academic function in children with learning disabilities, but neither method has yet to be supported by empirical research.

RESOURCES

International Dyslexia Association
40 York Road, 4th Floor, Baltimore, MD 21204
Phone: 410-296-0232
http://www.interdys.org

Learning Disabilities Association of America
4156 Library Road, Pittsburgh, PA 15234
Phone: 412-341-1515

National Center for Learning Disabilities
381 Park Avenue South, Suite 1401, New York, NY 10016
Phone: 215-545-7510
http://www.ncld.org

CHAPTER 10

Attention-Deficit/ Hyperactivity Disorder

Jason Bishop and Martin E. Block

Objectives

1. Describe the characteristics of attention-deficit/ hyperactivity disorder (ADHD)

2. Identify the three ADHD subtypes

3. Identify the causes and treatment of ADHD

4. Describe the key factors of including students with ADHD in the general physical education classroom

Physical education is Wang's favorite subject. He is a physically fit, active 7-year-old who can easily climb the jungle gym on the playground, throw a football the length of the gym, and run faster and longer than anyone else in his physical education class. Mrs. Nixon, Wang's physical education teacher, appreciates Wang's enthusiasm and athletic skills. However, Wang does cause some problems in physical education. First, children are supposed to walk into the gym calmly and find a place to sit on the floor in front of a whiteboard. Here, Mrs. Nixon quickly reviews the plan for the day and gives directions for the first activity. Wang usually runs or skips into the gym, and he often will run or jump around for several seconds before Mrs. Nixon has to remind him to sit down with the group. Once seated, Wang has trouble sitting and listening when Mrs. Nixon gives directions.

She is very good at keeping directions to a minimum, usually 2 minutes or less. Unfortunately, even 1 minute is too long for Wang to sit and wait, and he begins squirming in his place, touching other children, and raising his hand to ask questions. When it is time to get up and move, Wang's enthusiasm and athleticism shine as he quickly and smoothly moves about the gym playing tagging and fleeing games in warm-ups. Somewhat surprising though given Wang's athleticism is how often he bumps into other children, knocks over cones set up for boundaries, or just seems trip over his own feel and tumble into a heap on the floor. He is quick to get up, and everyone is used to hearing Wang say, "I'm okay." Another interesting thing about Wang is that none of his classmates want to be his partner or have him in their group. Again, he is very athletic, but Mrs. Nixon has noticed that Wang has trouble moderating his skills. For example, when tossing or kicking a ball back and forth with a peer, he usually throws or kicks the ball too hard or does not kick it accurately. He also wanders away from his partner or group and needs to be reminded to come back. It seems his peers prefer partners who can stay focused and can toss or kick balls back and forth nicely. Wang is beginning to notice that peers avoid selecting him as a partner or to be part of the group, and this has made him both sad and angry. A new behavior that is unsettling to Mrs. Nixon is Wang walking up to a group and kicking their ball away or even pushing a classmate. Whereas Wang's inattentiveness, hyperactivity, and clumsiness were

181

relatively minor issues for Mrs. Nixon, these new aggressive behaviors are more concerning. What should Mrs. Nixon do to help Wang?

Attention-deficit/hyperactivity disorder (ADHD) is a neurobehavioral disorder that typically begins before the age of 7 and often persists into adulthood (American Psychiatric Association [APA], 2013; Centers for Disease Control and Prevention [CDC], 2010a). According to the APA (2013), approximately 3%–7% of school-age children are diagnosed with ADHD; however, the CDC (2014c) reported estimates of more than 15% in some populations. Boys are twice as likely as girls to be diagnosed (Polanczyk, de Lima, Horta, Biederman, & Rohde, 2007). The essential feature of ADHD is a persistent pattern of inattention and/or hyperactivity-impulsivity that is more frequent and severe than that of a typically developing comparison peer (APA, 2013). Three subtypes distinguish the two primary features: primarily inattentive, primarily hyperactive/impulsive, and combined type. The combined type, the most common, is diagnosed when the individual presents symptoms of both features. Symptoms must manifest in two or more settings, such as home, school, and/or other social situations such as eating at a restaurant.

WHAT IS ATTENTION-DEFICIT/HYPERACTIVITY DISORDER?

The latest edition of the *Diagnostic and Statistical Manual of Mental Disorders* (*DSM-5*) of the American Psychological Association (APA, 2013) presents rich descriptions of symptoms related to ADHD. Children with ADHD often fail to give close attention to details or make careless mistakes in schoolwork or other tasks. Their work is often messy and performed carelessly. They have a difficult time sustaining attention in tasks or play activities and find it difficult to persist in completing tasks. They often appear as if their thoughts are elsewhere or they are not listening when spoken to. They frequently shift from one incomplete task to another and typically do not follow through on requests or instructions and often fail to complete chores, schoolwork, or other tasks. These children have difficulty organizing activities and tasks. Tasks that require sustained attention are reported to be unpleasant and aversive. It is not unusual for these children to avoid and markedly dislike activities that require sustained self-application, mental effort, close concentration, or a high level of organizational demands. These children are often distracted by irrelevant stimuli in the environment. They often forget details of daily activities such as keeping commitments or forgetting to bring their lunch to school.

Hyperactivity is frequently described as fidgeting or squirming in one's seat, getting out of the seat when expected to stay, picking up things that belong to others, or running or climbing when inappropriate. These children are often described as "driven by a motor." Other difficulties include blurting out answers before the question is asked, difficulty waiting one's turn, and frequently interrupting or intruding on others. These behaviors often lead to difficulties in gaining or maintaining appropriate friendships and meaningful relationships. Although all these symptoms are common among children (more so in boys than the behavioral "gold standard" set by girls), they manifest themselves more intensely, more frequently, and in longer duration in children with ADHD. The symptoms must not be better explained by another diagnosis such as intellectual disability, oppositional defiant disorder, or autism spectrum disorder. Symptoms will often vary according to setting and within a variety of situations within that setting (e.g., storytime, reading time). To meet diagnostic criteria, six or more symptoms of inattention and/or six or more symptoms of hyperactivity-impulsivity listed in the *DSM-5* must be present for 6 months prior to assessment.

Children with ADHD are more likely to develop conduct disorder during adolescence as well as antisocial personality disorder in adulthood (Mannuzza, Klein, Bessler, Malloy, & LaPadula, 1998). They have an increased risk of drug abuse, especially when comorbid with conduct disorder or antisocial personality disorder (Klein et al., 2012). About one fourth of children with ADHD also have conduct disorder (Willcutt et al., 2012).

CAUSES OF ATTENTION-DEFICIT/HYPERACTIVITY DISORDER

Research has not pinpointed a specific cause of ADHD, but it most likely results from a culmination of many factors. Many studies suggest that genes play a prominent role. Environment, brain injuries, and nutrition may also contribute to ADHD diagnosis.

Genetic Factors

Many international studies of twins indicate that ADHD runs in families (Faraone & Mick, 2010; Gizer, Ficks, & Waldman, 2009). In a study by Shaw et al. (2007), researchers found that children with ADHD who carry a specific version of a particular gene have thinner brain tissue in the prefrontal cortex. However, as the children in the study matured, their brains developed to a typical level of thickness, and their ADHD symptoms improved. Genetic variations such as duplication or deletion of segments of DNA known as "copy number variations" (CNVs) can include many genes. Some CNVs occur more often in people with ADHD, suggesting a possible role in the disorder (Elia et al., 2011).

Environmental Factors

Research studies have provided a correlational relationship between cigarette smoking and alcohol use during pregnancy (Millichap, 2008; Nomura, Marks, & Halperin, 2010) as well as exposure to lead (Froehlich et al., 2009) and a diagnosis of ADHD in children.

Brain Injuries

Children who have sustained a traumatic brain injury may display the inattention and/or hyperactivity characteristics of ADHD.

Nutrition

According to the National Institute of Mental Health, research has not validated the popular notion of sugar contributing to or increasing ADHD symptoms. However, children who abstain from a diet containing food additives (Millichap & Yee, 2012; Nigg, Lewis, Edinger, & Falk, 2012) may experience fewer symptoms of ADHD.

Treatments

Treatments aim at reducing the symptoms of ADHD as well as improving the completion of activities of daily living. Treatments usually include a combination of approaches, including medication and various types of psychotherapy, education, or training. Treatments help decrease symptoms, but there is no cure for ADHD. With appropriate treatment, most students can be successful in school and lead successful lives. Researchers are constantly working to develop safer, more effective treatments and interventions and are using new instruments such as brain imaging to better understand ADHD and find more ways to prevent and treat it.

Medication

The most common medication prescribed for treating ADHD is a neurological stimulant such as methylphenidate (e.g., Ritalin) or amphetamine (e.g., Adderall). Although it may appear to be unusual to treat a child with hyperactivity with a neurological stimulant, these prescription medications have a calming effect on children with ADHD. Other nonstimulant medications work in different ways in treating ADHD symptoms. For many children, ADHD medications help reduce impulsivity and hyperactivity and improve their ability to sustain attention, work, and learn. Table 10.1 provides a list of common ADHD medications.

Psychotherapy

Different types of psychotherapy are used to address ADHD symptoms. Behavioral therapy aims to help children modify their behavior to help organize tasks, complete schoolwork, or process difficult and emotional events such as such as losing a loved one, adjusting to a family move, or processing their parents' divorce. Behavioral therapy also teaches a child how to monitor and modify his or her own behaviors. Examples include learning to give oneself praise or a reward for acting in a certain way such as not interrupting, staying still, or controlling other

Table 10.1. List of common medications used to treat ADHD

Trade name	Generic name	Approved age
Adderall	amphetamine	3 and older
Adderall XR	amphetamine (extended release)	6 and older
Concerta	methylphenidate (long acting)	6 and older
Daytrana	methylphenidate patch	6 and older
Desoxyn	methamphetamine hydrochloride	6 and older
Dexedrine	dextroamphetamine	3 and older
Dextrostat	dextroamphetamine	3 and older
Focalin	dexmethylphenidate	6 and older
Focalin XR	dexmethylphenidate (extended release)	6 and older
Metadate ER	methylphenidate (extended release)	6 and older
Metadate CD	methylphenidate (extended release)	6 and older
Methylin	methylphenidate (oral solution and chewable tablets)	6 and older
Ritalin	methylphenidate	6 and older
Ritalin SR	methylphenidate (extended release)	6 and older
Ritalin LA	methylphenidate (long acting)	6 and older
Strattera	atomoxetine	6 and older
Vyvanse	lisdexamfetamine dimesylate	6 and older

From National Institutes of Health, National Institute of Mental Health. Retrieved from: http://www.nimh.nih.gov/health/topics/attention-deficit-hyperactivity-disorder-adhd/index.shtml#part_145449; adapted by permission.

impulses. Other examples include learning social skills such as how to wait one's turn, sharing toys or equipment, asking for help, or how to respond to teasing. Learning to read facial expressions and the tone of voice of others and how to respond appropriately to others are also goals of social skills training (National Institute of Mental Health, 2012).

CHARACTERISTICS OF ATTENTION-DEFICIT/HYPERACTIVITY DISORDER

Up to 52% of children with ADHD experience developmental delays (Barkley, 2006) when performing locomotor and object-control skills (Beyer, 1999; Harvey & Reid, 1997, 2005; Harvey et al., 2009). Obviously, not every child with ADHD experiences motor delays throughout his or her lifespan. Some children with ADHD acquire superior motor skills and are successful athletes as adults. For example, U.S. Olympic gold medalist Michael Phelps was diagnosed ADHD and used swimming during his youth for its therapeutic effects; Bruce Jenner, Pete Rose, and Terry Bradshaw are other examples of elite athletes diagnosed with ADHD (ADD/ADHD Foundation, n.d.). However, most children with ADHD, particularly those diagnosed with combined-type ADHD, experience motor delays (Harvey & Reid, 1997; Harvey et al., 2009; Harvey et al., 2007; Verret, Gardiner, & Beliveau, 2010). For example, Harvey et al. (2009) found that boys with ADHD performed poorer on locomotor and object controls skills than boys without ADHD. Yan and Thomas (2002) found that children with ADHD took more time in performing a rapid arm-movement task and were less accurate and more variable in completing the task than children without ADHD. Research indicates stimulant medication such as Ritalin has no effect on motor performance compared with children not taking medication (Harvey et al., 2007; Verret et al., 2010). However, it is recommended for children to take any prescription medication for ADHD approximately 1 hour prior to physical education.

Behavior Characteristics

Including students with moderate to severe ADHD symptoms in the general physical education classroom is a common challenge of physical education teachers (Bishop & Block, 2012). Often these children exhibit developmentally inappropriate behaviors that adversely affect their performance in all areas of learning, including academic (LeFever, Villers, Morrow, & Vaughn, 2002), social (Bagwell, Molina, Pelham, & Hoza, 2001), and motor

(Harvey & Reid, 2003). In addition, some students with ADHD often avoid motor skill practice opportunities in physical education and recreational activities (Kelly & Melograno, 2015).

Self-Perception Issues

One reason students with ADHD have a difficult time mastering motor skills is they hold a false belief about their motor skill competence and appear to have a unique *self-system* regulating their motivation. These children tend to have a *positive illusory bias* toward completing motor skills (Hoza, Pelham, Milich, Pillow, & McBride, 1993). The positive illusory bias is a condition in which individuals believe they are significantly better at completing a goal or task than they actually are. According to Harter's (1981) model of motivation, children's self-perceptions of competence and control contribute to their motivational orientation (Owens, Goldfine, Evangelista, Hoza, & Kaiser, 2007). In this model, children's self-efficacy toward completing a task is enhanced after successful practice trials, and they are motivated to engage in future challenging tasks. However, children who do not experience successful trials at a task often develop low self-efficacy toward that task and are less likely to pursue that task if given a choice not to participate.

Harter's (1981) model predicts that students with ADHD would be at risk for developing low levels of self-perceptions as they often experience failure in multiple domains. However, despite repeated failure when completing tasks, these students continue to report high levels of self-perceptions (Hoza, Dobbs, Owens, Pelham, & Pillow, 2002). Milich and Okazaki (1991) suggested that children with positive illusory bias may be more susceptible to failure as their inaccurate views likely prevent them from recognizing the need for improvement, acknowledging critical feedback, and modifying their approach to complete a task. Bishop (2013) found mixed results when investigating the presence of positive illusory bias in the motor domain of children with ADHD.

In addition to holding false beliefs toward completing motor skills, children with ADHD tend to give up more frequently when competing tasks and perform worse than their peers (Hoza, Pelham, Waschbushc, Kipp, & Owens, 2001; O'Neil & Douglas, 1991; Owens et al., 2007). Still, other reasons children with ADHD experience motor delays include cognitive immaturity, neuropsychological impairments, executive functioning impairments, and a marked unawareness of their impairments called the ignorance of incompetence hypothesis.

TEACHING STUDENTS WITH ATTENTION-DEFICIT/ HYPERACTIVITY DISORDER

Despite the motor learning delays of students with ADHD, positive illusory bias, and executive functioning impairments, many strategies are available to the physical education teacher to minimize learning delays.

Positive Feedback

Ohan and Johnson (2002) found that boys with ADHD lowered their exaggerated reports of self-competence when the teacher presented positive feedback during and after the completion of a task. It is thought that students with positive illusory bias try to protect their self-esteem by failing to acknowledge their inadequacies or by inflating their actual self-competence (Diener & Milich, 1997). Students may be more open to apply corrective motor skill feedback when learning a skill if they have received positive feedback by the instructor. Because of this relationship between positive feedback given by the physical education teacher and students applying corrective feedback, it is important for the teacher to be able to offer a positive feedback statement at any time during the physical education class, even when the student is misbehaving or having a bad day.

Provide Direct Instruction and Feedback

Children with ADHD tend to fail to acknowledge their inadequacies, including motor performances. One way to offer effective instruction is to provide skill-specific feedback. For example, if Manuel is boasting of his one-handed striking skills while continually hitting the ball into the net, the instructor should point out something he is doing correctly (e.g., "Good job of pointing your shoulders to the net") followed by skill-specific feedback (e.g., "Try starting the swing low and ending high").

Task Sheets

Sometimes, it is helpful to remove the instructor as the source of feedback. This can be accomplished by providing task sheets. A task sheet provides a progression of activities to be completed by the students and requires them to record the results of their practice attempts. After recording their scores for each task, the students turn in the task sheets at the end of class. The unique goal of the task sheet is to help the students asses their performance, acknowledge their lower scores, and recognize the need to improve their skills. To help students acknowledge their mistakes during motor skills practice, it may be helpful to create results-oriented (i.e., knowledge of results) tasks sheets before process-oriented task sheets. After a student understands his or her motor performance needs improvement, a process-oriented task sheet can be used.

Design Activities that Provide Immediate Feedback

Skills activities can often serve to provide feedback or be modified to do so. For example, in a one-handed-strike lesson, in which the goal is to return tennis balls over the net and in bounds, the net provides immediate feedback if a ball either hit the net or traveled over. Another activity that provides feedback is suspending a string from the basketball net when working on the backswing. In this scenario, students know they are successful in completing the backswing if they strike the suspended ball.

Token Economy or Point System

Token economies or point systems are structured agreements between the student and teacher in which the student earns rewards by meeting minimum expectations. For example, a student could earn a reward at the end of the month if he or she earns a predetermined amount of points. The amount and range of possible points earned are not dictated and can be negotiated. Some private schools choose a four-point Likert scale point system in which 0 represents complete failure to meet expectations or severe disrespect to self or others, 1 represents general disruptive behavior after several verbal and physical props or cues, 2 represents behavior approaching expectations after several props, and 3 represents behavior meeting expectations with minimal cues. Points can be allotted each class meeting or on multiple occasions during the same class meeting. For example, points can be earned three times a class period, once every 15 minutes. At the end of class, both the student and teacher initial the points earned. At the end of the month, the student may earn a reward of his or her choice from a selection of rewards provided by the teacher. Examples of rewards might include qualifying to referee a culminating activity, eating lunch with the physical education teacher, having extra free-choice time, or being responsible for distributing equipment for a physical education class. A *level system* is an extension of the point system in which the student earns greater rewards by earning additional points. Each "level" requires students to earn greater rewards but requires additional points. Again, the number of levels available to be earned is determined by the teacher. Many schools choose a four-level system. Students begin at Level 1 and move up according to their behavior and points earned. For example, in a physical education class that meets twice a week for 45 minutes and where points are allotted three times per class period (2 classes × 3 blocks × 4 weeks/month), the teacher may decide that a student must earn a total of 40 points a month for 2 consecutive months to advance to Level 2, 55 points to advance to Level 3, and 64 points to advance to Level 4.

The advantages of initiating a point-and-level system is that it communicates dignity, respect, and support from the instructor; provides additional motivation for the student to increase appropriate behaviors by rewarding good behavior instead of prescribing punishments for bad behavior; provides immediate external feedback; and helps students develop an external locus of control by holding the students accountable for their behavior.

RESOURCES

ADHD Aware
8 E Court Street, Doylestown, PA 18901
Phone: 215-348-0550
http://www.adhdaware.org

Attention Deficit Disorder Association (ADDA)
PO Box 7557, Wilmington, DE 19803
Phone: 800-939-1019
http://www.add.org

Children and Adults with Attention-Deficit/
  Hyperactivity Disorder (CHADD)
CHADD National Office
4601 Presidents Drive, Suite 200, Lanham,
  MD 20706
Phone: 301-306-7070
http://www.chadd.org

CHAPTER 11

Autism Spectrum Disorder

Sean Healy and Martin E. Block

Objectives

1. Understand the characteristics and causes of autism spectrum disorder

2. Know how to prepare the environment and the class for the inclusion of students with autism

3. Know how to modify instructional strategies suitable for students with autism

4. Know how to manage the behaviors of students with autism

5. Know how to adapt activities for students with autism

Brendan never walks into the gym with his third-grade class; he runs into it! He doesn't sit down with his classmates either but instead runs around the room squealing with joy. Although Mrs. Pritchard, his physical education teacher, loves Brendan's enthusiasm, she is not so excited about the way he enters the room. She knows Brendan has autism, and she knows Brendan has a teacher assistant with him throughout the day, including in physical education. However, she struggles to keep up with Brendan. With a little coaxing by his teacher assistant, he finally settles down and sits down among his peers. Unfortunately, he does not sit quietly and listen to Mrs. Pritchard's directions. Rather, he begins to rock back and forth and makes noises. Mrs. Pritchard does not talk very long, and the class is up and moving to music to warm up and review locomotor patterns. Brendan loves to move to music, but he does not change locomotor patterns (he only runs) and does not stop when Mrs. Pritchard stops the music. When the class makes a transition to stations to practice throwing at various targets, Brendan continues to run. When Mrs. Pritchard and his teacher assistant finally get Brendan over to a station, he just picks up a ball and throws it in the air and then jumps up and down about 20 times. This is all Brendan does at each throwing station: He tosses the ball up in the air and jumps up and down. His teacher assistant tells him to throw at the targets, but he does not seem to understand. The class concludes with a group game in which children are divided into teams and throw yarn balls at a large refrigerator box, trying to push it across the gym with their throws. The children really enjoy the activity and laugh and joke with each other. Brendan doesn't throw at the box like his peers, although he tends to hover around the box and his peers while dancing on his tiptoes with excitement. However, sometimes the loud laughing and sounds of balls hitting the box are too much for Brendan, and he will put his hands over his ears. Once, when playing with balloons in physical education a balloon popped, and this really scared Brendan, causing him to hit his teacher assistant and run out of the gym. Mrs. Pritchard wonders if Brendan is benefiting from her physical education class, and she wonders if there is anything she can do to get Brendan to focus more and to practice skills.

Esther also has autism and is in the same physical education class as Brendan, but her behaviors are very different from his. Esther does not have a teacher assistant. She walks into the gym quietly and calmly, and she happily sits down with her classmates waiting for instruction. When her peers get up to move to music, she gets up with the class. But then when her classmates are running, jumping, or galloping, Esther just walks around the gym. She will stop when the music stops when given an extra verbal reminder by a classmate or Mrs. Pritchard. At the throwing stations, Esther will pick up a ball, but she usually just holds the ball in her hand or taps the ball on her forehead. With encouragement by peers, she will walk up to the target and gently toss the ball or just drop the ball, but it really is not a throw. Like Brendan, Esther does not throw balls at the box in the final activity but rather just walks up to the box and touches the ball to the box. Unlike Brendan's behavior, Esther's behavior is not distracting for the other children or Miss Pritchard. However, Mrs. Pritchard does wonder if she is really helping her.

Physical education can be a dynamic, sensory stimulating, social, and physical environment; these attributes make it a cherished, enjoyable class for many students. Yet for some students with autism spectrum disorder (from here on referred to as simply autism), this environment can be challenging and can conflict with some of the characteristics of the disorder. The social nature of partner and group activities can aggravate the student who finds working and interacting with peers difficult; verbal instructions from the teacher can be ineffective for the student who prefers visual instruction; bright lights and loud noise can be agonizing for a student with sensory-processing issues; regular routine changes (e.g., moving from indoors to outdoors) can disrupt a student who likes consistency in his or her schedule; and the need to perform physical skills can pose problems for the student who has coordination issues.

It is clear that teaching a student with autism can be challenging for the physical education teacher. It requires proactive strategies such as preparing the environment, the equipment, the student, and his or her peers. It also demands reactive strategies such as managing challenging behavior and making adaptations to activities, communication techniques, and assessment methods. Yet with knowledge of the characteristics of autism and an understanding of specific strategies, the physical education teacher can enable the student with autism to enjoy and excel in physical education, thus providing the student with the skills that allows him or her to gain the multitude of benefits he or she needs and deserves. This chapter begins with an overview of autism, including characteristics associated with autism as well as its prevalence and causes. This is followed by a presentation of strategies that allow for the effective instruction and inclusion of the student with autism in general physical education. The chapter concludes with information on organizations related to physical education, sports, and physical activity for students with autism.

WHAT IS AUTISM SPECTRUM DISORDER?

Prevalence

Marking a 30% rise in prevalence rates since 2012, the Centers for Disease Control and Prevention (CDC, 2014e) now reports 1 in 68 American children to be on the autism spectrum. This prevalence rate remains constant across racial, ethnic, and socioeconomic groups. Boys are five times more likely than girls to have a diagnosis (1 in 54). As a physical educator, it is highly likely that you will have a student with autism in at least one of your classes.

CAUSES OF AUTISM SPECTRUM DISORDER

Autism is a neurodevelopmental disorder in which there exist impairments or irregularities in the growth and development of the brain. The actual cause of these impairments is uncertain, but it is likely that both genetics and the environment are influential. Hundreds of genes have now been linked to the disorder suggesting there are diverse genetic risk factors for autism (King et al., 2013). This is supported in twin studies; when one twin is affected, there is a 90% chance the other twin will also be on the autism spectrum (Rutter, 2005). Family studies also support the role of inheritance; in 10% of cases, a sibling of a child with autism will exhibit impairments consistent with autism (Boutot & Smith Myles, 2011). In addition, autism tends to occur more frequently than expected among individuals who have certain medical conditions such as fragile X syndrome, tuberous sclerosis, congenital rubella syndrome, and untreated phenylketonuria (PKU; Broyles, 2009). It is not known which specific genes contribute to susceptibility to the disorder, and research continues to try to shed more light on this area. Genetics does not, however, explain all occurrences of autism. The contribution of environmental factors to autism, which refer to influences other than changes in a gene's DNA, is also intensely researched. A study, the largest and most comprehensive to date, estimates heritability of autism to be 50%, with the other 50% explained by nonheritable or environmental factors (Sandin et al., 2014). How environmental factors interact with genetic susceptibility is a major focus of research, with factors such as toxins in our environment, parental age at conception, maternal nutrition, and infection during pregnancy all being examined (Grabrucker, 2012).

In 1998, a research paper now determined to be fraudulent claimed that autism spectrum disorders could be caused by the combined measles, mumps, and rubella (MMR) vaccine. Since then, some parents have expressed concerns regarding the issue of child vaccinations and autism. Particular concern was voiced regarding thimerosal, an ingredient previously found in some childhood vaccinations. There is now a consensus among researchers that no link exists between autism and vaccines. Reviews of the evidence by the CDC (n.d.), the American Academy of Pediatrics (n.d.), the Institute of Medicine (2011), and Demicheli, Jefferson, Rivetti, and Price (2005) all attest to this.

CHARACTERISTICS OF AUTISM

The use of the word *autism* has evolved over the last 100 years. Derived from the Greek word *autos*, meaning "self," the term was attributed to individuals who appeared removed from others or those who appeared isolated in one's self. Eugen Bleuler, a Swiss psychiatrist, was the first to coin the term, using it to categorize a group of schizophrenia symptoms. Thirty years later, the term was used by Leo Kanner, a researcher in the United States, to portray children who displayed social and emotional problems. Interestingly, at the same time and unknown to U.S. researchers, a German scientist, Hans Asperger, used the term *autistic* to describe similar characteristics in German children; these characteristics eventually became the criteria that defined Asperger syndrome (Silverman, 2011).

Until the 1970s, the term *autism* was largely regarded as a form of childhood schizophrenia. Increased research and an understanding of autism as a result of biological differences in brain development led to a distinction between autism and childhood schizophrenia. Objective criteria for diagnosing autism were defined in the 1970s, and the third edition of the *Diagnostic and Statistical Manual of Mental Disorders* (*DSM-III*) classified infantile

autism as a distinct disorder (American Psychiatric Association [APA], 1980). This category was later expanded and elaborated in the revised third edition, *DSM-III-R*, with diagnostic criterion provided for autistic disorder, which included three categories encompassing 16 symptoms, eight of which had to be present for a diagnosis. The three categories were 1) qualitative impairment in reciprocal social interaction, 2) qualitative impairment in verbal and nonverbal communication and in imaginative activity, and 3) markedly restricted repertoire of activities and interests as manifested by the following. In addition, such symptoms had to present during infancy or early childhood. The definition of autism expanded further in 1994 and 2000 with the *DSM-IV* and *DSM-IV-TR*, respectively, which both included five conditions under the umbrella term *pervasive developmental disorder (PDD)*: autistic disorder/autism, Asperger syndrome, Rett disorder, childhood disintegrative disorder, and PDD not otherwise specified.

The most recent changes in the *DSM-5* (APA, 2013) regarding autism were made in an attempt to clarify what a diagnosis entails and to increase consistency in diagnostics. The labels of Asperger syndrome, childhood disintegrative disorder, and PDD not otherwise specified are no longer used, and the group of conditions is now termed *autism spectrum disorder*. Psychologists and psychiatrists have been using the new *DSM-5* criteria and terms since May 2013. However, *DSM-IV* categories are also included and detailed here because, as a physical education teacher, you will be teaching children who have already been diagnosed with the older *DSM-IV* criteria. (Table 11.1 describes how students with autism may respond in physical education class.) The previous three categories of symptoms used to define autism are now collapsed into two categories in the *DSM-5*: social and communication skills and behaviors. A diagnosis of autism spectrum disorder is now given if a child fulfills the following criteria (see *DSM-5* for the exact definition of autism):

Ongoing impairments in social-communication and social interaction across many different settings, including the following:

- Significant impairments in social-emotional reciprocity—for example, unusual social quality of interactions when meeting and relating with others; diminished interests, emotions, or affect; inability to begin or respond to social interactions

- Significant impairments in nonverbal communicative behaviors used for social interaction, such as inadequate nonverbal and verbal communication, poor eye contact and body language,

Table 11.1.   **Students with autism in physical education**

Diagnostic criteria	Possible manifestations in the gymnasium
Deficits in social-communication and interaction	1. The student with autism may not share in the excitement shown by his or her teammates in an activity. 2. The student with autism may not respond to his or her peers' use of a high-five or pat on the back to signal "well done." 3. In waiting for physical education to begin, the student with autism may prefer to be alone rather than interacting and mixing with his or her peers.
Restricted and repetitive patterns of behavior, interests, or activities	1. The student with autism may like to practice behaviors such as flapping his or her hands or spinning in circles during physical education. He or she may also partake in atypical use of speech; for example, repeating what others say (echolalia) or saying a word that he or she likes repeatedly. 2. The student with autism may enjoy consistency in the structure of the physical education class. Changes in activities, equipment, or environment may agitate him or her. 3. The student with autism may have a particular interest that he or she likes to share with others (sometimes excessively) on a specific topic such as trains or dinosaurs. 4. The student with autism in physical education may be very sensitive to sensory input such as bright lights, children shouting, or heat from being physically active. In contrast, he or she may also be hyposensitive (e.g., not responding to a physical prompt unless it involves strong pressure).

Source: American Psychiatric Association (2013).

difficulty understanding and using gestures, and/or lack of facial expressions

- Significant impairments in developing, maintaining, and understanding relationships—for example, difficulty conforming to various social contexts, challenges with imaginative play or making friends, or lack of interest in peers

Limited and/or repetitive patterns of behavior, interests, or activities, as exhibited by at least two of the following:

- Repetitive or stereotypical movement patterns, use of objects, or speech (e.g., lining up toys, flipping objects, repeating words)

- Insistence on sameness and strict adherence and preference to rituals and routines expressed verbally and/or nonverbally, such as showing a strong need for consistency (e.g., eating the same food every night for dinner, following same bedtime routine) and displaying significant difficulties and distress with changes in these routines, transitions, and patterns of life

- Significant fixation in a few interests that are atypical in intensity or focus (e.g., unusually strong preoccupation or perseveration with a few objects to the detriment of focus on other things and people in the environment)

- Unusually strong sensitivity and reactivity to sensory stimulation as seen by either a hypersensitivity (gets upset with sounds or touch that would not bother others) or hyposensitivity (does not react to sensory input when others would respond). In addition, may display strange fascination with sensory aspects of the environment (e.g., indifference to pain/

temperature, inappropriate smelling or touching of objects, visual fascination with lights or movement)

- Symptoms must be present in the early childhood, although full display of the characteristics may not be apparent until later in life when social, academic, and environmental demands reach a level that becomes intolerable.

- Symptoms must be determined to cause clinically significant impairments in all major life domains of functioning, such as home, work, school, and the community.

- These unique characteristics cannot be explained by intellectual, developmental, or other behavior disability. It should be noted that intellectual disability and autism spectrum disorder are frequently comorbid diagnoses (i.e., a child may receive a diagnosis of both autism spectrum disorder and intellectual disability) (APA, 2013).

In addition to the new diagnostic criteria, new levels of severity have also been defined and included with the revised definition. The severity includes the following three levels (see *DSM-5* for the complete description of each level):

- *Level 3—Requiring very substantial support:* These children have severe impairments in verbal/nonverbal communication, social interactions, and inflexibility in behaviors, which lead to severe impairments in functioning.

- *Level 2—Requiring substantial support:* These children show marked impairments in verbal/nonverbal communication, social interactions, and inflexibility of behaviors that occur often enough and at a level that is obvious to even a casual observer and that interferes with functioning in a variety of contexts.

- *Level 1—Requiring support:* These children require minimal to moderate supports to successfully interact and engage in social settings, maintain flexibility in routines and activities, and moderate unusual behaviors.

Most important, we must remember that variability remains among children with a diagnosis of autism. Think of the example of Brendan and Esther in the case study at the opening of the chapter; clearly no two children with autism will present the same array or severity of symptoms. This variability is increased by the presence of secondary characteristics in many individuals with autism, as are outlined later in the chapter. As a physical educator, you should be aware if your students with autism have any of these conditions.

Motor Characteristics

It is particularly important for the physical educator to be aware of the unique motor characteristics associated with autism. It has been revealed that at least 63% of children with autism between the ages of 2 to 6 show some level of neurological motor impairment (Dowd, Rinehart, & McGinley, 2010). The presence and prevalence of motor impairments at a young age, often before social or communicative impairments are apparent, prompt a suggestion that motor characteristics may be a core feature of autism (Fournier, Hass, Naik, Lodha, & Cauraugh, 2010). Table 11.2 summarizes the array of potential motor impairments (or impairments that may appear as motor impairments) that a child with autism may present (Dowd et al., 2010; Fournier et al., 2010; Whyatt & Craig, 2012) and how these impairments may reveal themselves in physical education.

Despite these impairments, students with autism can experience a wealth of benefits from engaging in physical activity and physical education. "Increased aerobic exercise can significantly decrease the frequency of negative, self-stimulating behaviors. . .while not decreasing other positive behaviors" (Dawson & Rosanoff, 2009). Exercise can also deter students from engaging in self-injurious behaviors and improve their attention span (Dawson & Rosanoff, 2009). It has also been shown

Table 11.2.   Potential motor impairments

Motor impairment	Definition	Presentation in physical education
Fine motor skill impairments	Impairments in the coordination of small muscle movements	Difficulty in gripping a bat or tennis racquet, putting on a penny, tying laces
Sensory integration (or processing) issues	Sensory signals do not get organized into appropriate motor and behavioral responses	Can affect hearing, vision, touch, or multiple senses; for example, delayed response to verbal instruction (hearing), difficulty in predicted movement of teammates in team activities (vision), or inability to interpret a physical prompt (touch)
Poor coordination	Impairments in the ability to use different parts of the body together smoothly and efficiently	Difficulty in catching (two hands working together), throwing (stepping and arm movement), or combining skills (running and striking a ball)
Visual tracking impairments	Difficulties in visually following moving objects	Difficulty in tracking a ball prior to catching or striking
Slow reaction times	A delay between the presentation of a stimulus and the appropriate response	Difficulty in catching a ball or initiating a movement after receiving an instruction (verbal or visual) from the teacher or peer
Poor proprioception	An impaired ability to sense stimuli arising within the body regarding position, motion, and equilibrium	Difficulty in placing a hand or equipment piece (e.g., a tennis racquet) in the correct position, particularly when it is out of the line of sight (e.g., when completing an overhand throw or a tennis serve)
Bilateral integration impairments	The inability to use both sides of the body together in a coordinated way	Difficulty in running, skipping, catching with two hands, swimming, and so forth
Poor balance	The inability to maintain the line of gravity of the body with minimal postural sway	Difficulty in kicking, hopping, turning at a fast pace, and so forth
Dyspraxia	Impairments in the planning and coordination of fine and gross motor skills (also referred to as developmental coordination disorder or clumsy child syndrome)	Potential difficulty in all skills. Combinations of skills will be particularly challenging.

that impairments in locomotor and object control skills can be reduced with participation in a community-based adapted physical education program (DeBolt, Clinton, & Ball, 2010).

Health/Medical Problems

Large-scale studies have revealed that several medical conditions are significantly more prevalent in people with autism compared with the typical population (Kohane et al., 2012). Some of these conditions may present a direct challenge to the child's participation in physical education. For example, asthma, respiratory infections, severe headaches, migraines, and seizures (26% of adolescents with autism age 13 years or older are reported to have epilepsy; Viscidi et al., 2013) are all more prevalent in individuals with autism (Kohane et al., 2012). Such health conditions will have a direct impact on a student's ability to participate in physical education. In addition, a multitude of other medical issues such as allergic disorders, atypical immune function, gastrointestinal comorbidities, and autonomic nervous system dysfunction are also more prevalent in individuals with autism (Amaral, Geschwind, & Dawson, 2011). In addition to compromising general health, these conditions will affect the child's behavior and may present additional challenges to physical education participation. Table 11.3 provides a description of the possible manifestations of these conditions.

Additional Psychiatric Conditions

Some psychiatric conditions are also more prevalent in individuals with autism. These conditions will affect their participation in physical education. For example, anxiety disorders are more prevalent in individuals with autism; up to 35% of individuals with autism have generalized anxiety disorder, and up to 64% have specific phobias (Leyfer et al., 2006). In the physical education environment, this may manifest as anxiety about particular environments, equipment pieces, or activities. Chapter 6 provides information about using visual supports to decrease the impact of anxiety for the student with autism in physical education.

Obsessive-compulsive disorder (OCD) also frequently co-occurs with a diagnosis of autism. As suggested in the name, it is characterized by obsessive thoughts and compulsive actions. About 30% of individuals with autism also have OCD (Russell et al., 2013). Research also finds a high prevalence of attention-deficit/hyperactivity disorder (ADHD) in children with autism, with reports of comorbid

Table 11.3.　Possible manifestations

Condition	Manifestations
Seizure disorders	Seizure disorders (disturbed brain activity), when treated, can lead to significant improvements in language and autistic behaviors.
Allergic disorder	Food and inhalant allergies are common. Allergies have been shown to contribute to anxiety, irritability, fatigue, tics, and difficulty focusing.
Atypical immune function	Activation of the immune system can lead to functional changes in the nervous system and affect behavior, moods, personality, and cognitive functioning.
Gastrointestinal comorbidities	Gastrointestinal problems, such as diarrhea, constipation, and so forth, have been related to challenging behaviors, sensory overresponsivity, dysregulated sleep, anxiety, and irritability.

ADHD as high as 59% (Goldstein & Schwebach, 2004) and 78% (Lee & Ousley, 2006). In fact, ADHD is deemed the second most comorbid disorder in individuals diagnosed with an autism spectrum disorder (Simonoff, Pickles, Charman, Chandler, & Loucas, 2008). Although a dual diagnosis of ADHD and autism was not allowed under the *DSM-IV*, the new *DSM-5* has removed this prohibition.

Behavioral Characteristics

Many behaviors may be exhibited by students with autism that are derived from the core impairments of the disability or are the result of health and medical problems outlined previously. These behaviors often contribute to apprehension about teaching a student with autism and may lead to confusion for the child's peers who do not understand autism. As a teacher of a student with autism, you may expect behaviors related to the student's social and communication impairments, such as lack of ability to imitate and share with others, difficulty mixing with others, aloofness, lack of eye contact, peculiar speech tones, and echolalia (the repetition of words or phrases) (Boutot & Smith Myles, 2011). Behaviors relating to restricted repetitive behaviors may include possessiveness with certain equipment pieces and repetitive motor movements. Behaviors relating to the sensory processing issues a student with autism may have can include covering ears, peculiar reaction to touch, eating/chewing on equipment pieces, and self-injurious behavior (Hillman, Snyder, & Neubrander, 2014). Finally, behaviors as a result of the medical and health problems discussed previously may include tantrums

Table 11.4.   Common behaviors exhibited by individuals with autism

Behavior	Description
Lack of ability to imitate	An inability to copy the behavior of peers; often requires prompting by the teacher
Lack of ability to share	A failure to engage in the sharing of emotions or physical items (e.g., equipment pieces) with peers
Aloofness	An appearance of being distant, remote, or withdrawn
Peculiar speech tones	The use of atypical tone; for example, a high-pitched tone or monotone (flat tone)
Echolalia	Repeating words or phrases. The student with autism may repeat (often several times) a phrase you say or a phrase overheard from television.
Repetitive motor movements	The practice of behaviors such as hand flapping, spinning, and rocking; often, these behaviors will occur when the student is excited or upset.
Peculiar reaction to touch	Atypical tactile sensitivity wherein students with hypersensitivity may become agitated or upset when touched or may dislike certain equipment pieces touching their skin. Conversely, some students with hyposensitivity may seek deep-pressure touch (usually on their shoulders) from their teacher or their peers.
Self-injurious behavior	Behaviors causing injury to the self, such as head banging, hand biting, and excessive self-rubbing and scratching. The causes of these behaviors may be biomedical (the levels of some neurotransmitters are associated with the behavior; self-injurious behavior may increase production of certain endorphins), pain (e.g., head banging may be an attempt to reduce pain from an earache), sensory (e.g., self-scratching may be a form of self-stimulation), or frustration (perhaps due to the lack of ability to communicate).

and oppositional behavior, heightened anxiety, atypical locomotion patterns such as toe walking, vocal expressions such as moaning, and agitation, perhaps expressed though repeated pacing or jumping (Kohane et al., 2012). Table 11.4 lists some of these behaviors. Again, it is important to remember that the presence of these behaviors will vary from child to child. This will add to the uniqueness of each student with autism. It also should be noted that although some of these behaviors may derive from the presence of some medical conditions or psychiatric conditions, many of these behaviors are the student's unique response to the way he or she processes the immediate environment. How to prepare the environment and the student in order to minimize or manage the onset of these behaviors so that they don't conflict with the student's participation in physical education is discussed later in this chapter.

Cognitive Characteristics

Students with autism may present with a unique profile of cognitive strengths and weaknesses. Research has identified some of the cognitive features of autism such as impairments in paying attention to relevant information and cues; impairments in concept formation and abstract reasoning; and an inability to plan, organize, and solve problems (Gupta, 2004). In addition, activities that involve predicting the behavior of others based on the thoughts and feelings of others (also known as theory of mind) are difficult for many individuals with autism. These impairments may cause particular difficulties in

partner and group activities. Information later in the chapter will focus on how to adapt partner and group activities to overcome this challenge. Students with autism tend to do best on tasks that involve immediate memory or visual skills (Gabriels & Hill, 2002).

In addition, intellectual disabilities remain a highly prevalent co-occurrence with autism (Amaral et al., 2011), with approximately two thirds of those with autism having an intellectual disability (Waterhouse, 2013). In addition, 3%–6% of individuals with autism have fragile X syndrome, the most common inherited form of intellectual disability. Increasingly, intellectual disability and autism (as well as other disorders such as ADHD) are being identified as a feature of a shared brain development disorder (Owen, O'Donovan, Thapar, & Craddock, 2011) that is linked through multiple gene vulnerabilities.

TEACHING PHYSICAL EDUCATION TO STUDENTS WITH AUTISM

The characteristics of autism just described contribute to higher rates of obesity and inactivity among individuals with autism (Broder-Fingert, Brazauskas, Lindgren, Iannuzzi, & Van Cleave, 2014; Curtin, Anderson, Must, Bandini, 2010; Curtin, Jojic, & Bandini, 2014; Egan, Dreyer, Odar, Beckwith, & Garrison, 2013; Phillips et al., 2014). For example, in a review of thousands of medical records, researchers found that more than 23% of children with autism and 25% of those with Asperger syndrome were obese, whereas another 15% of children with autism and 11% with Asperger were overweight, whereas a little more than 6% of typically developing children were obese and 11% were overweight (Broder-Fingert et al., 2014). The responsibility on the physical educator to enable his or her students with autism to live physically active lives is great. Due to the variability within students with autism, as a physical educator, you must be willing and prepared to draw from a range of strategies that have been individualized to the student's needs and abilities. In this section, the challenges that you may face when including a student with autism in your class will first be outlined. Specific and practical strategies will then be offered to ensure safe and successful participation, such as strategies for preparing the student, his or her peers, and the environment; planning the curriculum; managing behavior; communicating with the student; and adapting activities.

Potential Challenges to Including a Student with Autism in Physical Education

Teachers (Obrusnikova & Dillon, 2012) and students with autism (Healy, Msetfi, & Gallagher, 2013) have shared the challenges that may arise in physical education. The following list of challenges is adapted from those revealed in research by Obrusnikova and Dillion (2011). As you read through the challenges that may arise in physical education, it is worth paying particular attention to the antecedents—that is, the events that occur within the physical education class that yield certain behaviors. Later, you will see that behavior management strategies are often focused on controlling, adapting, and minimizing these antecedents.

Inattention and Hyperactive Behaviors

Students with autism may have difficulty attending to instructions or tasks (Dodd, 2005), particularly when they demand prolonged attention and the environment contains external stimuli. This inattention may present as fidgeting, leaving the group/activity space, or exhibiting off-task behaviors such as running aimlessly around the gymnasium.

Impulsivity

Impulsivity has been defined as swift action without forethought or conscious judgment (Hinslie & Shatzky, 1940). Impulsivity is a common characteristic of individuals with autism (Amaral et al., 2011). The student with autism in physical education may exhibit impulsive behaviors such as blurting out questions or comments when instructions are being given or during other times that involve waiting. Impulsive physical behaviors may also present a challenge with the impulse to do an action overriding the desire to perform the correct components of the action/movement.

Social Impairments and Social Isolation

Teachers and students cite the social impairments related to autism as a challenge in physical education; the social nature of this environment may conflict with the social skills of the student (Healy et al., 2013). As the physical educator for students with autism, you will see many examples of how the social impairments of autism will present challenges for the student in interacting with his peers. For example, the social and communication impairments may affect the student's participation in group activities, sharing of equipment, and communication with the teacher and students. As communication is a key component of successful participation in team activities, an impairment may result in the student with autism disliking and avoiding activities that demand high levels of interaction with other students. It is not always the case that students with autism dislike being social; many students with autism want to interact with their peers but may lack the skills to appropriately do so. For example, in interacting with a peer, the student with autism may talk excessively about a certain topic, thus not allowing for back-and-forth communication. Similarly, the student with autism may not understand personal space or the body language of peers, which also may present a challenge to successful interactions. Research with students with autism revealed that bullying of students with autism also may occur in physical education (Healy et al., 2013).

Difficulties Understanding Instruction

Social and communication impairments are core characteristics of autism. This communication impairment makes verbal instructions alone often insufficient for a student with autism. To overcome this, the physical educator may use visuals to communicate with the student. An abundance of research demonstrates how teachers can use visual supports to effectively teach students with autism who struggle with social interactions, behavioral challenges, organization, transitions from one activity to another, and communication difficulties

(Arthur-Kelly, Sigafoos, Green, Mathisen, & Arthur-Kelly, 2009; Cohen & Sloan, 2007; Ganz & Flores, 2008). These visuals may be pictures, such as a visual of a clock to explain time is up; they may be physical objects, such as a poly spot or marker on the floor to show the student where to stand or step; they may be demonstrations by the teacher or a peer; or they may involve using videos to communicate.

Difficulties Performing Activities

The range of motor impairments in students with autism presents clear challenges for the physical education teacher. Table 11.2, shown earlier in the chapter, provides examples of the challenges that may arise due to motor impairments. Adaptations to instructions, equipment, and activities are often required to ensure the success of the student, and additional practice opportunities must also be provided.

Emotional Regulation Difficulties

Anxiety, aggression, and oppositional defiant behaviors are some of the emotion regulation difficulties that may arise in physical education for students with autism. Changes in routine, social situations, unsuccessful participation, competitiveness, an inability to communicate sufficiently, and sensory overload are just some of the reasons that emotional outbursts may occur. For example, a teacher might decide to take advantage of an unexpected warm winter day and take her students outside on the blacktop for physical education. For the past several weeks, the class has been inside, and the student with autism became used to this routine. A sudden change in routine can lead to anxiety, confusion, and ultimately unwanted behaviors such as a tantrum or hitting peers. Such behaviors may be troubling for the child, prevent his or her participation in activities, and can pose a distraction to the other classmates. This does not necessarily mean that a physical educator has to strictly keep with a particular routine the entire year. However, there are strategies that the physical educator can employ that will minimize the effects of emotion regulation difficulties.

Fixated Interests

The second diagnostic criteria category, "stereotyped or repetitive motor movements, use of objects, or speech," includes "highly restricted, fixated interests that are abnormal in intensity or focus" (APA, 2013). This characteristic can present various challenges in physical education. It is not uncommon for students with autism to become fixated on certain pieces of equipment or movements in physical education. For example, the student with autism may be fixated on the smell of a particular rubber ball or on the strings in a tennis racquet, distracting the student from the task the teacher wants him or her to perform.

Inflexible Adherence to Routines and Structure

Physical education is a dynamic environment. There are frequent changes of activities, tasks, locations, and equipment. In addition, games and team activities are often unpredictable. This inconsistency can present a challenge for the student with autism, which may lead to distraction from activities or off-task behavior. For example, some children with autism may be inflexible to changes to official rules of games and may get upset if rules are altered (e.g., allowing an extra strike in a softball game). Similarly, some children with autism will listen intently to instructions and rules presented in the beginning of class and expect strict adherence to these rules. However, a physical educator may decide to change rules and expectations in the middle of the class to make sure everyone is successful and challenged (e.g., allowing certain students to moving closer to the net when serving a volleyball and even using a beach ball in a volleyball game when using a regulation ball is too difficult). Although such midstream adjustments are good teaching practice, these unplanned changes may cause anxiety and behavioral issues for a child with autism who follows rules literally and strictly. Strategies are offered later in the chapter for how you may help keep maximum consistency in your classes and offer the students with autism support in dealing with the inevitable changes.

Strategies for Teaching Students with Autism

The previous section discussed an array of challenges that you may be presented with as the physical education teacher for a student with autism. The students with autism that you teach will each present with a unique combination of these behaviors and characteristics. Learning about these characteristics can be overwhelming and can make the thought of including a student with autism a daunting task. However, various strategies are at hand to allow you to successfully include the student with autism. Applying these skills will allow you to overcome the challenges discussed, resulting in an effective physical education class for all your students. These strategies are presented in four categories: preparing for inclusion, instructing the student, managing behaviors, and adapting activities.

Preparing for Inclusion

Know Your Student　Dr. Stephen Shore, a professor and author with Asperger syndrome, famously said, "If you've met one person with autism, you've met one person with autism" (Shore, Rastelli, & Grandin, 2006). A variety of combinations of symptoms can result in a diagnosis of autism. Social and communication deficits and restricted, repetitive patterns of behavior will present differently in each child. In addition, secondary comorbid characteristics will differ among children with autism. Knowing your student is essential for successful inclusion. Talk to the student, parents, teachers, and other professionals working with the child, such as speech, physical, and occupational therapists, to gain an accurate and comprehensive understanding of the student's needs, abilities, and preferences. For example, the speech therapist would be able to provide information on the child's ability to understand and communicate verbally and then provide strategies for presenting information verbally. Parents and special educators can provide specific information about the student's interests, reinforcers, sensory issues such as issues with loud noises, supports used (i.e., schedules, visual, communication systems, token economy system), past experiences in physical education, comorbid medical conditions, and so forth. Getting such information from individuals who know and have previously worked with the student with autism will greatly enhance your success in including him or her.

Prepare the Student　If the physical education environment is new or known to be anxiety inducing for the student, then preparing him or her for the environment is going to be essential. This can be done in a number of ways. Systematic desensitization, as outlined by Kamlesh (2011), may be one cognitive strategy for managing anxiety and fear in the physical education environment for students with autism. It involves gradually introducing the student to the environment. For example, the introduction sequence may involve showing pictures of the setting; showing videos of the setting; viewing a physical education class from the door of the gymnasium; watching from the periphery of the gym; and progressing to involvement in individual, partner, small-group, and finally large-group activities.

Previewing is also a useful technique for some students with autism. It involves using social stories or visual organizers to describe the setting that student will be part of and outlining appropriate responses (Grenier & Yealton, 2011). Such resources can be previewed by the student prior to class to assist the student in adjusting to the new social situation. A possible social story for preparing a student with autism prior to a class where he or she will be wearing pedometers is shown in Figure 11.1.

Visual schedules can also be created and presented to the student prior to class. Schedules are graphic organizers that provide an overview of the activities that the students will participate in. Schedules can be made in a variety of ways using pictures or words, but they should all be simple, one page long, and appropriate for the student's cognitive level. The student can then refer to the schedule throughout the class to assist in transitions between activities. See Chapter 5 for further information and an example of a schedule. Additional supports, such as a designated quiet space, can also be decided on, discussed, and introduced to the student prior to the physical education class.

Prepare the Student's Peers　Autism can be a difficult disorder for children to understand; the atypical behaviors, such as motor and verbal mannerisms, emotional outbursts, and intense interests, can be confusing to a child without knowledge

My name is _____. My classmates and I are wearing pedometers in physical education class this week. The pedometer will tell my teacher how much I move. My pedometer will attach to my pants. I will try to keep the pedometer on my pants. This is very important. My teacher will help me keep the pedometer on. My teacher likes it when I wear the pedometer.

Figure 11.1.　Pedometers.

of the disorder. To prevent this confusion from resulting in isolation of the student with autism and distraction for the students without autism, students should be informed about what autism is and the behaviors it may entail. Classmates should also be provided with direct and explicit guidelines about how to initiate contact and how to establish play with the children with autism. More important, this should occur with full support from the student and parents. See Chapter 6 for more details on preparing peers for the inclusion of classmates with disabilities.

Prepare the Environment   Now that the student with autism and the other classmates are prepared for inclusion, the environment should be assessed: Does it best facilitate successful participation of the students with autism? Most important, class layout should be as consistent as possible. For example, the student has a designated location where he or she waits while the class roster is called, receives instructions, watches demonstrations, and practices skills (i.e., physical activity stations). The consistency in being in a familiar space will help the student even if activities are changing. In addition, it may be beneficial that this space is located away from other distracters, such as windows. Second, the environment should be free from unnecessary equipment, and equipment should be laid out as consistently as possible (e.g., it may help for the ball or poly spots that the child uses to remain the same). The environment should also be adapted to best accommodate the student's sensory needs. For example, for students with hypersensitivity, bright lights and loud noise should be kept to a minimum. Equipment such as a baseball hat, sunglasses, or ear buds may help with this as well as thoughtful consideration of where the student is placed in the gym.

Instructing the Student with Autism

To cater for the diversity of abilities and preferences in communication of the student with autism, a hierarchy of instructional methods is presented here, sequenced from least intrusive to most intrusive (or least help to most help). As a physical educator, you must assess as to which instructional methods is most effective—that is, it provides adequate help, allowing for understanding and success, but limits the student's independence as little as possible.

Environmental Prompts   This method involves the intentional use of equipment to encourage specific behaviors or provide information. For example, poly spots can be used to direct the

student where to stand, a ball and target can inform the student of the planned activity, and other physical markers can outline the area an activity will be completed in. Equipment can also be used to make activities purposeful; this is very important for many students with autism. For example, instead of asking a student with autism to run around the length of the gymnasium, place bean bags at the end of the gym that the student must collect. In addition, equipment can be used to provide constraints that encourage the desired movement pattern. For example, if a student is having difficulty releasing the ball early enough when practicing the roll, the placement of a chair may encourage him or her to release earlier so that the ball goes under the chair.

Verbal Prompts   Verbal communication can be a challenge for students with autism. To overcome this, the following practices should be considered:

- Instruction should be concise, providing instructions one at a time, in as short a sentence as possible.

- Avoid negative sentences. For example, an instruction such as "step with your right leg" is better than "don't step with your left leg."

- Keep phrases and terms literal. For example, avoid phrases such as "keep your eye on the ball."

- Give adequate wait time. Students with autism may process auditory information more slowly than individuals without autism.

- Be consistent with language use and use one-word cues when teaching skills.

Visual Prompts   A variety of visual supports can be utilized to provide support and instruct the student with autism in physical education, taking advantage of the student's strength in visual processing. Schedules can provide an overview of the class's activities or can depict the steps in a particular activity. Pictures can also be used to explain specific actions, for example, a picture of an individual doing a jumping jack will demonstrate the correct body position of this exercise, or a picture of arrows on the wall will show which direction the student should move in. See Chapter 5 for more detailed information on using visual supports.

Video modeling is being increasingly used in the instruction of students with autism and may be a useful strategy for you to use in teaching the students specific motor skills or behaviors related to physical activity. It can be done using a videocamera, tablet, or smartphone. Video modeling involves the student with autism observing a target behavior being completed on video. Various types of video modeling can be used, including point-of-view modeling, wherein the action is played out as it would be seen by the participant. Video self-modeling involves the student themselves being the "model" in the video. Basic video modeling involves another individual as the model in the video.

As is true for all students, students with autism will also benefit from clear modeling of actions by the teacher or other students. Demonstration should be clear, repeated, coupled with verbal cues when appropriate, and show enough information for the student to attend to and process.

Physical Assistance For some students with autism, it may be necessary to provide physical assistance, which involves making physical contact with the student to encourage or teach a particular movement. This can be partial physical assistance, which may involve minimal physical guidance, for example, touching the student's hand to encourage the student to raise his or her hand to catch a ball or tapping the back of the student's foot to encourage him or her to step forward. Full physical guidance involves full hand-over-hand assistance. For example, this may be used to teach a student how to catch a ball and bring it into his or her chest. The teacher's hands are over the student's hands, guiding the student through the motion. It should be noted that some students with autism may respond differently to touch; some students will dislike any touch, whereas others react positively but only if it a very light touch or a very heavy touch is used. Through getting to know your student as well as speaking with the student's parents, you will learn the student's preferences and be able to offer support accordingly.

Peer Tutoring Research has shown peer tutoring is a viable and effective means for students with disabilities, including students with autism, to receive support in physical education (Klavina & Block, 2008; Lieberman, Dunn, van der Mars, & McCubbin, 2000; Temple & Lynnes, 2008). It has several benefits for the teacher and students involved: It is free, and it results in increased academic learning; increased physical activity levels; and improved social interaction, motivation, self-efficacy, and performance. Essential to the effectiveness of peer tutoring is trained tutors. This training should focus on disability awareness, communication techniques, instructional techniques (such as those listed earlier), scenario-based learning (e.g., providing tutors with scenarios of what tutoring a student with autism may involve and the appropriate responses), behavior management

strategies, and testing for understanding. The peer tutor program may take on various forms: one-to-one tutoring, a group of students rotating to tutor one student, classwide peer tutoring (all students are in pairs), and cross-age peer tutoring (an older student tutors a younger student). For more detailed information on implementing a peer tutoring program, see Cervantes, Lieberman, Magnesio, and Wood (2013).

Managing Behaviors/Motivational Strategies

Students with autism process the world differently than those without autism. Sounds, light, noises, time, and social behaviors are just some of the features of the world that students with autism may experience differently. These stimuli can trigger behaviors that conflict with the demands of a physical education class and that may distract other students in the class. Several strategies can be used in physical education to provide support to students with autism to help them to control their behaviors and participate in the class's activities. Refer to Chapter 19 for more information and strategies on preventing and dealing with challenging behaviors.

Identify Antecedents Antecedents are events that trigger a response. The responses may be positive, such as compliance with an instruction, or negative, such as making loud sounds. As the physical education teacher of a student with autism, you should take note of the antecedents that precede a student's behavior; dedicate a small notebook to making notes on the influential triggers in your class. Identify what triggers a desired behavior (e.g., you may notice that the student performs practice trials of a skill more effectively when he or she is working in the corner of the gymnasium) and work this into future classes. Conversely, identify what triggers a negative response (e.g., you may notice some equipment pieces cause the student to perform self-injurious behavior) and remove these triggers in later classes.

Incorporate the Student's Interests As referred to in the second diagnostic category, students with autism may have "highly restricted, fixated interests." Sometimes, these interests can be brought into the physical education class to motivate the student. For example, targets could feature a picture of the student's favorite cartoon character or a student interested in trains may roll the ball down the "train tracks" as marked on the floor with tape. With some imagination, nearly all interests can be incorporated into activities and can greatly aid a student's attention to the task. This strategy may not be appropriate when the student's interest is not age appropriate. If you are using a reward system, such as a token economy, the reward can incorporate the student's interest, which would ideally include a physical activity. For example, a student may earn the chance to shoot some baskets or bowl at the end of class as a reward for earning a certain amount of tokens.

Externalize the Authority A multitude of decisions must be made in a typical physical education class. For some students with autism, the acceptance of these decisions may be difficult and can result in problematic behavior, conflict with the teacher, and disengagement from activities. For example, decisions must be made regarding activity types, length of activities, number of practice repetitions, and team selection. The teacher or student may make these decisions. However, sometimes it is beneficial for authority to be placed outside of both parties, thus preventing the likelihood of conflict between teacher and student and increasing the likelihood of compliance by the student. Of course, the external object is always created, controlled, and implemented by the teacher so that the possible outcomes or decisions are predetermined to match the needs and goals of the student. The following methods can be used to achieve externality:

- Dice can be used to make a variety of decisions in physical education. For example, a couple dice can be thrown to determine the amount of practice repetitions. Dice can also be created to choose activity types for a student to practice.

- The selection of teams can be a difficult process for many students, and for those with behavior issues, it can be especially problematic. To put this decision out of the teacher's hands, the students can blindly choose bean bags from a bag; the color of the bean bag determines the team the student is on.

- Schedules (discussed previously) are typically used for assisting students with autism in making a transition between activities. However, schedules can also assist students who find it difficult to have teachers tell them what activities they should do. A schedule gives the impression that the activity format is predetermined and increases the chance of the students accepting it.

- A spinning wheel is another means of getting an external source to "decide" what activity or how many repetitions will be completed. The desired activities or numbers are simply drawn on the board, and the arrow is spun. Alternatively, the

physical education teacher can set up stations in the class, and a spinning arrow placed in the center of the gym can be used to determine where the student will work. After the child spins the arrow, he or she moves to the chosen station. Visuals here, as well as the equipment, will direct the student as to the skills he or she will work on.

- A timer can be used to decide on the time for a student to complete an activity or begin a new one.

Token Economy This behavior management strategy has been successfully applied to physical activity settings with individuals with autism and holds great potential for the effective management of behaviors of students with autism in physical education. It can be used to decrease off-task behaviors and increase positive behaviors. It consists of the following five steps:

1. *Identify behaviors:* As a physical educator, you must choose what behaviors you would like to increase. You should then define this behavior in an observable and measurable term (e.g., the student will place his or her equipment piece back in the equipment box after four out of five activities, when instructed to do so). Note the frequency at which this behavior is currently been done so as you may later assess the effectiveness of the token economy strategy.

2. *Choose reinforcers:* Using a token economy strategy, the student will work for tokens so as he or she can trade them for positive reinforcers; the reinforcer (e.g., an activity that the student is really motivated to work for, such as access to computer games, additional free time at the end of class, or time on the trampoline) as well as its "cost in tokens" should be set beforehand, and agreed upon by the student.

3. *Administer tokens:* Tokens (e.g., small printed cards, bingo chips, stickers) should be given to the student each time they engage in the desired behavior.

4. *Set trading rules:* Finally, allow the child to trade the token for the positive reinforcer when sufficient tokens are collected.

5. *Assess the effectiveness of the program:* Is the prevalence of the desired behavior increasing? If not, evaluate the strategy; are the reinforcements motivating enough? Does the student comprehend the desired behavior? Does the student need to be reminded of the token economy system that is in place?

The Premack Principle This principle states that an individual will perform a less-than-desired activity if it is followed by an activity he or she enjoys. Through thoughtful structuring of the class's activities, this simple strategy can be utilized in physical education to motivate students with autism to participate in activities that do not appeal to them. A first-then board (a simple schedule showing two activities, one to be done after the first is completed) may increase the success of the Premack principle by reminding the students of the activities that must be completed. Physical educators should ensure that this strategy does not alter the student's positive perspective of the "desired" activity.

Adapting Activities

The characteristics associated with autism will present differently in all students with autism. It is therefore beneficial for teachers to be aware that inclusion for children with autism, within the general physical education class, may occur on a spectrum. The inclusion spectrum (as outlined by Black & Williamson, 2011) offers teachers a framework for structuring classes to cater for diversity among students. The inclusion spectrum has five components, and depending on the social, physical, and cognitive abilities of the student, teachers can group students accordingly to maximize success for all. The five components are outlined here with examples of when they may be beneficial to students with autism.

Open Activities These activities are without modifications. Such a placement is useful when an activity allows for flexibility in movement patterns and individual student differences do not become barriers to participation. For example, a student with autism may successfully participate in a dance unit without modifications as he or she can choose how and with whom to move himself or herself. Another example is allowing children to travel (e.g., walk, run, gallop, slide) any way they want to music as part of a warm-up activity. This way, the child with autism will be successful by moving any way he or she chooses.

Modified Activities For some activities, modifications are necessary to enable the successful participation of students with autism. Modifications can be made using the STEP process (Roibas, Stamatakis, & Black, 2011), which represents modifications made to space, task, equipment, and people.

Space This involves modifying the area that the activity is being completed in. For example, a regular game of tag may not be conformable with the ability of a student with autism due to his dislike of being touched by other students. A space modification may rectify this by the teacher introducing a zone where students are tagged when the tagger comes within one meter of them while in this zone, thus eliminating the need for touching. Another simple modification of space may involve moving a student closer to a target to increase his or her success.

Task Modifications to the task may involve rule changes or additional rules imposed. For example, a rule change in basketball to increase participation may be that the ball must be passed to all team members before someone can shoot for a basket. To increase success, another rule change may be that hitting the backboard while using the correct shooting technique will earn one point. Similarly, rules may be applied to increase success for practicing skills. For example, when learning to bat, a rule may be enforced that states if a student misses two thrown balls, then they must hit the ball using a tee.

Equipment All equipment pieces can be adapted to increase learning and success for the students. One way to think about equipment adaptations is using the six Ss framework (Healy & Wong, 2012).

1. *Size:* Adaptations can be made to the size of the equipment piece. For example, using a bigger target may be better when practicing an overhand throw.

2. *Sound:* The sound of the equipment piece can also be adapted. For example, perhaps a student with autism dislikes the sound made when the bowling pins fall over. Placing the pins over carpeting will lessen the sound.

3. *Surface:* The surface of the equipment should be a consideration for some students. For example, some students may show a strong preference for equipment of a certain color.

4. *Speed:* Slowing down the speed of equipment pieces may also be necessary. For example, when practicing catching with a child with a delayed reaction, using a balloon will greatly enhance their success in learning the skills as the "ball" is now moving at a much slower pace.

5. *Support:* Equipment pieces, particularly balls, can also be supported to increase success for the

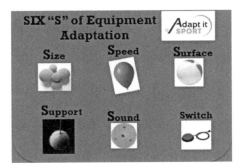

Figure 11.2. Six *S*s of equipment adaptation.

student with autism. For example, for a student with coordination difficulties or visual tacking impairments, it is advised that the ball is first supported on a tee or from a hanging rope while the student practices hitting it with the bat.

6. *Switches:* The final *S*, switches, refers to using switch-activated equipment pieces to allow for equipment use with minimal movement. This adaptation is primarily used for students with physical disabilities.

When teaching a student with autism, you may use the six *S*s framework to think about how the equipment pieces you are using can be adapted to maximize learning and success. See Figure 11.2 for some ideas about making adaptations.

People   Due to the social and communication impairments, an adaptation related to people may also be very beneficial when including a student with autism in modified activities. For example, reducing the number of players in a team activity may decrease anxiety for a student who dislikes large groups. Reducing the number of players will also increase the participation of each student involved.

Parallel Activities   Sometimes, it may be useful to separate the students into groups based on ability so that they can practice the same skills or do the same activities. For example, when practicing rolling, it may be useful for one group of students to practice using lighter balls, rolling from close proximity to the bowling pins. Another group of more skilled or experienced students may use larger, heavier balls and stand farther from the pins.

The teacher may allocate students to groups, allow students to choose groups themselves, or set criteria for group selection (e.g., if you miss all the pins once while part of the "expert" group, you move to the "training" group).

Separate Activities   Although students with autism must be given the opportunities to gain the social benefits of physical education, it will often be beneficial, and perhaps preferred by them, to sometimes work individually on their physical education goals. For example, some lifetime goals of students with autism may be individual activities, such as fitness goals or swimming, which may be best learned and practiced individually.

Disability Sports Activities   This component of the inclusion spectrum may benefit students by allowing for reverse mainstreaming, in which the students without disabilities participate along with the students with disabilities in sports designed or adapted for individuals with disabilities.

RESOURCES

Special Olympics
633 W 5th Street, Suite 2000, Los Angeles, CA 90071
Phone: 1-213-805-5231
http://www.specialolympics.org

Challenger Baseball
Phone: 570-326-1921
http://www.littleleague.org/learn/about/ divisions/challenger.htm

Surfers Healing
PO Box 1267, San Juan Capistrano, CA 92693
Phone: 877-966-SURF
http://surfershealing.org

Autism Speaks
1 East 33rd Street, 4th Floor, New York, NY 10016
Phone: 212-252-8584
http://www.autismspeaks.org

National Autism Association
1 Park Avenue, Suite 1, Portsmouth, RI 02871
Phone: 877-622-2884
http://nationalautismassociation.org

CHAPTER 12

Emotional Disturbance

Jason Bishop and Martin E. Block

OBJECTIVES

1. Understand the definition of emotional disturbance

2. Describe the characteristics and treatment of emotional disturbance

3. Identify the various disabilities associated with emotional disturbance

4. Describe the challenges of including students with emotional disturbance in physical education

5. Identify strategies to successfully include students with emotional disturbance in physical education

Jonathan, a seventh grader, often has trouble getting changed and out of the locker room for physical education. He quickly unlocks his locker and takes out his clothes. The trouble begins with how his clothes feel, starting with his socks. He puts on one sock and then takes it off, pausing for a second to look at the sock. He then puts the sock on again and then takes it off again. He repeats this pattern 40–50 times until the sock feels just right. Then he does the same thing with the other sock. Lacing up his sneakers leads to the same behavior of tying and untying his shoes countless times until it feels right. Finally dressed and ready to go, Jonathan closes his locker and spins the lock. He looks at the closed and locked locker, and then he reaches for the lock and gives it a pull just to make sure it is securely closed. He takes a step back, looks at the locker and lock one more time, and then reaches and pulls the locker again. This checking continues 30–40 times before Jonathan feels that the lock is truly secure. Getting dressed and out of the locker room has taken 20 minutes (most other students are out of the locker room in 5 minutes), and as a result, Jonathan's physical education teacher has once again marked him late for class.

Gabriela, a student in her first year of high school, is a little nervous and cautious by nature. She gets anxious very easily in new situations where she is not sure what to expect. Although many people get a little anxious in new situations, Gabriela's anxiety leads to faster-than-normal breathing even hyperventilating, sweating, and often feeling nauseous and faint. Although she has done pretty well in school, including in physical education, she has recently become more anxious with each new physical education unit. It has reached a point where Gabriela starts to feel sick and anxious at home on days she has physical education. If she makes it to school on these days, she has a lot of trouble focusing on her schoolwork because of the anticipation of going to physical education later in the day. When it is finally time for physical education and she walks into the locker room, she begins to hyperventilate, sweat profusely, and feel so faint that she has to sit down. Her physical educator sees how "sick" Gabriela appears, and she sends her to the school nurse. This pattern of symptoms leading to visits to the school nurse has happened several times, and Gabriela is now in jeopardy of failing physical education due to too many missed classes.

Unlike Gabriela, Chung's favorite class is physical education. He loves to run, he is strong and physically fit, and he is very athletic and skilled in many sports. He is popular in his fifth-grade physical education class, and everyone wants to be on Chung's team. Although Chung is a great athlete, he has trouble controlling his emotions. While he usually is the fastest, the strongest, and the best athlete in physical education activities, he does not always finish first. Just the other day, he was beaten by a peer when running laps during warm-up. This enraged Chung to the point where he hit his peer and was promptly sent to the office. A few days later, during a cooperative activity in which there were not supposed to be any winners or losers, Chung again lost his temper when his cooperative team took longer than other teams to solve the team movement problem set by the teacher. He yelled and cursed at his teammates and pushed and kicked two specific teammates who he felt were particularly at fault for his team taking so long to complete the challenge. This again led to a visit to the principal. It turns out that Chung's behaviors are not isolated to physical education; he has had several incidents of getting into fights on the playground during recess as well as in his classroom and in the lunchroom.

Jonathan, Gabriela, and Chung all have the label of "emotional disturbance," a population that comprises the fifth largest group of children receiving special education services under the Individuals with Disabilities Education Improvement Act (IDEA) of 2004 (PL 108-446; U.S. Department of Education, 2014b). Although the number of children with emotional disturbance increased from 446,000 in 1998 to 461,000 in 2007, the percentage of students (ages 8–21) with emotional disturbance remained constant at 7%. Many children have little quirks, are anxious in new situations, or get angry and even aggressive when things don't go as planned. However, if a persistent pattern of inappropriate and aggressive behavior is demonstrated, the child may be diagnosed with any of the myriad of diagnoses categorized as an emotional disturbance. Although many terms and diagnoses exist to capture the essence of the disability, we have chosen the term *emotional disturbance* in this book because it is the term used in IDEA 2004.

WHAT IS EMOTIONAL DISTURBANCE?

IDEA defines *emotional disturbance* as

a condition exhibiting one or more of the following characteristics over a long period of time and to a marked degree that adversely affects a child's education performance:

(A)   An inability to learn that cannot be explained by intellectual, sensory, or health factors.

(B)   An inability to build or maintain satisfactory interpersonal relationships with peers and teachers.

(C)   Inappropriate types of behavior or feelings under normal circumstances

(D)   A general pervasive mood of unhappiness or depression.

(E)   A tendency to develop physical symptoms or fears associated with personal or school problems (IDEA of 2004, 20 U.S.C. §§ 1400 *et seq.*)

Identifying children who have an emotional disturbance is challenging for school personnel, especially if the child has not been diagnosed with a specific behavioral or mood disorder. Bullis (1991) provided the following explanations for why school districts often underidentify students with emotional disturbance:

- Students are viewed as willful troublemakers rather than as people with a disability that affects their behavior.

- IDEA leads to constraints about disciplinary practices and due process protection.

- The large costs associated with special education may lead to a need for a residential school or hospital.

- There is a lack of sensitivity to mental health issues such as depression, anxiety, peer neglect and rejection, and affective disturbances, which often do not prompt teacher concern.

- A student's diagnosis is often based on subjectively determined conditions compared with those with obvious physical or mental disabilities.

- IDEA's definition of emotional disturbance is vague.

- Receiving a label of emotional disturbance is seen as stigmatizing.

Regardless of the prevalence of underidentification, the need to identify these children is especially important for the safety of the school environment. The increased media coverage of children acting out in a dramatic and/or violent fashion has increased national awareness of children who have emotional disturbance, how to identify these children, identification of appropriate therapeutic interventions, and increased funding to meet these children's needs. As the statistics indicate, the number of children who are at risk of an emotional disturbance is increasing, and it is important to understand the three requirements of identifying a child as emotional disturbed. The following three requirements are identified in the first sentence of the federal definition:

1. *Duration:* This requirement indicates that the behavior must be chronic, such as a persistent pattern of disruptive behavior that includes physical or verbal attacks on classmates, teachers, or school administration. The requirement excludes behaviors that are situational in nature and thus are understandable and expected. Such circumstances include divorce, a family's recent move to a new city, changing residences from one parent to another, a death in the family or of a close friend, or a similar crisis. These crisis situations could result in the child temporarily altering his or her behavior in a way that mimics an emotional disturbance; however, the aberrant behavior would need to persistent for more than 6 months to meet this qualifier (American Psychological Association [APA], 2013).

2. *Intensity:* The intensity and magnitude of the behavior is considered under this requirement. For example, confronting a classmate to resolve a conflict is a healthy behavior if executed respectfully and in a self-controlled manner. Some children may even resort to pushing and shoving to resolve the issue. However, the behavior would qualify under this criterion only if the child persistently resorts to physical and/or verbal attacks, which requires extensive crisis intervention from school personnel. The frequency and duration of time the student engages in a disruptive behavior is also important. For example, if the attacks occur frequently and for a long duration of time, the qualifier would be met.

3. *Adverse effects on educational performance:* To qualify for this requirement, school personnel, such as a classroom teacher, must provide evidence of a causal relationship between the child's behavior and his or her decreased academic performance. There are many ways to collect reliable and valid evidence, such as a discrepancy between the student's expected and actual performance. Another way is to correlate the time spent outside of the classroom due to managing the behavior and academic performance.

CAUSES OF EMOTIONAL DISTURBANCE

There are several factors responsible for emotional disturbance (Farrington, 2005). Some factors suggest a population-based difference in the prevalence of emotional disturbance. For example, boys are diagnosed about four times the rate of girls (Coutinho & Oswald, 2005; Russo & Beidel, 1994). Other factors include heredity, brain disorder, diet, stress, and family functioning.

Heredity Factors

Several biological factors may contribute to the etiology of emotional disturbance (Kauffman & Landrum, 2009). Some of these aberrations include brain injury or dysfunction, genetic anomalies, neuroendocrine imbalance, biochemical and neurotransmitter imbalance, negative temperament, nutritional deficiencies and allergies, physical disability or illness, and psychophysiological disorders. For example, Baskerville and Douglas (2010) reported that behavioral disorders are associated with a disruption in dopamine and oxytocin synthesis, distribution, and reception in the central nervous system. Cullinan (2007) proposed that brain disorders contribute to emotional and behavioral disorders through biological and physical influences. In addition, the Centers for Disease Control and Prevention (CDC) reported a link between sleep deprivation and increased risk of mental distress among adults (Gerber, 2014), which could also be a contributing factor to emotional disturbance among children. It is important to note that Kauffman and Landrum (2009) stipulated that the biological processes responsible for behavioral disorders only surfaced when the child engaged with environmental factors.

Family Functioning

Family factors such as parental inattention and separation/divorce can increase the likelihood of children displaying externalized or internalized challenging behaviors (Morgan, Farkas, & Wu, 2009). In addition, children of parents who use coercive discipline are more likely to develop behavioral disorders (Shaw, Gilliom, Ingoldsby, & Nagin, 2003). Broken homes; divorce; chaotic or hostile family relationships; absences of the mother or father; child abuse, including physical, verbal, and mental abuse; and parental or sibling separation are circumstances in which children are at risk for developing emotional disturbance. Many children find parental discord more injurious than separation from one or both parents (Loovis, 2011). Poverty is another contributing factor (Fujiura & Yamati, 2000). Research indicates a relationship between the number of risk factors and the development of emotional disturbance.

School Environment

Outside of the family unit, the school environment is the most significant socializing factor for children. During school days, children spend the majority of waking hours in transit to and from school and at school. For these reasons, the school environment is critical in preventing or facilitating the development of emotional disturbance. Kauffman and Landrum (2009) suggest that schools contribute to the development of emotional disturbance in the following ways:

- Insensitivity to the student's individuality
- Inappropriate expectations for the student
- Inconsistent management of behavior
- Instruction in nonfunctional and irrelevant skills
- Ineffective instructions in skills necessary for school success
- Destructive contingencies of reinforcement
- Undesirable models of school conduct

In addition, delayed early reading skills in kindergarten children are another risk factor (Morgan et al., 2009).

Cultural Discrepancies

More often than not, discrepancies exist between the values and expectations embraced by the child, family, and school. What might appear to be appropriate behavior at home for a child might not align with the social expectations and requirements of school. For example, Bandura's (1997) social learning theory suggests that children learn behaviors from watching older models they identify with, such as the child's father or mother. If the father of a boy exhibits physical and verbal violence to resolve issues, the child may learn that violence is an acceptable problem-solving method. However, this behavior is incompatible to a positive learning environment at school. As a result, there is an increased probability that the student will violate dominant cultural norms and be labeled defiant (Kauffman & Landrum, 2009). To this end, educators must intervene only when the behaviors are inconsistent with the achievement of core educational goals. It is important for educators to distinguish between behaviors that are inconsistent with educational goals and behaviors that do not conform to the educator's cultural mores.

Other cultural factors influencing behavior include the student's peer group, neighborhood characteristics, urbanization, ethnicity, and social class. These factors are only relevant when combined with other factors such as economic status and family conflict (Kauffman & Landrum, 2009). Prenatal exposure to drugs and alcohol affects children in at least two ways. First, both drugs and alcohol can cross the placenta and reach the fetus, causing chemical dependency, congenital aberrations, neurobehavioral abnormalities, and intrauterine growth delay (Loovis, 2011). Second, children of drug abusers are often exposed to chaotic family situations and may end up in the social services system moving from one substitute care situation to another. Research also indicates a relationship between prenatally drug-exposed children in Head Start programs and qualifying for special education services under emotional disturbance upon entering kindergarten.

CHARACTERISTICS ASSOCIATED WITH EMOTIONAL DISTURBANCE

The effects of emotional disturbance extend beyond the emotional domain. Depending on the severity of duration, degree, and adverse effects on educational performance, the mental disability can affect one's physical, social, and/or cognitive performance (National Dissemination Center for Children with Disabilities, 2010). Emotional disturbance is a mental illness and medical condition that disrupts a child's thinking, feeling, mood, ability to relate to others, and ability to complete activities of daily living. The accumulating effects often result in a diminished capacity for coping with daily trials (National Alliance on Mental Illness, 2010), including completing learning tasks in the general or adapted physical education classroom.

Maladaptive behaviors are often classified into two categories: *externalized* behaviors and *internalized* behaviors. Examples of externalized behaviors include acting out, aggression, or anger. Internalized behaviors include avoidance, social withdrawal, depression, and anxiety. In general, these children are not able to cope with their environment or peers. Children with severe cases may exhibit distorted thinking, excessive anxiety, bizarre movements, and dynamic mood swings. It is common for typical children to display mild to moderate levels of some of these behaviors at various times of development. However, children with an emotional disturbance display a persistent pattern of disruptive behavior. A combination of psychopharmacology and behavioral interventions are usually implemented for treatment.

Clinically speaking, children with an emotional disturbance may display any of a variety of behavioral characteristics depending on the specific type of emotional disturbance. For example, children with conduct disorder may display impulsive and aggressive behaviors and are often characterized by antisocial and/or violent behaviors (Frick, 1998). They tend to lose their temper, argue with adults and peers, defy or refuse to comply with rules and requests, deliberately annoy others beyond socially acceptable norms, blame their behavior on others, and be easily annoyed and often spiteful and vindictive (CDC, 2013). These children consistently ignore the basic rights of others and violate social norms. In the general physical education classroom, they are known to persistently argue with the physical educator and purposefully disrupt the flow of an activity. To illustrate, a middle school physical education class is engaging in a volleyball unit. During a miniscrimmage in which two games are played simultaneously and next to each other, a boy with conduct disorder purposefully spikes the ball toward a shy and smaller student on the other court. This behavior not only results in a lost point for his team but also disrupts the flow of the two games and threatens the emotional and physical safety of both the targeted child and other students. For children with conduct disorder, relationships with peers are often unstable and frequently result in conflict. Frick (1998) noted that children with conduct disorders often lack interest in social activities. The few social activities they do engage in tend to be superficial and temporary and require a minimum amount of immediate satisfaction to be maintained (Hill, 2002).

Children with other types of emotional disturbance might display completely different behaviors such as extreme withdrawal, tiredness and lack of interest in most things (e.g., depression), irrational thoughts that lead to not participating in activities (e.g., anxiety) or strange behaviors and rituals (e.g., obsessive-compulsive disorders [OCD]), and strange eating behaviors (e.g., anorexia/bulimia; Kauffman & Landrum, 2009). Often, children with these types of internalizing emotional disturbance are good at hiding these behaviors and can go unnoticed by peers, teachers, and even parents until a point where the behaviors result in a crisis such as a child with anorexia passing out and having to

be taken to the hospital or a child with anxiety or OCD refusing to leave the house. Some of the typical behaviors exhibited by these students include the following:

- *Hyperactivity*, which involves displaying a short attention span, leaving one's seat when sitting is expected, running or climbing in inappropriate situations, impulsiveness, frequent interruptions or intrusion on others, and picking up things that are not theirs. These children often appear to be driven by a "motor" that will not run out of gas, are restless, and have an inability to relax (APA, 2013). They may express strange, odd, or far-fetched ideas.

- *Aggression or self-injurious behavior*, which involves acting out and fighting; cooperative stealing; truancy; loyalty to delinquent friends; and disrespect for moral values, school rules, and public laws (Quay & Peterson, 1987)

- *Withdrawal*, which includes avoiding social interactions with others, excessive fear or anxiety when considering socializing with peers, increased self-consciousness, hypersensitivity, general fearfulness, anxiety, depression, and a perpetual disposition of depression.

- *Immaturity*, which includes inappropriate whining and crying, throwing temper tantrums when unrealistic expectations are not met (e.g., playing soccer *again* in general physical education class), poor coping skills, attention-seeking behavior, fighting, disruptiveness, repeating things over and over, and a tendency to annoy peers

- *Learning difficulties*, which include performing below grade level in academic and motor tasks

As mentioned previously, *emotional disturbance* is a generic umbrella term that encapsulates many mental health diagnoses. Disabilities categorized under this umbrella include (but are not limited to) the following.

Oppositional Defiant Disorder

A childhood disorder marked by a persistent pattern of developmentally inappropriate, negative, aggressive, and defiant behavior exhibited for more than 6 months. According to the *Diagnostic and Statistical Manual of Mental Disorders, fifth edition* (DSM-5; APA, 2013), the child must display at least four of eight behavioral categories during an interaction with at least one person who is not a brother or sister. For children 5 years of age or older, the behavior must occur at least once per week for at least 6 months. These children tend to lose their temper; argue with adults; and defy or refuse to follow rules, classroom and school expectations, and simple requests. They tend to deliberately annoy others, assume an external locus of control by blaming others for their own behavior, are easily annoyed, and are spiteful and/or vindictive. For example, a physical education class is developing soccer kicking skills. During a station activity, a game of two-touch is being played (the students kick a soccer ball against a wall, the next student has only two "touches" of the ball to return the kick to the wall for the next student). A student with oppositional defiant disorder might purposefully kick the ball three times (i.e., three touches) and expect not to be caught. However, several students notice and call the student's third touch to his attention. The student vehemently denies the third kick and refuses to perform the 10 jumping jacks to get back in the game. While the physical education teacher processes the behavior with the student, he blames his actions on another student who distracted him and delayed his response to get to the ball.

Conduct Disorder

Conduct disorder is marked by a persistent and consistent active disrespect of the basic rights of others and violation of social norms and rules. According to the *DSM-5*, a child must demonstrate three or more behaviors (e.g., often bullies, threatens, or intimidates others; physical cruelty to animals; setting fires to cause property or physical damage; breaking into someone else's house) throughout the previous 12 months with at least one exhibited in the past 6 months (APA, 2013). Kauffman and Landrum (2009) noted there are two major categories of conduct disorder. *Undersocialized, aggressive conduct disorder* is characterized by behaviors that isolate a child from peers and family and can include the following:

- Disobedience, stubbornness, being demanding
- Blaming others, arguing
- Swearing
- Bragging, showing off, teasing
- Being loud, threatening, or cruel
- Fighting, throwing temper tantrums, being aggressive, attacking others
- Exhibiting poor peer relationships

Socialized, aggressive conduct disorder is characterized by behaviors that are more likely to be displayed with others and can include the following:

- Alcohol and drug abuse
- Running away, truancy, joining a gang
- Stealing, arson
- Vandalism, being destructive
- Lying

When comorbid with attention-deficit/hyperactivity disorder or oppositional defiant disorder, conduct disorder often predicts later antisocial personality disorder, psychoactive substance abuse disorders, smoking, and bipolar disorder (Biederman et al., 2008).

Anxiety Disorder

Anxiety disorder is a family of disorders that share features of excessive fear and anxiety and similar disruptive behaviors. *Fear* is the emotional response to a real or perceived imminent threat, whereas *anxiety* is the emotional and physiological anticipation of a future threat. Although these two states overlap, fear is more often associated with autonomic responses necessary to confront a perceived threat or escape a perceived danger (i.e., fight or flight). Anxiety is characterized by muscle tension and prolonged intense anticipation of future danger (APA, 2013). According to the *DSM-5*, to qualify for an anxiety disorder, a child must demonstrate fear and anxiety more days than not for at least 6 months in a number of events or activities. The individual finds it difficult if not impossible to control the anxiety or worry. Anxiety is associated with three or more of the following six symptoms (note that only one symptom is required for diagnosis in children):

- Restlessness or feeling keyed up or on edge
- Being easily fatigued
- Difficulty concentrating or mind going blank
- Irritability
- Muscle tension
- Sleep disturbance (difficulty falling or staying asleep or restless, unsatisfying sleep)

The anxiety, worry, or physical symptoms cause clinically significant distress or impairment in social, occupational, or other important areas of functioning. In addition, the disturbance is not due to the direct physiological effects of a substance (e.g., a drug of abuse, a medication) or a general medical condition (e.g., hyperthyroidism) and does not occur exclusively during a mood disorder, a psychotic disorder, or a pervasive developmental disorder (APA, 2013). According to the National Survey of Children's Health (CDC, 2013), the prevalence of anxiety was higher in older children, children with lower socioeconomic status, boys (3.4% versus 2.6% for girls), and White non-Hispanic children.

Obsessive-Compulsive and Related Disorders

According to the *DSM-5* (APA, 2013), disorders grouped in this section have common behaviors in obsessive preoccupation and repetitive behaviors. Specific disorders identified in this group in the *DSM-5* include OCD, body dysmorphic disorder, trichotillomania (hair-pulling disorder), excoriation (skin-picking) disorder, and hoarding disorder. The most common of these disorders is OCD, which is characterized by the following two key behaviors:

Obsessions: Recurrent and persistent ideas, thoughts, impulses, or images that are intrusive and inappropriate. These obsessive thoughts often are perceived beyond an individual's control.

Compulsions: Also known as rituals, are repetitive, purposeful behaviors or mental acts that individuals perform to relieve, prevent, or undo the anxiety or discomfort created by obsessions or to prevent some dreaded event or situation

Obsessional symptoms, compulsive acts, or both must be present on most days for at least 2 successive weeks and be a source of distress or interference with activities. Either obsessions or compulsions (or both) are present on most days for a period of at least 2 weeks; cause marked distress; are time consuming (take more than 1 hour a day); or significantly interfere with the person's normal routine, occupational or academic functioning, or usual social activities or relationships (APA, 2013).

Adams (2004) noted common compulsions include cleaning/washing, checking/questioning, collecting/hoarding, counting/repeating, and arranging/organizing.

Depression and Suicidal Behavior

Depression is characterized by having at least five of the following nine symptoms present nearly every day and over a period of at least 2 weeks and that they represent a change from the person's baseline (APA, 2013). In addition, the following symptoms must result in impaired function in social, occupational, and/or educational situations:

- Depressed mood or irritable most of the day, nearly every day, as indicated by either subjective reports (e.g., feels sad or empty) or observations made by others (e.g., appears tearful)

- Decreased interest or pleasure in most activities, most of each day

- Significant weight change (5%) or change in appetite

- Change in sleep such as insomnia or hypersomnia

- Change in activity such as psychomotor agitation or retardation

- Fatigue or loss of energy

- Feelings of worthlessness or excessive or inappropriate guilt

- Diminished ability to think or concentrate or more indecisiveness

- Thoughts of death or suicide or has suicide plan

Depression can range from mild to severe and can be part of a major depressive disorder or an isolated episode. Limited research suggests physical activity may have a protective influence on the development of depression in children and adolescents (Brown, Pearson, Braithwaite, Brown, & Biddle, 2013; Strawbridge, Deleger, Roberts, & Kaplan, 2002).

Motor Characteristics Associated with Emotional Disturbance

Many children with emotional disturbance will not have any motor delays or impairments, particularly those with more mild symptoms. However, many others will exhibit specific motor issues that may be the result of lack of practice by choice (e.g., a child who is anxious or withdrawn) or by social rejection (e.g., overly aggressive children or children who peers perceive as odd or different). One group of researchers described the movement characteristics of children with more severe psychological disorders as wooden, clumsy, and less fluent with stereotypical movements and delayed gross motor skills (Bauman, Loffler, Curic, Schmidt, von Aster, 2004). Clinical observations suggest children with more severe emotional disturbance experience impaired motor performance and lower physical fitness scores. Emck, Bosscher, Beek, and Doreleijiers (2009) found that these children performed poorly in fundamental motor skills and fitness measures, including muscular strength and flexibility and in athletic speed, compared with normative data. Delayed motor coordination and balance control also have been reported for children with emotional disturbance (Erez, Gordaon, Sever, Sadeh, & Mintz, 2004; Stins, Ledebt, Emck, van Dokkum, & Beek, 2009; Vance et al., 2006). Studies indicated that socially anxious and impulsive children performed worse in motor skills compared with control groups (Dewey, Kaplan, Crawford, & Wilson, 2002; Kristensen & Torgersen, 2007). In a study by Green, Baird, and Surgden (2006), parents reported a strong association between social and emotional problems in children and delayed motor skills.

Smyth and Anderson (2000) reported that children with delayed motor coordination were less interactive in social play when playing on the playground and thus were at risk of becoming socially isolated. Emck, Bosscher, van Wieringen, Doreleijers, and Beek (2012) found that 65% of children of a small sample with gross motor delay met the criteria for psychiatric classification, suggesting a strong relationship between gross motor delay and psychiatric problems.

The issue is often compounded by the fact that children with emotional disturbance often cope with their motor and fitness impairments by avoiding activities in which they perceive they are incompetent. In this way, they protect their self-esteem by avoiding a potentially embarrassing failed practice attempt. Unfortunately, the lack of participation in practice attempts ultimately widens the motor performance gap between these children and their peers. As these children grow, they will have increasingly greater difficulty in participating in games and activities as a result of lack of practice. Consequently, they often lack the motor skills needed to participate in the more complex and demanding physical activities that their peers engage in. The *skill-learning gap* hypothesis states that as the majority of children within an age cohort develop proficiency in basic motor skills required to participate in physical activities, they learn, practice, and compete in increasingly more challenging activities. However, when children with motor delay try to participate, they find it difficult to play in a personally meaningful or developmental manner, thus exacerbating the difficulty to acquire the expertise to play in the activity (Wall, 2003). Not surprisingly, Cairney, Hay, Faught, Mandigo, and Flouris (2005); Cairney, Hay, Faught, Corna, and Flouris (2006); and Cairney, Hay, Faught, Wade, et al. (2005) also found that children with delays in motor skills participate less in physically active play and other physical activities than their peers, in part because of low generalized self-efficacy to successfully participate.

Health/Medical Problems Associated with Emotional Disturbance

There are no known health/medical conditions specifically associated with the label of emotional disturbance. Some conditions such as anorexia and bulimia can lead to severe health conditions such as extreme weight loss, malnutrition, and heart problems. Similarly, children who have severe anxiety disorder may refuse to eat certain foods or

participate in healthy exercise behaviors, which could lead to deteriorating health and secondary conditions such as Type 2 diabetes. However, as a general rule, there is no association between having an emotional disturbance and having specific health/medical conditions.

Cognitive Characteristics Associated with Emotional Disturbance

Cognitive assessments usually reveal an IQ above 85 with higher performance IQ than verbal IQ for children with emotional disturbance (Teichner & Golden, 2000). Despite the reported average intelligence, these children tend to have comorbid learning disabilities in many academic areas, including reading, spelling, writing, and math (Hill, 2000). Hill (2000) reports that many exhibit cognitive and executive functioning impairments. Coupled with these learning impairments and marked histories of failure experiences, children with emotional disturbance often develop low self-concept (Grande & Koorland, 1988). They tend to approach new tasks with a pessimistic attitude, which increases their probability of failure. As a result, these children tend to have an external locus of control and attribute success to luck rather than to skill proficiency (Grande & Koorland, 1988).

TEACHING PHYSICAL EDUCATION TO STUDENTS WITH EMOTIONAL DISTURBANCE

As teaching comprises instruction and class management (Graham, Holt-Hale, & Parker, 2013), effectively and efficiently managing student behaviors and improving motor performance and learning are obvious goals of the general physical education teacher. Without sufficient classroom management, instruction and learning are difficult at best. A poorly managed class results in physical educators spending more time attempting to address inappropriate behavior and less time on education, assessment, student practice, and instructional feedback. As more and more students with behavior problems, including emotional disturbance, are included in general physical education, it is essential for physical educators to be proficient in classroom management. Although a thorough discussion of positive behavior support to address the behavioral issues related to teaching children with emotional disturbance are addressed in Chapter 19, the following section focuses on specific strategies to prevent and appropriately respond to aggressive and threatening behaviors of children with emotional disturbance.

In *Poor Richard's Almanac*, U.S. founding father Benjamin Franklin popularized the saying "an ounce of prevention is worth a pound of cure." This cannot be truer when including students with emotional disturbance in the physical education classroom. Prevention begins with the physical education teacher's philosophy and attitude toward students with emotional disturbance in their class. Many physical education teachers do not feel adequately prepared to include students with disabilities into their classroom (Lienert, Sherrill, & Myers, 2001). Modifying one's philosophical approach and attitude is often the first step to successful inclusion. This philosophy toward inclusion must be applied to each individual student and constantly revisited to ensure the teacher is providing service in each student's best interests.

All students have the universal right to be treated with dignity and respect independent of their previous and/or current behaviors and attitudes. This right cannot be taken away and is guaranteed because of who they are, not what they do or do not do. An example of this philosophy is the use of person-first terminology (e.g., "a student with an emotional disturbance" as opposed to "an emotionally disturbed student"). By referring to a student as a person and not his or her disability, we communicate that people are affected by their abilities or disabilities but not defined by them. It is important to treat each student with dignity and respect.

Treating children with behavioral challenges consistently with dignity and respect can be very challenging for even the most skilled teachers. The first step toward conflict prevention is introspectively assessing our philosophy and attitude. Before we can be influential in helping children change their attitude and beliefs, we must first address our philosophy and attitude through our interactions with each student. For example, after interacting with a student, either nonverbally, verbally, or physically, it is often helpful to immediately reflect on the interaction by asking yourself, "Did I treat him or her with dignity and respect?" If not, ask yourself how you can improve and implement your answer during your next opportunity. When working with students with emotional disturbance, an important goal of the physical education teacher is to develop positive relationships (Pianta & Hamre, 2009), meet their needs, and help them develop dignity and respect for themselves and others. Abraham Maslow (1954) developed a conceptual model of hierarchical needs that must be met for us to be effective at accomplishing a task such as learning the forehand tennis strike. The model begins with basic human needs such as food, water, and shelter. This is followed by safety and security, including a consistent and predictable environment. Moving upward, the next needs are love and belonging, including healthy relationships with class peers, teachers, and staff. This is followed by the need for achievement, including goal pursuit and fun. The highest level in the hierarchy is self-actualization.

Two of Maslow's stages have particular applicability to physical education. Safety and security are provided by presenting a consistent and predictable class, curriculum, and teaching approach. For example, a student with an emotional disturbance will feel at greater ease knowing that in today's physical education class, students will first participate in a fitness-based warm-up followed by the introduction or review of a fundamental motor skill. Next, everyone will practice the skill, and finally, a cumulative noncompetitive game or activity will be followed by a review of the day's learning objectives. Only when a student feels physically, psychologically, socially, and emotionally safe and secure is he or she prepared to experience healthy relationships with peers and the physical education teacher. The "love and belonging" stage is associated with building healthy relationships based on trust and fidelity. It is at this stage where the student with emotional disturbance tends to struggle the most in physical education. For example, a physical education teacher may be presenting the overhead volleyball serve. After the skill presentation and some station work, the class stands between the attack line and the serving lines on each side, practicing serving to each other. A student with emotional disturbance may not feel secure in his or her relationships with his or her peers. To avoid looking "stupid" or "not good enough," this student will typically change his or her behavior to appear unmotivated or exhibit a behavior problem. Within school settings, children, particularly middle school children, who disobey the teacher hold a higher social status than those who try to complete tasks but "fail." One effective tactic for preventing this behavior is to use positive presence by using teacher proximity and offering positive feedback. The key is to use Maslow's hierarchy of needs to assess which level of the student's needs is not being met and then make the necessary adjustments to your teaching approach to meet those needs.

One key strategy to prevent conflict is to use the "RADAR" method (Mandt System Inc., 2010) to anticipate and prevent potential conflicts. The following components make up RADAR:

- *Recognize:* Use all senses (i.e., sight, hearing, smell, taste, and touch) to be aware of the environment and student behavior. When we are appropriately focused, the integration of our senses will often inform us (i.e., our "sixth sense") that something is wrong.

- *Assess:* Some common behaviors to look for to anticipate and prevent conflict include how a student is walking, the speed at which the student is walking and talking, the student's posture, and how the student holds his or her hands. The hands of a relaxed student are often held at the side or are engaged in an appropriate activity. Arms held close to the body or crossed with hunched shoulders may indicate defensiveness caused by fear and anxiety. Elbows flexed at about a 45-degree angle may indicate that the student is ready to either engage in a physical altercation or flee the environment (i.e., fight or flight).

- *Decide:* When you anticipate a conflict is surfacing, you will need to choose the most appropriate response. Each scenario is different and will often require difference responses. There are three categories of responses: nonphysical responses such as communication with the student or conflict management and resolution; general physical response such as physical proximity, body shifting, and so forth; and specific physical interaction such as a light touch on the shoulder.

- *Act:* This is the physical response of the decision, which can be either nonphysical, general physical, or specific physical interaction.

- *Review results:* Were your actions successful? What could you have done differently? What can be changed to prevent a future conflict?

The Mandt System is a comprehensive, research-based behavioral intervention that describes the steps students progress through as they engage in a crisis. Some stages are skipped as a student moves up or down the cycle. Each stage requires unique responses from the physical education teacher. The following is a description of each phase and the appropriate staff response:

- *Baseline phase:* This is known as the personal-best stage. In this phase, the emotional and physical security of each student is sufficient for learning. However, because of their difficulty in processing environmental stimuli and even mild demands, the baseline phase of students

with emotional disturbance is very close to the stimulus, or trigger, phase. While in this phase, the physical educator responds by maintaining the positive learning climate and building a relationship of trust with the student with emotional disturbance.

- *Stimulus, or trigger, phase:* In this phase, something upsetting has happened to the child. Possibilities include being teased by other students, being asked to do something or stop doing something, not getting enough attention, and so forth. Students with emotional disturbance will often enter the physical education classroom very close to this phase. The physical educator responds by removing the stimulus, such as separating two students, removing the student from the environment, or moving the class to a different location.

- *Escalation phase:* In this stage, the student is becoming more upset and tension between the student and the environment increases. The student may make demanding requests such as playing with different equipment, participating in a station, or joining a group that has earned an incentive. During this phase, it is recommended not to give in to this request as it will likely increase the difficulty of preventing future crises. Instead offer appropriate options and set limits to his or her behavior. Use as few words as possible during this phase and as the student gets more upset. Talking to the student is appropriate if he or she starts to calm down.

- *Crisis phase:* In this phase, the student physically acts on his or her emotions of anxiety, fear, anger, and frustration by kicking and/or throwing objects and screaming loudly. Because of the emotional intensity in the moment, the student is not able to access his or her reasoning resources of the prefrontal cortex. Emotions have taken over, and the student has lost the ability to cognitively evaluate the situation. For example, a student may physically assault another student and has been physically restrained by the physical education teacher. In this phase, the student is still trying to attack the student despite being restrained. However, physical restraint should be avoided unless the student is threatening physical harm to himself or others (including staff). In this phase, the teacher should respond by minimizing any engagement with the student, including talking, making eye contact, or gestures. The goal of the physical education teacher is to monitor the student for safety. Many crisis intervention strategy programs prohibit staff from physically intervening in this step unless the student is threatening physical self-harm (e.g., striking his head against a wall) or harm to others (e.g., attempting to strike another student). Never attempt to restrain someone who has fallen to the ground. It is difficult to attack another person from a prone or supine position. If the student engages in self-harm such as striking their head against the ground, place your hand between the student's head and the ground until you can replace your hand with protective equipment such as a pillow.

- *Deescalation phase:* During the crisis phase, a critical moment occurs when the student begins to use his or her cognitive resources to assess the situation and environment. For example, while being restrained, the student will begin to evaluate and strategize how to disengage, or he may simply ask, in a controlled manner, to be let go. The staff should respond by asking the student if he is ready to be let go or to walk with you to a safe place. When the student confirms he is ready, slowly disengage the restraint while assessing whether the student is trying to get out only to attack again. If so, the restraint may need to be reengaged. Once the restraint is released, the student may attempt to reengage in his previous attack. In this scenario, you may need to reengage the restraint if another noninvasive intervention, such as body position, is not effective. Occasionally you will need to engage in several sequential restraints. This is acceptable as long as the purpose is to protect people from physical harm. All precautions and prevention methods should be exhausted before engaging in a restraint, and the restraint should last as shortly as possible to support the student. The staff should offer alternative options such as going to a quiet place. The physical education teacher should remain positive during this stage, and a positive compliment might accelerate the deescalation process.

- *Stabilization phase:* In this phase, the student has cognitively returned and tries to return to a state where he or she can access his or her reasoning, compromising, and language skills. In a school setting, it is most likely that support staff have arrived and have escorted the student away from the physical education environment. Staff should engage in active listening and offer solutions to how students can get their needs met appropriately.

- *Postcrisis phase:* Crises are often extremely draining, both emotionally and physically. The student will often need to rest before rejoining his or her class.

It is important to understand that everyone follows a similar pattern when responding to stressful situations. For this reason, physical educators must constantly evaluate where students are on the crisis cycle when responding to a crisis. Teachers must always be at least one level below the student they are supporting. It is recommended that faculty remove themselves from the scenario by requesting additional support if they are unable to prevent themselves from moving close to crisis. The key to prevention is building a relationship with trust while the student is in the baseline phase.

Understanding Emotions, Stress, and Anger

Emotions

Emotions are what we feel, and behaviors are our actions or what we do. For example, anger is an emotion, and using profanity (e.g., cursing at the teacher) or striking the teacher is the behavior or action the student exhibits to communicate the emotion. Anger is a secondary emotion that follows more primary emotions such as fear, embarrassment, shame, or frustration. For example, a student may feel initial shame after failing to successfully make a shot on goal during a culminating soccer activity. In turn, he or she may feel anger because of his or her perceived failure. Anger itself is neither good nor bad, but it is emotional feedback that communicates to the student that something needs to change (Carter, 2002). Anger can be channeled to elicit positive behavioral change. An example is how the 2014 National Basketball Association (NBA) team the San Antonio Spurs used their emotions after losing the 2013 NBA Finals to increase their performance and defeat the Miami Heat in the largest average playoff point differential in NBA Finals history (14.1 points per game). However, instead of using anger as inspiration to increase their level of performance, some students instead choose to react negatively by engaging in a form of aggression such as verbal or physical aggression. A student who begins to escalate from the baseline to the stimulation phase may be trying to communicate that something is wrong. It is important that we pay attention and respond accordingly to meet the student's need. Some students will give a false impression of communicating a need to manipulate the physical education teacher to meet their needs of attention. When you suspect this, it is often recommended to address the student and then redirect his or her behavior. It is important to respond to student behaviors in a calm and controlled manner at each stage of the behavioral cycle even if our anxiety or anger increases or we are not physically safe from the student.

Stress

Stress is a natural physiological response to internal or external stimulation. The stimulation can be real or merely perceived. People experiencing high levels of stress experience physiological changes, including a rise in blood pressure, faster breathing, changes in skin color, and unnoticeable muscle contraction. They may experience tunnel vision by only being able to focus on the immediate source of stress. If the stress is high enough, the student may feel hopeless and refuse to listen to trusted adults. They may experience feelings of isolation, disassociation, and a feeling that they cannot trust others. Students with emotional disturbance will escalate up the crisis cycle if they are not able to appropriately channel and process the stress. Healthy relationships with the student can be nurtured when he or she initially experiences stress and before he or she accelerates into the escalation phase. The physical education teacher can help the student externalize emotions and replace hopelessness by offering options and a healthier perspective on the issue.

Anger

A student's anger cannot be controlled by the physical education teacher. However, the environment, teaching approach, and curriculum can be modified to provide the most positive environment available. Matheson and Jahoda (2005) found that children with developmental disabilities have difficulties in evaluating and responding appropriately to the emotions of other peers and adults. Specifically, children in the "aggressive" group experienced difficulty in associating important environmental cues that help identify the feelings of others. The Mandt System (2010) suggests that if children with emotional disturbance learn to assess their own feelings, such as anxiety and fear, and learn to communicate their needs to the physical education teacher or a teacher's aide, they will be less likely to use aggression. Fear is another instinct that heightens awareness and can prepare people to protect themselves. Students may act aggressively in response to fear. One way to address student aggression is to show that you accept the student's emotions without judgment and then suggest healthier ways for the student to express his or her feelings.

Fish! Philosophy

Another approach that has been successful in some private schools in serving students with emotional disturbance is the Fish! Philosophy (Cathcart, 2007). The basic premise of the Fish! Philosophy is to learn to love what you are doing in the moment, even if it is not what you prefer to do. For example, many collegiate basketball enthusiasts would prefer to watch the opening round of the National Collegiate Athletic Association Men's Basketball Tournament, which is often held during school hours on a Thursday and Friday in March. However, our professional obligation to teach physical education motivates us to go teach our classes instead of calling in sick to watch the games. There are four principles in the Fish! Philosophy that can be used to guide physical educators to increase their effectiveness in serving children with emotional disturbance and preventing crises:

1. *Choose your attitude:* The Fish! Philosophy states that we are responsible for how we view the world, our attitude, and how we choose to respond to daily tasks. This is important because working with children with emotional disturbance can be very challenging and draining. It is often easy to have an external locus of control and say things such as, "That student ruined my day." In this scenario, the teacher is choosing to be acted upon and to give control to the student when evaluating the quality of his or her day. While the student may have a particularly bad day requiring the teacher's patience and self-control, it is important to maintain an internal locus of control and choose a positive response and attitude. A healthier internal locus of control statement might be, "Johnny had a bad day that required a lot of focus and patience from me, and it was a very stressful day. However, I am glad that we were able to help him through his crises." In this scenario, the instructor acknowledges the fact that Johnny quickly escalated up the crisis cycle, which was very stressful and demanded a high level of focus and internal resources to resolve. However, no one was hurt during the crisis, and the instructor was able to make a positive difference in Johnny's life by providing a safe environment and intervention.

2. *Play:* Play is the premise of physical education and physical activity (Hawkings, 2011). We should do everything we can to make teaching fun and enjoyable. If we are happy, people around us, including our students with emotional disturbance, will be happier. In addition,

happiness and fun can be contagious. Students with emotional disturbance often deescalate down the crisis cycle in anticipation of a fun, safe physical education class. Likewise, an appropriate but quick and witty comment can help the student deescalate. For example, the author of this chapter once was supporting a student who was approaching a crisis after physical education class. After several minutes of engaging in active conflict resolution tactics and strategies, the author looked at the student and said, "I'm really tired today. Want to go to lunch and do this some other time?" The student thought the comment was humorous and calmed down. For this reason, it is important to self-assess our attitude and demeanor each day before arriving at work and prior to and during each physical education class.

3. *Make their day:* Teaching physical education is easier and more enjoyable when we focus on serving our students and making a positive impact in their lives. Striving to make another's day, particularly a student with emotional disturbance, helps us to forget about personal concerns and worries. Often, the smiles, laughter, and professional bonding relationships we develop with our students are the external reward that drives us to excel in our profession. In addition, the positive and professional resources we provide to our students with emotional disturbance may be a student's only authentic relationship and resource.

4. *Be there:* Sometimes, teachers are physically present but are emotionally and psychologically focused on other things during their classes. Many physical education teachers have additional school-related responsibilities, such as coaching, that are of concern. No matter what issues we may be facing during a physical education class, it is important to sustain focus and engagement in the present physical education lesson plan. Students sense when teachers are not engaged in a physical education class. This behavior results in decreased trust and security for students with emotional disturbance. In addition, a teacher's ability to use their RADAR is diminished, resulting in an increased likelihood of failing to prevent a crisis.

5. *Be a master of change:* While not a Fish! Philosophy, we want to constantly learn and grow by developing and refining our teaching philosophy, attitude, and approach. Research findings provide value-added knowledge of how

to increase our teaching effectiveness. School districts usually fund annual professional development workshops for teachers and faculty. Be committed to learning and applying as many new principles or approaches as feasible. Being a *master of change* is a great creed for teaching children with emotional disturbance, who often have difficulty processing environmental stress. Children with emotional disturbance need direct teaching of social skills and assistance in recognizing, labeling, processing, and appropriately responding to the behaviors of others.

Students with emotional disturbance often experience a heightened sense of fear, frustration, anxiety, and/or tension because of their difficulty in appropriately processing and understanding small everyday stressors. A simple request or a change in routine often results in a quick escalation to the stimulus phase. These children tend to experience a state of increased alertness for people or things that could cause harm, anticipate things going wrong, and experience constant perceptions of threat or fear.

RESOURCES

American Academy of Child and Adolescent Psychiatry
3615 Wisconsin Avenue NW, Washington, D.C. 20016
Phone: 202-966-7300
http://www.aacap.org

American Psychological Association
750 First Street NE, Washington, D.C. 200002
Phone: 800-374-2721
http://www.apa.org

National Institute of Mental Health
6001 Executive Boulevard, Rockville, MD 20852
E-mail: NIMHinfo@mail.nih.gov
http://www.nimh.nih.gov/index.shtml

National Alliance on Mental Illness
3803 N. Fairfax Drive, Suite 100, Arlington, VA 22203
Phone: 703-524-7600
http://www.nami.org

Anxiety Disorders Association of America
8701 Georgia Avenue, Suite 412, Silver Spring, MD 20910
Phone: 240-485-1001
http://www.adaa.org

Center of Positive Behavioral Interventions and Supports
http://www.pbis.org

Conduct Disorder
Style and Design, LLC
31878 Del Obispo Street, #118-335, San Juan Capistrano, CA 92675
Phone: 949-248-2682
http://www.conductdisorders.com

Encyclopedia of Mental Disorders
http://www.minddisorders.com/index.html

National Eating Disorders Association
165 West 46th Street, Suite 402, New York, NY 10036
Phone: 212-575-6200
http://www.nationaleatingdisorders.org

CHAPTER 13

Deafness or Hard of Hearing

M. Kathleen Ellis and Lauren J. Lieberman

OBJECTIVES

1. Define and successfully differentiate among the terms *Deaf, deaf,* and *hard of hearing*

2. Understand the various types and levels of hearing loss and the cause of each

3. Describe the different types of interventions common for each type of hearing loss

4. Understand the impact of hearing loss on the ability to successfully receive and interpret familiar speech and environmental sounds

5. Identify critical areas in which a teacher must make accommodations based on the impact of different levels of hearing loss

6. Understand the medical/pathological and cultural views of deafness

7. Understand the motor characteristics related to hearing loss

8. Understand the health/medical problems associated with hearing loss

9. Understand the cognitive characteristics associated with hearing loss

10. Understand the behavioral characteristics associated with hearing loss

11. Understand the cochlear implant and its impact on participation in physical education and sports

12. Understand the various factors that affect motor skill performance, physical fitness levels, and participation in sports and recreational activities by children with hearing loss

13. Understand how hearing loss affects physical education participation and how to ensure a successful learning environment

14. Understand how to use an interpreter in the physical education and sports environment

15. Understand how to make successful accommodations for children with hearing loss in the physical education and sports settings.

16. Identify sporting opportunities available to students with hearing loss, including the Deaflympics

Shakeera is a 12-year-old girl who is considered to be quiet and shy by her classmates and teachers. She is quite athletic, and she enjoys shooting baskets with her father and brother in the driveway and going for jogs with her mother and the family dog in the local park. Shakeera is deaf due to a congenital (i.e., prior to birth) sensorineural condition. She wears hearing aids, but these give her the ability to only hear sounds, not understand language. She often chooses not to wear hearing aids during physical education; she feels the gym is noisy, and the hearing aids only amplify the noise and do not help her in that setting. Shakeera knows sign language, and she has an interpreter with her during physical education. This can be good and also not so good for Shakeera. On the one hand, the interpreter helps Shakeera know what the physical education teacher is saying, and this helps Shakeera understand the directions and expectations for the class. The interpreter also picks up some, but very little, conversations of other children who are near Shakeera. On the other hand, the physical education teacher does not interact with Shakeera very much compared with other children. The teacher perceives the interpreter as not only someone who communicates with Shakeera but also an assistant who can help Shakeera with her skills. This is a common misunderstanding with interpreters in school settings; the reality is they are there to interpret what is said and not to teach. No one has taken the time to explain to the physical educator that Shakeera still needs him to provide instruction, feedback, and encouragement, and he also needs to help her be included and feel part of the group. Related to this last point, another not-so-good byproduct of the interpreter is that peers don't seem to be comfortable approaching Shakeera or inviting her to be their partner or in their group. Just the presence of an adult hovering around Shakeera is intimidating to her peers and makes them hesitant to approach Shakeera. This is unfortunate as some of her classmates have learned a little sign language and would love to interact with Shakeera and be her partner in physical education. The result of this lack of support from both the physical educator and Shakeera's peers has resulted in this athletic girl often looking lost and confused and unable to perform skills at the high levels she is capable of achieving. Not surprisingly, physical education is a lonely and unhappy time for Shakeera. What can be done to get this athletic girl to have a better physical education experience?

The term *deaf* is very unique in that it is viewed as meaning both a disability and a culture. From the disability perspective, *deaf* and *hard of hearing* are terms that are used to describe a range of hearing loss. There are also multiple definitions for these terms depending on the defining association. For example, Section 300.8.3 of the Individuals with Disabilities Education Act (IDEA) of 2004 (PL 94-142) defines the terms as follows: "Deafness means a hearing impairment that is so severe that the child is impaired in processing linguistic information through hearing, with or without amplification that adversely affects a child's educational performance" (U.S. Department of Education, 2014b). IDEA provides a separate definition under Section 300.8.5: "Hearing impairment means an impairment in hearing, whether permanent or fluctuating, that adversely affects a child's

educational performance but that is not included under the definition of deafness in this section" (U.S. Department of Education, 2014b).

To provide a contrast between these two definitions, the term *hearing impairment* as used by IDEA refers to any level of hearing loss, whether temporary or permanent, that may affect the child's ability to perform satisfactorily in the educational setting. This definition is in line with most references to the term *hard of hearing*.

However, deafness-specific organizations such as National Association of the Deaf provide the following definitions that are in line with the mission of their organization:

> D/deaf—we use the lowercase deaf when referring to the audiological condition of not hearing, and the uppercase Deaf when referring to a particular group of deaf people who share a language—American Sign Language—and a culture. (Padden & Humphries, 1988)

> Hard of Hearing—hard of hearing (HOH) can denote a person with a mild-to-moderate hearing loss. Or it can denote a deaf person who doesn't have/want any cultural affiliation with the Deaf community. Or both. The HOH dilemma: in some ways hearing, in some ways deaf, in others, neither. (Moore & Levitan, 2003)

In 1991, the World Federation of the Deaf voted to use the terms *deaf* and *hard of hearing* to designate individuals with varying forms of hearing loss. These terms are also preferred because they have no negative connotation. However, at one time, the term *hearing impaired* was considered politically correct and preferred to represent any individual with any form of hearing loss. Today, it is an outdated term and is no longer an acceptable term to use due to the negative denotation of the term *impairment*. It is important to be aware that although IDEA still uses the term *hearing impairment*, it is generally considered inappropriate for use with this population. Rather, the suggested terms are threefold and include *Deaf*, *deaf*, and *hard of hearing*. Therefore, the terms *deaf* and *hard of hearing* will be used in reference to hearing loss in this chapter.

Hearing loss can be categorized as being slight, mild, moderate, severe, or profound depending on the frequency and intensity of sound that a person is able to hear. The range of each level is listed in Table 13.1 and Figure 13.1 (Auditory Neuroscience, n.d.). The intensity of sound is how loud it is in decibels (dBs). For example, if a student has a 90-dB hearing loss, that means he or she is unable to hear the loudness or intensity of any sound below 90 dBs. In addition, with hearing loss, the ability to hear certain frequencies in hertz (Hz) is affected. Many individuals with hearing loss lose their ability to hear sound at high frequencies,

Table 13.1. Levels of hearing loss in decibels

Level of hearing loss	Decibel loss range
Typical hearing	−10–25 dB
Mild	26–40 dB
Moderate	41–55 dB
Moderately severe	56–70 dB[a]
Severe	71–90 dB[b]
Profound	91+ dB

[a]Level of hearing loss required for participation in deaf sports.
[b]Level of hearing loss setting lower limit for being classified as deaf.
From Clark, J.G. (1981). Uses and abuses of hearing loss classification. *ASHA, 23*(7), 493–500; adapted by permission.

which includes speech sounds such as /f/ and /s/. Therefore, it is important to be aware that hearing loss is not only about not being able to hear sound but also about the quality of sound that is affected.

In addition to levels of hearing loss, there are also three main types of hearing loss (Musiek & Baran, 2007). It is important for an educator to be aware of the type of hearing loss that the student has in order to better understand how to best accommodate the student's learning needs.

1. *Conductive hearing loss* occurs when there is a blockage or obstruction in the outer or middle ear. The outer ear consists of the external ear structure (pinna), whereas the middle ear refers to the auditory canal or pathway that sound must travel in order to reach the inner ear. Although conductive hearing loss usually does not result in severe loss of hearing, it can affect both the frequency and intensity of sound being heard. The most common cause of conductive hearing loss, which can be temporary, permanent, or fluctuating, is otitis media. Other causes include disease or obstructions such as ear wax. Many individuals with conductive hearing loss benefit from the use of a hearing aid and may also be helped medically (e.g., medicine to combat illness) or surgically (e.g., tubes in ears to drain fluids).

2. *Sensorineural hearing loss,* the most common type of permanent hearing loss, is more severe and results from irreversible damage to either the hair cells or the nerves of the inner ear. This type of hearing loss affects the ability to hear both the intensity and frequency of sound, even with amplification, leading to sound being distorted and undecipherable. Sensorineural hearing loss can range from mild to profound depending on the number of hair cells and/or nerves affected. Due to the impact of this type

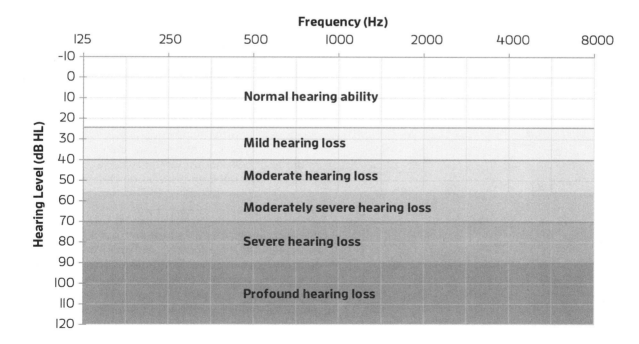

www.healthyhearing.com

Figure 13.1. Levels of hearing loss. (From Clason, D. [2015]. *How can I understand my hearing test results?* Retrieved from http://www.healthyhearing.com/report/41775-Degrees-of-hearing-loss; reprinted by permission.)

of hearing loss, the use of hearing aids is mostly ineffective. At this level, it is critical that students learn an alternative means for communicating, such as sign language. In some cases, surgical options such as a cochlear implant may be a viable means for enhancing the speech recognition of individuals with severe and profound sensorineural hearing loss. However, due to the various factors affecting success (e.g., presurgical speech recognition, usable hearing) and the stringent and lengthy speech and language training required, cochlear implants should not be considered as the best option for every individual with hearing loss.

3. *Mixed hearing loss* involves a combination of both conductive and sensorineural hearing losses. Individuals with this type of hearing loss pose unique challenges due to the involvement of both the outer/middle ear and the inner ear.

Figure 13.2 uses an image of the ear and its structures to provide a visual representation of where specific types of hearing loss may occur (Musiek & Baran, 2007).

Teachers should be aware of communication difficulties that a child may encounter due to the type and level of hearing loss that he or she possesses. For example, a child with 55-dB hearing loss, which is known as the critical range for effective communication, will have difficulty with any sounds lower than 55 dB in intensity. This includes all consonants and vowels. Because of this, a student with moderate to severe hearing loss (55 dB

Table 13.2.   Hearing loss implications

Level of hearing loss	Impact
Mild	• May miss 25%–40% of the speech signal • Usually results in problems with clarity
Moderate	• May miss 50%–75% of the speech signal • Problems with normal conversations • Problems with hearing consonants in words
Severe	• Difficulty in hearing in all situations • May miss 100% of the speech signal • Inability to have conversations except under the most ideal circumstances (i.e., face-to-face)
Profound	• May not hear speech at all • Forced to rely on visual cues instead of hearing as the main method of communication

Source: Associated Hearing of St. Paul, Inc. (n.d.).

and greater) will have difficulty in receiving at least 75% of the speech signal. For example, a student with this level hearing loss will most likely be unable to recognize /f/, /s/, /th/, /k/, /p/, /h/, and /b/ sounds (and many others) without the addition of some form of supplementary cues that help to identify the sound or word being used (e.g., cued speech, sign language). Table 13.2 identifies the impact of different levels of hearing loss and identifies critical areas in which a teacher must make accommodations.

It is important for teachers to be aware of not only the type of hearing loss that the student has but also the level of hearing loss. Knowing this information will allow teachers a better understanding of the challenges a student may have in their classroom and the accommodations that would enhance his or her overall communication and participation.

CAUSES OF DISABILITY

Hearing losses occur when any part of the ear is not working as expected and may be caused by a number of reasons, including illnesses, injury, noise, and heredity. However, each year, there are approximately 12,000 infants who are born with some form of hearing loss, most of which are from unknown causes (Centers for Disease Control and Prevention, 2014b). It has also been reported that 4–11 per 10,000 children have profound deafness of which more than 50% are known genetic causes (American Speech-Language-Hearing Association, n.d.).

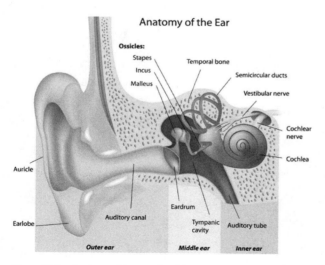

Figure 13.2.   Anatomy of the ear. (*MUSIEK, FRANK E.; BARAN, JANE A., THE AUDITORY SYSTEM: ANATOMY, PHYSIOLOGY, AND CLINICAL CORRELATES, 1st* Ed., ©*2007, p. 2.* Reprinted by permission of Pearson Education, Inc., New York, New York.)

Hearing loss can be either acquired or congenital. An *acquired* hearing loss means that the child became deaf or hard of hearing after birth. Causes of acquired hearing loss may include childhood diseases (e.g., measles, chicken pox, mumps), accidents causing head trauma, otitis media (i.e., ear infections such as fluid in ears), and noise. *Congenital* hearing losses are those that were present at birth and may also be caused by a number of reasons such as genetics, maternal illnesses, or complications during pregnancy (such as rubella, preeclampsia, gestational diabetes; Smith, Shearer, Hildebrand, & Van Camp, 2014).

Reports have indicated that 50%–60% of hearing loss is due to genetic causes, with approximately 20% of these cases also being diagnosed with a "syndrome" such as Down syndrome, CHARGE (coloboma, heart defect, atresia choanae, retarded growth and development, genital abnormality, and ear abnormality) syndrome, or Usher syndrome (Morton & Nance, 2006). In addition, approximately 25% of individuals with hearing loss are also diagnosed with developmental disabilities, such as cerebral palsy, intellectual disability, and vision loss to name a few (Bhasin, Brocksen, Avchen, & Braun, 2006). Because hearing loss is often present with other disabilities, the exact number of children who have hearing loss is unknown. It is possible that in many cases hearing loss is not considered the primary disability and thus is not reported statistically. Such discrepancies may account for the differences in numbers reported, as data from the Centers for Disease Control and Prevention indicate approximately 1–3 per 1,000 children have hearing loss, whereas other studies have reported anywhere from 2 to 5 per 1,000 children have hearing loss (Boulet, Boyle, & Schieve, 2009). The most reliable statistical data available is from the 1997–2008 National Health Interview Survey, which reported a prevalence of 5 per 1,000 children ages 3–17 classified as either deaf or hard of hearing (Boyle et al., 2011).

Once a child is diagnosed with a hearing loss, he or she may qualify for early intervention services under IDEA in the form of an individualized family service plan (IFSP). The purpose of such early intervention is to focus on aspects of the child's development that present delays, such as communication, reading, and social skills (U.S. Department of Education, 2014b). Regardless of the type, severity, and cause of hearing loss, it is critical that early detection is successful in order to allow for intervention related to the child's communication and language development (Hoff, 2013; Moeller, 2000).

DISABILITY VERSUS CULTURE?

As previously mentioned, deafness is the only condition that has been categorized as both a disability and a culture. There are two distinctive views of deafness, one from a medical/pathological perspective and one from a cultural perspective. The previous sections of this chapter focused on the medical/pathological perspective or deafness as a disability. The cultural perspective is the exact opposite and views deafness from a unique cultural perspective having its own community, language, beliefs, and values, among other things rather than as a disability. The cultural perspective views deaf people as a cultural and linguistic minority, similar to any other recognized cultural group. In this respect, their deafness is an identity rather than a disability or "impairment."

Deaf culture has a long history spanning more than 150 years. Individuals who identify within the American Deaf culture use American Sign Language as their primary means of communication and are involved in many different athletic, social, dramatic, religious, and literary organizations offering diverse cultural events. In fact, the Deaflympics, an elite sporting event solely for Deaf athletes, has competitions every 4 years with both summer and winter Deaflympics showcasing the athletic prowess of thousands of Deaf athletes on an international stage.

In addition to sporting organizations at the local, regional, national, and international levels, Deaf culture also has multiple other organizations and educational institutions:

- Gallaudet University: the first Deaf university in the United States
- National Theater for the Deaf: an internationally recognized theater production company
- National Association for the Deaf
- World Federation of the Deaf
- Miss Deaf American Pageant
- And many others!

The Deaf community has strong ties, social norms, beliefs, and values specific to its culture. However, approximately 90% of deaf children are born and raised by hearing parents and may have no introduction to Deaf culture until adulthood (National Institute on Deafness and Other Communication Disorders, 2014). This means that a small number of those in the Deaf culture actually acquire their cultural values and identity within the home, unless they are directly integrated into Deaf culture by their hearing parents. Most deaf children in public schools, however, learn about the whole new world of Deaf culture from their teachers, which makes Deaf culture an important topic for teachers to familiarize themselves with, especially for the opportunity of introducing students to Deaf sports.

MOTOR CHARACTERISTICS RELATED TO DISABILITY

There is no clear agreement on the impact of hearing loss on motor characteristics of deaf or hard-of-hearing children, with one exception being balance. A number of earlier studies reported that deaf or hard-of-hearing children demonstrated delayed development of motor skills (Boyd, 1967; Brunt & Broadhead, 1982; Butterfield, 1986, 1988; Butterfield & Ersing, 1988; Carlson, 1972; Wiegersma & Van der Velde, 1983). Some later studies have reported that their motor skill development is more in line with their hearing peers (Butterfield, Van der Mars, & Chase, 1993; Dummer et al., 1996). Butterfield and Ersing (1988) reported that deaf children demonstrated less mature fundamental motor patterns compared with those found among hearing children of the same age. The majority of research indicated both static and dynamic balance deficiencies of children with hearing losses when compared with their hearing counterparts (Crowe & Horak, 1988; Goodman & Hopper, 1992; Rine, 2009; Rine et al., 2000; Siegel, Marchetti, & Tecklin, 1991). This is especially true for children with sensorineural hearing loss due to vestibular function impact compared with those individuals with conductive hearing loss (Rine, 2009). In addition, a number of studies have reported that deaf children demonstrated delays in skills requiring balance as well as slower motor speeds due to greater time required to process motor skill information and complete the skill itself (Butterfield, 1986, 1988). The latter outcome was supported by a 2014 study that found that delays in sequence processing among deaf children may result in impairments in motor learning, which, in turn, may lead to impairments in a deaf child's overall motor development (Levesque, Theoret, & Champoux, 2014).

The role of vestibular function in balance and motor proficiency was investigated by Crowe and Horak (1988). The outcome of this study indicated that deaf or hard-of-hearing children with typical vestibular function demonstrated no impairments in either motor performance or balance. Furthermore, those deaf or hard-of-hearing children with vestibular deficiencies demonstrated typical motor performance accompanied by balance deficiencies. In addition, deaf or hard-of-hearing children were better able to compensate for their vestibular deficiencies through the use of visual input to better control for both static and dynamic balance, as indicated by their performance on balance skills requiring their eyes be open or closed.

For children without sensory impairments, including hearing loss, motor skill performance improves with increasing age due to maturation, experience, and, in some cases, heredity (Houwen, Hartman, & Visscher, 2009). This is indicative in that typically developing children are expected to demonstrate mature balance and postural control between the ages of 7 and 10 years (Rajendran & Roy, 2011). Most research has indicated that balance performance of deaf or hard-of-hearing children improves with age but typically remains lower than their hearing peers (Butterfield & Ersing, 1986; Siegel et al., 1991); however, it was also reported that when deaf or hard-of-hearing children were evaluated on static balance with eyes open, negligible differences were found between deaf or hard-of-hearing and hearing children with increased age (An, Yi, Jeon, & Park, 2009).

Because balance is a fundamental ability for motor development in children, it is critical that balance deficiencies are identified and steps are taken to negate the impact of such deficiencies on overall motor development and performance (De Kegel et al., 2010; Rajendran & Roy, 2011). Several studies have investigated the impact of intervention programs on balance deficiencies in deaf or hard-of-hearing children. Several studies incorporated programs designed to improve balance and body awareness (Lewis, Higham, & Cherry, 1985), specific static balance activities (Effgen, 1981), various object control and locomotor skills (Gursel, 2014), and exercise intervention involving enhancement of both visual-motor and somatosensory abilities (Rine et al., 2004). Although all programs led to increased balance skills, the exercise program supporting visual-motor and somatosensory ability enhancements demonstrated greater overall improvements in balance skill performance. This outcome indicates the importance for intervention programs to focus on specific deficiencies in order to prevent other areas of development from being affected (Dummer, Haubenstricker, & Stewart, 1996; Shumway-Cook & Woollacott, 1995).

Research has indicated that motor skill development, including balance, may be affected by factors other than hearing loss (Rajendran & Roy, 2011). Due to the varying outcomes of research investigating the motor skill performances of deaf or hard-of-hearing children, it may be reasonable to assume that such factors as school experiences, parents, communication, and sports opportunities may also play a significant role in differences found in motor skills of deaf or hard-of-hearing children.

Teachers who are aware of potential balance differences in deaf or hard-of-hearing students will be at an advantage in providing appropriate and effective programs for these students, especially given the connection between balance and development of mature motor skill patterns. Every limitation a deaf or hard-of-hearing student faces, whether it be a deficiency in balance or motor skill development, affects not only the inclusion of that student into the general physical education environment but also his or her effective participation in physical activities and communication with their peers. In addition, such cases may negatively affect a deaf or hard-of-hearing student's sense of competence, leading him or her to avoid participating with peers in any setting in which his or her differences in skills affect performance (Houwen et al., 2009).

HEALTH/MEDICAL PROBLEMS ASSOCIATED WITH DISABILITY

Although health/medical problems may not be directly associated with deafness per se, there are a number of studies that have focused on the health-related physical fitness of children who are deaf or hard of hearing. In relation to physical fitness levels, Ellis and Darby (1993) also investigated the impact of balance on maximal oxygen consumption that would directly affect the individual's ability to perform repeated motor movements over a period of time successfully, which validates the importance of ensuring a deaf or hard-of-hearing child demonstrates appropriate levels of both static and dynamic balance skills as part of any program designed to enhance physical and motor performance.

As with motor skill development, there are mixed results relating to health-related physical fitness of deaf or hard-of-hearing children with a number of studies reporting both outcomes. Some studies have reported that deaf or hard-of-hearing children demonstrate lower physical fitness than their hearing counterparts (Hartman, Houwen, & Visscher, 2011; Wiegersma & Van der Velde, 1983). Other studies have reported that the health-related physical fitness of deaf or hard-of-hearing children are in line with their hearing peers (Ellis, Butterfield, & Lehnhard, 2000; Goodman & Hopper, 1992; Winnick & Short, 1986) or have mixed outcomes wherein deaf or hard of hearing are higher on some skills and lower on others (Campbell, 1983; Pender & Patterson, 1982). However, given an equal opportunity to thrive in a physical activity setting, including learning various motor and sports skills required for successful

performance, there are no physical barriers preventing the deaf or hard-of-hearing child from excelling. Many of the studies that found deaf or hard-of-hearing children to have lower fitness levels came to that conclusion by comparing them to their hearing counterparts within the same school rather than national standardized norms. In other cases, deaf or hard-of-hearing children may be at a disadvantage due to lack of opportunity for involvement, perhaps due to environmental factors such as the educational environment or lack of understanding by parents (Dummer et al., 1996; Ellis, Lieberman, & Dummer, 2014).

COGNITIVE CHARACTERISTICS RELATED TO DISABILITY

Although deaf and hard-of-hearing students may demonstrate lower standardized test scores than their hearing peers, much of the variance may be explained due to below-average reading levels that many deaf or hard-of-hearing children exhibit (Luckner, Slike, & Johnson, 2012; Swanwick & Marschark, 2010). In addition to reading levels, other aspects of the child's education may be affected due to both learning and communication differences. It is important to be aware that in the absence of other associated disabilities being involved, hearing loss itself is not connected with differences in cognitive characteristics.

Communication plays an integral role in both academic achievement and participation in physical activities and sports. The deaf or hard-of-hearing student is automatically at a disadvantage because the loss of hearing, especially above 55 dB, prevents him or her from having meaningful communication with family, peers, teachers, and coaches unless alternative means are successfully incorporated. Using sign language has been found to enhance not only a deaf or hard-of-hearing child's academic success but also the child's overall educational and social experience (Luckner et al., 2012; Schultz, Lieberman, Ellis, & Hilgenbrink, 2013; Spencer, Bodner-Johnson, & Gutfreund, 1992; Spencer & Marschark, 2010; Swanwick & Marschark, 2010).

BEHAVIORAL CHARACTERISTICS RELATED TO DISABILITY

Imagine yourself in a situation where you are feeling left out and struggling to understand the communication being used. Now imagine that happening in all aspects of your life, at home, at school, with your friends, in sports, and so forth. Such conditions commonly lead to frustration and a desire to remove oneself from the situation. In this respect, deaf or hard-of-hearing students may not be able to express their feelings and frustrations about not being able to effectively understand and communicate in many areas of their lives (Hillburn, Marini, & Slate, 1997; Jambor & Elliott, 2005). Because of this, deaf or hard-of-hearing children may demonstrate behaviors that may appear to be misbehavior. It is up to the teacher to ensure clear communication and understanding both expressively and receptively in the child's preferred mode of communication. This includes children who may have a cochlear implant.

Cochlear implants have been increasingly seen as a way to treat severe and profound hearing loss in both children and adults. Cochlear implants involve invasive surgery under general anesthesia in which a receiver and magnet is inserted behind the ear where a portion of the aerated bone is removed to allow implantation. A small hole is then drilled in the cochlea to allow threading of the electrode array. The purpose of this device is to provide direct electrical stimulation of the auditory nerve in the inner ear through electrical impulses activated by the electrodes mimicking hair nerve stimulation, thus allowing for the perceived sensation of sound. Cochlear implants do not "restore" or "cure" hearing loss but rather provide the individual with sound stimulation sent to the brain via the auditory nerve for interpretation.

One of the anticipated benefits of cochlear implants is improved motor development given that previous research has hypothesized that the lack of auditory input could be a contributing factor for motor delays observed in deaf children (Savelsbergh, Netelenbos, & Whiting, 1991; Schlumberger, Narbona, & Manrique, 2004). However, limited research has been completed that evaluates the impact of cochlear implants on a deaf child's motor development and overall participation in physical activities and sports. Gheysen, Loots, and Van Waelvelde (2008) reported that deaf children with a cochlear implant did not demonstrate better motor development than did deaf children without a cochlear implant. However, it remains that cochlear implants destroy an individual's remaining hair cells and residual hearing, which play a role in vestibular function and in turn the development and control of balance skills.

An alternative option would be to raise the deaf child while incorporating sign language as a strategy for enhancing communication. There is some support that deaf individuals proficient in sign language demonstrate typical visual-motor skill patterns (Hauser, Cohen, Dye, & Bavelier, 2007). Early research has also reported a parallel connection between language and motor development milestones (Iverson, 2010). From this point, teaching deaf children sign language during infancy may lead to earlier development and meeting of motor milestones because infants have the capability to learn and use basic sign language skills 2–3 months before the equivalent spoken language (Bonvillian, Orlansky, & Novack, 1983). Even with the lack of research in the area, it makes sense from both the language and motor development perspective to incorporate sign language into a deaf child's life at a young age.

Teachers must be aware of some of the following contraindications that come with using a cochlear implant during physical activity:

- Many cochlear implants are not waterproof and cannot be worn in a situation where they will get wet from either direct water contact (swimming) or sweat (moderate or intense physical activity).

- Current technology has allowed children with cochlear implants to swim with the implant. The Nucleus Aqua Accessory is a single-use plastic enclosure that completely seals in the processing unit, cable and coil so that one can swim with the sound processor. It is designed to be used with rechargeable batteries. There are no wires or upgrades required, one slips the Aqua Accessory over the Nucleus 5 or 6 processor.

- Cochlear implants are breakable and must be removed during any activity in which they may get damaged, such as most contact sports in which a blow to the head could occur.

- Plastic equipment used during physical education and sports can cause static electricity, which can interfere with the mapping of the cochlear implant. Because of this, the cochlear implant must be removed before using any plastic equipment that may cause electrostatic discharge.

- Because of the many situations in which it is necessary to remove the external part of the cochlear implant to avoid harm to either the device or student, it is critical that the student has alternative means for communicating with others while in such a situation. This is a great reason for the deaf or hard-of-hearing student, as well as the student's parents, teachers, and peers, to learn and use sign language.

PARTICIPATION IN SPORTS AND RECREATION

In many cases, deafness is a "hidden disability" and not immediately apparent unless some form of communication difficulty, either receptive or expressive, arises. In sports such as basketball, a deaf or hard-of-hearing player may face certain disadvantages such as not being able to hear an official's whistle or coach's instruction during a game. Hearing difficulties are also compounded if the athlete is unable to wear his or her hearing aid or cochlear implant during the athletic competition due to sweat or possible impact. These are obstacles for the deaf or hard-of-hearing athlete to overcome as well as any loss of balance that he or she may have due to hearing loss.

Under international sporting criteria, to be eligible to compete in Deaf basketball competitions, all players must have at minimum hearing loss of 55 dBs in their best ear. In Deaf sports competition, hearing aids and cochlear implants are not allowed and must be removed, which evens the playing field for all Deaf athletes.

FACTORS THAT AFFECT MOTOR SKILL PERFORMANCE, PHYSICAL FITNESS LEVELS, AND PARTICIPATION IN SPORTS AND RECREATIONAL ACTIVITIES

Being deaf or hard of hearing itself has little impact on an individual's development of motor skills, physical fitness levels, and participation in sports and recreational activities. As mentioned previously, deficiencies in balance caused by improper vestibular function may affect the development of specific motor skills by deaf or hard-of-hearing children. This in turn may affect their participation in physical activities that lead to appropriate levels of physical fitness and enjoyment of lifelong physical activity.

However, there are a number of factors that may have a more direct impact on the deaf or hard-of-hearing child's performance and participation. One common impact is that of parental influence and involvement. In some cases, parental hearing status (i.e., deaf parents versus hearing parents) has had an impact on the deaf or hard-of-hearing child's participation in physical activity and their overall physical fitness levels. Two studies (Ellis, 2001; Ellis et al., 2014) indicated that deaf children of deaf parents were more physically active and demonstrated greater physical fitness levels than deaf children with at least one hearing parent. Other studies have indicated that deaf or hard-of-hearing children demonstrate similar levels of motor skill development regardless of their parents being deaf or hearing.

In addition, school placement can also have an impact on the deaf or hard-of-hearing child's performance and involvement (Butterfield et al., 1993; Ellis, 2001).

Finally, the use of peer tutors in inclusive settings may affect the deaf or hard-of-hearing child in a positive manner (Lieberman, Dunn, van der Mars, & McCubbin, 2000).

IMPLICATIONS FOR PHYSICAL EDUCATION

Students who are deaf/hard of hearing face several unique learning and communication challenges. Much of the learning environment is auditory in nature, putting the deaf or hard-of-hearing student at risk right off the bat. Teachers must remember that deaf or hard-of-hearing students are by nature visual learners and must be in the teacher's line of vision for all instruction and feedback. Some specific learning strategies/educational approaches best used for teaching deaf or hard-of-hearing students include the following:

- Communicate with the deaf or hard-of-hearing student using his or her preferred means of communication. This may mean several things. If the deaf or hard-of-hearing student is reliant on verbal communication, make sure that you give him or her a chance to become familiar with your verbalization habits. If the student relies on sign language, either learn the language yourself or incorporate a sign language interpreter into the classroom environment.

- When giving verbal instructions/directions, make sure the student can see your face clearly. Avoid obscuring your lips/face, and avoid unnecessary moving or pacing.

- When teaching a group how to complete a movement skill or a group exercise, teach while facing the class so that the student can mirror your movements. In addition, this will allow you to provide verbal instruction when needed by directly facing the deaf or hard-of-hearing student. When outdoors, make sure that the sun is to your face and not back so that the student is not looking into the sun.

- Make sure that you speak clearly and at a normal rate. Avoid overenunciating words as it does not benefit the deaf or hard-of-hearing student.

- Use visual aids that have images with descriptive words. Minimize the amount of written information presented by using visual pictures/images with your demonstration and one to two word cues to refer to specific movement patterns.

- Use a buddy system and peer tutoring, which can be effective for both the deaf or hard-of-hearing student and the hearing student alike (Lieberman et al., 2000).

- Turn on captioning or provide a transcript to the deaf or hard-of-hearing student when showing video/film in the classroom.

- Repeat comments or questions made by the student's classmates in order to clarify not only for the deaf or hard-of-hearing student but also for the whole class as well.

- Use a whiteboard or overhead projector to write down questions/answers discussed in class.

- Check for student understanding by having the deaf or hard-of-hearing student repeat directions/instructions and/or demonstrate the skill. Do not ask yes/no questions to verify understanding.

- When using an interpreter, make sure the interpreter is standing directly to your side so that the deaf or hard-of-hearing student can clearly see him or her. When communicating with the deaf or hard-of-hearing student, speak directly to the student, not at the interpreter.

- Do *not* treat the student as a second-class citizen just because he or she has a difference in hearing and communication needs. Patience is a virtue and affects the outcome of the student's success in your classroom.

One of the most important things an educator can do to assist deaf and hard-of-hearing students is learn sign language. Even if the deaf or hard-of-hearing student does not know sign language or is not yet fluent, it can be incorporated into the physical education curriculum (as well as other content areas). In addition, basic signs specific to physical education and socialization can be taught to both the deaf or hard-of-hearing student and his or her peers in order to enhance overall communication and socialization opportunities and reduce isolation for the deaf or hard-of-hearing student. It also gives the deaf or hard-of-hearing student the opportunity to share signs with their classmates, which can improve their self-confidence and self-esteem (Columna & Lieberman, 2011).

There are a number of web sites that provide learning opportunities to become familiar with American Sign Language, including the following:

1. Signing Online: https://signingonline.com
2. Life Print: http://www.lifeprint.com
3. ASL Pro: http://www.aslpro.com
4. Signing Savvy: http://www.signingsavvy.com

Guidelines for Using an Interpreter in the Physical Education Setting

When your deaf or hard-of-hearing student is reliant on a sign language interpreter for receptive and/or expressive communication, it is important to follow these guidelines when using an interpreter:

- Make sure that the interpreter is standing immediately to your side during instruction and both you and the interpreter are clearly visible to the deaf or hard-of-hearing student.

- Prior to class, it is helpful to preview specific language and terminology with the interpreter so that they can effectively translate content to the student.

- It is critical to remember that the interpreter is present to facilitate communication ONLY. They are not there to assist the deaf or hard-of-hearing student with performing skills or activities. It is inappropriate to ask them to be involved in any other way.

- When using an interpreter, speak directly to the deaf or hard-of-hearing student. Do not communicate with the interpreter and ask him or her to "ask the student" or "tell the student." Such behavior negates the student as a fully aware human being in your classroom.

- Prepare other students for the presence of the interpreter. Make sure that everyone is aware of how to use the interpreter and the role that he or she plays.

The bottom line is that the interpreter is there for a specific purpose: to enhance effective communication between the teacher and the student as well as the student and his or her peers. The interpreter is NOT an aide, assistant, or anyone who is in the classroom to assist with anything other than the effective facilitation of communication.

Accommodations to Make in Sports and Recreation

Just like their hearing counterparts, deaf individuals are interested in many different sports and recreational activities. In fact, there are many high-caliber elite deaf athletes who have been or are successful at the highest level of their sport. As with any athlete, deaf individuals need to work hard and practice to excel in their sport. However, they also require high-quality coaching and training to become the best at what they do. It is important for coaches to be qualified to work with deaf athletes and clearly understand their capabilities as well as their unique needs for success. Coaches of deaf athletes should keep the following guidelines in mind:

- Use visual cues to alert athletes of game start/stoppage or changes in strategy. For example, a red flag can be used to alert the deaf athlete that play has been stopped. A variety of colored flags or hand signals (or many other visuals) can be used to indicate specific plays or strategies during game play regardless of the sport.

- In some sports, such as track and field or swimming, sounds are used to start a race. In these events, a light can be used to flash in synchronization with the start of the race. Other less common ways to start races include having the referee wave his or her hand or drop a flag.

- Have alternative means to communicate with your deaf or hard-of-hearing athlete. It is preferable to learn sign language and teach everyone on the team so that there are no communication barriers present. This is a great team-building experience and one that will make the deaf or hard-of-hearing athlete feel like an important part of the team. It also assists tremendously with the socialization aspect among team members.

Fun Facts

In the early 1900s, the Gallaudet University football team was concerned about opposing teams stealing their plays due to everything being communicated in sign language. Because of this, players would huddle tightly together to discuss plays so that nobody would be able to see their hand movements. From this, the modern-day huddle was born.

Also involving the Gallaudet football team are the different means for communicating when the "hut" part was engaged so that the play on the field was activated. The team had an individual who would use a drum, with each beat referring to the hut call. For example, three beats meant "hut 1, hut 2, hut 3," and the deaf players could feel the vibrations from the drum and know which beat the play would start on. This was also used to "trick" the opposing team into being off sides when the number of huts appeared to be randomly changed.

Athletics is an arena in which many Deaf athletes excel. It is important that a teacher is aware of the many different opportunities that a deaf or hard-of-hearing student can participate in to advance his or her athletic skills. In addition, Deaf athletes may serve as inspiration and role models for deaf or hard-of-hearing students so that they can be aware of others "like them" who are already successful at such a high level. Some of the more well-known Deaf athletes include the following:

Luther Hayden Taylor: Professional baseball player for the New York Giants in the early 1900s. Nicknamed "Dummy" during a period when it was common for people to use offensive terms to refer to people with disabilities, Taylor was an integral part of the 1904 and 1905 championship teams. However, the more important storyline is that Taylor took exception when his teammates and coaches were not able to communicate with him, making this team one of the only professional sports teams to have all personnel and players learning sign language as a way to represent equality among players.

William "Dummy" Hoy: Outfielder in Major League Baseball. The hand signals which were developed so he could understand the umpires' calls are still being used today.

Gerry Hughes: Sailor who successfully sailed around the world solo.

Kitty O'Neal: Professional stunt woman in the 1980s.

Lou Ferrigno: Body builder and actor also known as The Incredible Hulk. In 1972, he was the youngest winner of Mr. Universe, which he won again in 1973. He starred in the series *The Incredible Hulk* from 1977 to 1982.

Ashley Fiolek: Four-time women's champion of the American Motorcyclist Association Motocross Championship. Also the youngest champion ever (men's and women's) in 2008.

Terrence Parkin: South African swimmer who won silver in the 200m breaststroke and finished fourth in the 100m breaststroke at the 2000 Olympics in Sydney.

Laurentia Tan: Equestrian silver medalist in the 2012 Paralympics. Tan also has cerebral palsy, which qualified her to compete in the Paralympics. She won four Paralympic medals in dressage.

Lee Duck-Hee: At the age of 15, Lee made waves on the junior tennis circuit, won several junior and senior titles, and competed in Wimbledon.

Matt Hamill: Ultimate Fighting Championship fighter. Nicknamed "the Hammer" after quickly winning his first ever wrestling match over a defending national champion. Hamill relies solely on sign language and visual cues to communicate.

Reed Doughty: Strong safety for the National Football League (NFL) who has played for the Washington Redskins since 2006.

Jim Kyte: First deaf player in the National Hockey League (NHL). Played 598 games for five teams in the NHL after being drafted 12th overall in 1982 by the Winnipeg Jets.

Lance Allred: First deaf player in the National Basketball Association. Wrote a book entitled *The Adventures of a Deaf Fundamentalist Mormon Kid and His Journey to the NBA.*

Tamika Catchings: Women's National Basketball Association (WNBA) forward for the Indiana Fever.

Emma Meesseman: WNBA player for the Washington Mystics.

Felicia Schroeder-Waldock: Star of the U.S. Deaf Soccer Team who was the first deaf player to play professionally in Europe.

Derrick Coleman: NFL fullback for the Seattle Seahawks. Coleman experienced repeated bullying as a child and was undrafted as a football player out of college. However, his confidence and determination led him to try out for and make the Seattle team that won the 2014 Super Bowl.

Derrick Coleman's experience is an excellent example for physical educators to remember when they have deaf or hard-of-hearing students in their classroom. It is important that deaf or hard-of-hearing students feel like they are equal members of the class, do not feel left out or an outcast, are given every opportunity to succeed, and are in a comfortable environment where communication barriers do not exist. In addition, they are being taught by an educator who not only believes in them but also shows it through his or her actions by encouraging their growth and adapting teaching to match the learning needs and style of each student.

SPECIAL SPORTS ORGANIZATIONS FOR INDIVIDUALS WITH HEARING LOSS

The following organizations focus specifically on Deaf sports:

- United States of America Deaf Sports Federation

- Committee des Sports des Sourds (international)

- Additional organizations can be found in the Resources section of this chapter

In order to qualify or compete in these Deaf sports organizations, athletes must have a minimum 55-dB hearing loss in better ear, without amplification. The web site of the United States of America Deaf Sports Federation (http://www.usadsf.org) lists the following 19 sports:

Aquatics	Badminton	Baseball
Basketball	Bowling	Cycling
Golf	Ice hockey	Shooting
Skiing (Nordic and alpine)	Snowboarding	Soccer
Team handball	Softball	Table tennis
Volleyball	Tennis	Track and field
	Wrestling	

There are several unique aspects about Deaf sports. First and foremost, Deaf sports not only represents a sporting arena for athletes who qualify, but it is also a social environment where the majority of participants, athletes, coaches, officials, administration, and organizers use sign language to communicate. Therefore, it is as much a social realm as it is a sporting event (Stewart, 1991).

The following web sites provide additional information about American Sign Language (ASL):

American Sign Language University (http://www.lifeprint.com): American Sign Language University is a resource site that contains various links to ASL vocabulary as well as sentence structure, grammar, syntax, phonology, and aspects of Deaf culture.

Signing Savvy (http://www.signingsavvy.com): Signing Savvy is a useful website for beginning to intermediate signers with videos depicting specific common vocabulary and fingerspelling in ASL.

USEFUL APPS

There are a number of apps that may be useful to deaf/hard-of-hearing students in the classroom or within the athletic arena. The following is a short list of apps that students and teachers might benefit from:

- *Speak It!* is a text-to-speech app that can be used to assist the student not only in learning to read or speak but also in communicating with peers and teachers when speech difficulties are involved. If the deaf/hard-of-hearing student experiences difficulties in expressive verbal communication skills, this app may be particularly useful in allowing the child to effectively communicate within the classroom and athletic settings.

- *Dragon Dictation* is an app used for students who have difficulty with writing. Research indicates that the average reading level for deaf/hard-of-hearing students is between the fourth- and sixth-grade levels (Luckner et al., 2012). However, many students are able to express themselves verbally in an effective manner, and this app allows students to communicate verbally by translating speech to written format.

- *Notability* is a note-taking app that is particularly useful in communicating verbal directions or instructions through written format. It can also be used in a variety of settings, such as in the classroom or on the field during sporting events.

This app works well with deaf/hard-of-hearing students because most are visual learners.

- *Draw Free for iPad* is similar to Notability but incorporates an artistic element. This can be quite useful when communicating movement patterns or offensive/defensive schemes on the playing field. For example, Draw Free allows individuals to draw shapes or other items in order to communicate such offensive or defensive schemes in sports.

RESOURCES

United States of America Deaf Sports Federation
PO Box 910338, Lexington, KY 40591
Phone: 605-367-5761
TTY: 605-367-5760 (voice)
http://www.usdeafsports.org

International Committee of Sports for the Deaf (Deaflympics/ICSD)
PO Box 91267, Washington, D.C. 20090
http://www.deaflympics.com

Deaf Digest Sports (news and updates)
http://deafdigestsports.com

Deaf Sports Academy
Phone: 951-208-6893 (voice/video phone)
http://www.dsastars.org

The Deaf Youth Sports Festival ("Mini Deaflympics"):
PO Box 421304, Indianapolis, IN, 46242
Phone: 317-493-0116 (video phone by appointment only)
Phone: 317-446-8095 (voice/text)
http://www.mdoyouth.org

CHAPTER 14

Visual Impairments and Deafblindness

Lauren J. Lieberman and Marla Runyan

Objectives

1. Understand the various causes of visual impairments

2. Understand the various visual abilities of different visual impairments

3. Understand the various guide running techniques

4. Understand what incidental learning is and how to ensure it happens during a class

5. Understand various teaching techniques for tactile instruction

6. Understand how to modify games, sports, and activities for individuals who are visually impaired

7. Understand the various sports offered by the United States Association of Blind Athletes and the International Blind Sports Federation

8. Understand the needs of individuals who are deafblind

9. Understand how to apply all these concepts for individuals who are deafblind

Charlotte Brown is a high school student who is blind. She has been an active member of her track team since she was in middle school. Charlotte came in fourth place in the Texas state high school track meet in the spring of 2014. She used a beeper where she planted her pole to guide her down the middle of the runway. She is a typical high school student, just one who cannot see. With the support of her family, coach, and the Texas State High School Athletic Association, she was able to reach her full potential in her chosen sport.

WHAT IS VISUAL IMPAIRMENT?

Visual impairment, including blindness, means an impairment in vision that, even with correction, adversely affects a child's educational performance. The term includes both partial sight and blindness (Individuals with Disabilities Education Act [IDEA] of 2004, § 300.8).

CAUSES OF COMMON VISUAL IMPAIRMENTS

There are multiple causes of vision loss. Some conditions are relatively mild and in many cases can be corrected (see Table 14.1). Most causes of more severe vision loss are associated with aging; however, occasionally, loss of vision occurs before or at birth (*congenital*), during childhood, or later in life (*adventitious*). Some causes of blindness are as follows.

Before Birth

Albinism is a total or partial lack of pigment causing abnormal optic nerve development; it may or may not affect skin color. People with albinism

Table 14.1. Common eye conditions affecting vision

Amblyopia, also known as lazy eye, is the loss or lack of development of central vision in one eye. Amblyopia can result from a failure to use both eyes together, and it is often associated with crossed eyes or a large difference in the degree of nearsightedness or farsightedness between the two eyes.

Astigmatism is a condition resulting from an irregular shape of the eye or a curvature of the lens inside of the eye that results in blurred vision.

Hyperopia, also known as farsightedness, is a condition in which objects in the distance are usually seen clearly, but objects close to the individual appear blurred.

Myopia, also known at nearsightedness, is a condition in which objects that are close to the individual can be seen clearly, but objects in the distance appear blurred.

Nystagmus is a condition in which the eyes make repetitive, uncontrolled movements, which may result in difficulty focusing.

Strabismus, also known as crossed eyes, is a condition in which both eyes do not look at the same place at the same time.

Source: American Optometric Association (2014).

may have one or more of the following conditions: decreased visual acuity, photophobia (sensitivity to light), high refraction error (the shape of the eye does not refract light properly so the image seen is blurred), astigmatism (blurred vision), nystagmus (uncontrollable eye movements that are involuntary, rapid, and repetitive), central scotomas (a blind or partially blind area in the visual field), and strabismus (the inability of one or both eyes to look directly at an object at the same time).

Leber congenital amaurosis (LCA) is a severe dystrophy of the retina affecting approximately 1 in 80,000. It is a genetic, inherited eye disease that appears at birth or in the first few months of life. Although the retina may initially appear normal, a pigmentary retinopathy reminiscent of retinitis pigmentosa is commonly seen later in childhood. Visual function is usually poor and often accompanied by nystagmus, sluggish or near-absent pupillary responses, photophobia, high hyperopia, and keratoconus. Visual acuity is rarely better than 20/400. LCA is associated with multiple genes, and as a result, the presentation of the condition varies from individual to individual (Perrault et al., 1999; Weleber, Francis, Trzupek, & Beattie, 2013).

Retinoblastoma is a malignancy of the retina in early childhood that usually requires removal of the eye and can occur in one or both eyes.

Retinopathy of prematurity (ROP) occurs in some infants who are born prematurely, resulting in reduced acuity or total blindness. ROP occurs when abnormal blood vessels grow and spread throughout the retina, the tissue that lines the back of the eye.

These abnormal blood vessels are fragile and can leak, scarring the retina and pulling it out of position. This causes a retinal detachment, which is the main cause of visual impairment and blindness in ROP. See the section on motor characteristics for more information on retinal detachments.

After Birth

Cataracts are opacities of the lens that restrict the passage of light and are usually bilateral. They reduce acuity, resulting in blurred vision, poor color vision, photophobia, and sometimes nystagmus. Visual ability fluctuates according to light. Please note that in some cases, children may be born with cataracts.

Cortical visual impairment (CVI) is caused by a brain disorder rather than an ocular problem. Children with CVI have variable vision, wherein visual ability can change day to day and minute to minute. One eye may perform significantly worse than the other, and depth perception can be very limited. Response time to visual stimuli may be significantly delayed and field of view may also be severely limited. Visual processing can take a lot of effort. A child with CVI may demonstrate a strong color preference, such as orange or yellow, and may be drawn toward light.

Glaucoma causes increased pressure in the eye because of blockage in the normal flow of the aqueous humor. Visual loss may be gradual, sudden, or present at birth. People with glaucoma may also have an increased sensitivity to light and glare. Peripheral vision loss may occur.

Macular degeneration is a progressive degeneration of the macula. Macular degeneration affects central vision, resulting in poor visual acuity, central blind spots or scotomas, and photophobia. Color vision may also be affected. Juvenile forms of macular degeneration include Stargardt disease and Best disease.

Retinitis pigmentosa is caused by a variety of inherited retinal defects, all of which affect the ability of the retina to sense light. It is a progressive disorder that causes loss of peripheral vision, night blindness, tunnel vision, decreased acuity and depth perception, spotty vision because of retinal scarring, and photophobia.

Teachers and support staff are encouraged to use the official United States Association of Blind Athletes (USABA) classification for visual impairment and a wealth of other information about how people with visual impairments participate in sports and other physical activities (see http://usaba.org/index.php/membership/visual-classifications).

MOTOR CHARACTERISTICS OF CHILDREN WITH VISUAL IMPAIRMENTS

Children with visual impairments are born with the same potential as their sighted peers. It is often due to lack of opportunities and overprotection that children with visual impairments experience delays and barriers to acquiring motor milestones and physical activity equal to their peers. The following are some of the issues that they may face without proper instruction and support.

Since children who are congenitally blind have no visual stimulus to spark their interest to move and investigate objects, they rely on auditory stimuli instead. People who are visually impaired develop the dependence of auditory cues to help them accomplish their activities of daily living. It is not surprising then that studies have shown that children with visual impairments are less physically active than recommended and less active than their sighted peers (Houwen, Hartman, Jonker, & Visscher, 2010; Houwen, Hartman, & Visscher, 2009; Lieberman, Byrne, Mattern, Watt, & Fernandez-Vivo, 2010).

In regard to physical activity levels, positive relationships have been found between motor skills and physical activity in children (Houwen et al., 2009). Children with visual impairments also demonstrate less developed motor skills than their sighted peers (Houwen et al., 2009; Houwen, Visscher, Lemmink, & Hartman, 2008; O'Connell, Lieberman, & Petersen, 2006; Wagner, Haibach, & Lieberman, 2013). For this population, motor skill proficiency is as important for daily living and sports activities as it is for any child (Houwen et al., 2010). Visual impairments may act as a constraint by slowing down motor skills acquisition; however, if a child with visual impairment has adequate levels of physical activity participation, he or she will likely have higher motor skill proficiency (Houwen et al., 2010; Houwen et al., 2009). It is due to these barriers that children with visual impairments will benefit from additional support and careful instructional planning during physical education.

Medical Characteristics

A visual impairment itself does not cause any specific medical conditions or health issues. There are some types of visual impairments that have contraindications associated with them. The following are some contraindications, or activities that are not recommended, for some eye conditions.

Glaucoma causes increased pressure in the eye. This pressure is often alleviated with eye drops and medication. Any activity that causes additional pressure on the head is not recommended. These activities include inversions such as handstands or headstands, or going deep under water such as the bottom of the pool in the deep end.

ROP may cause a retinal detachment. The retina is the part of the eye that attaches to the back of the eyeball and sends signals to the optic nerve and to the brain. If the retina becomes detached, the individual will lose more vision or may experience total vision loss. If a child has a detached retina, he or she must avoid being hit in the head or hitting other children. Making contact sports noncontact and using soft balls such as beach balls or balloons can alleviate this problem. An example of this is playing volleyball using a beach ball with only two people on each side. Another example is playing scooter hockey with a Frisbee as the puck and short sticks. Discussion with the student, parents, physician, and the vision teacher about the upcoming physical education units and potential modifications is recommended.

Cognitive Characteristics

A visual impairment itself does not affect the cognitive functioning of a child. The lack of seen experiences, expectations, and information may affect the child's knowledge of typical things. For example, if a child was not taught that napkins should be placed on the lap while eating, he or she may not know this is a custom. If a child is not explained the structure and function of the solar system, that child may not know the typical pattern of the earth and sun. *All* visual information must be explained to them intentionally, and all information that is available in print must also be available in braille. If the physical education teacher is giving out the history of lacrosse as a handout that students must learn, the printed information must be given to the teacher of the student who is visually impaired ahead of time to prepare a braille version. All information in print must be given to the child who is blind in braille at the *same* time as his or her peers if the student is expected to keep up with cognitive information.

Behavior Characteristics

Some children with visual impairments will display rocking, eye poking, or hand flapping behaviors. These behaviors are referred to as blindisms or self-stimulatory behaviors. There are several known causes of these behaviors, one of which is extreme prematurity combined with prolonged periods of hospitalizations (McHugh & Lieberman, 2003).

Most parents find that their child is more likely to participate in self-stimulatory behaviors when he or she is idle or stressed. Due to the fact that these little understood behaviors may inhibit social interaction and potential employment opportunities, some professionals feel that this behavior should be replaced by more acceptable behavior. Take the time to observe the types of self-stimulation that your student engages in and when the behavior is exhibited. Watch him or her and take notes about what you see and when you see it. Discuss this with your multidisciplinary team. Then work with the team and the child to see if there is any pattern to the self-stimulatory behaviors that would give you insight to the type or types of stimulation he or she prefers and the purpose it serves. At the same time, note and discuss with the child what types of activities he or she dislikes.

When you and the team have a good understanding about the student's preferences, begin to consider ways that you can offer other physical activities that will modify or expand on the preferred self-stimulation. Work with the team to analyze children of the same age and try to find toys or activities that may make the self-stimulatory behavior appear more "functional" (Murdoch, 1997).

Sometimes, a child's favorite self-stimulation activity can be modified or expanded in a way that will make it more socially acceptable. For example, Kyle, who is in third grade, rocks forward and backward in rhythm when he is bored. His teacher gave him a beaded jump rope cut in half. He swings it forward and backward when he rocks, and he is starting to develop the beginning patterns of jumping rope. As he gets older, he can be given a Wii remote and be permitted to play modified Wii games, kick a beeping soccer ball across a room, or hold an iPad to play music and dance.

TEACHING PHYSICAL EDUCATION TO STUDENTS WITH VISUAL IMPAIRMENTS

Physical Guidance and Tactile Modeling

A variety of instructional strategies can be used when teaching students with visual impairments, such as demonstration, verbal instruction, and tactile teaching (Lieberman & Cowart, 2011; Lieberman & Haibach, in press; O'Connell et al., 2006). For effective and pleasurable learning, teachers have to choose carefully which method to use depending on the student's learning preference and the skills being taught (Downing & Chen, 2011).

Figure 14.1. Physical guidance.

Two very common methods used with individuals who are blind are physical guidance and tactile modeling coupled with verbal explanation. Physical guidance is when an instructor or peer physically assists the child through a skill. This can be total support or a tap on the knee or elbow. This is more of a passive learning style but can be very effective (Cieslak, 2013). Tactile modeling is when an instructor or a peer models a skill and the student feels the motion of the movement. This is more of an active learning style and has some benefits as well. Research has shown that both of these techniques can be used effectively (O'Connell, 2000).

Incidental Learning

Incidental learning is the unplanned or "accidental" learning that occurs through observations of events within the natural environment. Knowledge and skills acquired through incidental learning by sighted children must be explicitly taught to children with visual impairments. Students with visual impairments are limited in acquiring information through incidental learning because they are often unaware of subtle activities in their environment. For example, the social skills that students who are blind need for daily life in school, at home, and in the community must be strategically taught and integrated into all aspects of their education.

Ensuring that children with visual impairments receive all visual information through other means is an important part of the instructor's responsibilities. A poster on the wall announcing tryouts for track, the rules for the gym, demonstrations of dance moves for a dance unit, or the color of various equipment around the room all must be intentionally conveyed to the child. Along these same lines, when there is a game going on, it is very important to either have an announcer to convey the game highlights or have the paraeducator or preferably a peer giving a play-by-play so that the student knows what is happening at all times. Do not assume that the child does not care or is not interested. Consistent relaying of information is the best way to ensure he or she knows what is happening at all times and is not left out of social situations. The last thing a child wants is to guess why people are cheering, laughing, or quiet.

Assessment of Children with Visual Impairments

The Test of Gross Motor Development III (TGMD III; Ulrich, 2015) is a validated gross motor test for children with visual impairments (Houwen et al., 2010) ages 6–12. The TGMD III covers six locomotor skills (running, galloping, hopping, leaping, jumping, and sliding) as well as six object control skills (striking, dribbling, catching, kicking, throwing, and rolling). The TGMD III can be modified in order to enable the children with visual impairments to perform all tasks (e.g., sound box for locomotor skills, fluorescent tape around bean bag for the leap, beep baseball for batting, wiffle ball with bells inside for the catch). It is important to note that this modified equipment can be used in classes with all children with no negative effect to the motor performance of the sighted peers (Lieberman, Haibach, & Wagner, 2014).

The Brockport Physical Fitness Test (BPFT; Winnick & Short, 2014) is a validated health-related fitness test that was developed to assess children with visual impairments in a similar manner to the Fitnessgram. The BPFT is valid for students ages 10–17 (although it can be used with children from age 6) and includes items in five areas of fitness. It provides a healthy fitness zone for children with

intellectual disabilities, visual impairments, and orthopedic impairments. Its validity has been determined using concurrent, construct, and content validity on each item with each disability involved (Winnick & Short, 2014).

Guide Running Techniques

The following is a list of guided running techniques for children who are visually impaired or blind. It is important to teach each technique to the child so he or she can choose the best one for each situation. Some children prefer one technique for shorter distances and one for longer distances or a different technique for a different surface.

- *Sighted guide:* The runner grasps the guide's elbow, shoulder, or hand depending on what is most comfortable for the runner and guide.
- *Tether:* The runner and guide grasp a tether (e.g., short string, towel, shoelace). This allows the runner full range of motion of the arms while remaining in close proximity to the sighted runner.
- *Guide wire:* The runner holds onto a guide wire and runs independently for time or distance. A guide wire is a rope or wire pulled tightly across a gymnasium or along a track. A rope loop, metal ring, or metal handle ensures that the runner will not receive a rope burn and allows for optimal performance. The runner holds onto the sliding device and runs independently for as long as desired. Guide wires can be set up permanently or temporarily.
- *Sound source from a distance:* The runner runs to a sound source such as a clap or a bell. This can be done as a one-time sprint or continued for a distance run.
- *Sound source:* The guide rings a bell or shakes a noisemaker for the runner to hear while running side by side. This works best in areas with limited background noise.
- *Circular running:* In a large, clear, grassy area, a 20- to 25-foot (6–8 m) rope is tied to a stake. The student takes the end of the rope, pulls it taut, and runs in circles. The circumference of the circle can be measured to determine the distance, or the athlete can run for time. A beeper or radio can be placed at the starting point to mark the number of laps completed.
- *Sighted guide's shirt:* The runner with partial vision runs behind a guide with a bright shirt. Ask the runner what color he or she can see best to ensure maximum vision. This must be done in areas that are not too crowded.

Figure 14.2. Running with a guide wire.

- *Independent running:* A runner with travel vision runs independently on a track marked with thick white lines.
- *Treadmill:* Running on a treadmill provides a controlled and safe environment. Select a treadmill with the safety feature of an emergency stop.
- *Wheelchair racing:* A person who is blind and in a wheelchair can use any of the previous adaptations as needed. Aerobic conditioning results from pushing over long distances, whether around a track, on neighborhood sidewalks, or along a paved path (From Lieberman, L.J. [2011]. Visual impairments. In J.P. Winnick [Ed.], Adapted physical education and sport [5th ed., pp. 233–248]. Champaign, IL: Human Kinetics.)

Modification Ideas

Children with visual impairments can play all the sports their sighted peers can play with some modifications. A modification may be as little as a baseball hat and sun glasses for a child with albinism when playing outside. It can also be the use of a beeping ball for baseball or kickball or the use of a sighted guide during a hockey unit or orienteering unit. A volleyball unit may be modified by allowing a catch of the ball, using a beach ball with bells inside, and allowing two bounces during each point. The player who is blind may also be allowed to walk up to the net and feel the net before throwing the ball over. No matter what age or unit, it is important to consider the objective of the game and the level of function of the student (Lieberman & Houston-Wilson, 2009). Modifications can be ongoing until the peers, student, and teacher feel comfortable with the level of play and challenge for everyone. It is perfectly okay to have two to three games going on in the gym with different levels of modifications if necessary. The key is to ensure the child with the visual impairment is fully included in class at all times. Preteaching is a big part of this, which is explained later in the chapter.

Expanded Core Curriculum

Physical activity and motor skills can help children with visual impairments to develop several of the areas from the *Expanded Core Curriculum (ECC)* first formulated by Hatlen in 1996 (Sapp & Hatlen, 2010). *ECC* is a generally accepted curriculum with nine areas of instruction that children with visual impairments need to be successful in school, the community, and the workplace (Sapp & Hatlen, 2010). Physical activity and motor skills can improve social interaction, independent living, self-determination, recreation and leisure, and orientation and mobility skills and concepts.

Physical activity and sports can positively influence orientation and mobility skills and concepts as well as independent living skills. Thus, helping children with visual impairments understand their own bodies and how to move as safely, efficiently, and independently as possible is imperative. For social interaction skills and recreational and leisure skills, sports and physical activity (e.g., such as clubs, teams, and program involvement) are often primary socialization environments and create an atmosphere of belonging (Movahedi, Mojtahedi, & Farazyani, 2011). Finally, self-determination skills refer to a person's right to decide freely and without undue influence how he or she wishes to live his or her life (Sapp & Hatlen, 2010). Physical activities and sports encourage students to become stronger at decision making, enabling the child to be more responsible and autonomous. At the same time that children learn to be more cooperative with others, they learn how to be less dependent on others, perceiving the fact that they are responsible for themselves and for the world in which they live (Movahedi et al., 2011).

Evidence-Based Practice

Physical education teachers who work with children with visual impairments should get to know and work collaboratively with the child's teacher(s) of the visually impaired and his or her orientation and mobility specialist. The teacher of the visually impaired will teach the child independence, socialization, and how to read in the preferred print medium whether it is braille, large print, or another format. The orientation and mobility specialist will teach the child how to navigate school and the community independently with his or her cane and will have great tips for the physical education environment. Physical educators can collaborate with these multidisciplinary team members on everything from skill acquisition strategies, to modification ideas, to ordering equipment on quota funds from American Printing House for the Blind.

The physical education teacher can also help these professionals by discussing the child's abilities in motor skills, fitness, and socialization as they occur in the physical education class. Collaborating together as a team will benefit all parties involved, including the child with the visual impairment and his or her family.

Preteaching

Children with visual impairments and blindness need more instruction and practice time in order to learn new concepts and movements (Lieberman, Ponchillia, & Ponchillia, 2013; Perkins, Columna, Lieberman, & Bailey, 2013). Part of the difficulty in learning new skills is a lack of background knowledge the student with a visual impairment often has related to the skills or content being taught. The teacher can meet the child where he or she is in understanding and begin to build the background knowledge related to the new sport or skill unit. Sapp and Hatlen (2010) suggest that children with visual impairments need preteaching, teaching, and reteaching in order to obtain *ECC* skills. This teaching cycle is also extremely important in learning skills and concepts related to physical education. Preteaching must be done before a new unit of instruction. The child must learn the perimeter of the court or field, which can be done with a tactile board.

The child must also learn the names of the positions or players, objective of the game, rules, scoring, equipment used, and the various levels of competition. Once these concepts are understood, the pace of the class and the concepts taught will be easier to acquire, and the student will be more successful.

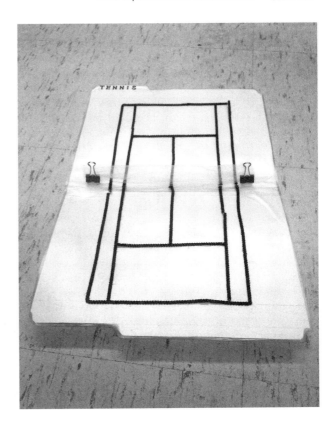

Figure 14.3. Tennis tactile board.

Preteaching can be done before school, after school, during orientation and mobility class, or at home. The professionals that can help with this are the physical education teacher, the orientation and mobility instructor, the teacher of the visually impaired, the paraeducator, or a peer or sibling. It is important that the physical education teacher provide the specific goals for the preteaching and the objectives of the unit to the person who delivers the preteaching of the lesson.

Training Paraeducators

Lieberman and Conroy (2013) found that paraeducators who worked with children with visual impairments had not been trained for the physical education class. However, trained paraeducators are instrumental in ensuring that specific component skills for the ECC are addressed during physical education. Trained paraeducators may be involved in ensuring that *ECC* skills are addressed in physical education and in monitoring a student's progress. It is the role of the teacher of the visually impaired along with the physical educator to design a student's program in these areas and to set and monitor progress toward individualized education program (IEP) goals with the support of the paraeducator.

Paraeducators can help monitor progress of the student toward the selected components of the *ECC* that are emphasized during physical education instruction. Changes to instruction can be made based on this performance data. In addition to the benefit of paraeducators, peer tutors may provide age-appropriate support in physical education and can be used in conjunction with paraeducators if necessary. Please see the Resource section of this chapter for paraeducator training programs.

Incorporating Trained Peer Tutors

As discussed earlier, trained peer tutors can assist in increasing socialization and motor skills for children with visual impairments by providing positive role models and honest feedback (Wiskochil, Lieberman, Houston-Wilson, & Petersen, 2007). With some planning and effort from physical education teachers and teachers of the visually impaired, peer tutors can be trained and utilized to reinforce instruction and provide feedback that will help the child with a visual impairment improve on the *ECC* components (Lieberman & Houston-Wilson, 2009).

Incorporating After-School Programming

It has been recommended that support for learning components of the *ECC* should extend to after-school programming (McDonough, Sticken, & Haack, 2006). In collaboration with visual impairment professionals, physical education teachers can continue to contribute to *ECC* components through school-based after-school physical activity and sport

programs (e.g., intramural sports, fitness clubs, or sport clubs). It is important for all school personnel who are involved in the education of students with visual impairments to work together in order to enhance the students' abilities during these activities. This team of professionals can determine adaptations and specific needs for the child with visual impairments, such as preteaching time (Conroy, 2012).

Quota Funds

Educating children with visual impairments requires additional funding for electronic equipment, educational materials, and products necessary for specific instruction. The American Printing House for the Blind (APH) is a government-funded agency that provides equipment and materials to educate children with visual impairments. Educational materials from APH are free for children with visual impairments up to a certain amount of money each year. Products available for physical education can be found in Table 14.2. In order to access these products, contact your teacher of the visually impaired or the orientation and mobility instructor of the children in your classes. Every product comes in large print, audio, or braille versions depending on the child's needs. The products can be found at APH's web site (http://www.APH.org).

Other Equipment/Material Adaptations

Table 14.3 reviews some common equipment and ways to modify them for use with children and youth with visual impairments.

Table 14.2. Physical activity products from the American Printing House for the Blind

Name of product	Description
Sound Balls	Hard foam sound balls in red or yellow that can be used universally in most ball sport units
Jump Rope Kit	A kit that comes with a ropeless jump rope, beaded jump ropes, plastic jump ropes, a foam mat to jump on, and a manual to help the child learn how to jump rope
30-Love Tennis Kit	A kit that comes with foam tennis balls, two racquets, blindfolds, and a tennis manual with rules of the game and modifications
Walk-Run for Fitness Kit	A kit that promotes walking and running. It comes with two talking pedometers, a guidewire, a tether, and a manual to teach children what to wear, how to use the different guide running techniques, advocacy, and so forth
Everybody Plays	A book for children from third through fifth grade that describes how children with visual impairments can play a variety of sports. It opens with a foreword by Erik Weihenmayer, a famous mountain climber who is blind, and ends with advice from elite athletes.
GAMES for People with Sensory Impairments	A book for parents and physical education teachers. It has a very long list of sports and games with specific modifications for children with visual impairments as well as children with multiple disabilities or deafblindness
Going Places	A transition guide for adolescents 14–21 years of age with visual impairments. It provides a curriculum to help these young adults decide what sports and recreational activities they would want to do when they graduate from school. It also provides extensive information on role models and advocacy approaches

Table 14.3. Equipment modifications

Equipment	Modification ideas
Balls	Tie a plastic bag around a ball to add sound. Use a bell ball. Use a beeping ball.
Jump ropes	Add sound by stringing the rope through one fourth of a Hula-Hoop so the hoop part creates a cadence when it hits the floor. Use a jump rope cut in half so the rope does not get tangled in a child's feet.
Goals or baskets	Put a beeper (see http://www.aph.org) to place behind soccer goals, archery targets, and basketball nets. Put bright-colored tape on top of a volleyball net.
Boundaries	Use bright cones, streamers, or rope on the floor with tape over it to mark clear boundaries.
Offensive players in a game	Ensure clear color differences when a child is playing on a team with pinnies. Have the players on the child's team wear bells or a specific color so that team members can be easily identified.

TEACHING CHILDREN WHO ARE DEAFBLIND

Not all children will only have a visual impairment. Some children may also have autism, cerebral palsy, or an intellectual disability. In those cases, combine suggestions from other relevant chapters with the recommendations in this chapter. In some instances, a child may have a dual sensory impairment. Unlike the famous Helen Keller, most individuals labeled deafblind will have some usable vision and hearing. The following suggestions for working with children who are deaflind are appropriate for all levels of sensory impairment (Erin, 2004; Huebner, Prickett, & Welch, 1995; McInnes, 1999; Sauerberger, 1993):

- Provide adequate time to explore the equipment and field dimensions. Make sure the student knows the purpose of the game or sport as well as the rules and strategies. This may take time, so allot adequate time for complete understanding before the unit. Please see the earlier section on preteaching for more information.

- Take the time to find out what methods of communication will be most comfortable and efficient for both you and the student. If you have difficulty establishing communication, ask for suggestions from other professionals who work closely with the student or from the student's family members.

- Discuss exactly how you will communicate during the activity or sport before it starts to ensure comfort, safety, and understanding.

Figure 14.4. Beep kickball used by children with and without visual impairments.

- Identify yourself each time you initiate interaction. It is easier to identify yourself if you have a signal or a designated name-sign that the deafblind person will recognize.

- Communicate directly with the person who is deafblind; do not direct your comments through another person.

- Before touching or moving students, be sure to communicate with them so they know you are approaching.

- Contact people who are deafblind on the hand, arm, or shoulder to avoid startling them. Or bring your hand up beneath the student's hand, so the back of your hand touches the student's palm. Use a light touch. To make it easier for the person to know where you are, leave your hand in contact with the person until he or she responds to you.

- Do not grab the student's wrist. Being grabbed or held is confining for a person who uses his or her hands to communicate.

- If you need to touch people who are deafblind somewhere besides the hand, arm, or shoulder (e.g., to point to something on their clothes or face) or to touch something they are holding, let them know what you are doing. One way to do this is to put your hand under theirs and then bring your hand toward them with their hand on yours.

- Be honest when you do not understand. Also, give the student opportunities to let you know when he or she is not sure what you meant, but do not ask repeatedly, "Do you understand?"

- Avoid placing the student's hand on objects. Pushing the student's hand onto an object is awkward and can be painful if the object is sharp or rough. Instead, tell the student you are putting your hand on the object while his or her hand is on yours. Then the student can find the object by sliding his or her hand off yours as you remove your hand.

- When students with restricted visual fields are watching you, do not move quickly to the side. If the student is trying to follow you or look at your signs and you move too quickly to the side, the student may lose sight of you. If the student cannot find you, you can let the student know where you are by touching an arm or hand.

- Do not misconstrue the student's normal speaking voice as a display of strong emotion. Some people conclude from the unusual voice inflections or the emphatic signs and facial expressions with which many people who are deaf and deafblind communicate that they are agitated or perturbed. It is important to realize that the voice may be the student's normal speaking voice and that eloquence in sign language usually involves dynamic, intense expressions.

SPORTS PROGRAMS FOR CHILDREN WITH VISUAL IMPAIRMENTS

In addition to modified equipment available, there are many programs that also promote sports and recreation for children with visual impairments. One of the programs that can be found nationally as well as internationally is Camp Abilities.

Camp Abilities is a developmental sports camp for children and adolescents with visual impairments, blindness, and deafblindness. The camp was founded at the College at Brockport at the State University of New York in 1996 by Dr. Lauren J. Lieberman and Dr. Monica Lepore. The first camp served 27 athletes and included 30 volunteer coaches. To date, the program has served more than 4,000 athletes at more than 25 locations across the United States and abroad (such as Canada, Costa Rica, Finland, Ireland, and Portugal). Each camp shares a similar structure and mission with the original Camp Abilities while adding unique aspects specific to the geographic region in which the camp is located.

Camp Abilities is built on the premise that instruction in a variety of physical activities and sport experiences improves the lives of students with visual impairments, blindness, and deafblindness. These activities are components of the three purposes of the program. The four major purposes of the program include 1) empowering students with visual impairments to be physically active members of their communities, 2) training preservice teachers from a variety of fields of study to teach physical activities to students with visual impairments, 3) providing a respite for families, and 4) to conduct much needed research in the field of physical activity and children with VI and deafblindness. Camp Abilities is successful in fulfilling its purposes through a unique programming structure, including providing high-quality teaching through one-to-one instruction by distinctively trained specialists and coaches. (For more information, please see Haegele, Lieberman, & Lepore, 2014.)

United States Association of Blind Athletes

USABA is a nonprofit membership organization that provides opportunities for participation and training and competition in the following sports for athletes who are blind, deafblind, or have low vision: athletics (track and field), tandem cycling, showdown, goalball, judo, powerlifting, Nordic and alpine skiing, swimming, wrestling, five-a-side-football, triathlon, archery, rowing, audio-darts, and 10-pin bowling. Its mission is to "enhance the lives of blind and visually impaired people by providing the opportunity for participation in sports and physical activity" (USABA, n.d.-b). The association also has a number of state affiliates across the United States called sports clubs. USABA members range from children with visual impairments who are just beginning to develop their sports skills, to youth who are participating on their school or local club teams, to adults running in a local 5K race, to elite athletes who train for international competitions such as the Paralympic Games. The USABA has reached thousands of individuals with visual impairments since its inception in 1976.

While not every child who is blind has the ability or desire to be a Paralympian, the skills learned through sports are beneficial in all aspects of daily living. Rather than focus on limitations, USABA aims to provide people who are blind and visually impaired the tools to know their abilities by experiencing success through sports and strives for a future in which all individuals who are visually impaired have the same opportunities to discover their potential and pursue their athletic dreams in the same way as anyone else.

The USABA arose as a result of the efforts of a few pioneers during and following the 1976 Paralympic Games in Toronto. The first meeting to organize USABA occurred in August 1976 in the days immediately following the Paralympics Games.

USABA has emerged as more than just a world-class trainer of blind athletes; it has also become a champion of the abilities of American athletes who are legally blind. USABA believes that athletes who are blind or visually impaired can and should compete alongside their sighted peers and against other athletes who are blind and visually impaired. Although many athletes who are blind or visually impaired have had great success, each year more than 50,000 youth with visual impairments are left on the sidelines in their school's physical education classes, and less than half have the opportunity to participate on either school or club sports teams. Through programs such as the USABA National Sports Education Camps Project (Ponchillia, Armbruster, & Wiebold, 2005) and Camp Abilities (see the previous section and the Camp Abilities web site at http://www.campabilities.org), USABA attempts to provide youth with the skills and confidence needed to participate not only in their physical education classes at school but also in sports teams alongside sighted youth. In addition to the Sport Education Camps, USABA provides clinics for youth and adults around the country in judo, tandem cycling, track and field, goalball, Nordic and alpine skiing, swimming, and powerlifting. USABA also hosts sports festivals in which participants are exposed to a variety of sports during clinic sessions, and at the conclusion of the festival, participants can compete in a sports competition that includes peers with visual impairments and sighted peers.

The USABA web site provides information for people who are interested in becoming involved with the organization's development camps (where participants work on improving their performance), trainings, and competitions, as well as information about the performance levels required to qualify for various competitions. USABA also provides information about upcoming sports events and the results of various competitions, including the USABA records for most sports, the results of past Paralympics, and the results of USABA-sanctioned goalball tournaments for the past several years. These records of the highest performance reached by athletes with visual impairments can serve as both goals and inspiration for young athletes. Of particular interest to coaches and teachers, from special educators to physical educators, are the descriptions of the adaptations necessary to make all the major sports activities accessible to athletes with visual impairments. The USABA web site also provides adaptations for sports for coaches who have participants with visual impairments on their sports teams. These tip sheets range from basketball, to wrestling, to football and provide instructional and equipment modification variables that can help with full inclusion of the participants with visual impairment with their sighted peers.

The USABA also serves military veterans who have come back from service with visual impairments. The USABA provides trainings and competitions for blinded veterans throughout the country (Lieberman et al., 2013).

RESOURCES

American Foundation for the Blind
2 Penn Plaza, Suite 1102, New York, NY 10121
Phone: 212-502-7600 or 800-232-5463
TDD: 212-502-7662
Fax: 212-502-7777
http://www.afb.org
E-mail: info@afb.org

American Printing House for the Blind
1839 Frankfort Avenue, PO Box 6085, Louisville, KY 40206
Phone: 502-895-2405 or 800-223-1839
http://www.aph.org
E-mail: info@aph.org

National Beep Baseball Association
5175 Evergreen Drive, North Olmsted, OH 44070
Phone: 440-779-1025
http://www.nbba.org

Beep Kickball Association
c/o Judy Byrd
4323 Big House Road, Norcross, GA 30092
Phone: 770-317-2035
http://www.beepkickball.com
E-mail: judybyrd@gmail.com

BOWLING

American Blind Bowlers Association
http://www.abba1951.org

PERKINS

Perkins
175 North Beacon Street, Watertown, MA 02472
http://www.Perkins.org

SPORTS CAMPS

Camp Abilities
Camp Abilities-Brockport, New York
The College at Brockport, State University of New York
350 New Campus Drive, Brockport, NY 14420
Phone: 585-395-5361
Fax: 585-395-2771
http://www.campabilitiesbrockport.org

Chapter 15

Physical Disabilities

Luke E. Kelly

OBJECTIVES

1. Understand the causes, incidence, treatment, health, and medical issues associated with spinal cord injuries and the implications for physical education

2. Understand the causes, incidence, treatment, health, and medical issues associated with spina bifida and the implications for physical education

3. Understand the causes, incidence, treatment, health, and medical issues associated with spinal column deviations and the implications for physical education

4. Understand the causes, incidence, treatment, health, and medical issues associated with cerebral palsy and the implications for physical education

5. Understand the causes, incidence, treatment, health, and medical issues associated with traumatic brain injuries and the implications for physical education

6. Understand the causes, incidence, treatment, health, and medical issues associated with amputations and the implications for physical education

Joy is a 7-year-old girl who loves to be color coordinated with her clothes. She has pink days and yellow days and green days. Joy also has cerebral palsy that affects her ability to walk smoothly. To help her walk, she has ankle-foot orthotics that help her keep her ankles locked and prevent her feet from dropping down. She also uses a walker to help maintain her balance and prevent falling. However, she still is prone to falling, and her parents have her wear kneepads similar to what volleyball players wear to make sure she does not hurt her knees when she does fall. Her parents have dyed her kneepads to match her daily outfits. So pink days include pink kneepads, green days have green kneepads, and so forth. Cute doesn't begin to describe Joy, and Mrs. Feeney, Joy's physical educator, certainly agrees that Joy is one of the cutest girls in her second-grade class. However, Mrs. Feeney is concerned with Joy's safety as well as the safety of the other students in the class. What if Joy gets knocked down? What if a peer gets hurt accidentally running into Joy's walker? How can Joy play games that require speed given how slow she moves?

Across town, another little girl is starting her first day of high school. Natalie is anxious like most adolescents making a transition from middle to high school. Even more anxious is Natalie's physical educator Mr. Flint because Mr. Flint just found out Natalie uses a wheelchair for mobility. Natalie was born with spina bifida, which resulted in paralysis in her legs. Mr. Flint is not sure how Natalie will be able to participate in activities such as soccer, basketball, volleyball, and lacrosse, all of which are key team sports that make up a large part of the high school curriculum. Furthermore, weightlifting and cardio equipment such as treadmills and elliptical trainers are used several times a year.

How will Natalie be able to use this equipment? What Mr. Flint does not realize is Natalie is quite the athlete. Her parents found out about Paralympics when she was younger, and she has participated in wheelchair basketball, wheelchair tennis, and wheelchair racing since she was 10 years old. Now at age 14, she is an accomplished and ranked junior wheelchair tennis player and wheelchair racer, and she is the youngest member of her wheelchair basketball team. She regularly goes to her local gym with her mother, father, and older brother to work out. How can Natalie and her parents communicate with Mr. Flint about Natalie's abilities and how she will be able to accommodate herself very successfully in general physical education?

Jamal is a middle school student who is returning to school after 2 weeks in the hospital and another 4 weeks at home and in rehabilitation. Jamal lost his leg from above his knee due to cancer that he has been battling for more than a year. Jamal is returning to school without a prosthesis, although there is a plan to fit him with a prosthesis in the next few months. Jamal will be participating in physical education and other classes using crutches. He actually is getting better with his crutches, but he still is slow and is prone to falling if bumped. Jamal is concerned with how he will be able to participate in physical education. How can Jamal's physical educator make sure he can safely and successfully participate in general physical education?

This chapter will address three categories of physical disabilities commonly found in children. The first category will address physical disabilities that result from damage to the spinal cord and column. These include traumatic spinal cord injuries (SCIs), spina bifida, and spinal column deviations. The second category includes physical disabilities that are caused by damage to various parts of the brain. The two most common types of this disability are cerebral palsy (CP) and traumatic brain injury (TBI). The third and final category will be amputations.

SPINAL CORD INJURIES

SCIs result from disease or injury of the vertebrae or the nerves in the spinal column. Spinal cord injuries are typically labeled by the location on the spinal column where they occurred (e.g., thoracic region at the sixth vertebrae would be T6) and whether the injury is complete or incomplete. In a complete injury, the cord is completely cut, which stops the transmission of any neural signals, preventing all movement and sensation below that point. In an incomplete injury, some nerves are still intact, allowing some sensation

Table 15.1.   Spinal column level and associated functions

Level	Function
C1–C4	Requires complete assistance with all activities of daily living; needs assistance to breathe
C5–C8	Can breathe independently and has some control of the arms and hands; requires some assistance with most activities of daily living
T1–T5	Good arm function and some control of chest, back, and abdominal muscles; can independently perform most activities of daily living
T6–T12	Good trunk control and balance in a seated position; can effectively use a manual wheelchair
L1–L5	Poor motor control and strength in hips and legs
S1–S5	Weakness in hips and legs but can generally walk

and motor function below the injury. Generally, the higher on the spine the injury occurs, the more severe the loss of function.

According to the Centers for Disease Control and Prevention (2010a), the most common causes of traumatic SCI are motor vehicle accidents (46%), falls (22%), violence (16%), and sports (12%). Eighty percent of SCIs occur in males, with 50%–70% of these injuries occurring between the ages of 15 and 35.

The amount of sensation and motor function lost due to SCI is a function of where on the spinal column the injury occurred and the severity of the damage to the spinal cord as shown in Table 15.1. Damage at T1 and above is classified as tetraplegia or quadriplegia, indicating that there is loss of function in all four limbs and the torso. Injuries below T1 are classified as paraplegia, indicating loss of function in the lower extremities. Individuals with both paraplegia and quadriplegia typically lack bowel and bladder control.

Students with SCI will almost always have some loss of motor functioning. The important questions are how significant the motor impairment is and whether the long-term needs of these students still align with the goals of the general physical education curriculum or if they will require adapted physical education curricula. In addition, it is important to realize that the greatest challenge for most of these students, as they return to school, will be accepting and learning to deal with the loss of previous abilities and learning to use the functional abilities they still have. With managed health care today, individuals with SCIs are moved through the hospital and rehabilitation treatment phases and returned to their homes relatively quickly.

Health and Medical Characteristics

While SCI in and of itself has clear implications to loss of movement and sensation, related health and medical issues are perhaps more critical for the long-term prognosis and quality of life of individuals with SCIs. Health and medical characteristics include three areas: secondary health issues, unique medical complications associated with exercise, and obesity.

Secondary Health Issues

There are a number of secondary health issues that are commonly associated with SCI that are likely to be experienced by students when they return to school. All these secondary conditions are preventable with proper precautions and treatment, including regular physical activity.

Pressure Sores   The first is a greater susceptibility to developing pressure sores or decubitus ulcers of the skin. These sores commonly occur in the buttocks and pelvis regions where boney prominences of their skeletal structure place greater pressure on the skin as the result of the lack of musculature to cushion these areas. Because they also lack sensation in these areas, they are not prompted to periodically shift their weight. To avoid developing pressure sores, these students need to regularly perform pressure releases or wheelchair pushups in which they slightly lift their weight off the seat of the chair and then lower it back down, thus redistributing their weight.

Skin Bruising   A second related issue is bruising of the skin. This can occur when limbs that are no longer innervated bump in to hard surfaces. For example, a student may bump his leg against a bench in the gym reaching for a piece of equipment or drag her foot on the ground because she is unaware it has slid off the footplate of her wheelchair. Although students may not feel pain as a result of these contusions and abrasions, the real problem is that these injuries are very slow to heal and are more prone to becoming infected due to the poor circulation in their lower limbs. The goal in physical education is to anticipate these problems and take preventive steps such as adding extra padding or Velcro strapping to prevent these injuries from occurring.

Contractures   When the SCI results in the loss of muscle function around a joint, the joint will no longer be naturally moved through its full range of motion during daily activities. In order to maintain the range of motion in affected joints, it is necessary for individuals with SCI to regularly passively move these joints through their full range of motion. If range of motion is not maintained, contractures (i.e., a permanent shortening of muscle, tendon, or scar tissue producing deformity and reduced range of motion) will occur, which can make many activities of daily living, such as dressing, more difficult to perform. In physical education, working on range of motion in affected joints can be built in as a component of these students' physical fitness routines.

Bladder and Bowel Function   A fourth health issue to be aware of is the need for individuals with SCI to manage their bladder and bowel functions. Bladder function is typically handled by a regular catheterization schedule. It is very important that this schedule be followed to avoid accidents (i.e., leakage) and more important to prevent urinary tract infections. Bowel function is controlled by a combination of diet, laxatives, and wearing adult diapers. Again, this can be a sensitive issue for many adolescents, and every effort should be made to address these issues to avoid any accidents or discomfort regarding these functions in relation to physical education.

Unique Medical Problems Associated with Physical Exercise

Individuals with SCI above T6 can also experience four unique problems, particularly when they perform physical fitness activities (National Center for Health Physical Activity and Disability, n.d.). The first is *hypotension*, or low blood pressure, during exercise due to the blood pooling in the lower limbs. Students should be encouraged to perform gradual warm-ups and cool-downs when exercising and to exercise in reclined positions to avoid becoming hypotensive. The second problem is *thermoregulation*, or the body's ability to regulate its internal temperature, during exercise. Precautions should be taken to avoid exercising in extremely hot and cold environments and to provide wet towels or cool compresses to assist in keeping the body from overheating. The third problem is *automatic dysreflexia*. This is a condition where there is a sudden and dangerously high increase in heart rate and blood pressure that can occur due to restrictive clothing cutting off circulation, bowel or bladder dissension, or skin irritation. Care must be taken to monitor for this condition and prevent conditions where it can be triggered. The last problem is a *reduction in maximum heart rate* due to damage to the nervous system. The maximum heart rate most individuals with SCI will be able to attain when exercising will be around 120 beats per minute. This is important for physical educators to understand before setting cardiorespiratory goals and when monitoring training effort during exercise.

Obesity as a Health Risk

The last health issue that is a critical issue for many individuals with SCI is obesity. Although the incidence of obesity has been increasing overall in our society, the prevalence of obesity is much higher in individuals with SCI. As a result of their injuries, individuals with SCI typically lose function of the large muscle groups in their lower limbs, which are the body's major calorie burners. They also tend to consume calories at the preinjury rate or in many cases increase their caloric intake as a coping mechanism while also becoming more sedentary and exercising less postinjury. Collectively, these factors often result in a loss of preinjury fitness levels, a rapid increase in body fat, and a poor prognosis for losing weight due to lower work capacity of the smaller muscle groups in their upper body and torso coupled with disproportional calorie intake. Once individuals with SCI become obese, they enter a negative health cycle. The heavier they become, the more difficult it is for them to move and perform their activities of daily living, and consequently, they move less, become less fit, and more sedentary. The longer they stay obese, the greater the likelihood of them developing other health risks such as diabetes, coronary heart disease, and metabolic syndrome. Research has shown that these negative health risks can be addressed by administering appropriate physical fitness programs for individuals with SCI (Phillips et al., 1998). As a result, it is very important that these issues be addressed in physical education, and appropriate physical activity goals should be included in the adapted physical education curricula to help students with SCI maintain and live an active healthy lifestyle.

Cognitive Characteristics

Although having a SCI does not directly affect an individual's cognitive ability or behavior, it may negatively affect their academic performance. Because the recovery time from injury to returning to school can take 3–6 months, it is not unusual for some of these students to lose a year. Couple this with how long it takes them to fully accept their injury, redefine their goals, and become motivated to excel in school again, some students with SCI will struggle academically after their injury. Teachers should be aware of these issues and the role physical education can play in helping students with SCI adjust to their injuries. For many students that were active in sports prior to their injury, sports can be used as way to make a transition back to normalcy. A popular activity for many individuals with

paraplegia could be wheelchair basketball or wheelchair tennis. The physical education teacher could contact some of the local wheelchair clubs in the community and arrange for the student with SCI to go watch a practice. Frequently being able to see other individuals who have sustained a similar injury and have accepted their injuries, are employed, live independently, can drive, and get together to play basketball can be very influential in helping individuals with SCI refocus on their potential as opposed to their limitations.

Psychological Characteristics

Physical education can play an important role in helping individuals with SCI make a transition back to school, accept their injury, and get refocused on maximizing their potential. A review of literature (Kawanishi & Greguol, 2013) revealed that there is a beneficial correlation between physical activity and quality of life and functional independence for individuals with SCI. It is therefore imperative that physical education optimize the physical and motor skill development of students so that they can fully engage in physical activity throughout their lives. To achieve these outcomes, the physical educator must assess not only the students' physical and motor capabilities but also a variety of other factors such as their attitude, acceptance of their condition, social support mechanisms, family support, and interests in physical activities. Many high school students with SCI fall behind academically and are separated from their peers when they have to repeat the previous year's courses. Students with SCI become further isolated from their friends because they can no longer independently go hang out with their friends or go to popular school events such as sporting events. At the same time, many of these students also realize that their injury has placed a tremendous burden on their families who now have to alter their plans and routines to take care of them. The end result is many of these students find themselves socially isolated at home where they feel guilty about the problems they have created for their families. Different students cope with these feelings in different ways such as withdrawing from everyone and becoming depressed or acting out and getting mad at everyone. Physical educators must select physical education goals that are reflective of the students' needs in these areas. Reengaging students with SCI back into physical activities that they enjoyed in the past is an effective strategy for initiating this transition process back to school. This information as well as input from the other members of the student's individualized education

Table 15.2. General recommendations for working with students with SCI

1. Allow a period of time for them to make a transition back to school. Initially when they return to school and see their friends, particularly in physical education, what many of them see and focus on is what their friends can still do that they can no longer do.

2. Take time to meet with the student, assess their interests in physical activity, and identify a few areas where the student can experience success.

3. Involve the student in setting the goals for the adapted physical education curriculum while also emphasizing the need for physical fitness and lifetime sports skills.

4. Within physical fitness, emphasize their need to work on range of motion to avoid contractures, cardiorespiratory endurance to burn calories, and nutrition to ensure they consume a balanced low-calorie diet.

5. For lifetime sports skills, pick sports that build on their interests, are readily available and accessible in the community, provide good role models of individuals who have adapted well to their injuries, and provide social outlets.

6. Develop their wheelchair or mobility skills so that they can maximize where they go and the activities they can participate in.

7. Start slow and initially break skills down into small learning steps so students can experience success and perceive that they are making progress.

8. Constantly look for ways the student can use the skills being learned and practiced in physical education in social and recreational settings.

program (IEP) team would then be used to determine what would be functional physical education goals for this student's adapted physical education curriculum and where this student should initially be placed for physical education. Although each individual with SCI would be unique, Table 15.2 summarizes a few additional recommendations for working with students with SCI.

SPINA BIFIDA

Spina bifida is the result of a congenital birth defect that occurs early in fetal development in which a portion of the neural tube does not close completely, causing the spinal column to develop improperly (National Institute of Neurological Disorders and Stroke, 2013). There are three main forms of spina bifida. The most severe form is meningomyelocele. In this form, meninges (the protective covering around the spinal cord), cerebral spinal fluid, and part of the spinal cord protrude through the opening, forming a visible sac on the back. This form is almost always associated with some neurological damage resulting in loss of sensation and motor control in the lower limbs and loss of bowel and bladder control. In the second form, meningocele,

only the spinal cord covering and cerebral spinal fluid protrude through the opening. This form of spina bifida is rarely associated with any loss of motor function. The third form, spina bifida occulta, is the most common and mildest form. In this form, the defect is present in the spinal column but nothing protrudes through the opening, resulting in no neurological damage.

Spina bifida occurs in approximately 3.5 out of every 10,000 live births (National Birth Defects Prevention Network, 2010) and can be detected by Week 16 by a combination of blood tests, amniocentesis, and sonograms. Although all the causes of spina bifida are unknown, deficits in folic acid in mothers have been found to be associated with spina bifida. As a result, in 1998, the U.S. Food and Drug Administration mandated folic acid to be added to all grain products. As a result of this intervention, the incidence of spina bifida has decreased from 5.22 in 1996 to 3.62 per 10,000 births in 2002 (Williams et al., 2002). If spina bifida is detected before birth, there are two treatment options available. Prenatal surgery can be performed on the fetus during Weeks 19–25 to close the opening in the neural tube, or the fetus can be delivered by Cesarean section at Week 37 and the defect surgically addressed soon after birth. The prenatal repair procedure (Adzick et al., 2011) is a revolutionary technique. Although it presents significant risks to the mother and fetus, it has shown very positive results related to improving motor function in the children.

Associated Health and Medical Conditions

The meningomyelocele form of spina bifida is commonly associated with three other health conditions that if left untreated can lead to serious medical complications. *Hydrocephalus* is a problem in which there is a buildup of cerebral spinal fluid in the ventricles of the brain. This condition is treated soon after birth by inserting a pressure-release valve in the ventricle and then draining the excess fluid off into the heart or abdomen. *Tethering of the spinal cord* describes a condition in which the spinal cord is attached to the spinal column at the site of defect. The tethering can stretch the spinal cord and reduce circulation in the cord that can result in additional loss of function. The negative effect of tethering frequently occurs during the adolescent growth spurt in approximately 60% of adolescents with spina bifida. When detected, the cord can be surgically untethered. *Chiari II malformation*, also referred to as Arnold-Chiari malformation (ACM), is a condition in which the lower brainstem is pulled down through the base of the skull into the top of the spinal column, further impairing function. This condition is surgically treated to decompress the brainstem.

Children with spina bifida are prone to a number of secondary health problems similar to those discussed under SCIs such as pressure sores, bruising, contractures, bowel and bladder issues, and obesity. The major difference is that children with spina bifida learn how to manage these issues as a natural part of growing up. That said, physical educators should be sensitive to their bowel and bladder issues because this is a sensitive subject for many children when they start school. Obesity can also be a major health risk for many students with spina bifida due to their reduced calorie-burning capacity and their tendency to both be sedentary and overeat. Physical education can help by developing their physical and motor skills and their overall physical fitness so that they can participate in a wide range of physical activities. When students with spina bifida become obese, they enter a negative health cycle. Obesity makes it more difficult to ambulate with crutches and in some cases leads to overuse joint problems in the wrists, elbows, and shoulders. When ambulation with crutches is no longer feasible, students with spina bifida move to a wheelchair, which can further reduce involvement and access to physical activities.

Finally, approximately 70% of children with spina bifida have been found to be allergic to *latex*. Although latex has been removed from most physical education equipment, physical educators should still make sure their equipment is latex free, particularly items such as rubber balls and balloons.

Cognitive Characteristics

Although most students with spina bifida fall in the typical IQ range, it is widely recognized that many students with spina bifida have mild to severe learning disabilities characterized by perceptual motor, comprehension, attention, memory, and organizational problems. It is therefore important for physical educators to work collaboratively with the IEP team so that they are aware of each student's specific learning needs and how these can be addressed in physical education.

Motor Characteristics

Students with spina bifida will require therapy and the use of assistive devices to position themselves so that they can parallel typical developmental positions experienced by children without disabilities, such as sitting, crawling, and standing. Particular attention must be paid to maintaining full range of motion in lower limb joints to avoid contractures and to stimulate circulation. With appropriate training, most children with spina bifida will learn to walk with a combination of leg braces and crutches but will experience significant delays (Teulier et al., 2009). It is very important that children with spina bifida are encouraged to stand and walk, at least during childhood and adolescence, because these weight-bearing activities stimulate bone growth and circulation in their lower limbs. However, wheelchair use as an adult may be a more functional means of mobility for those with spina bifida, particularly those with higher level spinal cord lesions.

As a general rule, students with spina bifida should be encouraged to ambulate with their crutches and to use their crutches as their primary means of moving both at home and in school. The one exception to this rule should be physical education. In many physical education activities, it will be important for students with spina bifida to be able to use their hands. When students use their crutches in physical education, their hands and arms are occupied for balance. However, if a wheelchair is substituted for locomotor skills, these children often can learn and perform all the typical skills taught in general physical education. Given that most students with spina bifida will enter kindergarten with some degree of motor development delay due to their disability and are likely to have some learning difficulties, most will qualify for adapted physical education services and require unique motor-related IEP goals. However, with reasonable accommodations, most students with spina bifida should be able to work on and achieve these unique goals within the general physical education program. In addition, many students with spina bifida have the potential to reach a level where they can be very functional and accommodate their own needs in general physical education and no longer need specialized adapted physical education services. In addition, some students with spina bifida may have the potential to be excellent wheelchair athletes if they are interested in competitive sports.

SPINAL COLUMN DEVIATIONS

Mild postural deviations of the spine are common in many children and adults. Fortunately, the majority of these are nonstructural and can be remediated by appropriate instruction, exercise, and practice. In more severe cases, the cause of the deviation is structural and can result in a permanent change if not treated. Unfortunately, the incidence of structural deviations is much more common in individuals with disabilities. The three most common deviations of the spine are kyphosis, lordosis, and scoliosis. *Kyphosis* is the result of an extreme concave curvature of the thoracic region of the spine, whereas *lordosis* is characterized by an extreme convex curve in the lumbar spine. The most common spinal cord deviation occurring in 2%–3% of children is scoliosis (National Scoliosis Foundation, n.d.). *Scoliosis* occurs between the ages of 10 and 16, and although the incidence is approximately the same in both boys and girls, cases in girls tend to be more severe and require more treatment.

Scoliosis

Most cases of structural scoliosis in children are labeled as idiopathic, which means the cause is unknown. For children with disabilities such as cerebral palsy, the cause of their scoliosis is typically labeled as neuromuscular. The treatment for scoliosis depends on the severity of the curve and typically follows three phases: observation, bracing, and surgery. In mild forms of scoliosis, where the curve is less than 25 degrees, the treatment is usually just to monitor the curve to make sure it does not get any worse. For curves greater than 25 degrees, the most common treatment is bracing. The purpose for wearing the brace is not to correct scoliosis but to hold the spine in correct alignment until the spine reaches skeletal maturity. Therefore, for bracing to be effective, the adolescent must consistently wear the brace for several years. Unfortunately, many adolescents are not compliant with wearing their brace, and their scoliosis gets worse. For curves greater than 40 degrees, the most common treatment is surgery. The surgery involves attaching rods to the sides of the affected vertebrae in the spine to prevent any further curvature of the spine.

Early detection of spinal deviations is important so the degree of deviation can be monitored and treatment is started when necessary. Because physical educators work on body awareness and posture and regularly assess the body alignment of students as they perform motor skills, they can play an important role in identifying potential spinal cord deviations.

Students with mild and moderate spinal column deviations typically can participate in most general physical education activities without any special modifications. When students are wearing a brace, the brace will generally be self-limiting—that is, the students should be encouraged to participate to the maximum extent that he or she can while wearing the brace. When students require surgery to treat their spinal column deviation, they will probably require adapted physical education until they fully recover from their surgery. They then should be slowly included back into the general physical education program.

There should be no major motor, health, cognitive, or behavior problems associated with the treatment of spinal column deviations. However, physical educators should be aware of the social ramifications that can be associated with an adolescent who has to wear a brace. Many adolescents are self-conscious about their appearance and how they are perceived by others, and wearing a brace is like wearing a sign that says, "Look at me, I am different!" This is particularly true when students need to change into gym clothes for physical education. As a result, some of these students may request to be excused from physical education or refuse to participate in physical education activities because of their condition. Physical educators should be sensitive to their concerns, particularly during the early phases when the students start wearing their braces, and make accommodations to transition them into being fully involved in the general physical education program. A recommended strategy is for the physical educator to meet with these students individually before each unit and discuss what skills will be worked on and what accommodations will be made to accommodate them so that they can fully participate.

CEREBRAL PALSY

Cerebral palsy (CP) is a nonprogressive disorder caused by damage to the developing brain. The condition is characterized by significant difficulties with physical movement and muscle coordination (http://cerebralpalsy.org/about-cerebral-palsy/definition). However, the official diagnosis does not even begin to suggest the variety of problems that can arise during the growth of a child and that need to be addressed over the course of therapeutic and education management. Movement problems are often seen as the biggest challenge in teaching children with CP in physical education classes.

Many classification systems of CP have been used by different authors over the years. The types of CP are usually defined according to the muscle tone and movement quality or according to the extent of involvement (McCarthy, 1992). For example, the topographical classification system describes how and where a child's body is affected by CP:

- *Hemiplegia:* The arm and leg on one side of the body are affected.
- *Diplegia:* The whole body is affected (but the legs more than arms).
- *Quadriplegia:* The whole body is affected.
- *Monoplegia:* Only one arm or, less frequently, only one leg is affected.
- *Paraplegia:* Only both lower limbs are affected.

Another classification system is based on the predominant neurological signs, including abnormalities in the definition of muscle tone:

- *Spastic CP* is characterized by increased muscle tone. Spastic CP is further classified depending on limb involvement as quadriplegia, hemiplegia, or diplegia.
- *Nonspastic CP* is characterized by decreased or fluctuating muscle tone. Multiple forms of nonspastic CP are each characterized by particular impairment: choreathetoid, ataxic, dystonic, hypotonic/atonic, and mixed.

Unfortunately, these classifications give little indication of the actual level of ability of the child. Some authors (Gowland, Boyce, Wright, Goldsmith, & Rosenbaum, 1995; Mutch, Alberman, Hagberg, Kodama, & Perat, 1992) have claimed that the concept of types of CP is artificial because most of the changes seem to develop with the growth of a child. It is not as important to distinguish the children by type of CP as by functional ability and their potential.

Health and Medical Characteristics

About half of all children with CP experience seizures. However, with a proper diagnosis and treatment plan, the frequency of certain seizure types can be controlled. In situations where seizures occur, teachers should protect the child from harm by monitoring the seizure and making the environment safe so that the child cannot be physically hurt. The teacher should not attempt to hold the child still or to prevent physical movement. It is important to remain with the child during the seizure. Also, children with CP may experience digestive symptoms such as diarrhea, vomiting, constipation, or bladder infections. In more severe conditions, children are not able to eat at all and require installation of temporary or permanent feeding tubes (Miller & Bachrach, 2006). Usually, a team of relevant health care professionals that can include a gastroenterologist, occupational therapist, speech therapist, dietitian, nurse, and psychologist helps family and education personnel to learn on how to manage feeding difficulties. Vision problems are also very common in children with CP and can include myopia, hyperopia, strabismus, amblyopia, and astigmatism (see Chapter 14 for more information about visual impairments and blindness; Hoon & Tolley, 2013).

Children with CP often have a lower activity level than typically developing children. When a child cannot participate in physical activities that require deep breathing, air passages are more likely to become infected and the muscles used for breathing aren't fully exercised. Because of the posture deformity, such as curvature of the spine, change in muscle tone may contribute to chest wall deformity, which in turn can lead to restricted lung function and the potential for unequal lung expansion.

Cognitive and Behavior Characteristics

About two thirds of children with CP have moderate to severe levels of intellectual (cognitive) impairment. It is common that a greater level of a physical impairment is associated with more severe intellectual disability. However, there might be a child who has a profound level of physical impairment and does not have an intellectual disability. Children with CP may present specific learning difficulties such as a short attention span, motor planning difficulties, and perceptual and language difficulties. Learning abilities may also be affected by restrictions in fine and gross motor skills. Students with CP need more time and effort to perform movements and follow the instructions of teachers than others, and they may tire more easily, too (Hoon & Tolley, 2013).

Children with CP may have behavioral issues that, in turn, may affect their psychological development and social interactions. One of most common problems is frustration. For example, when a child has difficulty completing a task due to motor difficulties, he or she may become depressed or angry. Teachers have to help the child feel a sense of success by assisting in the process yet still allowing him or her to complete the task. The communication restrictions also can cause behavior problems and increase dependence on adult assistants. For example, the child may demand the mother's or assistant teacher's continuous presence while limiting interactions with age-appropriate peers (Miller & Bachrach, 2006).

Motor and Fitness Characteristics

The most significant challenges children with CP face in physical education are related to weakness, muscle spasticity, and deficient balance. Teachers have to be aware of body movement restrictions and other physical barriers children with CP have to overcome. For example, they may have lower cardiovascular endurance; decreased maximal oxygen uptake (VO2max) values, which cause inefficient ventilation; and local fatigue in the spastic muscles (Hutzler, Chacham, Bergman, & Szeinberg, 1997).

Teaching Strategies for Children with Cerebral Palsy

Because children with CP vary regarding their individual needs in education, the strategies for teaching are different depending on the severity of individual student's symptoms. Most children with CP have difficulty staying focused or being able to follow multiple instructions. Therefore, physical education teachers should limit instructions to the key points so that students with CP can better follow along. Also, the teacher should use multiple instructional techniques, such as visual and verbal, so the student will have more resources to use. The teacher can ask other classmates to provide the peer with CP-individualized instructions or assist in some activities. Children with CP often benefit from short and clear instructions presented consistently. For example, the physical education teacher could write or illustrate in pictograms the list of activities so the student knows what is expected from him or her and can be consistent with those expectations and the consequences associated with them. The teacher can use simple cues such as tapping the student's hand or shoulder to prepare him or her in making a transition to another activity. Teachers also should facilitate the independence of students with CP by asking them to make choices (e.g., allowing them to choose the order in which they do certain tasks or who they want to choose as their partner for a given activity), which will help boost their self-confidence and contribute to their future independence. It is important that the teacher help students with CP build friendships and social interactions with other classmates. Some children with CP might use alternative communication devices, so teachers should make sure they have them switched on during physical education class. Physical education teachers should also show peers how to use the communication device so that they can converse with the student with CP.

The physical education teacher should be aware of the physical considerations that will benefit students' with CP when participating in physical education. For example, comfortable positioning in the wheelchair or in gait trainer will help students participate in activities. Also, the teacher might consider trying out different positions, such as sitting on the floor or lying down to prevent muscle tension and pain. Because students with CP might experience muscle stiffness, encourage them to stretch and move around as much as necessary. Students with CP typically have poor motor skills and might need assistance in holding objects (e.g., ball, tennis racket, baseball bat). Because of muscle fatigue, students with CP might tire easily and therefore should be allowed to rest when needed.

TRAUMATIC BRAIN INJURY

A traumatic brain injury (TBI) is defined as a nondegenerative, noncongenital insult to the brain from an external mechanical force, possibly leading to permanent or temporary impairment of cognitive, physical, and psychosocial functions, with an associated diminished or altered state of consciousness (Dawodu, Yadav, Talavera, Salcido, & Allen, 2013). According to the Centers for Disease Control and Prevention (CDC; 2014i) TBI is a significant problem in the United States. During 2010, TBI alone or in combination with other injuries accounted for more than 280,000 hospitalizations and 2.2 million emergency room visits. From 2001 to 2009, the rate for sports-related injuries diagnosed as a concussion or TBI rose 57% for children under the age of 19. The most common causes of TBI in school-age children are motor vehicle accidents, falls, sports-related injuries, and physical abuse.

After suffering a TBI, children receive acute care for their injuries in a hospital setting and then are transferred to a rehabilitation hospital where a team of medical doctors and therapists work collaboratively to further evaluate the impact of their injuries and begin the rehabilitation process. After the acute rehabilitation phase, children typically return home and continue therapy in outpatient clinics. As these students make a transition back to their homes and return to school, the school staff must work collaboratively with the parents and, whenever possible, the rehabilitation staff to ensure a smooth and consistent transfer of care.

Secondary Medical and Health Concerns

As with other orthopedic disabilities, students with TBI can have a variety of secondary disabilities such as contractures and obesity. One of the more serious secondary disabilities that can occur with TBI is seizures or epilepsy. Typically if the students only have one incident, it is referred to as a seizure; if they have repeated seizures, it is referred to as epilepsy. It is important to consult the medical records of students with TBI when they return to school to learn if they have epilepsy. If they do, the physical educator should talk to the parents and/or the student's physician to find out more about the type of seizure they have, what should be done during the seizure to assist the student, and what physical education activities (e.g., swimming) might be contraindicated. In most cases, the students will take antiepileptic medications to control their seizures. Physical educators should be aware of the side effects of these medications, such as fatigue and impaired balance, and how these factors may affect performance and safety in physical education.

Two important things to understand about TBI are that every injury is unique and that they typically involve various forms and combinations of physical, cognitive, and emotional impairments, as shown in Table 15.3. Students with TBI can exhibit many of the same motor characteristics as students with CP. These impairments are commonly labeled as ataxia (i.e., poor coordination), spasticity (i.e., abnormally high muscle tone), hypotonia (i.e., loose or low muscle tone), and apraxia (i.e., loss of ability to plan movement). These impairments can affect one or multiple limbs and range in severity from mild to severe. In addition,

students with TBI have the additional psychosocial challenges of dealing with the loss of their former motor abilities and the challenge of relearning motor skills. Unfortunately, learning capabilities and their ability to emotionally deal with all these challenges can also be adversely affected by their injuries.

Teaching Children with Traumatic Brain Injury

The transition back to school can be very challenging for many students with TBI. Often, seeing their friends reminds them of what they once could do. As a result, many students will be apprehensive about returning to school in general but specifically about returning to physical education. Typically, these students should start in adapted physical education where the teacher can assess their functional capabilities, interests, and where they are on learning to deal with accepting their condition. Many of these students will return to school with low fitness due to immobility from their injuries. Unfortunately, low fitness makes all movement more difficult, from performing simple everyday tasks such as getting dressed to moving between classes. Therefore, one of the essential goals when developing adapted physical education curricula for these students will be to find a physical activity that they are interested in. This goal should be selected to achieve multiple ends. First is simply getting them physically engaged in an activity and begin to improve their fitness. Second is developing their functional motor skills in the activity to further enhance their performance and confidence. Third is using the activity as a vehicle to include them back in general physical education and eventually out in the community where they can participate with their family and peers. For many students, starting with a physical activity or sport that they were successful at before their injury is effective in getting them to reengage. However, care should be taken if their TBI was associated with a sports injury. In these cases, it may be best to start with other physical activities or sports until they have adjusted to their injury and express an interest in the sport they were injured in. Depending on the severity of their TBI, these activities could range from relatively simple sports such as bowling to more complex activities such as wheelchair basketball or golf. As a rule, the general suggestions shown in Table 15.2 for SCIs should be followed with transitioning students with TBI back into physical education at school.

Table 15.3. Common physical, cognitive, and emotional impairments associated with TBI

Physical impairments	Cognitive impairments	Emotional impairments
Speech	Short-term memory impairments	Mood swings
Vision	Impaired concentration	Denial
Hearing	Slowness of thinking	Self-centeredness
Headaches	Limited attention span	Anxiety
Motor coordination	Impairments of perception	Depression
Muscle spasticity	Communication problems	Lowered self-esteem
Paralysis	Planning problems	Sexual dysfunction
Seizures	Writing problems	Restlessness
Balance	Reading problems	Lack of motivation
Fatigue	Judgment problems	Difficulty controlling emotions

From Brain Injury Association of America (n.d.). Retrieved from http://www.biausa.org/brain-injury-children.htm#symptoms; reprinted by permission.

AMPUTATIONS

In the United States, approximately 4 out of every 10,000 infants are born with an upper limb deformity and 2 out of every 10,000 infants are born with a lower limb deformity (CDC, 2014d). Limb deformities are also referred to as limb reductions and describe a limb that fails to form completely during fetal development. The cause of most congenital limb deformities is unknown but believed to be related to the mother being exposed to adverse factors such as viruses, drugs, and chemicals during pregnancy. Limb loss can also be acquired in children as a result of accidents and medical conditions such as cancer. Lawn mowers are the most common cause of traumatic injuries resulting in amputations in children under the age of 5 that involve loss of the lower limbs (Smith, 2006). Treatment of a limb deformity or amputation involves surgery designed to optimally prepare the limb in several ways: for weight bearing in the case of the lower limbs, prosthetic fitting, maximizing function, and appearance. Amputations are classified by the limb and level of the amputation into nine classes, as shown in Table 15.4.

The goal is to fit children with a prosthetic limb as soon as possible after an amputation so that it becomes part of their body image and they begin to learn to use it to explore their environment and learn to move. Children with amputations around birth are typically fitted with their first prosthetic upper limb around 6 months old and their first lower limb prosthetic around 12 months old. As children age, the limbs need to be replaced to adjust for growth and increase in sophistication to maximize function (Smith & Campbell, 2009). There has been a tremendous evolution in both the types of materials used to make prosthetic limbs and the technology incorporated in the limbs.

It is important for physical educators to understand that they need to encourage students to use their prostheses to the maximum extent they can while minimizing any risks of damaging the prostheses. Physical educators should also be aware that when children get a new prosthesis, there is an adjustment period where they need to learn how to use and become comfortable with the new device. During this period, they may have difficulty with performing some motor activities or become more easily frustrated.

Children with congenital amputations will likely experience some motor delays due to surgery, lack of function, and needing to learn how to use a prosthetic limb. In addition, they may be overprotected by their parents and restricted in their movement opportunities. Psychologically, they will also need to learn and understand that they may be perceived and treated differently by others (Novotny & Swagman, 1992).

Children with acquired amputations may also experience motor delays depending on their age and the nature of the amputation, but in many cases, their motor delays may be caused by psychological issues. This is because they typically need to deal with the loss of previous abilities as well as learn to deal with and learn how to use a new prosthetic limb. Physical educators should be especially sensitive to these issues for students with acquired amputations.

Health and Medical Problems

Two major health issues physical educators should be aware of when working with students that wear prosthetic limbs are stump pain and phantom limb pain. Stump pain is related to pain at the site where the surface of the limb interfaces with the prosthesis. This pain can be caused by a number of factors such as a poor fit between the stump and the prosthesis or a breakdown of the skin at the point of the interface with the prosthesis. Phantom pain refers to the person perceiving sensation of pain from the part of the limb that has been amputated. Many of these pain issues can be addressed by proper training on how to attach and wear the prosthesis. In more severe cases, the problem may be treated by medication or by surgery.

A second common health issue for individuals with above-the-knee lower limb amputations is obesity. The primary problems are the loss of the large muscles in the legs, which are the body's major calorie burners, and the tendency of many individuals with acquired lower limb amputations to not reduce their caloric intake after their injury.

Table 15.4. Amputation classifications

Class	Limbs involved	Location	Label
A1	Double leg	Above the knee	AK
A2	Single leg	Above the knee	AK
A3	Double leg	Below the knee	BK
A4	Single leg	Below the knee	BK
A5	Double arm	Above the elbow	AE
A6	Single arm	Above the elbow	AE
A7	Double arm	Below the elbow	BE
A8	Single arm	Below the elbow	BE
A9	Arm and leg	Combined lower and upper limbs	

Unfortunately, as an amputee's weight increases, more stress is placed on where their stump interfaces with the prosthesis. This creates a vicious cycle in which their increased weight produces increased pain and tissue break down, which further limits their physical activity and their ability to burn calories.

Implications for Physical Education

Many students with congenital amputations will have accepted and learned how to use their prostheses by the time they start school and will require little or only minor modifications to include them in general physical education. That said, physical educators should anticipate some possible motor skill delays and be sensitive to their potential sensitivity and frustration when learning new skills that involve their prosthesis or when they get a new prosthesis (Krebs, Edelstein, & Thornby, 1991). Physical educators should also anticipate that some students with amputations, particularly those that may have acquired their amputations, may not have fully accepted their condition or may not be fully proficient in using their prosthesis. The majority of these students should be included in general physical education but may require more significant modifications (e.g., use of a peer tutor) to be successful and make up for any delays in their skill development.

Regardless of whether the amputation is congenital or acquired, physical educators should always be sensitive to any changes in how these students interact with their classmates. At certain age levels (e.g., middle school), all students can become more aware of their physical characteristics and their differences. This may be particularly true for some students with amputations. When these situations arise, it may be appropriate to remind all the students in the class that they all have strengths and challenges and that their role as friends is to support and help each other.

The older students are when they acquire their amputation, the greater the potential challenges are for integrating them back into general physical education. As already discussed in this chapter for other acquired physical disabilities such as SCIs and TBI, accepting a permanent loss of function due to an injury can be devastating to many adolescents. The first step back to normalcy for these students is learning to accept their injury and understanding that they can still live a full, happy, and productive life. The second step is maximizing their physical and motor skills to enhance their overall quality of life. For many of these students, it may be appropriate to start them in adapted physical education when they return to school and then develop a plan to address their unique physical and motor needs. For some of these students, the appropriate goal will be to transition them back to the general physical education program, whereas for others, the goal may be to transition them to community-based physical activities such as weight training in a local fitness club. In all these cases, the initial goals will be assisting them in accepting their condition, learning to use their prosthesis when performing motor skills, and motivating them to become actively engaged in physical activity. For most students with a single-leg or a single-arm amputation, almost all common physical activities can be easily modified so that they can participate, and they should generally be encouraged to wear their prostheses in these activities. However, each case should be considered on an individual basis to determine if wearing their prosthesis hinders their performance (e.g., wearing a prosthetic arm while playing soccer) or unnecessarily places the prosthetic at a high risk of being damaged. For students with more complex amputations, such as double-leg amputees, it may be appropriate for them to learn to play some sports using a wheelchair even if they can ambulate and run proficiently with prosthetic legs.

As discussed for some of the other physical disabilities in this chapter, it is sometimes helpful for these students to participate in physical activities with other students who have similar disabilities but have already accepted them and are now reengaged in physical activity.

Special Sports Organizations for Individuals with Orthopedic Disabilities

- Disabled Sports USA (DSUSA; http://www .disabledsportsusa.org): DSUSA started by sponsoring national skiing competitions for individuals with disabilities in the 1960s and has grown and expanded over the years to serve more than 60,000 youth, wounded warriors, and adults in more than 100 communities in 37 states.

  - *Classification system:* For competitive sports, DSUSA uses the International Paralympic Committee functional classification system.

  - *Sports included:* DSUSA offers more than 40 sport development programs for individuals with SCIs, CP, and TBI such as alpine and Nordic skiing, snowboarding, biathlon, kayaking, water skiing, sailing, scuba, surfing, rafting, outrigger canoeing, fishing, hiking, golf, athletics, archery, cycling, running/wheeling, rock climbing, and equestrian.

- International Paralympic Committee (IPC; http://www.paralympic.org)

  - *Classification system:* The IPC uses a functional classification for each sport, which is described in detail on their web site (http://www.paralympic.org/classification/sport-specific).

  - *Sports included:* The following 28 sports are included in the Paralympics: alpine skiing, archery, athletics, biathlon, bocce, canoeing, cross-country skiing, cycling, equestrian, five-a-side football, seven-a-side football, goalball, ice sledge hockey, judo, powerlifting, rowing, sailing, shooting, swimming, table tennis, triathlon, volleyball (sitting), wheelchair curling, wheelchair basketball, wheelchair dance sport, wheelchair fencing, wheelchair rugby, and wheelchair tennis.

- Cerebral Palsy International Sport and Recreation Association (CPISRA; http://cpisra.org/main/)

  - *Classification:* Athletes with CP are classified into eight classes using a functional classification system developed by CPISRA, which can be found on their web site (http://cpisra.org/main/wp-content/uploads/2013/06/CPISRA-Classification-Rules-Release-9-October-27–2010.pdf).

  - *Sports included:* seven-a-side football, race running, track and field events, skiing, and table cricket

- National Wheelchair Basketball Association (NWBA; http://www.nwba.org)

  - *Classification system:* The NWBA classifies athletes into eight classes based on their functional ability. The eight classes are 1.0, 1.5, 2.0, 2.5, 3.0, 3.5, 4.0, and 4.5. The higher the classification, the greater the functional ability of the player. During a game, the maximum number of points (i.e., sum of the five players' classifications) cannot be more than 15.

  - *Sports included:* wheelchair basketball

- Wheelchair & Ambulatory Sports USA (WASUSA; http://www.wasusa.org)

  - *Classification system:* WASUSA uses a functional classification approach, and the classification system for each sport is described in detail in the rules book for each sport on their web site.

  - *Sports included:* archery, track and field, hand cycling, powerlifting, shooting, swimming, and table tennis

RESOURCES

Brain Injury Association of America
1608 Spring Hill Road, Suite 110, Vienna, VA 22182
Phone: 703-761-0750
http://www.biausa.org

Cerebral Palsy International Research Foundation
3 Columbus Circle, 15th Floor, New York, NY 10019
Phone: 212-520-1686
http://www.cpirf.org

Children's Hemiplegia and Stroke Association
4101 W. Green Oaks, Suite 305, #149, Arlington, TX 76016
http://www.chasa.org

Children's Neurobiological Solutions Foundation
1223 Wilshire Boulevard, #937, Santa Monica, CA 90403
Phone: 310-889.8611
http://www.cnsfoundation.org

Easter Seals
233 South Wacker Drive, Suite 2400, Chicago, IL 60606
Phone: 800-221-6827
http://www.easterseals.com

National Scoliosis Foundation
5 Cabot Place, Stoughton, MA 02072
Phone: 800-673-6922
http://www.scoliosis.org

National Spinal Cord Injury Association
Phone: 800-962-9629
http://www.spinalcord.org

March of Dimes
1275 Mamaroneck Avenue, White Plains, NY 10605
Phone: 914-997-4488
http://www.marchofdimes.com

Pedal-with-Pete Foundation (for Research on Cerebral Palsy)
PO Box 1233, Worthington, OH 43085
Phone: 614-527-0202
http://www.pedal-with-pete.org

Scoliosis Care Foundation
1085 Park Avenue, Suite 1E, New York, NY 10128
Phone: 800-391-8837
http://www.scoliosiscare.org

Scoliosis Research Society
555 East Wells Street, Suite 1100, Milwaukee, WI
  53202
Phone: 414-289-9107
http://www.srs.org

Spina Bifida Association
1600 Wilson Boulevard, Suite 800, Arlington, VA
  22209
Phone: 202-944-3285
http://www.spinabifidaassociation.org

Traumatic Brain Injury
2001 Market Street, Suite 2900, Philadelphia, PA
  19103
Phone: 866-930-8897
http://www.traumaticbraininjury.com

United Cerebral Palsy
1825 K Street NW, Suite 600, Washington, D.C.
  20006
Phone: 800-872-5827
http://ucp.org

United Spinal Association
75-20 Astoria Boulevard, East Elmhurst, NY 11370
718-803-3782
http://www.unitedspinal.org

CHAPTER 16

Other Health Impairments

Simon Driver and Alicia Dixon-Ibarra

Objectives

1. Describe the criteria for who qualifies for special education services within the other health impairment (OHI) category

2. Identify the most prevalent conditions within the OHI category

3. Describe the characteristics of children with specific OHIs

4. Identify the unique characteristics of children with OHI and how they influence participation in physical education

5. Identify appropriate modifications for children with OHI so they may safely and successfully participate in physical education

---

Growing up, Stacey would have loved to play soccer and basketball or even go bike riding with her friends, but because of her heart condition, she knew playing these active sports was not safe for her. Her physical educators also knew about her heart condition, and there were restrictions in physical education as well. Stacey is now 14 years old and moving from middle to high school. During summer orientation, she and her parents met with several teachers, including her physical educator, who listened to Stacey while she explained her heart condition. Although her physical educator clearly wants to do what is safe and appropriate for Stacey, he wonders what activities he could present to Stacy that would help her develop some lifetime leisure skills.

Michael is a classmate of Stacey's, but unlike Stacey, he has played sports growing up, and he plans on trying out for his high school's basketball and baseball teams. However, Michael has sickle cell anemia, and there are times when he has "episodes" in which he experiences severe pain throughout his whole body. Some of these episodes have reached a level of "crisis," resulting in Michael having to spend a few days in the hospital and, of course, missing school, practice, and games. Michael wonders how these episodes will affect his participation in high school physical education as well as his playing baseball and basketball for the high school team.

Daniel also is moving up from middle to high school. Daniel has always struggled with his weight, and in middle school, he really gained quite a bit of weight. One day during his last year of middle school, Daniel started to feel really strange during physical education and right before lunch; he was shaky, sweating profusely, had blurred vision, and then passed out. He was able to walk with assistance to the school nurse's office, and later, his mother took him to his pediatrician. Within a week, Daniel was diagnosed with Type 2 diabetes. Over the next few months, he changed his diet, started exercising, and started checking his blood sugar multiple times each day. Daniel wonders how he will do in high school physical education, and of course, Daniel's physical education teacher is wondering what restrictions Daniel might face.

Other health impairment (OHI) is one of the 14 categories of disability that is defined under the Individuals with Disabilities Education Act (IDEA; PL 108-446), which ensures eligible children receive services to appropriately meet their educational, developmental, and functional needs. IDEA includes multiple disability groups within "other" health impairments, so educators are challenged to provide adapted physical education services to a broad range of children with very different needs.

WHAT IS OTHER HEALTH IMPAIRMENT?

Specifically, Individuals with Disabilities Education Improvement Act of 2004 defines OHI as

> having limited strength, vitality, or alertness, including a heightened alertness to environmental stimuli, that results in limited alertness with respect to the educational environment, that—
>
> (i) Is due to chronic or acute health problems such as asthma, attention deficit disorder or attention deficit hyperactivity disorder, diabetes, epilepsy, a heart condition, hemophilia, lead poisoning, leukemia, nephritis, rheumatic fever, sickle cell anemia, and Tourette syndrome; and
>
> (ii) Adversely affects a child's educational performance. (IDEA of 2004, § 300.8[c][9])

What separates children with OHI from children with other identified disabilities is the chronic or acute medical nature of the conditions in this category, putting them more in line with disease versus disability. However, the effect of these conditions on education is still just as important as other IDEA categories when making decisions for inclusion in physical education (Winnick, 2011). Moreover, there are several important pieces of information to glean from the definition of OHI that may affect whether a child qualifies for adapted physical education services. First, the use of "such as" in IDEA's definition of OHIs suggests that the different diagnoses listed are by no means comprehensive. For example, cystic fibrosis and other childhood lung disorders are not listed but are unquestionably conditions that may affect a child's "strength and vitality," resulting in the need for adapted physical education services (as are early onset of multiple sclerosis, AIDS, HIV, and more). More so, this category in IDEA could be considered a catchall for those with conditions that limit participation in educational activities but are not identified specifically by the other 13 conditions. Many low-incidence disabilities/diseases can also

be included in this category. For example, a child with Dravet syndrome, a rare form of epilepsy, would certainly need adapted physical education services because seizures and behavioral and developmental delays would likely influence the student's performance in physical education.

On the other hand, having a medical diagnosis does not automatically guarantee that a child qualifies for special education services. Grice (2002) discussed a particular case in which a child had a medical condition but did not qualify as a student with a disability under IDEA. The child in question had asthma, took medication to control her asthma, and carried an inhaler in case she had an asthma attack. The school nurse and other key school personnel were aware of her condition and emergency procedures in the event of an asthma attack during school hours. However, her condition never affected her success in school, she never experienced asthma attacks at school, and she did not have any attendance problems. As a result, the hearing officer given her case determined she did not qualify for services under IDEA as a child with OHI because she showed no signs of limited alertness, strength, or vitality. Therefore, it is important to understand that OHI eligibility is made on a case-by-case basis and that the medical diagnosis is not necessary and not by itself sufficient evidence for OHI eligibility (Grice, 2002).

Due to the diverse needs of children within the OHI category, individualization is critical when developing an inclusive physical education experience. Many children within this category will have services that vary from term to term or from year to year as OHIs may be due to "chronic or acute health problems." The variation in health status presents a unique challenge and highlights the important role of adapted physical education. For example, a child with asthma may have difficulties during summer terms due to changes in humidity; however, during winter months, the child may be less affected by the condition and may be more able to participate in aerobic activities. In contrast, a child with cancer who is actively undergoing radiation treatments would need additional modifications to the type and intensity of activity and may even qualify for adapted physical education services (consultative to the general physical education teacher or even direct services to the child), whereas this same child a year later may be in cancer remission and need very different modifications for activity.

From a practical standpoint, when determining the extent to which a child with an OHI is included in physical education, it is important to consider the effect of the condition (e.g., limited strength, energy, alertness) on their performance (e.g., ability to participate in soccer drills followed by a small side game). Specifically, children with OHIs present their own unique characteristics as they relate to sports and physical activity participation. As long as you are aware of the contraindications of activity, physical activity can be beneficial to all children, including those with OHI. The following discusses conditions with greater incidence that are included in the OHI category and provides ways to include these children in your physical education classroom (see Table 16.1 for lower incidence OHIs).

Anemia

Anemia is typically an inherited condition in children that reduces their red blood cell count or limits the ability of the red blood cells to carry hemoglobin (which carries oxygen around the body). There are three main categories, which include anemia caused by 1) blood loss, 2) abnormal red blood cell production, and 3) the breakdown of red blood cells (WebMD, 2014). Iron deficiency, which is the most common type of anemia (Centers for Disease Control and Prevention [CDC], 2011a), affects an individual's ability to carry oxygen throughout the body as well as their muscles' ability to store and use oxygen. Sickle cell anemia is another common form of anemia that is named after the abnormal crescent or sickle shape of the red blood cell (CDC, 2014h). Due to the abnormal shape, the red blood cells are not able to pass through small blood vessels easily and may cause the individual sudden ("episode") or chronic pain ("crisis") that can range from mild to severe, cause pain throughout the whole body, and last indefinitely (CDC, 2014g). In addition, individuals may experience hand–foot syndrome, which is characterized by fever and swelling of the hands and feet, which in turn can effect participation in physical activity (CDC, 2014g). Depending on the type of anemia an individual has (there are hundreds of different types), it may be a short-term condition that is easily treated through diet and supplements or it may be a chronic condition that can become life threatening if not monitored appropriately. Diagnosis and treatment are managed by a physician and vary depending on the type of anemia.

Implications for Physical Education

There are several characteristics of anemia that are important to consider when including children into a physical education setting. For example, because hemoglobin is responsible for carrying oxygen from the lungs to the rest of the body, individuals with anemia may get shortness of breath quickly, have an unusually high heart beat during exercise, feel dizzy or weak, get headaches, and fatigue easily. In addition, individuals may experience periods of pain in the legs, arms, abdomen, and chest; this is especially true of children with sickle cell anemia due to the unusual shape of the red blood cell and hand–foot syndrome. As a result of the characteristics of anemia, there are several important implications for the physical education setting due to restrictions with "strength and vitality." However, it is important to note that regular exercise is still beneficial to endurance and overall fitness, so children with anemia should be included in physical education with appropriate modifications. Some considerations may include the following (Conley et al., 2014):

- High-intensity or long-duration activities may be challenging, so frequent rest periods should be incorporated into activities.

- Regular checks with the child on symptoms during activity to check for unusual heart rate, dizziness, or weakness. Heart rate monitors may be a good way to keep the child within a specific heart rate zone and may also be fun for the child to wear.

- Regularly check with the child and/or nurse and the classroom or special education teacher about any infections the child may have or had recently, which can increase the child's risk for crisis. If the child has an infection, then the intensity and duration of the activity should be reduced to avoid a crisis.

- Start the child with shorter activities and progress to longer activities over time as his or her endurance builds.

- Take regular water breaks during more intense activity or hot temperatures as dehydration may increase the risk of sickle cell pain crisis. For example, the crisis may cause pain throughout the whole body, requiring immediate stoppage of activity.

- Avoid activities that may involve collisions or impact, such as football, soccer, or basketball.

- Include the child in activities to the maximum extent possible to avoid feelings of isolation from the rest of the class.

- Assign a "buddy" to children with chronic anemia who may miss large portions of school so that they can "keep them in the loop" on what activities have been completed.

- If a child has a history of anemia and wants to play competitive sports, the National Athletic Trainers Association recommends that a preparticipation physical examination take place to measure hemoglobin and ferritin levels.

Table 16.1.   The characteristics and implications for physical education of less prevalent other health impairments

Other health impairment	Characteristics	Implications for physical education
Cystic fibrosis	• Inherited disease of secretory glands that make mucus and sweat • Mucus is thick and sticky and can build up in the lungs and sinuses, making it difficult to breath and increasing risk of infection. • Sweat can be very salty, leading to dehydration, reduced blood pressure, increased heart rate, fatigue, and weakness. • Symptoms can vary over time and range from mild to severe.	• Consider low-intensity activity and frequent breaks due to challenges with breathing and fatigue. • Take regular water breaks to ensure dehydration does not occur. • Check in regularly with the child to see if he or she is having difficulty breathing or is too hot. • Assign a peer buddy if the child has regular infections and misses school so that he or she is informed about what has been happening in class and feels part of the group. • If the child is working with a pulmonary rehabilitation specialist, check with the specialist to understand best practices and contraindications.
Hemophilia	• Inherited (type A or B; 80% are type A) • Usually males • Blood fails to clot easily. • External or internal bleeding in the joints	• Limit contact sports to avoid blunt force. • Contact physician to understand whether child is at risk for joint bleeding (knee, ankle) from running/jumping or repetitive upper body activities (elbow, wrist).
Epilepsy	• Two groups of seizures: primary generalized seizures and partial seizures • Typically a chronic issue caused by activity in the brain but may be controlled by medication or eventually outgrown • May feel strange sensations, display unusual emotions, or behave strangely • Can involve violent muscle spasms or loss of consciousness	• Inform peers of the child's seizure disorder and the steps to take should one occur. • Encourage a buddy system, promote group-based lifespan activities (e.g., baseball, biking with friends), and avoid contact sports. • Child may have cognitive or learning difficulties, so modified instructions may be required. • Fatigue or overexertion may induce a seizure, so strenuous activities should be performed with caution. • The individual may fall unexpectedly, so appropriate safety considerations should be made.
Tourette syndrome	• Tics, which are stereotyped, repetitive, or uncontrollable movements or verbalizations • Manifest as simple (e.g., twitching, grimacing, eye movement) or complex tics (e.g., neck twist and facial grimace, repetitive hopping or bending) • Some tics lead to self-harm (e.g., biting or punching self), shouting inappropriate words (e.g., swearing in public, which is known as coprolalia), or copying what other people say (known as echolalia).	• Overstimulation should be avoided (e.g., excitement, anxiety) as this may induce tics. • Educate peers about what tics the child may have and why they happen. • Understanding when the child takes medication is important as side effects include fatigue. • A small-group environment may be more appropriate to reduce overstimulation and social anxiety.
Nephritis	• Inflammation of the kidney(s) • Acute stages may only cause a temporary dysfunction; chronic inflammation can permanently impair renal tissues. • Severe cases will cause fatigue, anemia, itchy skin, and elevated blood pressure.	• Do not push child to exhaustion to avoid fatigue. • Build up activity slowly. • Avoid strenuous exercise, which could lead to renal distress.
Rheumatic fever	• Untreated strep throat caused by group A streptococcus Symptoms include fever, muscle aches, swollen and painful joints, inflammation of heart, and fatigue. • About half will have damage to the heart (rheumatic heart disease; see Table 16.2). Symptoms include shortness of breath, weight gain, dizziness, edema, and palpitations. • Can cause a temporary nervous system disorder known as chorea, which causes rapid, jerky, involuntary movements of the body	• Activity and sports may be restricted based on symptoms and physician recommendation, especially if carditis occurs. • Be aware of medications and their side effects. • Use a heart rate monitor to monitor intensity. • Avoid strenuous activity. • Provide ample rest intervals.
Human immunodeficiency virus infection/ acquired immune deficiency syndrome (HIV/AIDS)	• Not all people with HIV develop AIDS. • Disease may be spread by infected parent during childbirth, contact of open wounds with an individual with HIV/AIDS, sexual intercourse, or sharing needles • Acute symptoms include open sores, cough, and diarrhea. • Secondary conditions include hemophilia, developmental delays, and environmental deprivation effects.	• Precautions for handling biohazards • Modifications to reduce intensity for fatigue • Start at lower intensity and progress slowly. • Know how medication influences activity.

Cardiovascular Conditions

The majority of cardiovascular conditions are congenital (rather than acquired) in children, with an estimated 32,000 infants born with a defect each year in the United States (American Heart Association, 2013). However, there are many different cardiovascular conditions that affect children (e.g., Kawasaki disease, DiGeorge syndrome, heart murmurs, heart failure), all of which have very different physiological characteristics but similar effects on the child (see Table 16.2 for information on the major types of childhood cardiovascular conditions). For example, arrhythmias are an unusual heart rate that may speed up when inhaling and slow down when exhaling and result in the child feeling weak, lightheaded, or dizzy (American Heart Association, 2012). In contrast, cardiomyopathy is a type of heart disease that results in abnormalities in the muscle fibers involved with each heartbeat, which causes the child to feel fatigued and have reduced exercise capacity (American Heart Association, 2014). Thus, in general, cardiovascular conditions have a similar impact on the physical activity behaviors of children. It is also important to remember that some heart conditions may be secondary to primary conditions (e.g., Down syndrome, muscular dystrophy). For example, it is critical to know that if a child has a certain type of muscular dystrophy (e.g., Friedreich ataxia), then the child may also have related cardiomyopathy. Although many heart conditions are repaired at birth, especially for children with Down syndrome, it is important to know what surgeries have occurred before starting activity in physical education.

Implications for Physical Education

As cardiovascular conditions typically reduce the ability of the heart to supply the body with blood (and thus oxygen), the outcomes include fatigue, weakness, and dizziness, all of which will affect an individual's ability to be active. Although unique modifications are often required for children with cardiovascular conditions to participate successfully in physical education, activity should be promoted and will benefit the child's overall fitness and health. The following are some unique considerations for inclusion into physical education:

- Identify the exact heart condition and the child's physician's recommendations/contraindications for physical activity. In addition, consult with the child's physician (through the child's parents) to determine his or her appropriate heart rate range during physical activity as maximum heart rate may be contraindicated for some conditions.

- Schedule regular check-ins with the child to ask how he or she is feeling and watch for coughing, wheezing, discoloration of the skin, or lightheadedness (Braith, 2002).

- Use a heart rate monitor or check the child's heart rate periodically to assess intensity.

- Find out the child's medication related to the heart condition. Some medications for heart

Table 16.2. Common cardiovascular issues and symptoms

Heart condition	Part of heart affected	Typical symptoms
• Atrial or ventricular septal defect (congenital)	• Atria—hole in the septum between the atria • Ventricles—hole in the septum between the ventricles • Oxygenated blood mixes with deoxygenated blood.	• Size of defect affects symptoms • Poor appetite and growth • Shortness of breath and fatigue • Lung infections • If untreated, can lead to arrhythmia
• Rheumatic heart disease (acquired)	• Rheumatic fever may damage cardiac muscle and valves of heart. • Can be caused by untreated streptococcal infection	• Valve abnormalities may cause shortness of breath during activity or when lying down. • Cardiac abnormalities may lead to chest pain or swelling. • Joint pain and inflammation • Children who have had rheumatic fever are at greater risk of recurrent attack. • Some children may have no clear symptoms.
• Kawasaki disease (acquired)	• Damage to coronary arteries supplying the heart • Inflammation of heart muscle • Valve problems	• Joint pain • Low energy levels • Disease is characterized by rash, swelling of hands and feet, redness of eyes, inflammation of the mouth and throat, and fever. • Abnormal heart rhythm

Sources: Cardiovascular Disease in Children and Youth, 2014; Kawasaki Disease Symptoms, 2014; and Cardiovascular Conditions of Childhood, 2013.

conditions cause heart rate to remain low and stable and therefore will not rise as expected during activity. In such cases, the physical educator should use other forms of measurement such as the Borg Rating of Perceived Exertion scale, which estimates how hard someone thinks he or she is exercising. Ratings on this scale are related to heart rate (Physical Activity Line, n.d.).

- Competition (at times) should be avoided for some children following heart surgeries depending on residual effects. For example, following heart surgery, individuals may have sternal precautions while the incision heals, so stretching of those tissues or contact sports would be contraindicated. The physician may also have restrictions on how much weight a child can lift following heart surgery. Children without residual effects of surgery may be able to resume competitive sports (Durstine, 2009).

- Extend warm-up and cool-down time periods for students with chronic heart problems (Braith, 2002).

- Decrease intensity by modifying games and drills. For example, decreasing the length of the soccer playing area, playing seated versions of sport (e.g., sit volleyball), having the child play goalie or other less aerobic aspects of the game, or rotating the child into the game after ample rest intervals.

Asthma

Asthma is a common childhood condition (Rees, Kanabar, & Pattani, 2010). Although asthma affects people of all ages, it most often starts in childhood with greater incidence in boys than girls (National Heart, Lung, and Blood Institute, n.d.). In the United States, more than 24 million people have asthma; 7 million of these individuals are children (CDC, 2011d; National Heart, Lung, and Blood Institute, n.d.). To better understand how asthma occurs, it might be helpful to review how the airways function. Basically, the airways are tubes that carry air in and out of the lungs (National Heart, Lung, and Blood Institute, n.d.). For people with asthma, these airways become inflamed, making them swollen and sensitive to certain "triggers" that are either inhaled or body induced. When these airways react to a trigger, the muscle will tighten and narrow, limiting the amount of airflow into the lungs. Mucus may also be produced from the cells in the airways, further restricting airflow (Rees et al., 2010). Figures B and C in Figure 16.1 demonstrates typical versus asthma-restricted airways.

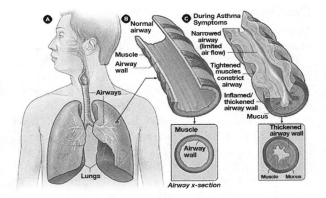

Figure 16.1.   Figure A shows the location of the lungs and airways in the body. Figure B shows a cross-section of a typical airway. Figure C shows a cross-section of an airway while asthma symptoms are present. (*Source:* National Heart, Lung, and Blood Institute; National Institutes of Health; U.S. Department of Health and Human Services.)

When airways become restricted, symptoms will occur and may initially include difficulty breathing and beginning to cough (National Heart, Lung, and Blood Institute, n.d.; Rees et al., 2010). Physical educators should recognize these initial symptoms to respond to the student's medication needs and prevent a more severe situation. Severe asthma attacks may require emergency care and can be fatal, so recognizing initial symptoms is very important. Other signs and symptoms may include wheezing and chest tightness (Rees et al., 2010).

There are multiple triggers to asthma attacks. Asthma is different for each person, but the most common triggers include allergens from dust, animal fur, cockroaches, mold, and pollens from trees, grasses, and flowers; irritants such as cigarette smoke, air pollution, chemicals, dust in the workplace, compounds in home décor products, and sprays (such as hairspray); medicines such as aspirin or other nonsteroidal anti-inflammatory drugs and nonselective β-blockers; sulfites in foods and drinks; and viral upper respiratory infections such as colds (Vernon, Wiklund, Bell, Dale, & Chapman, 2012). Physical activity is also a trigger for asthma (Naguwa, Afrasiabi, & Chang, 2012). It is estimated that 90% of individuals who have asthma have exercise-induced asthma (EIA; Naguwa et al., 2012). Therefore, it is likely that physical educators will have a student with EIA. Because physical activity is the primary trigger for EIA (Rees et al., 2010), Table 16.3 highlights important aspects of this condition.

Knowing the symptoms and having a plan to reduce the onset of asthma attacks is critical, as one study demonstrated that approximately 78% of physical education teachers, in a surveyed sample of 106, had students with asthma in their classes, with 41%

Table 16.3. What to know about exercise-induced asthma (EIA)

- *Asthma inhalers* or *bronchodilators* used 10 minutes prior to exercise can control and prevent symptoms.
- EIA symptoms usually peak at 8–15 minutes after cessation of exercise.
- A delayed asthmatic phase is seen in 30%–89% of individuals between 2 and 8 hours postexercise.
- Symptoms subside within 30–45 minutes.
- Warm-up that includes brief periods of intense activity and a proper cool-down is helpful in asthma prevention.
- Individuals with EIA are more sensitive to changes in the temperature and humidity in the air.
- High-risk sports include basketball, boxing, cycling, running, soccer, swimming, and winter sports (due to cold air).
- Low-risk sports include athletic field events, baseball, bowling, golf, softball, and tennis.
- Almost everyone with EIA can enjoy the mental and physical benefits of regular exercise.

Sources: Milgrom & Taussig (1999); Naguwa et al. (2012); Rees et al. (2010).

stating students had asthma attacks during a lesson (Sandsund, Thomassen, Reinertsen, & Steinshamn, 2011). Moreover, a plan of action might save a student's life, as severe asthma attacks, called status asthmaticus, can lead to respiratory failure without immediate medical attention (Karamessinis et al., 2011).

Implications for Physical Education

Physical educators should know which children in their classrooms have asthma. Moreover, the educator will want to know how asthma affects each individual student. For example, Johnny's fourth-grade physical educator should know his asthma triggers (e.g., moderate to vigorous activity, humid weather, other outdoor allergens such as pollen); that his initial symptoms are cough and wheezing; that he uses a fast-acting inhaler to stop the onset of severe symptoms, which include chest tightness, hyperventilating, and fainting; and that the inhaler will reduce symptoms within minutes.

There is a balance of understanding when a child with asthma is short of breath from activity and is beginning to accumulate symptoms of an asthma attack. Talk with the parents and medical personnel to differentiate activity fatigue and actual airway restriction. It can be a challenge to determine the difference as similar symptoms of wheezing and coughing can occur in children who are unfit or first-time exercisers. Beyond understanding the individuality of asthma for the student, the following are additional recommendations for physical education:

- Because young children might not be aware of their medication use, parents and teachers should document when medication is provided.

One example would be to use a notebook to write down the time of day and dosage of medication. This will allow parents and teachers to have a system of communication in place.

- Be understanding of children with asthma and accommodate activities around their triggers. For instance, avoid outdoor physical activity on humid days or reduce activity intensity for a student who has EIA.
- Gradual increase in physical activity over time may help the student with EIA tolerate more intense physical activity.
- Provide a proper warm-up and cool-down to reduce the incidence of breathing difficulties.
- Dehydration can also be a trigger for an attack. Make sure children with EIA are well hydrated and have ample water breaks to avoid dehydration.

Cancer

Cancer, although perceived as a single disease, has many different symptoms and influences on health and well-being based on the type and treatment. However, cancer typically has the same disease process, which includes cells growing abnormally and out of control in unusual sizes and shapes (Miller, 2010). These cells also ignore boundaries within the body and can destroy healthy neighboring cells, and if not treated quickly, cancer can spread to other tissues and organs. Unfortunately, as the cancer grows, it demands more of the body's energy stores, resulting in decreased strength, and makes children more vulnerable to other illnesses (Miller, 2010).

The types of cancers that occur most often in children are different from adults. Childhood cancers often are a result of changes in cells that occur prenatally or early in life (American Cancer Society, 2014a). Genetic factors may also increase the risk of cancer. For instance, individuals with Down syndrome are at increased risk of leukemia (Seewald, Taub, Maloney, & McCabe, 2012; Zipursky, Poon, & Doyle, 1992). Moreover, childhood cancers, unlike adult cancers, are not usually associated with lifestyle or environmental risk factors (American Cancer Society, 2014a).

Treatments of cancers have implications for how the child participates in everyday activities, including physical activity. The three treatment methods used for cancers include chemotherapy (the use of medical drugs to kill cancer cells), radiation (the use of radiant energy to kill cancer cells), and surgery (to remove cancerous cells or tumor; Miller, 2010). Prolonged hospital stays and the side effects from treatments may affect academic performance and development. Children may also experience pain, anemia, loss of hair, fatigue, nausea, fever/chills, muscle or joint pain, and numbness in the hands and feet, all of which would need additional consideration for physical education programming (American Cancer Society, 2014a).

Children with cancer often respond to cancer treatments better than adults, allowing them to resume previous activity; however, this is not always the case (American Cancer Society, 2014b; Wein & Contie, 2013). Posttreatment progress depends on the type and how much the child was able to maintain activity levels during treatment (American Cancer Society, 2014b). Long-term effects of these treatments may still be present and need to be acknowledged when including students recovering from cancer in physical education.

Implications for Physical Education

Physical activity and sports are important for young children with cancer. In particular, it can help them increase or maintain fitness before, during, and after treatments; help them maintain a healthy weight as treatment may cause the child to gain or lose weight; improve self-confidence; and improve their sense of belonging, especially with inclusion in team sports. Research findings suggest that exercise for children with cancer can lead to increased aerobic fitness, improved muscle strength and flexibility, reduced fatigue, and improved physical function (Huang & Ness, 2011). The following are some practical tips for physical activity for children with cancer. Specific guidelines for including these children should be obtained from the child's physician and parents.

- Be aware of blood and platelet counts. If hemoglobin counts are too low, the child will not be getting sufficient oxygen, and exercise may result in fainting or breathlessness. Low platelet counts, which is most important to consider, may increase the risk of bruising and bleeding. The American Physical Therapy Association contraindicates exercise when hemoglobin blood values are <8 g/dL, platelets are <20,000/mL, or white blood cells are <5,000/mm³. Physical educators should learn the importance of blood counts and talk with parents about this issue.

- If the child has an infection, do not pursue additional activity beyond routine daily activity. In addition, if the child has a fever, do not have him or her participate in activities.

- Observe the child for symptoms of fatigue. Provide a balance of rest and activity and know the child's limitations. A gradual increase in activity is a good way to overcome fatigue and increase energy.

- If the child is feeling unwell, or has new or unexplained pain, seek advice before allowing him or her to resume sports or exercise.

- For children with shunts in place to monitor intracranial pressure, avoid brain injury and prolonged periods of time lying on the back.

- Many children will have a central line fitted at some point during their treatment (i.e., a tube used to deliver chemotherapy). You should ask for specific advice about this, particularly in relation to swimming and other water sports.

- If the child has a prosthesis in place after surgery for bone cancer, it is very important that you seek advice from the child's physical therapist about which types of exercise would be considered appropriate.

- For children who are having difficulty returning to activity, try to maintain interest in sports and activities by including them through refereeing, coaching, or other sports management activities.

Diabetes Mellitus

Diabetes mellitus is a condition that affects how the body processes, stores, and uses glucose. Healthy glucose levels need to be maintained for the body to function properly (CDC, 2011b). To further understand this condition, it is important to understand the role of the pancreas. The pancreas secretes the insulin that is needed to break down glucose in the body and allow for storage in the liver (Durstine, 2009). Without the production of insulin (*hyperglycemia*), glucose is not broken down into glycogen and stored, which can result in damage to other organs (e.g., kidneys, eyes, heart, blood vessels). On the other hand, when there is too much insulin because of insufficient care of injections, food intake, or exercise, *hypoglycemia*, or low blood sugar, can occur. In severe cases, hypoglycemia can result in sudden coma (Durstine, 2009).

There are two types of diabetes. Type 1 is the most common type of diabetes and affects 90%–95% of children with diabetes. Type 1 is an autoimmune disease in which the body attacks healthy tissues and/or organs (i.e., insulin-producing cells in the pancreas; CDC, 2011b). Although historically not particularly common in children (CDC, 2011b), Type 2 diabetes is on the rise in the United States, mostly due to increased trends in obesity (Ginter & Simko, 2012).

It is important to know the warning signs for high or low blood sugar, as both can lead to serious medical conditions. Although hypoglycemia seems

Table 16.4. Characteristics of hypoglycemia and suggested treatments

Warning signs of hypoglycemia (insulin shock)	Treatment
• Shakiness • Nervousness or anxiety • Sweating, chills, and clamminess • Irritability or impatience • Confusion, including delirium • Rapid/fast heartbeat • Lightheadedness or dizziness • Hunger and nausea • Sleepiness • Blurred/impaired vision • Tingling or numbness in the lips or tongue • Headaches • Weakness or fatigue • Anger, stubbornness, or sadness • Lack of coordination • Seizures • Unconsciousness	1. Give child glucose tablets or simple carbohydrates. 2. Recheck blood glucose after 15 minutes. 3. If hypoglycemia continues, repeat. 4. Once blood glucose returns to normal, provide a small snack if their next planned meal or snack is more than an hour or two away. 5. Keep in mind that insulin shock can occur quickly. If the person loses consciousness, seek medical attention immediately.

Table 16.5. Characteristics of hyperglycemia and suggested treatment

Warning signs of hyperglycemia (diabetic coma)	Treatment
• Slower accumulation of symptoms over days • High blood glucose • High levels of sugar in the urine • Frequent urination • Increased thirst • Other signs of distress, such as irregular breathing and abdominal pain	• Seek immediate medical attention. Individuals with hyperglycemia may go into a diabetic coma.

Note. Symptoms for these characteristics may present themselves similarly. Talk with the child and parents to know specifically how these symptoms present themselves.

to be easily treated, prompt action needs to occur to prevent severe medical outcomes. Children with diabetes may not be as diligent in monitoring their blood sugar and may ignore early warning signs to continue participation. Therefore, as physical educators, you should be aware of the warning signs so prompt action can be taken. It is important to note that even a change in behavior could be a warning that the child has low blood sugar. Tables 16.4 and 16.5 outline the warning signs and treatment for hypo- and hyperglycemia.

Implications for Physical Education

As for all children, physical activity has numerous benefits for children with diabetes. Participating in physical activity and sports can help improve social skills, improve self-confidence, increase general fitness, and lower blood pressure and lipids. Activity also positively affects diabetes by improving insulin sensitivity, reducing glucose levels, and reducing long-term morbidity. For children with Type 2 diabetes, exercise helps to decrease fat and increase muscle mass, contributing to improved insulin sensitivity (Kollipara & Warren-Boulton, 2004).

The immediate effect of physical activity on glucose is important to understand in order to help manage students' diabetes before, during, and after activity. Usually, activity will lower glucose levels, making the body more sensitive to insulin (Kollipara & Warren-Boulton, 2004). At times

of more strenuous activity, glucose levels will increase due to the release of hormones during more intense activity. The change in glucose levels for activity is usually temporary, with the potential risk of delayed hypoglycemia occurring 12–16 hours following activity (Kollipara & Warren-Boulton, 2004).

The following factors should be considered when including a child with diabetes in physical education: food intake, insulin levels, and the amount of activity. According to the American Diabetes Association (2013), the response of blood glucose to physical activity will depend on the following:

- Blood glucose level before starting activity
- Food intake prior to activity
- Intensity of the activity
- Length of time of activity
- Changes to insulin doses
- Timing of insulin injection (avoid activity immediately after injection to avoid hypoglycemia)

A balance among food intake, insulin, and physical activity is needed to prevent hypo- and hyperglycemia during activity. In addition, each student with diabetes should have an action plan in place through his or her IEP if glucose levels drop or rise to unsafe levels. Make sure you are aware of these plans and act quickly when you see the warning signs. The following are tips and strategies for safely including a child with Type 1 diabetes in physical education (Dowshen, 2012; U.S. Department of Health and Human Services, 2010b):

- Monitor blood glucose. Allow the student to check blood glucose levels as outlined in the 504 Plan, IEP, or other education plan. It might be advantageous to check glucose levels prior to participating in physical education to determine the extent of the student's participation.

- Be prepared to recognize and respond to the signs and symptoms of hypoglycemia and hyperglycemia and take initial actions in accordance with the student's action plan for treatment.

- If the child does not feel well with high glucose levels and ketones, do NOT allow him or her to continue activity. Exercising when ketones are present may make blood glucose levels go even higher. Ketones are measured through blood or urine tests.

- Encourage the student to have personal monitoring supplies, glucose tablets, food, and so forth readily accessible in case glucose levels change suddenly during activity. If possible, physical educators should have fruit juice or candy bars readily accessible in case the student does not have them or is unable to communicate where they are located.

- Circulation may be affected. Some children with diabetes may have decreased sensation in the feet, so they can be unaware that abrasions are present. Thus, make sure there is special care with foot and skin health by avoiding barefoot activities. Socks, water slippers, and other types of footwear should be available to avoid risks of cuts, blisters, and other foot injuries.

SPECIAL SPORTS ORGANIZATIONS FOR INDIVIDUALS WITH OTHER HEALTH IMPAIRMENTS

Due to the diverse health issues and range of characteristics of children with OHI, there are no specific sports organizations for those with medical/health conditions. Children with medical conditions should, to the extent possible, be able to participate in sports with their peers without disabilities. In addition, sports organizations designed for people with disabilities (e.g., Special Olympics for athletes with intellectual and developmental disabilities, U.S. Association for Blind Athletes) would not be appropriate for children whose primary disabilities are medical.

Although including children with OHI in sports is recommended, understanding the specific needs and contraindication of activity individualized to the child is critical. Children within the OHI category will likely not fit a typical model for inclusive physical education and sports. Additional consideration of the child's medical needs

should be evaluated prior to including them into sports. For instance, it would not be appropriate to include a child with nephritis (i.e., inflammation of the kidneys) into a strenuous, full-court game of basketball due to the risk of renal distress. However, modifying the game by rotating athletes into the game every 2–3 minutes would allow the child with nephritis to participate with his or her peers while also having ample rest periods needed to reduce fatigue and strenuous activity.

RESOURCES

Anemia Resources

National Heart, Lung, and Blood Institute
NHLBI Health Information Center
PO Box 30105, Bethesda, MD 20824
Phone: 301-592-8573
http://www.nhlbi.nih.gov/health/health-topics/topics/anemia

Sickle Cell Disease Association of America, Inc.
3700 Koppers Street, Suite 570, Baltimore, MD 21227
Phone: 410-528-1555
http://www.sicklecelldisease.org

Sickle Cell for Kids Organization
http://www.sicklecellkids.org

American Sickle Cell Anemia Association
10900 Carnegie Avenue, Suite DD1-201, Cleveland, OH 44106
Phone: 216-229-8600
http://www.ascaa.org
http://www.ascaa.org/espanol.php

Sickle Cell Information Center
Grady Memorial Hospital, 80 Jesse Hill Jr. Drive SE, Atlanta, GA 30303
Phone: 404-616-3572
http://scinfo.org

Asthma Resources

National Heart, Lung, and Blood Institute
NHLBI Health Information Center, PO Box 30105, Bethesda, MD 20824
Phone: 301-592-8573
http://www.nhlbi.nih.gov/health/health-topics/topics/asthma

American Asthma Foundation
AAF Research Program, Box 0509, UCSF,
  San Francisco, CA 94143
Phone: 415-514-0730
http://www.americanasthmafoundation.org

Cancer Resources

American Cancer Society
250 Williams Street NW, Atlanta, GA 30303
Phone: 800-227-2345
http://www.cancer.org
http://www.cancer.org/cancer/cancerinchildren
  /index?sitearea
http://www.cancer.org/treatment/treatmentsand
  sideeffects/physicalsideeffects/chemotherapy
  effects/index

Nemours Foundation
1600 Rockland Road, Wilmington, DE 19803
Phone: 302-651-4046
http://kidshealth.org/parent/medical/cancer
  /cancer.html#a_About_Cancer

Cardiovascular Conditions Resources

American Heart Association
7272 Greenville Avenue, Dallas, TX 75231
Phone: 800-242-8721
http://www.heart.org/HEARTORG

The Society for Cardiovascular Angiography and
  Interventions
1100 17th Street NW, Suite 330, Washington, D.C.
  20036
Phone: 202-741-9854 or 800-992-7224
http://www.scai.org

Children's Heart Foundation
620 Margate Drive, Lincolnshire, IL 60069
Phone: 847-634-6474 or 888-248-8140
http://www.childrensheartfoundation.org

Diabetes Resources

Mayo Clinic
13400 E Shea Boulevard, Scottsdale, AZ 85259
Phone: 480-301-8000
http://www.mayoclinic.org/diseases-conditions
  /type-1-diabetes-in-children/basics/ definition
  /con-20029197

American Diabetes Association
1701 North Beauregard Street, Alexandria, VA
  22311
Phone: 1-800-DIABETES
http://www.diabetes.org
http://www.diabetes.org/living-with-diabetes
  /treatment-and-care/blood-glucose-control
  /hypoglycemia-low-blood.html#sthash
  .iE9EdJCG.dpuf

American National Red Cross
2025 E Street, NW, Washington, D.C. 20006
Phone: 1-800-RED CROSS
http://american.redcross.org/site/PageNavigator
  /SafetyNET/Feb_08/diabetes

EndocrineWeb
Vertical Health, LLC, 7 North Willow Street,
  Suite 7A, Montclair, NJ 07042
Phone: 973-783-0330
http://www.endocrineweb.com/guides/type
  -1-children/physical-activity-children-type
  -1-diabetes

National Center for Health Physical Activity and
  Disability
4000 Ridgeway Drive, Birmingham, AL 35209
Phone: 800-900-8086
http://www.nchpad.org/88/661/Diabetes

Other Resources

TheBody.com: The Complete HIV/AIDS
  Resource
730 3rd Avenue, 6th Floor, New York, NY 10017
Phone: 212-541-8500
http://www.thebody.com/index.html?ic=3001

National Center on Health, Physical Activity, and
  Disability
4000 Ridgeway Drive, Birmingham, AL 35209
Phone: 800-900-8086
http://www.nchpad.org/159/1197/Human
  ~Immunodeficiency~Virus~Acquired
  ~Immunodeficiency~Syndrome~~HIV~AIDS~

Shijiazhuang Kidney Disease Hospital
No. 5 Feiyi Road, Shijazhuang City, Hebei
  Province, China 050000
Phone +86-311-89261083
http://www.kidney-support.org/lupus-nephritis
  -basics/2081.html
http://www.kidneyabc.com/nephritis

Supporting Across Contexts

CHAPTER 17

Facilitating Social Acceptance and Inclusion

Martin E. Block, Aija Klavina, and Cathy McKay

Objectives

1. Discuss the importance of social inclusion

2. Describe the benefits of inclusion for children with and without disabilities as well as for physical educators

3. Describe some of the challenges to social inclusion

4. Describe several things the general physical educator can do to facilitate social aspects of inclusion

5. Describe several activities that can be implemented to prepare students without disabilities to be more accepting of peers with disabilities

6. Describe the Paralympic School Day and Get into It models of disability awareness

7. Describe how to prepare a paraprofessional to facilitate social aspects of inclusion

---

Ali is a fourth grader at Lewis Elementary School. Although Ali loves physical education, he appears to be different from his peers because he has Asperger syndrome, a disorder on the autism spectrum. He has brilliant skills in math and computers, and he is also obsessed with structure. Ali needs to stand next to particular peers, line up equipment in a certain way, and have teammates positioned properly around the ball before the game starts. He quickly becomes tremendously upset when things

are changed. He listens to his physical education teacher carefully and follows directions without hesitation. However, if the teacher suddenly changes activities during the class, Ali explodes, throwing a nearby object or screaming. When overwhelmed by noise and confusion, he often bites himself or picks at his nails. In addition, Ali does not understand the social rules and often says or does inappropriate things. For example, when approached by an overweight classmate, Ali said, "I do not want to play on your team because you are too fat." His peers view Ali as odd. They initially tried to talk to and include him in physical education activities, but after several attempts, his odd behaviors and social inappropriateness discouraged them. Worse, some of them have responded to him with rude comments. Ali's understanding of how to behave in society is muddled. This does not mean that Ali does not want to act more appropriately, to make friends, or be liked by his peers and teachers. Ali simply has trouble reading others' emotions, determining the social appropriateness of a situation, and dealing with change. Ali's behaviors make it hard for the teacher to meet his and other students' needs; she does not like seeing any of her students being left out and ostracized in her gymnasium. What can this physical education teacher do to get the class to understand Ali's challenges and stop the teasing? What can she do to encourage a few classmates to reach out and be friendly with Ali?

Martina is a 15-year-old girl with mixed spastic-athetoid cerebral palsy, and Diana is a 14-year-old girl with diplegic cerebral palsy. Martina and Diana have been good friends since preschool, and they are included in eighth-grade general physical education class at Greentown Middle School. Martina uses an electric wheelchair for mobility. Martina's movements are usually uncontrolled and tend to worsen with excitement or when under pressure. For example, it requires a great deal of effort for her to throw a ball to a peer or to shoot a ball at a lowered basket. Martina communicates by gaze, a few words, and facial expressions (usually grimaces when trying a skill). This results in others, particularly girls, underestimating her cognitive skills (she does not have any cognitive impairment) or making cruel comments. Because of her severe speech and motor limitations, Martina is assigned a teacher assistant who is helping her in many physical activities. Yet Martina has always struggled to find friends and be an equal and contributing player on a team. In contrast, Diana has no problems communicating or controlling her movements. She uses crutches and sometimes a manual wheelchair for games such as basketball. Peer rejection is not as evident in Diana's case, but her sensitivity for Martina's troubles prevents her from participating in activities with other classmates. In addition, Diana's classmates often give her less valued roles in games, such as being a goalie or retrieving balls. Thus, Martina and Diana do not have a wide circle of friends in school and tend to stay together most of the time. How can the general physical education teacher and teacher assistant promote more natural interactions between the students with and without a disability?

One of the greatest benefits of inclusion is the opportunity for social acceptance and interactions between students with and without disabilities. Inclusion can promote such social factors as learning how to interact with peers, playing cooperatively, taking turns, dealing with anger, following directions, listening quietly, staying on task, and generally behaving appropriately. For some children (e.g., those with behavior problems), social development is as important as motor and cognitive development and should be included in the child's individualized education program (IEP). In addition, peers without disabilities can learn that classmates who seem different on the outside might share similar interests, pleasures, problems, and concerns. Peers without disabilities can learn to be sensitive to, respectful of, and comfortable with differences and similarities with peers with disabilities. Finally, through appropriate interactions and contact, the opportunity for true acceptance, appreciation, and friendships between peers with and without disabilities becomes possible (Falvey & Rosenberg, 1995; Janney & Snell,

2016; Klavina & Block, 2008; Pearpoint, Forest, & O'Brien, 1996; Seymour, Reid, & Bloom, 2009).

Students with disabilities should never be placed in general physical education solely for social development (National Association for Sport and Physical Education, 1995a), and simply placing a child with a disability into general physical education does not ensure appropriate and meaningful social interactions and acceptance. Ali, Martina, and Diana all experience difficulties in their relationship with peers. They rarely interact with their peers, and when they do, their social behavior does not elicit ongoing social interaction. Although not all children with disabilities have difficulties interacting with their peers, many children without disabilities require specific training in order to interact with their peers with disabilities in a positive and age-appropriate manner. Unfortunately, physical educators often unwittingly create barriers to social interactions and acceptance rather than facilitate social growth and acceptance. What would happen if a physical educator did not tell peers that a child with behavior problems might get angry when his equipment is touched? How would peers feel if a physical educator did not explain why a child with intellectual disabilities and a heart problem does not have to run the mile like everyone else in class? In fact, placing children with disabilities into general physical education without preparing children without disabilities can lead to feelings of confusion and resentment.

The purpose of this chapter is to discuss ways in which general physical educators can remove barriers to social acceptance and foster interactions between students with and without disabilities. This chapter focuses on the two major players who can facilitate the social acceptance and inclusion of students with disabilities: 1) the general physical educator and 2) classmates. Examples of three common problems in general physical education classes that hinder social inclusion and some possible solutions are given.

TEACHER BEHAVIORS THAT FACILITATE SOCIAL INCLUSION

The general physical educator is perhaps the most important determinant in successful inclusion. General physical educators can either welcome students with disabilities or show disinterest. General physical educators can view a student with disabilities either as truly one of their students or as a visitor and someone else's burden. The attitude and commitment of the general physical educator will affect how classmates without disabilities accept

Table 17.1. Ways for teachers to facilitate social inclusion

- Have a positive attitude.
- Be the teacher for all students in your general education classes.
- Model appropriate behavior.
- Include the child in as many activities as possible.
- Individualize the curriculum and instruction.
- Reinforce positive interactions.
- Be knowledgeable about the child.

students with disabilities. Although general physical educators might not always feel prepared to work with students who have disabilities, they should always help all students feel welcome and a part of the group. The following are some suggestions on how to facilitate the social acceptance and inclusion of students with disabilities (see Table 17.1).

Have a Positive Attitude

It is very reasonable for general physical educators to feel nervous and even incompetent when working with children who have disabilities. Such feelings are quite common among general physical educators (Fejgin et al., 2005; Hersman & Hodge, 2010; Jerlinder, Danermark, & Gil, 2010; Lienert, Sherrill, & Myers, 2001; Sato & Hodge, 2009; Vickerman & Coates, 2009). However, general educators have noted that these fears tend to be based on misconceptions, misunderstandings, and general inaccurate preconceptions about their ability to teach students with disabilities. For example, Janney, Snell, Beers, and Raynes (1995) interviewed both general and special education teachers who had gone from segregated to inclusive classes. A high school general physical education teacher who was interviewed in the study suggested the following to other general physical educators dealing with inclusion for the first time:

> Well, I just, I would go in with an open mind, don't be closed-minded. . . . I think what's on every teacher's mind is the fact that, oh no, this is double the workload and double the problems that you might have. And I think the best thing they can do is wait, and talk it over and see the situation, and at least try. There are always modifications you can make if something is not working out. (Janney et al., 1995, p. 435)

Although feelings of apprehension and incompetence are common, general physical educators should commit themselves to giving inclusion their best shot by learning about the children with disabilities and experimenting with different ways to best include them into their general physical education program. There are plenty of resources in or around most school districts (e.g., special education

teachers, therapists, adapted physical education specialists, other general physical educators) who can help general physical educators with the mechanics of how to safely and successfully include children with disabilities. The first step is simply to be willing to try. General physical educators will be surprised how quickly they will become an expert on how to work with, motivate, and help particular students with disabilities in their general physical education program. In fact, many physical educators may find working with students who have disabilities to be more rewarding than working with students without disabilities. As another physical educator noted in Janney et al., "These kids seem to appreciate you a lot more. . .and that's a little pat on the back for the teacher" (1995, p. 435).

Take Responsibility for Teaching All Students in Your Class

It is common for general physical educators to feel that a child with a disability in their general physical education classes is not really one of their students. For example, some general physical educators have been heard to say, "I have 50 students in my third period physical education class plus Cassandra [the student with disabilities]. But Mrs. Jones [Cassandra's teacher assistant] works with Cassandra." General physical educators with this type of attitude often feel they are "hosting" a special visitor to their general physical education class and are thus not responsible for the child's education. When the general physical educator perceives his or her role as a host, it becomes the responsibility of someone else (e.g., paraprofessional, adapted physical education specialist) to work with and teach this student (Giangreco & Doyle, 2007). The general physical educator ends up having minimal contact with the student with disabilities.

Unfortunately, when the general physical educator chooses not to take responsibility for teaching the student with disabilities, major curricular and instructional decisions are left up to someone who is usually underqualified (e.g., paraprofessional, special education teacher).

It is important that general physical educators truly perceive themselves as the primary educator for all students who enter their gymnasiums, including students with disabilities. Although support personnel might accompany a child with disabilities to general physical education, the general physical educator should make key decisions about what the child with disabilities is doing, how he or she is doing it, and with whom he or she is doing it. This also means personally spending time with each student in the class, including the student with disabilities. "If you are successful teaching students without disabilities, then you have the skills to be successful teaching students with disabilities" (Giangreco & Doyle, 2007, p. 11).

Create an Atmosphere that Supports Contact Theory

Inclusive physical education programs should offer educational environments in which positive, equal-status contact experiences are created, sanctioned, and supported by the teacher. One way to offer such an environment is to create an atmosphere that supports Allport's (1954) contact theory. Allport first proposed the theory that social contact will improve relationships between members of majority and minority groups. This theory has been used to explain a great deal about human relations, particularly in terms of prejudice and difference. The general idea of contact theory states that contact with people different from oneself will lead to attitude change if contact is presented under the right conditions.

Creating a classroom setting that facilitates relationship building and equitable social interactions requires careful planning and preparation. Inclusive physical education programs can support behaviors of acceptance and place importance on the value of diversity by planning with the four necessary conditions for contact in Allport's contact theory in mind: 1) equal status, 2) cooperative pursuance of common goals, 3) personal interactions, and 4) identification and acceptance of social norms provided by authority.

The main condition of favorable contact proposed by Allport is based on equality. When groups have contact as equals in status, they are less likely to be antagonistic toward one another. If members of one group have an inferior role or status, it is likely that existing stereotypes will be reinforced. Creating a classroom atmosphere that supports equal status relationships among all students, in which all students are achieving success, is key.

In addition to creating an equal status environment, it is also important that the activities required with the contact are cooperative rather than competitive (Allport, 1954). For example, students working alongside peers to achieve group goals at a variety of activity stations support cooperative contact. Competitive contact should be avoided, as considerable research shows that a task-oriented climate that promotes learning compared with an egocentric-oriented climate that promotes competition leads to greater satisfaction for all students and prevents stereotyping and placing limited

value on those with fewer skills (including those with disabilities; e.g., Cunningham & Ping, 2008; Obrusnikova & Dillon, 2012; Schofield, 1995; Wang, Liu, Chatzisarantis, & Lim, 2010).

Allport (1954) suggested that the level of personal connection is significant to attitude change. A classroom atmosphere that supports exceptional personal contact is set up purposefully and designed with equity in mind. This atmosphere moves past typical and trivial contact. Exceptional and meaningful contact allows for individuals to really get to know one another, including shared interests and commonalities.

Finally, Allport suggested that changing attitudes through contact among group members relies on support of authority (including laws and customs), as support of authority establishes a norm of acceptance. Physical education teachers send a clear message to all students when they set up a classroom atmosphere that supports contact and sets high expectations of equitable social behaviors. Contact is more likely to be accepted and will have greater positive effects when it is socially supported.

Model Appropriate Behavior

Many children learn how to act around children with disabilities by modeling the behavior of respected adults. One of the simplest things you can do is welcome children with disabilities and model friendly behavior through your actions and words (David & Kuyini, 2012; Giangreco & Doyle, 2007). Greet and talk to the child with disabilities even if the child does not fully understand what you are saying. Pat the child with disabilities on the back, give high-fives, choose the child first, and recognize the child during activities (e.g., "Good throw, Billy!").

Include the Student in as Many Activities as Possible

Students with disabilities often spend a large portion of their time in general physical education away from their peers doing different activities. Time spent away from peers in general physical education inhibits learning and can lead to social isolation (Giangreco & Doyle, 2007). For inclusion to be successful, it is critical that the student with disabilities be included in as many general physical education activities as possible (although his or her goals might be different from peers). Although modifications may be necessary to safely and fairly include the child, the child should be part of the larger group as much as possible. For example, a child with intellectual disabilities who cannot keep up with the fast warm-up routine of a fifth-grade class can be encouraged to focus on three or four key warm-up movements rather than all the movements. Remember, "Where students spend their time, what they do, when, and with whom play major roles in defining affiliations and status within the classroom [and gymnasium]" (Giangreco & Doyle, 2007, p. 13).

Individualize the Curriculum and Instruction

Related to attitudes is a commitment by general educators to change the curricula and how information is presented to account for individual differences (Canadian Association of Health, Physical Education, and Recreation, 1994; Sherrill, 2004). Interestingly, many general education texts include passages about individualization in general physical education classes (e.g., Graham, Holt-Hale, & Parker, 2013; Mosston & Ashworth, 2008; Pangrazi & Beighle, 2015). Yet dealing with diversity and individualizing require a fundamental shift in philosophy and teaching style for many general physical educators. The inclusion of students with disabilities and the realization that all students have individual needs can make general physical educators better teachers. As noted by Ginny Popiolek, an adapted physical educator in Maryland who specializes in helping general physical educators with inclusion,

> The best thing that has happened with inclusion is that we have all become better physical education teachers. With inclusion, our regular physical education staff was forced to use a larger array of teaching strategies and materials to accommodate students with disabilities. These teachers quickly found that individualizing instruction and creating a variety of accommodations helped all the students in the physical education classes. These teachers have become aware of the fact that all students learn differently and that adaptations create a positive atmosphere and facilitate development in all their students. (personal communication, 1994)

It is also important to realize that some students with disabilities will learn differently from their peers without disabilities. Again, this realization can be difficult for general physical educators who are used to homogeneous groups. For example, students with severe attention-deficit/hyperactivity disorder or autism may be so distracted that they get only half the number of turns as peers when practicing throwing and catching in elementary school or sports skills such as basketball

shooting or hitting tennis balls in middle school. Yet given the child's limited focus and attention to the task, this child may be benefiting from physical education to the best of his or her abilities. Similarly, a child with autism might benefit from physical education if he or she interacts with peers, demonstrates appropriate behavior, and follows directions given in a large-group setting. Expectations should be high but individualized to meet the unique learning needs as well as the physical and motor needs of the student with disabilities.

Reinforce Positive Interactions

Encourage peers to befriend children with disabilities by being their partners, including them on their teams, and generally interacting with them during activities. When necessary, encourage peers to help the child with disabilities during physical education but have them avoid "mothering." This is particularly true for children with intellectual disabilities or autism who might not understand exactly what is going on. Do not tolerate teasing or negative interactions.

Be Knowledgeable About the Student

Although it is impossible to know everything about the child with disabilities, it is important to know medical and health information, how to communicate with the child, how to deal with behavior problems, and what activities the child really enjoys. This information can be obtained from the child's parents, special education teacher, therapists, and in some cases the child himself or herself (see Chapter 18). The key is to know as much as possible about the child so you can accommodate his or her unique needs and help peers understand why you are making certain modifications.

PREPARE CLASSMATES WITHOUT DISABILITIES FOR SOCIAL ACCEPTANCE AND INCLUSION

Peer acceptance can be the critical difference between successful and unsuccessful inclusion. Peer acceptance may lay the groundwork for successful inclusion of a peer with a disability and has the potential for playing a significant role throughout one's development (Odom, McConnell, & McEvoy, 1992). Without peer acceptance, the child with a disability is at a definite disadvantage, and rejection by peers can result in limited social learning opportunities. Peer rejection creates real barriers and inhibits the ability of the student with a disability to achieve independence, academic success, and his or her life goals. This can have powerful, far-reaching, long-term implications on the development of the individual with a disability.

Research suggests that many children without disabilities have positive attitudes toward including classmates with disabilities in physical education and sports activities (Block, 1995c; Block & Malloy, 1998; Block & Zeman, 1996; Brook & Galili, 2000; Gillespie, 2002; McKay, 2013b; Modell, 2007; Murata, Hodge, & Little, 2000; Obrusnikova, Block, & Dillon, 2010; Obrusnikova, Block, & Válková, 2003; Townsend & Hassall, 2007; Verderber, Rizzo, & Sherrill, 2003; Vignes et al., 2009). For example, Block and Malloy found that girls without disabilities ages 11–13 overwhelmingly accepted a child with a disability into their competitive, fast-pitch softball league. Furthermore, they were willing to allow modifications to make sure this peer was successful. However, the initial response of many peers without disabilities may be negative just because they have no experience with peers who have disabilities. Some will be scared of students with disabilities, particularly students with physical disabilities. Others will immediately reject students with disabilities because they feel that these students will slow down and disrupt their physical education program. Still others may be sympathetic toward students with disabilities and try to mother these students. Although none of these responses will facilitate successful inclusion, they are understandable given that most students without disabilities know very little about students with disabilities. Thus, an important part of the process of including students with disabilities is to prepare classmates.

Several authors have suggested ways in which teachers can help classmates without disabilities develop a more positive attitude toward students with disabilities (e.g., Auxter, Pyfer, Zittel, & Roth, 2010; Getskow & Konczal, 1996; Lieberman & Houston-Wilson, 2009), and research has supported the effects of such programs on promoting positive attitudes of children without disabilities toward peers with disabilities (e.g., Grenier, Collins, Wright, & Kearns, 2014; Kalyvas & Reid, 2003; Lindsay & Edwards, 2013; McKay, 2013b; Papaioannou, Evaggelinou, Barkoukis, & Block, 2013). The key is to help classmates become more knowledgeable about disability in general to avoid myths and stereotypes, learn how to view peers with disabilities in a positive manner, and learn how to interact with peers with disabilities during general physical education (see Table 17.2).

Table 17.2.   Preparing classmates without disabilities for social acceptance and inclusion

- Teach about circle of friends.
- Host guest speakers with disabilities who participate in sports or athletic activities.
- Conduct disability role-plays.
- Discuss the concept of rules and handicapping in sports.
- Lead a discussion on disabilities.
- Talk about famous people who have disabilities.
- Discuss the specific child who will be included.
- Provide ongoing information, encouragement, and support for everyone.

Published Disability Awareness Programs

Published disability awareness interventions tend to focus only on disability awareness without any reference to physical education or sports (e.g., Easter Seals, n.d.). Published disability awareness programs focusing on disability sports are less common. A basic Internet search indicates that published disability sports awareness programs have been created for specific countries (Australia: Sport Ability, Britain: Ability versus Ability, Belgium: School Project, Canada: Petro-Canada). One disability sports awareness program, Paralympic School Day (PSD), created by the International Paralympic Committee (IPC; n.d.-b), is designed for use internationally (including in the United States).

Paralympic School Day

PSD is a disability awareness program created to raise awareness and provide a platform for attitude change. According to the IPC (n.d.-b), the program was designed by specialists in Paralympic sport, pedagogy, and disability to create an educational opportunity for schools to increase awareness about and understanding of disability and disability sport. Similar to the components of Allport's (1954) contact theory, PSD is founded on the overall belief that youth without disability will increase their awareness and understanding when they are informed about the lives and actions of people with a disability, experiencing a realistic and holistic portrayal of disability sports and athletes who participate in disability sports (IPC, 2006).

The IPC's education goals are designed to integrate Paralympic ideals and values through educational activities that create awareness and understanding toward people with a disability (IPC, n.d.-b). According to the IPC, the aims of

Paralympic education are achieved through the following objectives:

- To increase knowledge and awareness of Paralympic sport
- To create a better understanding of practical application of inclusion in physical education/activity
- To inform about the different concepts in sport for people with an impairment
- To increase the usage of sport for people with an impairment for reverse integration
- To facilitate the change of perception and attitude towards persons with an impairment
- To promote scholarly research activities and studies about Paralympic education (IPC, n.d.-a)

The PSD curriculum is designed to reach these aims through a fun and lively set of activities that are appropriate for children ages 6–15 and through education about the Paralympics, about individual differences, and about acceptance (IPC, n.d.-b).

PSD materials were created with teacher flexibility in mind, providing a wealth of information to assist in the preparation and execution of a successful PSD while also allowing for creativity and individual adaptations based on the needs of the students (IPC, 2006). The PSD manual is divided into two sections. Section 1 covers the overall concept of PSD and information on planning a PSD, implementing a PSD, and following up after a PSD. Section 2 includes the history of the IPC and the Paralympic movement, information about the Paralympic Games, and general information about people with disabilities.

The PSD activity cards are divided into four categories. Each category represents one of the values of PSD: 1) respect for sporting achievement, 2) respect and acceptance of individual differences, 3) sports as a human right, and 4) empowerment and social support in sports (IPC, 2006). Activity cards are color coded by category, and within each category are three to seven activities from which teachers can choose when planning a PSD. Cards also include modification recommendations for a younger and older audience. At this time, the materials can be downloaded without IPC supervision, and the video resources can be found on the IPC YouTube Channel.

The PSD curriculum supports the components of Allport's (1954) contact theory. The PSD awareness intervention specifically calls for pleasant and meaningful interaction with a Paralympic athlete based on equal-status contact (IPC, 2006). The curriculum recommends that the athlete and the participants have equal and interactive discussions and provide and receive assistance from one another (IPC, 2006). In addition, PSD activities are purposely created to be cooperative in nature, as students work alongside Paralympic athletes to achieve group goals at the various activity stations. All PSD activity cards are cooperative in nature, creating opportunities for empowerment, awareness, knowledge acquisition, and teamwork experiences (IPC, 2006). Personal interactions are supported through PSD, as it is designed to include a variety of opportunities for personal interactions: 1) to hear an athlete's story about life experiences, 2) to learn from the athlete about sports as a human right, and 3) to ask questions and gain exposure to the successes and failures of the athlete (IPC, 2006). In addition, if the athlete is able to lead small-group simulation activities, increased personal interactions will occur. Finally, school leaders committed to planning and executing the PSD awareness intervention are indicating a level of support for meaningful and purposeful contact with Paralympic athletes. If the school already has a commitment to diversity through programming, values, and expected behaviors, the norm of acceptance is likely already strong. In addition, active participation during PSD by school leaders and teachers helps to establish the expectation of inclusivity and contact and shows direct support from authority (McKay, 2013a).

Special Olympics: "Get into It"

Get into It is an interactive, age-appropriate service-learning curriculum designed to advance students' civic knowledge and skill development and promote acceptance and understanding of people's differences to motivate them to become advocates for and together with all people. It is not a curriculum for special education classrooms. Rather, it is a set of resources that educators across all subject areas can use to address their core curriculum requirements, infuse character education into their classrooms, and help implement meaningful service-learning projects that can have a lasting impact among students (Special Olympics, n.d.-a). Specific goals of the program include the following:

- Educate, motivate, and activate young people to better understand the issue of diversity as it relates to people with intellectual disabilities.
- Demonstrate the similarities and differences among people with and without intellectual disabilities.
- Promote better understanding and acceptance of individuals with intellectual disabilities.
- Foster participation in Special Olympics.

- Motivate sustainable change among students and activate them as champions of an important social movement. (Source: Special Olympics [2011].)

The revised, web-based program includes fun, interactive activities; inspiring athlete stories; tools for antibullying/teasing campaigns; and experiential role-play activities all with a service-learning focus. Activities are aligned with educational curricular standards, including language arts, social studies, health, civics, government, technology, history, and cross-curricular extensions. Types of activities include students self-reflecting on their attitudes and behaviors toward those with intellectual disabilities, evaluating levels of tolerance and inclusion within their school and community, developing and delivering messages of support to athletes, creating a product that models inclusion and acceptance, and involvement as a coach, playing partner, or fan in the Special Olympics movement.

Circle of Friends

Circle of friends is a systematic way of identifying and outlining all the friends, acquaintances, and key people in a student's life (Falvey & Rosenberg, 1995; Pearpoint et al., 1996). Most children without disabilities have an extensive network of friends. Some children with disabilities do not have any friends at all. The circle-of-friends process can help children without disabilities realize how important friends are in their life and how children who do not have friends must feel. Through this process, children without disabilities often have a greater appreciation of the importance of accepting and befriending peers with disabilities.

The circle-of-friends process begins with a "social scan." This gives a picture of key people in a person's life. This also helps children without disabilities see very clearly who might be involved in certain activities and what circles need to be filled. The process involves each student in the class drawing four concentric circles (see Figure 17.1). Each child is told that he or she is in the center of the circles. Students are then prompted to fill in the people who are in each of the four circles. The first circle, *circle of intimacy*, lists the people most intimately connected to a student's life—that is, those people the student could not imagine living without (e.g., parents, siblings, grandparents). The second circle, *circle of friendship*, lists each student's good friends. The third circle, *circle of participation*, lists people, organizations, and networks in which the student might be involved (e.g., sports teams, clubs, scouts). Finally, the fourth and outer circle, *circle of exchange*, lists people who are paid

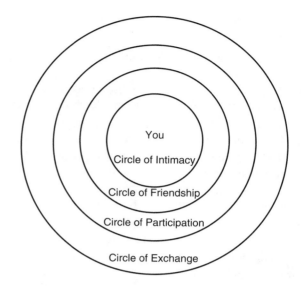

Figure 17.1. Circle of friends. (From Pearpoint, J., Forest, M., & O'Brien, J. [1996]. MAPs, Circles of Friends, and PATH: Powerful tools to help build caring communities. In S. Stainback & W. Stainback [Eds.], *Inclusion: A guide for educators* [Fig. 3, p. 75]. Baltimore, MD: Paul H. Brookes Publishing Co.; adapted by permission.)

to provide services to the student (e.g., teachers, medical professionals, barbers; Falvey & Rosenberg, 1995; Pearpoint et al., 1996).

Once all students have finished their social scan, lead a discussion about the results, focusing on the circles of students with disabilities. Students will quickly see that students with disabilities have fewer names in their circle of friends and circle of participation and more names in their circle of exchange. The process concludes with ways members of the class can help this student have more friends and participate in more activities (Pearpoint et al., 1996).

To apply this process to general physical education, the general physical educator can ask students to draw and then fill in three circles: 1) who they play with and interact with during physical education daily, 2) who they play and interact with in class occasionally, and 3) who they never play or interact with. Students can become more aware through this process that they only interact with some children and not others and that some children rarely interact with anyone during physical education. Through discussion and prompting, the teacher can then help children realize that some children might be very lonely and isolated in physical education. Finally, the general physical educator can help children realize that this situation can change if classmates make an effort to interact with and befriend more students during physical education, including the child with disabilities.

Guest Speakers

Guest speakers with disabilities can change attitudes through their powerful and moving stories of personal success and fulfillment through sports. Inviting guests who participate in adapted and Paralympic sports such as wheelchair racing, wheelchair basketball, sit skiing, sled hockey, or goalball can dispel stereotypes and increase awareness of the powerful manner in which sports can unite and connect athletes of all abilities. Local sports organizations with national affiliations (e.g., United States Association of Blind Athletes, Paralympic Sport Clubs, National Wheelchair Sports Association, Special Olympics) are excellent resources for recruiting speakers.

Role Playing

Another method for changing attitudes is role playing in which students without disabilities are given a disability. This technique has been used for years in Red Cross adapted aquatics classes as well as in inclusive physical education programs (Mizen & Linton, 1983). In physical education, students can be blindfolded and asked to move through an obstacle course, sit in chairs to play volleyball or basketball, or have one arm tied up while trying to hit a softball. The teacher should facilitate discussions regarding how a peer with a disability might feel when he or she is trying to participate in these activities. Discussions should also include how in some situations a person with a disability is at an advantage. Auxter et al. (2010) have provided a list of role-playing activities (see Table 17.3).

Sports Rules Discussion

Attitudes can also change by discussing the purpose of sport rules and how these rules can be modified to successfully include all students.

Discussion should include the concept of disabling (i.e., making rule modifications) in order to equalize competition. Encourage students to discuss ways of disabling to equalize competition in physical education. For example, a student who is blind might have difficulty hitting a pitched ball and running to first base. A fair modification for this student might include allowing him to hit a ball off a tee. When he must run to first base, a peer can guide the student. Because it takes longer for the student to run to first base, the base can be moved closer to home plate. When students are involved in the process of developing modifications to accommodate students with different abilities, they are more likely to accept them.

Lead a Discussion on Differences and Similarities

A discussion on differences and similarities can help children understand that all people are different in some ways and similar in others. Have children name similarities and differences in their classmates, and point out that differences are a natural part of life. For example, have everyone who was born in the state raise their hands; then have those born in another state raise their hands. Have everyone who brings lunch to school raise their hands; then have everyone who buys lunch raise their hands. Repeat with other types of contrasts. After several of these scenarios, point out how some students are like others in some ways and some students are different in some ways. Conclude by noting that children with disabilities are probably a lot more alike than different from their classmates.

Lead a Discussion on Disabilities

It is helpful to discuss disabilities in general. Talk about why people might have a disability (some are

Table 17.3.   Role-playing ideas to teach children about disabilities

- Walk with a piece of paper between your knees and try to run (simulates cerebral palsy).
- Try to write your name or throw a ball using your opposite hand (simulates coordination problems).
- Close your eyes and, in a safe area, run toward a peer who is clapping his or her hands; holding a string between your hand and a peer's, close your eyes and then try to run slowly (simulates a visual impairment).
- Sit in a chair (wheelchair if available) and try to do a chest pass to a peer or shoot a basketball into a basket (simulates use of a wheelchair).
- Hold your hands over your ears and have a classmate very softly give verbal directions to do a multitask motor activity such as dribbling and then shooting a jump shot in basketball or sliding from one cone to another and then running back to the first cone (simulates a hearing impairment).
- Try to walk while balancing a tennis ball on a spoon and while peers are clapping their hands in your ears and waving their hands in your face (simulates autism or attention-deficit/hyperactivity disorder).
- Tie your arm to your body and try to run, catch a ball, or hit a baseball off a tee (simulates having only one arm).

born with a disability and others acquire it). Ask students who have a family member, friend, or neighbor with a disability to share their experiences. Or have students answer a questionnaire about children with disabilities (including questions such as "Would you pick a child who uses a wheelchair to be on your team?") and discuss their answers as a group. Make sure the children understand that there are no right or wrong answers. Rather, explain to the students that their answers reveal how they feel about classmates with disabilities. The group discussion can explore stereotypes and fears as well as why some children have more favorable attitudes toward children with disabilities. Two tools that lend themselves to these types of discussions can be found in Figures 17.2 and 17.3.

Talk About Famous People Who Have Disabilities

Talk about famous people who have disabilities (Center for Disability Information and Referral, 2012).

Choose several names from the list in Appendix at the end of this chapter and ask children to write down the first thing that they think of when they hear each name. Then explain to the children that each of these famous people has a disability but is recognized for their individual talents and abilities. Finally, discuss what the class has learned about people with disabilities and how this will affect their treatment of classmates with disabilities.

Use Movies to Dispel Stereotypes

Some movies offer realistic portraits of people with disabilities. Choose a movie from the list in Table 17.4 and play a segment to the class showing the challenges the main character with a disability had to face or stereotyping behavior of the characters without a disability. Ask the children what makes the main character in the movie different from others and what behaviors were inappropriate. Then ask the children to rewrite the script to portray the person with disabilities in a more appropriate manner.

Disabilities Feelings Survey

For each statement below, check the box that best describes how you feel. There are no right or wrong answers! Just think about how you feel, and then answer honestly.

	Yes	No	Maybe
1. I feel okay around people who have disabilities.	___	___	___
2. I think people who have disabilities should live and work with everybody else.	___	___	___
3. I have seen people with disabilities who are employed at local businesses.	___	___	___
4. People with disabilities are able to ride bicycles, drive cars, and participate in sports.	___	___	___
5. A person who has a disability can marry a person who does not have a disability.	___	___	___
6. People who have disabilities can be good parents.	___	___	___
7. Kids who have disabilities should go to the same schools as everyone else.	___	___	___
8. Kids who have disabilities can be just as smart as those who do not have disabilities.	___	___	___
9. Kids who have disabilities can have many friends.	___	___	___
10. I would like to make friends with someone who has a disability.	___	___	___
11. During recess on the school playground, I would play with kids who have disabilities.	___	___	___
12. I would invite someone who has a disability over to my house to play.	___	___	___
13. Kids who have disabilities are the same as me in many ways.	___	___	___
14. Kids who have disabilities can be as happy as those who do not have disabilities.	___	___	___
15. Kids who have disabilities can live on their own when they grow up.	___	___	___

Review your answers. Then, bring in newspaper or magazine articles that support your point of view about disabilities, and share the articles with your class.

Figure 17.2. Disability feelings survey. (From Getskow, V., & Konczal, D. [1996]. *Kids with special needs: Information and activities to promote awareness and understanding* [p. 34]. Santa Barbara, CA: Learning Works; reprinted by permission.)

Questions from the Children's Attitude Toward Intergrated Physical Education–Revised

Okay, let me tell you about **Mike**. He is the same age as you, but he cannot walk. Mike likes playing the same games you do, but he does not do very well in the games. Even though Mike can move around, he is slower than you and tires easily. Mike can throw a ball but not very far. He can catch balls that are tossed straight to him, and he can hit a baseball off a tee, but he cannot shoot a basketball high enough to make basket. Because Mike's legs do not work well, he has difficulty kicking a ball.

Let's get started. Listen to the following statement and think about Mike. Answer each with yes, probably **yes, probably no,** or **no**. Remember, there are no right or wrong answers. Your answers will depend on your feelings and will probably be different from other kids in your class.

	Yes	Probably Yes	No	Probably No
1. It would be okay having Mike come to my PE class.				
2. Because Mike cannot play sports very well, he would slow down the game for everyone else.				
3. If we were playing a team sport such as basketball, it would be okay having Mike on my team.				
4. PE would be fun if Mike were in my PE class.				
5. If Mike were in my PE class, I would talk to him and be his friend.				
6. If Mike were in my PE class, I would like to help him practice and play the games.				
7. Mike could hit a ball placed on a batting tee.				
8. Someone could tell Mike where to run when he hits the ball.				
9. The distance between home and first base could be shorter for Mike.				
10. Someone could help Mike when he plays in the field.				
11. If the ball was hit to Mike, the batter could only run as far as second base.				

Figure 17.3. Questions from the Children's Attitude Toward Integrated Physical Education–Revised (CAIPE-R) Inventory. The CAIPE-R was designed for children in 5th through 12th grades. After reading the following vignette about a child with a disability, have students respond to the series of statements regarding how they feel about having this child in their physical education class and how they feel about specific modifications to a sport to facilitate inclusion. (Adapted, with permission, from G.S.D. Morris and J. Stiehl, 1999, Development and validation of the Children's Attitudes Toward Integrated Physical Education-Revised [CAIPE-R] inventory," Adapted Physical Activity Quarterly 12[1]: 64–65.)

Explain How to Interact with Specific Children

Many children may want to interact with a child who has a disability, but they are not quite sure if it is okay or how to approach the child. For example, peers sometimes see a teacher assistant helping the child with disabilities and think that they are not supposed to interact with the child. Explain to peers that it is great to talk to and play with this child and how important it is for this child to really feel like part of the class. Then explain how to talk to the child (if the child has unique communication techniques), how to include the child in activities (what simple modifications might work), and specific ways to befriend the child. For example, many elementary students love to learn basic sign language.

Similarly, it can be fun and challenging for peers to figure out the best way to modify various physical education activities to include peers with disabilities. Providing some suggestions on how to interact with classmates who have disabilities will help peers be more understanding and welcoming to these children. Note that these discussions may need to take place several times during the school year. For example, children may be very friendly and helpful to a child with intellectual disabilities in the beginning of the school year. However, after several months, children may begin to ignore the child or forget that the child needs modifications to activities to participate successfully. In such cases, you may need to remind the group of the child's needs.

Provide Ongoing Information, Encouragement, and Support for Acceptance

Preparing peers for inclusion is important and should be ongoing. Too often students with disabilities

Table 17.4. Movies featuring disabilities

Name of movie	Year released	Director	Actor
Cognitive disability/Down syndrome			
I Am Sam	2001	Jessie Nelson	Sean Penn
The Other Sister	1999	Garry Marshall	Juliette Lewis
The Eighth Day (Le Huitième jour)	1997	Jaco van Dormael	Pascal Duquenne
Forrest Gump	1994	Robert Zemeckis	Tom Hanks
Autism			
Rain Man	1988	Barry Levinson	Dustin Hoffman
What's Eating Gilbert Grape	1993	Lasse Halström	Leonardo DiCaprio
The Boy Who Could Fly	1988	Nick Castle	Jay Underwood
Backstreet Dreams	1990	Rupert Hitzig & Jason O'Malley	John Vizzi
Miracle Run	2004	Gregg Champion	
Schizophrenia/mental illness			
A Beautiful Mind	2002	Ron Howard	Russell Crowe
Shine	1996	Scott Hicks	Geoffrey Rush
Benny and Joon	1993	Jeremiah S. Chechik	Mary Stuart Masterson
Cerebral palsy			
My Left Foot	1989	Jim Sheridan	Daniel Day-Lewis
Dwarfism			
Simon Birch	1998	Mark Johnson	Ian Michael Smith
Deafness			
Mr. Holland's Opus	1995	Stephen Herek	
Immortal Beloved	1994	Bernard Rose	Gary Oldman
Sound and Fury	2000	Josh Aronson	
Blindness			
Scent of a Woman	1992	Martin Brest	Al Pacino
Blink	1994	Michael Apted	Madeleine Stowe
At First Sight	1999	Irwin Winkler	Val Kilmer
The Miracle Worker	2000	Nadia Tass	Hallie-Kate Eisenberg

are ignored in physical education because their classmates do not know how to interact or assist the student with a disability (Block & Brady, 1999). Provide ongoing encouragement to peers (through both modeling and direct suggestion) to talk to the student with disabilities, to provide feedback and positive reinforcement, and to ask the student if he or she needs assistance (but not assume assistance is needed without asking). The entire class should take responsibility for ensuring every student feels included, and students should be continuously prompted and reinforced for interacting with the student with disabilities. As classmates begin to feel more comfortable with the student who has a disability, then interactions will become more spontaneous.

COMMON BARRIERS TO SOCIAL INCLUSION IN GENERAL PHYSICAL EDUCATION AND POSSIBLE SOLUTIONS

Unfortunately, the social aspects of inclusion are rarely addressed in general physical education. Simply placing a child with disabilities in general physical education will not ensure socialization. Furthermore, many physical educators unknowingly create situations that prevent the social development of students with disabilities. Five problems primarily prevent socialization in inclusive physical education: 1) when teacher assistants try too hard, 2) when usual activities are inappropriate, 3) when peers serve only as tutors and not as friends, 4) when students with disabilities are grouped together, and 5) when peers are being exclusive and unkind to students with disabilities.

Problem 1: Teacher Assistants Are Trying Too Hard

Students with more severe disabilities often come to general physical education with a teacher assistant. These teaching assistants often know a lot about the student with disabilities but very little about physical education. Furthermore, these well-meaning teacher assistants feel compelled to assist the student as much as possible. Some students even consider their teacher assistants to be their closest friend. Although close ties between students with disabilities and teaching staff are not necessarily negative, these ties may prevent the students from learning appropriate social skills needed to make relationships with classmates. Teacher assistants who hover over a student with a disability unwittingly prevent interaction with peers without disabilities (Malmgren & Causton-Theoharis, 2006).

Similarly, peers often feel uncomfortable approaching the student with disabilities when a teacher assistant is working with the student. For example, at a throwing station, a teacher assistant is instructing the student with a disability how to throw overhand. She also retrieves beanbags for this student to throw. Peers seeing this interaction may not want to interfere with the instruction that is taking place. The student also becomes very dependent on the teacher assistant in this activity.

Solution: Provide Awareness Training for Teacher Assistants

Teacher assistants want to do what is best for their students with disabilities, and they want to be useful. Simply explaining that you want to encourage more interactions between the student with disabilities and his or her peers without disabilities is a good beginning. Explain how their presence could prevent important social interactions with peers. Show the teacher assistant how he or she can move away and help other students while still keeping an eye on the student with disabilities. In fact, a teacher assistant can be assigned a group of students that includes the student with disabilities.

Teacher assistants also can be given specific examples of how to promote interactions between peers with and without disabilities. For example, the teacher assistant can encourage peers to choose the child with disabilities as a partner. When a child

needs assistance to retrieve balls or go to another station, the teacher assistant can encourage peers to help the child. When playing group games, the teacher assistant can encourage peers to help the child know where to stand and what to do. The teacher assistant may need to be in the general area for safety reasons, but he or she does not need to hover around the student with disabilities the entire period. By backing off, the student is given a greater opportunity for interaction with peers and a chance to become more independent.

Problem 2: Student Cannot Participate in the General Activity

In some cases, students with disabilities cannot participate in a particular activity because of health or safety issues. Although it may be appropriate to have the child off to the side doing a more appropriate activity, such separation from peers encourages isolation and prevents social interactions. For example, it may be unsafe for a 10th grader with cerebral palsy who uses an electric wheelchair to play soccer with his peers or for a third grader with Down syndrome to participate in forward rolls during a tumbling unit. Yet sitting off to the side and watching or playing by himself or herself is not an appropriate solution to the problem.

Solution: Utilize Peers without Disabilities

One relatively simple solution is to have peers rotate over to the student with a disability and participate with him or her in an alternative activity. Continuing with the soccer example, each player in the soccer game is given a number from 1 to 6. Because there are 30 students in the class, five players will have the number 1, five will have the number 2, and so forth. At the start of the soccer game, players with the number 1 will be off to the side working with the student with cerebral palsy in an alternative activity. In keeping with the theme of soccer, students practice dribbling as quickly as they can through cones or pass a ball back and forth with a partner. The student with cerebral palsy practices maneuvering his wheelchair through the cones or pushing a ball off his lap tray to a partner. After about 3 minutes, the ones rotate in and the twos rotate out. Having peers at the alternative activity creates opportunities for social interactions.

Another way to promote more interactions with peers is to add more activities. For example, if a child with Down syndrome cannot do forward rolls due to the possibility of a neck injury, set up another area of the gym with mats for other tumbling activities such as log rolls and crab walks. Have all students rotate through all stations, except for the child with Down syndrome, who rotates only through the last two stations. With this setup, the child with Down syndrome is working on motor and fitness skills but also has an opportunity to interact with peers, to wait his turn, and to observe appropriate behavior.

Problem 3: Peers Are Tutors but Not Friends

Using peers as tutors to facilitate inclusion has been promoted (e.g., Klavina & Block, 2008, 2013; Lieberman & Houston-Wilson, 2009) because peers are a free, readily available source of support for students with disabilities who need extra attention or extra help. However, if peers only serve in the role of tutor, then there is an imbalance in the relationship. This imbalance promotes a feeling that students with disabilities always need help and are somehow less than students without disabilities. Such imbalanced relationships can lead to lower self-esteem in students with disabilities (Carter, Asmus, & Moss, 2013; Sherrill, 2004).

Solution: Utilize Reciprocal Rather than One-Way Peer Tutoring

Although you still can use peers as tutors to help students with disabilities, create situations in which students with disabilities can serve as tutors. Known as the reciprocal style of teaching (Mosston & Ashworth, 2008), the student with disabilities and a peer take turns serving as tutor and tutee. This works particularly well with students with mild disabilities such as learning disabilities or behavior problems. As tutee, the student with disabilities learns how to listen and accept feedback. As a tutor, the student with disabilities learns how to carefully observe others and to provide feedback in a nice way. Furthermore, taking turns as tutor and tutee leads to more interactions and discussions between the two students. For example, a fourth grader who does not follow directions, is hyperactive, and can be belligerent is paired with a peer in a throwing activity. Students are given a score sheet with the components of the overhand throw. The student with the behavior problem starts as the tutor. She is encouraged by the tutee to watch her throw, paying particular attention to her stepping with the opposite foot. The tutor watches the throw and gives immediate feedback following a script written out by the teacher: "Good throw, you stepped with the opposite foot." After

five throws, the students switch roles. The student with a behavior problem now gets to throw and receive feedback, but the student has seen a model of how to stay on task, how to listen to feedback, and how to accept feedback properly.

Alternate Solution: Utilize Peers as Friends as Well as Tutors

Another solution to the imbalance of peer tutoring is to set up situations in which peers are simply friends. For example, a ninth grader with fetal alcohol syndrome has motor delays (about 3 years delayed compared with peers) as well as behavior problems (short attention span, impulsive, hyperactive, lies). In the past, this student has been assigned a peer to help him stay on task, follow directions, and stay with the group. However, the physical education teacher decides to have the entire class look out for the student as his friends. All are assigned responsibility for helping the student stay on task and behave more appropriately in physical education. The class discusses this new model and their new roles as friends. For example, when students line up in squads for roll call and for warm-ups, peers in this student's squad call the student over to say hi and then remind him to line up. During warm-ups, peers in his squad remind him when it is time to change to a new warm-up activity, and several peers try to be his partner during sit-ups. When the teacher is giving instructions, peers around the student provide gentle reminders to sit and listen quietly. During the basketball game, teammates guide the student on where to stand and who to pass to and warn him not to play too rough on defense. The other team, aware that the student is not as skilled, allows him a little more room to pass and to shoot, and they do not call traveling unless it is blatant. This more subtle approach to helping this student provides more dignity and promotes a more natural delivery of support. Furthermore, the student has a chance to interact with all his classmates rather than just one peer tutor.

Problem 4: Students with Disabilities Are Grouped Together

Despite the opportunities for social interaction, evidence suggests that without adult intervention, students with disabilities tend to interact more frequently with their peers with disabilities in social situations (Sainato & Carta, 1992). Ellis, Wright, and Cronis (1996) found that when an entire self-contained special education class of 11 students was included in general physical education, they tended to maintain their group identity rather than interact with the rest of the class. In a similar study, Place and Hodge (2001) found that even three students with disabilities placed together in the same general physical education class were significantly more likely to interact with each other than with peers without disabilities.

Solution: Provide Teacher-Mediated Interaction

Recall from Chapter 2 that one of the basic premises of inclusion is the *principle of natural proportions* (placing only one or two students with disabilities into a general physical education class of 20–25 students). Although special education teachers find it easier to bring a larger portion of the class (or even the entire class) to general physical education, this creates a setting ripe for failure. If two or more students with disabilities absolutely have to be included in one class, then designing inclusive environments to facilitate the social behavior of children with disabilities is paramount. The general physical educator should take into account the severity or level of disability of each child and the number of socially competent peers available for interaction. Dividing the class into small groups with only one student with a disability in each group would create an environment conducive to social interactions between students with and without disabilities. If the principle of natural proportions is not being met, the general physical educator should also consider a full-class disability awareness experience to better educate the students and create an atmosphere for successful inclusive attitudes.

Problem 5: Peers Are Being Exclusive and Unkind to Students with Disabilities

Research related to the success of inclusion in the physical education setting offers mixed results. Students with disabilities report having experiences that range from isolation to involvement, from ridicule to compliments, and from limited involvement to active involvement (Asbjørnslett & Hemmingsson, 2008; Blinde & McCallister, 1998; Bredahl, 2013; Goodwin, 2001; Goodwin & Watkinson, 2000; Herold & Dandolo, 2009; Spencer-Cavaliere & Watkinson, 2010). For example, Goodwin and Watkinson (2000) categorized student experiences into two categories: 1) good days, which include feeling a sense of belonging, shared benefits, and skillful participation, and 2) bad days, which include restricted participation, questioned competence, and social isolation. Socialization is often

argued to be a benefit of inclusive physical education (Block, 2007); however, research cited earlier seems to indicate that at least part of the time students with disabilities experience limited social interaction, limited social learning experiences, and few friends in physical education.

Solution: Provide Disability Education and Awareness Experiences

Attitude is considered one of the keys to changing behaviors toward people who are different, and these improved behaviors are essential to adapted physical education and inclusion (Hutzler, 2003). Peers without disabilities were found to be the most significant support system for students with disabilities in a study by Hutzler, Fliess, Chacham, and Van den Auweele (2002), and peer education was recommended.

As noted earlier, preparing peers without disabilities for the inclusion of peers with disabilities is viewed as one key factor in successful inclusion practice (Klavina & Block, 2013; Lieberman & Houston-Wilson, 2009; McKay, 2013b). The manner in which students without disabilities are prepared for the inclusion of their peers with disabilities is essential. Blinde and McCallister (1998) emphasize that sensitivity and empathy toward the needs of others should be covered. Murata, Hodge, and Little (2000) emphasize that diversity appreciation and disability awareness should be covered. Block (2007) notes that specific training is needed for children without disabilities in order for them to interact with peers with disabilities in a positive and age-appropriate manner. Wilhite, Mushett, Goldenberg, and Trader (1997) write that emphasizing the *ability* of individuals with disabilities can result in positive and practical outcomes for students taking part in awareness education training activities. Awareness programs such as the PSD curriculum discussed earlier in this chapter can be easily introduced in the general physical education setting, creating an opportunity for ongoing education and tolerance activities that helps support equal-status relationships and positive peer contact.

SUMMARY

Perhaps the greatest benefit to including students with disabilities into general physical education is the opportunity it creates for children with disabilities to interact with peers, make friends, and feel like a member of the group. Yet such benefits will not occur if children with disabilities are simply placed in general physical education. The general physical education teacher and peers without disabilities have to welcome the child into general physical education by learning about the child, by working to genuinely include the child in as many general physical education activities as possible, and by showing the child that he or she is welcome and a true member of the class.

Although it is never appropriate to include a child in general physical education just for socialization, social inclusion and acceptance is an important goal in any classroom. Quality physical education should promote motor, cognitive, and *social development*. This can be particularly important for students with disabilities.

Famous People with Disabilities

ATHLETES

Jim Abbott *(baseball)* Physical disability (hand amputation)

Muhammad Ali *(boxing)* Brain injury

Lance Armstrong *(cycling)* Cancer

Larry Brown *(football)* Hearing impairment

Harold Connelly *(track and field)* Physical disability (left arm)

Tom Dempsey *(football)* Physical disability (congenital foot deformity)

Jim Eisenreich *(baseball)* Tourette syndrome

Sean Elliot *(basketball)* Kidney disease

Pete Gray *(baseball)* Physical disability (had one arm)

Nancy Hogshead *(swimming)* Asthma

Catfish Hunter *(baseball)* Diabetes, amyotrophic lateral sclerosis

Bruce Jenner *(track and field)* Learning disability

Magic Johnson *(basketball)* HIV

Jackie Joyner-Kersee *(track and field)* Asthma

Tony Lazzeri *(baseball)* Epilepsy

Greg Louganis *(diving)* Asthma, HIV

Walter Payton *(football)* Kidney disease

Wilma Rudolph *(track and field)* Physical disability (birth defects and polio)

Ron Santo *(baseball)* Diabetes, physical disability (leg amputation)

O.J. Simpson *(football)* Learning disability

Kenny Walker *(football)* Deafness

Kristi Yamaguchi *(figure skating)* Asthma

POLITICIANS

Winston Churchill Learning disability

Robert Dole Physical disability (right arm)

John F. Kennedy Physical disability (back injury), Addison disease

Abraham Lincoln Depression, Marfan syndrome (a connective tissue disorder)

George Patton Learning disability

Ronald Reagan Alzheimer disease

Franklin D. Roosevelt Physical disability

Woodrow Wilson Learning disability

ACTORS

Chris Burke Down syndrome

Cher Dyslexia (Cher uses a reading coach to learn television, movie, and commercial scripts.)

Tom Cruise Dyslexia (Cruise uses a reading coach to learn scripts.)

Sammy Davis, Jr. Visual impairment

Walt Disney Learning disability (Disney did not learn how to read until he was 9. He drew pictures to help him remember what he was learning.)

287

Michael J. Fox   Parkinson disease

Annette Funicello   Parkinson's disease

Danny Glover   Learning disability (Glover was placed in a class for students with intellectual disabilities until he was in high school, and he did not learn how to read or write until after he graduated from school.)

Whoopi Goldberg   Dyslexia (Goldberg uses a reading coach to help her learn scripts.)

James Earl Jones   Communication disability (stuttering) (Jones did not speak in school because he was so embarrassed. He learned to speak without stuttering by reading poetry. Poetry has a rhythm to it, and people who stutter often can sing or read poetry.)

Marlee Matlin   Deafness

Richard Pryor   Multiple sclerosis

Christopher Reeve   Quadriplegia

MUSICIANS

Beethoven   Deafness

Ray Charles   Blindness

Jacqueline du Pré   Multiple sclerosis

John Lennon   Learning disability

Freddie Mercury   AIDS

Itzhak Perlman   Physical disability

Stevie Wonder   Blindness

OTHER FAMOUS PEOPLE

Hans Christian Andersen *(writer)*   Learning disability

Agatha Christie *(writer)*   Learning disability

Thomas Edison *(inventor)*   Deafness

Albert Einstein *(physicist and Nobel laureate)*   Learning disability

Stephen Hawking *(physicist and writer)*   Amyotrophic lateral sclerosis

Helen Keller *(writer)*   Deafness and blindness

Darci Kistler *(ballerina)*   Diabetes

Sources: Appenzeller (1983); Getskow and Konezal (1996); Zygmunt, Larson, and Tilson (1994)

CHAPTER 18

Making Inclusive Physical Education Safe

Martin E. Block and Mel Horton

<hr />

OBJECTIVES

1. Define and differentiate liability versus negligence

2. Define and differentiate the following terms: *malfeasance*, *misfeasance*, *nonfeasance*, and *foreseeability*

3. Understand the following considerations as they relate to safety: how to find out necessary medical information about the student, how to conduct an assessment of the student and the environment, key aspects of the environment and equipment you need to analyze for safety, safe teaching techniques, and the key components of an emergency plan

<hr />

Not many things scare Mr. Strawberry. At 6 feet, 4 inches and weighing 275 pounds, most people are a little scared of Mr. Strawberry, especially the kindergartners who meet him for the first time. Truthfully, Mr. Strawberry is a teddy bear who loves teaching physical education to elementary school children. He has been teaching elementary physical education for 10 years and is one of the few veteran teachers who really look forward to coming back to school each fall.

But Mr. Strawberry is not looking forward to returning to school this fall because of a little girl named Angel. Angel and her parents just moved to town. Over the summer, Mr. Strawberry received a call from the special education teacher at Perry Creek Elementary School briefly explaining some of Angel's

medical conditions. Angel is on a respirator for oxygen. She is fed via a feeding tube. She uses a wheelchair for mobility, but she needs someone to push it for her. Due to severe scoliosis and frequent hip dislocations, several different straps and wedges on her wheelchair help her stay in the correct position. Angel is also considered deaf and blind. She wears hearing aids, which allow her to hear sounds. She wears very thick glasses, which help her identify large images and people directly in front of her. She is nonverbal and has intellectual disabilities, so it is difficult for her to communicate and to understand what others want.

Mr. Strawberry was told that Angel would attend general physical education with the support of a full-time nurse. Separate programming was not an option, at least not for the first few months of school, to determine if Angel would be successful in general physical education. Reports from her previous school said that Angel successfully attended general physical education.

Mr. Strawberry wants to do what is best for Angel, but he is scared that she might have a medical crisis in the gymnasium. He is also unclear about how to ensure the safety of someone who seems so fragile in a gymnasium where balls and kids are constantly flying around. Mr. Strawberry has a plan for getting the kids out of the gym when there is a fire drill, and he has a basic first-aid kit for cuts and scrapes. But a more extensive emergency plan seems to be needed for Angel. Yes, despite his size, Mr. Strawberry is definitely scared of Angel and all the challenges that she presents. What should Mr. Strawberry do?

Gallahue and Cleland-Donnelly noted, "The very nature of physical education classes, which take place in the gymnasium, swimming pool, or playground, exposes the teacher to greater liability for accidents and injuries than any other area of the school curriculum" (2003, p. 397). Safety issues in physical education are compounded when children with disabilities are included in general physical education programs. There are three major safety concerns for students with disabilities who are included in general physical education. First, safety is a problem for students with disabilities who do not have the same level of speed, strength, stamina, balance, or coordination as their peers without disabilities. In addition, many students with disabilities have cognitive and perceptual impairments that can add to their confusion and inability to react to situations as quickly as their peers. Such differences can easily lead to injuries. For example, in a dodging/fleeing activity, a child with cerebral palsy who is very unstable in standing could easily be knocked down. Similarly, a child who has intellectual disabilities may not know that he or she is standing too close to the batter during a softball game. The student could be in danger of getting hit by the ball or the bat.

Second, safety is an issue for children who have medical conditions that can lead to emergency complications. For example, many children with asthma at times require emergency medical attention (National Institutes of Health [NIH], 2012). Similarly, changes in diet and exercise patterns can have severe consequences for children who have diabetes (Smart, Alesander-van Vliet, & Waldron, 2009). Of even greater concern are children with disabilities who are medically dependent for life support, such as tracheostomies for children who need oxygen for breathing, gastrostomy tubes for children with feeding problems, shunts for children with hydrocephalus, and colostomies and ileostomies for children with bowel and bladder problems. Children with such severe medical conditions used to be in hospital and special schools; however, a greater number of these children are being placed in general school settings (Porter, Branowicki, & Palfrey, 2014). In fact, the Supreme Court of the United States ruled that public schools must provide a wide array of medical care for children with disabilities in public school settings, including general physical education (Biskupic, 1999).

Third, including students with disabilities in general physical education poses dangers to students without disabilities. For example, a student who uses a wheelchair may be involved in a game of tag. During the excitement of the game, a child without a disability could easily run into the child's wheelchair. Similarly, a child with crutches could accidentally hit or trip another student during a soccer game, or a child with an artificial arm could accidentally bump into and hurt a peer during movement exploration activities.

Safety certainly should be a priority in physical education for students with and without disabilities, and there are some cases in which children with disabilities cannot safely be included in general physical education. However, safety concerns should not be used as a blanket excuse to separate all students with disabilities into separate physical education classes. As noted in Chapters 1 and 2, placements need to be made on a case-by-case basis. Only when the setting is deemed unsafe or inappropriate after attempts at making it safe and appropriate through supplementary aids and supports can the student be placed in a separate setting (Block, 1996; Individuals with Disabilities Education Improvement Act (IDEA) of 2004, 20 U.S.C. § 1412[a][5][A]; *Oberti v. Board of Education of the Borough of Clementon School District*, 1992).

The purpose of this chapter is to share strategies that can be used to make general physical education settings and activities safe for all students. First, liability and negligence are discussed. This is followed by a brief discussion of six key aspects of making inclusive settings safe: 1) the student with disabilities, 2) the general environment, 3) the equipment, 4) class organization, 5) content, and 6) emergency procedures. It is understood that some students in some activities and environments may not be able to participate safely and should receive physical education in an alternative setting. This process allows general physical educators to make more objective decisions about which children need alternative programs or placements. However, this process allows most students with disabilities, including those with severe disabilities, to be safely accommodated within general physical education.

A PRIMER ON LEGAL LIABILITY

Liability

From a legal standpoint, legal or *tort liability* refers to someone being at fault—with this "fault" leading to or causing an injury or death and that "someone" being legally responsible for the injury or death (Appenzeller & Appenzeller, 1980; Black, 2014; Dougherty, Golderberger, & Carpenter, 2007). With regard to physical education, a student can hold a physical education teacher liable (at fault) for injuries received during physical education class. For example, a child with a visual impairment is knocked down during a dodging and fleeing game. Her parents sue the physical education teacher for their child's injuries. Although the parents have the right to hold the physical education teacher liable for their daughter's injuries, the court must show that the cause of the child's injuries was the physical education teacher's "negligence."

Negligence

Fault that results in personal injury is also known as *negligence*. Negligence is defined as failure on the part of the physical education teacher to act in a manner that is judged to be reasonable, careful, and prudent for someone with that level of training or status (Appenzeller, 1983; Dougherty et al., 2007). This is also known as the "prudent or reasonable person principle" (Dougherty et al., 2007)—that is, would another reasonably prudent physical education teacher placed in that same situation have done the same thing to ensure the safety of the child who was injured? A physical educator who places children in unnecessarily risky situations or who does not provide proper supervision of activities may be considered negligent. Appenzeller (1983), Gallahue and Cleland-Donnelly (2003), and Pangrazi and Beighle (2015) noted that negligence must be proven in a court of law and that the following five factors must be shown if negligence is to be established:

1. *Duty:* It must be determined that the defendant (i.e., the physical education teacher) had a responsibility to provide for the safety and welfare of the plaintiff (i.e., the student). If the injured party is a student in the defendant's physical education class, then established duty is a foregone conclusion. It is important to note that the licensed physical education teacher has the duty to provide for the safety and welfare of all students who enter his or her physical education program, including children with disabilities and even when the child with a disability is accompanied by a teacher assistant, volunteer, or peer tutor. In fact, the licensed physical education teacher is responsible for the safety of teacher assistants, volunteers, and peer tutors who enter the physical education setting as well.

2. *Breach of duty:* It must be shown that the defendant failed to provide the standard of service that could be reasonably expected of a professional under similar circumstances. A duty can be breached by "nonfeasance" or "act of omission" (i.e., failure to do something that a prudent physical educator should have done, such as providing alternative instruction to students who are deaf), "malfeasance" or "act of commission" (i.e., doing something that a prudent physical educator should not have been doing, such as allowing a child with Down syndrome who tested positive for atlantoaxial instability, which can lead to paralysis if pressure is placed on the neck, to do forward and backward rolls with the other children), or "misfeasance" (i.e., following proper procedures but not to the required standard of conduct expected by a prudent physical education teacher, such as supervising children in a game of tag but having too small a space and too many children moving at once, causing a child with low vision to collide with another child).

3. *Foreseeability:* It must be shown that the physical education teacher could have been able to predict the likelihood of an accident or injury occurring due to the specific circumstance or situation. For example, could the physical education teacher have foreseen that a third-grade peer tutor did not have the strength or control to safely push a child in a wheelchair down a steep hill? Could the physical education teacher have foreseen that a child prone to asthma attacks might have an asthma attack when running a mile on a hot June day?

4. *Damage:* Damage refers to actual injury or loss. The plaintiff has to prove damage to receive compensation from the defendant. Damages could be things such as medical expenses, rehabilitation, psychological stress, and time away from school. Compensation for damages then could be in the form of monetary compensation for medical expenses, psychological counseling, home tutoring, and any medical discomfort experienced by the defendant.

5. *Proximate cause:* If a breach of duty has been established, then the plaintiff must prove that there was a reasonable relationship between the defendant's breach of duty and the student's injury. In other words, was it the physical education teacher's specific breach of duty that led to the damage incurred by the student? If, for example, a child with intellectual disabilities who was properly supervised and instructed got hurt due to "an act of God" (e.g., the child trips over his own feet and breaks an ankle while

working at a basketball station), then the physical education teacher is not necessarily liable. As noted by Appenzeller,

> The fact that an accident occurs does not necessarily mean the teacher or coach is negligent or liable for damages. It must be proved that the injury is reasonably connected with negligence. . . .No court has held a defendant liable where there was substantial evidence that the defendant acted with prudence and caution in the performance of his duties. (1983, p. 183)

When an Injury to a Student Is Not Negligence

A physical education teacher could be found not negligent in relation to an injury incurred by a student during physical education class under the following circumstances: contributory negligence, act of God, and proximate cause (Appenzeller, 1983; Dougherty et al., 2007; Pangrazi & Beighle, 2015).

1. *Contributory negligence:* This refers to the plaintiff (i.e., the student) being held partially or wholly responsible for the injury he or she received. Note that a court will take into consideration a student's age, physical capabilities (both mental and physical), and training before it rules. In other words, the defense tries to prove that the activity and equipment were familiar to the student, that the student received training in the activity or with the equipment, and that the injured student did not follow proper safety procedures that would be expected of other students his or her age and with his or her capabilities. For example, a 16-year-old boy who uses a wheelchair, has no intellectual impairments, and has been in the same school in the same gymnasium for 3 years wheels his chair into the wall while playing basketball and sustains a broken leg and a concussion. The court could reasonably rule that this child was old enough and capable enough to move his wheelchair safely within the confines of the gymnasium and that running into the wall was at least partially the student's own fault. In some states, the concept of "comparative negligence" is used, which means that fault for a given situation is portioned out based on the information presented to the court (e.g., the physical education teacher is 30% at fault, whereas the student is 70% at fault). In such cases, the student can still receive compensation for damages but at a prorated basis.

2. *Proximate cause:* As noted previously, this suggests that the injury was not caused by the negligence of the physical education teacher. There must be a close relationship between the breach of duty by the teacher and the resulting injury to the student. For example, a teacher sets up five stations for children to work on their physical fitness. The teacher would normally move around the room supervising the various stations but not directly assisting any of the children (i.e., they all could do all the fitness activities independently). However, at one point during class, a therapist comes into the gym to ask the physical education teacher a "quick question." While the physical education teacher is talking to this therapist, a child who uses crutches but has excellent upper body strength strains to do one more pull-up. With her last effort, she slips off the bar and hits the back of her head on a mat on the floor. This causes the child to have a concussion and bruised spinal cord. Even if the physical education teacher was watching this child as he normally would, the child still could have fallen and hurt herself. Therefore, although it could be argued that the physical education teacher was not providing proper supervision, this lack of supervision was not the proximate cause of this child's injury.

3. *Act of God:* This suggests that the injury occurred due to an event that was completely unexpected or could not be foreseen. In other words, something happened that caused an accident that was beyond the reasonable control of the teacher. For example, while playing outside, a sudden gust of wind knocks down a child who has muscular dystrophy, causing him to break several bones. To prove an "act of God," the defense must show that the accident still would have occurred even though reasonable action had been taken.

In summary, teachers who act responsibly, with common sense, and with an aim to create the safest possible setting while still allowing children to be actively involved in movement and fitness activities should not be scared of liability and negligence. Always ask yourself, what would a prudent physical educator do in this situation? Also, think of worst-case scenarios in an attempt to foresee potential safety concerns. It is important to learn as much as you can about each child so you can anticipate any possible problems, provide proper supervision and instruction, make sure equipment is in proper working order, and provide activities and progressions that are appropriate for each child's abilities.

SAFETY ISSUES SPECIFIC TO STUDENTS WITH DISABILITIES

Many students with disabilities have visible impairments that present an immediate concern to the physical educator (e.g., students who use wheelchairs or students who are blind). Others have hidden disabilities (e.g., seizure disorder, asthma, diabetes, HIV/AIDS). Hidden disabilities are particularly dangerous because special educators and parents often forget to inform physical education staff about conditions that can result in injury. Being unaware of a student's health/medical problems can lead to participation in unsafe activities in unsafe ways and possible lawsuits. Ultimately, you as the physical educator are responsible for the safety of all the students you serve (Aufsesser, 2003; Cotton, 1994; Dougherty et al., 2007).

The first step is to simply identify children with health problems and/or specific disabilities by carefully reviewing the medical records of all the students you serve (Pangrazi & Beighle, 2015). An easier way is to review the emergency cards on file in the main office. These cards usually highlight children with special health problems such as asthma, diabetes, or allergies and any medications taken, among other things. In addition, you can ask the school nurse or each classroom teacher to identify students with special health problems or disabilities.

Once you have identified students with health problems and/or disabilities, examine their medical records and cumulative folders, both of which should be available in the main office. If for some reason, detailed records are outdated or not available, then contact the child's parents to obtain more information. Another relatively simple way to obtain information about children with special health problems or disabilities is to send home a checklist for parents and/or a physician to fill out (see Figure 18.1). Some school districts may even require such forms to be filled out before a child with a disability can participate in physical education. Detailed information on each child with special health problems or disabilities can then be stored in a database and updated yearly. A database allows you to sort children based on necessary precautions (e.g., having an inhaler or other medicine available, not doing strenuous exercise in the fall during heavy pollen season).

Although this may seem like a tremendous task, it is critical that you know as much as possible about each child with special health concerns or disabilities in order to ensure safe participation in general physical education. Physical activity can lower blood sugar in children with diabetes, which can cause a hypoglycemic reaction (Petray, Freesemann, & Lavay, 1997; Smart et al., 2009; U.S. Department of Health and Human Services, 2010b). Many children with spina bifida have shunts to drain fluid from their brains, and most physicians recommend some restrictions in physical education activities (French, Keele, & Silliman-French, 1997). Children with exercise-induced asthma are particularly sensitive to continuous exercise (NIH, 2012). A physical educator who is not aware of these and other conditions could put a child into dangerous situations.

Another way to get this and other information is to participate in the individualized education program (IEP) meeting. All critical team members, including parents, attend this meeting and share information about the child with disabilities. This meeting also is a great place to educate IEP team members about your program and what you know about the child. You can share information such as the child's fitness level, gross motor skills, perceptual motor abilities, skills in specific activities, and general motivation and behavior during physical education. Once team members begin to understand your program, the unique aspect of the physical education environment, and the gross motor/fitness skills of the student, they can provide more specific suggestions to make your program safe.

Having updated medical and health information is imperative. You also need to know about each child's physical fitness level, body and space awareness, balance, eye–hand coordination, and other motor abilities and how these might affect safe participation in physical education. For example, if a child has problems with eye–hand coordination, you should plan accommodations during dodging, catching, rebounding, and striking activities, such as using foam balls. Similarly, you could allow children who have balance problems, including children who use walkers or canes, to move in a special zone so that they will not get bumped or knocked down during chasing and fleeing activities. Figure 18.2 provides a list of questions regarding a child's fitness level and gross motor abilities.

Finally, you need to find out about each child's communication skills and behavior problems. Again, you can get much of this information at the IEP meeting by listening to and talking with parents, general and special education teachers,

Physical Education Information Form

I. General information (to be filled out by parent/guardian)

Child's name: _____ Date of birth: _____

Parent/guardian: _____ Telephone: _____

II. Medical information (to be filled out by parent/guardian and/or doctor)

A. Nature of disability (If your child does not have a disability, skip to B.)

What type of disability(ies) does the child have: _____

_____

_____

Please describe in more detail the characteristics of the child's disability(ies): _____

_____

_____

Is there anything I should be aware of in physical education? _____

_____

_____

B. Specific health conditions (If your child does not have any health conditions, skip to C.)

Asthma _____ yes _____ no

If you answered yes, is there an inhaler at school? _____ yes _____ no

If you answered yes, where is it located? _____

Bee sting allergies _____ yes _____ no

If you answered yes, is there a bee sting kit at school? _____ yes _____ no

If you answered yes, where is it located? _____

Diabetes _____ yes _____ no

If you answered yes, does your child take insulin? _____ yes _____ no

If you answered yes, where is it located? _____

Heart problems _____ yes _____ no

If you answered yes, please explain in more detail.

_____

_____

Other health conditions

Are there any other health conditions we should be aware of?

_____

_____

_____

(page 1 of 3)

Figure 18.1. Physical education information form. (*Sources:* Fairfax County Public Schools, 1994; Kelly & Wessel, 1986; Markos & Jenkins, 1994.)

Figure 18.1. *(continued)*

Physical Education Information Form

C. Medications

Does your child take any medications? _____ yes _____ no

If you answered yes, what are the names of the medications, and what are they used for?

_____

_____

_____

_____

When are the medications administered? _____

_____

_____

_____

Do they have any effects on physical/motor performance? _____

_____

_____

Are there any specific concerns regarding medications that I should be aware of in physical education including any activities that the child should not do? _____

_____

_____

III. PE activities that may be inappropriate (to be filled out by parent, physical therapist, and/or doctor)

Some activities can be dangerous for children with particular disabilities. Please place an X next to any activity that you have concerns about and explain why, along with any accommodations that would allow the student to participate safely in the activity.

ELEMENTARY SCHOOL (K-5)

Locomotor skills	Manipulative skills	Body management	Fitness
Running	Throwing	Twisting	Continuous running
Jumping	Catching	Turning	Sprinting
Galloping	Striking	Stretching	Stretching
Hopping	Kicking		Push-ups/pull-ups
Skipping	Dribbling (with feet)		Sit-ups
Bouncing			Rope climbing
			Aerobic dance
			Weight lifting
			Stationary bike

Tumbling	Games	Water activities
Balance beam	Chasing/fleeing	Getting wet
Log roll	Dodging	Standing in water
Forward roll	Tag	Floating
Backward roll	Racing	Basic strokes
Head/hand stand	Team sports	Lap swimming
Vaulting	Skating	Diving
Pyramids	Jumping rope	
Rope climbing		

(page 2 of 3)

(continued)

Figure 18.1. *(continued)*

Physical Education Information Form

MIDDLE/HIGH SCHOOL

Team sports	**Individual sports**	**Gymnastics**	**Dance**
Basketball	Golf	Rings	Aerobic
Softball	Tennis	High bar	Square
Volleyball	Archery	Parallel bars	Folk
Soccer	Bowling	Vault	Modern
Flag football	Badminton	Floor exercise	
Floor hockey	Wrestling		
Lacrosse			

Comments on activities that you have concerns about for this student:

_____
_____
_____
_____
_____
_____
_____
_____
_____
_____
_____
_____
_____
_____
_____
_____

Name(s) of person(s) who filled out this form and their relationship to the child:

_____
_____
_____
_____

Signature: _____ Date: _____

Signature: _____ Date: _____

Signature: _____ Date: _____

Signature: _____ Date: _____

(page 3 of 3)

Safety Inventory

Child's name: _____ Date of birth: _____

Person filling out this form: _____

Relationship to child: _____

Does the child have specific problems in space awareness? _____ yes _____ no

Activities that might be affected _____

Possible solutions/modifications _____

Does the child have specific problems with body awareness? _____ yes _____ no

Activities that might be affected _____

Possible solutions/modifications _____

Does the child have specific problems with upper body strength? _____ yes _____ no

Activities that might be affected _____

Possible solutions/modifications _____

Does the child have specific problems with lower body strength? _____ yes _____ no

Activities that might be affected _____

Possible solutions/modifications _____

Does the child have specific problems with endurance? _____ yes _____ no

Activities that might be affected _____

Possible solutions/modifications _____

Does the child have specific problems with flexibility? _____ yes _____ no

Activities that might be affected _____

Possible solutions/modifications _____

Does the child have specific problems with speed? _____ yes _____ no

Activities that might be affected _____

Possible solutions/modifications _____

Does the child have specific problems with eye-hand coordination? _____ yes _____ no

Activities that might be affected _____

Possible solutions/modifications _____

Does the child have specific problems with balance? _____ yes _____ no

Activities that might be affected _____

Possible solutions/modifications _____

Figure 18.2.   Safety inventory.

therapists, and teacher assistants. For example, the general and special educator can note behaviors that could create safety problems (e.g., aggressive behaviors, tendency to run away), and the speech therapist can note how much verbal information the child understands. Figure 18.3 provides questions to guide you when meeting with these professionals.

CREATING A SAFE TEACHING ENVIRONMENT

Making the general physical education environment safe for students with disabilities is very similar to recommended practices in making physical education safe for all students.

Space

First and foremost, the general physical educator should consider the amount of teaching space available. The area in which students will be working should allow for movements that are free from restrictions (Graham, Holt-Hale, & Parker, 2013). This is particularly true for students with intellectual disabilities or learning disabilities who may not be very aware of their personal space. For example, if a student with intellectual disabilities is working on striking with a bat, there should be enough space to freely swing the bat without harming peers. If a child who uses a wheelchair is involved in a warm-up activity such as a chasing and fleeing game, extra space may be needed to ensure safety. An example from an actual case involved a 16-year-old student with quadriplegia (Aufsesser, 2003). This student (who used an electric wheelchair) was playing basketball in a general physical education class. One of the students without disabilities was hurt when he ran into the wheelchair. As a result, the student using the wheelchair was removed from the general physical education class. This error in lack of safety precautions relative to spatial relations created an unfortunate, yet preventable, circumstance for all those involved.

Boundaries and Equipment Setup

The teaching environment should have boundaries that separate activity and hazardous areas. You may need to highlight boundaries for children with low vision, perceptual motor concerns, or attention-deficit/hyperactivity disorder (ADHD). Students with visual impairments might benefit from brightly colored cones or tape (Lieberman, Ponchillia, & Ponchillia, 2013). Peers can provide extra physical assistance and verbal cues to students with autism, visual impairments, or intellectual disabilities who may not be aware of safe boundaries (Klavina & Block, 2013).

Working space should be organized to ensure safe participation. One of the easiest yet most effective safety measures is to keep extraneous equipment out of the activity area. Large equipment such as volleyball standards and gymnastics equipment should be placed off to the side of the activity area. Smaller equipment to be used that day should be kept out of the way until needed. Although this may be a little inconvenient, it will make the environment much safer for all children.

Unique Environment Considerations

Some students present unique concerns in terms of creating a safe environment. For example, it is necessary to familiarize students who have visual impairments with the surroundings. This includes identifying where equipment is set up; where boundaries are; and where extraneous equipment such as chairs, tables, water fountains, steps, and ramps are (Lieberman et al., 2013). Similarly, it will be necessary for students who use walkers or wheelchairs to have an uncluttered environment through which to move (Auxter, Pyfer, Zittel, & Roth, 2010). As noted, extraneous equipment should be off to the side until needed. Finally, for students with asthma or other respiratory disorders, the teaching environment should be well ventilated and the temperature set at a comfortable level. In addition, the gym should be as dust-free as possible. Request that ductwork and support beams be cleaned annually. Finally, you may need to allow students who are sensitive to pollen to stay inside during days when the pollen count is high.

Adapted Equipment

Equipment should accommodate the unique movement needs of each student. This can be accomplished by varying the size, weight, and texture of catching and throwing objects, striking implements, and other manipulative equipment. For example, a catching station should have balls ranging in size from small to large, light to heavy, and foam to rubber. At a striking station, balloons may be more appropriate for children with limited object control skills; beep balls would assist children who are blind. In addition, peers need to be sensitive to the motor skills of classmates with disabilities by varying such components as speed, distance, and force. For example, when tossing a ball to a partner

Communication, Behaviors, and Reinforcement Inventory

Child's name: _____ Date of birth: _____

Person filling out this form: _____

Relationship to child: _____

Communication skills

1. Does the child understand simple verbal directions? _____ yes _____ no

2. If no, do you have suggestions to facilitate communication? _____

_____

_____

3. Can the child convey his or her wishes and/or needs? _____ yes _____ no

4. If no, do you have any suggestions regarding how I might know what the student wants or needs?

_____

_____

Behaviors

1. Does the child understand simple rules of games? _____ yes _____ no

2. If no, do you have suggestions to help the student play safely? _____

_____

3. How does the child handle conflicts, such as being on the losing team?

_____

_____

4. Is the child ever aggressive? _____ yes _____ no

5. If yes, what do you do when this happens? _____

_____

6. Does the child have a hard time paying attention and staying on task? _____ yes _____ no

7. If yes, what do you do when this happens? _____

_____

Reinforcers

1. What activities, objects, and/or people does the child like?

_____

_____

2. What activities, objects, and/or people does the child dislike?

_____

_____

Figure 18.3. Communication, behaviors, and reinforcement inventory.

with intellectual disabilities and limited catching skills, students should use light force and stand closer to the catcher.

When adapting equipment, it also is important to consider the developmental level of the student with disabilities. Just as it would be unsafe for kindergartners to practice striking using regulation-size tennis rackets, it would be unsafe for a student with Down syndrome who has small hands to use a regulation-size softball bat when striking. Instead, he or she should strike with his or her hand and then progress to small, light foam paddles. Grips of such implements may also need to be altered for some children. If you are not sure how the child is supposed to use special equipment, whether special equipment is fitted properly, or whether special equipment is in good repair, consult with the child's physical/occupational therapist, special education teacher, or parent (Canadian Association of Health, Physical Education, and Recreation [CAHPER], 1994).

Teaching How to Use Equipment Properly

Perhaps the greatest concern for students with disabilities, particularly students with intellectual disabilities and emotional disturbance, is teaching safe and appropriate use of equipment. For example, some children with intellectual disabilities may not be aware of safe ways to use physical education equipment, such as looking around before swinging a golf club or a racket. Children with behavior problems may exhibit inappropriate behavior with equipment, such as using improper force when throwing balls to peers. Children with ADHD may be so impulsive with equipment that they do not take the time to think of the consequences of their actions. Similarly, a child with autism who sees a brightly colored cage ball may run and try to jump on the ball, not realizing that his forceful action is going to cause the ball to slide across the gym floor, resulting in the student falling and banging his chin on the floor. In all the cases described, it is important to teach these students how to use equipment safely.

SAFE TEACHING TECHNIQUES

Quality physical education presumes that general techniques regarding safety are common practice among physical educators. Teachers have a responsibility for providing appropriate instruction, proper supervision, and conducting activities in a safe manner (Nichols, 2001; Pangrazi & Beighle, 2015).

Establish Safety Rules

The first safe teaching technique is to establish and review safety rules with the class. Although you do not need to have hundreds of safety rules and regulations, it is important to establish a few critical safety rules such as establishing stop/start signals, maintaining good personal space, adhering to set boundaries, avoiding equipment that is off limits, and encouraging safe use of equipment. These rules should be posted in a visible place and reviewed frequently with all students. Focus special attention on students with intellectual disabilities, ADHD, or emotional disturbance who may tend to forget or ignore these rules. In addition, frequently remind other students to move cautiously around students who use wheelchairs or walkers or who are blind.

Supervision

Because physical educators are legally responsible for everything that goes on in the physical education setting, it is imperative that they observe all that is going on in the class, particularly when students with disabilities are included. Observing the entire class involves establishing a position such as the "back-to-the-wall" technique and scanning, which allows you to see all students at all times (Graham et al., 2013). Halsey (2012) noted that the level of supervision provided to a specific child depends on that child's ability to understand the dangers of the activity, judge his or her skill level as it relates to the activity, and follow the established safety procedures related to the activity. This is particularly important for children with intellectual disabilities or autism. For example, a child with autism can participate in a golf unit in high school, but extra supervision is needed to help this student understand the dangers of swinging golf clubs. In such a situation, a peer, community volunteer, or even teacher assistant could be used to ensure the safe participation of this student in this activity.

Also, always be aware of children who have impulsive tendencies, children who can be aggressive, and children who wander away. When possible, place these students close to you. If this is not possible, utilize peers, community volunteers, or teacher assistants. When opting to utilize peers or aides, provide them specific precautions and outline their responsibilities in assisting the child (Klavina & Block, 2013).

Delivery of Instructional Cues

Proper instruction is an important part of creating a safe physical education program (Halsey, 2012).

The delivery of instructional cues should be provided in such a manner that everyone understands directions and safety cues. Do not assume that all students in your class understand verbal cues. For example, children who have hearing impairments may need visual aids such as demonstrations or pictures to understand complex directions. Children with intellectual disabilities or autism or children who are blind may need physical assistance. Even children with relatively mild disabilities such as specific learning disabilities may benefit from extra demonstrations. If students do not understand directions and safety cues, there is a greater chance of injury.

Another factor in the delivery of instructional cues involves positioning children. Children with visual impairments who have some residual vision might benefit from demonstrations if they are positioned at the front of the class. Similarly, children with hearing impairments should be positioned so that they can read lips and have a better vantage point for picking up visual cues. Finally, children with ADHD, emotional disturbance, or autism should be positioned away from antagonizing peers, extraneous equipment, and markings on the floor. Children who are prone to physically attacking peers (e.g., biting, hitting, scratching) should be positioned close to you.

Warm-Up

One of the most important teaching techniques in preparing students for physical activity is a warm-up activity. For students with disabilities, this is particularly important. For example, a student with cerebral palsy needs to stretch hamstrings and groin muscles prior to walking with a walker during a movement exploration activity. Similarly, children with autism often need to experience repetition in warm-ups before they can be expected to participate in new activities.

Although most students with disabilities can participate in the same warm-up activities as their peers, some students might need special warm-up activities. For example, the student with cerebral palsy might need to work on special leg stretches designed by the physical therapist and carried out by a teacher assistant while peers work on different stretches. Similarly, children with limited strength can be allowed to do modified sit-ups and push-ups, and children with asthma can be allowed to alternate between walking and running laps. Such individualization can be implemented with minimal disruption to your regular program.

Activities

It is important to plan activities that are progressive in nature (Halsey, 2012). When activities are progressive, injuries can be avoided (CAHPER, 1994; Pangrazi & Beighle, 2015). To illustrate, consider a student with low muscle tone who is working on handstands. This student could receive a serious injury because he or she is not ready to support total body weight on his or her hands. Instead, there should be various levels of weight transfer at this station that eventually lead to a handstand. This student may simply need to work on transferring weight from feet to hands before focusing on an actual handstand.

Many unsafe practices can be avoided with careful planning that allows for the foreseeability of accidents (Gray, 1995; Grosse, 1990; Pangrazi & Beighle, 2015). For example, extra precautions should be taken from the start when planning high-risk activities such as gymnastics, aquatics, or the rope climb. To illustrate, during an aquatics session, the teacher can arrange for peers to assist students who use walkers and might need extra help walking around the pool area. At the same time, a student with a seizure disorder may need a "buddy" in case the student has a seizure while in the water. In tumbling or gymnastics, students with ADHD, autism, or intellectual disabilities may not be aware of the inherent risks of using the equipment without supervision. A child might run over and try to swing on the uneven bars or try to climb on the rope unsupervised. When you have children with impulsive behaviors, you should constantly review safety rules with them, assign peers to assist in preventing them from inappropriate use of the equipment, and in extreme cases, assign a teacher assistant to the student. In all cases, each student's unique characteristics must be considered (CAHPER, 1994).

Attitude

Safe teaching techniques include having a positive attitude toward teaching children with disabilities. This involves serving as a role model for students without disabilities on how to interact with, assist, and befriend students with disabilities. Peers can be a tremendous resource in terms of making the environment safe, but peers will not know what to do unless you show them by example. Although safety should be of utmost concern, care should be taken to not be overly protective. All students should be allowed certain experiences without the hindrance of exorbitant safety concerns (CAHPER, 1994). For example, children who use wheelchairs often are excluded from team sports such as basketball and soccer. Although participation in such activities can pose a risk to the student in the wheelchair as well as peers, with proper modifications and careful review of safety rules, many of these children can participate safely in team sports. An excellent way to illustrate how modifications to team sports might work is to invite an athlete from the community who participates in wheelchair sports such as wheelchair basketball to come speak to students (McKay, 2013a).

CONTENT

One of the biggest misconceptions with inclusion is that students with disabilities have to follow the same content at the same level as their peers without disabilities. Actually, all students should be presented with physical activities that are individualized to meet their unique needs. In some cases, these needs can be met by following the general curriculum with simple modifications; in other cases, an alternative curriculum will need to be followed. In either case, forcing a child with or without a disability to participate in an activity that he or she is not physically, mentally, and/or emotionally ready for can lead to injury. Therefore, it is important to determine if the content that you present is appropriate for the student's abilities and, if not appropriate, determine what adjustments (or alternatives) will be needed to ensure safe participation in physical education.

SPECIFIC DISABILITIES AND SAFE ACTIVITIES

It is important to remember that physical activity is often recommended in treating a variety of conditions. Because the benefits of exercise are numerous, worries about safety issues should not be a reason to keep students with disabilities from participating in general physical education. To illustrate, an increased awareness of diabetes and new ways to manage it in children have resulted in increased participation in physical activity (U.S. Department of Health and Human Services, 2010b). Implications of this for the safety-conscious physical educator include allowing a student to check blood glucose levels, recognizing changes in a student's behavior that could be related to changes in blood glucose, creating an action plan in the event of a hypoglycemic or hyperglycemic episode, and providing access to a fast-acting form of glucose by taping it to a clipboard when participating in outdoor activities. Such solutions can assist a child with diabetes in participating safely in a variety of activities that require any type of energy output.

The job of the physical educator is to encourage physical activity and participation in sports for all students, with safety for all as the utmost concern.

Emergency Procedures

Make sure you have an emergency plan in place and that all staff are familiar with and have practiced this plan in the unlikely event of an injury (Clements, 2000; Halsey, 2012; see Table 18.1). First and foremost, you should know CPR and first aid

Table 18.1.   Emergency procedures: Action plan

Preparation

1. Identify kinds of injuries, emergencies, and health incidents that might occur.
2. Learn emergency care for each of these incidents.
3. Create an incident surveillance system to track all incidents for a particular student, for the facility, or for the program.
4. Examine medical information and talk to parents and other professionals for clues to possible medical situations for particular students with disabilities.

Plan

1. Create a written emergency action plan.
2. The plan should include, but not be limited to, the identification of the injured person, recognition of injury or medical need, initiation of first aid, and the obtaining of professional help.
3. Detailed protocols for seeking assistance and talking with medical personnel should be posted in appropriate places.

Learn and rehearse

1. Each employee and classmate knows his or her role in the emergency plan.
2. First aid, rescue, and emergency equipment are adequate, routinely checked, and ready for use.
3. Staff members know how to use all equipment.
4. The system has been created with input from community emergency medical crews.
5. The plan is rehearsed with the staff and with community emergency medical crews. Approximate times required to reach a facility are determined by each of these agencies.
6. Rehearsals are conducted periodically and whenever new staff are employed.
7. Records of all practice and those involved are prepared and retained.

Follow-up

1. Follow-up procedures for seriously injured persons exist and are used.
2. Parents are notified in a uniform fashion.
3. A means of working with the media exists and is used.
4. The entire system is known by all, rehearsed often, and periodically monitored for flaws.
5. Legal counsel and insurance representatives are invited to review the entire system.

From Clements, A. (2000, March). *Emergency action plans.* Paper presented at the American Alliance for Health, Physical Education, Recreation and Dance, Orlando, FL.

(Halsey, 2012; Hawkins, 2012; Pangrazi & Beighle, 2015). In addition, familiarize yourself with universal precautions for handling blood (Bailey, 2012; Brown & Richter, 1994). Rubber gloves, gauze, and other essentials should be placed into a first-aid kit and readily available. Also, fill an ice cooler with ice and bags each morning. The school nurse and the child's parents can help formulate special emergency procedures. For example, there may be a special way to handle a student who has a particular type of seizure disorder. If your school does not have a school nurse, have a plan in place for emergencies such as contacting a rescue squad or doctor's office that is close to the school.

Have emergency cards on all students. In addition, notations can be made on your roll book to signify students who have medical problems such as asthma, diabetes, seizures, and allergies. For example, a child who is stung by a bee might be allergic to bee stings. By noting this allergy on an emergency card or in your roll book, you will know right away to immediately contact the nurse for assistance. Similarly, you may be more sensitive to a child who you know has asthma and is wheezing after a tag activity.

You will need to establish special emergency plans for some children with health problems or disabilities such as a plan for removing children who are in wheelchairs from the gymnasium in the event of a fire or other emergency. Children with health problems may need to bring emergency materials to physical education to be prepared in the event of an emergency. For example, children who are prone to asthma attacks should bring an inhaler with them to physical education, and orange juice and insulin should be available for children with diabetes. Although you may not feel comfortable with medical procedures such as giving insulin,

you should have these materials available when qualified personnel arrive. Finally, notify the office in the event of a medical emergency or injury, and complete a student accident report immediately (see Pangrazi & Beighle, 2015).

SUMMARY

Safety is the most important part of any quality physical education programming. Physical educators should follow safety procedures and conduct safe physical education programs for all children who enter their gymnasium. Inclusion of children with disabilities heightens awareness of safety issues, but rarely does it result in major changes to physical education programs. However, there are some things that should be examined to ensure the safety of children with disabilities in general physical education. When children with disabilities are included in general physical education, find out as much as possible about each child, including medical and health information, motor and fitness skills, and learning and behavioral characteristics. Carefully examine the physical education environment as well as the equipment that you use to make sure it safely meets the needs of students with disabilities. Critique your classroom management techniques, teaching practices, and content that you plan on presenting to the class to ensure that they match the learning style and individualized goals of students with disabilities. Finally, have an emergency plan in place, including special plans for children with unique health concerns. Safety concerns should be addressed, and necessary modifications, including the use of support personnel, should be implemented. However, safety should not be the sole reason for excluding students with disabilities from general physical education.

CHAPTER 19

Positive Behavior Support of Children with Challenging Behaviors

Martin E. Block, Hester Henderson, and Barry Lavay

OBJECTIVES

1. Understand major types of behavior problems

2. Explain laws related to behavior problems and discipline

3. Define two major approaches to treatment

4. Describe the ABC approach to behavior management

5. Demonstrate the ability to create a functional, positive behavior plan

6. Explain differences between positive and negative reinforcement

7. Explain punishment and what and when mild forms of punishment (e.g., time-out) are appropriate

---

Mrs. McCray, a seventh-grade physical education teacher, has had her share of students with behavior problems. She was always able to handle them until she met James and Mike Jones, twins who have severe behavior problems. Both repeated kindergarten and third grade and were much older than their seventh-grade peers. They were suspended multiple times in elementary and middle school, mostly for fighting and vandalism. In addition, both have had run-ins with the law: James for stealing a car and taking it for a ride and Mike for trying to steal CDs and clothes from a local Walmart. James and

Mike have been labeled as emotionally disturbed, with a secondary diagnosis of attention-deficit/hyperactivity disorder (ADHD). Both are taking medication for their ADHD.

Last year in sixth grade, it did not take long for the boys to begin to cause problems in Mrs. McCray's sixth-grade physical education class. First, neither boy brought his gym uniform for the first 2 weeks of school, so they both had to sit out and watch. Rather than just sit, they constantly talked to each other or yelled and teased their peers. Mrs. McCray tried to ignore this behavior, but the boys became louder and more aggressive. Mrs. McCray then warned the boys that they would have to go to the office if they continued to disrupt her class; this warning did not seem to help. She eventually sent the boys to the office, but they returned the next day unfazed. Once the boys remembered to bring their uniforms, they continued to bully their peers by yelling at them and pushing them. Mrs. McCray put the boys in time-out and again threatened to send them to the office. This resulted in a fair amount of cursing and posturing at Mrs. McCray. She was not one to be intimidated by a couple of middle school boys and again sent them to the office. The next day, they were back and doing their best to disrupt the class, threaten classmates, and taunt Mrs. McCray.

Mrs. McCray thought that something was going on with Mike and James that might be contributing to their acting out. Perhaps someone at home or at school was triggering these bullying behaviors. Could the boys be embarrassed by the fact that they are both overweight, have low levels of fitness, and have difficulty performing motor skills? Maybe they never learned how to appropriately make friends and socialize with peers. Whatever the cause, Mrs. McCray felt that traditional behavior management techniques such as time-out, being sent to the office, and suspension were not effective and did not address the cause of the boys' problem. Mrs. McCray, in a quest to understand these boys and develop and implement a behavior program, arranged to meet with the special education teacher.

The importance of teachers effectively and efficiently managing student behaviors and improving performance and learning is obvious. Without these skills, instruction and learning are difficult. A chaotic class results in physical educators spending more time dealing with inappropriate behavior and less time on instruction and student practice. Because of this, teachers consistently mention behavior management as an area in which they need more training (Lavay, French, & Henderson, 2007a; Lavay, Henderson, French, & Guthrie, 2012; Maag, 2001). This is particularly true when general physical educators teach in an inclusive environment (Lavay, French, & Henderson, 2007b). More and more students with emotional or behavioral disorders, traumatic brain injuries, ADHD, or autism spectrum disorder are being placed in general physical education settings. Although not all students with these diagnoses will demonstrate behavior problems, they do tend to display behaviors that can make teaching physical education difficult and their behaviors can negatively influence the learning environment for all students (Lavay et al., 2007b; Smith & Rivera, 1995). See Table 19.1 for a list of common disabilities and their related behaviors.

HISTORY OF APPROACHES

Unfortunately, physical educators who are just starting out may lack the knowledge and skill to manage students' behaviors in such heterogeneous classes. Even veteran physical educators who are competent in employing a variety of techniques to manage student behavior may need to go beyond traditional behavioral techniques. They are being asked to move toward positive approaches that teach students new self-management skills. There are several approaches to managing student behavior, but the psychodynamic approach and behavior modification have been the most widely used in educational settings.

With the *humanistic or psychodynamic approach*, the focus is on the psychotherapeutic or underlying reasons the behavior is or is not being demonstrated (Hellison, 2011; Watson & Clocksin, 2013). It is assumed in this approach that most behavior problems are a result of an unconscious motivation (i.e., power, attention). The approach is student centered and facilitates a strong connection through communication between the teacher and student. This approach has been used successfully for many years by Hellison and colleagues in variety of physical activity settings and with different

Table 19.1.   Common disabilities and related behaviors that can affect learning

- *Attention-deficit/hyperactivity/disorder (ADHD)* is made up of three subtypes. First subtype is Predominantly Inattentive. Students have difficulty sustaining physical or motor tasks and often appear to be daydreaming or not listening. The second subtype is Predominantly Hyperactive-Impulsive, in which students demonstrate the inability to stay on their attendance spot, are not able to wait for their turn, or blurt out answers or questions when the physical educator is giving instructions. The third subtype is the Combined Type. In all three types, students have chronic problems in internally regulating their attention, impulses, and activity level.

- *Autism spectrum disorder (pervasive developmental disorder)* is a disability noted by problems with social interacting, language used in social interaction, play skills, repetition, or stereotyped patterns of behavior. Common characteristics of students with this disorder include making inappropriate sounds, making inappropriate gestures, having inappropriate affect (e.g., laughing when no one else is laughing), being withdrawn, being anxious in new and different situations, and running away.

- *Emotional (behavioral) disorder* is a condition involving one or more of the following behaviors over a long period of time, which must adversely affect educational performance: (a) inability to learn, which cannot be explained by intellectual, sensory, or health factors; (b) inability to build or maintain satisfactory interpersonal relationships; and (c) demonstrating inappropriate behavior or feelings, such as a general pervasive mood of unhappiness or depression or a tendency to develop physical symptoms or fears. Common characteristics for students with this disorder vary widely based on the specific type of emotional disability, ranging from juvenile delinquency, depression, obsessive-compulsive disorder, eating disorders, and bipolar disorders.

- *Intellectual disabilities* refers to substantial limitations in personal capabilities manifested as significantly subaverage intellectual functioning occurring with significant deficits in adaptive behavior (e.g., self-help skills, communication, working, academics). Common characteristics of students with intellectual disabilities vary based on the specific cause and level of functioning. For example, many students with fetal alcohol syndrome are impulsive and hyperactive, while students with Down syndrome tend to have trouble understanding and following complex directions.

- *Traumatic brain injury* refers to a permanent damage caused by concussion, contusion, or hemorrhage. In many cases, this condition may cause severe impairments in perception, emotion, cognition, and motor function. Again, common characteristics vary widely based on the extent and location of the brain injury.

populations. Techniques such as character education, teaching personal and social responsibility, the talking bench, and self-talk are just some techniques used within this humanistic approach (Glover & Anderson, 2003; Hellison, 2011; Lavay, French, & Henderson, 2016; Watson & Clocksin, 2013).

In *behavior modification*, the focus is on what in the environment is causing the behavior to occur or not occur. This approach is based on the principle of operant conditioning that is often referred to as the ABC paradigm. In this paradigm, there is a stimulus or antecedent (A) that precedes the behavior (B), which is followed by a positive and/or negative consequence (C) that results in an increase or decrease of the behavior (Lavay et al., 2016). Physical educators who use this approach generally manipulate the events that occur just before (A) or after (C) the behavior is exhibited in hopes of increasing appropriate behaviors or preventing or decreasing inappropriate behaviors (B). The consequences can be reinforcement of appropriate behavior or ignoring/punishment of inappropriate behaviors.

Leveling systems offer a way to overlap traditional behavior modification with the humanistic approach within physical activity environments (Hellison, 2011; Lavay et al., 2016). Hellison's model presents five levels of personal and social responsibility. Students are placed on one of a series of clearly defined steps based on their present level of performance. Moving up a step is contingent on reaching specific, observable behaviors, goals, and objectives based on the specified criteria. In Levels 1–3, the focus is personal responsibility, and in Levels 4 and 5, the focus is more on social responsibility:

Beginning Levels 1, 2, and 3 (Personal Responsibility)

Level 1—Respecting the rights and feelings of others: Individuals maintain self-control and do not let their lack of control affect the learning of others.

Level 2—Effort and cooperation: Individuals are self-motivated to participate. They explore and try new tasks. They get along and maintain respect for others.

Level 3—Self-direction: Individuals are given responsibility to work independently. They set goals with progressions and work on them without supervision.

Advanced Levels 4 and 5 (Social Responsibility)

Level 4—Helping others and leadership: Individuals act with care and compassion. They are sensitive and responsive to the well-being of others.

Level 5—Transfer outside the gym: Individuals take their sense of personal and social responsibility (Levels 1–4) and apply these ideas in other areas of life, practicing them at home, on the playground, and in the community.

It is important to note that Hellison's levels are meant to be guidelines and are to be adjusted to specific teaching situations. It is not a cookbook approach in which "one size fits all." Although this model is based on the humanistic approach, it also uses techniques such as time-out and the Premack principle, which are integral components of the traditional behavior modification approach. The Premack principle recommends making a high-frequency behavior contingent on completing a low-frequency behavior. For instance, a student does not like to participate in the warm-up jogging activity (low frequency or less preferred). He does love to play basketball (high frequency or more preferred). If the student jogs during the warm-ups for a week, he earns the privilege to play 5 minutes of basketball.

Historically, the behavior modification approach has been the most widely used in both general and adapted physical education environments. This is clearly reflected by the amount of information focused on behavior modification in textbooks regarding elementary (Hastie & Martin, 2006; Pangrazi & Beighle, 2015), secondary (Darst, Pangrazi, Sariscsany, & Brusseau, 2012), and adapted physical education (Hodge, Lieberman, & Murata, 2012; Loovis, 2011; Seaman, DePauw, Morton, & Omoto, 2007). The trend is to use behavior modification along with other approaches, particularly the humanistic approach. For instance, Bambara, Janney, and Snell (2015) stated that there needs to be a movement away from traditional behavior practices and toward behavior interventions grounded in person-centered values such as the following:

- To develop respect and trust among students, teachers, staff, and parents

- To provide suitable opportunities for students, whenever appropriate, to interact with their peers not only in the school but also in the community environment

- To focus on prevention or the reduction of situations that could involve failure and increase situations that involve success

- To focus on the instruction of communication and social interaction skills

- To eliminate the "one-size-fits-all approach" and emphasize the development of individualized support for students that is positive

Positive behavior support (PBS) continues to be an effective, evidence-based intervention for use in numerous settings with people of any age (Bambara et al., 2015; Buchanon, Hinton, & Rudisill, 2013; Crone, Hawken, & Horner, 2015; Hellison, 2011; Hodge et al., 2012; Lavay et al., 2016). PBS combines some behavior modification techniques such as analyzing what might be causing an inappropriate behavior and creating a plan to prevent the behavior from occurring with the humanistic approach of determining why a child displays a behavior, teaching more appropriate ways to interact with the environment, and teaching the child to self-manage his or her behavior.

A POSITIVE APPROACH TO BEHAVIOR MANAGEMENT

As noted earlier, traditional approaches to dealing with unwanted behaviors focused on eliminating behaviors by using negative consequences without concern for why the behavior occurred. For example, after physical education class, a child with autism hits a classmate while waiting in line to get a drink of water. As a result, the child is sent to time-out and told "no hitting." In contrast, the PBS approach seeks to understand the underlying cause (i.e., triggers) and purpose of the behavior, tries to create an environment to prevent triggers, and then teaches the child alternative, more appropriate behaviors (Bambara et al., 2015; Positive Behavioral Interventions and Support, 2015; Scheuermann & Hall, 2012). In the previous example, the child might be sensitive to touch and close spaces, and waiting in line being bumped by peers makes the child feel uncomfortable and anxious. Due to the child's limited language, he cannot tell his peers to give him some space, and his way of communicating his discomfort is to hit his peers. A teacher engaged in PBS might quickly see the situation and take the child out of line and assist the child in touching a picture on a "feelings board" expressing "anxious" and "need a break." Then the child is allowed to walk to a different water fountain to get a drink. The teacher knows to make sure the child has more space when waiting or even step out of line to wait to prevent the behavior. She also knows to give the child the "feelings board" when waiting in line and to practice and teach the child to use the board when he feels anxious.

Clearly, PBS is designed to not only eliminate unwanted behaviors but also prevent unwanted

behaviors, teach more appropriate behaviors, and respond to unwanted behaviors in a more positive approach. PBS has been recommended as the most effective, most appropriate, and most ethical behavioral model for children with challenging behaviors (Bambara et al., 2015; Crone et al., 2015; Positive Behavioral Interventions and Support, 2015).

PBS emphasizes collaborative problem solving, prevention through effective educational programs, teaching students more appropriate alternative behaviors, and supporting the student through systematic planning rather than trial and error. When using PBS, the use of reinforcement to strengthen behaviors and punishment to reduce behaviors play a smaller part than in more traditional behavioral management approaches (Bambara et al, 2015; Jackson & Panyan, 2001; Positive Behavioral Interventions and Support, 2015).

Goals of PBS include helping students develop new communication, social, and self-control skills; form more positive relationships with classmates, teachers, and community members; and take a more active role in their classrooms, schools, and communities. The success of PBS is judged not only by whether a target behavior has been reduced but also by whether students have learned new skills and ways to control their behaviors so that their lifestyle has been improved (Bambara et al., 2015; Bambara & Knoster, 2009; Crone et al., 2015).

As the name suggests, the heart of the model is the provision of positive behavior supports that prevent students from displaying unwanted behavior and teach them new, more appropriate behaviors. These supports can include the following (Bambara et al., 2015; Bambara & Knoster, 2009; Crone et al., 2015):

- Individualized education program (IEP) accommodations (e.g., place to calm down, additional adult supervision during transitions, extending time for completing tasks)

- Curricular adaptations (e.g., simplified curriculum or one that emphasizes functional skills)

- Instruction in social skills or self-management techniques, changes to the classroom environment (e.g., preferential seating, a quiet place to study or read), scheduling changes (e.g., placement in classes with particular peers, placement in heterogeneous classes, alternating between easy and difficult subjects or courses)

- More assistance in doing an assignment or task and the support of peer buddies, partners, or tutors

Another important aspect of PBS is the recognition that all behaviors serve a purpose. These purposes include social-communication functions such as getting attention, escape or avoidance, or getting something tangible and sensory functions such as self-regulation and play or entertainment (Bambara et al., 2015; Jackson & Panyan, 2001).

The following, modified from Bambara et al. (2015), outlines the key components of developing a behavior plan using the PBS model: 1) identify a behavior, 2) examine antecedents for possible causes, 3) examine possible functions of behavior, 4) explore the consequences, 5) consider simple alternatives that might prevent/reduce the behavior, and 6) create the behavior plan (see Table 19.2). It is important that each step in the PBS model be followed in order to develop the most appropriate and effective plan possible.

Table 19.2.   Creating a behavior plan

1. *Identify the behavior in objective, measurable terms.*
   a. Describe what the student is doing.
   b. Describe how the student is acting.
   c. Record the behavior.
2. *Examine antecedents for possible causes.*
   a. When does behavior usually occur?
   b. Where does behavior usually occur?
   c. What is usually happening when behavior occurs?
3. *Examine possible functions of behavior.*
   a. Does the student want attention?
   b. Does the student want to be involved?
   c. Is the student angry?
   d. Is the student frustrated?
   e. Is the student in pain or discomfort?
   f. Does the student need help with something?
   g. Other possible reasons
4. *Explore the consequences.*
   a. What happened when the behavior occurred?
   b. When did the consequences take place (immediate/delayed)?
   c. How did the student react to the consequences?
5. *Consider simple alternatives that might prevent/reduce the behavior*
   a. Move student.
   b. Rearrange the environment.
   c. Change the activity.
   d. Give the student a partner.
   e. Regroup the class.
6. *Create the behavior plan.*
   a. Clearly state targeted behavior on measurable terms.
   b. Outline procedures for increasing appropriate behaviors.
   c. Outline procedures for preventing/reducing the behavior.
   d. Outline consequences for dealing with the behavior if it occurs.

Source: Bambara, Janney, & Snell (2015).

Identify the Behavior

Identifying the behavior(s) seems like a simple task. However, all too often physical educators have trouble specifying exactly what behavior is bothersome. Some examples of unhelpful identification and helpful identification of behaviors are the following:

Unhelpful identification	*Helpful identification*
"He is always in my face."	"Every day, when Bill enters the gym, he comes directly to me and wants to know what exactly we will be doing in class."
"He is constantly in motion."	"Reggie cannot stay on his attendance spot on the bench when his team is at bat or while I am explaining an activity for more than 20 consecutive seconds."
"She is destroying my gym."	"Alyssa will come to class and immediately begin to move the equipment at each station for the obstacle course lesson."
"The devil sent this student to torture me."	"Bruno is the class bully. He pushes and hits students in class daily. The students complain about him, and this is occurring more often than I observe."

Certainly conveying emotions is very important, but even more important to determining a behavior plan is identifying the student's actual behavior. The physical educator, with help from other professionals, needs to carefully examine what the student is doing and document the behaviors in measurable, objective terms.

Being able to measure the behavior will allow physical educators to chart progress. There are several common ways to measure behaviors in physical education. If the physical educator can watch the student the entire class period, he or she can use either *frequency recording* or *duration recording*. In frequency recording, the physical educator records the number of times a behavior is exhibited in a given period of time. For example, a physical educator might record how many times a student inappropriately touches other students during a 30-minute class period. In duration recording, a physical educator records how long a behavior is exhibited each time it occurs. For example, a physical educator might record how long a student is off task during physical education class.

If the physical educator cannot watch the student all the time during the class period, he or she can use either *interval recording* or *time sampling*. In interval recording, the physical educator divides the class period into intervals and records either the frequency or duration of a behavior during each interval. For example, during a 60-minute class the teacher would randomly select three 5-minute intervals to observe. The teacher counts either the number of times the behavior occurs (frequency) or the amount of time the behavior occurs (duration) during the 5-minute intervals. The frequency or duration of that behavior then could be predicted for the entire 60-minute class by multiplying by 4 because there were three 5-minute intervals for a total observation of 15 minutes. Sixty minutes divided by 15 equals 4.

Time sampling is used for duration recording when the physical educator is trying to predict the percentage of time the selected behavior occurs during a specified period of time. For example, the physical educator randomly selects a specific number of times to observe the student during the class to determine whether the student is performing the selected behavior or not. If the desired behavior is *participation in the activity*, the physical educator may choose to observe every 2 minutes during the 30-minute class (and look up at those specified times and mark down on a chart if the student is participating or not). Then the number of times the student is participating is divided by the total number of observations to determine the percentage of time the behavior is occurring. So if the student is participating in 8 out of the 15 observations, we can say that the student is participating 53% of the time. Figure 19.1 provides examples of frequency, duration, interval, and time sampling recording.

The type of recording mechanism used needs to be based on the nature of the behavior. Behaviors that occur frequently but for short duration (e.g., touching peers) should be recorded using frequency recording. Behaviors that do not occur frequently but last a long time (e.g., crying) need to be measured using duration recording. When a student cannot be observed during the entire class period, the physical educator can use either interval recording or time sampling. The information gathered during these recording procedures can be used to determine baseline data and, after the intervention is employed, to determine if the behavior intervention used was effective (i.e., increase or reduction in the behavior).

Examine Antecedents for Possible Causes

Once the behavior has been identified, defined, and measured, the next step in the process is to examine what environmental factors might be causing the behavior. Many times, something in the

Event recording: How many times does the student talk back in 30 minutes?

Day	Tally count per day	Total
Day 1	1 1 1 1 1 1 1 1 1 1 1 1 1 1 1 1 1 1 1 1	20
Day 2	1 1 1 1 1 1 1 1 1 1 1 1 1 1 1 1	16
Day 3	1 1 1 1 1 1 1 1 1 1 1 1 1 1 1 1 1	17
Day 4	1 1 1 1 1 1 1 1 1 1 1 1 1 1 1 1 1 1	18

Average: 17.75 occurrences

Duration recording: How long does the student choose to pout in the corner of the gym?

Day	Duration of each episode of pouting			Total time pouting
Day 1	2:00	4:00	1:00	7:00 minutes
Day 2	3:00	3:30		6:30 minutes
Day 3	2:00			2:00 minutes
Day 4	5:00	1:30		6:30 minutes

Average: 5:30 minutes per 30-minute class

Interval recording: How much is the student touching other students?

Day	30 minutes, broken into 2-minute intervals	Number of incidences in interval
Day 1	y n y y y y n y n y n n y n y y	9/15
Day 2	n n y y y y y n y y y n n n y y	9/15
Day 3	y y n n n y y n n n n n n y y	6/15

Average # of intervals per 30 minutes: 8/15

Figure 19.1. Ways to measure behavior in general physical education: Example for a student off task. (From Albemarle County Public Schools. [n.d.]. Functional behavior assessment form 80.01, adapted with permission.)

environment may be triggering the behavior. For example, having to sit and wait while the teacher takes attendance might cause a student with ADHD to get antsy and start talking loudly to peers. Similarly, a student with autism who does not like loud noises might yell and try to scratch and bite his teacher assistant just before the music used for warm-ups is played. In both cases, something in the environment seems to be causing the behavior. Through careful analysis of antecedents surrounding the behavior, the physical educator might be able to detect what is causing the student's inappropriate behaviors. This process is often referred to as a *functional behavior assessment*. An example of a form used to collect data for a functional behavior assessment is provided in Figure 19.2.

Factors to consider in the functional behavioral assessment can be divided into four categories of questions:

1. *Who* is present when the behavior occurs? In other words, are particular adults or peers in the environment triggering the behavior? Is there a particular peer or group of peers that seems to trigger behaviors, or perhaps the behaviors escalate when there is a particular teacher assistant or specialist with the student.

2. *When* does the behavior usually occur? Does the behavior seem to occur more at the beginning, middle, or end of class? Maybe making a transition from the classroom to physical education (beginning of class) or making a transition from physical education to the classroom (end of class) triggers behaviors.

3. *Where* does the behavior usually occur? Is the behavior more likely to appear in the locker room, in the hallway while going to or leaving the gym, in particular parts of the gym, or perhaps more when you are outside with the class?

4. *What* is usually happening when the behavior occurs? Do behaviors appear more or less frequently during warm-ups compared with other parts of the lesson? Does waiting seem to cause an escalation of behaviors? How about making a transition from one activity to another, such as moving to a different station? Does individual game play cause more behaviors compared with partner activities?

Although the cause of behaviors cannot always be determined by analyzing the antecedents in the environment, such an analysis may reveal what may have triggered the student to display certain inappropriate behaviors.

Examine Possible Functions of Behavior

Once the environment has been analyzed for possible causes of the behavior, the next step is to examine why the student might be displaying the behavior—that is, what does the student want or what does the student hope to accomplish by displaying the inappropriate behavior? Rarely does a student display inappropriate behavior without a goal in mind, even if the student does not really understand the goal. For example, a student with autism might suddenly strike out at his teacher assistant or peer for no apparent reason. However, a close examination of antecedents and some guess work by the physical educator reveals that the student is avoiding playing with balloons. Perhaps the student is afraid of the sound of balloons when they pop or of the way they feel. But for whatever reason, the student clearly gets agitated when balloons are mentioned or introduced. Scratching and screaming is how this student communicates his fear of balloons. With this information, the behavior plan might include having the student do a different activity at the other end of the gymnasium when peers are playing with balloons. Other possible reasons a student is displaying inappropriate behavior include the following: attempting to gain attention; wanting to be involved; anger against another student, teacher, or situation; frustration; pain or discomfort; needing help with something; needing to go to the bathroom; and/or not liking the peers he or she has been assigned. As with antecedents, it may not be possible to fully understand why a student is displaying particular behaviors. However, such a functional analysis in many cases will help the physical educator begin to see why some students do what they do.

Explore the Consequences

What happens to the student after he or she displays a behavior is known as a consequence, and determining the effects of the consequence can be as important as analyzing antecedents and functions. Consequences may be the reason the student is displaying the behavior in the first place. For example, a student does not want to participate in physical education during a particular unit so he displays noncompliant behavior and talks back to the teacher, resulting in time-out during physical education. This is what the student wanted all along! Consequences can make the behavior stronger or weaker

Functional Behavior Assessment

Student: _____   School: _____

Disability: _____   Evaluator(s): _____

Today's date: _____   Student's date of birth: _____

This functional behavior assessment is being conducted because (check all that apply):

_____ Student exhibits persistent behavior problem(s) that impedes the learning of peers.

_____ Traditional supports/interventions/consequences have not been effective.

_____ Assessment is in response to disciplinary actions by school personnel.

_____ Alternative services or programs are being considered.

I. Analyze the situation.

1. **What is/are the student's problem behavior(s)?** (Write in measurable terms.)

   _____

   _____

2. **Describe the behavior in detail** (frequency, duration, and level of intensity [distracting, disturbing, or destructive]).

   _____

   _____

3. **What are the student's strengths** (e.g., interests, skill level, support systems)?

   _____

   _____

4. **What seems to trigger the student's behavior(s)?**

   Who? _____

   What? _____

   Where? _____

   When? _____

   Other? _____

5. **What other factors at home or at school appear to adversely influence the student's behaviors?**

   _____

   _____

6. **What happens to the student immediately after he or she engages in the problem behavior(s)?**

   _____

   _____

Figure 19.2.   Functional behavior assessment.

Figure 19.2. *(continued)*

Functional Behavior Assessment

7. **Why might the student be acting this way** (e.g., attention, escape/avoidance, getting something, self-regulation)?

   a. What might he or she get by behaving this way?

   _____

   _____

   _____

   b. What might he or she be avoiding by behaving this way?

   _____

   _____

   _____

   _____

II. Develop a hypothesis statement.

Use this format: When (antecedent event, see Item 4) happens in (specific setting), he or she does (problem behavior, see Item 1) in order to (perceived function, see Item 7).

   _____

   _____

   _____

   _____

III. Develop a plan.

What teaching strategies would you use to teach the student more appropriate, functional behaviors?

   _____

   _____

   _____

   _____

What prevention strategies would you use to keep the student from displaying the targeted behavior?

   _____

   _____

   _____

   _____

In the event the student displays the targeted behavior at a high intensity, how would you respond?

   _____

   _____

   _____

   _____

   _____

(page 2 of 2)

Behavioral Observation Data Sheet

Student's name: _____
Person filling out this form: _____
Date: _____   Student's age: _____
Behavior: how is the student acting? Describe in measurable terms. _____
Examine antecedents: what in the environment might be causing inappropriate behaviors?
When does the behavior usually occur?

_____
_____
_____
_____

Where does the behavior usually occur?

_____
_____
_____
_____

What is usually happening when the behavior occurs?

_____
_____
_____
_____

Who is in the environment when the behavior occurs?

_____
_____
_____
_____

Examine function: what might the student be trying to communicate?
_____ does the student want attention?
_____ does the student want to tell you something?
_____ does the student want a particular piece of equipment?
_____ does the student want to be with a particular friend?
_____ does the student not want to do the activity?
_____ does the student need to go to the bathroom?
_____ does the student want to escape the situation?
_____ is the student angry?
_____ is the student frustrated?
_____ is the student in pain or discomfort?
_____ does the student need help with something?
_____ other possible reasons:

_____
_____

Examine selected negative consequences: check the selected negative consequences, and explain how the student reacted to them.

Consequence	*Reaction*
_____ received angry look	_____
_____ teacher moved closer to student	_____
_____ received verbal warning	_____
_____ received verbal reprimand	_____
_____ told to tell peer he or she was sorry	_____
_____ told to clean up mess	_____
_____ lost equipment privileges	_____
_____ changed partner or group	_____
_____ given a time-out	_____
_____ received physical assistance	_____
_____ was physically restrained	_____
_____ was sent to principal	_____
_____ other	_____

Suggestions for plan: _____
_____
_____
_____

Figure 19.3. Behavioral observation data sheet. (*Source:* Bambara et al., 2015.)

depending on how the student reacts to the consequences. Consider the following three questions when examining potential consequences:

1. What happened immediately after the behavior occurred? For example, a boy who has been known to be mean to other students pulled a girl's hair that resulted in her crying. This made him laugh. Even being verbally reprimanded by the teacher and then sent to time-out was not enough of a deterrent compared with the reinforcement of hearing the girl cry.

2. When was the consequence presented (i.e., was it immediately or delayed)? If a consequence is delayed for too long, the student might forget why he or she is receiving the consequence in the first place.

3. How did the student react to the consequence? Did the student happily gallop off to time-out, or did the student curse and yell at the physical educator? Did the student apologize to the peer whom she pushed, or did she fold her arms and choose to go to time-out? Again, how the student reacts to the consequence that results from the behavior may provide insight as to why the student displayed the behavior in the first place and what consequences will and will not work in the future (see Figure 19.3 for a behavior observation data sheet to collect information).

PROCEDURES TO PREVENT INAPPROPRIATE BEHAVIORS

With information about the behavior, antecedents, possible functional causes, and results of consequences, the physical educator and other team members are ready to discuss ways to prevent inappropriate behaviors. These strategies should be based on the previous analyses of what might trigger the behavior (antecedents), reactions to the behavior (consequences), and the function or purpose of the behavior. The following reviews several strategies that can be used to prevent and respond to unwanted behaviors as well as strategies to teach more appropriate behaviors and self-management skills.

Establish Class Rules

Having rules, consequences, and a clear consistent class structure will prevent many students (including students with disabilities) from displaying inappropriate behaviors. In developing the class rules by yourself or with your students, always consider cultural diversity. For example, teachers need to clearly identify expectations, what is considered appropriate and inappropriate behaviors, and realize their own cultural beliefs can influence and constitute what is considered acceptable and unacceptable behavior (Hodge et al., 2012). Class rules for all students should be clearly defined and established during the beginning of the school year in an orientation session and subsequently reviewed when needed throughout the year (Lavay et al., 2016). The consequences should not be entirely negative. There can also be positive consequences for following the rules, such as a popcorn party for all students who have followed the class rules. These activities should reflect the goals and objectives within the class unit or theme. Rules and consequences could be laminated and posted on various walls, on a clipboard, on a fence, on a chair, on large cones, or on equipment carts (Seaman et al., 2007). In addition, most physical educators review the rules with the class at the beginning of the school year and as needed during the school year. Some will ask students to repeat the rules either verbally or in a written quiz in order to determine their understanding. Others send the rules home in a written format for parents to review, sign, and send back. It is generally recommended to not have more than four to six rules (Lavay et al., 2016). Some of the traditional rules and consequences used in physical education can be found in Table 19.3.

Table 19.3. Traditional rules and consequences used in physical education

Rules for physical education	
Raise your hand.	Listen to instructions.
Be quiet when others talk.	Enter and exit the room quietly.
Remain on your spot.	Show respect to your classmates/teachers.
Practice assigned task.	Take care of equipment.
Follow directions.	Throw chewing gum away before class.

Consequences used in physical education	
For following the rules	*For not following the rules*
Free play at end of period or week	First warning
Choice of activity (e.g., parachute)	Second warning
Game at end of class	Three-minute time out
Choice of music during activity	Letter home to parents (negative)
Stickers or stamps	Send back to classroom teacher
Letter home to parents (positive)	Send to principal

Enforce Consequences

In addition to establishing class rules and consequences, it is critical that these rules and consequences be consistently enforced. If students perceive that some students can get away with misbehavior whereas others cannot, then students will become confused and angry. This does not mean that you cannot establish some alternative rules and consequences for students with disabilities. Just make it clear to all the students why such an alternative is necessary. For example, a student with intellectual disabilities often tries to talk to peers when the teacher is giving instructions. Rather than sending the student to time-out, peers have been instructed to gently and quietly remind the student not to talk while the teacher is talking. Later, peers talk to the student on the way to a station or at other times when it is appropriate.

Add Support

Some behaviors can be prevented by *adding support* such as increasing the number of people (e.g., peers), adding new places to the student's schedule (e.g., going outside for a walk a few times during the day), or changing activities (e.g., adding some highly reinforcing physical activities such as shooting baskets or riding a scooter board).

Avoid Antecedents

Other behaviors can be prevented by *avoiding antecedents* known to trigger the behavior such as changing who the student sits next to, what activities are presented, or when activities are presented. For instance, a student with autism has trouble making a transition from his classroom to the gymnasium. His behaviors have escalated (he often hits peers or his teacher when walking down the hall to the gym) ever since the physical educator started doing a different activity for warm-ups each day. The special educator suggested that the physical educator have the students do the same thing every day upon entering the gym. This simple change has helped this student feel more confident when he comes to the gym. Although he still displays inappropriate behaviors at times during physical education, the transition from the classroom to the gym is no longer a problem.

Other Prevention Techniques

Other simple changes that might work immediately with some students include moving the student closer to you (i.e., teacher proximity) or away from particular peers, changing the environment such as not putting out equipment until you are ready to use it, changing the activity from competition to cooperation (or at least making this a choice for some students), having a special colored ball or mark on the floor that the student knows is his or hers, or giving the student a partner. See Table 19.4 for more suggested techniques for preventing behavior problems.

Consider Teaching New Behaviors

If prevention strategies are not successful and inappropriate behaviors are still occurring, it is time to teach new, alternative skills as well as social and self-management skills that allow the student to interact with his or her environment in more appropriate, functional ways. Strategies for teaching alternative, more appropriate skills might include modeling (demonstrating the appropriate behavior), prompting or cuing (reminder of when to perform a desired behavior), shaping (reinforcing attempts at, or approximations of, the behavior), behavioral rehearsal (repeated practice of the appropriate behavior), and incidental learning (highlighting and reinforcing the behavior when it occurs naturally; Bambara et al., 2015). Strategies for teaching social and self-management skills include student checklists, picture schedules, self-reinforcement, self-talk, problem solving, anger control, and relaxation training (Bambara et al., 2015)

Consider Responding Strategies

Students need to be reinforced when they demonstrate appropriate, recently learned, positive behaviors, or appropriate self-management skills. If a student displays an unwanted behavior, then the teacher and others around the student must respond in a manner that does not reinforce the student for displaying the behavior (e.g., not chasing after a student who runs away to get attention). Proper responding can lead to immediate reduction in the frequency, duration, or intensity of the unwanted behavior (e.g., student only runs a few feet before he realizes that no one is chasing after him) and ultimately to the extinction of the unwanted behavior.

Positive responding strategies include nonreinforcement (not responding in a way that allows behavior to work/achieve its purpose) and redirection (redirecting the student to an alternative behavior and then reinforcing the alternative behavior). Punitive strategies to reduce a behavior include removal of a pleasurable stimulus (e.g., extinction,

Table 19.4. Techniques for preventing behavior problems

1. *Determine cause of behavior* (try and determine what might be causing the unwanted behavior and then try to rearrange the environment or the situation to prevent the behavior from reoccurring)
2. *Tune into your class* (be aware of what is going on; pay particular attention to students who have a history of problem behavior)
3. *Set the right pace* (lesson should run so there is a smooth flow from activity to activity; have a comfortable pace—one that is not too fast or too slow)
4. *Manage time efficiently* (reduce non-teaching time to prevent misbehavior that occurs when students are bored or waiting)
5. *Encourage clarification of instructions* (make sure students understand instructions by repeating instructions, asking students to repeat instructions back to you, or giving some students extra cues or help from peers)
6. *Set realistic goals* (set goals or help students set goals that are realistic for them that are both achievable and challenging; students get bored if activities are too easy and frustrated if they are too hard)
7. *Make sure students are appropriately placed* (some students cannot handle large classes or classes that are very competitive. Either try and place the student in a smaller or less competitive class or separate the class into smaller groups with some playing competitive activities and others cooperative activities)
8. *Involve the entire group* (organize the class to encourage maximum, active participation – avoid waiting in line, elimination games, and sharing equipment)
9. *Hold students accountable for what is taught* (make sure students know what they are supposed to be working on and what is expected of them, then hold them accountable for their performance)
10. *Keep the class attentive* (use creative techniques to keep students' attention such as unique equipment, novel games, and having high school or college athletes come and help teach an activity)
11. *Keep the students motivated* (be aware of the motivational level of the class and individual students—note that it is better to stop an activity when students are still enjoying it rather than wait until they become bored)
12. *Be assertive but gentle* (face problems immediately, do not ignore them; be direct yet calm when dealing with students who display behavior problems)
13. *Use humor* (use humor to reduce tension and defuse stressful situations)
14. *Appeal to your students' values* (appeal to students' sense of fairness, their commitment to the group's code of behavior, and to the positive relationship you have and want to continue to have with them)
15. *Generate enthusiasm* (show your students genuine enthusiasm about physical activity and about how you care about their success by cheering, clapping hands, and generally having a good time)
16. Know your stuff (students respect and want to learn from teachers who are competent in the skills and activities being taught. Make sure you are prepared for your lessons, and get experts in the community to help you with units you do not feel comfortable with)
17. *Take responsibility for managing behavior* (try to deal with students' behavior problems in the gymnasium rather than always sending students to the principal)
18. *Establish a consistent behavior management plan* (develop your plan for physical education with plan used in other parts of the building by other professionals)
19. *Use proximity control* (students will be less likely to misbehave if you stand closer to them)
20. *Take an interest in your students* (students are more willing to cooperate with a teacher who shows interest in them by discussing their interests, asking about their weekend, noting their achievements, etc.)
21. *Be a good role model* (since many students imitate their teacher, model appropriate dress, talk, and conduct including showing self-control in heated discussions when you get angry or a student gets angry at you)
22. *Redirect disruptive behavior* (try and redirect disruptive or dangerous situations into more productive tasks)
23. *Provide vigorous activities* (help students release their anger and frustration through vigorous activity such as sprints, volleyball spiking, hitting a softball, or aerobics)
24. *Befriend a disliked student* (a teacher who befriends a disliked student often helps other students accept him or her)
25. *Use nonverbal cues* (teach and then use simple gestures such as finger to the lips, the time-out sign, or simply giving direct eye contact to deal with minor disruptions)
26. *Establish class rules early* (establish and review class rules and consequences from the first day of class; post the rules in a conspicuous place, and review the rules often)
27. *Grade fairly* (establish clear and fair criteria for grades; explain the grading system on the first day of class and keep careful records of progress for calculating grades)
28. *Avoid nagging* (continually nagging can make students anxious or may cause them to "tune out" the teacher—give one warning or reminder, then give a negative consequence)
29. *Develop an appropriate physical environment* (create an environment that promotes enthusiasm, learning, and participation; make sure the environment is as comfortable as possible; ensure that students have enough space for a given activity; try and limit auditory and visual distractions in the environment)
30. *Place a large laminated poster* at the entrance and exit doors to the class that can easily be touched by the students. At the top of the poster place a happy face, in the center a neutral face, and at the bottom a frowning face. As the students come into class have the students "tap in" and "tap out" of class touching the picture that best describes their present state of mind. This will give the physical educator an idea of how a specific student or the general class is feeling.

From Henderson, H.L., & French, R.W. (1993). *Creative approaches to managing student behavior* (2nd ed.). Park City, UT: Family Development Resources; adapted by permission.

response cost, time-out); presentation of an aversive stimulus (direct discussion, silent look, verbal reprimand); and requiring an aversive behavior (physical activity, overcorrection; Bambara et al., 2015; Lavay et al., 2016).

PROCEDURES TO MAINTAIN OR STRENGTHEN A BEHAVIOR

Many techniques within the PBS approach are based on the principles of operant conditioning or the ABC approach. In operant conditioning, a systematic application of consequences is presented following a behavior in order to maintain, strengthen, or weaken a behavior. When something is presented or taken away with the purpose of increasing the likelihood that the behavior will be repeated, it is known as *reinforcement*. When something is presented or taken away that decreases the likelihood that the behavior will be repeated, it is known as *punishment* (Lavay, French, & Henderson, 2015; Loovis, 2011).

Reinforcement

Reinforcement refers to consequences of behavior that increase the future rate of that behavior occurring. Reinforcement can be positive, negative, or nonreinforcement. In a survey of Nationally Certified Adapted Physical Education Teachers, the most frequently used reinforcement methods to maintain or increase appropriate behaviors were verbal positive statements, prompting, positive pinpointing, tangible reinforcement, Premack principle, and physical activity reinforcement (Lavay, Henderson, & Guthrie, 2014).

Positive reinforcement involves the presentation of a positive stimulus following a particular response with the goal of maintaining or increasing that response. For example, allowing students to ride scooter boards (positive reinforcer) after completing their warm-ups without complaining (targeted response behavior) may increase the likelihood that the students will do their warm-ups without complaining. The key is to use the least amount of intervention or begin at the most natural level of reinforcement and move along the continuum until a reinforcer works for the student or class. For example, if a social praise such as a "high-five" is effective with the student, then there is no need to use a reward such as a sticker, decal, or stamp. It is also important to match the type of reinforcement to the student's developmental level. For example, a student with severe disabilities is limited in cognition and will not understand sophisticated delayed schedules of reinforcement such as a token economy. At first, these students

Table 19.5. Guidelines for using reinforcement

1. Make sure the student is performing the target behavior before you provide reinforcement.
2. Reinforce the behavior immediately after it occurs.
3. Be specific in your praise. For example, tell the student "good swinging your leg when you hop" rather than "good job."
4. When students are first learning to perform a skill or display a behavior appropriately, make sure you reinforce that skill or behavior every time it is done correctly.
5. After a skill or behavior has been learned, then you, the physical educator, need only reinforce that skill or behavior periodically.
6. If social praise is effective in maintaining or increasing a behavior, do not use other rewards. Only use more tangible rewards when social praise is not effective.
7. If a tangible reinforcer has to be introduced, pair it with social praise and then gradually fade away the use of the tangible reinforcer.
8. Make sure that what you are using as a reward for the student is truly reinforcing. Each student might find different things rewarding.

From Henderson, H.L., & French, R.W. (1993). *Creative approaches to managing student behavior* (2nd ed.). Park City, UT: Family Development Resources; adapted by permission.

will require primary reinforcers such as food paired with a social reinforcer of verbal praise. Table 19.5 provides the reader with general guidelines for administering reinforcement.

Remember a one-size-fits-all approach when selecting a reinforcer generally is ineffective because the reinforcer selected depends on the unique preferences of the student or situation. A student will respond better when he or she has a variety of reinforcers to choose from (i.e., reinforcement menu with a visual display of reinforcers). Ways to identify potential reinforcers are observing students and seeing what types of activities they enjoy, asking the students to list or point to activities they enjoy, having the class list activities on the board, using a reinforcement preference survey (see Figure 19.4), and asking other teachers or parents.

Intrinsic Reinforcement

Intrinsic reinforcement occurs when the activity itself is reinforcing. The goal is to have all students so interested in the activities in the physical education class that they are engaged and performing because they are intrinsically motivated to do so (French, Henderson, Lavay, & Silliman-French, 2014). For example, a student happily joins his or her peers when a tetherball activity is about to begin and does not need external motivation or reinforcement (e.g., certificate, sticker). Playing with a tetherball is reinforcing in and of itself.

Reinforcement Survey

For each activity, please mark an X in the column that most explains your feelings.

	Like very much	Like	Dislike
Do you like juice?	_____	_____	_____
Do you like fruit?	_____	_____	_____
Do you like candy?	_____	_____	_____
Do you like sports equipment of your own?	_____	_____	_____
Do you like to rollerblade?	_____	_____	_____
Do you like soccer?	_____	_____	_____
Do you like basketball?	_____	_____	_____
Do you like football?	_____	_____	_____
Do you like softball?	_____	_____	_____
Do you like recess?	_____	_____	_____
Do you like to be a squad leader?	_____	_____	_____
Do you like to demonstrate a skill?	_____	_____	_____
Do you like to play in groups?	_____	_____	_____
Do you like activities that you can do alone?	_____	_____	_____
Do you like your teacher to ask you for help?	_____	_____	_____
Do you like to win at relays and games?	_____	_____	_____
Do you like certificates and awards?	_____	_____	_____
Do you like to help other students?	_____	_____	_____
Do you like to play music during class?	_____	_____	_____
Would you like to talk to a sports star?	_____	_____	_____

Please answer the following questions:

What is your favorite activity at home? _____

_____

What is your least favorite activity at home? _____

_____

What is your favorite activity at school? _____

_____

What is your least favorite activity at school? _____

_____

What is your favorite activity in physical education? _____

_____

What is your least favorite activity in physical education? _____

_____

Figure 19.4. Reinforcement survey. (*Source:* Walker, Shea, & Bauer, 2003.)

Social Praise

Social praise is providing positive feedback for good behavior or performance. When you see good behavior, acknowledge it or "catch them being good." This is also known as positive pinpointing. This can be done verbally or nonverbally through a nod, a smile, a high-five, or a thumbs-up (French, Henderson, Lavay, & Silliman-French, 2013). The important thing is to effectively communicate to the student that you are pleased with some aspect of his or her performance or behavior. Social reinforcement is the most common and easiest form of reinforcement used in physical education, and it can be quite effective. Although social praise can be overly used, it generally is not used enough with students who are learning to behave or who first master a new task. Some types of social praise are gestures (e.g., look of pleasure, a grin), statements (e.g., "good keeping your eyes on the ball," "I like how you helped Billy up when he fell"), or a pat on the shoulder. Another type of social recognition is public posting. This technique involves posting in public view (e.g., physical education bulletin board or web site) names of students who have mastered an individual challenge or the "Physical Education Student of the Week" (Lavay et al., 2016).

Physical Activity

A favorite physical activity can be used as a reward for demonstrating an appropriate behavior. In physical education, using physical activity as a positive reinforcer is highly appropriate and beneficial to the student and the program (Lavay et al., 2016). In fact, physical activity itself may be a behavioral intervention as there is a positive relationship between exercise and emotional health, particularly in reducing depression and anxiety (Marcus & Forsyth, 2003; Sallis & Owen, 1999). Some other benefits include no extra cost to the physical education budget, the availability of many types of equipment and games, and the potential of physical activity to improve the student's level of physical fitness and motor skills as well as self-esteem and self-confidence (Lavay, 1984).

Sensory Stimuli

Sensory stimuli, or auditory, visual, or kinesthetic sensations, can also be presented as reinforcement for appropriate behaviors. This technique is particularly effective with students on the autism spectrum (Alexander & Schwager, 2012). For example, allowing a student with autism to swing (vestibular stimulation) after he or she completes a warm-up routine can be very reinforcing. Music is also very reinforcing. While riding a stationary bike or walking on a treadmill, music can be played or stopped contingent on the student staying on task and within his or her target heart rate zone. When provided in an age-appropriate manner, sensory stimuli can be an effective reinforcer for older students. For example, listening to music on an iPod (auditory stimulation) or going for a brisk walk or jog (kinesthetic/vestibular stimulation) is performed daily by millions of people in the United States.

Tangibles

Tangibles are objects and edibles given to a student to reinforce a behavior. Objects include stickers, stamps, certificates, award ribbons, patches, trophies, and plaques. Objects can potentially become expensive, so when possible, use inexpensive reinforcers such as watching a favorite video clip on a tablet or receiving a certificate. Certificates can be generated on the computer with many examples located on various web sites (Lavay et al., 2016). Edibles should only be used if the student is not motivated by other methods, and you should always provide healthy choices. When using tangible rewards, make sure they are age appropriate and similar to rewards that are used in other school settings. For example, giving a doll to an 18-year-old female is not age appropriate and only makes this student look unusual in the eyes of her peers. A better solution is giving this student a magazine such as *Seventeen*.

Other Methods to Increase Appropriate Behaviors

Group Contingencies

Group contingencies refer to the presentation of a reinforcer to a group of students based on the group's following an appropriate set of rules to meet the desired behavior. For example, if all the students sit quietly in their squad while the teacher takes roll, then the squad gets to choose one warm-up activity. Each squad member exerts peer pressure to control the behavior of the other squad members. This technique has proven to be very successful in the physical education environment, and in certain instances, it is superior to the individual reinforcement technique in managing behavior, especially with older students at the middle and high school levels who seek and desire peer approval. This method can also effectively build team spirit and camaraderie among individuals working together to meet a common goal (Glover & Anderson, 2003).

Group contingencies can be categorized into three basic types (Kauffman, Mostert, Trent, & Hallahan, 1998). First, there is the *dependent group contingency* in which a target student must earn the desired reinforcer for the entire group. To ensure that undue peer pressure is not placed on the student, the teacher must be certain the target student is capable of earning the reinforcement. For example, if the group can get Marcus (a student with Down syndrome who often refuses to walk or run on the track) to run one lap, then the group gets to play a game of soccer.

Second is an *independent group contingency* in which a squad goal is stated, and students work on their own individualized goals to earn the desired reinforcer. This eliminates the competitiveness because, for example, everyone in the squad completes their own prescribed number of push-ups and sit-ups. When everyone in the squad completes their push-ups and sit-ups, the squad gets to shoot baskets for a specified number of minutes.

Third is *interdependent group contingency* in which the desired reinforcer is dependent on the behavior of the entire squad or class (Vogler & French, 1983). Note that if one student constantly ruins the chances of the entire group to earn the desired reinforcer, an individual behavior management technique may need to be implemented within the group contingency procedure.

The Good Behavior Game (Lavay et al., 2016; Vogler & French, 1983) is an example of an interdependent group contingency. For example, the physical educator places the students in various squads and explains that they will earn 10 minutes of activity time to play basketball if the squad members are on task and performing the activities at the fitness stations. The physical educator will look at all the squads 10 different times during the class period. If a squad at the end of the class has earned 8 or more points by being on task at least 8 of the 10 times, then activity time will be awarded to practice basketball. Those squads that have fewer than 8 points remaining continue with the fitness class activity. It is possible that all squads can win because they are not competing against each other. It is beneficial if activity time means the students select from a menu of activities that focus on daily or weekly instructional goals and objectives of the teacher.

Token Economy

The *token economy* is a delayed method of reinforcement where individuals receive a token immediately following successful performance of the desired behavior. Later, they exchange the tokens for a reward. Tokens are symbolic rewards used as temporary substitutes for more substantial reinforcers. Tokens may take the form of checkmarks, points, poker chips, colored strips of paper, or play money ("PE Bucks") that have a predetermined value and are earned for performing specific behaviors. Be sure when selecting tokens that they are age appropriate, easy to dispense, and easily recorded (Lavay et al., 2016). An advantage of a token system is that the symbolic rewards can be presented immediately following the demonstration of the appropriate behavior or task with minimal interference in the ongoing activity. In addition, these rewards can easily be added to contracts. Paraprofessionals and peers can assist in providing the tokens to students (Alstot, 2012).

Contracts

Contracts are written agreements between at least the physical educator and the student regarding improvement in behavior or task performance (see Figure 19.5).

This is an agreement between Shawn Jackino and his physical education teacher. This contract begins on September 1, 2015, and will be reviewed daily by the physical education teacher.

I, Shawn Jackino, agree to discuss my behavior with the physical education teacher each day immediately after class. At that time, we will determine whether I earned a point in each of four categories: 1) class attendance, 2) class participation, 3) appropriate interaction with peers, and 4) use of appropriate language. A maximum of four points per day can be earned. A weekly behavior chart will be used to keep track of my points. Once I have earned enough points, I can choose from the reinforcement menu I have developed with my physical education teacher (shown below).

Shawn Jackino, Student   Date: 8/3/15

George McCall, General Physical Education Teacher   Date: 8/3/15

Jennifer E. Austin, Licensed School Psychologist   Date: 8/3/15

Reinforcement menu	Points needed
Free time with peer (e.g., shooting baskets)	10
Opportunity to be teacher's aide	10
Opportunity to choose class activity	10
Opportunity to lead daily stretching activities	5
Sports drink	5

Figure 19.5. Token economy contract.

Billy will pay attention in physical education this week. He will earn the right to choose the class activity from four choices on Monday.

_____
Billy Smith, Student　　　　　　　　　　　Date

_____
John Matthews, General Physical Educator　　Date

Figure 19.6. Teacher-controlled contract.

Contracts are adaptable to a variety of behaviors and situations (Lavay et al., 2016). There are three basic types of contracts. First, there is the *teacher-controlled contract* in which the educator determines the target behavior and the reinforcers (see Figure 19.6). This type of contract is commonly referred to as a *proclamation*. Second, there is the *student-controlled contract* in which the student determines the task and the reinforcer (see Figure 19.7). Third, there is a *mutual contract* in which both the physical educator and the student work together to determine the terms of the contract (see Figure 19.8). Perhaps the most appealing feature of the latter two contracts is that the student takes some ownership, learns self-management skills, and takes responsibility for his or her own behavior. It also removes the onus of responsibility from the physical educator's shoulders. See guidelines for designing and implementing contracts in Table 19.6.

My physical education contract for success:

I, Jeramias Williams, promise to

• Follow teacher directions

• Participate in all physical education activities without arguing 4 of 5 days per week

• Get dressed for physical education and do all activities Monday through Thursday

• Not fight with other students

• Not curse in class
_____
If I do all of the above, I will be rewarded by

• Not having to get dressed for physical education on Fridays

• Passing physical education

_____
Jeramias Williams, Student　　　　　　　　　Date

_____
Clarence Thompson, General Physical Educator　Date

_____
Sallie H. Swisher, Licensed School Psychologist　Date

Figure 19.7. Student-controlled contract.

Michelle will dress for class for the next 15 class periods. After Michelle reaches the 15th class period, coach Morales will reward Michelle with a shirt with a logo of her favorite soccer team.

_____
Michelle Roberson, Student　　　　　　　　Date

_____
Anthony Morales, Coach　　　　　　　　　Date

Figure 19.8. Mutual contract.

Prompts

Prompts are cues that help the student identify and also remember target behaviors. There are three major types of prompts (Alexander & Schwager, 2012). First are *visual prompts* such as placing a cone on the gymnasium floor where you want the student to stand or charts on the wall to remind the class of the rules or routines. Second are *auditory prompts* such as a verbal cue or verbal directions. The third type of prompt is *physical guidance* in which the physical educator may hold the student's hand or put his or her hand on the student's shoulder when walking to make a transition from one activity to the next. Prompts can help students who are hesitant to perform a skill and can also aid in the student being successful. For example, using a visual prompt of where to stand and a physical prompt to assist them with how to hold a bat and hit a ball off a tee may make a student with intellectual disabilities to be more willing to try the activity because he knows he will be successful.

Table 19.6. General guidelines in designing and implementing contracts

1. Read and explain the conditions of the contract aloud with the student.
2. Make sure the contract is fair for all persons.
3. Design the contract in a positive manner.
4. Design the contract in small approximations that leads to the target behavior or skill.
5. Allow for frequent reinforcement that is given immediately following successful achievement.
6. Be consistent and systematic in using a contract.
7. Whenever possible, all persons concerned should sign and receive a copy of the contract.
8. Renegotiate contract if it is not effective.
9. Start the contract as soon as possible after signing.

From Jansma, P., & French, R. (1994). *Special physical education: Physical activity, sports, and recreation* (p. 385). Upper Saddle River, NJ: Prentice Hall; reprinted by permission.

Shaping

Shaping refers to the development of a new behavior that at first may be too difficult to complete by reinforcing a series of behaviors that are gradually and progressively leading up to the target behavior. This is also referred to as *reinforcing successive approximations* (Cooper, Heron, & Heward, 2007). For example, the target behavior for a student is to come into the gym and go directly to his squad. However, this student tends to run directly to the equipment and start playing until the physical educator literally pulls him away and takes him to his squad. Rather than waiting for the student to display the target behavior, the physical educator may reinforce this student when he comes in, runs over to the equipment but does not touch it, and then goes and sits down in his squad. Reinforcing successive approximations rather than waiting until the student has completely mastered the entire skill will more likely result in the student eventually achieving mastery.

Chaining

Chaining is a procedure of identifying a series of steps needed to perform a specific target behavior and taking the student through the steps. In this procedure, each step might be taught separately, and then the separate responses are linked together or each step would be taught then linked to the next step (Cooper et al., 2007). There are two types of chaining: backward and forward chaining. *Backward chaining* involves teaching the steps to perform a target behavior in the reverse order it would normally occur. For example, in backward chaining, a student would practice the last step (e.g., the follow-through in the overhand throw) first. Then working backward, the student would practice releasing the ball and following through and then trunk rotation, releasing the ball, and following through. The other two steps of extending his arm backward and side orientation would be similarly chained until the student was performing all five steps. Another method of backward chaining is to assist the student through all the steps of the movement except the last step. Then the physical educator assists with all components except the last two, and so forth. Backward chaining at times may be more motivational than forward chaining because the last part of the skill (i.e., results or consequences) is the most motivational. In contrast, *forward chaining* involves teaching the steps to perform a target behavior in the order they typically occur.

Negative Reinforcement

Negative reinforcement refers to taking something aversive away to maintain or increase a behavior. Negative reinforcement is a less commonly used method of behavior management (Henderson & French, 1989; Loovis, 2011), but it can be another effective means of reinforcing a desired behavior. There are two major procedures involved in negative reinforcement. The first is the *avoidance procedure*. This is when a person increases a desired behavior in order to avoid something aversive. For example, the physical educator may state that all students who run a mile in less than 10 minutes will not be required to run the mile the next day. Because most students do not want to run the mile during a second day (an aversive stimulus), they will attempt to run the mile in less than 10 minutes. The second is the *escape procedure*. This is when a person increases a desired behavior in order to escape having to do an aversive behavior. Using this procedure, a high school basketball coach says that all players have to run across the court and back in 10 seconds or less or else everyone must run again (aversive stimulus). Players will increase their effort to escape having to run again (escaping the aversive stimulus).

Because positive reinforcement is more appropriate and effective in physical education than negative reinforcement, there needs to be some caution when using negative reinforcement (Lavay et al., 2016; Rizzo & Zabel, 1988), especially in ensuring that it not be confused with punishment. Punishment is focused solely on decreasing a certain behavior, whereas negative reinforcement, like positive reinforcement, promotes the increase of a certain behavior. For example, a student with intellectual disabilities who is overweight does not want to dress out for physical education when the class is doing the mile run. He is a slow runner, and he knows he cannot run the entire way. The physical educator realizes that the student will not participate if she makes him run the entire mile. She decides to tell the student that he only needs to run as far as he can and then walk the rest of the way (takes away the threat of having to run a mile). The student feels less threatened, dresses out for physical education, and runs farther and faster than he ever did before.

Sometimes, a physical educator may inadvertently cause inappropriate behaviors to increase in the class through negative reinforcement. For example, when the class is running wind sprints and Danielle does not want to run wind sprints, she may throw a ball at another student and go to time-out to avoid having to run the wind sprints. The next time winds sprints are on the agenda not only Danielle but also Nicole and Penny now act up in order to go to time-out. They are negatively reinforced for acting up by not having to run wind sprints (aversive behavior), so acting up behavior will increase unless the physical educator is aware of this and makes sure that when time-out is over, the students are still required to run the wind sprints before taking part in the other class activities.

PROCEDURES TO REDUCE OR ELIMINATE BEHAVIORS

Even when physical educators have been proactive and have implemented prevention techniques to decrease inappropriate behaviors, they may still occur. There are two main methods that a physical educator can use to reduce or eliminate behaviors: differential reinforcement and punishment. These methods need to be carefully implemented, and consequences should be as natural, as logical, and as educationally appropriate as possible (Bambara et al., 2015).

Differential Reinforcement

There are four general differential reinforcement strategies: differential reinforcement of low rates of behavior (DRL), differential reinforcement of omission of behaviors (DRO), differential reinforcement of alternative behaviors (DRA), and differential reinforcement of incompatible behaviors (DRI; Alberto & Troutman, 2005; Lavay et al., 2016).

Differential Reinforcement of Low Rates of Behavior

This procedure uses a specific schedule of reinforcement to decrease the rate of a challenging behavior that may be tolerable or even desirable at low rates but inappropriate when it occurs too often or too rapidly. There are two types of DRL reinforcement delivery schedules based on the frequency, intensity, and duration of the challenging behavior. First, there is the *class DRL* in which the total number of inappropriate responses that occur during the entire class is compared with a preset criterion. A reinforcer is given if the occurrences of the challenging behavior are at or below the predetermined criterion. For example, a physical educator is frustrated because students are talking to each other throughout the entire physical education class. After collecting baseline data, it is determined that the talking behavior occurs for 40 minutes out of the 60-minute class. The physical educator has spoken to the class and asked the students to please decrease their conversation to at most 15 minutes so that they have more time to participate in the class activities. When the students achieve that criterion of 15 or fewer minutes of talking, they are rewarded by getting to play a soccer game on Friday.

When reinforcement is needed more often to keep the behavior at a low rate, *interval DRL* can be used. This technique involves dividing the class period into an activity or time interval where the inappropriate behavior is occurring across numerous intervals. This approach could be used if the problem occurs during various times in the class period and it is believed that reinforcement will be effective only if it is awarded at various times during the class rather than waiting until the end of the class. For example, there could be time periods after each activity within a lesson (i.e., dressing out, roll taking, instruction, warm-up, activity, cool-down, closure). At the completion of each activity, the students are given a reward if the number of inappropriate responses in a specified period of time was less than or equal to a prescribed limit. As the challenging behavior dissipates, the number of activities in which appropriate behavior is reinforced increases. The procedure is then gradually removed when the inappropriate behaviors are at an acceptable rate.

Differential Reinforcement of Omission of Behaviors

This differential reinforcement strategy involves a reinforcer being delivered contingent on the inappropriate behavior not being demonstrated for a specific period of time. For example, if Tracy is making duck noises during class, the physical educator might tell her that those noises are distracting and ask her to stop making them. Then Tracy would be reinforced for a specified period of time, perhaps 10 minutes, for not making duck noises during those 10 minutes. The time set is dependent on the frequency of the occurrence of that behavior at baseline. Whereas DRL is used to reinforce a gradual reduction of a challenging behavior, DRO is only used to reinforce zero occurrences of the behavior for a specified period of time.

Differential Reinforcement of Alternative Behaviors

In this strategy, a reinforcer is provided when the student displays an alternative and acceptable behavior instead of the inappropriate behavior. For example, Hayden gets mad when he misses a basket and throws the ball as hard as he can against the wall. The physical educator tells Hayden why that behavior is inappropriate and suggests that he take a self-time-out and run around the gym twice when he misses a shot. He is then reinforced for performing the alternative behavior.

Differential Reinforcement of an Incompatible Behavior

In this procedure, a behavior is reinforced that is incompatible with the inappropriate behavior. Incompatible means you cannot do the two behaviors at the same time. For example, a student receives reinforcement for standing on his spot or for being quiet in line, which is incompatible with standing in the wrong spot or being disruptive in line. Similarly, students are reinforced for clapping their hands to the music, which is incompatible with inappropriate hand-waving behavior. This procedure has been reported to be quite effective in reducing aggressive behavior and other inappropriate behaviors (Goldstein, 1995).

Punishment

The term *punishment* is used here as a technical descriptor for several common behavior techniques used in public schools such as time-out, taking away equipment from a child, or giving a child a stern look. These mild punishment techniques described may be needed to decrease the inappropriate behavior only after first using strategies to prevent behaviors. Whenever possible, always use positive and preventive techniques before using negative or punishment methods. We do not advocate any type of punishment that demeans or causes any physical or emotional harm to the student.

Punishment is defined as the removal of a pleasurable stimulus, presentation of an aversive stimulus, or requiring an aversive behavior as a consequence immediately following an inappropriate behavior in order to decrease the occurrence of that behavior in the future. In a survey of Nationally Certified Adapted Physical Education Teachers, the most frequently used punishment methods to decrease inappropriate behaviors were time-out, extinction, and verbal reprimands (Lavay et al., 2014). If punishment is used appropriately, it can make positive differences. However, experts caution that punishment may undermine the prosocial values that physical educators are attempting to teach (Deci, Koestner, & Ryan, 2001; Kohn, 1998; Loovis, 2011; Weinberg & Gould, 2011).

Removal of a Pleasurable Stimulus

Extinction

There are students whose main goal is to upset, frustrate, or anger teachers and others. These students are reinforced in two ways. First, they receive attention from the teacher or other students. Second, they get revenge. One way to reduce or eliminate this type of behavior is to use an extinction procedure (Lavay et al., 2016). In this method, the physical educator eliminates or extinguishes inappropriate behaviors by simply ignoring them. Extinction is one of the most effective ways to permanently remove an inappropriate behavior (Lavay et al., 2014) and is most effective, as with other punishers, when combined with positive reinforcement. Extinction can be difficult to implement, as it takes a great deal of self-control on the part of the physical educator and peers to ignore a behavior. Also, when the behavior is ignored, it often increases before it decreases because the student is trying even harder to get the attention he or she wants. Extinction should never be used with inappropriate behaviors that are harmful to the student or others. See guidelines for using extinction in Table 19.7.

Response Cost

This procedure refers to the removal from a student of a specific quantity of reinforcement that has been previously earned such as minutes of time to perform an activity, loss of equipment, or points taken away from a grade. This system of punishment is used in most traditional sports. For instance, if a player inappropriately hits another player, the penalty will cost the team valuable yardage in football or even possession of the ball in basketball. In using this type of punishment, the physical educator

Table 19.7.   Guidelines when using an extinction procedure

A. Generally combine with other methods such as strategies related to differential reinforcement.

B. Be consistent and do not occasionally reinforce the problem behavior.

C. Practice not responding to the misbehavior.

D. Be aware of what is termed *extinction bursts*. After the extinction procedure is initiated, the inappropriate behavior may occur more often, more vigorously, or for longer periods of time by the student in an effort to gain attention. Eventually, the extinction burst will fade and the problem behavior gradually diminishes.

E. Do not give eye contact, verbal cues, verbal contact, or physical contact.

F. Some form of punishment may be the procedure of choice if the problem behavior intensifies over a long period of time.

must consider the following: the magnitude of the cost in relation to the challenging behavior exhibited, the provision of opportunities to regain the lost privilege or points when the appropriate behavior has replaced the inappropriate behavior, and ensuring that the student understands the rules for the removal of the reinforcing event (Jansma & French, 1994).

Time-Out

This technique involves the removal of the student from positive reinforcement for a fixed period of time. There are different thoughts on the length of the time-out period. Some authorities suggest it should be no longer than 2 or 3 minutes. Others believe the student should stay in time-out for the equivalent of 1 minute for each year of his or her age. There are four general forms of time-out (Lavay et al., 2016). First is *observational time-out* in which the student is removed from the activity but allowed to view the activity. Second is *seclusion time-out* in which the student is required to sit or stand away from the activity or in a corner within the physical education environment where he or she cannot see students participating in the activity from which he or she was removed. Third is the *exclusion time-out* in which the student must leave the environment and go to a setting that is supervised and not more reinforcing than the environment that he or she left. The fourth is a *self-time-out* in which the student, who feels that he or she is going to respond inappropriately to a situation, can select an appropriate activity that will calm him or her down such as taking 10 deep breaths, doing sit-ups, or running around the track. This technique can be highly effective with students with disabilities when they are "melting down" and need to regain control and is valuable for teaching students self-management skills (Alexander & Schwager, 2012).

Time-out is simple to implement in a short amount of time and has been shown to be effective in decreasing many undesirable student behaviors. The major disadvantage is that the student is not participating in the planned activities and is not learning the skills. Also, as a precaution, some students who want to avoid participating in physical education find time-out reinforcing. It is important then that when the student is out of time-out, he or she must perform the activities that the class was doing when the time-out occurred. Check with your school district regarding the type of time-out procedures that are acceptable.

Presentation of an Aversive Stimulus

Direct Discussion

When a student performs an inappropriate behavior, the first step is almost always having a direct discussion with the student about the behavior. In a calm and concerned manner, the physical educator will ask the student why he or she performed that behavior. A majority of the time, this discussion is all that is needed to get the behavior to decrease.

Silent Look

As a mild punisher, a silent or stern look by the physical educator when a student exhibits an inappropriate behavior can sometimes be effective. This gesture may stop the recurrence of the behavior. For example, if a student is talking while the teacher is trying to give directions, the teacher may stop giving directions and look at the student. The student then realizes he is disturbing the teacher and stops talking. Consider combining the silent look with teacher proximity in which you stand near the student.

Verbal Reprimand

Verbal reprimands are used widely and, in many cases, effectively in physical education. The verbal reprimand has three steps. The first step is to tell the student that "what" they did was inappropriate (e.g., "Bouncing the ball when I am giving instructions is not acceptable"). The second step is to explain "why" it is inappropriate (e.g., "When you bounce the ball, others cannot hear my instructions"). The third step is to give an "alternative behavior" (e.g., "Please hold the ball when I am talking"). It is key to always address the inappropriate behavior and not the student. The following illustrates inappropriate ways to use verbal reprimands: "You can't do anything right!" or "Can't you control yourself and act your age!"

Requiring an Aversive Behavior

Physical Activity

Often in physical activity settings, students are made to perform physical activities when they display inappropriate behaviors. For example, coaches often have the players run sprints when they come late to practice. Teachers may have the students do push-ups when they are talking instead of listening to instructions. If our goal as physical educators is to create a lifelong desire to be physically active, we should not use physical activity as a punisher (French, Lavay, & Henderson, 1985).

Overcorrection

Overcorrection is a technique in which an individual is required to perform an action that teaches a lesson associated with the inappropriate behavior. There are two basic types of overcorrection. First, *restitutional overcorrection* refers to a process by which a student is required to make amends for an inappropriate behavior by returning the environment to an improved state. For example, if a student put his chewing gum on top of his locker, he would be required to clean his gum off his locker plus all the gum that others have put on their lockers. Second, *positive practice overcorrection* refers to the technique in which a student is required to repeatedly practice a positive behavior in the correct manner. For example, suppose the physical educator sees a student running in the locker room. In positive overcorrection, the student may be required to practice correctly at the required speed for five consecutive times. The teacher then rewards him for the appropriate behavior by patting him on the back and verbally praising him.

Cautions When Using Punishment

Although punishment is usually effective in decreasing inappropriate behaviors, it also can be abusive, leading to withdrawal, anger, frustration, and even further misbehavior from the student. Therefore, punishment should *only* be used when positive techniques have not been effective. When punishment is used, it is all too easy to focus on decreasing or eliminating an inappropriate behavior and forget the importance of teaching positive, alternative behaviors. It is critical to remember to address behavior pairs, targeting both the behavior to increase and the behavior to decrease. For example, by reinforcing Frank for walking directly to his squad, his goofing-off behavior when coming into the gym decreases.

If it is determined that punishments must be used, it is important that certain guidelines be followed (see Table 19.8). Again, if punishment must be used, use the least amount of intervention or mildest form possible, making sure it is a natural

Table 19.8.   Guidelines for the use of punishment

1. Always talk to the student privately first to determine the cause of misbehavior.
2. Establish classroom rules so students know beforehand what the punishable behaviors are and what their consequences will be.
3. Post the rules in the gym and go over them with the students.
4. Send a list of the rules of unacceptable behaviors and consequences home to the parents so they know what is expected of their child.
5. Provide models of acceptable behavior so students know appropriate ways of behaving.
6. Do not allow a student to exhibit an inappropriate behavior for too long a period of time so that it increases in intensity before you attempt to intervene. Punishment must occur immediately after the behavior is first observed. Afterward, it is important that you provide opportunities for the student to behave appropriately and to receive positive reinforcement for this appropriate behavior.
7. Distinguish between intentional and unintentional disruptions. Do not treat students who make accidental mistakes the same way as those who misbehave on purpose. For instance, a student who accidentally throws a ball that hits another person should be treated differently that a student who throws a ball with the intention of hitting someone. Make the punishment suit the behavior.
8. Do not lose control over your own emotions. The problem will only become worse if both the student and the teacher have lost control.
9. Avoid confrontations with the student, especially in front of peers. Secondary-level students, in particular, tend to function as a member of a group and are quite protective of each other. By confronting one student, you may lose respect of the other students as well.
10. Avoid the use of sarcasm. Some teachers use sarcasm to chastise or demean a student in an attempt to control behavior. Using words as weapons of control can alienate all students in the class. Many times the teacher unconsciously slips into using this technique or considers it a form of joking to get the point across. Sarcasm is generally not considered funny by the students, and could negatively affect their self-image and status with their peers. It is not a recommended way to manage behaviors.
11. Be consistent in your use of punishment. What is wrong today must be wrong tomorrow, and the consequences must be the same.
12. Be fair. Behavior that is wrong for Tommy to exhibit must also be wrong for Mary to exhibit.
13. When a student does misbehave, make sure that in your reprimand you specify that it is the behavior, NOT the student, of which you disapprove. For example, do not say, "You are a bad person, and I will not tolerate you in my class," but rather, "That behavior is inappropriate, and I will not tolerate that behavior in this class."
14. Avoid touching a student when you are angry. Physical restraint, however, may be appropriate with aggressive, self-destructive, or dangerous behaviors when the teacher is unable to successfully use a more gradual, positive approach due to the possibility that the student may cause harm to himself or to others. When using physical restraint, hold the student firmly but not roughly, to give the student a sense of protection – not punishment. The preferred technique is for the teacher to stand behind the student and hold the student's wrists with the student's arms crossed over his or her chest.
15. Never hit a student. Hitting is totally inappropriate for a teacher. There are too many negative side effects of hitting a student for it ever to be an approved management technique. In addition to all of the negative repercussions of hitting a student, there is an issue of legal liability.

From Henderson, H.L., & French, R.W. (1993). *Creative approaches to managing student behavior* (2nd ed.). Park City, UT: Family Development Resources; adapted by permission.

punishment and paired with teaching appropriate behaviors.

SOME FINAL THOUGHTS ON ADDRESSING BEHAVIOR PROBLEMS

The previous sections presented a great deal of information on how to understand and help students who display behavior problems in general physical education using the PBS model. The following provides some final points related to the application of the PBS model that need to be considered when working with students with behavior problems.

Plan on Teaching Appropriate Behaviors

The management of behavior problems should be treated in the same way as the management of instructional problems. For example, if a student makes an error in performing a motor task, a correction procedure is implemented and the student is provided more practice and review. If the problem is not corrected, the physical educator reassesses the problem and rearranges the practice session. However, when an inappropriate behavior occurs, the student typically is given a reminder of the disregarded rule or expected behavior and administered a penalty for exhibiting the inappropriate behavior. Too frequently, appropriate behaviors are not taught. This is a crucial component of behavior management. Appropriate behavior must be systematically and consistently taught, and when necessary, there needs to be follow-up to ensure students are continuing to perform the appropriate behavior.

Communicating with Students

Communication is vital to develop positive interactions with students that lead to trust and acceptance. In physical education programs where there is a great deal of communication, students are more likely to do what teachers ask of them. Just relating by talking to or listening to students will help. Some authorities have suggested that physical educators should interact in some way with each student in class during each class period. This could include verbal or nonverbal communication. In large classes, this may take two class periods or more, and the instructor will need to keep track of the students with whom they have interacted (French et al., 2013; Hellison, 2011). One useful technique is meeting students at the door when they are entering or leaving the gym. Another technique is standing near students during the daily

activity and providing feedback on their behavior and/or performance. For instance, if students are jogging, position yourself in one corner of the gym so you can provide a friendly look, a high-five, or a word of encouragement as they pass by. Table 19.9 presents techniques to consider when communicating with students.

Communicating with Parents

Keep parents abreast of how well the student is doing in all school settings, including physical education. This is particularly true for students who have a history of displaying inappropriate behaviors. Communication with parents can be by school

Table 19.9. Techniques to consider when communicating with students

1. Focus on behaviors, not on the student. Do not say "that behavior problem student"; say "the student with a behavior problem."

2. Listen to the student as long as the student is not using the opportunity to control the physical educator. For example, a primary-grade student during an elementary physical education class kept coming up to the teacher and holding her hand. The physical educator, in attempt to manage and instruct the class of 28 students, kept asking the student to go back to his spot or station. This behavior continued throughout the class period. After school, the physical educator went to the classroom teacher to see if this behavior also occurred in the classroom. The physical educator was informed that the night before the young student had upset his father and the father had forced the student to sleep alone outside the home that night. It would have been better if the physical educator was informed of this information earlier.

3. Understand your feelings toward the student. With heterogeneity in the levels of behavior and learning of students, teachers must modify traditional teaching styles. If a student has a cognitive deficiency, techniques must be implemented to ensure the student understands the instructions. If this does not occur, the teacher may become constantly frustrated because this student is continually in the wrong place and talking to other students to figure out what he is supposed to do in class.

4. Accentuate students' strengths. With large classes, it seems that it is a constant chore just to "put out fires." Focusing on a student's appropriate behavior and learning and not just their deficiencies may decrease many of the problems that are being exhibited in class. Students who are never reinforced may not be supportive of this environment.

5. Respect students' legitimate opinions. When a student provides his or her opinion, reinforce that you support students' opinions when they are honest and not negative. Many times these opinions can improve instruction. Sometimes a student states that it is too cold out, that he or she is bored of the activity, or that he or she never gets to play a certain position during a game; the student may not be the only one to feel this way. Maybe the physical educator should be listening and making the appropriate modifications, not ignoring.

6. Assist in developing positive peer relationships.

Source: Pangrazi (2004).

web site, telephone, e-mail, or notes. Communication ought to include times when the student has displayed appropriate behaviors as well as times the student has had problems. Also, contact parents and other team members if you notice changes in the student's behavior. Sometimes you will learn that the student's medication is being changed or there are changes in the home situation. For example, a student may be starting a new medication to combat a seizure disorder, and the medication may be affecting his or her coordination and stamina in physical education. Similarly, a student who seems very depressed and does not want to dress out for physical education might be dealing with his or her parents' divorce.

The key is to view parents as allies in developing the most appropriate behavior management program and to keep the lines of communication always open. Remember that many parents have had very poor experiences throughout their child's education, including in physical education, leading to negative attitudes toward their child's teachers. This negative attitude needs to be changed in order to earn their support for your program. The following are some ways to communicate with parents:

- Using the school web site, newsletters, or e-mail to explain all class rules, routines, and consequences (e.g., appropriate dress, class procedures, what activities are being worked on)

- Developing behavioral awards that are sent home (e.g., a note that reads, "Your child is student of the week in physical education!")

- Posting pictures of the students who had a significant behavioral improvement either in the gym, on a bulletin board, or on the class web site. Be sure to check with your school regarding the policy for posting pictures

- Having parent conferences or meetings

- Having a family play day, perhaps during back-to-school night

Communicating with Administrators

Developing positive relationships with administrators is extremely beneficial. Talking to the administrators about district and school policies and also how they would like you to deal with behaviors often opens the lines of communication and shows the administrators that you are concerned about creating an environment conducive to learning. Often, administrators do not want physical educators sending students with challenging behaviors to the office frequently and instead want these issues dealt with in class. However, you cannot ignore serious problems. A good rule before interacting with the administrator is to show that you have made an effort to deal with and have documented student misbehavior, particularly safety and legal problems. Try not to focus on teacher inconvenience. In addition, do not walk into the administrator's office with only the problem; be prepared to share your thoughts on possible solutions. This demonstrates to the administrator that the issue has been well thought out. Remember that most administrators have years of experience and could be excellent mentors.

Utilize a Team Approach

For challenging behaviors to be modified, collaboration among administrators, faculty, staff, parents, and the community may be required. This is especially important when designing a behavior intervention plan (BIP). Include as many team members as possible in the diagnosis of the problem and development of a plan. This needs to include a consensus on how the plan will be implemented and who is responsible for each part of the plan. For example, a teacher assistant might not be needed to accompany a student with an emotional disability to physical education every day, but she may be asked to be available in emergencies. Similarly, in large high schools that have several vice principals, the team should decide which assistant principal is in charge of behavior problems for particular students.

Schoolwide and Communitywide Behavior Programs

Behavior management plans that are developed independently by one teacher and implemented in only one setting are rarely effective for dealing with students with behavior problems. Many schoolwide programs have expanded to include parents as active partners. And in some small towns, there is communitywide involvement including storekeepers, police, firefighters, and park and recreation staff. Physical educators teaching students with disabilities must become an integral part of the schoolwide behavior management system. A schoolwide system needs to be infused into the more comprehensive programs used in settings with students with disabilities, such as leveling systems. This will enable students reaching the upper steps of the leveling system to make a transition into more fully inclusive settings if they have practiced and learned to effectively function in the schoolwide program.

Teaching Personal and Social Responsibility Through Physical Education

It is important that all students in class learn to respect and value others. For some students, this must be taught through knowledge and experiences. Physical educators may want to reanalyze the games and activities they use, focusing on rewarding points for appropriate behaviors, and respecting/including peers instead of rewarding in the traditional manner by the number of runs scored or baskets made. One system that infuses this concept into traditional physical educator's games and activities is referred to as points modification (Davis & French, 1986). For example, in traditional relay races, the team that finishes first receives the most points, and then the second-place team earns points, and so forth. Points can be added to each team not only for placing but also for demonstrating appropriate behaviors. For instance, a physical educator can add points to the teams that are participating cooperatively (e.g., not starting a game until a classmate gets back from the bathroom, staying in line, helping an opponent up, not yelling at another player). This technique will increase group cooperation and respect for others.

As another example, in an elementary physical education class, Jodie is student who has poor motor skills and also demonstrates some inappropriate behaviors. The other students do not interact with her or include her in activities. The physical educator is just beginning a volleyball unit and decides to incorporate the points modification approach. She decides that when Jodie is one of the players who touches the ball, her team automatically earns a point. This modification encourages peers to include Jodie more as a team member during the game.

Another approach that is supported by Hellison (2011) and Watson and Clocksin (2013) is class meetings to solve intra- and interpersonal problems that may affect the valuing of self or others. This approach is designed to develop social relationships and to teach students how to resolve conflicts within a physical education environment.

Know the Laws

It is now stated in the Individuals with Disabilities Education Improvement Act (IDEA) of 2004 (PL 108-446) that schools are required to conduct functional behavioral assessments and provide behavioral services to students who are disciplined beyond 10 days (IDEA 2004, § 300.536). Furthermore, schools are required to continue providing services that enable students who are disciplined

to participate in the general curriculum and to meet their IEP goals. For example, under most circumstances a student with a disability cannot be expelled from school unless a trained and knowledgeable group of individuals first determine whether the student's misconduct is related to his or her disabling condition. This is commonly termed *manifestation determination*. The second is the creation of a BIP. The following, summarized from the U.S. Department of Education (2006), explains these two key concepts regarding discipline under IDEA:

1. *Understand the term* disciplinary action: Within 10 days after the date disciplinary action is taken against a student with a disability, the school district must conduct a review of the relationship between the student's disability and the behavior that is the subject of the disciplinary action. This stipulation is for students who do not carry weapons or illegal drugs to school. The 504 or IEP committee may determine that the student's behavior was or was not a manifestation of the student's disability. This determination must be based on the evaluation and diagnostic results, observations of the student, and a review of the appropriateness of the student's IEP and placement.

   If it is determined that the student's disability did not impair his or her ability to understand the impact and consequences of the behavior subject to the disciplinary action, the student can be disciplined in the same manner as students without disabilities. However, if the student is suspended or expelled, then the district must continue to provide the student a free appropriate public education to decrease the possibility of educational regression. This provision does not apply to students without disabilities who were suspended or expelled for the same inappropriate behavior.

   If the behavior is determined to be a manifestation of the student's disability, the student cannot be disciplined for the behavior. Instead, the district must attempt to remediate the deficiency in the student's 504 plan or IEP and/or its implementation. This could mean the 504 or IEP committee may need to develop or revise a BIP. There are some exceptions. If the student with a disability carries a weapon to school or a school function or knowingly possesses or uses illegal drugs or sells or solicits the sale of a controlled substance while in school or at a school function, then he or she may be placed in an alternative education setting, determined by the 504 or IEP committee, for the same amount of time a student without a disability would be sanctioned, but for no more than 45 days. In addition, if school officials believe that a student with a disability is substantially likely to injure himself or herself or others in the student's general placement, they can ask an impartial hearing officer to order the student be removed to an interim alternative educational setting for a period of up to 45 days. It is important to note that if the student is served under IDEA 2004, he or she is protected from zero tolerance rules (i.e., you cannot expel the student). However, this protection does not apply to students who receive services under Section 504.

2. *Develop a BIP:* This plan contains strategies to address specific behaviors exhibited by a student who interferes with his or her own performance or with the learning of others. This plan must include strategies, consequences (i.e., rewards and punishers), and educational supports to increase the student's performance and learning. This plan is designed by a student's IEP committee, which includes a student's general education teacher. For any student who has committed a drug or weapon offense, the IEP committee must meet no later than 10 days after the offense to develop a functional behavior assessment plan review and modify an existing BIP (or develop a new one) for the student.

    For example, Sam is a ninth grader who just began attending high school. His IEP committee determined that he has emotional disorder and is exhibiting behaviors that negatively affect his education performance. Although he has the capacity to understand school rules, he will not follow them. Specifically, Sam has frequent unexcused tardiness, uses inappropriate language, verbally interrupts, and does not complete assignments. He appears to respond well to responsibility and opportunities to participate in activities that set him apart from the rest of the class. Various behavior management techniques have been implemented. Some have been a little effective (e.g., parent conference, loss of privileges) and others not effective (e.g., detention, suspension). The IEP team decided to develop and implement a BIP to accompany Sam's IEP.

Crisis Management

Some students demonstrate aggressive or violent behavior to a point where it is referred to as a "crisis." Teachers and specialists who deal with such students need to be trained in crisis management techniques that often include some form of personal restraint. When students hurt themselves or others, the behavior needs to be stopped immediately. The purpose of a crisis management plan is to protect the student from harming himself or herself as well as others and to help the student calm down and deescalate the problem (Bambara et al., 2015). The crisis plan should be developed and practiced by all school members who are in contact with the student. With this plan, there is a better chance for human dignity and recovery for the student in crisis and safety for all involved. Janney and Snell (2000) outlined five steps that are useful in managing a behavioral crisis:

1. *Ignore* the behavior problem when possible.
2. *Protect* the individual or others from physical consequences of challenging behavior.
3. *Momentarily restrain* the individual when exhibiting challenging behavior.
4. *Remove* anyone who is in danger from the area where the crisis is occurring.
5. *Introduce cues* that evoke positive behavior.

Specific procedures should be used to protect the student and the teacher. Physical educators must be trained to use the appropriate restraint techniques. Most important, restraint techniques must never be used without written parental permission, and they must be supported by the school administrators as a part of the school district's policy. If you do not have experience with crisis management techniques, it is highly recommended that you attend a district-approved restraint program. This may also protect you. Teachers who try to restrain a student without knowing the appropriate techniques sometimes find themselves in lawsuits in which parents claim that the educator caused physical harm to their child. In addition, a number of national programs exist to train teachers and accommodate school districts in crisis intervention (Crisis Prevention Institute, 2015).

Begin with Simple Techniques

Once the teacher knows the possible causes and reasons for a student's inappropriate behavior, the teacher can begin with the simplest technique, or the least amount of intervention. Some techniques could be just using cues, prompts, or social praise. This may be all that is required to put the student on task. Simple cues or prompts may help some students refocus on the task at hand. Simple hand signals such as the following can be used to cue and prompt children:

- One hand over head means the student immediately goes to his or her spot.
- Two hands over head means freeze.
- Two hands locked together over head means stop.
- Two hands over mouth means quiet.
- A clicker or whistle means go.

  Verbal cues such as the following can also be used:

  - "One, two, three, clap."
  - "Eyes on me."

Another simple technique is *name-dropping*. Name-dropping involves saying a student's name when that student is off task. Sometimes just hearing one's name helps a student to get back on task. For instance, when speaking to the class say, "You can see, Bill, we are still working on our throwing skills." If cues and prompts are not effective, use praise when the student is demonstrating the appropriate behavior. Another strategy is to use teacher proximity and stand near or next to the student.

CONCLUSIONS

Some physical educators feel frustration, isolation, and lack of understanding when teaching students with severe behavior or learning disabilities. For general physical educators to be effective with these students, at least four major factors must be considered. First, the physical educator has to set a positive supporting tone for the entire class by demonstrating a caring yet firm affect. The physical educator must be a good communicator with all the students, be consistent, have good rapport, be sensitive and understanding yet firm, and have a fair and consistent code of conduct. If a physical educator is unorganized and lacks consistent and fair behavior management skills, then the students may become angry, depressed, and feel helpless. In turn, students may react with fear and hostility.

Second, know your students. Physical educators have to learn as much as possible about students with disabilities who are in their classes before they can plan appropriate behavior management programs. What reinforces each student?

When does the student display particular behaviors? What seems to set the student off? What might the student be trying to accomplish by displaying inappropriate behaviors? How does the student react to consequences? Answers to these and other questions from the classroom teacher and parents will aid the physical educator in developing a behavior program that matches each student's unique abilities and needs.

Third, preservice and in-service training are a critical initial step in helping general physical educators meet their professional responsibilities for educating students with behavior problems who are included in their classes (Lavay et al., 2007a; Lavay et al., 2012; Lavay et al., 2014). When this training is provided, two factors must continually be considered: change is slow, difficult, and gradual and should not be expected in a one-shot in-service program. It is important to provide continued support and follow-up after initial training.

Fourth, think about your philosophies, values, and goals before you attempt to develop your behavior management plan for your students. Consider a 10-step plan, such as the following, to assist you in areas in which you as an educator may need improvement:

Step 1: Examine your philosophy of teaching and behavior management.

Step 2: Based on your philosophy, establish your teaching and behavior management goals.

Step 3: Evaluate the effectiveness of your current teaching practices.

Step 4: Implement the changes you have determined need to be made and analyze the results.

Step 5: Decide what remaining problems you need to deal with.

Step 6: Examine the challenging behavior and then make an earnest attempt to determine its cause.

Step 7: Design an intervention to change the challenging behavior.

Step 8: Implement the intervention and then evaluate its effectiveness.

Step 9: Repeat steps 6–8 for the other behaviors you listed.

Step 10: Repeat the entire process at least annually.

CHAPTER 20

Including Students with Disabilities in Community-Based Recreation

Martin E. Block, Andrea Taliaferro, and Thomas E. Moran

Objectives

1. Understand laws related to community recreation and sport for individuals with disabilities

2. Identify barriers to community recreation and sport for individuals with disabilities

3. Describe the empowerment model for overcoming barriers

4. Describe the steps needed to implement an inclusive approach to recreation for individuals with disabilities

5. Describe unique community-based sports programs

6. Describe special sports organizations that provide sports programs for individuals with disabilities

Chris plays youth football and youth baseball for a local parks-and-recreation league. One day, before Chris's practice, his younger brother Nathan, who has Down syndrome, looked at their mom and said, "Me play?" The mother responded, "Sorry, Nathan, you can't play." Chris looked up at his mom and asked, "Why can't Nathan play? He gets to watch me. I wish he could play too!" The mother saw the sincere look on Chris' face and began to wonder if there was a way for Nathan to participate or if she could find a program in the area that offered recreational opportunities for individuals with disabilities. As a physical educator, what can you do to become an advocate for Nathan? How can you help his mom or convince her that Nathan could and should participate in recreation programs?

WHY PARTICIPATE

Many children with disabilities such as Nathan see brothers and/or sisters playing sports and want to play too. They may engage in activities in their physical education or adapted physical education classes, but individual and/or parental fears may limit engagement in community-based programming. This is unfortunate as there are many reasons why children with disabilities should participate in extracurricular or recreational pursuits (see Cooper, 2013; Johnson, 2009; Mactavish & Schleien, 2000, 2004; Potvin, Snider, Prelock, Kehayia, & Wood-Dauphinee, 2013; Schleien, Meyer, Heyne, & Brandt, 1995; Schleien, Ray, & Green, 1997; and Smith, Austin, Kennedy, Lee, & Hutchison, 2005, for more detail on benefits). Some reasons include the following:

- Participation in leisure activities is related to increases in skills in other curricular areas. For example, research shows that problem-solving skills, personal-social behavior, social interaction skills, social knowledge, self-determination skills, gross and fine motor skills, and even reading comprehension and mathematics improve when students participate in leisure activities (Cory, Dattilo, & Williams, 2006; Dattilo & Schleien, 1994; Kunstler, Thompson, & Croke, 2013; Voeltz & Apffel, 1981; Wehman & Schleien, 1981). It has been suggested that students with disabilities are more receptive to instruction in these areas when participating in an enjoyable leisure activity (Cory et al., 2006; Dattilo & Schleien, 1994; Wehman & Schleien, 1981).

- An increase in appropriate play and leisure skills leads to decreases in inappropriate behavior. It is thought that unstructured "downtime" may lead to boredom, which in turn can lead to students with disabilities engaging in self-stimulatory behavior, excess behavior (e.g., overeating), acting out, and even self-injurious behavior. However, constructive use of leisure time has been shown to decrease such negative behavior when implemented as part of a positive behavior support program (Gaylord-Ross, 1980; Mahoney & Stattin, 2000; Meyer & Evans, 1989; Schleien, Kiernan, & Wehman, 1981; Sigafoos, Tucker, Bushell, & Webber, 1997).

- Constructive use of leisure time also is related to success in living in the community, including improved employment, self-esteem, and social skills (Kunstler et al., 2013). Again, downtime leads to boredom and dissatisfaction with one's place in the community. Parents often report that they are unhappy with how their child uses his or her leisure time when living in an independent or supported community living arrangement, noting that their child seems to need constant supervision and is unable to entertain himself or herself (Katz & Yekutiel, 1974). Teaching students with disabilities to fill their leisure time with appropriate, active recreation pursuits can help them feel more positive about their lives in the community and also reduce the need for such supervision (Duvdevany & Arar, 2004; Schleien et al., 1997).

- Finally, having a repertoire of enjoyable leisure activities is essential for quality of life (Abells, Burbidge, & Minnes, 2008; Badia, Orgaz, Verdugo, Ullán, & Martínez, 2011; Duvdevany & Arar, 2004; Sylvester, Voelkl, & Ellis, 2001). For many people, the most satisfying and enjoyable part of the day is recreation time, including after-school clubs or athletic programs; playing tennis or golf or going hiking with friends on the weekends; or relaxing, working out, or taking the dog for a walk in the evening. People (whether with or without disabilities) who do not have enjoyable leisure activities to fill their free time

are more likely to become bored, lonely, and depressed (Badia et al., 2011; Schleien et al., 1995). Thus, it is important to teach students with disabilities appropriate recreation and leisure skills so they can use their leisure time in a satisfying, fulfilling way.

Given the importance of recreation and leisure in the lives of individuals with disabilities and the problems with access to community recreation programs, the purpose of this chapter is to discuss ways of making community recreation and sports programs available to individuals with disabilities. The first part of this chapter reviews the legislation that provides access to recreation programs for individuals with disabilities. The second part of this chapter discusses the individual, programmatic, and external barriers that affect successful participation and provide a model to combat discussed barriers. The third part of this chapter outlines an eight-step process for creation and/or implementation of successful participation in community-based recreational programming for individuals with disabilities. And finally, the chapter concludes with a review of several community sports programs that have been specially designed for individuals with disabilities.

LAWS REGARDING PARTICIPATION IN SCHOOL AND COMMUNITY SPORTS PROGRAMS

Americans with Disabilities Act

On July 26, 1990, President George H.W. Bush signed into law the Americans with Disabilities Act (ADA; PL 101-336), arguably the most extensive civil rights legislation since the Civil Rights Act of 1964. ADA was designed to prevent people with disabilities from being treated differently solely because of their disability and to eliminate the discrimination of individuals with disabilities from participating in all aspects of life that most of us consider basic rights of being an American (Imber & Van Geel, 2001; U.S. Department of Justice, 2001, 2009, 2010). The law protects individuals with disabilities in a wide range of public and private services such as education, transportation, housing, employment, and recreation (Carpenter, 2000; Epstein, McGovern, & Moon, 1994; Fried, 2005; Sullivan, Lantz, & Zirkel, 2000). Sports and recreation activities and facilities are covered under ADA (Block, 1995b).

It is important to note that ADA was not designed to be an affirmative action program. There are no quotas stating that a certain amount of one's employees or club members must have disability. Rather, it ensures equality of opportunity and full participation. As such, the law prohibits individuals with disabilities from being excluded from jobs, services, activities, or benefits based solely on their disability (Stein, 1993; U.S. Department of Justice, 2001). For example, it would be a violation of the ADA to tell a child with intellectual disabilities that he could not play Little League Baseball.

Who Is Protected?

The ADA does not identify specific disabilities. Rather, the ADA provides the following general description of who is covered: an otherwise qualified individual who 1) has a physical or mental impairment that substantially limits one or more of the major life activities of the individual (i.e., seeing, hearing, speaking, walking, breathing, performing manual tasks, learning, caring for oneself, and working), 2) has a record of such an impairment (e.g., a person who is recovering from cancer, mental illness, or an alcohol problem), or 3) is regarded as having such an impairment (e.g., limits major life activities as the result of the negative attitudes of others toward those with disabilities such as severe burns, HIV/AIDS, epilepsy, facial abnormalities, or alcoholism; U.S. Department of Justice, 2001, 2009, 2010). Individuals with minor conditions that can be corrected, for example, those with glasses or hearing aids, are generally not covered in the act. Similarly, conditions that affect a person for a short period of time (e.g., sprain, broken limb, or the flu) are not considered "disabling conditions" under this act (U.S. Department of Justice, 2001).

ADA regulations are waived for an individual who is a direct threat to the health or safety of others that cannot be alleviated by appropriate modifications or aids (Appenzeller, 2000, 2005; Block, 1995b; Imber & Van Geel, 2001). Three criteria must be met before one can exclude a person based on health and/or safety factors: 1) The threat must be real, 2) the threat should be based on objective and unbiased information, and 3) attempts must be made to reduce or eliminate the risk (Appenzeller, 2000, 2005). For example, a community soccer league would not have to enroll a player with severe autism who has a well-documented history of unpredictable, violent behavior when placed in a group setting. However, the league would have to enroll a player with HIV/AIDS whom a doctor has determined not to be dangerous to others if those around this individual take universal precautions when handling blood.

Note that an individual with a disability cannot be denied participation in an activity solely because someone feels the activity is too dangerous for that person. It is the right of all Americans to choose activities, including those that involve a certain level of risk (Block, 1995b). While recreation program staff can tell a participant about the risks involved in a particular activity, in the end, it is the person's decision (with consult from the child's parents and physician) whether or not to participate in a recreation program (Block, 2005).

The ADA is divided into five major titles: Employment, Public Service, Public Accommodations, Telecommunications, and Other Provisions (U.S. Department of Justice, 2001, 2009). Title III, Public Accommodations, includes recreation. According to Title III, it is illegal to discriminate against a person with disabilities by denying him or her full and equal enjoyment of goods, services, facilities, privileges, advantages, or accommodations that are available to the general public. This includes hotels, restaurants, banks, business offices, convention centers, retail stores, libraries, schools, and recreation facilities. For example, a county recreation program must make sure that all facilities it uses are accessible to individuals who use wheelchairs. Similarly, a local basketball league must make sure it does not have any policies or practices that discriminate against individuals with disabilities.

Reasonable Accommodation and Undue Hardship

Two important parts of the ADA are reasonable accommodations and undue hardships. The ADA defines a *reasonable accommodation* as an adaptation to a program, facility, or workplace that allows an individual with a disability to participate in the program or service or perform a job. Accommodations also may consist of changes in policies, practices, or services and the use of auxiliary aids (Carpenter, 2000; Imber & Van Geel, 2001). Examples of reasonable accommodations include qualified interpreters for deaf people in a community soccer league, bowling guide rails at a local bowling alley, and flotation devices at a community swimming pool. Reasonable accommodations also can include making a facility more accessible, adding more staff, and providing extra staff training. Note that these accommodations should not fundamentally alter the nature of the activity, give the participant with a disability an unfair advantage, or cause undue hardship to the recreation program (Block, 1995b; Paciorek & Jones, 2001; Stein, 2005).

Undue hardship refers to actions that are considered significantly difficult, costly, extensive, substantial, disruptive, or that fundamentally alter the nature of the program. Factors to be considered include the following: nature and cost of the accommodation; overall financial resources of the facility, including number of individuals employed; and type of operation of covered entity, including the composition, structure, and function of work force (U.S. Department of Justice, 2001). For example, it may be an undue hardship (e.g., significantly expensive, fundamentally alters the activity) for a golf course to make all its sand traps and greens accessible to people who use wheelchairs. It would be reasonable (known as "readily achievable" according to ADA) to allow a golfer to use a regular golf cart to get around the course and facilities, allow the golfer to hit from the golf cart, allow the golfer some rule modifications such as free lift from the sand trap, and allow the golfer to use a special golf cart that does not damage the greens. Determining what is an undue hardship or what fundamentally alters the nature of a game can be very tricky. This concept was the heart of *PGA Tour, Inc. v. Martin*. Casey Martin argued that riding a golf cart would not fundamentally alter the game of golf, whereas the PGA Tour felt that walking was fundamental to competitive golf and would give Martin an advantage. The Supreme Court ruled in favor of Martin (Lane, 2001; Paciorek & Jones, 2001).

What Must Recreation Programs Do to Meet the Mandate of the Americans with Disabilities Act?

The following sections, modified from Block (1995b) and updated regarding more recent legislation, including the ADA Amendments Act of 2008 (PL 110-335) and the *2010 ADA Standards for Accessible Design* (U.S. Department of Justice, 2010), highlight key things community recreation programs must do to meet ADA mandates.

Opportunity to Participate   Publicly or privately controlled recreation facilities that are open to the general public must provide people with disabilities the opportunity to participate in their general recreation programs that have no other criteria (e.g., no skill criteria). For example, a local soccer league accepts all soccer players who live in the county, are of a certain age, and pay the entrance fee. This soccer league could not deny a child who is blind the chance to participate in this league if the child otherwise meets the stated league requirements. In addition, the league would have to allow reasonable accommodations (e.g., allowing the child's dad to assist him during practices and during the game). Even recreation programs that

have special skill criteria (e.g., travel soccer team) must provide an opportunity for individuals with disabilities to try out or qualify for a place on the team.

Even if a specialized recreation program is offered in a particular community or by a particular agency, the community recreation program still must provide opportunity for an individual with a disability to participate in their regular programs. For example, a community might offer Special Olympics soccer. Nevertheless, an individual with intellectual disabilities may choose to participate in the community-based soccer program rather than Special Olympics.

Facilities   Publicly or privately owned recreation programs that are open to the general public must make facilities accessible to individuals with disabilities if such accommodations are readily achievable and do not cause an undue hardship (Fried, 2005; Paciorek & Jones, 2001; U.S. Department of Justice, 2010). In many cases, reasonable accommodations mean that a portion of existing facilities needs to be made accessible. For example, it would be reasonable to have one "accessible" stall in the bathroom rather than changing all the stalls. Similarly, one or two soccer fields in a multifield complex should be accessible to individuals who use wheelchairs (see Fried, 2005, for simple, inexpensive ways of modifying facilities to meet ADA mandates). Note that any structure built after 1993 must be fully accessible to individuals with disabilities. ADA regulations contain a wide range of relatively moderate measures that may be taken to remove barriers, including installing ramps, making curb cuts, repositioning shelves, rearranging tables, repositioning telephones, adding Braille markings on doorways and elevators, and creating designated parking spaces (Fried, 2005; U.S. Department of Justice, 2001, 2010)

Revised regulations released by the Department of Justice in 2010 contain updated requirements to the ADA for Title II (State and Government Services) and Title III (Public Accommodations and Commercial Facilities). The *2010 ADA Standards for Accessible Design* (U.S. Department of Justice, 2010) establishes minimum requirements for state and local government facilities, public accommodations, and commercial facilities (including swimming pools, golf courses, and exercise facilities) so that they are readily accessible and usable by individuals with disabilities. This includes requirements that programs, services, and activities are accessible to individuals with disabilities unless doing so results in a fundamental alteration to the program or undue burden (U.S. Department of Justice, 2010).

Among these revisions are standards on accessibility for swimming pools, wading pools, and spas. The requirements ensure that individuals with disabilities will be able to participate in and enjoy activities and conveniences available to individuals without disabilities such as swim meets, swimming lessons, and recreational swimming. Although there are some exceptions, the regulations provide requirements for structural changes to address program accessibility. For example, the 2010 standards include specifications regarding the number, type, and means of accessible pool entry and exit such as ramps, pool lifts, transfer systems, sloped entries, and stairs. Furthermore, it is recommended that staff be provided with training regarding instruction on available accessible features, maintenance, and safety considerations (U.S. Department of Justice, 2012)

All public entities and public accommodations must comply with the 2010 standards as required under Title II (Program Accessibility) and Title III (Readily Achievable Barriers Removal Requirements) effective as of March 15, 2010, for all existing, newly constructed, or altered facilities and after January 31, 2013, for pools, wading pools, and spas (U.S. Department of Justice, 2012). More information regarding the *2010 ADA Standards for Accessible Design* (U.S. Department of Justice, 2010) can be found at http://www.ada.gov/regs2010/2010ADAStandards/2010ADAStandards.pdf.

FITNESS AND ATHLETIC EQUITY FOR STUDENTS WITH DISABILITIES ACT

In the state of Maryland, the Fitness and Athletic Equity for Students with Disabilities Act (2008) is groundbreaking legislation resulting from a federal court case of discrimination regarding a high school athlete with spina bifida who was not allowed to compete on her high school track team. Tatyana McFadden, an athlete who uses a wheelchair, was told by the Maryland Public Secondary School Athletic Association she was not allowed to participate on her high school track team due to safety concerns as well as having an unfair advantage. In a 2007 court case (*McFadden v. Grasmick*), the U.S. Supreme Court ruled in favor of Ms. McFadden, and she was allowed to compete on her track team, at the same time, with her peers. In 2008, the Maryland legislature passed the Fitness and Athletic Equity for Students with Disabilities Act. This landmark

law requires boards of education to develop policies to include students with disabilities in their physical education classes and athletic activities. The law requires schools to provide students with reasonable accommodations to participate, the chance to try out for school teams, and access to alternative sports opportunities. The Maryland law was the first state law of its kind in the nation and has served as a model for other state and federal legislation.

This legislation indicates the following:

(b) "Adapted program or corollary sports" means a program that is developed for a student with a disability.

(c) "Allied sports or unified program" means a program that is specifically designed to combine groups of students with and without disabilities together in physical activity.

(d) "Mainstream athletic program" means intramural or interscholastic athletic activity that is developed and offered to students in accordance with criteria established by the State Board. (Maryland Fitness and Athletic Equity for Students with Disabilities Act of 2008)

In addition, the law requires schools to provide the opportunity for students with disabilities to participate in extracurricular or interscholastic competition, as demonstrated by either of the following:

(i) Equivalent opportunities for participation in extracurricular or interscholastic athletic programs; or

(ii) Evidence indicating that the interests and abilities of students with disabilities have been fully and effectively accommodated by the county board's implemented programs. (Maryland Fitness and Athletic Equity for Students with Disabilities Act of 2008)

Dear Colleague Letter

On January 24, 2013, the Office for Civil Rights issued a "Dear Colleague Letter" clarifying requirements of schools under the Rehabilitation Act of 1973 (PL 93-112) to provide extracurricular athletic opportunities for students with disabilities. Similar to the Maryland law discussed, the letter presents guidance for how schools can include students with disabilities into mainstream athletic programs and create adapted programs for students with disabilities. Some have referred to the Dear Colleague Letter as Title IX for students with disabilities, but minimally it sends a clear message to public schools that students with disabilities must be provided opportunities for physical activity and sports equal to those afforded to students without disabilities (Lakowski, 2013). What is important to remember is that this Dear Colleague Letter is not a new mandate but rather a clarification of, and guidance for, the existing regulations and statutes under the Rehabilitation Act of 1973. The Rehabilitation Act protects the rights of students with disabilities in schools, and it includes a provision that requires equal opportunity for participation in extracurricular activities. Not all schools have always met that obligation.

The 2013 Dear Colleague Letter clarifies the responsibility of schools under Section 504 of the Rehabilitation Act and calls for schools to act broadly and proactively to include students with disabilities in athletic programs. Policies apply to all levels of education including both interscholastic and intercollegiate athletics. This means that any educational institution that receives federal funding must adhere to these rules, from elementary schools to colleges and universities (Lakowski, 2013). The letter clarifies when and how schools must include students with disabilities in mainstream athletic programs and defines what true equal treatment means. This section of the letter discusses how schools must provide reasonable accommodation for students with disabilities using common sense modifications that allow a student with disabilities to participate without giving them a competitive advantage or changing the fundamental nature of the sport. For example, a deaf student who wants to try out for the lacrosse team at her high school would be given an interpreter for tryouts to ensure that the coach focuses on the student's ability in the sport and not her communication challenges. Similarly, an athlete with a visual impairment who wants to run cross-country at his high school should be allowed to have a guide runner with him on the course, an athlete should be allowed to play tennis from her wheelchair in competitions with her community college tennis team, and an athlete who has only one leg and uses crutches should be allowed to use his crutches when playing soccer for his college team. Note that none of the accommodations suggested provide a competitive advantage or fundamentally change the nature of the game.

The letter also noted there are many students with disabilities who cannot participate in mainstream sports without changing the fundamental nature of the sports (e.g., children who use power wheelchairs cannot play on a grass soccer field and may pose a danger to other players who may inadvertently run into the wheelchair). In cases such as these, schools districts need to offer students with disabilities adapted opportunities for athletic activities, such as creating a power rugby team or other adapted sports opportunities (Lakowski, 2013). The

Maryland model is a great example of how such adapted sports can be created and implemented. The adapted/corollary sport model brings students with a variety of disabilities, such as intellectual disabilities, autism, or multiple disabilities, from one school to play sports such as softball or bocce against other schools. The Maryland Public Secondary School Athletic Association has sanctioned these adapted sports offering regional- and state-level tournaments. The allied/unified approach would allow athletes with and without disabilities to play together in an adapted sports program. This is a great model when there are not enough athletes with disabilities to form a team. For example, a high school may have two to three students with physical disabilities who want to play sitting volleyball. In order to make a team that could compete against other high schools, three to four athletes without disabilities are recruited to play, but everyone plays sitting down following the rules of sitting volleyball. The Georgia High School Athletic Association (GHSAA) also has successfully used this model with support from the American Association for Adaptive Sports Programs. GHSAA has gone as far as allowing athletes with and without disabilities from different high schools within and even across school districts to come together to form teams for sports such as wheelchair basketball.

BARRIERS TO PHYSICAL ACTIVITY IN STUDENTS WITH DISABILITIES

The *2008 Physical Activity Guidelines for Americans* (U.S. Department of Health and Human Services [DHHS], 2008) recommend that children and youth have 60 minutes of physical activity of moderate and vigorous intensity daily in three types of activities: aerobic activities, muscle-strengthening activities, and bone-strengthening activities. Furthermore, the guidelines suggest adults with disabilities engage in at least 150 minutes of moderate intensity physical activity per week (DHHS, 2008). The guidelines include a brief mention of children and youth with disabilities:

> Children and adolescents with disabilities are more likely to be inactive than those without disabilities. Youth with disabilities should work with their healthcare provider to understand the types and amounts of physical activity appropriate for them. When possible, children and adolescents with disabilities should meet the Guidelines. When young people are not able to participate in appropriate physical activities to meet the Guidelines, they should be as active as possible and avoid being inactive. (DHHS, 2008, p. 19)

Unfortunately, individuals with disabilities tend to not meet recommended levels of physical activity (DHHS, 2010a). There are several reasons why there are limited opportunities for students with disabilities to participate in active community recreation programs. In this chapter, the barriers are classified into three main types: participant, programmatic, and external. Within each category, specific examples are mentioned to highlight some of the problems individuals with disabilities face regarding community-based physical activity opportunities:

Participant

Students with disabilities often lack the physical and/or cognitive skills needed to participate in regular community sports programs (Schleien et al., 1995; Smith et al., 2005; Spencer-Cavaliere & Watkinson, 2010). For example, although Meghan, a paraplegic who uses a wheelchair for mobility, is very skilled in moving her wheelchair on hard, level surfaces or for short distances, she may lack the physical strength and/or endurance to maneuver her chair up and down a grass field to successfully play youth soccer. Randy, a middle school student with autism who has a deep love and enthusiasm for sports, currently does not possess the necessary motor skills, speed, or level of cognitive understanding of sports such as basketball or soccer to be successful.

Individuals with disabilities have expressed the fear of being unable to accomplish the skills most other children could, making them reluctant to even try (Spencer-Cavaliere & Watkinson, 2010). Often individuals with disabilities have low self-efficacy toward their ability to successfully participate in community-based programming, and they question whether instructors will be able to address their unique needs (Burns & Graefe, 2007; Moran, Taliaferro, & Pate, 2015; Stephens, Neil, & Smith, 2012).

Programmatic

There are a lack of options for organized physical activity for people with disabilities in both school and community settings (Kleinert, Miracle, & Sheppard-Jones, 2007; Stephens et al., 2012). For instance, some children with disabilities (e.g., learning disabilities) may be skilled enough to play for their community little league, whereas others (e.g., children with significant physical disabilities) may need more specialized programming. For those who are unable to play the "typical" game or play under "typical" rules, they still may be capable of playing baseball/softball if the game is slightly modified. A couple of examples of simple modifications could be allowing a student with a congenital arm amputation to hit off a tee when he or she experiences extreme difficulty hitting off the pitcher or allowing a child with autism to have a base coach to help him or her run to the appropriate base. These modifications could be key to the participants' success because specialized programs are not as readily available as programs geared toward people without disabilities, especially in rural areas or communities with limited resources. The lack of available programs coupled with the instructors' lack of training and participants' fears makes it clear why physical activity participation is limited among individuals with disabilities.

In addition, an emphasis tends to be placed on specialized leisure programs and environments. Many communities offer typical sports programs for very skilled athletes and special sports programs for individuals with disabilities (e.g., Special Olympics). Unfortunately, communities rarely offer something in between that allows less skilled individuals without disabilities and individuals with disabilities to participate together (Badia, Orgaz, Verdugo, & Ullán, 2013; Schleien et al., 1995). For example, if an individual cannot play in a traditional five-on-five basketball league where the game is played at a fast pace but does not want to play Special Olympics basketball, where he or she might only compete in skill-specific stations and never get to play in a modified game setting, the individual or family may become frustrated as there are no "middle" options to play organized basketball in the community.

Physical education programs, particularly middle and high school programs, often emphasize nonlifetime sports such as football, soccer, and basketball. These sports require a high level of skill to be successful in community-based programs, and they are not readily available for young adults in most communities. Sports that would be more beneficial to students with disabilities across the lifespan include bowling, tennis, golf, hiking, and weight training.

Coaches and community-based instructors may lack the necessary training, knowledge, and instructional support to allow all individuals to successfully participate (Johnson, 2009; Martin, 2004; Moran & Block, 2010; Spencer-Cavaliere & Watkinson, 2010). Organizations may reach out to special education teachers, who can provide disability expertise but who do not have formal training in teaching physical activity–related skills. For example, most special educators feel uncomfortable trying to teach students with disabilities the skills necessary to play basketball or golf. As a result, most special education teachers do not get involved in recreation and sports programs unless they have an interest or are highly skilled in specified activities.

External

Participation in community recreation and sports programs requires money, transportation, and specialized equipment (Rimmer, Rubin, & Braddock, 2000). For example, purchasing golf clubs, getting to the golf course, and then paying for green fees can be very expensive, especially for an adult with a disability who is making minimum wage. In addition, participants with disabilities may not have the necessary support groups (e.g., peers, parents, coworkers) who are interested in participating in active community recreation and sports programs (Davis & Sherrill, 2004; Krueger, DiRocco, & Felix, 2000).

Gaps in knowledge, training, and resources of instructors often produce a strong fear on the part of the parents when it comes to community-based sports participation for their children with disabilities (Spencer-Cavaliere & Watkinson, 2010). This fear of failure by parents causes them to predict that their child will experience far more failure and frustration than success. Often parents will not enroll their child with a disability in community sports programs due to these fears (Moran & Block, 2010).

A variety of surfaces (e.g., grass versus hard court; level versus uneven field), inaccessible facilities (e.g., stairs leading to gym in a YMCA built before 1990), and other challenges out of the control of the participant are all external barriers to participation. For example, many parents and coaches may feel that a wheelchair is unsafe in an environment such as baseball, as the chair presents a safety concern for the other players on the field and not just for the individual, who may not be able to get out of the way of a ball or oncoming base runner.

EMPOWERMENT MODEL: SYSTEMATIC PROCESS TO COMBAT BARRIERS AND CHALLENGES IN COMMUNITY-BASED RECREATION PROGRAMS

The empowerment model proposed by Moran et al. (2015) uses a multitiered continuum approach of training, support, and programming to address these barriers to physical activity programming for people with disabilities (see Figure 20.1).

Training

The training component of the model is designed to give professionals, coaches, and community instructors/organizations the specific knowledge and skills they need to successfully implement developmentally appropriate and differentiated instruction. This occurs through training modules that are sequential in nature and that prepare instructors and coaches with information on common disabilities,

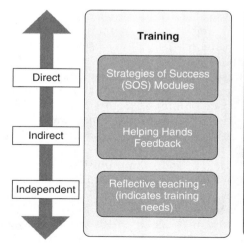

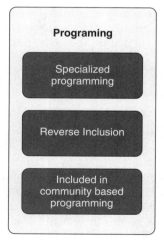

Figure 20.1. The tiered continuum of the empowerment model. (From T.E. Moran, A.R. Taliaferro, J.R. Pate [2014]. Confronting Physical Activity Programming Barriers for People with Disabilities: The Empowerment Model. *Quest 66* [4], 396–408, reprinted by permission of the National Association for Kinesiology in Higher Education [http://www.NAKHE.org].)

provide an understanding of learner and environmental constraints that affect performance, and offer specific strategies to differentiate instruction.

Support

In the empowerment model, support is offered in two ways: directly or indirectly. This support is provided by an individual (mentor) who is trained and willing to provide support to the participant with a disability or to the coach/instructor. This trained mentor might provide support to the participant with a disability, such as by accompanying a child with cerebral palsy to a basketball practice and offering assistance as the child participates in activities or providing the child with modified equipment or pertinent visual or auditory cues. The mentor could also support the instructor. For example, in the case of a child with autism who is participating in a baseball program in the community, the mentor might work alongside the coach and help him or her learn how to address communication needs for the child, present content in meaningful ways, provide prompts to keep the child on task, and structure the practice to assist the student with autism while providing support to the child as necessary. If the instructor or child does not require direct support during programming, the mentor could provide consultation, such as by discussing specific strategies with the instructor ahead of time or tracking participant progress and success from the sidelines. The degree of mentor support will vary depending on the type of programming; abilities of the participant; and level of self-efficacy, knowledge, experience, and comfort of the instructor.

Programming

Programs developed and implemented using the empowerment model are designed to meet the needs of children with disabilities as well as any typically developing peers who are invited or decide to participate in the program. These programs are classified by two categories: group dynamic and environmental context. Group dynamic ranges from specialized programs that are organized solely for individuals with disabilities and include trained coordinators and support (such as Miracle League Baseball), reverse inclusion programs that are organized for individuals with disabilities but include a limited number of peers without disabilities as well (such as TOPSoccer), and inclusion or programs that are organized for equal numbers of participants who have and do not have disabilities (such as Special Olympics Unified Sports or traditional community

recreation programs). Environmental context varies from community-based dependent (led by a trained specialist) to community-based independent (led by typical program staff). The range of program offerings allows participants to select both the programming and the environment appropriate for their needs and also allows a continuum of options from specialized to full inclusion.

Interacting Continuums

The continuums of training, support, and programming overlap and interact with each other, promoting the success of instructors and participants and addressing common barriers to physical activity participation. For example, one instructor can be directly provided with training and also provided with a mentor to provide support to both the instructor and the child during a gymnastics program. Another instructor in the same community gymnastics program might, however, be further along the continuum and only request indirect support from a mentor to provide suggestions on how to modify the skills for a child who uses a wheelchair.

Ultimately, the goal of the tiered empowerment continuum is move populations progressively through the continuum to more independent levels of training, support, and programming. On the training continuum, for example, the goal is to move instructors from needing direct training to a level of independence where they are able to reflect on their own instruction and seek further training based on their specific needs. On the programming continuum, the goal is to move, if appropriate, as many participants as possible from successful participation in specialized programs to reverse inclusion and, ultimately, to full inclusion into community-based programming.

IMPLEMENTATION PROCESS FOR INCLUSIVE, COMMUNITY-BASED RECREATION PROGRAMS

Sarah, a high school freshman who has autism, has enjoyed learning some new lifetime sports activities in her physical education class this year. Because the summer is near, Sarah's parents are interested in signing her up for a recreation program in the community to stay busy. However, they are not sure what the first step is and what programs are even offered in their community. Furthermore, they are concerned that the staff at these community recreation programs won't know how to work with Sarah or be able to make appropriate accommodations so that she can successfully participate.

Table 20.1. Implementation process for inclusive recreation

Step 1: Initial contact, data gathering, and registration process
Step 2: Accommodations
Step 3: Training
Step 4: Participation
Step 5: Follow-up
Step 6: Evaluation
Step 7: Documentation of progress

From Wagner, G., Wetherald, L., & Wilson, B. (1994). A model for making county and municipal recreation department programs inclusive. In M.S. Moon (Ed.), *Making school and community recreation fun for everyone: Places and ways to integrate* (p. 182). Baltimore, MD: Paul H. Brookes Publishing Co.; adapted by permission.

How can Sarah's parents find information regarding appropriate programs in their community? How will they know which activities Sarah will enjoy most and which programs will be a good fit?

Chapter 4 outlines a systematic process for developing and implementing an inclusive physical education program for children with disabilities. A similar model was suggested by Wagner, Wetherald, and Wilson (1994; see Table 20.1). The following sections detail the key steps and components of this model.

Step 1: Initial Contact and Registration Process

Assessing the Student's Interests

The first step in the process is identifying the recreational activity and then assisting the student and/or the student's parents in signing up for the program. Wagner et al. (1994) suggested that the first component of this step is to assess the student's interests in various community-based recreation programs. When possible, simply ask the student what types of recreation programs he or she enjoys. For example, one student might talk at length about basketball, whereas another student might express an interest in hiking, inline skating, or weightlifting. Figure 20.2 provides an example of a survey that can be used to determine a student's leisure interests (Schleien et al., 1997).

When a student cannot clearly articulate his or her interests, various recreation activities can be presented to the student. The student then could be observed participating in each activity to gauge his or her reaction and interest when participating in these activities.

For example, a physical education teacher is trying to decide what community-based recreation activities might be of interest to a student who has autism who is moving from middle to high school.

This physical educator knows from reports from the middle school physical educator and other members of the student's individualized education program (IEP) team (including the student's parents) that the student does not like being in crowds or in places where there are loud noises. The student also likes routines and repetitive activities. However, even with this knowledge, the IEP team does not know what recreation activities are available in the community or what recreation activities might be of interest to the student. The high school physical educator decides to spend the first several weeks of the semester assisting the student in sampling various appropriate recreation activities in the community. This includes taking the student to the tennis courts to try to hit tennis balls off a tee or with a gentle toss, to an open field to hit golf balls (similar to hitting balls at a driving range), to shoot baskets on the playground (student could shoot baskets by himself or with a roommate in the driveway of his group home), riding a stationary bike and weightlifting in the school's weight room (similar to a weight room available in the community), and hiking through the woods that surround the school (similar to hiking trails available in the community). Some activities were crossed off the list after initial consideration because of this student's unique characteristics. These included bowling (environment tends to be very loud); Special Olympics sports (all sports, even individual sports, are practiced and competed with too many other participants); skating and swimming (facilities are not available in the community); and basketball, soccer, softball, and volleyball (too unpredictable and too many participants).

Assessing Parent Interests

In addition to the student's interests, it also is important to determine parents'/caregivers' recreation interests. Parents tend to have the greatest influence on the type of recreation activities their children participate in as well as whether their children participate in segregated or inclusive recreation programs (Mayer & Anderson, 2014; Modell & Imwold, 1998). Parents also can promote recreation programming for their child as well as advocate for recreation programs in their community (Heyne & Schleien, 1997). Therefore, determining parents' recreational interests is an important part of the process.

Other Factors to Consider

In addition to student and parent interests, choosing an activity also depends on what recreation activities are popular with similar-age peers without

Leisure Activity Selection Checklist

Date: _____

Name: _____

Age: _____ Sex: _____ Telephone: _____

Address: _____

Activity	Currently do	Interested in	Activity	Currently do	Interested in
Team sports			**Arts and crafts (continued)**		
Bowling	_____	_____	Crocheting	_____	_____
Softball	_____	_____	Latch hook	_____	_____
Basketball	_____	_____	Ceramics	_____	_____
Soccer	_____	_____	Other (specify) _____	_____	_____
Tee ball	_____	_____	**Table games**		
Football	_____	_____	Cards	_____	_____
Hockey	_____	_____	Checkers	_____	_____
Other (specify) _____	_____	_____	Chess	_____	_____
Music			Dominoes	_____	_____
Singing	_____	_____	Scrabble	_____	_____
Playing instruments	_____	_____	Puzzles	_____	_____
Attending concerts	_____	_____	Billiards	_____	_____
Other (specify) _____	_____	_____	Table tennis	_____	_____
Dance			Other (specify) _____	_____	_____
Folk	_____	_____	**Outdoor/leisure/social**		
Modern	_____	_____	Hiking	_____	_____
Square	_____	_____	Gardening	_____	_____
Aerobic	_____	_____	Camping	_____	_____
Tap	_____	_____	Barbeques/picnics	_____	_____
Ballet	_____	_____	Skiing	_____	_____
Jazz	_____	_____	Canoeing	_____	_____
Other (specify) _____	_____	_____	Other (specify) _____	_____	_____
Individual sports			**Day trips**		
Gymnastics	_____	_____	Historical	_____	_____
Jogging/running	_____	_____	Cultural	_____	_____
Tennis	_____	_____	Sporting	_____	_____
Archery	_____	_____	Shopping/restaurants	_____	_____
Swimming	_____	_____	Other (specify) _____	_____	_____
Golf	_____	_____	**Social clubs**		
Badminton	_____	_____	Scouts	_____	_____
Horseback riding	_____	_____	Photography	_____	_____
Fishing	_____	_____	Travel	_____	_____
Bike riding	_____	_____	Gourmet cooking	_____	_____
Walking	_____	_____	Card playing	_____	_____
Other (specify) _____	_____	_____	Other (specify) _____	_____	_____
Arts and crafts					
Painting	_____	_____			
Knitting	_____	_____			

(page 1 of 2)

From Schleien, S.J., Ray, M.T., & Green F.P. (1997). *Community recreation and people with disabilities: Strategies for inclusion* (2nd ed., pp. 224–225). Baltimore, MD: Paul H. Brookes Publishing Co.; adapted by permission.
In *A Teacher's Guide to Adapted Physical Education: Including Students with Disabilities in Sports and Recreation, Fourth Edition,* by Martin E. Block. Copyright © 2016 by Paul H. Brookes Publishing Co., Inc. All rights reserved.

Figure 20.2. Leisure interest survey.

_____

(continued)

Figure 20.2. *(continued)*

Leisure Activity Selection Checklist

My leisure experiences usually are:

_____Physical	_____Individual	_____Structured
_____Active	_____Planned	_____Expensive
_____Mental	_____Social	_____Nonstructured
_____Passive	_____Long term	_____Spontaneous
_____Inexpensive		

With whom do you usually engage in leisure experiences?

_____Alone   _____A friend(s)

_____Family member(s)

During what time of day do you participate in leisure activities?

_____Morning   _____Afternoon

_____Evening

Do any of the following prevent you from participating in leisure activities?

_____Financial difficulties	_____Lack of transportation
_____Facility not accessible	_____No one to participate with
_____Geographic location	_____Disability/lack of skill
_____No motivation	_____Child care problems
_____Other (specify) _____	

Please check any special needs or considerations that may affect your participation.

_____Physical

_____Mental

_____Social

_____Other (specify) _____

Would you be interested in serving as a member of a community leisure advisory board on recreation for people with disabilities?

_____yes   _____ no

Would you attend an open organizational meeting to assist us in planning leisure services for people with disabilities in your community?

_____yes   _____ no

From Schleien, S.J., Ray, M.T., & Green F.P. (1997). *Community recreation and people with disabilities: Strategies for inclusion* (2nd ed., pp. 224–225). Baltimore, MD: Paul H. Brookes Publishing Co.; adapted by permission.
In *A Teacher's Guide to Adapted Physical Education: Including Students with Disabilities in Sports and Recreation, Fourth Edition,* by Martin E. Block. Copyright © 2016 by Paul H. Brookes Publishing Co., Inc. All rights reserved.

disabilities and what recreation activities are readily available in the community. For example, it does not make sense to teach a student to play golf if his or her parents, siblings, and peers have no interest in golf. Similarly, it does not make sense to teach a student how to roller-skate if no one in the community roller-skates. And finally, it does not make sense to teach a student to ice skate or snow ski if such activities are not available in the community (see Chapter 4 for more detail on selecting an activity).

Still, an activity that is readily available in the community may be inappropriate for a particular student. For example, even though soccer is popular and readily available in a particular community, and even though a student loves soccer, playing soccer may be beyond the abilities of a child with severe cerebral palsy. Or, even though a child expresses an interest in playing golf in the community, the IEP team may decide that the cost of golf is too expensive when compared with how much this student makes at his part-time job and how much he receives in Supplemental Security Income (SSI). However, the IEP team should be careful when dismissing recreation programs that are available in the community. Although the student with cerebral palsy cannot play soccer in the community, he may enjoy and get exercise benefits from kicking a ball around with his friends at his group home in the future or with his parents after school. Although golfing at a golf course is expensive, hitting plastic golf balls in the backyard is very inexpensive yet enjoyable for a particular student and his peers. The IEP team should think creatively about how a student who really loves a particular recreation activity can participcate in or access that activity. See Figure 20.3 for factors to consider when selecting a recreation activity (Schleien et al., 1995).

Step 2: Identify a Suitable Program

With an appropriate recreation activity selected, the next step is to identify suitable programs in the community. The key to finding a suitable recreation program is to determine the student's abilities in the targeted recreation activity, the student's interest in participating in an inclusive program or a special program, how flexible the community program is regarding accepting and perhaps modifying the program to include a student with a disability, cost (how expensive), transportation (how far), and time (when offered) factors related to the program (see Figure 20.3 and Part I-A of Figure 20.4).

Finding suitable recreation programs will most likely be easier in larger communities. Many larger communities will offer a variety of programs at many different levels ranging from high-level teams that compete nationally to recreation leagues where participants play for fun. In addition, these communities may offer a variety of specialized programs such as different levels of Special Olympics softball for people with intellectual disabilities (from highly competitive, inclusive team play to individual skill competitions), beep baseball for people with visual impairments, and Challenger Baseball for children with varying disabilities. In such communities it would be easy to find a match for a student with almost any type of disability who really wants to play softball. Smaller communities, however, may only offer fairly high-level softball team play with no lower level recreation softball programs or special softball/baseball programs. This makes finding a suitable program more challenging.

One solution is to create lower level recreation programs or special programs in smaller communities in order to provide the necessary program for students with disabilities. For example, three rural counties come together to create the first Tri-County Softball League, which is designed for people interested in playing recreation softball with a focus on having fun. Though each county individually may not have enough interest to create a recreation league, pooling all interested participants across the three counties results in the creation of a six-team league. Because this is a recreation program, the teams accept players of all abilities (including players with disabilities), and the league is willing to be flexible with rules (e.g., allowing players to hit a ball off a tee) to ensure the success and fun of all participants.

Observe Community Programs

With a recreation program identified, the next component of Step 2 is to observe the community program. This observation can be conducted by staff at the student's school and/or by the student's parents. Whenever possible, the student should observe the program to further validate his or her interest in the particular program. For example, tee-ball is targeted for a bright 6-year-old girl with cerebral palsy (she uses crutches to aid her when she walks). She loves to play catch with her dad and older sister, and she loves to hit a ball off a tee. However, when she goes with her dad and sister to watch a tee-ball game, she quickly realizes that there is a lot of standing and waiting. She observes that most children only get two or three turns to hit a ball off a tee during the entire game (she gets to hit 20–30 balls off a tee in 15 minutes when playing with her dad and sister in her backyard).

Leisure Activity Selection Checklist

Participant: _____ Date: _____

Completed by: _____

For each activity, circle *yes* or *no* for each criterion. Tally the number of yes responses for each of these subsections and record them on the appropriate line. Tally the overall score for each activity. Activities that receive a score of 11–14 points are generally considered appropriate for instruction.

Lifestyle: Select activities that are socially valid and will facilitate typical play and leisure behaviors, as well as provide opportunities for increasingly complex interactions.

	Activity 1		Activity 2		Activity 3	
1. *Age appropriateness:* Is this activity something a peer without disability would enjoy during free time?	yes	no	yes	no	yes	no
2. *Attraction:* is this activity likely to promote the interest of others who frequently are found in the participant's leisure-time environments?	yes	no	yes	no	yes	no
3. *Environment flexibility:* Can this activity be used in a variety of potential leisure-time situations on an individual and group basis?	yes	no	yes	no	yes	no
4. *Degree of supervision:* Can the activity be used under varying degrees of caregiver supervision without major modifications?	yes	no	yes	no	yes	no
5. *Longitudinal application:* Is the activity appropriate for both an adolescent and an adult?	yes	no	yes	no	yes	no

Individualization: Issues related to logistical and physical demands of leisure activities on current and future environments and free-time situations

	Activity 1		Activity 2		Activity 3	
1. *Skill level flexibility:* Can the activity be adapted for low- to high-entry skill levels without major modifications?	yes	no	yes	no	yes	no
2. *Prosthetic capabilities:* Can the activity be adapted to various disabilities?	yes	no	yes	no	yes	no
3 *Reinforcement power:* Is the activity sufficiently novel or stimulating to maintain interest?	yes	no	yes	no	yes	no
4. *Preference:* Is the participant likely to prefer and enjoy the activity?	yes	no	yes	no	yes	no

Environmental: Challenges and accommodations to leisure activities related specifically to the individual so that he or she can be successful in current or future free-time situations

	Activity 1		Activity 2		Activity 3	
1. *Availability:* Is the activity available (or can it easily be made so) across the participant's leisure environments?	yes	no	yes	no	yes	no
2. *Durability:* Is the activity likely to last without need for major repair or replacement of parts for at least a year?	yes	no	yes	no	yes	no
3. *Safety:* Is the activity safe (i.e., would not pose a serious threat to harm the participant, others, or the environment if abused or used inappropriately)?	yes	no	yes	no	yes	no
4. *Noxiousness:* Is the activity not likely to be overly noxious (noisy, space consuming, distracting) to others in the participant's leisure environments?	yes	no	yes	no	yes	no
5. *Expense:* Is the cost of the activity reasonable?	yes	no	yes	no	yes	no

Scores	Activity 1	Activity 2	Activity 3
1. Lifestyle	_____	_____	_____
2. Individualization	_____	_____	_____
3. Environmental	_____	_____	_____
TOTAL ACTIVITY SCORES	_____	_____	_____

Figure 20.3. Leisure activity selection checklist. (From Schleien, S.J., Meyer, L.H., Heyne, L.A., & Brandt, B.B. [1995]. *Lifelong leisure and lifestyles for persons with developmental disabilities* [p. 245]. Baltimore, MD: Paul H. Brookes Publishing Co.; adapted by permission.)

I. SKILL SELECTION CONSIDERATIONS/FACILITY DESCRIPTION
A. Appropriateness of leisure skill facility
1. Is skill or facility selected appropriate for individuals without disabilities of the same chronological age?
2. Has the individual with disabilities previously acquired any skills related to the activity?
3. If the particular responses would be difficult to perform, are material/procedural adaptations available to enhance participation?
4. Does the individual with disabilities have access to the facility or materials (e.g., distance from home, transportation concerns)?
5. Is the cost prohibitive? Are there other resources to help pay for the cost of the facility (e.g., reduced fee, waived fee, sponsorship)?
6. Has the individual with disabilities expressed interest in this particular activity?

B. Description of leisure skills: environmental inventory/discrepancy analysis
1. See Figure A20.1 in the appendix at the end of this chapter.

C. Description of leisure facility or environment
1. Provide a general description of leisure facility or environment.
2. Conditions under which the participant will be required to participate and interact (who else will be there, noise level, other distractions, etc.)?
3. Provide a diagram of facility or environment.

D. Description of social environment
1. What social interactions with peers, supervisors, and others are required in the immediate environment?
2. What is the typical dress for the environment.

II. ANALYSIS OF COMPONENT SKILLS AND ADAPTATIONS FOR FULL/PARTIAL PARTICIPATION
A. List of required equipment and materials
1. Provide a detailed listing (and description, as needed) of all the equipment and materials that a person may come in contact with in the environment.

B. Physical considerations: gross motor, fine motor, fitness
Describe each motor response using the following as a guideline:
1. Number and complexity of coordinated movement patterns?
2. What strength is required to perform the activity or to manipulate materials?
3. What body positions and flexibility are required to perform the activity?
4. What speed is required to perform the activity?
5. What levels of endurance are required to perform the activity?
6. What are the minimal health conditions necessary to participate in the activity?

C. Perceptual considerations: visual, auditory, body awareness
1. What visual skills (including discrimination) are needed in the environment and in the activity?
2. What auditory skills (including discrimination) are needed in the environment and in the activity?
3. What body awareness skills are needed in the environment and in the activity?

D. Interpersonal interaction considerations: exchange between participants
1. What typical types of interactions occur in the environment (e.g., turn taking, cooperating, unstructured)?
2. What optional interactions might you expect (e.g., getting a drink)?
3. What are the language requirements in the environment? (List typical nouns, verbs, cues, and statements used in activity.)

E. Functional academics: reading, writing, math/scoring, time telling
1. What reading skills are needed? Can they be bypassed with modifications?
2. What writing skills are needed? Can they be bypassed with modifications?
3. What math skills are needed? Can they be bypassed with modifications?
4. What time telling skills are needed? Can they be bypassed with modifications?

F. Decisions/judgments necessary for successful participation
1. What time and situation judgments may have to be made by the person with a disability to successfully participate in the leisure activity?

G. Specific adaptations/adjustments needed for partial participation
When making suggestions for adaptations, keep the following in mind:
1. Whenever possible, activities should not be altered to make the individual stand out.
2. Whenever possible, adaptations should be considered temporary.
3. Adaptations should be made on an individual basis (as opposed to making modifications for the entire group when only one person needs modification).

III. ANALYSIS OF SUPPORTIVE SKILLS
A. Preparation prior to participation in leisure activity
1. Can the student prepare him- or herself for participation (e.g., choose appropriate clothes; eat appropriately; bring correct amount of money; bring ID card, towel, and lock)? If not, who will assist student in preparation?

B. Transportation
1. What mode of transportation will be used?
2. Does the student have mobility skills needed to independently use this type of transportation? If not, who will assist student?

C. Informed consent
1. Has the student and/or parent/guardian signed consent form participation in program?
2. Does student have insurance?

From Certo, N.J., Schleien, S.J., & Hunter, D. (1983). An ecological assessment inventory to facilitate community recreation participation by severely disabled individuals. *Therapeutic Recreation Journal, 17*(3), 29–38; adapted by permission.
In *A Teacher's Guide to Adapted Physical Education: Including Students with Disabilities in Sports and Recreation, Fourth Edition*, by Martin E. Block, Copyright © 2016 by Paul H. Brookes Publishing Co., Inc. All rights reserved.

Figure 20.4. Outline for developing a community-referenced leisure skill inventory.

She also observes that most children never get to touch the ball, let alone throw it during the game (again, playing with her dad and sister she gets lots of turns to throw). So after watching tee-ball a few times, she decides that she does not want to play tee-ball but instead expresses interest in wheelchair tennis. She has seen wheelchair tennis when watching the Paralympics on television, and she thinks she could really enjoy that sport. She also saw how some wheelchair tennis players practiced and played with able-bodied peers, and one girl even played on her high school tennis team. She decides that she would like to check out what tennis programs are available in her community.

Discuss Client with Staff

After observing the program, the next component in Step 2 is to discuss the student with the staff of the recreation program. It would be unfair to the staff and to the student to simply have the student show up the first day to the program without giving the staff a "heads up," information on the student, and some training. At this step in the process, you simply want to inform the staff of the recreation program that a student with a disability is interested in participating in the program. Then after providing some general information about the student and his or her abilities/disabilities, allow the staff to ask questions. The staff may need several days to generate questions about the student.

For example, a 14-year-old student who uses a wheelchair may want to join a local health club. The student's parents arrange a meeting with one of the managers of the health club to introduce and discuss the student's abilities and needs. When asked if she had any questions, the manager simply said no. However, after talking to other managers of the club, she e-mailed the student's mom with several questions.

Help Register the Participant

The last component of Step 2 is to help register the participant for the program. When appropriate, the participant should register himself or herself. However, even participants who can register themselves may need help reading over the registration materials and contracts. For example, health clubs are notorious for getting people to sign up for upgraded or lengthy contracts. The participant may benefit from help in navigating the various options offered by the health club (full club membership versus the weight and cardio rooms) and the length of the contract ($300 for a 1-year membership when paid up front versus $20 per month for a 3-year contract). This may be a place to negotiate a reduced fee for participants with low income. For example, a student with autism plans on going to the driving range and hitting a bucket of golf balls twice each week (the driving range is an easy bus ride from his parent's house). It costs $5 for a bucket of balls, which totals $40 per month. The student's mother explains that although this is not much for most people, this is a significant expense for this student (he does not have a job, he is not yet eligible for SSI, and his mom is a single parent who does not have a lot of extra money). The driving range is pretty quiet between 3:00 p.m. and 4:00 p.m. (the time when this student plans on going to the range), and the manager realizes that this student will be a consistent client throughout the year. He is willing to reduce the cost to $2.50 per bucket.

Step 3: Data Gathering

The next step in the process is to prepare the student and his or her parents for participation in the program. This step involves sitting down with the family and discussing the student's participation in the program. This is a chance for the student and his or her parents to ask questions about participation. Table 20.2 presents several questions that parents/students might ask regarding participation in community recreation programs.

Table 20.2.   Questions parents ask about community recreation programs

What children and/or adults participate in this program (e.g., novice, recreation level, competitive, very skilled)?

Where is the program located?

How much will the program cost?

What equipment or clothing will I need?

What transportation will be provided to the program, or do parents provide transportation?

When and how many times per week does the program take place?

Are any of the student's friends or classmates participating in this program?

What safety precautions and emergency plans are in place in the event the student has a medical problem (see Chapter 10)?

How will the staff at the program react to having a student with a disability in the program?

How will the staff and other participants be prepared for this student?

What accommodations are anticipated to allow for the student's safe, successful, and meaningful participation in the program?

Step 4: Accommodations

Step 4 focuses on determining specific accommodations the student needs to successfully and safely participate in the community recreation program. Hopefully, potential accommodations were discussed with the manager or leader of the recreation program earlier in the process. For example, it would not make sense at this point in the process to spring the idea of not allowing defensive players to steal the ball from a child with intellectual disabilities and allowing him free shots in a basketball game. What if the league commissioner says these types of accommodations would fundamentally alter the game? Therefore, although specific accommodations are created at this point in the process, a preliminary discussion of accommodations needs to be discussed earlier in the process.

Determining specific accommodations to a recreational program should follow a systematic process. Certo, Schleien, and Hunter (1983) created a model for analyzing the various aspects of a recreation program in order to determine the need for specific accommodations (see Figure 20.4). The focus of this model starts with an environmental inventory with a discrepancy analysis (see Table 4.3 in Chapter 4 and Figure A20.1 in the Appendix at the end of this chapter). This allows the physical educator and the community recreation provider an opportunity to analyze all the steps of the program and then determine specific accommodations a student needs to be successful. For example, there are several important activities related to the subenvironment of "driving range shop" (see Figure 20.5).

Although this student can do many of the activities in the subenvironment independently, the ones that require communication and waiting require some accommodations. With the help of this student's speech therapist and special education teacher, it is decided that relatively simple accommodations (e.g., having the counter worker do some simple prompting, substituting a written note for speaking) can help this student become independent in this subenvironment.

		Subenvironment: Driving range clubhouse
Name: Bart Atkins		Date of birth: March 26, 2006
Evaluator: Martin Block		Date: September 7, 2015

Activities	Assistance currently needed	Accommodations
1. Opens door to club house	I	None needed
2. Walks to counter	I	None needed
3. Waits turn (if necessary)	V	Counter worker knows to tell person to wait
4. Asks counter worker for a medium bucket of balls to hit	V	A child has a card that says he wants to hit a medium bucket of balls.
5. Waits for response by counter worker	I	None needed
6. Takes money out of wallet	V	Cue by counter worker
7. Gives counter worker money for bucket	I	None needed
8. Waits for change (if necessary)	V	Cue by counter worker
9. Waits for bucket	V	Cue by counter worker
10. Takes bucket and thanks counter worker	I	None needed
11. Takes bucket and walks to door	I	None needed
12. Opens door and walks out of club house	I	None needed

Figure 20.5.   Sample of ecological inventory for hitting a bucket of golf balls. (*Key:* I, independent; V, verbal cues or reminder; P, physical assistance.)

Other areas that should be carefully analyzed to determine the need for any accommodations include gross and fine motor skills (types and complexity of coordinated movements), fitness requirements (minimal strength, endurance, and flexibility required to participate in the activity), perceptual requirements (any visual, auditory, or body awareness skills that are needed for the activity), interpersonal skills and appropriate behavior/etiquette (turn taking, typical interactions, language requirements), functional academics (any reading, writing, math, or time-telling skills needed for the activity), financial assistance (cost of program, equipment, and transportation), and transportation (how will student get to and from recreation program; Certo et al., 1983; see Figure 20.4 for more detail).

Step 5: Training

Training staff is the last step before the student is included in the community recreation program. This is a critical yet often missing step in the process. Without proper training, staff who take the student to the recreation program as well as the staff who work at the recreation program will not be able to facilitate meaningful inclusion. In addition, training prevents the staff from making assumptions about the participant based on the participant's label (Fink, 2001). For example, the recreation program for a 16-year-old girl with Down syndrome involves going to a local health club to lift weights and walk on a treadmill. The program has been carefully planned with several modifications to help the student be successful. Unfortunately, no one has prepared the teacher assistant who will take the student to this health club. The assistant struggles to figure out how to help this student independently check in to the health club and change in the locker room, so she ends up doing much more for the student than is necessary. Staff at the health club assume that strenuous activities are probably dangerous for people "like her" and choose to restrict the student from using the elliptical trainer or using the free weights and only allowing this girl to walk slowly on the treadmill. The teacher assistant does not know how to help the student use the weight machines and is afraid of the student being injured, so the student does not do any weightlifting. As a result, this student rides a stationary bike (something she does not like to do) and then sits in the health club café, drinking a cola and eating a bagel.

Clearly, training is a critical final step, but it does not have to be a particularly difficult step. The

person accompanying the student to the recreation facility should be trained on the following information: the goal of the program, the student's particular abilities/needs, any medical or behavioral issues and programs, how to teach skills (e.g., verbal cues versus demonstrations versus physical assistance as well as how to teach specific parts of a motor skill or how to use equipment), how to collect data, and how and who to ask for help. This training should be a collaborative effort conducted by the special education teacher (behaviors, how to teach the student in general), therapists (communication, physical considerations and contraindications, safety), and the physical educator (how to teach specific sports skills, rules of the game, social etiquette of the game).

Training the staff at the recreation facility (e.g., league commissioners, coaches, staff at recreation centers) should include the following information: goals of the program (why is this student in your recreation program), background on the student's abilities/disabilities and how these have been accommodated, medical/health problems and emergency plans (if needed), student's social and behavioral skills and problems, what behaviors you might see from the student and what tends to upset the student, and how the staff at the recreation program can prevent behavior problems, the importance of facilitating social interactions between the student and other participants and how such interactions can be facilitated, and how they can help the student be successful in the program.

Step 6: Participation

The student is now ready to be included in the recreation program. All the preplanning involved in Steps 1–5 has increased the odds that the student will have a successful experience in the program. However, things do not always go smoothly, especially the first few sessions. First, the student may be apprehensive of the new facility, new people, new routine, and new expectations (even individuals without disabilities get a little anxious when starting a new recreation program). However, with time, support, and successful experiences, most students settle into a routine and enjoy the program. Second, the staff (both those who assist the student and those associated with the recreation program) need time to learn about the student and how best to help the student have a successful experience. Again, time and continued support from the IEP team (parents, teachers, therapists) will help the staff learn about the student and how to successfully include the student into the program.

An important part of this step is to collect ongoing data to determine how well the student is doing in the program. How does the student seem to be enjoying himself or herself? How are the student's behaviors? Is the student interacting with peers? How successful is the student in the program? How are coaches and recreation staff feeling about the student's inclusion? Are there adjustments needed to the program to make the student more successful? These questions can be answered with simple checklists created by the student's IEP team.

For financial and transportation reasons, it may be difficult to take a student to community recreation programs more than once per week. Nevertheless, the student needs a great deal of practice if he or she is going to acquire the key skills needed to be successful in the community recreation program. Creating a simulated environment back at school can help the student acquire these key skills. Although not the same as practicing at the community recreation facility, practicing key parts of the activity in a simulated setting such as the school gymnasium can help the student be more successful when the student actually goes to the community facility. For example, the physical educator can set up a driving range on a grassy area behind the school, a bowling alley in the gymnasium, and a health club in the school's weight room. Key motor skills such as placing the ball on the tee and then hitting the ball, walking up to the foul line and rolling the ball, and properly using weightlifting equipment can be practiced and mastered in these simulated settings. Whenever possible, this simulated setting should mirror the community-based setting as much as possible. For example, the bowling setting in the gymnasium should include chairs to sit on to wait one's turn, a place to retrieve the ball from the ball return, a second lane next to the student's lane (with other students bowling), and a foul line. This way skills learned in the practice sessions in the simulated settings will have the greatest opportunity to transfer to the community-based setting.

Step 7: Follow-Up

Hopefully, the preparticipation process has created a setting that has allowed the student to have a meaningful and successful community recreation experience. To be sure everything is going as planned once the student has begun participation in the program, it is important to follow up with the staff who are implementing the program, the student, and the staff at the community recreation facility. This can be an e-mail or telephone call, or it can involve a face-to-face meeting. The important point is to not assume that the program is being implemented as planned and that the student is successful. So many things (anticipated and unanticipated) can derail a well-planned community recreation program. For example, a student who initially expressed interest in working out at a health club finds the targeted club too busy and noisy at the times he planned on working out. As a result, the student does not work out at the club as planned. Or, a retired golfer from the community who said he would be a golfing buddy to a student with a disability (playing nine holes of golf once per week) suddenly is too busy to play more than once per month. Without the support of this buddy (transportation, helping the student check in at the club house, helping the student on the golf course), this student is unable to play golf.

Follow-up discussions or meetings can lead to solutions and get the student's recreation program back on track. These follow-up discussions can include discussions of the student's success and how the student feels about the program, problems that have arisen and potential solutions to any problems, or adjustments to the program to make it even more successful. Again, these discussions can be as simple as a telephone call or e-mail. However, a visit to observe the student participating in the activity at the recreation facility is the best way to truly find out how the student is doing. And as noted, these discussions should include the staff or volunteers implementing the program, the student, and the staff at the community recreation program.

Step 8: Evaluation

Toward the end of the program, it is important to conduct a formal evaluation of the program. This allows the staff who implemented the program, the student (when appropriate), and the staff at the community recreation program to reflect on what went well in the program, what did not go so well in the program, and recommendations to improve the program for the next time they implement a similar program for this student or other students with disabilities. This evaluation can be a written survey with open-ended questions, a more detailed written survey with several yes/no questions about the program, an e-mail, or a face-to-face interview. Figure 20.6 provides an example of a simple participant satisfaction survey that can be administered to a student with a disability after completion of the program.

It is important that this step is completed in order to get a fair evaluation of the program and to make improvements for future programming. Too

Participant Satisfaction Survey

Name: _____

Support staff: _____

Name of activity: _____ Date: _____

1. Was the recreation facilitator helpful in finding activities in which you were interested?   ___ yes   ___ no

2. Did you get a chance to express your preferences before activities were identified for you?   ___ yes   ___ no

3. Did you enjoy the activity/program in which you participated?   ___ yes   ___ no

4. Was the recreation facilitator helpful in assisting you to participate in the activity to your fullest ability?   ___ yes   ___ no

5. Did you make any new friends while participating in the program?   ___ yes   ___ no

6. Did you develop any new interests as a result of participating in the program?   ___ yes   ___ no

7. Were the other participants and program staff/volunteers friendly and helpful?   ___ yes   ___ no

8. Will you continue to participate in this activity or another similar one?   ___ yes   ___ no

9. Would you like more support in participating in this or another similar activity?   ___ yes   ___ no

_____

Recommendations/comments:_____

_____

_____

_____

From Moon, M.S., Stierer, C.L., Brown, P.J., Hart, D., Komissar, C., & Friedlander, R. (1994). Strategies for successful inclusion in recreation programs. In M.S. Moon (Ed.), *Making school and community recreation fun for everyone: Places and ways to integrate* (pp. 33–53). Baltimore, MD: Paul H. Brookes Publishing Co.; reprinted by permission.
In *A Teacher's Guide to Adapted Physical Education: Including Students with Disabilities in Sports and Recreation, Fourth Edition,* by Martin E. Block, Copyright © 2016 by Paul H. Brookes Publishing Co., Inc. All rights reserved.

Figure 20.6.   Participant satisfaction survey.

often, community recreation programs are implemented, but no one takes the time to conduct an end-of-program analysis. The staff and the student may know whether the program was successful, but without a formal evaluation, no one may know why the program was or was not a success. For example, a student indicates on the participant satisfaction survey that she does not plan to play youth soccer in the spring. Clearly something about the program must have had a negative effect on this student. But the staff that helped implement the program as well as the program staff (the coach) did not sense any problems. However, after answering questions on a postparticipation survey, they realized that the child really did not interact with peers that much. In fact, they now recall that interactions with peers, although pretty good at the beginning of the program, were almost nonexistent at the last few games. By looking at the student's satisfaction with the program as well as helping the staff analyze the program, the team was able to pinpoint what went wrong toward the end of the program. They now realize that the discussion they presented to the other players on the team at the beginning of the soccer season (who the child was, how to interact with her, the importance of making her feel a part of the team) needed to be repeated halfway through the season.

Step 9: Documentation of Progress

This final step in the process involves sending a report home to the student's parents as well as to other team members who may not have had firsthand experience with the community program. Parents will want to know if their child was successful in the program, what specific skills the student acquired as a result of the program, if the student is now more independent with the activity, and what is recommended for future community recreation pursuits. Similarly, other staff members who may have helped design the program but who did not participate in the implementation of the program will want to know if the program was successful and what adjustments might need to be made in the future for this student or for other students with disabilities.

Figure 20.7 provides a sample of a progress report for a 12-year-old girl with autism who participated in an after-school softball program. This type of progress report provides the key information that Lakeisha's parents and the other members of the IEP team need to understand how well she did in this program. The program described was an intramural/interscholastic program offered to all girls at all the middle schools in the school district. The adapted physical education specialist thought this girl would benefit from the sport's setting, which provided many opportunities to improve her motor skills, interact with peers, and practice appropriate behaviors. The IEP team agreed with the idea, but they realized the girl would need support to be successful due to her limited motor skills and her behaviors. The adapted physical education specialist contacted the local university's volunteer program, which matches students from the university with various community needs. The university recommended a junior who was a physical education major looking to volunteer for Special Olympics or some similar program. After receiving training from the adapted physical education specialist and working with Lakeisha during adapted physical education a few times, Ron was on his own, assisting Lakeisha during all practices (once each week) and during all games (once each week).

SPECIAL COMMUNITY-BASED SPORTS PROGRAMS FOR STUDENTS WITH DISABILITIES

Consider again the scenario with Nathan at the beginning of this chapter. What potential sports programs would Nathan be eligible to participate in? As Nathan's physical education teacher, how can you help Nathan and his mom find a suitable sports program in the community to participate in? The ideal is to have individuals with disabilities participate in general community recreation and sports programs. However, there are circumstances in which special sports programs might be more appealing. For example, even with modifications some athletes with disabilities just do not have the skill level to compete with athletes without disabilities. Also, some athletes with disabilities (and their parents) may want to have a more readily accessible program without as much work to carve a place for the student, and often times, special sports programs tend to be more accommodating. Finally, some athletes just feel more comfortable and seek a sense of camaraderie with peers who have similar abilities. For those athletes with disabilities interested in special sports programs, there are several special sports programs designed for individuals with disabilities. The first two—Challenger Baseball and TOPSoccer or VIP Soccer—are designed for children with a variety of disabilities. The other sports associations discussed are for children and adults with specific disabilities.

Name: Lakeisha Jefferson	Activity: Softball
Support: Ron Carter (community volunteer)	Date: 5/31/15
Staff person: Kari Johnston, CAPE (APE specialist)	

Lakeisha has been playing softball with a local softball team of 12- and 13-year-olds for the past 8 weeks. Lakeisha was really excited to join the team, and she has made some very good progress during the season. Below is a description of her progress in the key softball skills we targeted for her this season. In addition, there is a description of her improvement in social skills and behaviors during the season. Ron Carter (a volunteer from the University of Virginia who has helped Lakeisha during the season) did a great job assisting her while still allowing Lakeisha to become more independent as the season progressed.

Object control skills

Lakeisha has worked on the two-hand strike and the catch during the season. Activities used to help Lakeisha included practicing with a peer, receiving direct physical assistance on how to hold the bat and how to position herself to catch, and using a lighter bat and hitting off a tee (she was allowed to hit off a tee during games after trying to hit three tossed pitches). The following describes Lakeisha's progress this season. Note that 0 indicates <u>not observed in at least three of four trials</u> and 1 indicates <u>observed in at least three of four trials</u>.

	2/27/15	5/25/15
<u>Two-hand strike</u>		
1. Dominant hand grips bat above nondominant hand	0	1
2. Nondominant side of body faces the tosser	0	1
3. Hip and spine rotation	0	0
4. Weight is transferred by stepping with front foot	0	1
5. Hits ball off tee consistently	1	1
6 Hits pitched ball (tossed from 5 feet away) consistently	0	0
<u>Catch</u>		
1. Preparation phase where elbows are flexed and hands are in front of body	0	1
2. Arms extend in preparation for ball contact	0	1
3. Ball is caught and controlled by hands/mitt only	0	0
4. Elbows bend to absorb force	0	0
5. Catches softball when tossed from 5 feet away directly to her	1	1
6. Catches softball when tossed from 10 feet away directly to her	0	1
7. Catches softball when tossed from 15 feet away directly to her	0	0

Behaviors/interaction with peers

Important goals included helping Lakeisha learn how to wait her turn, follow directions, and generally get along with peers. We have helped Lakeisha work on these goals by reminding her of appropriate behaviors, praising her for appropriate behaviors, preparing her for situations when she will have to wait her turn or interact with peers, and removing her from the group and allowing her to sit down for a few minutes in order to help her calm down. The following describes Lakeisha's progress during the season:

	2/27/15	5/25/15
1. Waits turn for up to 30 seconds without getting out of line	0	1
2. Follows verbal directions after first verbal cue	0	0
3. Follows demonstrations after first demonstration	0	1
4. Attends to peers for 30 seconds in partner activities	0	0
5. Plays in the games with assistance but without crying, hitting, or running away.	0	1

We are pleased with Lakeisha's progress, and we anticipate seeing similar progress if she chooses to play softball again next year. She seemed to enjoy both practices and the games (practices more than games, as she gets a little bored with all of the waiting in the games), and she seemed to enjoy the interactions with her teammates. Her teammates really did a nice job of befriending Lakeisha and really trying to make her a part of the team.

Kari Johnston, CAPE (APE specialist)	Parent signature

Figure 20.7. Sample progress report.

Challenger Division of Little League of America

Little League of America offers a special baseball program for boys and girls ages 4–22 with disabilities. The Challenger Baseball program is offered in many localities throughout the United States where Little League Baseball is played. More than 30,000 individuals with disabilities participate in more than 900 challenger divisions in 10 countries worldwide (Little League of America, n.d.). The Challenger division differs from traditional Little League Baseball in that it is not a competitive program. Teams play against each other, but there are no winners and losers. Rather, the goal of games is for active participation, to learn about baseball, and to have fun.

There are several modifications in Challenger Baseball. First, each player is assigned a "buddy" to assist the player during the game. This buddy can be a parent, sibling, or volunteer. Second, Challenger players do not pitch, although a player is assigned to field the pitcher's mound. Third, players are given six swings and the option of hitting off a tee. Fourth, all team members (which can be up to 15–20 players) get to bat when their team is up. In addition, all team members play in the field at least half of the game. Finally, games are typically one to two innings and are an hour long (Little League of America, n.d.).

American Youth Soccer Organization VIP and U.S. Youth Soccer TOPSoccer Programs

The American Youth Soccer Organization (AYSO) VIP and U.S. Youth TOPSoccer programs provide a quality soccer experience for children and adults whose physical or mental disabilities make it difficult to successfully participate on mainstream teams. AYSO's VIP (very important players) program carries the philosophy "everybody plays" (AYSO, n.d.). Program goals include players have fun, understand the fundamentals of the game, learn teamwork and fair play, increase positive self-esteem, become more physically fit, and meet and become comfortable with new people.

U.S. Youth Soccer TOPSoccer (The Outreach Program for Soccer) is a community-based training and team placement program for young athletes with disabilities, organized by youth soccer association volunteers. The program is designed to give children who have a mental or physical disability the opportunity to learn and play soccer and become valued and successful members of the U.S. Youth Soccer family (U.S. Youth Soccer, 2014). Each program is very much like regular soccer with the following key modifications (Lavay & Semark, 2001):

- Buddies assist players on the field in playing the game.
- Teams can have as few as five players.
- Teams may be coed.
- Teams are balanced with players rated by size and physical ability.
- Older and younger players form their own divisions when numbers allow.
- Teams play on smaller fields, but the field is part of the regular soccer league field.
- Rules are relaxed (e.g., no offside calls, latitude on throw-ins, no side changes at halftime).
- Buddies can assist as necessary but are faded away when possible.

Special Olympics

Special Olympics is an international organization dedicated to empowering individuals with intellectual disabilities to become physically fit, productive, and respected members of society through sports training and competition. Special Olympics offers children and adults with intellectual disabilities year-round training and competition in 34 Olympic-type summer and winter sports (see Table 20.3). There is no charge to participate in Special Olympics (Special Olympics, n.d.-b). Special Olympics also offers three unique programs: the Motor Activities Training Program (MATP), Unified Sports, and Youth Athletes. MATP is for individuals with severe limitations who do not yet possess the physical and/or behavioral skills necessary to

Table 20.3. Special Olympics sports

Alpine skiing	Cricket	Floorball	Judo	Open water	Softball
Aquatics	Cross-country skiing	Football (soccer)	Kayaking	swimming	Speed skating
Athletics	Cycling	Golf	Motor activity training	Power lifting	Table tennis
Badminton	Equestrian	Gymnastics (artistic	program	Roller skating	Tennis
Basketball	Figure skating	and rhythmic)	Netball	Sailing	Unified sports
Bocce	Floor hockey	Handball		Snowboarding	Volleyball
Bowling				Snowshoeing	

participate in official Special Olympics sports. Unified Sports promotes social inclusion by bringing together athletes with and without intellectual disabilities to train and compete together on the same teams. It was inspired by a simple principle: Training together and playing together is a quick path to friendship and understanding. In Unified Sports, teams are made up of people of similar age and ability, which makes practices more fun and games more challenging and exciting for all. Young Athletes is a unique sports and play program for children ages 2½–7.

Special Olympics serves 4.2 million people with intellectual disabilities in more than 200 programs in more than 170 countries (Special Olympics, 2014). To be eligible to participate in Special Olympics, one must be identified by an agency or professional as having one of the following conditions: intellectual disabilities, cognitive delays as measured by formal assessment, or significant learning or vocational problems due to cognitive delay that require or have required specially designed instruction (Special Olympics, 2014).

Special Olympics sports programs follow the same rules as regular Olympics sports programs. However, there are accommodations that make Special Olympics different. First, athletes compete among those of equal abilities through the "10% rule." Athletes are pretested on their individual or team skill level. Results of these pretests are used to "heat" athletes or teams against athletes or teams of similar abilities. For example, 10 athletes all have been pretested on the 50-meter dash with scores (in seconds) as follows: 8, 9, 10, 11, 13, 14, 15, 20, 22, and 24. Three heats would be created with Heat 1 consisting of the four athletes with times of 8, 9, 10 and 11 seconds; Heat 2 consisting of three athletes with times of 13, 14, and 15 seconds; and Heat 3 consisting of 20, 22, 24 seconds. Each heat is competed as a separate competition so that the person who finishes first in Heat 1 would get gold medal, the person who wins heat Heat 2 would get a gold medal, and the person who wins Heat 3 would get a gold medal. This way everyone, no matter how skilled, has a reasonable chance of getting a medal in his or her heat.

As noted, no fees are charged to athletes to train or compete in any Special Olympics program. Although this may seem like a small thing, Special Olympics is one of the only sports programs that does not charge fees to its athletes. In addition to no fees, Special Olympics provides awards to all participants. Even if a child does not come in first, or even second or third, the athlete receives a ribbon for finishing in the top eight or for participating in the event.

Special Olympics also conducts a random draw for advancement to higher levels of competition. To advance from a local competition to a state competition, a local program randomly selects athletes rather than picking the best athletes. Similarly, advancing from state level to national or international competition is done randomly, with all athletes who received a gold medal at the state level eligible to be randomly selected to compete at the national or international level (Special Olympics, 2014).

United States Association of Blind Athletes

The mission of the United States Association of Blind Athletes (USABA) is to increase the number and quality of sport opportunities for Americans who are blind or have visual impairments. This is achieved by providing athletes and coaches information on programs, support, and sports training and competition programs at the state and national levels and representation at the international levels. One important value stressed by USABA is the opportunity to demonstrate through sports the abilities of people who are blind and visually impaired (USABA, n.d.-c).

Since its founding in 1976, the USABA has reached more than 100,000 blind individuals. Sports under USABA include archery, bowling, biathlon, cycling, equestrian, goalball, golf, gymnastics, judo, outdoor recreation, power lifting, rowing, sailing, Nordic and alpine skiing, showdown, swimming, track and field, and wrestling.

In addition to its mission of providing individuals who are blind or visually impaired with athletic opportunities, USABA is trying to change society's negative stereotypes concerning the abilities of individuals who are blind. The organization has emerged as more than just a world-class trainer of athletes with visual impairments—it has become a champion of the abilities of Americans who are legally blind. Although an athlete may be blind, he or she has the ability to compete alongside his or her sighted peers. In fact, USABA athletes have competed in the regular Olympics. Marla Runyan qualified for the 2000 Olympic Team in the 1,500-meter race event and made the finals. She also finished as the top American in the Boston and New York Marathons (USABA, n.d.-a).

As was discussed in Chapter 14, one unique aspect of sports for people who are blind is the use of athlete classification based on each athlete's functional visual abilities and limitations. The USABA created four classifications of blind athletes to make competition as equitable as possible (see http://usaba.org/index.php/membership/visual-classifications).

Wheelchair and Ambulatory Sports, USA

Wheelchair and Ambulatory Sports, USA (WASUSA) was founded in 1956 as the National Wheelchair Athletic Association. Its mission was to serve athletes with disabilities—mostly World War II veterans—who wanted to participate in sports other than basketball. Wheelchair basketball was popular at U.S. veterans' hospitals in the 1950s. During these early days, many wheelchair basketball players saw participation in individual wheelchair sports as supplementary training for their primary interest in basketball.

> However, the WASUSA program appealed to even greater numbers of athletes with disabilities because it was able to incorporate women and quadriplegics (those with paralysis in upper as well as lower extremities), two populations that basketball could not reasonably accommodate at that time. (WASUSA, n.d.)

Since the early 1970s, additional efforts have been undertaken to organize WASUSA programs at the local and regional levels throughout the United States. The organization has expanded to include athletes who are ambulatory, hence the name change to Wheelchair and Ambulatory Sports, USA. WASUSA is organized geographically into three regional point organizations that collectively oversee 34 individual chapters. Each chapter is responsible for developing local wheelchair and ambulatory sports programs and for conducting qualifying meets for the National Wheelchair Games.

Europe's first organized wheelchair sports program was introduced in 1948 by well-known neurosurgeon Dr. Ludwig Guttman, founder of the Spinal Injury Center in Stoke Mandeville, England. The first Stoke Mandeville Games included only a handful of participants (26) and few events (shot put, javelin, club throw, and archery), but growth in both the number of events and participants came quickly. In 1952, a team from the Netherlands was invited to compete with the British team. This was the first International Stoke Mandeville Games, an event that has been held annually ever since.

As of 2014, WASUSA offers archery, hand cycling, powerlifting, shooting, swimming, table tennis, and track/field (WASUSA, n.d.). WASUSA expanded its offerings to junior athletes. The WASUSA Junior National Championships, the organization's largest annual event, was first held in July 1984. This event provided the first national program of competitions for junior athletes. Since that time, athletes ages 7–21 with spinal cord injuries, cerebral palsy, visual impairments, amputations, limb deficiencies, and other congenital abnormalities compete in Olympic-style events. Chosen athletes can also compete in the International Wheelchair and Amputee Sports World Junior Games.

PARALYMPIC CLUB SPORTS

Since 2007, U.S. Paralympics, a division of the United States Olympic Committee, has partnered with community organizations from across the country to create a network of Paralympic Sport Clubs. Paralympic Sport Clubs are community-based programs developed to involve youth and adults with physical and visual disabilities in sports and physical activity, regardless of skill level (U.S. Paralympics, 2014). All Paralympic Sport Club programs and activities are based in the community and are run by the local organization. The local organization could be a parks and recreation department, nonprofit organization, rehabilitation hospital, school system, college/university, or other community-based organization that has the interest, expertise, and resources to successfully plan and implement a program. The Paralympic Sport Club program is designed to be implemented within an organization's menu of programs.

The objectives of Paralympic Sport Club program include the following:

- Developing community-based sports clubs that recruit and involve youth and adults with physical and visual disabilities in sports and physical activity regardless of skill or interest level.

- Developing a comprehensive, community-based Paralympic Sport Club network as a foundation for a Paralympic athlete pipeline.

- Providing community-based sport program opportunities for injured service members and veterans to continue sport participation upon their integration back into their home communities.

- Creating a national, unified, community-based Paralympic Sport Club network that provides a "grassroots" branding campaign to educate Americans on the opportunities and benefits inherent in sport and physical activity as practiced by people with physical and visual disabilities. (U.S. Paralympics, 2014)

DISABLED SPORTS USA: NETWORK OF SPORTS PROGRAMS

Disabled Sports USA utilizes a community-based chapter network, a grassroots approach that supports local chapters in identifying the needs of the communities they serve. Disabilities include those with visual impairments, amputations, spinal cord injury, multiple sclerosis, brain injury, cerebral palsy, other neuromuscular/orthopedic conditions, autism, and related intellectual disabilities (Disabled Sports USA, n.d.).

Through their nationwide network, Disabled Sports USA serves more than 60,000 youths, wounded veterans, and adults annually through a nationwide network of more than 100 community-based chapters in 37 states nationwide in more than 40 different sports (for a list of included sports, please see Table 20.4; Disabled Sports USA, n.d.). Since 1967, Disabled Sports USA's mission is to provide national leadership and opportunities for individuals with disabilities to develop independence, confidence, and fitness through participation in community sports, recreation, and educational programs.

Table 20.4.   Disabled Sports USA sports

- Alpine and Nordic skiing
- Snowboarding
- Biathlon
- Kayaking
- Water skiing
- Sailing
- Scuba
- Surfing
- Rafting
- Outrigger canoeing
- Fishing
- Hiking
- Golf
- Athletics
- Archery
- Cycling
- Running/wheeling
- Rock climbing
- Equestrian

From United States Association of Blind Athletes (n.d.). *IBSA visual classifications.* Retrieved from http://www.usaba.org/Pages/sports information/visualclassifications.html; reprinted by permission.

SUMMARY

Community sports and recreation programs are such an important part of childhood and growing up, and participation in these programs can teach students so much more than the skills of the game. Because of this, one important goal of all physical education programs is to help students acquire the skills and behaviors needed to be successful in community sports and recreation programs. Most students without disabilities will acquire these skills and have many different community sports and recreation opportunities readily available to them. Unfortunately, this is not the case with students with disabilities. Students with disabilities often do not have the requisite skills, knowledge, or behaviors needed to be successful even with entry-level recreation and sports programs. Also, students with disabilities often need extra support to be successful in community sports and recreation programs. As a result, students with disabilities often never have the chance to participate in and gain the benefits from community sports and recreation programs. One way to help students with disabilities move into community sports and recreation programs is to carefully plan and support students in acquiring the skills to be successful in these programs.

When skills are beyond a student's abilities, accommodations can be implemented to the program to allow the student to participate successfully. And when accommodations to regular sports cannot be achieved, special community sports and recreation programs should be explored. The important point is that community sports and recreation can be such a wonderful experience, and students with disabilities should be given every opportunity to participate in these programs.

Sample Community-Referenced Leisure Skill Inventory

I SKILL SELECTION CONSIDERATIONS/ FACILITY DESCRIPTION

Adaptive Skiing, Wintergreen Resort

A. Appropriateness of leisure skill facility

1. *Is skill or facility selected appropriate for individuals without disabilities of the same chronological age?* Yes. Skiing is a great workout and tons of fun for all ages and ability levels (with or without disabilities). Skiing can also be a wonderful self-confidence builder for an individual with a disability. This activity can also be a wonderful social outlet.

2. *Has the individual with disabilities previously acquired any skills related to the activity?* Yes. Maura is able to stand, walk, and jog on her own.

3. *If the particular skills would be difficult to perform, are material/procedural adaptations available to enhance participation?* Yes. Wintergreen has adapted equipment to help any individual be successful on the slopes. Wintergreen also provides at least one trained volunteer per student.

4. *Does the individual with disabilities have access to the facility or materials (distance from home, transportation concerns)?* Yes.

Maura's family has a house at Wintergreen Resort, so she is able to come to Wintergreen for 2 weeks over Christmas break and on most weekends throughout the skiing season. However, this is obviously not possible for all individuals with disabilities. Individuals who need transportation can contact Wintergreen and find out if any volunteer drivers live in their vicinity.

5. *Is the cost prohibitive? Are there other resources to help pay for the cost of the facility (e.g., reduced fee, waived fee, sponsorship)?* Wintergreen provides ski instruction, a lift ticket, and adapted or regular equipment from 10 a.m. to 4 p.m. for $75, or $40 from 1 p.m. to 4 p.m. An individual who does not need instruction and can ski independently may obtain half-price tickets and rental equipment. Skiing is an extremely expensive sport, but Wintergreen will help those with disabilities in need of financial help.

6. *Has the individual with disabilities expressed interest in this particular activity?* Yes. Maura loves the thrill of skiing. She is only 14 years old, but she has already made it clear that she wants to ski for the rest of her life. She has Down syndrome and cannot compete with her peers in most other physical activities, but on the slopes with the appropriate equipment and support, she is probably a better skier than 60% of her peers.

B. Description of leisure skills: environmental inventory and discrepancy analysis

Wintergreen Adapted Skiing (WAS)

    Student's name: Maura McDonald

    Student's birth date: 1/26/03

    Teacher: Harmony Craft

    Environment: APE Skiing

    Dates of unit: Skiing season

    Suggested assistant: Any WAS volunteer or employee

See Figure A20.1 for an environmental inventory and discrepancy analysis.

C. Description of leisure/facility environments

1. *General description of leisure environment:* Wintergreen Ski Resort is located at an altitude of 4,000 feet on the eastern slope of the Blue Ridge Mountains and has beautiful views of the local scenery. The resort's main attraction in the winter is skiing and snowboarding, but there are also snowtubing, banquet halls, restaurants, bars, and an exercise and spa center. At other times in the year, the resort has the attractions of a golf course, horseback riding, tennis, mountain biking, outdoor swimming pools, hiking trails, and youth outdoor camps. The mountain has five beginner slopes, four intermediate slopes, six expert slopes, and a total of four lifts. The lift that provides transportation for the majority of the beginner slopes at Wintergreen, often the most crowded area of the mountain, is only a few years old and runs at a high speed while holding six people per chair.

2. *Conditions under which the participant will be required to participate and interact (who else will be there, noise level, other distractions)?* At times, especially around the holidays and on weekends, the ski slopes can be extremely crowded, with many individuals who know how to ski and many who do not know how to ski. Thus, there may be skiers/snowboarders of all ages and sizes flying down the mountain completely out of control. On a busy day, the mountain probably houses at least 1,000 people, most of whom will be on the beginner slopes. Another huge obstacle at Wintergreen are the snow blowers, which are strategically placed on many slopes and make a horribly loud noise while shooting manmade snow in the faces of any skier passing by. These snow blowers cause skiers' vision to be temporarily blurred, and at worst can completely blind a skier for several seconds, until he or she moves through the blower's area. Maura seems to do fine with all of these obstacles. She is completely bundled up (face covered and eyes protected by goggles) in preparation for the snow blowers, and her WAS instructor always watches out for her safety in the crowds.

3. *A diagram of facility or environment is usually included in a community-referenced leisure skill inventory.*

D. Description of social environment

1. *What social interactions with peers, supervisors, and others are required in the immediate environment?* Maura will interact with multiple WAS volunteers, other students of all ages and various disabilities, lift attendants, people in lift lines and on the lifts, and any individual on the slope whom she may run into or who may run into her (hopefully neither will occur). Overall, Maura has to be okay with having many people around her at all times, which she seems to enjoy.

2. *What is the typical dress for the environment?* The typical dress for skiing is a long underwear top and bottom, followed by multiple layers of fleeces, sweatshirts, and more long underwear. It is important to have many layers so that if a person gets too hot, he or she can just remove a layer. If possible, it is best to not wear cotton (especially on the layer directly against the skin) because cotton absorbs a person's sweat and becomes damp. The final layer on both the top and bottom should be something waterproof or water resistant because it is important not to get wet. If a person's underlayers become wet, the person can quickly become cold, which if not taken care of can quickly lead to hypothermia. Additional dress requirements include warm gloves or mittens (preferably waterproof or water resistant), warm socks that can be pulled up onto the shins, a warm hat, a helmet, and goggles/sunglasses. Other optional dress includes scarves, facemasks, vests, and any other warm clothing that an individual prefers.

Subenvironment	What are the steps of the activity that a person without disabilities uses?	What assistance does the student with disabilities currently need?	What adaptations or levels of assistance might help this student?
Parking lot/ entrance	Get out of car.	I	Usually her mom, dad, or sibling accompanies her.
	Walk from car to the Wintergreen Adapted Skiing (WAS) house.	I	Usually her mom, dad, or sibling accompanies her.
	Open WAS house door and enter building.	I	Usually her mom, dad, or sibling accompanies her.
WAS building	Find a seat so that she is not in the way of others (the building is extremely small).	V	Remind Maura to sit down and wait for someone to help her with her equipment.
	Check to make sure she has all of her ski clothes (i.e., pants, gloves, hat, jacket).	V	WAS volunteer will remind Maura if she forgets to check something.
	Begin putting on ski clothing.	PP	WAS volunteer will assist Maura with clothing.
	Check to make sure that all clothing is on properly (i.e., gloves tucked under jacket, hat not blocking vision, socks pulled up and put under/over ski pants).	PP	WAS volunteer will double check everything to make sure that nothing is uncomfortable and that Maura will be warm/cool enough, depending on the weather for the day.
	Get prepared to go outside (e.g., put on helmet, goggles, ski boots).	PP	WAS volunteer will check to make sure that the helmet fits properly, goggles are not too tight/ loose, and ski boots are buckled and snug/ loose enough so that they can be functional but not painful.
On ski slope directly outside of WAS building	Stand up and depart from building.	I/PP	Maura is good at walking in her ski boots, but it is important that someone, usually the WAS volunteer, is close by in case she loses her balance.
	Open door to deck of building.	I/PP	Someone may have to help Maura open the door.
	Walk down steps to the slope.	I/PP	Someone will need to make sure that Maura is not going to trip and fall while going down the steps.
	Walk on the slope to where her equipment will be waiting for her.	V/PP	Maura will receive the verbal cue of "heel to toe," which is how she is supposed to walk in her ski boots on the snow. A WAS volunteer will need to be nearby Maura, in case she loses her balance.
	Put skis on.	V/PP	WAS instructor will tell Maura, "Put your toe in the binding first and then step down hard to smash the bug!" Maura knows what this means, but someone will still have to physi- cally guide the boot to the correct placement in the binding. Sometimes several tries may be necessary.

Figure A20.1.   Sample environmental inventory and discrepancy analysis for adapted skiing for Maura. (*Key:* I, independent; V, verbal cues or reminder; PP, partial physical assistance; P+, physical assistance [student tries to help]; P, physical assistance [student is passive].)

(continued)

Figure A20.1.   *(continued)*

Subenvironment	What are the steps of the activity that a person without disabilities uses?	What assistance does the student with disabilities currently need?	What adaptations or levels of assistance might help this student?
On ski slopes	Begin skiing down the slope.	I/V	WAS instructor will remind Maura to make her "pizza pie" with the skis and slowly begin down the hill.
	Ski down the slope.	I/V	Maura is a capable skier on the two beginner slopes, but she does like to follow the WAS instructor. The WAS instructor often skis backwards, making large turns across the slope, verbally cuing Maura to push out with her right ski to make a good left turn and vice versa. When Maura goes on an intermediate slope, she becomes very timid and forgets the skills that she knows so well. Often, when Maura makes this transition, she needs a lot of coaching and encouragement to overcome her fear.
	After falling, getting up and/or putting her skis back on (if they have come off), and begin going down the hill again.	V/P+/P	The most important thing for Maura to do when she falls is to place her skis perpendicular (across) to the slope. Putting skis on when on the hill is much more difficult than when they are on a flat surface. The WAS instructor will gather anything that Maura may have lost in the fall (e.g., gloves, skis) and will say to Maura, "Put your skis across the hill." Then the WAS instructor will stand downhill from Maura, help her stand up and put on her skis again (with same verbal cues as before when putting on skis). Sometimes Maura may be extremely helpful in this entire process and sometimes she is dead weight and has to be physically picked up and manipulated by the instructor.
	Stop at the bottom of the hill.	V/PP	WAS instructor will give Maura verbal cue to "make a big pizza pie and turn across the hill (or open space below the lift) to stop."
Ski lift	Get in ski lift line.	P+	Maura does not have poles, so it is hard for her to move on flat ground. She is pulled by her instructor to the line but does try to help by trying to move her feet/skis forward.
	Get on lift.	V/PP	Give Maura verbal cues: "Wait at the cones (line); then go forward when the chair passes in front of you; stop at the next set of cones (line); look behind you and watch your chair come toward you; and sit down when the chair gets to you, just like you would sit down on a normal chair." Even with these cues, Maura will need someone beside her telling her when to stop/go and helping her move forward.
	Ride on lift.	V	WAS instructor will give Maura verbal cues: "Lean back while we put the bar down and try to put your feet on the foot rest."
	Prepare to get off the lift.	V	WAS instructor will tell Maura, "Lean back, move skis off of foot rests, put bar up, and point ski tips upward."
	Get off lift.	I/V/PP	WAS instructor will tell Maura, "Make large pizza pie with your skis, put skis down on snow, lean forward and stand up, let the hill take you down, then keep your pizza pie until you come to a stop, and turn to the left or right to stop." Maura is capable of doing all of this by herself but likes to have the safety of the instructor by her side. (Sometimes the instructor has to help Maura stand up when exiting the lift.)

Figure A20.1.   *(continued)*

Subenvironment	What are the steps of the activity that a person without disabilities uses?	What assistance does the student with disabilities currently need?	What adaptations or levels of assistance might help this student?
Ending the skiing day	Go down slope to WAS house.	I/V	WAS instructor will say, "Keep pizza pie, make good turns (push out with right ski to turn left and push out with left ski to turn right), make sure to follow me."
	Get to WAS house.	I/V	WAS instructor will remind Maura, "Remember to stop in front of the WAS house. Turn across the hill by the stairs, remember to start turning before you get there—it is okay to stop early."
	Walk up the stairs, open the door, and enter the WAS house.	I/PP	Have someone near Maura to make sure that she does not lose her balance and to help her open the door.
	Take off ski equipment and clothing (e.g., gloves, hat, helmet, boots, jacket)	I/V/PP	WAS instructor will ask Maura, "What do you need to take off now that we are inside?" Someone can help her take off her ski equipment and clothing, but she usually can do it by herself.
Exit/parking lot	Put regular shoes back on, open door, leave WAS house, and walk to parking lot.	I/PP	Maura may need help with her shoes. At this point, someone from her family will be at the WAS house to walk with her out to the car.
	Get in car and drive home.	I	Maura can walk with her family member and ride home with them.

II ANALYSIS OF COMPONENT SKILLS AND ADAPTATIONS FOR FULL/PARTIAL PARTICIPATION

A. List of required equipment and materials

1. *What equipment and materials might a person come in contact with in the environment? Provide a detailed listing (and description as needed).*

   a. Snow
   b. Skis, boots, poles, snowboards
   c. Adapted ski equipment
      i. *Bi-ski:* A sit-down form of ski that has two large skis stabilizing the "chair" portion of the ski
      ii. *Mono-ski:* A sit-down form of ski that has one large ski stabilizing the chair portion of the ski
      iii. *Outriggers:* Ski poles that have tips of skis attached at the bottom; used so that a person with poor balance (or a person who has lost part of a leg) can ski with more stability (used with regular skis as well as with sit-down skis)
      iv. *Ski-bra:* A device that holds the tips of skis together
      v. *Tail pipe:* A device that goes behind the boots in ski bindings and functions to keep the skis from wandering too far apart in the back.
   d. Snow blowers—machines that shoot manmade snow onto the ski slopes
   e. Ski lifts

B. Physical considerations: manipulatory, motoric, health

Describe each motor response:

1. *Number and complexity of coordinated movement patterns?* 1: skiing (very complex)—includes balance, coordination, strength, and body weight transition
2. *What strength is required to perform the activity/manipulate materials?* Lower body strength is extremely important in making turns, stopping, and overall just supporting the body. The quadriceps muscles are constantly being used because the proper position for skiing is with knees bent and the body leaning downhill. This position can be extremely tiring on the quadriceps and butt muscles. The calf muscles are also used often because when making a turn on skis, it is important to put pressure on the foot (ball of the foot) on the opposite ski of

whatever direction the turn is going. This process is initiated by flexing the calf muscle. Also, when an individual falls, it takes a lot of lower and upper body strength to get back up.

3. *What body positions and flexibility are required to perform the activity?* Stretches: Stretching is not commonly done, but stretching the calf muscles, the quadriceps, the back, and the hamstrings before and after skiing will save a person from muscle soreness and/or possible injuries. The main position for skiing is a semi-squat, which constantly works the quadriceps, calves, and butt muscles.

4. *What speed is required to perform the activity?* Speed is arbitrary. As long as skiers have control, they can go as slow or as fast as their hearts desire.

5. *What levels of endurance are required to perform the activity?* A high level of muscular endurance and low level of cardiovascular endurance are needed.

6. *What are the minimal health conditions necessary to participate in the activity?* A skier must be healthy with no chance of having a seizure and no atlantoaxial instability.

C. Perceptual considerations: visual, auditory, body awareness

1. *What visual skills (including discrimination) are needed in the environment and in the activity?* It is definitely important to have good vision when skiing, but if vision is a problem, it can be worked around. Vision is important so that an individual can avoid obstacles, such as trees; snow blowers; ski lift poles; and the most important obstacle, the many other people on the slopes. However, even a blind person can ski with the help of a WAS instructor. As long as an individual has someone with him or her, telling him or her about the surroundings and which way to turn, the individual can ski.

2. *What auditory skills (including discrimination) are needed in the environment and in the activity?* Auditory skills are not necessary when skiing. However, it is extremely helpful to know if someone is coming, either by hearing the noise of snow moving or by hearing him or her yell.

3. *What body awareness skills are needed in the environment and in the activity?* An individual needs to know where he or she is in relation to other people on the slopes and always needs to know that he or she is responsible for not running into someone downhill from him or her. Again, however, this can be supplemented by a WAS instructor informing the individual of his or her location in relation to others.

D. Interpersonal interaction considerations: exchange between participants

1. *What are the typical types of interactions that occur in the environment (e.g., turn taking, cooperating, unstructured)?* It is important to wait one's turn in the lift line. WAS skiers and instructors do get to cut in the public line but still have to wait their turn at the ski school. It is important to sometimes wait to take one's turn because one can see that someone is coming into the space that you were going to turn into.

2. *What optional interactions might you expect (e.g., getting a drink)?* Maura might get cold and want to go the cafeteria to get some hot chocolate (which she loves). This can be an excellent form of motivation. She may be thirsty for some water or hungry for a snack. Maura may be too hot or too cold, in which case we would go back to the WAS house and rethink the clothing situation.

3. *What are the language requirements in the environment (list typical nouns, verbs, cues, and statements used in the activity)?* "Turn right/left," "Push out with your right/left ski," "Put pressure on your right/left foot," "Bend your knees," "Try to lean forward," "Make your pizza pie bigger/smaller," "Turn across the hill and stop," "Look behind you," "Sit down when the lift gets here," "Stop now," "Smash the bug," "Toe in the binding and step straight back with all your weight," "One more good run and then we will go in to get some hot chocolate," "Follow me," "You lead, I'm going to follow," "Try to speed up/slow down," "Watch out for the person on your right/left," "Lean back—I'm putting the bar down/up," "Put your ski tips up and make your pizza pie-get ready to get off," "And up."

E. Functional academics: reading, writing, math/scoring, time telling

1. *What reading skills are needed? Can they be bypassed with modifications?* No reading skills are needed, as long as the skier can read the color code of green being the easiest slopes, blue being intermediate, and black being the hardest. In Maura's case, she is always with someone telling her where to go.

2. *What writing skills are needed? Can they be bypassed with modifications?* None

3. *What math skills are needed? Can they be bypassed with modifications?* The only math skill needed is the ability to have basic money skills. Maura always has someone with her who takes care of money.

4. *What time telling skills are needed?* None, except if a person is supposed to meet someone else at a specific time. Again, Maura always has someone doing this for her.

F. What decisions/judgments are necessary for successful participation?

1. *What time and situation judgments may have to be made by the person with a disability to successfully participate in the leisure activity?* It is important for a person with a disability to make sure that he or she has contacted WAS about what day he or she will be coming. If WAS is not contacted in advance, WAS most likely will not have anyone available to work with the individual for the day.

G. What specific adaptations/adjustments are needed for partial participation?

1. *When making suggestions for adaptations, keep the following in mind:*
   - *Whenever possible, activities should not be altered to make the individual stand out.*
   - *Whenever possible, adaptations should be considered temporary.*
   - *Adaptations should be made on an individual basis (as opposed to modifica-*

tions for the entire group when only one person needs modification).

The only modifications for Maura are the following:

   - *Maura is placed with a WAS instructor who has a jacket identifying himself or herself as such.*
   - *Maura does not use poles, but many other able skiers also do not use poles.*
   - *Maura has a ski-bra keeping the tips of her skis together and a tail pipe keeping the backs of her skis from drifting too far apart.*

III. ANALYSIS OF SUPPORTIVE SKILLS

A. Leisure preparation prior to participation in leisure activity

1. *Can the student prepare him/herself for participation? If not, who will assist the student in preparation?* Maura receives help from her family when choosing what clothes and money to bring for the day and what to eat for breakfast. Once Maura is at the WAS house, the instructors make sure that she is dressed appropriately for the day and that she stops skiing if she is cold, hungry, or tired.

B. Transportation

1. *What mode of transportation will be used?* Maura's family will bring her to and from the WAS house.

2. *Does the student have the mobility skills needed to independently use this type of transportation? If not, who will assist student?* Yes, she will be with her family.

C. Informed consent

1. *Has the student and/or parent/guardian signed consent form for participation in program?* Yes, when a student participates with WAS, his or her parents must sign a consent form. If he or she is over 18, then he or she must sign the consent.

2. *Does student have insurance?* Maura is currently covered by her parents' insurance coverage.

CHAPTER 21

Multicultural Education and Diversity Issues

Ana Palla-Kane and Martin E. Block

OBJECTIVES

1. Understand multicultural education and diversity issues in adapted physical education

2. Explore multicultural education strategies and practices that are considered essential in physical education settings

3. Critically analyze the issues related to disability and diversity by exploring ableism and people with disabilities as a minority group

4. Increase awareness of people with disabilities from culturally diverse backgrounds (e.g., race and ethnicity, gender, English as a second language, religion, poverty)

5. Understand the views of people with disabilities in our society, including the misrepresentations of people with disabilities in the media

6. Explore strategies to increase diversity proficiency in general and adapted physical education specialists

Tamika is an 11-year-old African American girl with multiple disabilities. She comes from a poor family and lives with her grandmother and three siblings. She has been included in a general elementary school since preschool. Mrs. Wolf, Tamika's adapted physical education specialist, thought it would be good to videotape Tamika before defining

her goals and accurately measuring her progress. Mrs. Wolf sent a letter home to request guardian authorization. Weeks passed by, but no letter was returned. Mrs. Wolf decided to call Tamika's grandmother. In that conversation, the grandmother said that she did not want any videotape made of Tamika but refused to give a reason via telephone. So Mrs. Wolf set up a time in which she could meet with Tamika's grandmother at her home. While driving to the grandmother's house, Mrs. Wolf became concerned about how the interaction would go. She knew that the grandmother was an older African American woman who was the guardian of four grandchildren. In contrast, Mrs. Wolf was White, young, and came from an upper middleclass upbringing.

Mrs. Wolf arrived at their very simple home. Tamika's grandmother opened the door, invited Mrs. Wolf in, and offered her coffee; in that moment, all Mrs. Wolf's concerns disappeared and she was glad she came. Mrs. Wolf and the grandmother spoke for more than an hour. The grandmother explained that in the past, people had videotaped Tamika and used her images inappropriately, and she did not want it to happen again. She was not against Mrs. Wolf or the school; she just did not want them to videotape her granddaughter. She was very supportive and grateful for all that Mrs. Wolf and the school had provided her granddaughter, and she asked Mrs. Wolf to use other ways to assess Tamika. As Mrs. Wolf said goodbye, she was happy and very satisfied. She was able to fully understand

367

and respect Tamika and her family and to establish goals and assessment tools that most suited the family's wishes and needs.

Mario is a sixth-grade Hispanic student with intellectual disabilities. His family has recently arrived in the United States from Peru, and they do not speak English. They are facing difficulties with his placement in public school. He attended a special school in Lima, and the U.S. regulations, individualized education programs (IEPs), and placements are very confusing to them. Communicating with teachers and specialists is difficult, but they also don't understand how the educational system is organized and the services that are available. Mario qualifies to receive adapted physical education services once a week, and he also is scheduled to be in general physical education twice a week. Mr. Taylor, the adapted physical education specialist, is having problems with Mario's motivation and willingness to participate in adapted physical education and general physical education. He has refused to participate in any physical education class, and he does not like to change in front of the other students in the locker room. Mr. Taylor wonders if Mario is simply confused as to what to do because of his language barrier or if there are other factors affecting his participation. Mr. Taylor sent a note home to Mario's parents, but he never received a response. Mr. Taylor found out later that Mario's parents could not read English and probably were unable to read his note. In an attempt to communicate with Mario's parents during the IEP meeting, Mr. Taylor and the special education team brought in an interpreter. Mario's mother came to the meeting and said that when Mario is not at school, he stays home watching television or playing with his siblings. She could not understand why he is refusing to participate in adapted and general physical education. She also did not know if he had physical education back in Lima. Even though she seemed to be very interested in learning how Mario was doing in school, she didn't provide information that could help Mr. Taylor. After the meeting, Mr. Taylor was confused and frustrated. He did not know how to define Mario's IEP goals and was very concerned about the coming school year.

Fatima is a 14-year-old girl whose parents are from Saudi Arabia. She has been in the United States from birth, and her parents continue to practice traditional Islam, including having all girls and women in the family wear clothing that covers their entire body, neck, and head. Fatima has never had a problem with the way she dresses, and her friends have never ridiculed or teased her about the clothes she wears to school. Fatima actually is very popular at her middle school and participates in a variety of school-related activities, including band and student council. She is getting ready to move to high school in the fall, and she is worried about dressing out for physical education. In middle school, dressing out was optional. However, at high school, all students have to dress out. Her religion does not allow her to dress in front of others (even other girls), and she is not allowed to show her legs or arms or head or neck when in public. Should Fatima be allowed to wear clothing to cover her body while in physical education, or should she be forced to dress out like everyone else in physical education?

Racial, economic, cultural, religious, language, and educational differences are present in almost all interactions that teachers have with students, parents, and colleagues. Our society is becoming more and more diverse. According to the 2010 U.S. Census, approximately 36.3% of the population belongs to a racial or ethnic minority group: American Indian or Alaska Native, Asian American, Black or African American, Hispanic or Latino, and Native Hawaiian or Other Pacific Islander (Centers for Disease Control and Prevention, 2014f). The number of minority students is even greater in special education, with 49.6% of students with disabilities coming from backgrounds considered "other than White" (IDEA Data Center, 2012; see Table 21.1). This diversity contributes to the challenge of teaching children with disabilities and requires educators to take drastic steps in making education multicultural with not only the curricula and learning resources but also the instructional techniques and strategies (Chepyator-Thomson, 1994).

Adapted and general physical educators are expected to teach a wide range of learners with disabilities (Sutherland & Hodge, 2001). Unfortunately,

Table 21.1. Racial/ethnic composition of students with disabilities, ages 6–21, served under IDEA in all environments, as of 2012

	American Indian or Alaska Native	Asian	Black or African American	Hispanic/ Latino	Native Hawaiian Pacific Islander	Two or more races	White
Number	40,245	74,866	579,073	686,545	17,149	78,374	1,499,754
Percentage	1.4%	2.5%	19.5%	23.1%	0.6%	2.6%	50.4%

Source: IDEA Data Center (2012).

research in adapted and general physical education has not considered the impact of multiculturalism on attitudes toward people with disabilities. A lot of attention has focused on including students with disabilities in general physical education based on their disabilities and level of performance. However, no attention has been given to inclusion strategies to accommodate students with disabilities who come from different backgrounds or represent a minority.

The purpose of this chapter is to highlight and discuss the most common issues that adapted and general physical education teachers deal with when teaching students with disabilities from culturally diverse backgrounds. We start with a review of multicultural education and why multicultural awareness is important. This is followed by a look inside the culture of the most prevalent minority groups of students in public schools in the United States (e.g., African Americans, Asian Americans, Hispanics, low-income families, English language learners). The chapter concludes with an examination of how people with disabilities have been treated in American society, as disability itself is considered a minority group. Misunderstanding, stereotyping, prejudice, and discrimination toward students with disabilities still persist in our society. We invite you to look to your background, professional experiences, and views of disability. Overall, teachers are not aware of the impact of their culture and their biases toward students from minority groups, and the majority of teachers are White, female, and from a Christian background (Lynch & Hanson, 2011; Zamora-Duran & Artiles, 1997). By approaching inclusion from a multicultural education perspective, we expand our view and our abilities to offer quality education and physical education for all students.

WHAT IS MULTICULTURAL EDUCATION?

A multicultural approach is essential, considering the diversity of American schools and their students. A multicultural perspective and culturally responsive instruction are needed to meet the needs of children of varied backgrounds and cultures (Sparks, 1994). It is important to embrace diversity and to perpetuate the notion that all students have the right to educational equity and access to educational programs. Banks and Banks defined multicultural education as an idea or concept, an education reform movement, and a process:

> Multicultural education incorporates the idea that all students—regardless of their gender or social class

and their ethnic, racial or cultural characteristics—should have an equal opportunity to learn in school. Another important idea in multicultural education is that some students, because of these characteristics, have a better chance to learn in schools as they are currently structured than do students who belong to other groups or have different cultural characteristics. (2010, p. 3)

Banks and Banks continue, "Multicultural education is also a reform movement that is trying to change the schools and other educational institutions so that students from all socioclass, gender, racial, language, and cultural groups will have an equal opportunity to learn" (2010, p. 4).

Adams, Bell, and Griffin (1997) explained that learning about diversity and social justice enables teachers and students to become conscious of their operating worldview and be able to critically examine alternative ways of understanding the world and social relations. In multicultural education and education for social justice, there is the expectation that individuals learn to critique current social relations and to envision more just and inclusive possibilities for social life, including educational settings. One of the challenges is to make schools more efficient in working with children, families, and the community. Educators need to recognize the diversity in the classrooms and create more suitable educational environments if they expect all children to do well at school (Zhang, Katsiyannis, Ju, & Roberts, 2014). A multicultural education approach is needed to guarantee the success of students with disabilities in general or adapted physical education as well.

Multicultural Education in General and Adapted Physical Education

Multicultural education strategies and practices have been discussed with reference to physical education (e.g., Chepyator-Thomson, 1994; Harrison & Worthy, 2001; Kahan, 2003; McCollum, Civlier, & Holt, 2004). However, there is a lack of information and virtually no resources concerning multiculturalism and diversity as they relate to adapted physical education. Resources in multicultural education and physical education focus mainly on incorporating games and dances of different countries and cultures into the physical education curriculum. Although including such activities into physical education is a good start, it is a far cry from truly embracing a multicultural education approach.

Sparks advocated for a culturally sensitive pedagogy in physical education, stating, "Teachers have a moral responsibility to be culturally responsive or to design curricular programs that are responsive to the educational needs of learners from diverse cultural backgrounds" (1994, p. 35). In our view, multicultural education is designed to meet the needs of a socially diverse, changing, global society by promoting the understanding and appreciation of the principles of social diversity and cultural pluralism. "Multicultural education is designed to empower all teachers and students to become knowledgeable, caring, and active citizens in a deeply troubled and ethnically polarized nation and world" (Banks & Banks, 2010, p. 7).

In order to effectively integrate multicultural education, general and adapted physical educators need to 1) develop the knowledge and skills to be able to promote social justice and equality for all people (e.g., students, their families, colleagues), 2) foster positive attitudes toward diverse groups among students, and 3) promote an environment in which students can be successful. A lack of successful physical activity experiences in school can contribute to a lack of interest in physical education and sports in adolescents and throughout adulthood (Beveridge & Scruggs, 2000). As teachers attempt to become more responsive to the demographics of a changing world, they must understand the effect of culture on the ongoing development of children's attitudes and values. Values are determined by culture, which influences behavior and decisions (Sparks, 1994).

A multicultural education context in physical education is important to ensure students' achievement. Although there is agreement on the relevance of diversity in education, issues such as race and culture often make people uncomfortable. Teachers and students have a variety of feelings, experiences, and awareness with these issues (Adams et al., 1997). There is a need to create opportunities for teachers to express their views and share their personal experiences about diversity because fear, distrust, anger, denial, guilt, ignorance, and naiveté can prevent teachers from truly becoming multicultural (Adams et al., 1997).

Integration of multicultural concepts within a physical education (or adapted physical education) program is more than an introduction of different cultural games—it is the acquisition of informed social attitudes through the creation of a knowledge base that conveys the desirability and value of diversity. For multicultural instructional units that foster well-informed, nonprejudicial attitudes to be developed and promoted in teaching practices, teachers at all levels must gain an understanding and appreciation of diversity. Culturally responsive pedagogy in physical education would help eliminate discriminatory practices and promote multicultural understanding. Physical education, because of its strength in social orientation, can lead in this process. (Chepyator-Thomson, 1994, p. 32)

Wessinger (1994) also defended the idea of a multicultural education as one that fosters cultural pluralism and equal opportunity for all in physical education. She pointed out a list of knowledge, attitudes, and skills needed to address ethnicity in general and adapted physical education classes:

- *Knowledge*

  Understanding prejudice, stereotyping, and discrimination and the definitions of ethnicity and culture

  Learning about different cultures

  Recognizing diversity and pluralism as strengths

  Learning how various cultures contribute to a pluralistic society

  Discovering one's own roots, as well as others', in the community

- *Attitudes*

  Appreciating the value of cultural diversity and human rights

  Accepting one's own differences

  Appreciating others' experiences

  Being prepared to take action on behalf of others

- *Skills*

  Cooperating, sharing, and the human relations skills of self-awareness

  Interpersonal communication

  Group process, problem solving, and decision making

  Seeing from different perspectives

It is extremely important that both adapted and general physical educators purposely structure physical education and create teaching strategies that promote high levels of active participation across diverse groups (Beveridge & Scruggs, 2000). Banks and Banks (2010), Beveridge and Scruggs (2000), Butt and Pahnos (1995), and Sparks (1994) identified several strategies for building a culturally responsive and multicultural physical education program.

Constantly Develop Your Relationships and Build Trust

- Create ways to show that you are interested and that you want to establish a relationship with your students, their parents, and your colleagues.

- Create a practice where you acknowledge your students, their family, your colleagues, and yourself. It is important that you recognize and be proud of your achievements.

- Let students know that their efforts are valued and will be rewarded.

- Learn the names of your students and how to pronounce them. If necessary, use name tags in the beginning. Students will have fun in creating name tags. Ask your students how they self-identify: African American, Black, African, Hispanic, Latino, Asian, Asian American, or something else.

- Include games that reflect the culture of your students.

- Share your accomplishments with your colleagues; it will give you the opportunity to share what is working in your teaching and to contribute.

- Use a collaborative approach with your IEP team and colleagues. As you face a problem with your students, share with your colleagues and be open to assisting them when they need your help. Being open to others' contributions and support decreases feelings of loneliness and isolation when dealing with a problem student.

- Be in communication every time you are facing a challenging situation. Avoid hiding what is happening and hoping that everything will be fine.

- Read about cultures and share information with your class during discussions or by creating bulletin boards with cultural information. You can identify favorite sports and physical activities in different cultures, select a list of athletes, gather their pictures, and share them with the class.

- Identify cultures present in your class and assign students to do research about physical activities and sports in that culture, country, or region. You can start with the city that you are in and expand to other parts of the world.

- Introduce new units of instruction through games or activities that provide cultural and historical perspectives.

- Travel to different places and areas within your community, your state, the country, or even internationally. As you experience life in different communities and lifestyles, you will start appreciating the differences in the way that people approach life. You can find completely different cultures even in a small town. Search for them and have fun even if you feel uncomfortable. Everything new tends to be uncomfortable at first.

- Participate in activities with people from different cultures. You will be able to expand your ability to share yourself and to understand about other groups' cultures and routines. Be open to personally experience and participate in different sports and games that are not part of American culture.

Expand Your Cultural Knowledge and Become Culturally Literate

- Learn about your students' backgrounds (e.g., the language they speak, characteristics of culture and country they come from, traditions, interaction styles, social values). A lot of this information cannot be found in books; ask your students and their parents. Each one has a unique culture, and you will never get to a point where you know enough.

- Learn about your background and share your findings with your students.

- Observe students in settings outside of school. Get to know their families. Make home visits. Talk to parents on the phone.

- Learn a few words from the vocabulary of your non–English-speaking students.

- Ask your students and their parents about typical and cultural parties/events and participate.

Create New and Transform Current Methodological Approaches

- Learn about the different learning styles of children from different cultures (e.g., organization level; visual, tactile, or auditory style; working alone rather than in groups).

- Vary your instructional approach. Use visual learning (e.g., instructor or student demonstrations, visual displays, films), tactile learning (e.g., reciprocal peer instruction and feedback by physically assisting each other, or instructor physically assisting and guiding student through movement), auditory learning (e.g., develop good listening skills, use sounds as cues for activities or changes or to guide activity/skill rhythm).

- Do not assume that a student from a different culture has particular academic or athletic interests. Encourage broad participation and ask students about their preferences.

- Use music in your activities. It can give you an opportunity to share your music preferences and to ask students to bring music that is representative of their cultures. Be aware of appropriate language.

- Learn individual student needs. Remember that assessment tools are traditional and norm-referenced and that by using a functional or ecological approach (see Chapter 4), you will have assessment tools that are effective for your diverse group of students.

- Provide in your lessons culturally relevant, student-centered activities and cooperative opportunities. Use more cooperative activities and games, placing less emphasis on competition.

- Create classes where you can have students working on different activities in different groups. Creating stations might be a good idea to accommodate students who prefer to work alone or with whom you need to practice a skill.

- Consider student preferences by allowing them to participate in the decision process when selecting among several different activities.

- Have a variety of activities. It will give your students the opportunity to make choices.

- Give yourself time to implement new strategies. It is okay if a new strategy did not work as you expected. Give yourself and your students time to get used to a new methodology. It is common for students to show resistance to new activities in the beginning.

- Teach personal and social responsibility skills. Practice them during class. For example, teach students to use integrity principles (e.g., keeping their word regarding agreements they made to follow the rules, be on time, be honest about issues that might come up). Create a community of respect (e.g., speaking when given the opportunity, respecting others, thanking and offering help, understanding and respecting differences, speaking up when disappointed or upset). These principles are important and easy to implement.

- Create an environment where students feel comfortable communicating with you regarding any issue that might come up. If there is not enough class time for discussion, ask them to visit you after class or write you a letter or email.

- Review the instructional resources, curriculum, support materials, and activities with each new class.

- Ensure that materials, equipment, and teaching strategies include perspectives from different cultural and ethnic groups. Do not assume that a student knows how to use certain pieces of equipment.

- Remember that physical education and sports have a rich heritage that has evolved from cultures throughout the world. Use these resources and highlight different racial or ethnic contributions or the unique contributions made by women.

- Use reward systems to encourage and promote full participation. Negotiate with students what they would like to have as a reward (e.g., give students an opportunity to choose activities; use a favorite physical education activity, equipment, or game as a reward to be given at end of class; create stickers, cards, or medals with students' names and goals achieved).

- Increase physical activity time and opportunities and provide developmentally and age-appropriate activities and equipment.

Use Activities that Promote Critical Thinking and that Give Students the Opportunity to Express Their Views

- Offer a variety of activities and variations within each activity so that students can choose. By providing variety and choice in your curriculum, you promote recognition of your students' diverse cultures, promote decision making, and respect students' individuality. You might have classrooms where it is not possible to offer different activities, so try to vary levels of intensity, equipment, and rules within the same activity. Make sure students participate in the creation process.

- Promote discussion about games and activities before they start. Discuss rules and create new rules with students.

- Have students develop mental images or verbalize physical skills as they are taught. Ask them to create variations of the skill and then play with those variations.

- Have students teach other students. As students give instruction and feedback, they also learn and process the components of skills learned.

- Use problem-solving approaches. Avoid giving "the answer" on how to execute basic or complex skills. Let students come up with options and experience them. Change rules or basic forms of equipment (e.g., move or lower basketball goals, play with balls of different sizes and shapes). A football might be completely different for some students. Explore the use of a football in other sports. Create games with elementary school students where they can use their imagination and use metaphors when performing basic skills (e.g., ford a river, crawl through a cave, climb a small hill, walk like a bear).

Provide Effective Feedback and Instruction

- Give concrete and specific feedback. In teaching a physical skill, focus on the specific qualities of the skill or activity being taught.

- Give feedback that is positive, specifically corrective, and of equal quality for all students regardless of race or ethnicity.

- Emphasize that performance of skills is individual and discourage comparison of any nature. Avoid comparing a current class with classes that you have taught in the past. Remember that you are teaching a class of students with different body types and shapes, height and weight, past experiences in activities, families and cultures, and so forth. Even if they all come from similar backgrounds, each student has his or her own uniqueness. Avoid generalizing and comparing your students.

- Avoid stereotypical, racist, or gender-biased language such as "Throw like a girl," "Sit like an Indian," and "You guys." Avoid assertions such as "This is the way it should be," "This is the right and only way to do it," and "You should do it like so-and-so." Be open and flexible in your teaching. Do not assume that students coming from other cultures have had experience with basic activities typically taught in Western cultures. For example, students from South America, Asia, or Africa might never have experienced or even seen baseball, softball, American football, or lacrosse.

- Keep in mind that teachers also communicate things in nonverbal ways. Be aware of negative body language.

Create Positive Relationships with Your Students' Parents and Families

- Build relationships with your students' parents and families.

- Communicate with parents or guardians to acknowledge students' successes. Do not wait until students are having difficulties to communicate with parents.

- Be in communication with parents and ask about students' strengths, weaknesses, and family activities and interests and use them to plan your

activities. For your students with disabilities, make sure that parents fully participate in the creation of your student's IEP goals and objectives. Create a structure where you can be in frequent communication with parents (phone, letters, e-mail, or meetings). For parents who do not speak English, it may be best to avoid communication by phone; use letters or email, or meet in person. Use an interpreter as needed (e.g., family members can be interpreters).

- Be partners with parents because you share common objectives for your students' success.

- Get to know the siblings of your students with disabilities. They can be great support during classes, after school, and helping their brothers and sisters with "physical education homework" (e.g., you might ask the student to practice activities at home or to start creating an active routine with activities). Siblings can help you to define what is important to their brothers and sisters based on their life experience.

Distinguish and Recognize Your Prejudices and Biases

Teachers have control of the classroom and will choose whether to implement a culturally responsive approach. Teachers can build sensitivity to diversity in numerous ways. However, they must first face their own biases, stereotypes, prejudices, and behaviors before helping children recognize and address their own (Butt & Pahnos, 1995; see Table 21.2 for an exercise on bias awareness).

Table 21.2. Bias awareness exercise

It is important to know yourself and the assumptions that you "automatically" make about a student. Be honest with yourself when answering the following questions:

    What are my expectations toward my students?

    Am I challenging one student more than the others?

    What are the assumptions I am making?

    What can I do to include all students?

It is important to remember that it is not about "you" discriminating against your students. In our society and the culture of your school and community, some groups of students have more privileges than other groups. By recognizing your views about students with disabilities who come from certain backgrounds, you will be aware of those views and have the ability to change those views.

Always consider that you likely have some biases and preexisting ideas toward your students and their families. They come from your education, upbringing, values, and past experiences. If you are struggling to be successful relating to a particular student, take time to discuss the issues with your peers, supervisor, or school counselor.

Source: IDEA Data Center (2012).

Teachers can directly influence how students are treated in their classrooms. Although teachers try to be fair to all students, there is evidence that teachers differentiate among them (Hutchinson, 1995). To recognize and eliminate stereotypes, teachers must acknowledge that they exist and look closely at the ways in which they encourage or discourage certain groups (e.g., girls, children with disabilities, African Americans, Asian, Hispanics, others) during physical education classes. It is important for teachers to reflect on their own behaviors and how these behaviors influence their teaching strategies (Hutchinson, 1995). Also, by observing the interactions among students, teachers can determine how to structure lesson plans and include activities that promote cooperation and interaction among and between diverse groups (Hutchinson, 1995).

DISABILITY AND DIVERSITY

People with disabilities are the largest minority group in the United States. About 56.7 million people (19% of the population) had a disability in 2010 (United States Census Bureau, 2014). However, not until the Rehabilitation Act of 1973 (PL 93-112) were those with disabilities considered a class of people. Typically, their rights and privileges are associated with their cultural and/or gender group (Bryan, 1999).

An examination of the U.S. Census data on the population with disabilities (age 5 and older) by race shows that African Americans shared the highest disability rate (22.3%), followed by Hispanics with 17.8% and Asian Americans with the lowest disability rate of 14.5% (IDEA Data Center, 2012). Table 21.1 shows the number and percentage of students with disabilities by racial and ethnic groups served in 2012 under the Individuals with Disabilities Education Improvement Act (IDEA) of 2004 (PL 108-446). People with disabilities who are members of a racial minority group must be considered from two perspectives when considering cultural diversity (Bryan, 1999). Multicultural education helps educators within the special education team (including the adapted physical education specialist) become more responsive and sensitive to the needs of students with disabilities from culturally diverse backgrounds.

Professionals often ignore diversity and cultural characteristics, and individuals with disabilities may end up not receiving appropriate services. The combination of disability and ethnicity, race, and/or cultural background often results in a double form of discrimination. Individuals with disabilities who are members of minority ethnic, racial, or cultural groups frequently experience more discrimination disproportionately than their White counterparts (Bryan, 1999).

One group's standards, values, belief system, and morals will often become the dominant culture in any society. This fact is neither good nor bad but simply a fact of how society has been organized. However, the extent to which the dominant culture extends itself to include or exclude other belief systems, values, and standards as a significant part of overall society causes the dominant group's motives and actions to be considered oppressive or exclusive (Banks, 1999).

Euro-American culture has been the dominant culture in America for several hundred years, and its domination has been so encompassing that practically all other cultures have been suppressed, assimilated, or eliminated. Wehrly explained how immigrants were induced to adopt a pattern of determined Euro-American values:

For a time, it was thought that the United States would become a melting pot of all the cultures brought by the immigrants and an idealized, blended national culture would emerge. As more and more immigrants came to United States in the late 19th and early 20th centuries, the white European men in power became concerned about the different values and behaviors brought by immigrants, and so the norm was changed from the melting pot to that of assimilation. Cultural assimilation, as practiced in United States, is the expectation by the people in power that all immigrants and all people outside the dominant group will give up their ethnic and cultural values and adopt the values and norms of the dominant society—the white, male Euro-Americans (Wehrly, 1995, p. 12).

Many discriminatory acts have been ruled unconstitutional and have been replaced by humane and empowering laws such as the Civil Rights Act of 1964 (PL 88-352), the Americans with Disabilities Act (ADA) of 1990 (PL 101-336), and IDEA. Those with professional as well as personal concerns regarding education, employment, counseling, and other health and social issues, such as rehabilitation, human relations, and human resource development, began to pay close attention to the issues of cultural diversity in the population with disabilities.

Noncultural Factors

Gender

Physical educators tend to have very specific stereotypes about boys and girls. Beveridge and Scruggs (2000) argued that boys and girls are influenced into behaving according to specific social and cultural roles and that parental and cultural expectations for physical activity and sport engagement are usually higher for boys than for girls. Limitations are imposed on girls when physical educators do not recognize that they may be treating their female students differently than their male students. In a case study, Palla and Block (2004) found that the adapted physical education specialists expressed bias based on a student's gender. One teacher said, "The other day I felt frustrated with one of my students, he was being so stubborn, and crying . . . so I left him alone in the class. I hope he learned a lesson" (Palla & Block, 2004, p. 57). When the teacher was asked if he would have left a girl alone, the teacher smiled, expressed embarrassment, and said, "I would not. I can see that I am hard on him and that the fact that he is a boy probably influenced my reaction . . . but I am not sure" (Palla & Block, 2004, p. 57).

Hutchinson (1995) reminded that we cannot forget gender discrimination and inequalities in our classrooms, in physical education programs, and in sports. She approaches gender discrimination in physical education as a socially constructed issue, noting that perpetuating gender differences helps to continue inequalities in instruction, participation, and opportunities for girls. Several central misconceptions about women's and girls' participation in sports and physical activity can influence the way teachers treat and plan for girls with disabilities. For example, some teachers consider certain activities inappropriate for girls, such as vigorous and competitive sports that are believed to make women develop masculine traits and are potentially harmful to women's ability to have children. These conceptions and stereotypes support the view of women as weak and fragile. Physical education curricula and experiences must be implemented in ways that convey equitable messages about sport and physical activity for girls and boys (Hutchinson, 1995).

English as a Second Language

Imagine preparing to attend an IEP meeting knowing that everyone you meet with will be speaking Chinese. How would you feel? How well do you think you would understand what is being said, and how well do you think the others would understand what you are saying? This is how parents and students who have limited English proficiency (LEP) or speak English as a second language (ESL) feel when they step into an American school.

The Virginia Department of Education (2005), like many states, uses the definition of LEP found in the No Child Left Behind Act of 2001 (PL 107-110; see Table 21.3). Enrollment of LEP students across

Table 21.3. Definition of students with limited English proficiency (LEP)

An LEP student is classified as one:

A. who is age 3 through 21;

B. who is enrolled or preparing to enroll in an elementary or secondary school;

C. (i) who was not born in the United States or whose native language is a language other than English; and who comes from an environment where a language other than English is dominant.

OR

(ii) (I) who is Native American or Alaska Native, or native resident of outlying areas; and

(II) who comes from an environment where a language other than English has had a significant impact on the individual's level of English language proficiency.

OR

(iii) who is migratory, whose native language is a language other than English, and who comes from an environment where a language other than English is dominant.

AND

D. whose difficulties speaking, reading, writing, or understanding English language may be sufficient to deny the individual—

(i) the ability to meet the State's proficient level of achievement on State assessments described in section 1111(b)(3)

(ii) the ability to achieve successfully in classrooms where the language of instruction is English; or

(iii) the opportunity to participate fully in society.

From No Child Left Behind Act of 2001, PL 107-110, Title IX, Part A, § 9101(25).

the country has grown. For example, in Virginia, the number of LEP students has grown from about 19,000 in 1994 to 67,000 in 2004. These numbers are no doubt higher in states that attract a high number of immigrants, such as New York, California, Texas, and Arizona. Although Spanish is the predominant language of most LEP students, more than 120 different languages were spoken by LEP students in Virginia in 2002 (Virginia Department of Education, 2005).

Lynch and Hanson (2011) pointed out that language is the primary means of access to understanding, relationships, and services. Whenever someone is speaking a language other than the majority language (English in the United States), they are putting more effort into their communication. These difficulties in communication often lead to frustration. Even if family members speak and understand English, the language used in typical IEP meetings by school personnel and specialists is often highly technical. When family members do not speak English, they must rely on interpreters who do not always provide accurate information. Unfortunately, interpreters may lack the language abilities or technical expertise to translate special education jargon accurately, and more than likely, some languages do not have adequate translations. Many times, younger or extended family members are asked to interpret, and their own concerns may shape the information being transmitted (Lynch & Hanson, 2011). For example, a daughter may be hesitant to tell her parents that their son (her brother) has been diagnosed with intellectual disabilities or may need special services.

Being able to understand and being understood by others is critical in situations such as IEP meetings where interpersonal relationships and interactions are important. This includes both verbal and nonverbal means of communication. Some nonverbal gestures that seem subtle and innocuous may be offensive. Both sending and understanding messages are prerequisites to effective interpersonal interactions. Because language and culture are so closely tied together, communicating with families from different cultural backgrounds is very complex (Lynch & Hanson, 2011). Working with students and their families who have limited English skills can be particularly challenging for both general and adapted physical educators (Lucas, 2011). Information presented in Table 21.4 provides strategies for general and adapted physical educators when teaching students with LEP.

Religion

With more immigration from around the world, our schools are becoming more religiously diverse. It is not uncommon to teach children whose religious affiliations vary from Islam to Hindu to Buddhism. Such religious diversity should be not only tolerated but also embraced. However, the United States and, in turn, public schools were founded under a Judeo-Christian belief system, and the majority of students in public schools continue to be Christian (Lynch & Hanson, 2011). For the physical education teacher, challenges include issues with dressing out for students who for religious reasons are forbidden from showing their legs in public (Muslim and Hindu), challenges with boys and girls participating in physical activity together (Muslim), and challenges with dietary rules such as month-long fasting (Muslim; Kahan, 2003; Lucas & Block, 2008). In addition, public school calendars take days off for most Christian holidays, and many physical educators incorporate popular Christian (e.g., Christmas, Easter) and pseudo-Christian (Halloween) holidays into their physical education programs. Such practices may be disrespectful of religious beliefs. The important point is that physical educators should be aware of children who come from religious backgrounds

Table 21.4. Strategies for teaching students with limited English proficiency

Use computer software for English-to-Spanish translation for instructional aids, cognitive assessments, parent info, individualized education program (IEP) forms, and authorization for assessment.

Learn basic words in other languages to use during adapted physical education classes and assist with classroom management and communication.

Invite peers to support students during class.

Call students by their correct names.

Learn to read the student. Body language, gestures, and facial expressions can often communicate intent and feelings better than verbal language.

Minimize the use of verbal language and rely on demonstrations, gestures, and body language for communication.

Post the physical education rules in other languages relevant to your class as well as in English.

Use commands for addressing an individual student and the verb form of locomotor, nonlocomotor, and manipulative skills (as well as enunciation).

Use instructional strategies that foster social interactions (e.g., peer teaching, cooperative learning).

Use a buddy system (e.g., pair the student with limited English proficiency with a student who understands some of the language or is bilingual).

Use instructional aids (e.g., pictures, keywords for the day, directional arrows).

Use visual demonstrations along with verbal explanations of learning task. Include activities from a variety of cultural and ethnic backgrounds to appeal to the diversity of your class.

When using music for starting and stopping activity, get creative. Consider music with a Latin rhythm or play a march or perhaps a tribal drum beat.

Give words typically used in the physical education setting to the English-language teacher to teach the students with limited English proficiency before they come to physical education.

Source: McCollum et al. (2004).

different from theirs and different from the community norm and allow these children to honor their religious practices as they relate to physical education participation. This might include allowing children who are fasting for the month of Ramadan to be excused from overly vigorous activity, allowing excused absences for students who are observing important holidays for their faith (e.g., Yom Kippur and Rosh Hashanah for Jewish students), creating private dressing areas in the locker room and relaxing showering rules for students whose religion prohibits public nudity (Muslim, Hindu), and having flexible dress codes for students such as allowing Muslim girls to wear a long-sleeve shirt and loose sweats under their physical education uniform as well as a *hijab* to cover their head, neck, and ears (Kahan, 2003; Lucas & Block, 2008).

Socioeconomic Status

Living in poverty means that one has the minimum or less than the minimum required for basic survival, including housing, clothing, food, transportation, and access to quality health care. The United States calculates poverty based on a formula that combines annual income, overall family size, and number of related children under 18 years. For example, in 2010 (latest census data) the threshold for a single person younger than age 65 to be considered as "living in poverty" is $11,344, whereas the threshold for a family of four that includes two related children younger than the age of 18 is $22,133. Based on this definition, in 2010, 15.1% of all people in the United States lived in poverty. The poverty rate in 2010 was the highest since 1993 (between 1993 and 2000, the poverty rate fell each year reaching a low of 11.3% in 2000). Children represent a disproportionate share of the people who are poor in the United States; they account for 24% of the total population but 36% of the poor population. In 2010, 16.4 million children, or 22%, lived in poverty (National Center for Children in Poverty, n.d.).

Families living in poverty tend to exhibit the following qualities (Hanson & Lynch, 2013):

- Be headed by a single parent, typically a mother

- Have at least one wage earner whose wages are insufficient to move the family out of poverty

- Live in the central or core area of a city

- Live in the South

- Be White in terms of absolute numbers, although a considerably larger percentage of Latino and African American families are poor compared with the percentage of White families

- Be undereducated, with the best educated parent having less than a high school education

According to the 2010 U.S. Census, about 28.6% of people ages 15–64 with severe disabilities were living in poverty (United States Census Bureau, 2014). Just as the earnings and income are lower for people with disabilities, poverty rates were also higher. Approximately 25% of children with disabilities in United States live in poverty (United States Census Bureau, 2014). Low-income families are almost 50% more likely to have a child with a disability compared with higher income families. Compared with higher income single mothers, low-income single mothers are more likely to have disabilities (29% versus 17%) and have considerably higher rates of severe disability (17% versus 5%; Lee, Sills, & Oh, 2002). These data are not surprising given that children who live in poverty are more likely to be subjected to factors related to disability, including low birth weight, chronic health problems, limited access to health care, inadequate nutrition, and trauma (Hanson & Lynch, 2013). In addition, children who grow up in poverty are more likely to be abused, have lower quality health care, be exposed to various environmental toxins, and have parents who abuse drugs (Lawrence, Chau, & Lennon, 2004). Finally, there appears to be a relationship between growing up in poverty and various child outcomes, including teenage pregnancy, low academic achievement and learning disabilities, juvenile delinquency, and social-emotional difficulties (e.g., conduct disorder, anxiety, depression; see Hanson & Lynch, 2013, for a review of these studies).

Clearly, poverty is an issue in the lives of many children with and without disabilities in the United States. What are the implications for general and adapted physical educators? First and foremost, physical educators can have a more empathetic understanding of what it must be like to grow up in poverty. Children who grow up in poverty may not have a house to live in and may not know where their next meal will come from. These children likely will not have regular access to a television or a computer, will not have parental or peer support to help with homework, and will not have opportunities to play community sports programs. These children may have to wear the same clothes several days in a row during the week, and they will have a difficult time purchasing basic school supplies, let alone luxury items such as soccer shoes or a lacrosse stick. Just being aware of these facts and understanding the challenges children in poverty face daily may help you understand and more compassionately deal with some of the physical, emotional, and cognitive problems these children bring with them to the gymnasium. This new awareness might include finding some extra clothes for a child who wears the same clothes to school every day, creating general rules for your physical education classes that encourage interacting with everyone in class and discourage teasing and isolating children, and giving away extra physical education equipment that you might have received for free or that you planned on discarding anyway.

Physical educators should also understand the issues that face the child's family and try to support and help the families as much as possible. This does not necessarily mean giving things to parents, although finding a used pair of soccer shoes or a used lacrosse stick will surely be welcomed. A large part of supporting families who live in poverty is to help parents feel that they can have a big impact on their child's education and welfare. This includes helping parents understand that they can provide stimulating and supportive environments (both scholastically and athletically) for the child; that they can and should have the same academic, behavioral, and athletic expectations as other parents; and that they can help their child (Hanson & Lynch, 2013). For example, you might send home a jump rope along with a note to a child's parents saying that you have been working on teaching Samantha (a second-grade girl with mild intellectual disabilities) how to jump rope. In your note, you can say that Samantha has learned how to jump rope, but she still needs lots of practice to become more consistent. You then can ask the parents if they would use the rope you provided to encourage Samantha to jump rope at home. They can keep the rope as long as they want, as long as they practice with Samantha.

Lewis (2001) suggested several things that all schools can do to help children who live in poverty and/or who come from underprivileged backgrounds:

- Help parents understand how children's social and learning abilities develop.

- Increase the emphasis on cognitive skills, especially the development of early literacy.

- Make sure transitions between grades and between schools are as seamless and smooth as possible for children and parents.

- Gather data on the evaluation of children's academic progress and achievement. Provide remedial support early and check for biases that could prematurely label children.

- Set academic success (including success in physical education) for all students as the school's mission. Provide no opportunity to use excuses for underachievement.

- Include everyone (teachers, parents, and students) in setting and carrying out this mission.

- Cultivate a philosophy within the school of respecting and cultivating family cultural values and traditions.

- Make sure students and families are aware of community-based services that are available.

- Provide support for creating professional learning environments for teachers (in-services).

- Oppose both retention and social promotion: The goal must be to ensure all students are meeting, at the minimum, grade-level standards, no matter what it takes.

- Use the diversity of students, their families, and neighborhoods/communities to make the curriculum relevant to students.

- Adopt fair discipline policies and apply them consistently.

- Publicize progress.

Refugees

The refugee student is an individual who is outside his or her country and is unable or unwilling to return to that country because of well-founded fear that he or she will be persecuted because of race, religion, nationality, political opinion, or membership in a particular social group. This does not include persons displaced by natural disasters or persons who, although displaced, have not crossed an international border or persons commonly known as "economic migrants," whose primary reason for flight has been a desire for personal betterment rather than persecution. (Virginia Department of Education, 2005)

There are 9 million stateless people around the globe. Between 2009 and 2011, the United States accepted the largest number of refugees for resettlement, with 56,384 people emigrating mostly from Burma, Bhutan, Iraq, Somalia, Cuba, Eritrea, Iran, Congo, Ethiopia, Haiti, and Afghanistan (United Nations High Commissioner for Refugees, 2013). Refugee children are usually enrolled in school as soon as possible after arrival. Many are enrolled in school without speaking any English and often experience a drastic culture shock. Newly arriving students are generally placed in a grade on the basis of age and previous academic study. Children speaking little English may be placed initially in a lower grade. Students with no English or poor English skills tend to be placed into ESL but included in art, music, and physical education classes. Some children may need 2–5 years to adjust fully to life in their new community (Center for Applied Linguistics, Cultural Orientation Resource Center, 1996).

Teachers often refer refugee students for adapted physical education because cultural and language problems often make these children seem delayed when compared with their American peers. Some of the students may come from completely different cultures, in which being instructed to be physically active was not part of their lifestyle. Be aware of the child's needs and be sensitive to cultural differences when choosing assessment tools and deciding on goals and placement. Running laps, using the locker room, use of appropriate clothing and shoes, specific games and sports, and engaging in physical activity with certain equipment might be completely unfamiliar for a lot of refugee children. Detailed planning might be needed. Understanding class rules in physical education as well as basic instruction will be a challenge for ESL refugee students. Initially, students might be confused and refuse to participate in physical education. Written tests and health education classes bring an extra challenge. Also, seek support from local refugee agencies in your community to learn more about the student's background and ways to accommodate the student in your program (Palla & Block, 2004).

DISABILITY AS A MINORITY GROUP

Membership in the world of disability has no boundaries. Anyone, regardless of race, gender, ethnicity, socioeconomic status, or age is subject to become a member at any time in his or her life. Equity of inclusion notwithstanding, people with disabilities make up the largest open-class group in the world (Bryan, 1999).

As the population of America has increased, the rate of disabilities has also increased. There were 56.7 million people with some type of long-lasting condition or disability living in the United States in 2010 (United States Census Bureau, 2014). Gaining equal access to the benefits and opportunities in our society has long been a challenge of people with disabilities. Historically, people with disabilities have faced serious and persistent forms of discrimination, segregation, exclusion, and sometimes elimination. People with disabilities have struggled to establish their place in society and secure their basic civil rights. The passage of the ADA was the result of the efforts of a cross-disability coalition that took root in the early 1970s. The ADA asserts the equality of people with disabilities and opens the door to the benefits and responsibilities of full participation in society (Adams et al., 1997).

Data from the U.S. Department of Education (2013) show that more than 6.4 million children between ages 3 and 21 were served under IDEA in the 2011–2012 academic year. The majority of children are served in general education schools with different amounts of time in the general education classroom. IDEA, along with the inclusion movement, has given students with disabilities new opportunities. Today, more and more students with disabilities are included in general education settings. Unfortunately, people with disabilities are still generally viewed unfavorably in society. The cultural and societal system of oppression against people with disabilities can be defined as *ableism*.

What Is Ableism?

People with disabilities are often viewed as inadequate to meet expected social and economic roles. The term *ableism* is used to describe the exclusionary policies and attitudes of institutions, groups, and individuals against those with mental, emotional, or physical disabilities. Ableism could be said to be perpetuated by the media, both public and private, and reflects our society's deeply rooted beliefs about human health, beauty, and the value of human life (Rauscher & McClintock, 1997).

Because many people do not know how to deal with people with disabilities, they try to avoid contact with or even talking about people with disabilities. One reason for this avoidance is the fear of being around someone who is so different from oneself (Henderson & Bryan, 1997). Also, lack of knowledge can lead to lack of interest, ignoring, concern, anxiety, and/or withdrawal. People without disabilities have mixed feelings when they encounter a person with disabilities (Sherrill, 2004). As a result of unanswered questions and unexpressed concerns or fears, people without disabilities begin to create their own assumptions and rationalizations, which are often used to comfort, protect, and justify themselves.

One of the many roots of ableism is the fear of becoming disabled. Disability reminds us of the fragility of life and confronts us with questions about our mortality. Yet, disability remains a normal part of human experience. Every racial, ethnic, and religious group has people with disabilities. In fact, everyone who lives long enough will have some form of disability.

Prejudice and discrimination against people with disabilities have been perpetuated through language. Using language to talk about disability, the experience of being disabled, and people who have disabilities is sometimes difficult and has gone through many changes. Terms once used to describe people with disabilities in the 19th and 20th centuries have fallen into disfavor (e.g., *crippled*, *deformed*, *deaf and dumb*, *insane*, *idiot*). Terms acceptable just a few years ago, such as *retardation*, *handicap*, or *mental illness*, have been replaced with terms such as *developmental disability* and *emotional disability*. The increased use of person-first language (e.g., *a person with a disability*) encourages viewing people who have disabilities as people first and disabled second. These different uses of language reflect the different perspectives held by people with disabilities and the evolution of thinking about disabilities. The term *people with disabilities* is most commonly used by the disability rights movement (Rauscher & McClintock, 1997).

Images of People with Disabilities in the Media

The media are powerful in perpetuating stereotypes of people with disabilities.

The culturally and socially predetermined stereotypes toward people with disabilities may affect each one of us. For example, if as a teacher we see the student as a victim or someone who needs help, it might limit our view of what the student can accomplish. In turn, this stereotype might determine how much we challenge the student in physical education. The image of people with disabilities in the media is often as people to be feared, pitied, and avoided. People with disabilities often are characterized as victims who possess undesirable social skills and personal qualities. When depictions of disability are present, they usually are accompanied by circumstances with some sort of stress, trauma, overcompensation, character flaw, or bizarre behavior tendencies (Donaldson, 1981).

Lester and Ross (2003), in their book *Images that Injure: Pictorial Stereotypes in the Media*, reported negative stereotypes of different groups in the United States, including people with disabilities. They stated that stereotypes of people with disabilities fit a pattern that is represented in the media and reflected in social interactions. Nelson (2003) listed six major stereotypes of people with disabilities in our society: a victim, a hero, a threat, someone unable to adjust, one to be cared for, and as one who should not have survived (see Table 21.5). Negative stereotypes can influence educators' views, attitudes, and behaviors and can affect how they plan and teach their classes. For example, teachers may choose infantile toys, activities, or music because they see these students as childlike. Most of the stereotypes of people with disabilities show that the disability is the central focus of a person's life. However, having a disability does not in any way limit people from having meaningful and valuable

Table 21.5. Pattern of stereotypes in the media toward people with disabilities

The Victim

People with disabilities are seen as childlike, incompetent, needing total care, nonproductive, and a drain on taxpayers. This image of people with disabilities as a victim, a cripple, and confined in a wheelchair is kept alive by shows such as telethons and fund-raising campaigns, where pity is used by featuring stories to get money. In these cases, they are rarely seen as people who manage to live happy and productive lives despite having a disability. Their accomplishments are rarely pointed out.

The Hero

The word *super crip* describes this stereotype. The common inspiring story is of someone who faces the trauma of a disability and, through courage and stamina, rises above it or surrenders heroically. It shows the person with a disability as a hero when succeeding in college, business, relationship, or sports. It diminishes the much-needed attention to access, transportation, jobs, and housing issues, and for the movement to improve the status of all individuals with disabilities. This stereotype perpetuates the view that a lot of ordinary people with disabilities feel like failures if they have not done something extraordinary.

A Threat

People with disabilities look as if they are evil and warped. They are a threat and represent evil characters in the movies, whose presence implies danger. This stereotype is frequently represented in portrayals of villains whose evil is exemplified by some obvious physical limitations such as the lack or addition of a limb, a hook for a hand, a black patch over the eye, a hunchback, or a facial deformation. These representations play on and reinforce subtle and deeply held fears and prejudices. "These attitudes have been nurtured by Hollywood portrayals and carry over into attitudes toward others with similar limitations in real life" (Nelson, 2003, p. 178).

The One Unable to Adjust

This is the image of a person with disabilities who ended up maladjusted, unable to handle the trauma of his or her problem, and bitter and full of self-pity. The message is that people with disabilities need a friend or family member to set the "pitiable person" straight. The message is often "just buck up and take control of your life." It perpetuates the idea that the person without the disability understands the problem better than the person with the disability. It implies that people with disabilities are helpless and do not really understand their situations and are unable to make sound judgments themselves.

The One to Be Cared For

People with disabilities are seen as a burden. This is one consistent representation of a person with disabilities as the frail person who needs to be cared for or as a burden on family and society. As a "dramatic device" (Nelson, 2003, p. 179), the depiction shows the noble intent and generosity of those who furnish the care, which makes the person with a disability little more than a prop rather than a human capable of interacting with others to the profit of both.

The One Who Should Not Have Survived

One of the cruelest stereotypes of people with disabilities comes under the heading of the better-off-dead syndrome.

"This comes from the attitude that those with a serious disability would really be better off if they hadn't survived. It echoes the belief that anyone with a serious physical impairment cannot live a fulfilling and happy life and, therefore, might as well not be alive" (Nelson, 2003, p. 180).

This stereotype perpetuates the fear and aversion some people feel for people with disabilities. It frightens and reminds people of their own mortality and vulnerability.

Source: Nelson (2003).

lives or from contributing to their families, work, and communities.

What Are Other Views of People with Disabilities in Our Society?

Lester and Ross (2003) presented some perspectives regarding how individuals with disabilities are represented in the media. How are people with disabilities seen in our media and our society? What are the views of your peers, family, and co-workers about disability? The images of people with disabilities in society have evolved over time. Professionals and students need to continue to explore their views and the perspectives presented by the media.

Watching movies, talks, and commercials that portray individuals with disabilities can be an effective strategy for expanding the awareness of current and future general physical education and adapted physical education teachers about disability. Watching movies, commercials, and talks is a fun and engaging strategy for being exposed to a variety of views and perspectives about individuals with disabilities. Some perspectives are more empowering than others, but after being exposed to new perspectives, there is the opportunity for reflection or discussion.

Table 17.4 in Chapter 17 includes a list of movies that portray individuals with disabilities. Table 21.6 includes a list of links of commercials and TED Talks that portray individuals with disabilities that can be used to lead such discussions. After professionals identify their personal views, and the pervasive views in their environment, there is an opportunity to change the automatic, inherited views into designed, empowering views of individuals with disabilities.

Altering the Image of People with Disabilities

In the past 30 years, attitudes toward minorities have shifted. Attitudes toward those with disabilities, however, still need some major shifts. New images seem to be developing, but many of the negative attitudes of the past that viewed people with disabilities as invisible or unworthy of notice remain. The impact of the image and stereotypes of people with disabilities in television and movies cannot be overestimated, and as the Internet and social media take a central role in people's lives, there is also a vast promise of what they can do to alter attitudes toward people with disabilities (Lester & Ross, 2003).

Table 21.6.   Commercials and TEDTalks portraying individuals with disabilities

Commercials

Walmart: Work Is a Beautiful Thing: Meet Patrick (http://youtu.be/O-J_lXR3oZM)

Guinness: basketball commercial (http://youtu.be/Au8Y98Rgxbk)

Duracell: Trust Your Power—NFL's Derrick Coleman, Seattle Seahawks (http://youtu.be/u2HD57z4F8E)

P&G: Thank You, Mom | Tough Love | Sochi 2014 Paralympic Winter Games (http://youtu.be/7RR-r2n5DLw)

Nike: Warhawk Matt Scott in Nike "No Excuses" Commercial (http://youtu.be/UtsnpyCSX5Q)

TEDTalks

Stella Young: I'm Not Your Inspiration, Thank You Very Much (April 2014; http://www.ted.com/talks/stella_young_i_m_not_your_inspiration_thank_you_very_much)

Maysoon Zayid: I Got 99 Problems...Palsy Is Just One (December 2013; http://www.ted.com/talks/maysoon_zayid_i_got_99_problems_palsy_is_just_one)

Aimee Mullins: The Opportunity of Adversity (October 2009; http://www.ted.com/talks/aimee_mullins_the_opportunity_of_adversity)

Phil Hansen: Embrace the Shake (February 2013; http://www.ted.com/talks/phil_hansen_embrace_the_shake)

Sue Austin: Deep Sea Diving...in a Wheelchair (December 2012; https://www.ted.com/talks/sue_austin_deep_sea_diving_in_a_wheelchair)

Keith Nolan: Deaf in the Military (April 2011; http://www.ted.com/talks/keith_nolan_deaf_in_the_military)

Caroline Casey: Looking Past Limits (Dec 2010; https://www.ted.com/talks/caroline_casey_looking_past_limits)

As adapted and general physical education teachers and coaches, we live in a culture in which people with disabilities have been defined by stereotypes and labels. Although labels of disabilities are important for administrative and funding purposes, they can lead to negative stereotyping of students and tend to focus attention on students' disabilities rather than their abilities. It is crucial to understand students' abilities and functioning level when planning for a successful and meaningful physical education curriculum (Sutherland & Hodge, 2001). It is our job to create strategies and generate conversations (in IEP meetings, with our colleagues, with parents, with your classroom, with friends, and with your family) that minimize the restrictive and oppressive views of people with disabilities. Speaking effectively about people with disabilities can transform the environment in your class, then in your school, and perhaps throughout your community.

A significant segment of people with all types of disabilities have reclaimed and redefined the terms *disability* and *disabled* in a positive way.

They reject the notion that being disabled is an inherently negative experience or in any way descriptive of something broken or abnormal. From this perspective, *disability* is a positive term. Proponents of this perspective take pride in the differences in their bodies and minds and strive to make others aware of their experiences and accomplishments. Many people with disabilities take part in an ongoing struggle against the oppressive social, economic, and environmental forces that limit their ability to achieve their full potential (Rauscher & McClintock, 1997). Adapted and general physical education teachers coming from this perspective can empower their students with disabilities and their families toward accomplishing goals and maximizing the positive view of disability inside their communities.

Teachers' Attitudes Toward Teaching Students with Disabilities

Block, Griebenauw, and Brodeur (2004) reviewed research examining attitudes of physical educators and coaches toward working with children with disabilities in general physical education and sports settings (Block & Rizzo, 1995; Conatser, Block, & Lapore, 2000; Kozub & Porreta, 1998; Rizzo, Bishop, & Tobar, 1997; Rizzo & Vispoel, 1991; Theodorakis, Bagiatis, & Goudas, 1995). Attitudes of teachers and coaches toward students with disabilities varied based on the number of students with disabilities in the classroom and the individual student's personal characteristics and disability label. For example, research has shown that physical educators have more favorable attitudes toward children with learning disabilities compared with children with intellectual disabilities. And physical educators had more favorable attitudes toward people with mild to moderate disabilities than people with severe disabilities. Two factors found to have a positive impact on physical educators' attitudes toward individuals with disabilities were training and experience. Teachers and coaches who had received training in adapted physical education or special education, who had positive experiences working with students with disabilities, and/or who perceived themselves to be competent when working with students with disabilities had more favorable attitudes toward students with disabilities compared with physical educators who had no extra training, less experience, and/or had lower perceived competence.

Related to this idea of positive experience influencing attitudes toward students with disabilities

is the *contact theory* (Sherrill, 2004). When interactions between teachers or coaches and students with disabilities are frequent, pleasant, and meaningful, the interactions produce positive attitudes (Sherrill, 2004). In other words, the more positive interactions and experiences an adapted or general physical educator has with students with disabilities, the more likely this teacher will have a positive attitude toward students with disabilities.

Increasing Diversity Among Adapted Physical Education Specialists

Federal legislation suggests "efforts within special education must focus on bringing a larger number of minorities into the profession in order to provide appropriate practitioner knowledge, role models, and sufficient manpower to address the clearly changing demography of special education" (Individuals with Disabilities Education Act (IDEA) Amendments of 1997, p. 40). There is a need for finding creative ways to increase the proportion of African Americans and other ethnic and culturally diverse graduate students in the adapted physical education profession (Webb & Hodge, 2003).

The number of African Americans in both general and adapted physical education teacher education programs is small. Today, the majority of general and adapted physical educators are White. Less than 5% of all physical education professionals are people of color, and an even smaller percentage choose adapted physical education as part of their major (Webb & Hodge, 2003). Webb and Hodge (2003) evaluated the factors that influence career choices of African American students. They found that participants who chose adapted physical education as a profession 1) enjoyed working with individuals with disabilities and 2) had satisfying practical experiences with individuals with disabilities. The ones who did not chose adapted physical education as a profession said that they 1) did not have interest in adapted physical education and 2) had no professional preparation in the area of adapted physical education. These data do not indicate whether the lack of such preliminary exposure was due to the choice of the undergraduate students or if this type of exposure was absent in the participants' current professional preparation programs.

The most obvious solution is to make sure undergraduate students from ethnic and culturally diverse backgrounds are provided with early exposure to adapted physical education coursework, including positive practical experiences with people with disabilities. The effectiveness of adapted physical education services relies on teachers' successful interactions with students, parents, and team members. More than any time in the history of education in the United States, students, parents, and team members are likely to come from different backgrounds (e.g., different race, ethnicity, culture, religion, socioeconomic status, educational level). As a result, today's physical education classes include a large number of students who more than likely look different from the physical education teacher and different from many of their peers. Some students may look different but share a common language or religion. Some may look the same but speak a different language or have a different cultural heritage. Consequently, there is a need for multicultural education resources, training, and support for both general and adapted physical education teachers.

CONCLUSIONS

Physical educators have a tremendous commitment toward teaching all students and, as professionals teaching in a very diverse classroom, they face challenges regarding finding the best strategies to ensure that all students are successful. It is time for each of us to start looking closely at aspects that affect one's perception of self and others. Adapted physical education requires the collaboration of professionals, families, and students with and without disabilities. As we begin to see people beyond our limited views shaped by stereotypes and labels, we see that these views limit what is possible for our students and our fulfillment as teachers. It will require a daily effort and willingness to look at yourself, to ask for help, to work in collaboration, and to stand for equality in your classroom, your school, and your communities.

References

Abells, D., Burbidge, J., & Minnes, P. (2008). Involvement of adolescents with intellectual disabilities in social and recreational activities. *Journal on Developmental Disabilities, 14*(2), 88–94.

Academy for Certification of Vision Rehabilitation and Education Professionals. (2005). *Scope of practice for orientation and mobility specialists.* Retrieved from https://www.acvrep.org/ascerteon/control/certifications/coms

Adams, G.B. (2004). Identifying, assessing, and treating OCD in school-age children. *TEACHING Exceptional Children, 37*(2), 46–53.

Adams, M., Bell, L.A., & Griffin, P. (1997). *Teaching for diversity and social justice: A sourcebook.* New York, NY: Routledge.

Adapted Physical Education National Standards. (2014a). *APENS history.* Retrieved from http://www.apens.org/history.html

Adapted Physical Education National Standards. (2014b). *Certification.* Retrieved from http://www.apens.org/certification.html

ADD/ADHD Foundation. (n.d.). *What is ADD/ADHD.* Retrieved from http://addadhdfoundation.com/?page_id=13

Adzick, N.S., Thom, E.A., Spong, C.Y., Brock, J.W., III, Burrows, P.K., Johnson, M.P.,. . .Farmer, D.L. (2011). A randomized trial of prenatal versus postnatal repair of myelomeningocele. *New England Journal of Medicine, 364*(11), 993–1003.

Akuffo, P.B., & Hodge, S.R. (2008). Roles and responsibilities of adapted physical education teachers in an urban school district. *Education and Urban Society, 40,* 243–268.

Alberto, P.A., & Troutman, A.C. (2005). *Applied behavior analysis for teachers* (7th ed.). Columbus, OH: Merrill.

Alexander, M., & Schwager, S. (2012). *Meeting the physical education needs of children with autism spectrum disorder.* Champaign, IL: Human Kinetics.

Allport, G.W. (1954). *The nature of prejudice.* Reading, MA: Addison Wesley.

Alstot, A.E. (2012). The effects of peer-administered token reinforcement on jump rope behaviors of elementary physical education students. *Journal of Teaching in Physical Education, 31*(3), 261–278.

Amael, A., Benoit, L., & Pascale, D. (2013). Cooperative group, risk-taking and inclusion of pupils with learning disabilities in physical education. *British Educational Research Journal, 39*(4), 677–693.

Amaral, D., Geschwind, D., & Dawson, G. (2011). *Autism spectrum disorder.* London, United Kingdom: Oxford University Press.

American Academy of Pediatrics. (n.d.). *Autism facts: What parents should know about measles-mumps-rubella (MMR) vaccine and autism.* Retrieved from http://www2.aap.org/immunization/families/autismfacts.html

American Association for Physical Activity and Recreation & National Consortium for Physical Education and Recreation for Individuals with Disabilities. (2010). Position paper: Highly qualified adapted physical education teachers. Reston, VA: American Alliance for Health, Physical Education, Recreation, and Dance. Retrieved from http://www.shapeamerica.org/advocacy/positionstatements/loader.cfm?csModule=security/getfile&pageid=5850

American Association on Intellectual and Developmental Disabilities. (2010). *Intellectual disability: Definition, classification, and systems of supports* (11th ed.). Washington, DC: Author.

American Cancer Society. (2014a). *Cancer in children.* Retrieved from http://www.cancer.org/cancer/cancerinchildren/index?sitearea

American Cancer Society. (2014b). *Chemotherapy effects.* Retrieved from http://www.cancer.org/treatment/treatmentsandsideeffects/physicalsideeffects/chemotherapyeffects/index

American Diabetes Association. (2013). *Exercise and type 1 diabetes.* Retrieved from http://www.diabetes.org/food-and-fitness/fitness/exercise-and-type-1-diabetes.html

American Heart Association. (2012). *Children and arrhythmia.* Retrieved from http://www.heart.org/HEARTORG/Conditions/Arrhythmia/UnderstandYourRiskforArrhythmia/Children-and-Arrhythmia_UCM_301982_Article.jsp

American Heart Association. (2013). *Cardiovascular conditions of childhood.* Retrieved from http://www.heart.org/HEARTORG/Conditions/More/CardiovascularConditionsofChildhood/Cardiovascular-Conditions-of-Childhood_UCM_314135_SubHomePage.jsp

American Heart Association. (2014). *Pediatric cardiomyopathies.* Retrieved from http://www.heart.org/HEARTORG/Conditions/More/CardiovascularConditionsofChildhood/Pediatric-Cardiomyopathies_UCM_312219_Article.jsp

American Occupational Therapy Association. (2015). *What is occupational therapy?* Retrieved from http://www.aota.org/About-Occupational-Therapy/Professionals.aspx

American Optometric Association. (n.d.). *Glossary of all eye and vision conditions*. Retrieved from http://www.aoa.org/patients-and-public/eye-and-vision-problems/glossary-of-eye-and-vision-conditions?sso=y

American Physical Therapy Association. (2014). *APTA background sheet 2005: The physical therapist.* Retrieved from http://www.apta.org/PTCareers/RoleofaPT

American Psychiatric Association. (1980). *Diagnostic and statistical manual of mental disorders* (3rd ed.). Arlington, VA: Author.

American Psychiatric Association. (2013). *Diagnostic and statistical manual of mental disorders* (5th ed.). Arlington, VA: Author.

American Speech-Language-Hearing Association. (n.d.). *Causes of hearing loss in children*. Retrieved from http://www.asha.org/public/hearing/disorders/causes.htm

American Speech-Language-Hearing Association. (2015). *Fact sheet: Speech-language pathology.* Retrieved from http://www.asha.org/Students/Learn-About-the-CSD-Professions

American Therapeutic Recreation Association. (2015). *Frequently asked questions about therapeutic recreation.* Retrieved from https://www.atra-online.com/what

American Youth Soccer Organization. (n.d.). *VIP.* Retrieved from http://www.ayso.org/For_Families/AYSO_Soccer_Programs/VIP.htm

Americans with Disabilities Act of 1990, PL 101-336, 42 U.S.C. § 12101 *et seq.*

Ammah, J.O., & Hodge, S.R. (2006). Secondary physical education teachers' beliefs and practices in teaching students with severe disabilities: A descriptive analysis. *High School Journal, 89*(2), 40–54.

An, M.H., Yi, C.H., Jeon, H.S., & Park, S.Y. (2009). Age-related changes of single-limb standing balance in children with and without deafness. *International Journal of Pediatric Otorhinolaryngology, 73*(11), 1539–1544.

Anardag, M., Arikan, H., Yilmaz, I., & Konukman, F. (2013). Physical fitness levels of young adults with and without intellectual disability. *Kinesiology, 45*(2), 233–243.

André, A., Deneuve, P., & Louvet, B. (2011). Cooperative learning in physical education and acceptance of students with learning disabilities. *Journal of Applied Sport Psychology, 23*, 474–485.

Appenzeller, H. (1983). *The right to participate.* Charlottesville, VA: Miche.

Appenzeller, H., & Appenzeller, T. (1980). *Sports and the courts.* Charlottesville, VA: Miche.

Appenzeller, T. (2000). *Youth sport and the law: A guide to legal issues.* Durham, NC: Carolina Academic Press.

Appenzeller, T. (2005). Youth sports and the law. In H. Appenzeller (Ed.), *Risk management in sports: Issues and strategies* (2nd ed., pp. 131–142). Durham, NC: Carolina Academic Press.

Arbogast, G., & Lavay, B. (1986). Combining students with different ability levels in games and sports. *Physical Educator, 44*(1), 255–259.

Arnold, J.B., & Dodge, H.W. (1994). Room for all. *American School Board Journal, 181*(10), 22–26.

Arthur-Kelly, M., Sigafoos, J., Green, V., Mathisen, B., & Arthur-Kelly, R. (2009). Issues in the use of visual supports to promote communication in individuals with autism spectrum disorder. *Disability and Rehabilitation, 31*(18), 1474–1486.

Asbjørnslett, M., & Hemmingsson, H. (2008). Participation at school experienced by teenagers with physical disabilities. *Scandinavian Journal of Occupational Therapy, 15*(3), 153–161.

Assistance to States for the Education of Children with Disabilities, 34 C.F.R. § 300 (2006).

Assistive Technology Act Amendments of 2004, PL 108-364, 29 U.S.C. § 3001 *et seq.*

Auditory Neuroscience. (n.d.). *Sensitivity to sound.* Retrieved from http://www.auditoryneuroscience.com/acoustics/clinical_audiograms

Aufsesser, P.M. (1991). Mainstreaming and the least restrictive environment. How do they differ? *Palaestra, 7*(2), 31–34.

Aufsesser, P.M. (2003). Liability considerations for placement of students with disabilities in general physical education classes. *Palaestra, 19*(1), 40–43, 58.

Auxter, D., Pyfer, J., Zittel, L., & Roth, K. (2010). *Principles and methods of adapted physical education and recreation* (11th ed.). New York, NY: McGraw-Hill.

Ayvazo, A. (2010). Assessment of classwide peer tutoring for students with autism as an inclusion strategy in physical education. *Palaestra, 25*(1), 4–7.

Badia, M., Orgaz, B.M., Verdugo, M.A., Ullán, A.M., & Martínez, M.M. (2011). Personal factors and perceived barriers to participation in leisure activities for young and adults with developmental disabilities. *Research in Developmental Disabilities, 32*(6), 2055–2063.

Badia, M., Orgaz, M.B., Verdugo, M.A., & Ullán, A.M. (2013). Patterns and determinants of leisure participation of youth and adults with developmental disabilities. *Journal of Intellectual Disability Research, 57*(4), 319–332.

Bagwell, C.L., Molina, B.S.G., Pelham, W.E., Jr., & Hoza, B. (2001). Attention-deficit hyperactivity disorder and problems in peer relations: Predictions from childhood to adolescence. *Journal of the American Academy of Child and Adolescent Psychiatry, 40*(11), 1285–1292.

Bailey, T.R. (2012). Blood-borne pathogens. In H. Appenzeller (Ed.), *Risk management in sport: Issues and strategies* (3rd ed., pp. 193–198). Durham, NC: Carolina Academic Press.

Bambara, L.M., Janney, R., & Snell, M.E. (2015). *Teachers' guides to inclusive practices: Behavior support* (3rd ed.). Baltimore, MD: Paul H. Brookes Publishing Co.

Bambara, L.M., & Knoster, T.P. (2009). *Designing positive behavior support plans* (2nd ed.). Washington, DC: American Association on Intellectual and Developmental Disabilities.

Bandura, A. (1997). *Self-efficacy: The exercise of control.* New York, NY: Freeman.

Banks, J.A. (1999). *An introduction to multicultural education.* Boston, MA: Allyn & Bacon.

Banks, J.A., & Banks, C.A.M. (2010). *Multicultural education: Issues and perspectives* (7th ed.). Hoboken, NJ: John Wiley & Sons.

Barbetta, P.M., Miller, A.D., Peters, M.T., Heron, T.E., & Cochran, L.L. (1991). Tugmate: A cross-age tutoring program to teach sight vocabulary. *Education and Treatment of Children, 14,* 19–37.

Barkley, R.A. (2006). *Attention-deficit hyperactivity disorder: A handbook for and treatment* (3rd ed.). New York, NY: Guilford Press.

Barnes, T.L., Howie, E.K., McDermott, S., & Mann, J.R. (2013). Physical activity in a large sample of adults with intellectual disabilities. *Journal of Physical Activity and Health, 10*(7), 1048–1056.

Barwick, R.B., Tillman, M.D., Stopka, C.B., Dipnarine, K., Delisle, A., & Sayedul Huq, M. (2012). Physical capacity and functional abilities improve in young adults with intellectual disabilities after functional training. *Journal of Strength and Conditioning Research, 26*(6), 1638–1643.

Baskerville, T.A., & Douglas, A.J. (2010). Dopamine and oxytocin interactions underlying behaviors: Potential contributions to behavioral disorders. *CNS Neuroscience and Therapeutics, 16*(3), 92–123.

Bateman, B.D. (2012). *Better IEPs: How to develop legally correct and educationally useful programs* (5th ed.). Longmont, CO: Sopris West Educational Services.

Bateman, B.D., & Chard, D.J. (1995). *Legal demands and constraints on placement decisions.* In J.M. Kauffman, J.W. Lloyd, D.P. Hallahan, & T.A. Astuto (Eds.), *Issues in educational placement* (pp. 285–316). Mahwah, NJ: Lawrence Erlbaum Associates.

Bateman, B.D., & Herr, C.M. (2003). *Writing measurable IEP goals and objectives.* Verona, WI: IEP Resources.

Bauman, C., Loffler, C., Curic, A., Schmidt, E., von Aster, M. (2004). Motor skills and psychiatric disturbance. *Psychiatrische Praxis, 31,* 395–399.

Beirne-Smith, M., Patton, J.R., & Hill, S. (2015). *An introduction to intellectual disabilities* (8th ed.). Upper Saddle River, NJ: Pearson.

Bernard-Opitz, V., & Häußler, A. (2011). *Visual support for children with autism spectrum disorders: Materials for visual learners.* Shawnee Mission, KS: AAPC.

Beveridge, S., & Scruggs, P. (2000). TLC for better PE: Girls in elementary physical education. *Journal of Physical Education, Recreation & Dance, 71*(8), 22–27.

Beyer, R. (1999). Motor proficiency of boys with attention deficit hyperactivity disorder and boys with learning disabilities. *Adapted Physical Activity Quarterly, 16*(4), 403–414.

Bhasin, T.K., Brocksen, S., Avchen, R.N., & Braun, K.V.N. (2006). Prevalence of four developmental disabilities among children aged 8 years—Metropolitan Atlanta Surveillance Program, 1996 & 2000. *Surveillance Summaries, 55*(SS01), 1–9.

Biederman, J., Petty, C.R., Doaln, C., Hughes, S., Mick, E., Monuteaux, M.C., & Faraone, S.V. (2008). The long-term longitudinal course of oppositional defiant disorder and conduct disorder in ADHD boys: Findings from a controlled 10-year prospective longitudinal follow-up study. *Psychological Medicine, 38*(7), 1027–1036.

Bishop, J.C. (2013). *Learning effects of a positive illusory bias intervention in the motor domain of children with attention-deficit/hyperactivity disorder* (Unpublished doctoral dissertation). University of Virginia, Charlottesville, VA.

Bishop, J.C., & Block, M.E. (2012). The positive illusory bias in children with ADHD in physical education. *Journal of Physical Education, Recreation & Dance, 83*(9), 42–48.

Biskupic, J. (1999, March 4). Disabled pupils win right to medical aid. *Washington Post,* p. A01.

Black, H.C. (2014). *Black's law dictionary* (10th ed.). St. Paul, MN: Westlaw.

Blinde, E.M., & McCallister, S.G. (1998). Listening to the voices of students with physical disabilities. *Journal of Physical Education, Recreation & Dance, 69*(6), 64–68.

Black, K., & Williamson, D. (2011). Designing inclusive physical activities and games. In A. Cereijo-Roibas, E. Stamatakis, & K. Black (Eds.), *Design for sport* (pp. 195–224). Farnham, United Kingdom: Gower.

Block, M.E. (1991). The motor development of children with Down syndrome: A review of the literature. *Adapted Physical Activity Quarterly, 8,* 179–209.

Block, M.E. (1992). What is appropriate physical education for students with profound disabilities? *Adapted Physical Activity Quarterly, 9,* 197–213.

Block, M.E. (1994). Why all students with disabilities should be included in regular physical education. *Palaestra, 10*(3), 17–24.

Block, M.E. (1995a). Development and validation of Children's Attitudes Toward Integrated Physical Education, Revised (CAIPE-R) Inventory. *Adapted Physical Activity Quarterly, 12,* 60–77.

Block, M.E. (1995b). Impact of the Americans with Disabilities Act (ADA) on youth sports. *Journal of Physical Education, Recreation & Dance, 66*(1), 28–32.

Block, M.E. (1995c). Using task sheets to facilitate peer tutoring of students with disabilities. *Strategies, 8*(7), 9–11.

Block, M.E. (1996). Modifying instruction to facilitate the inclusion of students with disabilities in regular physical education. *Strategies, 9*(4), 9–12.

Block, M.E. (1999). Did we jump on the wrong bandwagon? Problems with inclusion in physical education. *Palaestra, 15*(3), 30–38.

Block, M.E. (2005). The preparticipation physical examination. In H. Appenzeller (Ed.), *Risk management in sport: Issues and strategies* (2nd ed., pp. 191–210). Durham, NC: Carolina Academic Press.

Block, M.E. (2007). *A teacher's guide to including students with disabilities in general physical education* (3rd ed.). Baltimore, MD: Paul H. Brookes Publishing Co.

Block, M.E., & Brady, W. (1999). Welcoming students with disabilities into regular physical education. *Teaching Elementary Physical Education, 10*(1), 30–32.

Block, M.E., & Burke, K. (1999). Are your students receiving appropriate physical education? *TEACHING Exceptional Children, 31*(3), 18–23.

Block, M.E., & Conatser, P. (1999). Consultation in adapted physical education. *Adapted Physical Activity Quarterly, 16,* 9–26.

Block, M.E., Griebenauw, L., & Brodeur, S. (2004). Psychological factors and disability: Effects of physical activity and sport. In M. Weiss (Ed.), *Developmental sport and exercise psychology: A lifespan perspective* (pp. 429–455). Morgantown, WV: Fitness Information Technology.

Block, M.E., & Krebs, P.L. (1992). An alternative to the continuum of the least restrictive environments: A continuum of support to regular physical education. *Adapted Physical Activity Quarterly, 9*(2), 97–113.

Block, M.E., & Malloy, M. (1998). Attitudes of girls towards including a child with severe disabilities in a regular fast-pitch softball league. *Mental Retardation, 36,* 137–144.

Block, M.E., Oberweiser, B., & Bain, M. (1995). Utilizing classwide peer tutoring to facilitate inclusion of students with disabilities in regular physical education. *Physical Educator, 52*(1), 47–56.

Block, M.E., & Obrusnikova, I. (2007). A research review on inclusion of students with disabilities in general physical education. *Adapted Physical Activity Quarterly, 24,* 103–124.

Block, M.E., Provis, S., & Nelson, E. (1994). Accommodating students with special needs in regular physical education: Extending traditional skill stations. *Palaestra, 10*(1), 32–35.

Block, M.E., & Rizzo, T.L. (1995). Attitudes and attributes of GPE teachers associated with teaching individuals with severe and profound disabilities. *Journal of the Association for Persons With Severe Handicaps, 20,* 80–87.

Block, M.E., & Taliaferro, A. (2014). Assessment and the IEP process. In M. Grenier (Ed.), *Physical education for students with autism spectrum disorders* (pp. 47–62). Champaign, IL: Human Kinetics.

Block, M.E., Taliaferro, A., & Moran, T.E. (2013). Physical activity and youth with disabilities: Benefits, barriers and supports. *Prevention Researcher, 20*(2), 18–20.

Block, M.E., & Vogler, E.W. (1994). Including children with disabilities in regular physical education: The research base. *Journal of Physical Education, Recreation & Dance, 65*(1), 40–44.

Block, M.E., & Zeman, R. (1996). Including students with disabilities into regular physical education: Effects on nondisabled children. *Adapted Physical Activity Quarterly, 13*(1), 38–49.

Blubaugh, N., & Kohlmann, J. (2006). TEACCH model and children with autism. *Teaching Elementary Physical Education, 17*(6), 16–19.

Bluechardt, M.H., Wiener, J., & Shephard, R.J. (1995). Exercise programmes in the treatment of children with learning disabilities. *Sports Medicine, 19,* 55–72.

Bondy, A., & Frost, L. (2011). *A picture's worth: PECS and other visual communication strategies in autism* (2nd ed.). Bethesda, MD: Woodbine House.

Bonvillian, J.D., Orlansky, M.D., & Novack, L.L. (1983). Developmental milestones: Sign language acquisition and motor development. *Child Development, 54*(6), 1435–1445.

Boswell, B. (2011). Rhythmic movement and dance. In J.P. Winnick (Ed.), *Adapted physical education and sport* (5th ed., pp. 461–480). Champaign, IL: Human Kinetics.

Boulet, S.L., Boyle, C.A., & Schieve, L.A. (2009). Health care use and health and functional impact of developmental disabilities among U.S. children, 1997–2005. *Archives in Pediatric and Adolescent Medicine, 163*(1), 19–26.

Boutot, E.A., & Smith Myles, B. (2011). *Autism spectrum disorders: Foundations, characteristics and effective strategies.* New York, NY: Pearson.

Boyd, J. (1967). *Motor behavior in deaf and hearing children* (Unpublished doctoral dissertation). Northwestern University, Evanston, IL.

Boyle, C., Boulet, S., Schieve, L., Cohen, R., Blumberg, S., Yeargin-Allsopp, M.,...Kogan, M. (2011). Trends in the prevalence of developmental disabilities in U.S. children, 1997–2008. *Pediatrics, 127*(6),1034–1042.

Bradley, C.B., & Drowatzky, J.N. (1997). Time intervals of five successive steps in children with learning disabilities and children without learning disabilities. *Clinical Kinesiology, 51*(3), 58–61.

Braith, R.W. (2002). Exercise for those with chronic heart failure: Matching programs to patients. *Physician and Sportsmedicine, 30*(9), 29–38. doi: 10.3810/psm.2002.09.436

Brandon, J.E., Eason, R.L., & Smith, T.L. (1986). Behavioral relaxation training and motor performance of learning disabled children with hyperactive behaviors. *Adapted Physical Activity Quarterly, 3,* 67–79.

Brasher, B., & Holbrook, M.C. (1996). Early intervention and special education. In M.C. Holbrook (Ed.), *Children with visual impairments: A parent's guide* (pp. 175–204). Bethesda, MD: Woodbine House.

Bredahl, A. (2013). Sitting and watching the others being active: The experienced difficulties in PE when having a disability. *Adapted Physical Activity Quarterly, 30*(1), 40–58.

Breslin, C.M., & Rudisill, M.E. (2011). The effect of visual supports on performance of the TGMD-2 for children with autism spectrum disorder. *Adapted Physical Activity Quarterly, 28*(4), 342–353.

Bricker, D. (1995). The challenge of inclusion. *Journal of Early Intervention, 19*(3), 179–194.

Broder-Fingert, S., Brazauskas, K., Lindgren, K., Iannuzzi, D., & Van Cleave, J. (2014). Prevalence of overweight and obesity in a large clinical sample of children with autism. *Academic Pediatrics, 14*(4), 408–414.

Brook, U., & Galili, A. (2000). Knowledge and attitudes of high school pupils towards children with special health care needs: An Israeli exploration. *Patient Education and Counseling, 40*(1), 5–10.

Brown, H.E., Pearson, N., Braithwaite, R.E., Brown, W.J., & Biddle, S.J.H. (2013). Physical activity interventions and depression in children and adolescents: A systematic review and meta-analysis. *Sports Medicine, 43*(3), 195–206.

Brown, J., & Beamish, W. (2012). The changing role and practice of teachers of students with visual impairments: Practitioners' views from Australia. *Journal of Visual Impairment & Blindness, 106*(2), 81–92.

Brown, J.D., & Richter, J. (1994). How to handle blood and body fluid spills. *Strategies, 7*(7), 23–25.

Brown, L. (1994, December). *Including students with significant intellectual disabilities in regular education.* Paper presented at the annual conference of the Association for Persons With Severe Handicaps, Atlanta, GA.

Brown, L., Branston, M.B., Hamre-Nietupski, S., Pumpian, I., Certo, N., & Gruenewald, L. (1979). A strategy for developing chronological-age-appropriate and functional curricular content for severely handicapped adolescents and young adults. *Journal of Special Education, 13*(1), 81–90.

Brown, L., Long, E., Udvari-Solner, A., Schwarz, P., VanDeventer, P., Ahlgren, C., . . .Jorgensen, J. (1989). Should students with severe intellectual disabilities be based in regular or in special education classrooms in home schools? *Journal of the Association for Persons With Severe Handicaps, 14*(1), 8–12.

Brown, L., Schwarz, P., Udvari-Solner, A., Kampschroer-Frattura, E., Johnson, F., Jorgensen, J., et al. (1991). How much time should students with severe intellectual disabilities spend in regular education classrooms or elsewhere? *Journal of the Association for Persons With Severe Handicaps, 16*, 39–47.

Brown v. Board of Education, 347 U.S. 483 (1954).

Broyles, B. (2009). *Clinical companion for pediatric nursing.* Independence, KY: Cengage Learning.

Bruininks, R.H. (1978). *Bruininks-Oseretsky Test of Motor Proficiency: Examiner's manual.* Circle Pines, MN: American Guidance Service.

Bruininks, V., & Bruininks, R.H. (1977). Motor proficiency of learning disabled and nondisabled students. *Perceptual and Motor Skills, 44*, 1131–1137.

Brunt, D., & Broadhead, D.B. (1982). Motor proficiency traits of deaf children. *Research Quarterly for Exercise and Sport, 53*(3), 236–238.

Bryan, W.V. (1999). *Multicultural aspects of disabilities: A guide to understanding and assisting minorities in the rehabilitation process.* Springfield, IL: Charles C Thomas.

Buchanon, A., Hinton, V., Rudisill, M. (2013). Using positive behavior support in physical education. *Journal of Physical Education, Recreation & Dance, 84*(5), 44–50.

Burden, R. (2005). *Dyslexia and self-concept.* Philadelphia, PA: Whurr.

Burns, R.C., & Graefe, A.R. (2007). Constraints to outdoor recreation: Exploring the effects of disabilities on perceptions and participation. *Journal of Leisure Research, 39*(1), 156–181.

Butt, K.L., & Pahnos, M.L. (1995). Why we need a multicultural focus in our schools. *Journal of Physical Education, Recreation & Dance, 66*(1), 48–53.

Butterfield, S.A. (1986). Gross motor profiles of deaf children. *Perceptual and Motor Skills, 62*(1), 68–70.

Butterfield, S.A. (1988). Deaf children in physical education. *Palaestra, 6*(4), 28–30.

Butterfield, S.A., & Ersing, W.F. (1986). Influence of age, sex, etiology, and hearing loss on balance performance by deaf children. *Perceptual and Motor Skills, 62*(2), 659–663.

Butterfield, S.A., & Ersing, W.F. (1988). Influence of age, sex, hearing loss and balance on catching development by deaf children. *Perceptual and Motor Skills, 66*, 997–998.

Butterfield, S.A., Van der Mars, H., & Chase, J. (1993). Fundamental motor skill performance of deaf and hearing children ages 3–8. *Clinical Kinesiology,47*(1), 2–6.

Cairney, J., Hay, J., Faught, B.E., Corna, L.M., & Flouris, A. (2006). Developmental coordination disorder, age, and play: A test of the divergence in activity-deficit with age hypothesis. *Adapted Physical Activity Quarterly, 23*(3), 261–276.

Cairney, J., Hay, J.A., Faught, B.E., Wade, T.J., Corna, L., & Fouris, A. (2005). Developmental coordination disorder, generalized self-efficacy toward physical activity, and participation in organized free play activities. *Journal of Pediatrics, 147*, 515–520.

Cairney, J., Hay, J.A., Faught, B.E., Mandigo, J.L., & Flouris, A. (2005). Developmental coordination disorder, self-efficacy toward physical activity, and play: Does gender matter? *Adapted Physical Activity Quarterly, 22*(1), 67–82.

Calders, P., Elmahgoub, S., de Mettelinge, T., Vandenbroeck, C., Dewandele, I., Rombaut, L., & Cambier, D. (2011). Effect of combined exercise training on physical and metabolic fitness in adults with intellectual disability: A controlled trial. *Clinical Rehabilitation, 25*(12), 1097–1108.

Cammisa, K.M. (1994). Educational kinesiology with learning disabled children: An efficacy study. *Perceptual and Motor Skills, 78*(1), 105–106.

Campbell, M.E. (1983). *Motor fitness characteristics of hearing impaired and normal hearing children* (Unpublished master's thesis). Northeastern University, Evanston, IL.

Canadian Association of Health, Physical Education, and Recreation. (1994). *Moving to inclusion: Introductory binder.* Gloucester, Canada: Author.

Cantwell, D.P., & Baket, L. (1991). Association between attention deficit-hyperactivity disorder and learning disorders. *Journal of Learning Disabilities, 24*(2), 88–95.

Carlson, B.R. (1972). Assessment of motor ability of selected deaf children in Kansas. *Perceptual and Motor Skills, 34*(1), 303–305.

Carmeli, E., Bar-Yossef, T., Ariav, C., Levy, R., & Liebermann, D.G. (2008). Perceptual-motor coordination in persons with mild intellectual disability. *Disability and Rehabilitation, 30*(5), 323–329.

Carpenter, L.J. (2000). *Legal concepts in sport: A primer* (2nd ed.). Reston, VA: American Alliance of Active Lifestyles and Fitness.

Carter, E.W., Asmus, J., & Moss, C.K. (2013). Fostering friendships: Supporting relationships among youth with and without developmental disabilities. *Prevention Researcher, 20*(2),14–17.

Carter, L. (2002). *Good 'n' angry: How to handle your anger positively.* Grand Rapids, MI: Baker.

Cathcart, R. (2007). FISH! At the reference desk. *Reference Librarian, 48*(1), 95–97. doi:10.1300/j120v48n99_07

Causgrove, J., & Dunn, J. (2006). Psychosocial determinants of physical education behavior in children with movement difficulties. *Adapted Physical Activity Quarterly, 23,* 293–309.

Causgrove, J., & Watkinson, E.J. (2002). Perceptions of self and environment as mediators of participation in physical activity: Considering motivation theory in the study of developmental coordination disorder. In S.A. Cermak & D. Larkin (Eds.), *Developmental coordination disorder* (pp. 185–199). Albany, NY: Delmar.

Causton, J., & Theoharis, G. (2014). *The principal's handbook for leading inclusive schools.* Baltimore, MD: Paul H. Brookes Publishing Co.

Center for Applied Linguistics, Cultural Orientation Resource Center. (1996). *Welcome to the United States: A guidebook for refugees.* Retrieved from http://www.culturalorientation.net/providing-orientation/toolkit/welcome

Center for Disability Information and Referral. (2012). *Famous people with disabilities.* Retrieved from http://www.iidc.indiana.edu/cedir/kidsweb/famous.html

Cerebral Palsy Alliance. (2014). How does cerebral palsy affect people? Retrieved from https://www.cerebralpalsy.org.au/what-is-cerebral-palsy/how-cerebral-palsy-affects-people

Centers for Disease Control and Prevention. (2010a). Increasing prevalence of parent-reported attention-deficit/hyperactivity disorder among children—United States, 2003 and 2007. *Morbidity and Mortality Weekly Report, 59*(44), 1439–1443.

Centers for Disease Control and Prevention. (2010b). *Spinal cord injury (SCI): Fact sheet.* Retrieved from http://www.cdc.gov/TraumaticBrainInjury/index.html

Centers for Disease Control and Prevention. (2010c). *The association between school-based physical activity, including physical education, and academic performance.* Atlanta, GA: U.S. Department of Health and Human Services.

Centers for Disease Control and Prevention. (2011a). *Iron and iron deficiency.* Retrieved from http://www.cdc.gov/nutrition/everyone/basics/vitamins/iron.html

Centers for Disease Control and Prevention. (2011b). *National diabetes fact sheet: National estimates and general information on diabetes and prediabetes in the United States.* Atlanta, GA: Author.

Centers for Disease Control and Prevention. (2011c). Unhealthy sleep-related behaviors—12 states, 2009. *Morbidity and Mortality Weekly Report, 60,* 233–238.

Centers for Disease Control and Prevention. (2011d). Vital signs: Asthma prevalence, disease characteristics, and self-management education: United States, 2001–2009. *Morbidity and Mortality Weekly Report, 60*(17), 547–552. doi:mm6017a4 [pii]

Centers for Disease Control and Prevention. (2013). Mental health surveillance among children—United States, 2005–2011 [Supplement]. *Morbidity and Mortality Weekly Report, 62*(2), 1–35.

Centers for Disease Control and Prevention. (2014a). *Adolescence and school health: Physical activity facts.* Retrieved from http://www.cdc.gov/healthyyouth/physicalactivity/facts.htm

Centers for Disease Control and Prevention. (2014b). *Annual data early hearing detection and intervention (EHDI) program.* Retrieved from http://www.cdc.gov/ncbddd/hearingloss/ehdi-data.html

Centers for Disease Control and Prevention. (2014c). *Attention-deficit/hyperactive disorder (ADHD).* Retrieved from http://www.cdc.gov/ncbddd/adhd/data.html

Centers for Disease Control and Prevention. (2014d). *Facts about upper and lower limb reductions defects.* Retrieved from http://www.cdc.gov/ncbddd/birthdefects/ul-limbreductiondefects.html

Centers for Disease Control and Prevention. (2014e). Prevalence of autism spectrum disorders among children aged 8 years—Autism and Developmental Disabilities Monitoring Network, 11 sites, United States, 2010. *Morbidity and Mortality Weekly Report, 63*(2), 1–21.

Centers for Disease Control and Prevention. (2014f). *Racial and ethnic minority populations.* Retrieved from http://www.cdc.gov/minorityhealth/populations/remp.html

Centers for Disease Control and Prevention. (2014g). *Sickle cell disease (SCD): Complications and treatments.* Retrieved from http://www.cdc.gov/ncbddd/sicklecell/treatments.html

Centers for Disease Control and Prevention. (2014h). *Sickle cell disease (SCD): Facts about sickle cell disease.* Retrieved from http://www.cdc.gov/ncbddd/sicklecell/facts.html

Centers for Disease Control and Prevention. (2014i). *Traumatic brain injury in the United States: Fact sheet.* Retrieved from http://www.cdc.gov/traumaticbraininjury/get_the_facts.html

Centers for Disease Control and Prevention. (n.d.). *Immunization and safety and autism.* Retrieved from http://www.cdc.gov/vaccinesafety/00_pdf/CDC-StudiesonVaccinesandAutism.pdf

Certo, N.J., Schleien, S.J., & Hunter, D. (1983). An ecological assessment inventory to facilitate community recreation participation by severely disabled individuals. *Therapeutic Recreation Journal, 17*(3), 29–38.

Cervantes, C.M., Lieberman, L.J., Magnesio, B., Wood, J. (2013). Peer tutoring: Meeting the demands of inclusion in today's general physical education settings. *Journal of Physical Education, Recreation & Dance, 84*(3), 43–48.

Chadsey-Rusch, J. (1990). Social interactions of secondary-aged students with severe handicaps: Implications for facilitating the transition from school to work. *Journal of the Association for Persons With Severe Handicaps, 15*(2), 69–78.

Chaves, I.M. (1977). Historical overview of special education in the United States. In P. Bates, T.L. West, & R.B. Schmerl (Eds.), *Mainstreaming: Problems, potentials, and perspectives* (pp. 25–41). Minneapolis, MN: National Support Systems Project.

Chen, A. (2001). A theoretical conceptualization for motivation research in physical education: An integrated perspective. *Quest, 53*(1), 35–58.

Chepyator-Thomson, J. (1994). Multicultural education: Culturally responsive teaching. *Journal of Physical Education, Recreation & Dance, 65*(9), 31–32.

Childre, A., & Chambers, C.R. (2005). Family perceptions of student-centered planning and IEP meetings. *Education and Training in Developmental Disabilities, 40*(3), 217–233.

Cieslak, F. (2013). *Instructional preferences in aquatics for children with visual impairments and their instructors* (Unpublished master's thesis). State University of New York, Brockport, New York.

Civil Rights Act of 1964, PL 88-352, 20 U.S.C. § 241 *et seq.*

Clark, S. (2000). The IEP process as a tool for collaboration. *TEACHING Exceptional Children, 33*(2), 56–66.

Clements, A. (2000, March). *Emergency action plans.* Paper presented at the American Alliance for Health, Physical Education, Recreation, and Dance (AAHPERD), Orlando, FL.

Coates, J., & Vickerman, P. (2010). Empowering children with special educational needs to speak up: Experiences of inclusive physical education. *Disability and Rehabilitation, 32*(18), 1517–1526.

Cohen, M., & Sloan, D. (2007). *Visual strategies for people with autism.* Bethesda, MD: Woodbine House.

Cohen, M.J., & Sloan, D.L. (2008). *Visual supports for people with autism: A guide for parents and professionals.* Bethesda, MD: Woodbine House.

Cole, D.A. (1988). Difficulties in relationships between nonhandicapped and severely mentally retarded children: The effect of physical impairments. *Research in Developmental Disabilities, 9*, 55–72.

Combs, S., Elliott, S., & Whipple, K. (2010). Elementary physical education teachers' attitudes towards the inclusion of children with special needs: A qualitative investigation. *International Journal of Special Education, 25*(1), 114–125.

Conatser, P.K., Block, M.E., & Lapore, M. (2000). Aquatic instructors' attitudes toward teaching students with disabilities. *Adapted Physical Activity Quarterly, 17*(2), 173–183.

Condon, M.E., York, R., Heal, L.W., & Fortschneider, J. (1986). Acceptance of severely handicapped students by nonhandicapped peers. *Journal of the Association for Persons With Severe Handicaps, 11*(3), 216–219.

Conley, K.M., Bolin, D.J., Carek, P.J., Konin, J.G., Neal, T.L., & Violette, D. (2014). National athletic trainers' association position statement: Preparticipation physical examinations and disqualifying conditions. *Journal of Athletic Training, 49*(1), 102–120. doi:10.4085/1062-6050-48.6.05

Conroy, P. (2012). Supporting students with visual impairments in physical education. *Insight: Research and Practice in Visual Impairment and Blindness, 5*, 3–7.

Cooper, J.O., Heron, T.E., & Heward, W.L. (2007). *Applied behavior analysis* (2nd ed.). Columbus, OH: Merrill.

Cooper, R. (2013, March). Fringe benefits. *Sports and Spokes,* 22–28.

Cory, L., Dattilo, J., & Williams, R. (2006). Effects of a leisure education program on social knowledge and skills of youth with cognitive disabilities. *Therapeutic Recreation Journal, 40*(3), 144–164.

Cotton, D. (1994). Courtside students acting as teachers: Who is liable? *Strategies, 8*(1), 23–25.

Council for Exceptional Children. (n.d.). *Selected job profiles in special education.* Retrieved from http://www.cec.sped.org/Professional-Development/Job-Profiles-in-Special-Education

Council for Exceptional Children. (1975). What is mainstreaming? *Exceptional Children, 42*, 174.

Council for Exceptional Children. (1999). *IEP team guide.* Reston, VA: Author.

Council for Learning Disabilities. (1986). Use of discrepancy formulas in the identification of learning disabled individuals: A position statement by the board of trustees of the Council for Learning Disabilities. *Learning Disability Quarterly, 9*, 245.

Council on Physical Education for Children. (1992). *Developmentally appropriate physical education practices for children.* Reston, VA: National Association of Sport and Physical Education.

Coutinho, M.J., & Oswald, D.P. (2005). State variation in gender disproportionality in special education. *Remedial and Special Education, 26*(1), 7–15.

Covey, S.R. (1989). *The seven habits of highly effective people.* New York, NY: Fireside/Simon & Schuster.

Cowden, P.A. (2010). Social anxiety in children with disabilities. *Journal of Instructional Psychology, 37*(4), 301–305.

Craig, S.E., Haggart, A.G., & Hull, K.M. (1999). Integrating therapies into the educational setting: Strategies for supporting children with severe disabilities. *Physical Disabilities: Education and Related Services, 17*(2), 91–110.

Crisis Prevention Institute. (2015). *CPI's nonviolent crisis intervention training program: General information and empirical support.* Milwaukee, WI: Author. Retrieved from http://www.crisisprevention.com/Blog/May-2011/CPI-s-Nonviolent-Crisis-Intervention-Program-Gener

Crone, D.A., Hawken, L.S., & Horner, R.H. (2015). *Building positive behavior support systems in schools: Functional behavior assessment* (2nd ed.). New York, NY: Guilford Press.

Crowe, T., & Horak, F. (1988). Motor proficiency associated with vestibular deficits in children with hearing impairments. *Physical Therapy, 68*(10), 1493–1499.

Cullinan, D. (2007). *Students with emotional and behavioral disorders* (2nd ed.). Upper Saddle River, NJ: Pearson.

Cullinan, D., Sabornie, E.J., & Crossland, C.L. (1992). Social mainstreaming of mildly handicapped students. *Elementary School Journal, 92*, 339–352.

Cunningham, G.B., & Ping, X. (2008). Testing the mediating role of perceived motivational climate in the relationship between achievement goals and satisfaction: Are these relationships invariant across sex? *Journal of Teaching in Physical Education, 27*(2), 192–204.

Curtin, C., Anderson, S.E., Must, A., & Bandini, L. (2010). The prevalence of obesity in children with autism: A secondary data analysis using nationally representative data from the National Survey of Children's Health. *BMC Pediatrics, 10*(11), 1471–2431.

Curtin, C., Jojic, M., & Bandini, L.G. (2014). Obesity in children with autism spectrum disorder. *Harvard Review of Psychiatry, 22*(2), 93–103.

Darst, P.W., Pangrazi, R.P., Sariscsany, M.J., & Brusseau, T.A. (2012). *Dynamic physical education for secondary school students* (7th ed.). San Francisco, CA: Benjamin Cummings.

Dattilo, J., & Schleien, S. (1994). Understanding leisure services for individuals with mental retardation. *Mental Retardation, 32*(1), 53–59.

David, R., & Kuyini, A.B. (2012). Social inclusion: Teachers as facilitators in peer acceptance of students with disabilities in regular classrooms in Tamil Nadu, India. *International Journal of Special Education, 27*(2), 157–168.

Davids, K., Button, C., & Bennett, S. (2008). *Dynamics of skill acquisition.* Champaign, IL: Human Kinetics.

Davis, R. (2011). *Teaching disability sport* (2nd ed.). Champaign, IL: Human Kinetics.

Davis, R., & French, R. (1986). Managing student behaviors in physical education through a positive modified scoring system. *Directive Teacher, 8*(1), 15.

Davis, R.W., & Sherrill, C. (2004). Sports recreation and competition: Socialization, instruction, and transition. In C. Sherrill (Ed.), *Adapted physical activity, recreation, and sport: Crossdisciplinary and lifespan* (6th ed., pp. 413–440). New York, NY: McGraw-Hill.

Davis, W.E., & Burton, A.W. (1991). Ecological task analysis: Translating movement behavior theory into practice. *Adapted Physical Activity Quarterly, 8*(2), 154–177.

Dawodu, S.T., Yadav, R.R., Talavera, F., Salcido, R., & Allen, K.L. (2013). *Traumatic brain injury (TBI): Definition, epidemiology, pathophysiology. Medscape Reference.* Retrieved from http://emedicine.medscpate.com/article/326510-Overview

Dawson, G., & Rosanoff, M. (2009). *Sports, exercise, and the benefits of physical activity for individuals with autism.* Retrieved from http://www.autismspeaks.org/science/science-news/sports-exercise-and-benefits-physical-activity-individuals-autism

De Kegel, A., Dhooge, I., Peersman, W., Rijckaert, J., Baetens, T., Cambier, D., & Van Waelvelde, H. (2010). Construct validity of the assessment of balance in children who are developing typically and in children with hearing impairments. *Physical Therapy, 90*(12), 1783–1794.

DeBolt, L.S., Clinton, E.A., & Ball, A. (2010). The effects of an adapted physical education program on children with autism: A case study. *Kentucky Newsletter for Health, Physical Education, Recreation & Dance, 47*(1), 24–27.

Deci, E.L., Koestner, R., & Ryan, R.M. (2001). Extrinsic rewards and intrinsic motivation in education: Reconsidered once again. *Review of Educational Research, 71*(1), 1–27.

Delquadri, J., Greenwood, C.R., Whorton, D., Carta, J.J., & Hall, E. (1986). Class-wide peer tutoring. *Exceptional Children, 52,* 535–542.

Demicheli, V., Jefferson, T., Rivetti, A., & Price, D. (2005). Vaccines for measles, mumps and rubella in children. *Cochrane Database of Systematic Reviews, 19*(4). doi:10.1002/14651858.CD004407

DePaepe, J. (1985). The influence of three least restrictive environments on the content, motor-ALT and performance of moderately mentally retarded students. *Journal of Teaching in Physical Education, 5*(1), 34–41.

DePaepe, J.L. (1984). Mainstreaming malpractice. *Physical Educator, 41*(1), 51–56.

Dewey, D., Kaplan, B.J., Crawford, S.G., & Wilson, B.N. (2002). Developmental coordination disorder: Associated problems in attention, learning and psychosocial adjustment. *Human Movement Science, 21*(5–6), 905–918.

Diamond, A. (2013). Executive functions. *Annual Review of Psychology, 64*(1), 135–168.

Diamond, A., & Taylor, C. (1996). Development of an aspect of executive control: Development of the abilities to remember what I said and to "Do as I say, not as I do." *Developmental Psychobiology, 29*(4), 315–334.

Diener, M.B., & Milich, R. (1997). Effects of positive feedback on the social interactions of boys with attention deficit hyperactivity disorder: A test of the self-protective hypothesis. *Journal of Child Clinical Psychology, 26*(3), 256–265.

Dietz, S., & Montague, M. (2006). Attention deficit hyperactivity disorder comorbid with emotional and behavioral disorders and learning disabilities in adolescents. *Exceptionality, 14*(1), 19–33.

Disabled Sports USA. (n.d.). *Our story.* Retrieved from http://www.disabledsportsusa.org/about-us/our-story

Dodd, S.M. (2005). *Understanding autism.* New York, NY: Elsevier.

Donaldson, J. (1981). The visibility and image of handicapped people on television. *Exceptional Children, 47*(6), 413–416.

Dore. (2014). *What is the Dore program?* Retrieved from http://www.doreusa.com/programme

Dougherty, N.J., Golderberger, A.S., & Carpenter, L.J. (2007). *Sport, physical activity and the law* (3rd ed.). Champaign, IL: Sagamore.

Doulkeridou, A., Evaggelinou, C., Mouratidou, K., Koidou, E., Panagiotou, A., & Kudlacek, M. (2011). Attitudes of Greek physical education teachers towards inclusion of students with disabilities in physical education classes. *International Journal of Special Education, 26*(1), 1–11.

Dowd, A.M., Rinehart, N.J., & McGinley, J. (2010). Motor function in children with autism: Why is this relevant to psychologists? *Clinical Psychologist, 14*(3), 90–96.

Dowda, M., Sallis, J.F., McKenzie, T.L., Rosengard, P., & Kohl, H.W. (2005). Evaluating the sustainability of SPARK physical education: A case study of translating research into practice. *Research Quarterly for Exercise and Sport, 76*(1), 11–19.

Downing, J.E. (1996). *Including students with severe and multiple disabilities in typical classrooms: Practical strategies for teachers.* Baltimore, MD: Paul H. Brookes Publishing Co.

Downing, J.E. (2002). *Including students with severe and multiple disabilities in typical classrooms: Practical strategies for teachers* (2nd ed.). Baltimore, MD: Paul H. Brookes Publishing Co.

Downing, J.E., & Chen, D. (2011). Using tactile strategies with students who are blind and have severe disabilities. *TEACHING Exceptional Children, 36*(2), 56–60.

Dowshen, S. (2012). *KidsHealth: Sport, exercise, and diabetes.* Retrieved from http://kidshealth.org/parent/diabetes_center/living_diabetes/sports_diabetes.html

Doyle, B.A., & Higginson, D.C. (1984). Relationships among self-concept and school achievement, maternal self-esteem and sensory integration abilities for learning disabled children, ages 7 to 12 years. *Perceptual and Motor Skills, 58*, 177–178.

Doyle, M.B. (2008). *The paraprofessional's guide to the inclusive classroom: Working as a team* (3rd ed.). Baltimore, MD: Paul H. Brookes Publishing Co.

Dummer, G.M., Haubenstricker, J.L., & Stewart, D.A. (1996). Motor skill performance of children who are deaf. *Adapted Physical Activity Quarterly, 13*, 400–414.

Dunn, J., & Leitschuh, C. (2010). *Special physical education* (9th ed.). Dubuque, IA: Kendall/Hunt.

Dunn, J.C., & Dunn, J.G.H. (2006). Psychosocial determinants of physical education behavior in children with movement difficulties. *Adapted Physical Activity, 23*, 293–309.

Durstine, J.L. (2009). *ACSM's exercise management for persons with chronic diseases and disabilities* (3rd ed.). Champaign, IL: Human Kinetics.

Duvdevany, I., & Arar, E. (2004). Leisure activities, friendships, and quality of life of persons with intellectual disability: Foster homes vs. community residential settings. *International Journal of Rehabilitation Research, 27*(4), 289–296.

Easter Seals. (n.d.). *Friends who care.* Retrieved from http://www.easterseals.com/explore-resources/making-life-accessible/friends-who-care.html

Education for All Handicapped Children Act of 1975, PL 94-142, 20 U.S.C. § 1400 *et seq.*

Education of the Handicapped Act Amendments of 1986, PL 99-457, 20 U.S.C. § 1400 *et seq.*

Effgen, S.K. (1981). Effect of an exercise program on the static balance of deaf children. *Physical Therapy, 61*, 873–877.

Egan, A.M., Dreyer, M.L., Odar, C.C., Beckwith, M., & Garrison, C.B. (2013). Obesity in young children with autism spectrum disorders: Prevalence and associated factors. *Childhood Obesity, 9*(2), 125–131.

Eichstaedt, C.B., & Lavay, B.W. (1992). *Physical activity for individuals with mental retardation.* Champaign, IL: Human Kinetics.

Elementary and Secondary Education Act of 1965, PL 89-10, 20 U.S.C. § 241 *et seq.*

Elia, J., Glessner, J.T., Wang, K., Takahashi, N., Shtir, C.J., Hadley, D.,. . .Hakonarson, H. (2011). Genome-wide copy number variation study associates metabotropic glutamate receptor gene networks with attention deficit hyperactivity disorder. *National Genetics, 44*(1), 78–84.

Elliott, S. (2008). The effect of teachers' attitude toward inclusion on the practice and success levels of children with and without disabilities in physical education. *International Journal of Special Education, 23*(3), 48–55.

Ellis, D.N., Wright, M., & Cronis, T.G. (1996). A description of the instructional and social interactions of students with mental retardation in regular physical education settings. *Education and Training in Mental Retardation and Developmental Disabilities, 31*(3), 235–241.

Ellis, K., Lieberman, L., & LeRoux, D. (2009). Using differentiated instruction in physical education. *Palaestra, 24*(4), 19–23.

Ellis, M.K. (2001). Influence of parental hearing levels and school placement on the health-related physical fitness and community sports involvement of children who are deaf. *Palaestra, 17*(1), 44–49.

Ellis, M.K., & Darby, L.A. (1993). The effect of balance on the determination of peak oxygen consumption for hearing and nonhearing female athletes. *Adapted Physical Activity Quarterly, 10*(3), 216–225.

Ellis, M.K., Butterfield, S.A., & Lehnhard, R. (2000). Grip strength performances by 6- to-19-year-old children with and without hearing impairments. *Perceptual and Motor Skills, 90*, 279–282.

Ellis, M.K., Lieberman, L.J., & Dummer, G.M. (2014). Parent influences on physical activity participation and physical fitness of deaf children. *Journal of Deaf Studies and Deaf Education, 19*(2), 270–281.

Ellmo, W., & Graser, J. (1995). *Adapted adventure activities.* Dubuque, IA: Kendall/Hunt.

Emck, C., Bosscher, R., Beek, P., & Doreleijiers, T. (2009). Gross motor performance and self-perceived motor competence in children with emotional, behavioral, and pervasive developmental disorders: A review. *Developmental Medicine and Child Neurology, 51*(7), 501–517.

Emck, C., Bosscher, R.J., van Wieringen, P.C., Doreleijers, T., & Beek, P.J. (2012). Psychiatric symptoms in children with gross motor problems. *Adapted Physical Activity Quarterly, 29*(2), 161–178.

Epstein, R.S., McGovern, J., & Moon, M.S. (1994). The impact of federal legislation on recreation programs. In M.S. Moon (Ed.), *Making school and community recreation fun for everyone: Places and ways to integrate* (pp. 87–96). Baltimore, MD: Paul H. Brookes Publishing Co.

Erez, O., Gordaon, C.R., Sever, J., Sadeh, A., & Mintz, M. (2004). Balance dysfunction in childhood anxiety: Findings and theoretical approach. *Journal of Anxiety Disorders, 18*(3), 341–356.

Erin, J. (Ed.). (2004). *When you have a visually impaired student in your classroom with multiple disabilities: A guide for teachers.* New York, NY: American Foundation for the Blind.

Ernst, M., & Byra, M. (1998). Pairing learners in the reciprocal style of teaching: Influence of student skill, knowledge, and socialization. *Physical Educator, 55*(1), 24–37.

Escobar, L., Sanders, M.E., Lawson, D., & Benitez, C. (2013). A case study: Mobility and health impact of an aquatic fitness program for a woman with intellectual and physical disabilities. *International Journal of Aquatic Research and Education, 7*(2), 147–156.

Etzel-Wise, D., & Mears, B. (2004). Adapted physical education and therapeutic recreation in schools. *Intervention in School and Clinic, 39*(4), 223–232.

Faison-Hodge, J., & Porretta, D.L. (2004). Physical fitness and exercise training of individuals with mental retardation. *Medicine and Science in Sports and Exercise, 25,* 442–450.

Falvey, M.A., & Rosenberg, R.L. (1995). Developing and fostering friendships. In M.A. Falvey (Ed.), *Inclusive and heterogeneous schooling* (pp. 267–284). Baltimore, MD: Paul H. Brookes Publishing Co.

Faraone, S.V., & Mick, E. (2010). Molecular genetics of attention deficit hyperactivity disorder. *Psychiatric Clinics of North America, 33*(1), 159–180.

Farrington, D.P. (2005). Childhood origins of antisocial behavior. *Clinical Psychology and Psychotherapy, 12*(3), 177–190.

Fawcett, A.J., & Nicolson, R.I. (1995). Persistent deficits in motor skill of children with dyslexia. *Journal of Motor Behavior, 27*(3), 225–240.

Federal Register. (1977, August 23). *Education of Handicapped Children: Implementation of Part B of the Education of the Handicapped Act.* Vol. 42, No. 163, Part II, pp. 42474–42518.

Fejgin, N., Talmor, R., & Erlich, I. (2005). Inclusion and burnout in physical education. *European Physical Education Review, 11*(1), 29–50.

Ferguson, D.L. (1995). The real challenge of inclusion: Confessions of a "rabid inclusionist." *Phi Delta Kappan, 77*(4), 281–306.

Fink, D.B. (2001). Carlton plays tee-ball: A case study in inclusive recreation. *Parks and Recreation, 36*(8), 54–58.

Fittipaldi-Wert, J., & Mowling, C.M. (2009). Using visual supports for students with autism in physical education. *Journal of Physical Education, Recreation & Dance, 80*(2), 39–43.

Fitzgerald, H. (2005). Still feeling like a spare piece of luggage? Embodied experiences of (dis)ability in physical education and school sport. *Physical Education and Sport Pedagogy, 10*(1), 41–59.

Fitzgerald, H., & Stride, A. (2012). Stories about physical education from young people with disabilities. *International Journal of Disability, Development and Education, 59*(3), 283–293.

Fletcher, J.M., Barth, A.E., & Stuebing, K.K. (2011). A response to intervention (RTI) approach to SLD identification. In D.P. Flanagan & V.C. Alfonso (Eds.), *Essentials of specific learning disability identification* (pp. 155–144). Hoboken, NJ: John Wiley & Sons.

Flores, M., Musgrove, K., Renner, S., Hinton, V., Strozier, S., Franklin, S., & Hill, D. (2012). A comparison of communication using the Apple iPad and a picture-based system. *Augmentative and Alternative Communication, 28*(2), 74–84.

Fluegelman, A. (1976). *New games book.* New York, NY: Doubleday.

Fluegelman, A. (1981). *More new games! And playful ideas from the New Games Foundation.* New York, NY: Dolphin Books/Doubleday.

Foley, J.T. (2006). *Exploring the physical activity levels of students with mental retardation and students without disabilities in both school and after-school environments* (Unpublished doctoral dissertation). Oregon State University, Corvallis, OR.

Forest, M., & Lusthaus, E. (1989). Promoting educational equality for all students: Circles and maps. In S. Stainback, W. Stainback, & M. Forest (Eds.), *Educating all students in the mainstream of regular education* (pp. 43–58). Baltimore, MD: Paul H. Brookes Publishing Co.

Fournier, K.A., Hass, C.J., Naik, S.K., Lodha, N., & Cauraugh, J.H. (2010). Motor coordination in autism spectrum disorders: A synthesis and meta-analysis. *Journal of Autism and Developmental Disorders, 40,* 1227–1240. doi:10.1007/s10803-010-0981-3

Freeman, C., & Dennison, G. (1998). *I am the child: Using brain gym with children who have special needs.* Ventura, CA: EDU-Kinesthetics.

French, R., Henderson, H., Lavay, B., & Silliman-French, L. (2013). Opportunities for recognition can improve learning and performance. *Journal of Physical Education, Recreation & Dance, 84*(7), 51–55.

French, R., Henderson, H., Lavay, B., & Silliman-French, L. (2014). Use of intrinsic and extrinsic motivation in adapted physical education. *Palaestra, 28*(3), 32–37.

French, R., Keele, M., & Silliman-French, L. (1997). Students with shunts: Program considerations. *Journal of Physical Education, Recreation & Dance, 68*(1), 54–56.

French, R., Lavay, B., & Henderson, H. (1985). Take a lap. *Physical Educator, 42*(4), 180–185.

Frey, G.C., McCubbin, J.A., Hannigan-Downs, S., Kasser, S.L., & Skaggs, S.O. (1999). Physical fitness of trained runners with and without mild mental retardation. *Adapted Physical Activity Quarterly, 16*(2), 126–137.

Frey, G.C., Stanish, H.I., & Temple, V.A. (2008). Physical activity of youth with intellectual disability: Review and research agenda. *Adapted Physical Activity Quarterly, 25*(2), 95–117.

Frick, P.J. (1998). *Conduct disorders and severe antisocial behavior.* New York, NY: Plenum.

Fried, G.B. (2005). ADA and sport facilities. In H. Appenzeller (Ed.), *Risk management in sport: Issues and strategies* (2nd ed., pp. 289–302). Durham, NC: Carolina Academic Press.

Froehlich, T.E., Lanphear, B.P., Auinger, P., Hornung, R., Epstein, J.N., Braun, J., & Kahn, R.S. (2009). Association of tobacco and lead exposures with attention-deficit/hyperactivity disorder. *Pediatrics, 124*(6), e1054–1063.

Fuchs, D., & Fuchs, L.S. (2001). Responsiveness-to-intervention: A blueprint for practitioners, policymakers, and parents. *TEACHING Exceptional Children, 38*(1), 57–61.

Fujiura, G.T., & Yamati, K. (2000). Trends in demography of childhood poverty and disability. *Exceptional Children, 66*(2), 187–199.

Furney, K.S., & Salembier, G. (2000). Rhetoric and reality: A review of the literature on parent and student participation in the IEP and transition planning process. In D.R. Johnson & E.J. Emanuel (Eds.), *Issues* influencing the future of transition programs and services in the United States (pp. 111–126). Minneapolis, MN: University of Minnesota.

Gabbard, C. (2011). *Lifelong motor development* (6th ed.). Upper Saddle River, NJ: Pearson.

Gabriels, R.L., & Hill, D.E. (2002). *Autism: From research to individualized practice.* London, United Kingdom: Jessica Kingsley.

Gallahue, D.L., & Cleland-Donnelly, F.C. (2003). *Developmental physical education for all children* (4th ed.). Champaign, IL: Human Kinetics.

Gallahue, D.L., Ozmun, J.C., & Goodaway, J. (2012). *Understanding motor development: Infants, children, adolescents, adults* (7th ed.). New York, NY: McGraw-Hill.

Gallegos, J., Langley, A., & Villegas, D. (2012). Anxiety, depression, and coping skills among Mexican school children: A comparison of students with and without learning disabilities. *Learning Disability Quarterly, 35*(1), 54–61.

Ganz, J.B., & Flores, M.M. (2008). Effects of the use of visual strategies in play groups for children with autism spectrum disorders and their peers. *Journal of Autism and Developmental Disorders, 38,* 926–940. doi:10.1007/s10803-007-0463-4

Gaustad, J. (1993). Peer and cross-age tutoring. *ERIC Digest, 79,* 1–5.

Gaylord-Ross, R. (1980). A decision model for the treatment of aberrant behavior in applied settings. In W. Sailor, B. Wilcox, & L. Brown (Eds.), *Methods of instruction for severely handicapped students* (pp. 135–158). Baltimore, MD: Paul H. Brookes Publishing Co.

Gerber, L. (2014). Sleep deprivation in children: A growing public health concern. *Nursing Management, 45*(8), 22–28.

Getchell, N., & Gagen, L. (2006). Adapting activities for all children: Considering constraints can make planning simple and effective. *Palaestra, 22*(1), 20–27.

Getchell, N., McMenamin, S., & Whitall, J. (2005). Dual motor task coordination in children with and without learning disabilities. *Adapted Physical Activity Quarterly, 22,* 21–38.

Getskow, V., & Konczal, D. (1996). *Kids with special needs.* Santa Barbara, CA: Learning Works.

Geuze, R., & Borger, H. (1993). Children who are clumsy: Five years later. *Adapted Physical Activity Quarterly, 10,* 10–21.

Gheysen, F., Loots, G., & Van Waelvelde, H. (2008). Motor development of deaf children with and without cochlear implants. *Journal of Deaf Studies and Deaf Education, 13*(2), 215–224.

Giangreco, M.F., & Doyle, MB. (2000). Curricular and instructional considerations for teaching students with disabilities in general education classrooms. In. S. Wade (Ed.), *Inclusive education: A case book of readings for prospective and practicing teachers* (Vol. 1, pp. 51–69). Hillsdale, NJ: Lawrence Erlbaum Associates.

Giangreco, M.F., & Doyle, M.F. (2007). *Quick-guides to inclusion: Ideas for educating students with disabilities* (2nd ed.). Baltimore, MD: Paul H. Brookes Publishing Co.

Giangreco, M.F., & Putnam, J.W. (1991). Supporting the education of students with severe disabilities in regular education environments. In M.H. Meyer, C.A. Peck, & L. Brown (Eds.), *Critical issues in the lives of people with severe disabilities* (pp. 245–270). Baltimore, MD: Paul H. Brookes Publishing Co.

Gillespie, M. (2002). Attitudes of university students toward an integrated campus recreation program. *Palaestra, 18*(3), 27–31.

Ginter, E., & Simko, V. (2012). Diabetes type 2 pandemic in 21st century. *Bratislava Medical Journal, 111*(3),134–137.

Givner, C.C., & Haager, D. (1995). Strategies for effective collaboration. In M.A. Falvey (Ed.), *Inclusive and heterogeneous schooling: Assessment, curriculum, and instruction* (pp. 41–57). Baltimore, MD: Paul H. Brookes Publishing Co.

Gizer, I.R., Ficks, C., & Waldman, I.D. (2009). Candidate gene studies of ADHD: A meta-analytic review. *Human Genetology, 126*(1), 51–90.

Glover, D.R., & Anderson, L.A. (2003). *Character education.* Champaign, IL: Human Kinetics.

Goldstein, L.S. (1995). *Understanding and managing students' classroom behavior.* New York, NY: John Wiley & Sons.

Goldstein, S., & Schwebach, A.J. (2004). The comorbidity of pervasive developmental disorder and attention deficit hyperactivity disorder: Results of a retrospective chart review. *Journal of Autism and Developmental Disorders, 34*(1), 329–339.

Goodman, J., & Hopper, C. (1992). Hearing impaired children and youth: A review of psychomotor behavior. *Adapted Physical Activity Quarterly, 9*(3), 214–236.

Goodwin, D.L. (2001). The meaning of help in PE: Perceptions of students with physical disabilities. *Adapted Physical Activity Quarterly, 18*(3), 289–303.

Goodwin, D.L., & Watkinson, E.J. (2000). Inclusive physical education from the perspective of students with physical disabilities. *Adapted Physical Activity Quarterly, 17*(2), 144–160.

Gowland, C., Boyce, W.F., Wright, V., Goldsmith, C.H., & Rosenbaum, P.L. (1995). Reliability of the Gross Motor Performance Measure. *Physical Therapy, 75*(7), 597–602.

Grabrucker, A.M. (2012). Environmental factors in autism. *Front Psychiatry, 3*(1), 118. Retrieved from http://www.ncbi.nlm.nih.gov/pmc/articles/PMC3548163

Graham, G., Holt-Hale, S., & Parker, M. (2013). *Children moving: A reflective approach to teaching physical education* (9th ed.). Boston, MA: McGraw-Hill.

Grande, C.G., & Koorland, M.A. (1988). A complex issue: Special education in corrections. *Children and Youth Services Review, 10*(4), 345–350.

Grandin, T. (2006). *Thinking in pictures, expanded edition: My life with autism.* New York, NY: Vintage Books.

Gray, G.R. (1995). Safety tips from the expert witness. *Journal of Physical Education, Recreation & Dance, 66*(l), 18–21.

Green, A., & Sandt, D. (2013). Understanding the Picture Exchange Communication System. *Journal of Physical Education, Recreation & Dance, 84*(2), 33–39.

Green, D., Baird, G., & Surgden, D. (2006). A pilot study of psychopathology in developmental coordination disorder. *Child: Care, Health, and Development, 32*(6), 741–750.

Greenwood, C.R., & Todd, N.M. (1988). *The frequency interaction recording system: FIRS.* In M. Hersen & A.S. Bellack (Eds.), *Dictionary of behavioral assessment techniques* (pp. 228–230). New York, NY: Pergamon.

Gregory, G.H., & Chapman, C.M. (2013). *Differentiated instructional strategies.* Thousand Oaks, CA: Corwin.

Grenier, M., Collins, K., Wright, S., & Kearns, C. (2014). Perceptions of a disability sport unit in general physical education. *Adapted Physical Activity Quarterly, 31*(1), 49–66.

Grenier, M.A. (2006). A social constructionist perspective of teaching and learning in inclusive physical education. *Adapted Physical Activity Quarterly, 23*(3), 245–260.

Grenier, M., & Yealton, P. (2011). Previewing: A successful strategy for students with autism. *Journal of Physical Education, Recreation & Dance, 82*(1), 28–32.

Grenier, M.A. (2011). Co-teaching in physical education: A strategy for inclusive practice. *Adapted Physical Activity Quarterly, 28*(2), 95–112.

Grice, K. (2002). Eligibility under IDEA for other health impaired children. *School Law Bulletin, 33*(3), 7–12.

Grineski, S. (1996). *Cooperative learning in physical education.* Champaign, IL: Human Kinetics.

Groft-Jones, M., & Block, M.E. (2006). Strategies for teaching children with autism in physical education. *Teaching Elementary Physical Education, 17*(6), 25–28.

Grosse, S. (1991). Is the mainstream always a better place to be? *Palaestra, 7*(2), 40–49.

Grosse, S.J. (1990). How safe are your mainstreamed students? *Strategies, 4*(2), 11–13.

Gupta, V.B. (2004). *Autistic spectrum disorders in children.* Boca Raton, FL: CRC Press.

Gursel, F. (2014). Inclusive intervention to enhance the fundamental movement skills of children without hearing: A preliminary study. *Perceptual and Motor Skills, 118*(1), 304–315.

Gutkin, T.B., & Curtis, M.J. (1982). School-based consultation: Theory and techniques. In C.R. Reynolds & T.B. Gutkin (Eds.), *The handbook of school psychology* (pp. 796–828). New York, NY: John Wiley & Sons.

Haegele, J., Lieberman, L.J., & Lepore, M. (2014). A service delivery model for physical activity: Camp abilities. *Journal of Visual Impairment & Blindness, 108,* 473–483.

Hallahan, D.P., & Cruickshank, W.M. (1973). *Psychoeducational foundations of learning disabilities.* Englewood Cliffs, NJ: Prentice-Hall.

Halsey, J.J. (2012). Risk management for physical educators. In H. Appenzeller (Ed.), *Risk management in sport: Issues and strategies* (3rd ed., pp. 93–102). Durham, NC: Carolina Academic Press.

Hanft, B.E., & Place, P.A. (1996). *The consulting therapist.* San Antonio, TX: Therapy Skill Builders.

Hanson, M.J., & Lynch, E.W. (2013). *Understanding families: Supportive approaches to diversity, disability, and risk* (2nd ed.). Baltimore, MD: Paul H. Brookes Publishing Co.

Harrison, L., & Worthy, T. (2001). "Just like all the rest": Developing awareness of stereotypical thinking in physical education. *Journal of Physical Education, Recreation & Dance, 72*(9), 20–24.

Harter, S. (1981). A model of intrinsic mastery motivation in children: Individual differences and developmental change. In W.A. Collins (Ed.), *Minnesota symposium on child psychology* (Vol. 14, pp. 215–255). Hillsdale, NJ: Lawrence Erlbaum Associates.

Hartman, E., Houwen, S., & Visscher, C. (2011). Motor skill performance and sports participation in deaf elementary school children. *Adapted Physical Activity Quarterly, 28*(2), 132–145.

Harvey, W.J., & Reid, G. (1997). Motor performance of children with attention-deficit hyperactivity disorder: A preliminary investigation. *Adapted Physical Activity Quarterly, 14*(3), 189–202.

Harvey, W.J., & Reid, G. (2003). A review of fundamental movement skill performance and physical fitness of children with ADHD. *Adapted Physical Activity Quarterly, 14,* 189–202.

Harvey, W.J., & Reid, G. (2005). Attention-deficit hyperactivity disorder: Ways to improve APA research. *Adapted Physical Activity Quarterly, 20,* 1–25.

Harvey, W.J., Reid, G., Bloom, G.A., Staples, K., Grizenko, N., Mbekou, V.,. . .Joober, R. (2009). Physical activity experiences of boys with and without ADHD. *Adapted Physical Activity Quarterly, 26*(2), 131–150.

Harvey, W.J., Reid, G., Grizenko, N., Mbekou, V., Ter-Stepanian, M., & Joober, R. (2007). Fundamental movement skills and children with ADHD: Peer comparisons and stimulant effects. *Journal of Abnormal Child Psychology, 35,* 871–882.

Hastie, P.A., & Martin, E.H. (2006). *Teaching elementary physical education: Strategies for the classroom teacher.* San Francisco, CA: Benjamin Cummings.

Hauser, P.C., Cohen, J., Dye, M.W., & Bavelier, D. (2007). Visual constructive and visual-motor skills in deaf native signers. *Journal of Deaf Studies and Deaf Education, 12*(2), 148–157.

Hawkings, A. (2011). Kinesiology for humans. *Quest, 63*(3), 250–264.

Hawkins, J.D. (2012). Emergency medical preparedness. In H. Appenzeller (Ed.), *Risk management in sport: Issues and strategies* (3rd ed., pp. 259–264). Durham, NC: Carolina Academic Press.

Haywood, K., & Getchell, N. (2014). *Lifespan motor development* (6th ed.). Champaign, IL: Human Kinetics.

Haywood, K., Roberton, M.A., & Getchell, N. (2012). *Advanced analysis of motor development.* Champaign, IL: Human Kinetics.

Healthy Hearing. (n.d.). *Home page.* Retrieved from http://www.healthyhearing.com.

Healy, S. (2013). Adapting equipment for teaching object control skills. *Palaestra, 27*(4), 37–42.

Healy, S., & Wong, J. (2012, May). *Adapt It Sport: Adapting equipment for inclusion of all students.* Workshop presented at the European Congress of Adapted Physical Activity, Killarney, Ireland.

Healy, S., Msetfi, R., & Gallagher, S. (2013). "Happy and a bit nervous": The experiences of children with autism in physical education. *British Journal of Learning Disabilities, 41*(3), 222–228.

Heitman, R., Erdmann, J., Gurchiek, L., Kovaleski, J., & Giley, W. (1997). Constant versus variable practice in learning a motor task using individuals with learning disabilities. *Clinical Kinesiology, 51*(3), 62–65.

Hellison, D. (2011). *Teaching personal and social responsibility through physical activity* (3rd ed.). Champaign, IL: Human Kinetics.

Henderson, G., & Bryan, W.V. (1997). *Psychological aspects of disability.* Springfield, IL: Charles C Thomas.

Henderson, H., & French, R. (1989). Negative reinforcement or punishment? *Journal of Physical Education, Recreation & Dance, 60*(5), 4.

Henderson, S.E., May, D.S., & Umney, M. (1989). An exploratory study of goal-setting behavior, self-concept and locus of control in children with movement difficulties. *European Journal of Special Needs Education, 4*(1), 1–15.

Herkowitz, J. (1978). Developmental task analysis: The design of movement experiences and evaluation of motor development status. In M. Ridenour (Ed.), *Motor development: Issues and applications* (pp. 139–164). Princeton, NJ: Princeton Book.

Herold, F., & Dandolo, J. (2009). Including visually impaired students in physical education lessons: A case study of teacher and pupil experiences. *British Journal of Visual Impairment, 27*(1), 75–84.

Heron, T.E., & Harris, K.C. (1993). *The educational consultant: Helping professionals, parents, and mainstreamed students* (3rd ed.). Austin, TX: PRO-ED.

Hersman, B.L., & Hodge, S.R. (2010). High school physical educators' beliefs about teaching differently abled students in an urban public school district. *Education and Urban Society, 42*(6), 730–757.

Heyne, L., & Schleien, S.J. (1997). Teaming up with parents to support inclusive recreation. *Parks and Recreation, 32*(5), 76–81.

Higbee, J.L. (2008). Institutional transformation: Some concluding thoughts. In J.L. Higbee and E. Goff (Eds.), *Pedagogy and student services for institutional transformation: Implementing universal design in higher education* (pp. 481–484). Minneapolis, MN: Regents of the University Minnesota.

Hill, J. (2002). Biological, psychological and social processes in the conduct disorders. *Journal of Child Psychology and Psychiatry, 43*(1), 133–164.

Hill, W.M. (2000). Investigating school-related behavior disorders: Lessons learned from a thirty-year research career. *Exceptional Children, 66*(2), 151.

Hillburn, S., Marini, I., & Slate, J.R. (1997). Self-esteem among deaf versus hearing children with deaf versus hearing parents. *Journal of the American Deafness and Rehabilitation Association, 30*, 9–12.

Hillman, J., Snyder, S., & Neubrander, J. (2014). *Childhood autism: A clinician's guide to early diagnosis and integrated treatment.* London, United Kingdom: Routledge.

Hinslie, L., & Shatzky, J. (1940). *Psychiatric dictionary.* New York, NY: Oxford University Press.

Hodge, S.R., & Akuffo, P.B. (2007). Adapted physical education teachers' concerns in teaching students with disabilities in an urban public school district. *International Journal of Disability, Development and Education, 54*(4), 399–416.

Hodge, S.R., Ammah, J.O.A., Casebolt, K.M., LaMaster, K., Hersman, B., Samalot-Rivera, A., & Sato, T. (2009). A diversity of voices: Physical education teachers' beliefs about inclusion and teaching students with disabilities. *International Journal of Disability, Development and Education, 56*(4), 401–419.

Hodge, S.R., Lieberman, L.J., & Murata, N.M. (2012). *Essentials of teaching adapted physical education: Diversity, culture, and inclusion.* Scottsdale, AZ: Holcomb Hathaway.

Hodge, S.R., Murata, N.M., & Porretta, D.L. (1999). Enhancing motor performance through various preparatory activities involving children with learning disabilities. *Clinical Kinesiology, 53*(4), 76–82.

Hoff, E. (2013). *Language development* (5th ed.). Belmont, CA: Wadsworth.

Hollis, J., & Gallegos, E. (1993). Inclusion: What is the extent of a school district's duty to accommodate students with disabilities in the regular classroom? *Legal Digest, 9*(9), 1–8, 17.

Hoon, A.H., & Tolley, F. (2013). Cerebral Palsy. In M.L. Batshaw (Ed.), *Children with disabilities* (7th ed., pp. 423–450). Baltimore: Paul H. Brookes Publishing Co.

Horton, M. (2001). Utilizing paraprofessionals in the general physical education setting. *Teaching Elementary Physical Education, 12*(6), 22–25.

Horton, M., Wilson, S., & Gagnon, D. (2003). Collaboration: A key component for successful inclusion in general physical education. *Teaching Elementary Physical Education, 14*(3), 13–17.

Horvat, M., Block, M.E., & Kelly, L. (2007). *Developmental and adapted physical activity assessment.* Champaign, IL: Human Kinetics.

Houston-Wilson, C., Dunn, J.M., van der Mars, H., & McCubbin, J. (1997). The effects of peer tutors on the motor performance in integrated physical education classes. *Adapted Physical Activity Quarterly, 14*, 298–313.

Houston-Wilson, C., Lieberman, L., Horton, M., & Kasser, S. (1997). Peer tutoring: A plan for instructing students of all abilities. *Journal of Physical Education, Recreation & Dance, 68*(6), 39–44.

Houwen, S., Hartman, E., Jonker, L., & Visscher, C. (2010). Reliability and validity of the TGMD-2 in primary-school-age children with visual impairments. *Adapted Physical Activity Quarterly, 27*, 143–159.

Houwen, S., Hartman, E., & Visscher, C. (2009). Physical activity and motor skills in children with and without visual impairments. *Medicine and Science in Sports and Exercise, 41*(1), 103–109. doi:10.1249/ MSS.0b013e318183389d

Houwen, S., Visscher, C., Lemmink, K.A.P.M., & Hartman, E. (2008). Motor skill performance of school-age children with visual impairments. *Developmental Medicine and Child Neurology, 50,* 139–145. doi:10.1111/j.1469-8749.2007.02016.x

Hoza, B., Dobbs, J., Owens, J.S., Pelham, W.E., Jr., & Pillow, D.R. (2002). Do boys with attention deficit/hyperactivity disorder have positive illusory self-concepts? *Journal of Abnormal Psychology, 111,* 268–278.

Hoza, B., Pelham, W.E., Milich, R., Pillow, D., & McBride, K.(1993). The self-perceptions and attributions of attention deficit hyperactivity disordered and nonreferred boys. *Journal of Abnormal Child Psychology, 21,* 271–286.

Hoza, B., Pelham, W.E., Waschbushc, D.A., Kipp, H., & Owens, J.S. (2001). Academic task persistence of normally achieving ADHD and control boys: Performance, self-evaluations, and attributions. *Journal of Consulting and Clinical Psychology, 69,* 271–283.

Huang, T.T., & Ness, K.K. (2011). Exercise interventions in children with cancer: A review. *International Journal of Pediatrics, 2011,* 461–512. doi:10.1155/2011/461512

Huebner, K.M.,Prickett, J.G., & Welch, T.R. (1995). *Hand in hand: Essentials of communication and orientation and mobility for your students who are deaf-blind.* New York, NY: American Foundation for the Blind.

Huebner, T.A. (2010). Differentiated instruction. *Educational Leadership, 67*(5), 79–81.

Hurley, R., & Turner, C. (1991). Neurology and aquatic therapy. *Clinical Management: The Magazine of the American Physical Therapy Association, 11*(1), 26–29.

Hutchinson, G.E. (1995). Gender-fair teaching in physical education. *Journal of Physical Education, Recreation & Dance, 66*(1), 42–47.

Hutzler, Y. (2003). Attitudes toward the participation of individuals with disabilities in physical activity: A review. *Quest, 55*(4), 347–373.

Hutzler, Y., Chacham, A., Bergman, U., & Szeinberg, A. (1997). Effects of exercise on respiration in children with cerebral palsy. *Palaestra, 13*(4), 20–24.

Hutzler, Y., Fliess, O., Chacham, A., & Van den Auweele, Y. (2002). Perspectives of children with physical disabilities on inclusion and empowerment: Supporting and limiting factors. *Adapted Physical Activity Quarterly, 19,* 300–317.

IDEA Data Center. (2012). *IDEA Part B Child Count and Education Environments.* Retrieved from https://inventory.data.gov/dataset/8715a3e8 -bf48-4eef-9deb-fd9bb76a196e/resource/a68a23f3 -3981-47db-ac75-98a167b65259

Imber, M., & Van Geel, T. (2001). *A teacher's guide to education law* (2nd ed.). Mahwah, NJ: Lawrence Erlbaum Associates.

Improving America's Schools Act of 1994, PL 103-382, 20 U.S.C. § 630 *et seq.*

Individuals with Disabilities Education Act Amendments of 1997, PL 105-17, 20 U.S.C. § 1400 *et seq.*

Individuals with Disabilities Education Act (IDEA) of 1990, PL 101-476, 20 U.S.C. § 1400 *et seq.*

Individuals with Disabilities Education Improvement Act (IDEA) of 2004, PL 108-446, 20 U.S.C. § 1400 *et seq.*

Individuals with Disabilities Education Improvement Act, Part B Regulations, 34 C.F.R. § 300. 530–536 (2004b).

Institute of Medicine. (2011). *Adverse effects of vaccinations: Evidence and causality.* Retrieved from http://www.iom.edu/Reports/2011/Adverse-Effects-of-Vaccines-Evidence-and-Causality.aspx

International Paralympic Committee. (n.d.-a). *Education.* Retrieved from http://www.paralympic.org/ the-ipc/education

International Paralympic Committee. (n.d.-b). *Paralympic school day.* Retrieved from http:// www.paralympic.org/TheIPC/WWD/Paralympic SchoolDay

International Paralympic Committee. (2006). *Paralympic school day.* Retrieved from http://www .paralympic.org/the-ipc/paralympic-school-day

Iverson, J.M. (2010). Developing language in a developing body: The relationship between motor development and language development. *Journal of Childhood Language, 37,* 229–261.

Jackson, L., & Panyan, M.V. (2001). *Positive behavioral support in the classroom: Principles and practices.* Baltimore, MD: Paul H. Brookes Publishing Co.

Jambor, E., & Elliott, M. (2005). Self-esteem and coping strategies among deaf students. *Journal of Deaf Studies and Deaf Education, 10*(1), 8–17.

Janney, R., & Snell, M.E. (2006). *Teachers' guides to inclusive practices: Social relationships and peer support* (2nd ed.). Baltimore, MD: Paul H. Brookes Publishing Co.

Janney, R., & Snell, M.E. (2013). *Teachers' guides to inclusive practices: Modifying schoolwork* (3rd ed.). Baltimore, MD: Paul H. Brookes Publishing Co.

Janney, R.E., & Snell, M.E. (2016). Designing and implementing instruction for inclusive classes. In F.E. Brown, M.E. Snell, & J.J. Mcdonnell (Eds.), *Instruction of students with severe disabilities* (8th ed., pp. 190–222). Old Tappan, NJ: Pearson.

Janney, R.F., Snell, M.E., Beers, M.K., & Raynes, M. (1995). Integrating students with moderate and severe disabilities into general education classes. *Exceptional Children, 61,* 425–439.

Jansma, P., & Decker, J. (1990). *Project LRE/PE: Least restrictive environment usage in physical education.* Washington, DC: Department of Education, Office of Special Education.

Jansma, P., & French, R. (1994). *Special physical education.* Upper Saddle River, NJ: Prentice-Hall.

Jerlinder, K., Danermark, B., & Gill, P. (2010). Swedish primary-school teachers' attitudes to inclusion: The case of PE and pupils with physical disabilities. *European Journal of Special Needs Education, 25*(1), 45–57.

Johnson, C.C. (2009). The benefits of physical activity for youth with developmental disabilities: A systematic review. *American Journal of Health Promotion, 23*(3), 157–167.

Johnson, D.W., & Johnson, R.T. (1999). *Learning together and alone: Cooperation, competition, and individualization* (7th ed.). Needham Heights, MA: Allyn & Bacon.

Johnson, M., & Ward, P. (2001). Effects of classwide peer tutoring on correct performance of striking skills in 3rd grade physical education. *Journal of Teaching in Physical Education, 20*(3), 247–263.

Johnston, T., & Wayda, V.K. (1994). Are you an effective communicator? *Strategies, 7*(5), 9–13.

Kahan, D. (2003). Islam and physical activity: Implications for American sport and physical educators. *Journal of Physical Education, Recreation & Dance, 74*(3), 48–54.

Kalkowski, P. (2001). *Peer and cross-age tutoring.* Portland, OR: Education Northwest.

Kalymon, K., Gettinger, M., & Hanley-Maxwell, C. (2010). Middle school boys' perspectives on social relationships with peers with disabilities. *Remedial and Special Education, 31,* 305–316.

Kalyvas, V., & Reid, G. (2003). Sport adaptation, participation and enjoyment of students with and without disabilities. *Adapted Physical Activity Quarterly, 20,* 182–199.

Kamlesh, M.L. (2011). *Psychology in physical education and sport.* New Delhi, India: Khel Sahitya Kendra.

Kamps, D.M., Greenwood, C., Arreaga-Mayer, C., Veerkamp, M.B., Utley, C., Tapia, Y.,. . .Bannister, H. (2008). The efficacy of classwide peer tutoring in middle schools. *Education and Treatment of Children, 31*(2), 119–152.

Karagiannis, A., Stainback, W., & Stainback, S. (1996). Rationale for inclusive schooling. In S. Stainback & W. Stainback (Eds.), *Inclusion: A guide for educators* (pp. 3–16). Baltimore, MD: Paul H. Brookes Publishing Co.

Karamessinis, L., Sala, K., Tang, Y., Spinella, P., Zucker, A., & Carroll, C. (2011). Respiratory failure in children with status asthmaticus: A review of the virtual PICU database. *American Journal of Respiratory and Critical Care Medicine, 183,* A6279.

Kasser, S.L. (1995). *Inclusive games.* Champaign, IL: Human Kinetics.

Kasser, S.L., & Lytle, R.K. (2005). *Inclusive physical activity: A lifetime of opportunities.* Champaign, IL: Human Kinetics.

Kasser, S.L., & Lytle, R.K. (2013). *Inclusive physical activity: Promoting health for a lifetime* (2nd ed.). Champaign, IL: Human Kinetics.

Kassing, G., & Jay, D.M. (2003). *Dance teaching methods and curriculum design.* Champaign, IL: Human Kinetics.

Katz, S., & Yekutiel, E. (1974). Leisure time problems of mentally retarded graduates of training programs. *Mental Retardation, 12,* 54–57.

Kauffman, J.M. (1993). How we might achieve the radical reform of special education. *Exceptional Children, 60,* 294–309.

Kauffman, J.M., & Landrum, T.J. (2009). *Characteristics of emotional and behavioral disorders of children and youth* (9th ed.). Upper Saddle, NJ: Merrill.

Kauffman, J.M., Mostert, M.P., Trent, S.C., & Hallahan, D.P. (1998). *Managing classroom behavior* (2nd ed.). Boston, MA: Allyn & Bacon.

Kavale, K., & Mattson, P.D. (1983). "One jumped off the balance beam": Meta-analysis of perceptual-motor training. *Journal of Learning Disabilities, 16*(3), 165–173.

Kawanishi, C.Y., & Greguol, M. (2013). Physical activity, quality of life, and functional autonomy of adults with spinal cord injuries. *Adapted Physical Activity Quarterly, 30,* 317–337.

Kelly, L.E. (1991). National standards for adapted physical education. *Advocate, 20*(1), 2–3.

Kelly, L.E. (2011). *Designing and implementing effective adapted physical education programs.* Urbana, IL: Sagamore.

Kelly, L.E., & Melograno, V.J. (2015). *Developing the physical education curriculum: An achievement-based approach* (2nd ed.). Long Grove, IL: Waveland Press.

Kelly, L.E., & Wessel, J.A. (1986). *Achievement-based curriculum development in physical education.* Philadelphia, PA: Lea & Febiger.

Kelly, L.E., Wessel, J.A., Dummer, G., & Sampson, T. (2010). *Everyone can!: Elementary physical education curriculum and teaching resources.* Champaign, IL: Human Kinetics.

Kerr, R., & Hughes, K. (1987). Movement difficulty and learning disabled children. *Adapted Physical Activity Quarterly, 4,* 72–79.

King, I.F., Yandava, C.N., Mabb, A.M., Hsiao, J.S., Huang, H.-S., Pearson, B.L.,. . .Zylka, M.J. (2013). Topoisomerases facilitate transcription of long genes linked to autism. *Nature, 501*(7465), 58–62.

King-Sears, M., Janney, R., & Snell, M.E. (2015). *Teachers' guides to inclusive practices: Collaborative teaming* (3rd ed.). Baltimore, MD: Paul H. Brookes Publishing Co.

Klavina, A., & Block, M.E. (2008). The effect of peer tutoring on interaction behaviors in inclusive physical education. *Adapted Physical Activity Quarterly, 25,* 132–158.

Klavina, A., & Block, M.E. (2013). Training peer tutors to support children with severe, multiple disabilities in general physical education. *Palaestra, 27*(2), 26–32.

Klavina, A., Jerlinder, K., Kristen, L., Hammar, L., & Soulie, T. (2014). Cooperative oriented learning in inclusive physical education. *European Journal of Special Needs Education, 29*(2), 119–134. doi:10.1080/08856257.2013.859818

Klein, R.G., Mannuzza, S., Olazagasti, M.A., Belsky, E.R., Hutchison, J.A., Lashua-Shriftman, E., & Castellanos, F.X. (2012). Clinical and functional outcome of childhood ADHD 33 years later. *Archives of General Psychiatry, 69*(12). 1295–1303.

Kleinert, H., Miracle, S., & Sheppard-Jones, K. (2007). Including students with moderate and severe intellectual disabilities in school extracurricular and community recreation activities. *Intellectual and Developmental Disabilities, 45* (1), 46–55.

Kline, F.M., Silver, L.B., & Russell, S.C. (Eds.). (2001). *The educator's guide to medical issues in the classroom.* Baltimore, MD: Paul H. Brookes Publishing Co.

Kohane, I.S., McMurry, A.,Weber, G., MacFadden, D., Rappaport, L., Kunkel, L.,. . .Churchill, S. (2012). The co-morbidity burden of children and young adults with autism spectrum disorders. *PLOS ONE, 7*(4). Retrieved from http://journals.plos.org/plosone/article?id=10.1371/journal.pone.0033224

Kohn, A. (1998). *What to look for in the classroom.* San Francisco, CA: Jossey-Bass.

Kollipara, S., & Warren-Boulton, E. (2004). *Diabetes and physical activity in school.* Retrieved from http://ndep.nih.gov/media/SNN_May_2004.pdf

Kovaleski, J.F., van der Heyden, A.M., & Shapiro, E.S. (2013). *The RTI approach to evaluating learning disabilities.* New York, NY: Guilford Press.

Kozub, F.M. (2001). Adapted physical activity programming within the family: The family systems theory. *Palaestra, 17*(3), 30–38.

Kozub, F.M., & Porreta, D.L. (1998). Interscholastic coaches' attitudes toward integration of adolescents with disabilities. *Adapted Physical Activity Quarterly, 15,* 328–344.

Krebs, D.E., Edelstein, J.E., & Thornby, M.A. (1991). Prosthetic management of children with limb deficiencies. *Physical Therapy, 71,* 920–934.

Krebs, P.L., & Block, M.E. (1992). Transition of students with disabilities into community recreation: The role of the adapted physical educator. *Adapted Physical Activity Quarterly, 9,* 305–315.

Kristensen, H., & Torgersen, S. (2007). The association between avoidant personality traits and motor impairment in a population-based sample of 11–12-year-old children. *Journal of Personality Disorders, 21,* 87–97.

Krueger, D.L., DiRocco, P., & Felix, M. (2000). Obstacles adapted physical education specialists encounter when developing transition plans. *Adapted Physical Activity Quarterly, 17,* 222–236.

Kudláček, M., Ješina, O., Štěrbová, D., & Sherrill, C. (2008). The nature of work and roles of public school adapted physical educators in the United States. *European Journal of Adapted Physical Activity, 1*(2), 45–55.

Kunstler, R., Thompson, A., & Croke, A. (2013). Inclusive recreation for transition-age youth: Promoting self-sufficiency, community inclusion, and experiential learning. *Therapeutic Recreation Journal, 47*(2), 122–136.

Kurpius, D.J., & Rozecki, T.G. (1993). Strategies for improving interpersonal communication. In J.E. Zins, T.R. Kratochwill, & S.N. Elliott (Eds.), *Handbook of consultation services for children* (pp. 137–158). San Francisco, CA: Jossey-Bass.

Lacy, A.C. (2010). *Measurement and evaluation in physical education and exercise science* (6th ed.). Upper Saddle River, NJ: Benjamin Cummings.

Lahtinen, U., Rintala, P., & Malin, A. (2007). Physical performance of individuals with intellectual disability: A 30-year follow-up. *Adapted Physical Activity Quarterly, 24,* 125–143.

Lakowski, T. (2013). U.S. Department of Education orders sports access for students with disabilities: A watershed moment for students with disabilities. *Palaestra, 27*(2), 6–8.

LaMaster, K., Gall, K., Kinchin, G., & Siedentop, D. (1998). Inclusion practices of effective elementary specialists. *Adapted Physical Activity Quarterly, 15,* 64–81.

Lane, C. (2001, March 30). Disabled pro golfer wins right to use cart. *Washington Post,* A01.

Latash, M.L. (1992). Motor control in Down syndrome: The role of adaptation and practice. *Journal of Developmental and Physical Disabilities, 4,* 227–261.

Lavay, B. (1984). Physical activity as a reinforcer in physical education. *Adapted Physical Activity Quarterly, 1,* 315–321.

Lavay, B., & DePaepe, J. (1987). The harbinger helper: Why mainstreaming in physical education doesn't always work. *Journal of Physical Education, Recreation & Dance, 58*(7), 98–103.

Lavay, B., French, R., & Henderson, H. (2006). *Positive behavior management in physical activity settings* (2nd ed.). Champaign, IL: Human Kinetics.

Lavay, B., French, R., & Henderson, H. (2007a). Do PERD professionals get enough training in behavior management and supervision in physical activity settings? *Journal of Physical Education, Recreation & Dance, 78*(2), 11–12.

Lavay, B., French, R., & Henderson, H. (2007b). A practical plan for managing the behavior of students with disabilities in general physical education. *Journal of Physical Education, Recreation & Dance, 78*(2), 41–48.

Lavay, B., French, R., & Henderson, H. (2016). *Positive behavior management in physical activity settings* (3rd ed.). Champaign, IL: Human Kinetics.

Lavay, B., Henderson, H., French, R., & Guthrie, S. (2012). Behavior management instructional strategies and content of college/university physical education teacher education programs. *Physical Education and Sport Pedagogy, 17*(2), 195–210.

Lavay, B., Henderson, H., & Guthrie, S. (2014). The behavior management training and teaching practices of adapted physical education teachers. *Palaestra, 28*(1), 24–31.

Lavay, B., & Semark, C. (2001). Everyone plays: Including special needs children in youth sports programs. *Palaestra, 17*(4), 40–43.

Lawrence, S., Chau, M., & Lennon, M.C. (2004). *Depression, substance abuse, and domestic violence.* New York, NY: National Center for Children in Poverty, Columbia University.

Lazarus, J.C. (1994). Evidence of disinhibition in learning disabilities: The associated movement phenomenon. *Adapted Physical Activity Quarterly, 11,* 57–70.

LDOnline. (2010). *What is a learning disability?* Retrieved from http://www.ldonline.org/ldbasics/whatisld

Le Masurier, G., & Corbin, C. (2006). Top 10 reasons for quality physical education. *Journal of Physical Education, Recreation & Dance, 77*(6), 44–53.

Lee, D.O., & Ousley, O.Y. (2006). Attention-deficit hyperactivity disorder symptoms in a clinic sample of children and adolescents with pervasive developmental disorders, *Journal of Child and Adolescent Psychopharmacology, 16*(1), 737–746.

Lee, S., Sills, M., & Oh, G. (2002). *Disabilities among children and mothers in low-income families. Research-in-brief.* Washington, DC: Institute for Women's Policy Research. Retrieved from http://www.iwpr.org/publications/pubs/disabilities-among-children-and-mothers-in-low-income-families

LeFever, G.B., Villers, M.S., Morrow, A.L., & Vaughn, E.S. (2002). Parental perceptions of adverse educational outcomes among children diagnosed and treated for ADHD: A call for improved school/provider collaboration. *Psychology in the Schools, 39*(1), 63–71.

LeFevre, D. (2012). *Best new games* (updated ed.). Champaign, IL: Human Kinetics.

Lepore, M. (2011). Aquatics. In J.P. Winnick (Ed.), *Adapted physical education and sport* (5th ed., pp. 481–501). Champaign, IL: Human Kinetics.

Lepore, M., Gayle, G.W., & Stevens, S.F. (2007). *Adapted aquatics programming: A professional guide* (2nd ed.). Champaign, IL: Human Kinetics.

Lerner, J.W., & Johns, B. (2014). *Learning disabilities and related disabilities: Strategies for success* (13th ed.). Independence, KY: Cengage Learning.

Lester, P.M., & Ross, S.D. (2003). *Images that injure. Pictorial stereotypes in the media.* Westport, CT: Greenwood.

Levesque, J., Theoret, H., & Champoux, F. (2014). Reduced procedural motor learning in deaf individuals. *Frontiers in Human Neuroscience, 8,* 1–6.

Levinson Medical Center for Learning Disabilities. (n.d.). *Famous dyslexics mean that you are not alone and you can succeed.* Retrieved from http://www.dyslexiaonline.com/basics/famous_dyslexics.html

Lewis, A. (2001). *Add it up: Using research to improve education for low-income and minority students.* Washington, DC: Poverty and Race Research Action Council.

Lewis, R.B., & Doorlag, D.H. (1991). *Teaching special students in the mainstream* (3rd ed.). New York, NY: Macmillan.

Lewis, S., Higham, L., & Cherry, D.B. (1985). Development of an exercise program to improve the static and dynamic balance of profoundly hearing impaired children. *American Annals of the Deaf, 130,* 278–283.

Leyfer, O.T., Folstein, S.E., Bacalman, S., Davis, N.O., Dinh, E., Morgan, J.,. . .Lainhart, J.E. (2006). Comorbid psychiatric disorders in children with autism: Interview development and rates of disorders. *Journal of Autism and Developmental Disorders, 36,* 849–861.

Lieberman, L.J. (Ed.). (2007). *A paraprofessional training guide for physical education.* Champaign, IL: Human Kinetics.

Lieberman, L.J. (2011). Visual impairments. In J.P. Winnick (Ed.), *Adapted physical education and sport* (5th ed., pp. 233–248). Champaign, IL: Human Kinetics.

Lieberman, L.J., Byrne, H., Mattern, C., Watt, C., & Fernandez-Vivo, M. (2010). Health-related fitness in youth with visual impairments, *Journal of Visual Impairments & Blindness, 104,* 349–359.

Lieberman, L.J., & Conroy, P. (2013). Paraeducator training for physical education for children with visual impairments. *Journal of Visual Impairment & Blindness, 107,* 17–28.

Lieberman, L.J., & Cowart, J. (2011). *Games for people with sensory impairments* (2nd ed.). Louisville, KY: American Printing House for the Blind.

Lieberman, L.J., Dunn, J.M., van der Mars, H., & McCubbin, J. (2000). Peer tutors' effects on activity levels of deaf students in inclusive elementary physical education. *Adapted Physical Activity Quarterly, 17,* 20–39.

Lieberman, L.J., & Haibach, P. (in press). *Motor development for children with visual impairments.* Louisville, KY: American Printing House for the Blind.

Lieberman, L.J., Haibach, P., & Wagner, M. (2014). Let's play together: Sports equipment for children with and without visual impairments. *Palaestra, 28,* 13–15.

Lieberman, L.J., & Houston-Wilson, C. (2009). *Strategies for inclusion: A handbook for physical educators* (2nd ed.). Champaign, IL: Human Kinetics.

Lieberman, L.J., Lepore, M., & Haegele, J. (2014). Camp Abilities: A sports camp for children with visual impairments. *Palaestra, 28*(4), 37–43.

Lieberman, L.J., Newcomer, J., McCubbin, J., & Dalrymple, N. (1997). The effects of cross-aged peer tutors on the academic learning time of students with disabilities in inclusive elementary physical education classes. *Brazilian International Journal of Adapted Physical Education Research, 4*(1), 15–32.

Lieberman, L.J., Ponchillia, P.E., & Ponchillia, S.V. (2013). *Physical education and sports for people with visual impairments and deafblindness: Foundations of instruction.* New York, NY: American Foundation for the Blind.

Lienert, C., Sherrill, C., & Myers, B. (2001). Physical educators' concerns about integrating children with disabilities: A cross-cultural comparison. *Adapted Physical Activity Quarterly, 18,* 1–17.

Lindsay, S., & Edwards, A. (2013). A systematic review of disability awareness interventions for children and youth. *Disability and Rehabilitation, 35*(8), 623–646.

Lipsky, D.K., & Gartner, A. (1987). *Beyond separate education: Quality education for all.* Baltimore, MD: Paul H. Brookes Publishing Co.

Lipsky, D.K., & Gartner, A. (1998). *Inclusion and school reform: Transforming America's classrooms.* Baltimore, MD: Paul H. Brookes Publishing Co.

Lipton, D. (1994, April). *The full inclusion court cases: 1989–1994.* Paper presented at the Wingspread Conference, Racine, WI.

Little League of America. (n.d.). *Challenger division.* Retrieved from http://www.littleleague.org/learn/about/divisions/challenger.htm

Logan, K.R., Jacobs, H.A., Gast, D.L., Murray, A.S., Daino, K., & Skala, C. (1998). The impact of typical peers on the perceived happiness of children with profound multiple disabilities. *Journal of the Association for Persons with Severe Handicaps, 23,* 309–318.

Longhurst, G.K., Coetsee, M.F., & Bressan, E.S. (2004). A comparison of the motor proficiency of children with and without learning disabilities: Research article. *South African Journal for Research in Sport, Physical Education and Recreation, 26*(1), 79–88.

Loovis, E.M. (2011). Behavior management. In J.P. Winnick (Ed.), *Adapted physical education and sport* (5th ed., pp. 155–172). Champaign, IL: Human Kinetics.

Lovering, J.S., & Percy, M. (2007). Down syndrome. In I. Brown & M. Percy (Eds.), *A comprehensive guide to intellectual and developmental disabilities* (pp. 140–172). Baltimore, MD: Paul H. Brookes Publishing Co.

Lucas, M.D. (2011). Working with students with English as a second language in physical education. *Virginia Journal, 32*(1), 13–15.

Lucas, M.D., & Block, M.E. (2008). What adapted physical educators should know about Islam. *Palaestra, 21*(2), 28–34.

Luckner, J.L., Slike, S.B., & Johnson, H. (2012). Helping students who are deaf or hard of hearing succeed. *TEACHING Exceptional Children, 44*(4), 58–67.

Luvmour, J., & Luvmour, B. (2013). *Everyone wins: Cooperative games and activities* (2nd ed.). Gabriola Island, Canada: New Society.

Lynch, E.W., & Hanson, M.J. (2011). *Developing cross-cultural competence: A guide for working with children and their families* (4th ed.). Baltimore, MD: Paul H. Brookes Publishing Co.

Lytle, R., Lavay, B., & Rizzo, T. (2010). What is a highly qualified adapted physical education teacher? *Journal of Physical Education, Recreation & Dance, 81*(2), 40–44, 50.

Maag, J.W. (2001). Reward by punishment: Reflections on the misuse of positive reinforcement in schools. *Exceptional Children, 67*(2), 173–186.

MacDonald, C., & Block, M.E. (2005). Self-advocacy in physical education for students with physical disabilities. *Journal of Physical Education, Recreation & Dance, 76*(4), 45–48.

Mactavish, J.B., & Schleien, S.J. (2000). Exploring family recreation activities in families that include children with developmental disabilities. *Therapeutic Recreation Journal, 34* (2), 132–153.

Mactavish, J.B., & Schleien, S.J. (2004). Re-injecting spontaneity and balance in family life: Parents' perspectives on recreation in families that include children with developmental disability. *Journal of Intellectual Disability Research, 48*, 123–141.

Madden, N.M., & Slavin, R.E. (1983). Mainstreaming students with mild handicaps: Academic and social outcomes. *Review of Educational Research, 53*, 519–569.

Mahoney, J.L., & Stattin, H. (2000). Leisure activities and adolescent antisocial behavior: The role of structure and social context. *Journal of Adolescence, 23*(2), 113–127.

Malmgren, K.W., & Causton-Theoharis, J.N. (2006). Boy in the bubble: Effects of paraprofessional proximity and other pedagogical decisions on the interactions of a student with behavioral disorders. *Journal of Research in Childhood Education, 20*(4), 301–312.

Maloney, M. (1994). Courts are redefining LRE requirements under the IDEA. *Inclusive Education Programs, 1*(1), 1–2.

Mandt System, Inc. (2010). *The Mandt System®: Reducing workplace violence through positive behavior supports.* Unpublished manuscript.

Mannuzza, S., Klein, R.G., Bessler, A., Malloy, P., & LaPadula, M. (1998). Adult psychiatric status of hyperactive boys grown up. *American Journal of Psychiatry, 155*, 493–498.

Marcus, B.H., & Forsyth, L.H. (2003). *Motivating people to be physically active.* Champaign, IL: Human Kinetics.

Margolis, H., & Fiorelli, J. (1987). Getting past anger in consulting relationships. *Organization Development Journal, 5*(1), 44–48.

Margolis, H., & McCabe, P.P. (1988). Overcoming resistance to a new remedial program. *Clearing House, 62*(3), 131–134.

Markos, N., & Jenkins, A. (1994). *Medical information form: Broadus Woods Elementary School.* Earlysville, VA: Author.

Martin, B. (2004). *I know I can do it: Sports are for disabled children, too.* Retrieved from http://www.cureourchildren.org/sports.htm#'I%20Know%20I%20Can%20Do%20It

Martin, N.R.M. (2005). *A guide to collaboration for IEP teams.* Baltimore, MD: Paul H. Brookes Publishing Co.

Maryland Fitness and Athletic Equity for Students with Disabilities Act of 2008, Ann. Code of Maryland § 7–4B-02 et seq.

Maslow, A. (1954). *Motivation and personality.* New York, NY: Harper.

Mason, C., Field, S., & Sawilowsky, S. (2004). Implementation of self-determination activities and student participation in IEPs: Practices and attitudes of educators. *Exceptional Children, 69*, 441–451.

Matheson, E., & Jahoda, A. (2005). Emotional understanding in aggressive and nonaggressive individuals with mild and moderate mental retardation. *American Journal on Mental Retardation, 110*(1), 57–67.

Mayer, W.E., & Anderson, L.S. (2014). Perceptions of people with disabilities and their families about segregated and inclusive recreation involvement. *Therapeutic Recreation Journal, 48*(2), 150–168.

Mayes, S.D., Calhoun, S.L., & Crowell, E.W. (2000). Learning disabilities and ADHD: Overlapping spectrum disorders. *Journal of Learning Disabilities, 33*, 417–424.

Mayo Clinic. (2014). *Kawasaki disease: Symptoms.* Retrieved from http://www.mayoclinic.org/diseases-conditions/kawasaki-disease/basics/symptoms/con-20024663

Mazzocco, M.M., & Holden, J.J.A. (2007). Fragile X syndrome. In I. Brown & M. Percy (Eds.), *A comprehensive guide to intellectual and developmental disabilities* (pp. 173–188). Baltimore, MD: Paul H. Brookes Publishing Co.

McCarthy, G.T. (1992). *Physical disability in childhood: An interdisciplinary approach to management.* New York, NY: Churchill Livingstone.

McCollum, S., Civalier, A., & Holt, A. (2004). Equitable learning for Spanish speaking students in elementary physical education. *Strategies, 17*(6), 21–23.

McCollum, S., Elliott, S., Burke, S., Civalier, A., & Pruitt, W. (2005). PEP up your P.E. program: Writing and implementing a PEP grant. *Teaching Elementary Physical Education, 16*(4), 44–52.

McCubbin, J., Jansma, P., & Houston-Wilson, C. (1993). The role of the adapted (special) physical educator: Implications for educating persons with serious disabilities. In P. Jansma (Ed.), *Psychomotor domain training and serious disabilities* (4th ed., pp. 29–40). Lanham, MD: University Press of America.

McDonough, H., Sticken, E., & Haack, S. (2006). The expanded core curriculum for students who are visually impaired. *Journal of Visual Impairment & Blindness, 100*(10), 596–598.

McGuire, J., Scott, S., & Shaw, S. (2006). Universal design and its application in educational environments. *Remedial and Special Education, 27*, 166–175.

McFadden v. Grasmick, 485 F. Supp. 2d 642 (D. Md. 2007).

McHugh, B.E., & Lieberman, L.J. (2003). The impact of developmental factors on incidence of stereotypic rocking among children with visual impairments. *Journal of Visual Impairment & Blindness, 97* (8), 453–474.

McInnes, J.M. (1999). *A guide to planning and support individuals who are deafblind.* Toronto, Canada: University of Toronto Press.

McKay, C. (2013a). Paralympic School Day: A disability awareness and education program. *Palaestra, 27*(4). 14–19.

McKay, C. (2013b). *The impact of Paralympic School Day on student attitudes toward inclusion in physical education* (Doctoral dissertation). Available from ProQuest Dissertations and Theses database. (UMI No. 3571557)

Meegan, S., & MacPhail, A. (2006). Irish physical educators' attitude toward teaching students with special educational needs. *European Physical Education Review, 12*(1), 75–97.

Metzler, M. (2011). *Instructional models for physical education* (3rd ed.). Scottsdale, AZ: Holcomb Hathaway.

Meyer, L.H., & Evans, I.M. (1989). *Nonaversive intervention for behavior problems: A manual for home and community.* Baltimore, MD: Paul H. Brookes Publishing Co.

Milgrom, H., & Taussig, L.M. (1999). Keeping children with exercise-induced asthma active. *Pediatrics, 104*(3), e38.

Milich, R., & Okazaki, M. (1991). An examination of learned helplessness among attention-deficit hyperactivity disordered boys. *Journal of Abnormal Child Psychology, 19*(5), 607–623.

Miller, F., Bachrach, S.J. (2006). *A complete guide for caregiving* (2nd ed.). Baltimore, MD: Johns Hopkins Press.

Miller, R.E. (2010). *KidsHealth: Childhood cancer.* Retrieved from http://kidshealth.org/parent/medical/cancer/cancer.html#a_About_Cancer

Miller, S.R., & Miller, P.F. (1995). Cross-age peer tutoring: A strategy for promoting self-determination in students with severe emotional disabilities/behavior disorders. *Preventing School Failure, 39*(4), 32–38.

Millichap, J.G. (2008). Etiologic classification of attention-deficit/hyperactivity disorder. *Pediatrics, 129*(2), e358–e365.

Millichap, J.G., & Yee, M.M. (2012). The diet factor in attention-deficit/hyperactivity disorder. *Pediatrics, 129*(2), 330–337.

Mills v. Board of Education of District of Columbia, 348 F. Supp. 866 (D. DC. 1972).

Mizen, D.W., & Linton, N. (1983). Guess who's coming to P.E.: Six steps to more effective mainstreaming. *Journal of Physical Education, Recreation & Dance, 54*(8), 63–65.

Modell, S.J. (2007). Student perceptions about sports for persons with physical disabilities: An exploratory study. *Palaestra, 23*(3), 32–37.

Modell, S.J., & Imwold, C.H. (1998). Parental attitudes toward inclusive recreation and leisure: A qualitative analysis. *Parks and Recreation, 33*(5), 88–93.

Moeller, M.P. (2000). Early intervention and language development of children who are deaf and hard of hearing. *Pediatrics, 106*(3), e43.

Molinar, S., & Doprotka, B. (2014). School of breakfalls: Where safety and falling meet. *Palaestra, 28*(2), 31–35.

Moore, M.S., & Levitan, L. (2003). *For hearing people only* (3rd ed.). Rochester, NY: Deaf Life Press.

Moran, T.E., & Block, M.E. (2010). Barriers to participation of children with disabilities in youth sports. *TEACHING Exceptional Children Plus, 6*(3), 1–13.

Moran, T.E., Taliaferro, A.R., & Pate, J.R. (2015). Confronting physical activity programming barriers for people with disabilities: The empowerment model. *Quest, 66*(4), 396–408. doi:10.1080/00336297.2014.948687

Morgan, P.L., Farkas, G., & Wu, Q. (2009). Kindergarten predictors of recurring externalizing and internalizing psychopathology in the third and fifth grades. *Journal of Emotional and Behavioral Disorders, 17*(3), 67–79.

Morris, G.S.D., & Stiehl, J. (1999). *Changing kids' games* (2nd ed.). Champaign, IL: Human Kinetics.

Morton, C.C., & Nance, W.E. (2006). Newborn hearing screening: A silent revolution. *New England Journal of Medicine, 354*, 2151–2164.

Mosston, M., & Ashworth, S. (2002). *Teaching physical education* (5th ed.). Upper Saddle River, NJ: Benjamin Cummings.

Movahedi, A., Mojtahedi, H., & Farazyani, F. (2011). Differences in socialization between visually impaired student-children and non-children. *Research in Developmental Disabilities, 32*, 58–62. doi:10.1016/j.ridd.2010.08.013

Munk, D.D., & Dempsey, T.L. (2010). *Leadership strategies for successful schoolwide inclusion: The STAR approach.* Baltimore, MD: Paul H. Brookes Publishing Co.

Murata, N.M., Hodge, S.R., & Little, J.R. (2000). Students' attitudes, experiences, and perspectives on their peers with disabilities. *Clinical Kinesiology, 54*, 59–66.

Murdoch, H. (1997). Stereotyped behaviours: How should we think about them? *British Journal of Special Education, 24*, 71–75.

Musiek, F.E., & Baran, J.A. (Eds.). (2007). *Auditory system: The anatomy, physiology, and clinical correlates.* Upper Saddle River, NJ: Pearson.

Mutch, L., Alberman, E., Hagberg, B., Kodama, K., & Perat, M.V. (1992). Cerebral palsy epidemiology: Where are we now and where are we going? *Developmental Medicine and Child Neurology, 34*, 547–551.

My Child. (2014). *Neurologic health.* Retrieved from http://cerebralpalsy.org/information/neurologic-health

Naguwa, S., Afrasiabi, R., & Chang, C. (2012). Exercise-induced asthma. In M.E. Gershwin & T.E. Albertson (Eds.), *Bronchial asthma: A guide for practical understanding and treatment* (pp. 251–266). New York, NY: Springer.

National Alliance on Mental Illness. (2010). *What is mental illness: Mental illness facts.* Retrieved from http://www.nami.org/Content/NavigationMenu/Inform_Yourself/About_Mental_Illness/About_Mental_Illness.htm

National Association for Sport and Physical Education. (1992). *Outcomes of quality physical education programs.* Reston, VA: American Alliance for Health, Physical Education, Recreation, and Dance.

National Association for Sport and Physical Education. (1995a). *Including students with disabilities in physical education.* Reston, VA: Author.

National Association for Sport and Physical Education. (1995b). *Moving into the future: National standards for physical education. A guide to content and assessment.* St. Louis, MO: Mosby.

National Association for Sport and Physical Education. (2004). *Moving into the future: National standards for physical education* (2nd ed.). Reston, VA: Author.

National Association for Sport and Physical Education & American Heart Association. (2012). *Shape of the nation report: Status of physical education in the USA.* Reston, VA: American Alliance for Health, Physical Education, Recreation, and Dance.

National Birth Defects Prevention Network. (2010). *Spina bifida prevalence.* Retrieved from http://www.cdc.gov/ncbddd/features/spina-bifida-study.html

National Center for Children in Poverty. (n.d.). *Poverty in the United States: Frequently asked questions.* Retrieved from http://npc.umich.edu/poverty

National Center for Health Physical Activity and Disability. (n.d.). *Spinal cord injury and exercise.* Retrieved from http://www.nchpad.org/111/860/Spinal~Cord~Injury~and~Excercise

National Center for Learning Disabilities. (2014). *Learning disabilities: What they are and aren't.* Retrieved from https://www.understood.org/en/learning-attention-issues/getting-started/what-you-need-to-know/learning-disabilities-what-they-are-and-arent

National Consortium for Physical Education and Recreation for Individuals with Disabilities. (2006). *Adapted physical education national standards* (2nd ed.). Champaign, IL: Human Kinetics.

National Dissemination Center for Children with Disabilities. (2010). *NICHCY Disability Fact Sheet #5.* Retrieved from http://www.parentcenterhub.org/repository/specific-disabilities

National Heart, Lung, and Blood Institute. (n.d.). *What is asthma?* Retrieved from http://www.nhlbi.nih.gov/health/health-topics/topics/asthma

National Institute of Mental Health. (2008). *Introduction: Mental health medications.* Retrieved from http://www.nimh.nih.gov/health/publications/mental-health-medications/index.shtml#pub8

National Institute of Mental Health. (2012). *Attention-deficit hyperactivity disorder (ADHD)* (DHHS Publication No. 12-3572). Washington, DC: Government Printing Office.

National Institute of Neurological Disorders and Stroke. (2013). *Spina bifida fact sheet.* Retrieved from http://www.ninds.nih.gov/disorders/spina_bifida/detail_spina_bifida.htm#261953258

National Institute on Deafness and Other Communication Disorders. (2014). *Quick statistics.* Retrieved from http://www.nidcd.nih.gov/health/statistics/Pages/Default.aspx

National Institutes of Health. (2012). *Asthma and physical activity in school* (NIH Publication No. 12–3651). Washington, DC: Author. Retrieved from http://www.nhlbi.nih.gov/health/public/lung/asthma/phy_asth.pdf

National Scoliosis Foundation. (n.d.). *Information and support.* Retrieved from http://www.scoliosis.org/info.php

Nelson, J.A. (2003). The invisible cultural group: Images of disability. In P.M. Lester & S.D. Ross (Eds.), *Images that injure: Pictorial stereotypes in the media* (pp.175–184). Westport, CT: Greenwood.

Newell, K.M. (1986). Constraints on the development of coordination. In M.G. Wade & H.T.A. Whiting (Eds.), *Motor development in children: Aspects of coordination and control* (pp. 341–360). Boston, MA: Martinus Nijhoff.

Newell, K.M., & Jordan, K. (2007). Task constraints and movement organization: A common language. In W.E. Davis & G.D. Broadhead (Eds.), *Ecological task analysis and movement* (pp. 5–24). Champaign, IL: Human Kinetics.

Nichols, B. (2001). *Moving and learning: The elementary physical education experience* (3rd ed.). Madison, WI: WCB/McGraw-Hill.

Nigg, J.T., Lewis, K., Edinger, T., & Falk, M. (2012). Meta-analysis of attention-deficit/hyperactivity disorder or attention deficit/hyperactivity disorder symptoms, restriction diet, and synthetic food color additives. *Journal of American Academic Child Adolescent Psychiatry, 51*(1), 86–97.

Nirje, B. (1969). The normalization principle and its human management implications. In R.B. Kugel & W. Wolfensberger (Eds.), *Changing patterns in residential services for the mentally retarded* (pp. 179–195). Washington, DC: Government Printing Office.

No Child Left Behind Act of 2001, PL 107-110, 115 Stat. 1425, 20 U.S.C. § 6301 *et seq.*

Nomura, Y., Marks, D.J., & Halperin, J.M. (2010). Prenatal exposure to maternal and paternal smoking on attention deficit hyperactivity disorders symptoms and diagnosis in offspring. *Journal of Nervous Mental Disability, 198*(9), 672–678.

Northern, J.L., & Downs, M.P. (2002). *Hearing in children* (5th ed.). Baltimore, MD: Lippincott Williams & Wilkins.

Novotny, M., & Swagman, A. (1992). Caring for children with orthotic/prosthetic needs. *American Academy of Orthotists and Prothetists, 4*(4), 191–195.

Oberti v. Board of Education of the Borough of Clementon School District, 995 F.2d 1204 83 Ed. Law Rep. 1009 (3rd Cir. 1993).

O'Brien, J., Forest, M., Snow, J., & Hasburg, D. (1989). *Action for inclusion*. Toronto, Canada: Frontier College Press.

Obrusnikova, I. (2008). Physical educators' beliefs about teaching children with disabilities. *Perceptual and Motor Skills, 106*(2), 637–644.

Obrusnikova, I., Block, M., & Dillon, S. (2010). Children's beliefs toward cooperative playing with peers with disabilities in physical education. *Adapted Physical Activity Quarterly, 27*(2), 127–142.

Obrusnikova, I., Block, M.E., & Válková, H. (2003). Impact of inclusion in GPE on students without disabilities. *Adapted Physical Activity Quarterly, 20,* 230–245.

Obrusnikova, I., & Dillon, S.R. (2012). Students' beliefs and intentions to play with peers with disabilities in physical education: Relationships with achievement and social goals. *Journal of Teaching in Physical Education, 31*(4), 311–328.

Obrusnikova, I., Dillon, S.R., Block, M.E., & Davis, T.D. (2012). Validation of the Children's Beliefs and Intentions to Play With Peers With Disabilities in Middle School Physical Education Scale. *Journal of Developmental and Physical Disabilities, 24*(1), 35–51.

O'Connell, M.E. (2000). *The effect of physical guidance and brailling on self-efficacy during goal ball for children who are blind* (Unpublished master's thesis). State University of New York, Brockport, New York.

O'Connell, M., Lieberman, L., & Petersen, S. (2006). The use of tactile modeling and physical guidance as instructional strategies in physical activity for children who are blind. *Journal of Visual Impairment & Blindness, 100*(8), 471–477.

Odom, S.I., McConnell, S.R., & McEvoy, M.A. (1992). Peer-related social competence and its significance for young children with disabilities. In S.I. Odom, S.R. McConnell, & M.A. McEvoy (Eds.), *Social competence of young children with disabilities: Nature, development and intervention* (pp. 3–35). Baltimore, MD: Paul H. Brookes Publishing Co.

Ohan, J.L., & Johnson, C. (2002). Are the performance overestimates given by boys with ADHD self-protective? *Journal of Clinical Child Psychology, 31,* 230–241.

O'Neil, M.E., & Douglas, V.L. (1991). Study strategies and story recall in attention-deficit disorder and reading disability. *Journal of Clinical Child Psychology, 19,* 691–692.

Opitz, D.L., & Block, L.S. (2006). Universal learning support design: Maximizing learning beyond the classroom. *Learning Assistance Review, 11*(2), 33–45.

Orelove, F.P., Sobsey, D., & Silberman, R.K. (Eds.). (2004). *Educating children with multiple disabilities: A collaborative approach* (4th ed.). Baltimore, MD: Paul H. Brookes Publishing Co.

Orlick, T. (2006). *Cooperative games and sports: Joyful activities for everyone* (2nd ed.). Champaign, IL: Human Kinetics.

Osborne, A.G. (1996). *Legal issues in special education*. Boston, MA: Allyn & Bacon.

Osgood, R.L. (2007). *The history of special education: A struggle for equality in American public schools*. Westport, CT: Praeger.

Oswald, D.P., & Coutinho, M.J. (2001). Trends in disproportionate representation in special education: Implications for multicultural education policies. In C.A. Utley & F.E Obiakor (Eds.), *Special education, multicultural education, and school reform: Components of a quality education for students with mild disabilities* (pp. 53–73). Springfield, IL: Charles C Thomas.

Owen, M.J., O'Donovan, M.C., Thapar, A., & Craddock, N. (2011). Neurodevelopmental hypothesis of schizophrenia. *British Journal of Psychiatry, 198*(3) 173–175.

Owens, J.S., Goldfine, M.E., Evangelista, N.M., Hoza, B., & Kaiser, N.M. (2007). A critical review of self-perceptions and the positive illusory bias in children with ADHD. *Clinical Child and Family Psychological Review, 10,* 335–351.

Özer, D., Nalbant, S., Ağlamiş, E., Baran, F., Samut, P.K., Aktop, A., & Hutzler, Y. (2013). Physical education teachers' attitudes towards children with intellectual disability: The impact of time in service, gender, and previous acquaintance. *Journal of Intellectual Disability Research, 57*(11), 1001–1013.

Paciorek, M.J., & Jones, J.A. (2001). *Disability sport and recreation resources* (3rd ed.). Traverse City, MI: Cooper.

Padden, C., & Humphries, T. (1988). *Deaf in America: Voices from a culture*. Cambridge, MA: Harvard University Press.

Paige, R. (2003). *No child left behind: A toolkit for teachers*. Washington, DC: U.S. Department of Education.

Palla, A., & Block, M. (2004, October 28–30). *Impact of multiculturalism and diversity on adapted physical educator's teaching: A case study*. Poster session presented at North American Federation of Adapted Physical Activity (NAFAPA), Thunder Bay, Canada.

Pan, C. (2008). School time physical activity of students with and without autism spectrum disorders during PE and recess. *Adapted Physical Activity Quarterly, 25*(4), 308–321.

Pangrazi, R.P., & Beighle, A. (2015). *Dynamic physical education for elementary school children* (18th ed.). San Francisco, CA: Benjamin Cummings.

Pangrazi, R.P. (2007). *Dynamic physical education for elementary school children* (15th ed.). San Francisco, CA: Benjamin Cummings.

Papaioannou, C., Evaggelinou, C., Barkoukis, V., & Block, M.E. (2013). Disability awareness program in a summer camp. *European Journal of Adapted Physical Activity, 6*(2), 19–28.

Pearpoint, J., Forest, M., & O'Brien, J. (1996). MAPs, Circle of Friends, and PATH: Powerful tools to help build caring communities. In S. Stainback & W. Stainback (Eds.), *Inclusion: A guide for educators* (pp. 67–86). Baltimore, MD: Paul H. Brookes Publishing Co.

Peck, C.A., Donaldson, J., & Pezzoli, M. (1990). Some benefits nonhandicapped adolescents perceive for themselves from their social relationships with peers who have severe handicaps. *Journal of the Association for Persons With Severe Handicaps, 15*, 211–230.

Pedron, N.A., & Evans, S.B. (1990). Modifying classroom teachers' acceptance of the consulting teacher model. *Journal of Educational and Psychological Consultation, 1*, 189–200.

Peleg, O. (2009). Test anxiety, academic achievement, and self-esteem among Arab adolescents with and without learning disabilities. *Learning Disability Quarterly, 32*(1), 11–20.

Pellegrini, A.D., & Smith, P.K. (1998). Physical activity play: The nature and function of a neglected aspect of play. *Child Development, 69*, 577–598.

Pender, R.H., & Patterson, P.E. (1982). A comparison of selected motor fitness items between congenitally deaf and hearing children. *Journal of Special Educators, 18*(4), 71–75.

Pennell, R.L. (2001). Self-determination and self-advocacy. *Journal of Disability Policy Studies, 11*(4), 223.

Pennsylvania Association for Retarded Children v. Commonwealth of Pennsylvania, 334 F. Supp. 1257 (E.D. Pa. 1971).

Percy, M. (2007). Factors that cause or contribute to intellectual and developmental disabilities. In I. Brown & M. Percy (Eds.), *A comprehensive guide to intellectual and developmental disabilities* (pp. 125–148). Baltimore, MD: Paul H. Brookes Publishing Co.

Perkins, K., Columna, L., Lieberman, L.J., & Bailey, J. (2013). Parental perceptions toward physical activity for their children with visual impairments and blindness. *Journal of Visual Impairment & Blindness, 107*, 131–142.

Perrault, I., Rozet, J., Gerber, S., Ghazi, I., Leowski, C., Ducroq, D.,. . .Kaplan, J. (1999). Leber congenital amaurosis. *Molecular Genetics and Metabolism, 68*, 200–208.

Petray, C., Freesemann, K., & Lavay, B. (1997). Understanding students with diabetes: Implications for the physical education professional. *Journal of Physical Education, Recreation & Dance, 68*(l), 57–64.

Phillips, K.L., Schieve, L.A., Visser, S., Boulet, S., Sharma, A.J., Kogan, M.D.,. . .Yeargin-Allsopp, M. (2014). Prevalence and impact of unhealthy weight in a national sample of US adolescents with autism and other learning and behavioral disabilities. *Maternal and Child Health Journal, 8*(9), 145–151.

Phillips, W.T., Kiratli, B.J., Sarkarati, M., Weraarchakul, G., Myers, J., Parkash, I., & Froelicher, V. (1998). Effect of spinal cord injury on the heart and cardiovascular fitness. *Current Problems in Cardiology, 11*, 641–716.

Physical Activity Line. (n.d.). Rating of Perceived Exertion Scale. Retrieved from http://physical activityline.com/pdf_files/pal-doc-perceived exertionscale.pdf

Physical and Health Education Canada. (2014). *What is physical literacy?* Retrieved from http://www. phecanada.ca/programs/physical-literacy/what-physical-literacy

Pianta, R.C., & Hamre, B.K. (2009). Conceptualization, measurement, and improvement of classroom processes: Standardized observation can leverage capacity. *Educational Researcher, 38*(2), 109–119.

Piletic, C.K., & Davis, R. (2010). A profile of the introduction to adapted physical education course within undergraduate physical education teacher education program. *Journal of Research in Health, Physical Education, Recreation, Sport & Dance, 5*(2), 26–32.

Pitetti, K.H., & Fernhall, B. (2004). Comparing the run performance of adolescents with mental retardation, with and without Down syndrome. *Adapted Physical Activity Quarterly, 21*, 219–228.

Pitetti, K.H., & Yarmer, D.A. (2002). Lower body strength of children and adolescents with and without mild mental retardation. *Adapted Physical Activity Quarterly, 19*, 68–77.

Pitetti, K.H., Yarmer, D.A., & Fernhall, B. (2001). Cardiovascular fitness and body composition of youth with and without mental retardation. *Adapted Physical Activity Quarterly, 18*, 127–141.

Place, K., & Hodge, S.R. (2001). Social inclusion of students with physical disabilities in GPE: A behavioral analysis. *Adapted Physical Activity Quarterly, 18*, 389–404.

Polanczyk, G., de Lima, M.S., Horta, B.L., Biederman, J., & Rohde, L.A. (2007). The worldwide prevalence of ADHD: A systematic review and metaregression analysis. *American Journal of Psychiatry, 165*(6), 942–948.

Ponchillia, P., Armbruster, J., & Wiebold, J. (2005). The National Sports Education Camps Project: Introducing sports skills to students with visual impairments through short-term specialized instruction. *Journal of Visual Impairment & Blindness, 99*, 685–695.

Pope, M., Liu, T., Breslin, C., & Getchell, N. (2012). Using constraints to design developmentally appropriate movement activities for children with autism spectrum disorders. *Journal of Physical Education, Recreation & Dance, 83*(2), 35–41.

Porter, S.M., Branowicki, P.A., & Palfrey, J.S. (2014). *Supporting students with special health care needs: Guidelines and procedures for schools* (3rd ed.). Baltimore, MD: Paul H. Brookes Publishing Co.

Positive Behavioral Interventions and Support. (2015). *Home page*. Retrieved from http://www.pbis.org

Potvin, M.C., Snider, L., Prelock, P., Kehayia, E., & Wood-Dauphinee, S. (2013). Recreational participation of children with high functioning autism. *Journal of Autism and Developmental Disorders, 43*(2), 445–457. doi:10.1007/s10803-012-1589-6

Price, L.A., Wolensky, D., & Mulligan, R. (2002). Self-determination in action in the classroom. *Remedial and Special Education, 23*, 109–116.

Pyfer, J.L., & Carlson, R. (1972). Characteristic motor development of children with learning disabilities. *Perceptual and Motor Skills, 35*, 291–296.

Quay, H.C., & Peterson, D.R. (1987). *Manual for the revised behavior problem checklist*. Coral Gables, FL: University of Miami.

Rainforth, B., York, J., & MacDonald, C. (1992). *Collaborative teams for students with severe disabilities: Integrating therapy and educational services*. Baltimore, MD: Paul H. Brookes Publishing Co.

Rainforth, B., & York-Barr, J. (1997). *Collaborative teams for students with severe disabilities: Integrating therapy and educational services* (2nd ed.). Baltimore, MD: Paul H. Brookes Publishing Co.

Rajendran, V., & Roy, F.G. (2011). An overview of motor skill performance and balance in hearing impaired children. *Italian Journal of Pediatrics, 37*, 33. Retrieved from http://www.ijponline.net/content/37/1/33

Ratey, J., & Hagerman, E. (2008). *SPARK: The revolutionary new science of exercise and the brain.* New York, NY: Little, Brown.

Rauscher, L., & McClintock, M. (1997). Ableism curriculum design. In M. Adams, L.A. Bell, & P. Griffin (Eds.), *Teaching for diversity and social justice: A source book* (pp. 198–229). New York, NY: Routledge.

Rees, J., Kanabar, D., & Pattani, S. (2010). *ABC of asthma.* Hoboken, NJ: John Wiley & Sons.

Rehabilitation Act of 1973, PL 93-112, 29 U.S.C. § 701 *et seq.*

Revie, G., & Larkin, D. (1993). Task-specific intervention with children reduces movement problems. *Adapted Physical Activity Quarterly, 10*, 29–41.

Rimmer, J.H., Rubin, S.S., & Braddock, D. (2000). Barriers to exercise in African American women with physical disabilities. *Archives of Physical Medicine and Rehabilitation, 81*, 182–187.

Rine, R.M. (2009). Growing evidence for balance and vestibular problems in children. *Audiological Medicine, 7*(3), 138–142.

Rine, R.M., Cornwall, G., Gan, K., LoCascio, C., O'Hare, T., Robinson, E., & Rice, M. (2000). Evidence of progressive delay of motor development in children with sensorineural hearing loss and concurrent vestibular dysfunction. *Perceptual and Motor Skills, 90*(3), 1101–1112.

Rintala, P., & Loovis, E. (2013). Measuring motor skills in Finnish children with intellectual disabilities. *Perceptual and Motor Skills, 116*(1), 294–303.

Rizzo, J.V., & Zabel, R.H. (1988). *Educating children and adolescents with behavior disorders: An integrative approach.* Boston, MA: Allyn & Bacon.

Rizzo, T.L., Bishop, P., & Tobar, D. (1997). Teaching students with mild disabilities: What affects attitudes of future physical educators. *Adapted Physical Activity Quarterly, 12*, 205–216.

Rizzo, T.L., & Vispoel, W.P. (1991). GPE teachers' attributes and attitudes toward teaching students with handicaps. *Adapted Physical Activity Quarterly, 8*, 4–11.

Rohnke, K. (1977). *Cowtails and cobras: A guide to ropes courses, initiative games, and other adventure activities.* Hamilton, MA: Project Adventure.

Rohnke, K. (2010). *Silver bullets: A revised guide to initiative problems, adventure games, stunts, and trust activities.* Dubuque, IA: Kendall/Hunt.

Rohnke, K., & Butler, S. (1995). *Quicksilver: Adventure games, initiative problems, trust activities, and a guide to effective leadership.* Dubuque, IA: Kendall/Hunt.

Roibas, A.C., Stamatakis, E., & Black, K. (2011). *Design for sport.* Farnham, United Kingdom: Gower.

Roizen, N.J. (2013). Down syndrome. In M.L. Batshaw, N.J. Roizen, & G.R. Lotrecchiano (Eds.), *Children With disabilities* (7th ed., pp. 307–318). Baltimore, MD: Paul H. Brookes Publishing Co.

Rousselle, C., & Wolff, P.H. (1991). The dynamics of bimanual coordination in developmental dyslexia. *Neuropsychologia, 29*(9), 907–924.

RTI Action Network. (n.d.). *What is RTI?* Retrieved from http://www.rtinetwork.org/learn/what/whatisrti

Russell, A.J., Jassi, A., Fullana, M.A., Mack, H., Johnston, K., Heyman, I.,. . .Mataix-Cols, D. (2013). Cognitive behavior therapy for comorbid obsessive-compulsive disorder in high-functioning autism spectrum disorders: A randomized controlled trial. *Depression and Anxiety, 30*(8), 697–708.

Russo, M.F., & Beidel, D.C. (1994). Comorbidity of childhood anxiety and externalizing disorders: Prevalence, associated characteristics and validation issues. *Clinical Psychology Review, 14*, 199–221.

Rutter, M. (2005). Aetiology of Autism: Findings and questions. *Journal of Intellectual Disability Research, 49*(4), 231–238.

Sailor, W., Gee, K., & Karasoff, P. (1993). Full inclusion and school restructuring. In M.E. Snell (Ed.), *Instruction of students with severe disabilities* (4th ed., pp. 1–30). New York, NY: Merrill.

Sainato, D.M., & Carta, J.J. (1992). Classroom influences on the development of social competence in young children with disabilities. In S.I. Odom, S.R. McConnell, & M.A. McEvoy (Eds.), *Social competence of young children with disabilities: Nature, development and intervention* (pp. 93–109). Baltimore, MD: Paul H. Brookes Publishing Co.

Sallis, J.F., & Owen, N. (1999). *Physical activity and behavioral medicine.* Thousand Oaks, CA: Sage.

Sandin, S., Lichtenstein, P., Kuja-Halkola, R., Larsson, H., Hultman, C.M., & Reichenberg, A. (2014). The familial risk of autism. *JAMA: The Journal of the American Medical Association, 311*(17), 1770–1777.

Sandsund, M., Thomassen, M., Reinertsen, R.E., & Steinshamn, S. (2011). Exercise-induced asthma in adolescents: Challenges for physical education teachers. *Chronic Respiratory Disease, 8*(3), 171–179. doi:10.1177/1479972310397676

Sapp, W., & Hatlen, P. (2010). The expanded core curriculum: Where we have been, where we are going, and how we can get there. *Journal of Visual Impairment & Blindness, 104*(6), 338–348.

Sato, T., & Hodge, S.R. (2009). Asian international doctoral students' experiences at two American universities: Assimilation, accommodation, and resistance. *Journal of Diversity in Higher Education, 2*(3), 136.

Sato, T., Hodge, S.R., Murata, N.M., & Maeda, J.K. (2007). Japanese physical education teachers' beliefs about teaching students with disabilities. *Sport, Education and Society, 12*(2), 211–230.

Sauerberger, D. (1993). *Independence without sight or sound: Suggestions for practitioners working with deaf-blind adults.* New York, NY: American Foundation for the Blind.

Savelsbergh, G.J., Netelenbos, J.B., & Whiting, H.T. (1991). Auditory perception and the control of spatially coordinated action of deaf and hearing children. *Journal of Child Psychology and Psychiatry, 32,* 489–500.

Savner, J.L., & Myles, B.S. (2000). *Making visual supports work in the home and community: Strategies for individuals with autism and Asperger syndrome.* Shawnee Mission, KS: Autism Asperger.

Scbnoes, G., Reid, R., Wagner, M., & Marder, G. (2006). ADHD among students receiving special education services: A national study. *Exceptional Children, 72,* 483–496.

Scheuermann, B.K., & Hall, J.A. (2012). *Positive behavioral support for the classroom* (2nd ed.). Upper Saddle River, NJ: Pearson.

Schleien, S.J., Kiernan, J., & Wehman, P. (1981). Evaluation of an age-appropriate leisure skills program for moderately retarded adults. *Education and Training of the Mentally Retarded, 16*(1), 13–19.

Schleien, S.J., Meyer, L.H., Heyne, L.A., & Brandt, B.B. (1995). *Lifelong leisure and lifestyles for persons with developmental disabilities.* Baltimore, MD: Paul H. Brookes Publishing Co.

Schleien, S.J., Ray, M.T., & Green, F.P. (1997). *Community recreation and people with disabilities* (2nd ed.). Baltimore, MD: Paul H. Brookes Publishing Co.

Schlumberger, E., Narbona, J., & Manrique, M. (2004). Non-verbal development of children with deafness with and without cochlear implants. *Developmental Medicine and Child Neurology, 46,* 599–606.

Schnorr, R.F. (1990). "Peter? He comes and goes...": First graders' perspective on a part-time mainstreamed student. *Journal of the Association for Persons With Severe Handicaps, 15,* 231–240.

Schofield, J.W. (1995). Improving intergroup relations among students. In J.A. Banks & C.A.M. Banks (Eds.), *Handbook of research on multicultural education* (pp. 635–646). New York, NY: Simon & Schuster.

Schultz, J., Lieberman, L.J., Ellis, M.K., & Hilgenbrink, L. (2013). Including your deaf students into general physical education: Teaching strategies. *Journal of Physical Education, Recreation & Dance, 84*(5), 51–56.

Seaman, J.A., DePauw, K.P., Morton, K.B., & Omoto, K. (2007). *Making connections: From theory to practice in adapted physical education* (2nd ed.). Scottsdale, AZ: Holcomb Hathaway.

Seewald, L., Taub, J.W., Maloney, K.W., & McCabe, E.R. (2012). Acute leukemias in children with down syndrome. *Molecular Genetics and Metabolism, 107*(1), 25–30.

Semmel, M.I., Gottlieb, J., & Robinson, N.M. (1979). Mainstreaming: Perspectives on educating handicapped children in the public school. *Review of Research in Education, 7,* 223–279.

Seymour, H., Reid, G., & Bloom, G.A. (2009). Friendship in inclusive physical education. *Adapted Physical Activity Quarterly, 26*(3), 201–219.

Shapiro, B.K., & Batshaw, M.L. (2013). Developmental delay and intellectual disability. In M.L. Batshaw, N.J. Roizen, & G.R. Lotrecchiano (Eds.), *Children with disabilities* (7th ed., pp. 291–306). Baltimore, MD: Paul H. Brookes Publishing Co.

Shaw, D.S., Gilliom, M., Ingoldsby, E.M., & Nagin, D. (2003). Trajectories leading to school-age conduct problems. *Developmental Psychology, 29,* 189–200.

Shaw, L., Levine, M.D., & Belfer, M. (1982). Developmental double jeopardy: A study of clumsiness and self-esteem in children with learning problems. *Journal of Developmental and Behavioral Pediatrics, 3*(4), 191–196.

Shaw, P., Gornick, M., Lerch, J., Addington, A., Seal, J., Greenstein, D.,...Rapoport, J.L. (2007). Polymorphisms of the dopamine D4 receptor, clinical outcome, and cortical structure in attention-deficit/hyperactivity disorder. *Archives of General Psychiatry, 64*(8), 921–931.

Sherrill, C. (2004). *Adapted physical activity, recreation, and sport: Crossdisciplinary and lifespan* (6th ed.). New York, NY: McGraw-Hill.

Sherrill, C., Heikinaro-Johansson, P., & Slininger, D. (1994). Equal-status relationships in the gym. *Journal of Physical Education, Recreation & Dance, 65*(1), 27–31.

Shore, S., Rastelli, L.G., & Grandin, T. (2006). *Understanding autism for dummies.* Hoboken, NJ: John Wiley & Sons.

Shumway-Cook, A., & Woollacott, M.H. (1995). *Motor control: Theory and practical applications.* Baltimore, MD: Williams & Wilkins.

Siedentop, D. (2004). *Introduction to physical education, fitness, and sport* (5th ed.). New York, NY: McGraw-Hill.

Siegel, J.C., Marchetti, M., & Tecklin, J.S. (1991). Age-related balance changes in hearing-impaired children. *Physical Therapy, 71,* 183–189.

Sigafoos, J., Tucker, M., Bushell, H., & Webber, Y. (1997). A practical strategy to increase participation and reduce challenging behavior during leisure skills programming. *Mental Retardation, 35*(3), 198–208.

Sigmon, S. (1983). The history and future of educational segregation. *Journal for Special Educators, 19,* 1–13.

Silla, V.A., & Burba, B. (2008). Using visual supports to decrease functional exclusion in physical education for students with autism. *Pennsylvania Journal of Health, Physical Education, Recreation and Dance, 78*(2), 37–42.

Silverman, C. (2011). *Understanding autism: Parents, doctors and the history of a disorder.* Princeton, NJ: Princeton University Press.

Simonoff, A., Pickles, T., Charman, S., Chandler, T., & Loucas, G. (2008). Baird psychiatric disorders in children with autism spectrum disorders: Prevalence, comorbidity, and associated factors in a population-derived sample, *Journal of the American Academy of Child and Adolescent Psychiatry, 47*(1), 921–929.

Skowronski, W., Horvat, M., Nocera, J., Roswal, G., & Croce, R. (2009). Eurofit special: European fitness battery score variation among individuals with intellectual disabilities. *Adapted Physical Activity Quarterly, 26*(1), 54–67.

Smart, C., Aslander-van Vliet, E., & Waldron, S. (2009). Nutritional management in children and adolescents with diabetes. *Pediatric Diabetes, 10*(Suppl. 12), 100–117.

Smith, D. (2006). Congenital limb deficiencies and acquired amputations in children. *inMotion, 19*(1), 1–4.

Smith, D., & Campbell, K.M. (2009). Prostheses for children with limb differences: Issues and expectations. *inMotion, 19*(2), 1–5.

Smith, D.D., & Rivera, D.P. (1995). Discipline in special education and general education settings. *Focus on Exceptional Children, 27*(5), 1–14.

Smith, R.J.H., Shearer, A.E., Hildebrand, M.S., & Van Camp, G. (2014). *Deafness and hereditary hearing loss overview.* Retrieved from http://www.ncbi.nlm.nih.gov/books/NBK1434

Smith, R.W., Austin, D.R., Kennedy, D.W., Lee, Y., & Hutchison, P. (2005). *Inclusive and special recreation: Opportunities for persons with disabilities* (5th ed.). New York, NY: McGraw-Hill.

Smyth, M.M., & Anderson, H.I. (2000). Coping with clumsiness in the school playground: Social and physical play in children with coordination impairments. *British Journal of Developmental Psychology, 18,* 389–413.

Snell, M.B., Martin, K., & Orelove, F.P. (1997). Meeting the demands for specialized teachers of students with severe disabilities. *Teacher Education and Special Education, 20*(3), 221–233.

Snell, M.E. (1988). Gartner and Lipsky's "Beyond special education: Toward a quality system for all students.": Messages for TASH. *Journal of the Association for Persons With Severe Handicaps, 13,* 137–140.

Snell, M.E. (1991). Schools are for all kids: The importance of integration for students with severe disabilities and their peers. In J.W. Lloyd, N.N. Singh, & A.C. Repp (Eds.), *The regular education initiative: Alternative perspectives on concepts, issues, and models* (pp. 133–148). Sycamore, IL: Sycamore.

Snell, M.E., & Drake, G.P. (1994). Replacing cascades with supported education. *Journal of Special Education, 27,* 393–409.

Snell, M.E., & Eichner, S.J. (1989). Integration for students with profound disabilities. In F. Brown & D.H. Lehr (Eds.), *Persons with profound disabilities: Issues and practices* (pp. 109–138). Baltimore, MD: Paul H. Brookes Publishing Co.

Society of Health and Physical Educators (SHAPE). (2014). *National standards and grade level outcomes for K–12 physical education.* Reston, VA: Author.

Spann, S.J., Kohler, F.W., & Soenksen, D. (2003). Examining parents' involvement in and perceptions of special education services: An interview with families in a parent support group. *Focus on Autism and other Developmental Disabilities, 18,* 228–237.

SPARK Physical Education Curriculum. (n.d.). Retrieved from http://www.sparkpe.org/what-is-spark/we-provide/

Sparks, W.G., III. (1994). Culturally responsive pedagogy: A framework for addressing multicultural issues. *Journal of Physical Education, Recreation & Dance, 65*(9), 33–36, 61.

Special Olympics. (n.d.-a). *Get into it.* Retrieved from https://getintoit.specialolympics.org

Special Olympics. (n.d.-b). *Sports and games.* Retrieved from http://www.specialolympics.org/sports.aspx.

Special Olympics. (n.d.-c). *Unified Sports®.* Retrieved from http://resources.specialolympics.org/Sections/Sports-and-Games/Unified_Sports.aspx

Special Olympics. (n.d.-d). *What we do.* Retrieved from http://www.specialolympics.org/Sections/What_We_Do/About_Special_Olympics.aspx

Special Olympics. (n.d.-e). *Young Athletes toolkit.* Retrieved from http://resources.specialolympics.org/Topics/Young_Athletes/Young_Athletes_Toolkit.aspx

Special Olympics. (2005). *Special Olympics Motor Activities Training Program: Coaches Guide.* Retrieved from http://media.specialolympics.org/soi/files/sports/MATP+Coaching+Guide.pdf

Special Olympics, Connecticut (n.d.). *Unified Sports® Fitness Clubs.* Retrieved from http://www.soct.org/sports-and-fitness-programs/unified-sports-fitness-clubs

Spencer, E.S., & Marschark, M. (2010). *Evidence-based practice in educating deaf and hard-of-hearing students.* New York, NY: Oxford University Press.

Spencer, P., Bodner-Johnson, B.A., & Gutfreund, M.K. (1992). Interacting with infants with hearing loss: What we can learn from mothers who are deaf? *Journal of Early Intervention, 16*(1), 64–78.

Spencer-Cavaliere, N., & Watkinson, J.E. (2010). Inclusion understood from the perspectives of children with disability. *Adapted Physical Activity Quarterly, 27*(4), 275–293.

Stainback, S., & Stainback, W. (1985). *Integration of students with severe handicaps into regular schools.* Reston, VA: Council for Exceptional Children.

Stainback, S., & Stainback, W. (1987). Educating all students in regular education. *TASH Newsletter, 13*(4), 1, 7.

Stainback, S., & Stainback, W. (1990). Inclusive schooling. In W. Stainback & S. Stainback (Eds.), *Support networks for inclusive schooling* (pp. 3–24). Baltimore, MD: Paul H. Brookes Publishing Co.

Stainback, W., & Stainback, S. (1991). A rationale for integration and restructuring: A synopsis. In J.W. Lloyd, N.N. Singh, & A.C. Repp (Eds.), *The regular education initiative: Alternative perspectives on concepts, issues, and models* (pp. 225–239). Sycamore, IL: Sycamore.

Stainback, W., Stainback, S., & Bunch, G. (1989). A rationale for the merger of regular and special education. In W. Stainback, S. Stainback, & M. Forest (Eds.), *Educating all students in the mainstream of regular education* (pp. 15–28). Baltimore, MD: Paul H. Brookes Publishing Co.

Stein, J.U. (1993). The Americans with Disabilities Act: Implications for recreation and leisure. In S.J. Grosse (Ed.), *Leisure opportunities for individuals with disabilities: Legal Issues* (pp. 1–11). Reston, VA: American Alliance for Health, Physical Education, Recreation, and Dance.

Stein, J.U. (2005). Accommodating individuals with disabilities in regular sports programs. In H. Appenzeller (Ed.), *Risk management in sports: Issues and strategies* (2nd ed., pp. 389–398). Durham, NC: Carolina Academic Press.

Stephens, C., Neil, R., & Smith, P. (2012). The perceived benefits and barriers of sport in spinal cord injured individuals: A qualitative study. *Disability and Rehabilitation, 34*(24), 2061–2070.

Stephens, T.L., Silliman-French, L., Kinnison, L., & French, R. (2010). Implementation of a Response-to-Intervention System in General Physical Education. *Journal of Physical Education, Recreation & Dance, 81*(9), 47–53.

Stewart, D.A. (1991). Deaf sport: The impact of sports within the deaf community. Washington, DC: Gallaudet University Press.

Stiehl, G.S., Morris, D., & Sinclair, C. (2008). *Teaching physical activity: Change, challenge and choice.* Champaign, IL: Human Kinetics.

Stins, J.F., Ledebt, A., Emck, C., van Dokkum, E.H., & Beek, P.J. (2009). Patterns of postural sway in high anxious children. *Brain and Behavioral Functions, 5*(1), 42.

Strawbridge, W.J., Deleger, S., Roberts, R.E., & Kaplan, G.A. (2002). Physical activity reduces the risk of subsequent depression for older adults. *American Journal of Epidemiology, 156*(4), 328–334. doi:10.1093/aje/kwfo47

Sullivan, K.A., Lantz, P.J., & Zirkel, P.A. (2000). Leveling the playing field or leveling the players? Section 504, the Americans with Disabilities Act, and Interscholastic sports. *Journal of Special Education, 33,* 258–267.

Suomi, J., Collier, D., & Brown, L. (2003). Factors affecting the social experiences of students in elementary physical education classes. *Journal of Teaching in Physical Education, 22*(2),186–202.

Sutherland, S. (1999). Special Olympics' unified sports, partners club, and sports partnership models. In P. Jansma (Ed.), *The psychomotor domain and serious disabilities* (5th ed., pp. 333–340). Lanham, MD: University Press of America.

Sutherland, S.L., & Hodge, S.R. (2001). Inclusion of a diverse population. *Teaching Elementary Physical Education, 12*(2), 18–21.

Swanwick, R., & Marschark, M. (2010). Enhancing education for deaf children: Research into practice and back again. *Deafness and Education International, 12*(4), 217–235.

Sylvester, C., Voelkl, J.E., & Ellis, G.D. (2001). *Therapeutic recreation programming: Theory and practice.* State College, PA: Venture.

Tannehill, D., MacPhail. A., Halbert, G., & Murphy, F. (2013). *Research and practice in physical education.* London, United Kingdom: Routledge.

Taylor, S.J. (1988). Caught in the continuum: A critical analysis of the principle of the least restrictive environment. *Journal of the Association for Persons With Severe Handicaps, 13,* 41–53.

Teichner, G., & Golden, C.J. (2000). The relationship of neuropsychological impairment to conduct disorder in adolescence: A conceptual review. *Aggression and Violent Behavior, 5,* 509–528.

Temple, V.A., & Lynnes, M.D. (2008). Peer tutoring for inclusion. *ACHPER Australia Healthy Lifestyles Journal, 55*(2–3), 11–21.

Teulier, C., Smith, B.A., Kubo, M., Chia-Lin, C., Moerchen, V., Murazko, K., & Ulrich, B.D. (2009). Stepping responses of infants with myelomeningocele when supported on a motorized treadmill. *Physical Therapy, 89,* 60–72.

Theodorakis, Y., Bagiatis, K., & Goudas, M. (1995). Attitudes toward teaching individuals with disabilities: Application of the planned behavior theory. *Adapted Physical Activity Quarterly, 12,* 151–160.

Thomas, C.A., & Wehman, P. (2010). *Getting the most out of IEPs: An educator's guide to the student-directed approach.* Baltimore, MD: Paul H. Brookes Publishing Co.

Thompson, L.P., Boufard, M., Watkinson, E.J., & Causgrove Dunn, J.L. (1994). Teaching children with movement difficulties: Highlighting the need for individualized instruction in regular physical education. *Physical Education Review, 17*(2), 152–159.

Tinning, R., & Glasby, T. (2002). Pedagogical work and the "cult of the body": Considering the role of HPE in the context of the "new public health." *Sport, Education and Society, 7*(2), 109–119.

Tomlinson, C.A. (2001). *How to differentiate instruction in mixed-ability classrooms* (2nd ed.). Alexandria, VA: Association for Supervision and Curriculum Development.

Townsend, M., & Hassall, J. (2007). Mainstream students' attitudes to possible inclusion in unified sports with students who have an intellectual disability. *Journal of Applied Research in Intellectual Disabilities, 20*(3), 265–273.

Tremblay, M.S., Inman, J.W., & Willms. J.D. (2000). The relationship between physical activity, self-esteem, and academic achievement in 12-year-old children. *Pediatric Exercise Science, 12,* 312–324.

Tripp, A., & Rizzo, T. (2006). Disability labels affect physical educators. *Adapted Physical Activity Quarterly, 23*(3), 310–326.

Turnbull, H.R. (1990). *Free appropriate public education: The law and children with disabilities* (3rd ed.). Denver, CO: Love.

United States Census Bureau. (2014). *Facts for Features: Anniversary of Americans with Disabilities Act: July 26.* Retrieved from http://www.census.gov/prod/2012pubs/p70–131.pdf

U.S. Department of Education. (2006). *Building the legacy of IDEA 2004: Topic—discipline.* Retrieved from http://idea.ed.gov/explore/view/p/%2Croot%2Cdynamic%2CTopicalBrief%2C6%2C

U.S. Department of Education. (2011). *Creating equal opportunities for children and youth with disabilities to participate in physical education and extracurricular athletics.* Washington, DC: Author. Retrieved from http://www2.ed.gov/policy/speced/guid/idea/equal-pe.pdf

U.S. Department of Education. (2013). *Digest of education statistics 2012.* Washington, DC: Author. Retrieved from http://nces.ed.gov/pubs2014/2014015.pdf

U.S. Department of Education. (2014a). *Building the legacy: IDEA 2004.* Retrieved from http://idea.ed.gov/explore/view/p/,root,regs,300,A,300%252E8

U.S. Department of Education. (2014b). *35th annual report to congress on the implementation of the Individuals with Disabilities Education Act, 2013.* Washington, DC: Author. Retrieved from http://www2.ed.gov/about/reports/annual/osep/2013/parts-b-c/35th-idea-arc.pdf

U.S. Department of Health and Human Services. (2008). *2008 physical activity guidelines for Americans.* Washington, DC: Government Printing Office. Retrieved from http://www.health.gov/paguidelines

U.S. Department of Health and Human Services. (2010a). *Healthy people 2020: Improving the health of Americans.* Washington, DC: Government Printing Office.

U.S. Department of Health and Human Services. (2010b). *Helping the student with diabetes succeed: A guide for school personnel.* Retrieved from http://ndep.nih.gov/media/NDEP61_SchoolGuide_4c_508.pdf

U.S. Department of Justice. (2001). *Americans with Disabilities Act: Questions and answers.* Retrieved from http://www.ada.gov/qandaeng.htm

U.S. Department of Justice. (2009). *A guide to disability rights laws.* Retrieved from http://www.ada.gov/cguide.htm

U.S. Department of Justice. (2010). *2010 ADA standards for accessible design.* Retrieved from http://www.ada.gov/regs2010/2010ADAStandards/2010ADAStandards.pdf

U.S. Department of Justice. (2012). *ADA requirements: Accessible pools: Means of entry and exit.* Retrieved from http://www.ada.gov/pools_2010.htm

U.S. Government Accountability Office. (2010, June). *Students with disabilities: More information and guidance could improve opportunities in physical education and athletics* (GAO-10–519). Washington, DC. Author. Retrieved from http://www.gao.gov/products/GAO-10-519

U.S. Paralympics. (2014). *Paralympic sport clubs.* Retrieved from http://www.teamusa.org/US-Paralympics/Community/Paralympic-Sport-Clubs

U.S. Youth Soccer. (2014). *TOPSoccer.* Retrieved from http://www.usyouthsoccer.org/programs/topsoccer

Ulrich, D. (2000). *Test of gross motor development* (2nd ed.). Austin, TX: Pro-Ed.

Ulrich, D. (in press). *Test of gross motor development* (3rd ed.). Austin, TX: Pro-Ed.

Ulrich, D.A. (1985, August). *Current assessment practices in adapted physical education: Implications for future training and research activities.* Paper presented at the annual meeting of the National Consortium on Physical Education and Recreation for the Handicapped, New Carrollton, MD.

United Nations High Commissioner for Refugees. (2013). *Statistics and operational data.* Retrieved from http://www.unhcr.org/pages/49c3646c4d6.html

United States Association of Blind Athletes. (n.d.-a). *About us.* Retrieved from http://usaba.org/index.php/about-us

United States Association of Blind Athletes. (n.d.-b). *Mission and vision.* Retrieved from http://usaba.org/index.php/about-us/mission-and-vision

United States Association of Blind Athletes. (n.d.-c). *Visual classifications.* Retrieved from http://usaba.org/index.php/membership/visual-classifications

Valentini, N.C., & Rudisill, M.E. (2004). An inclusive mastery climate intervention and the motor skill development of children with and without disabilities. *Adapted Physical Activity Quarterly, 21,* 330–347.

Vance, A., Arduca, Y., Sanders, M., Karamitsios, M., Hall, N., & Hetrick, S. (2006). Attention deficit hyperactivity disorder, combined type, dysthymic disorder and anxiety disorders: Differential patterns of neurodevelopmental deficits. *Psychiatric Research, 143,* 213–222.

Vandercook, T., & York, J. (1990). A team approach to program development and support. In W. Stainback & S. Stainback (Eds.), *Support networks for inclusive schooling: Interdependent integrated education* (pp. 95–122). Baltimore, MD: Paul H. Brookes Publishing Co.

van de Vliet, P., Rintala, R., Fröjd, K., Verellen, J., van Houtte, S., Daly, D.J., & Vanlandewijck, Y.C. (2006). Physical fitness profile of elite athletes with intellectual disability. *Scandinavian Journal of Medicine & Science in Sports, 16,* 417–426.

van Rossum, J.H.A., & Vermeer, A. (1990). Perceived competence: A validation study in the field of motoric remedial teaching. *International Journal of Disability, Development and Education, 37*(1), 71–81.

Verderber, J.M.S., Rizzo, T.L., & Sherrill, C. (2003). Assessing student intention to participate in inclusive physical education. *Adapted Physical Activity Quarterly, 20,* 26–45.

Vernon, M.K., Wiklund, I., Bell, J.A., Dale, P., & Chapman, K.R. (2012). What do we know about asthma triggers?: A review of the literature. *Journal of Asthma, 49*(10), 991–998.

Verret, C., Gardiner, P., & Beliveau, L. (2010). Fitness level and gross motor performance of children with attention-deficit hyperactivity disorder. *Adapted Physical Activity Quarterly, 27,* 337–351.

Vickerman, P., & Coates, J.K. (2009). Trainee and recently qualified physical education teachers' perspectives on including children with special educational needs. *Physical Education and Sport Pedagogy, 14*(2), 137–153.

Vignes, C., Godeau, E., Sentenac, M., Coley, N., Navarro, F., Grandjean, H., & Arnaud, C. (2009). Determinants of students' attitudes towards peers with disabilities. *Developmental Medicine and Child Neurology, 51*(6), 473–479.

Virginia Department of Education. (2005). *English as a second language.* Retrieved from http://www.doe.virginia.gov/instruction/esl

Viscidi, E.W., Triche, E.W., Pescosolido, M.F., McLean, R.L., Joseph, R.M., Spence, S.J., & Morrow, E.M. (2013). Clinical characteristics of children with autism spectrum disorder and co-occurring epilepsy. *PLOS ONE, 8*(7), 1–11.

Voeltz, L.M. (1980). Children's attitudes toward handicapped peers. *American Journal of Mental Deficiency, 84*(5), 455–464.

Voeltz, L.M. (1982). Effects of structured interactions with severely handicapped peers on children's attitudes. *American Journal of Mental Deficiency, 86,* 380–390.

Voeltz, L.M., & Apffel, J.A. (1981). Leisure activities curricular components for severely handicapped youth. Why and how? *Viewpoints in Teaching and Learning, 57,* 82–93.

Vogler, E.W., & French, R. (1983). The effects of a group contingency strategy on behaviorally disordered students in physical education. *Research Quarterly for Exercise and Sport, 54,* 273–277.

Wagner, G., Wetherald, L., & Wilson, B. (1994). A model for making county and municipal recreation department programs inclusive. In M.S. Moon (Ed.), *Making school and community recreation fun for everyone: Places and ways to integrate* (pp. 181–192). Baltimore, MD: Paul H. Brookes Publishing Co.

Wagner, M., Haibach, P.S., & Lieberman, L.J. (2013). Gross motor skill performance in children with and without visual impairments: Research to practice. *Research in Developmental Disabilities, 34,* 3246–3252.

Walker, H.M., & Bullis, M. (1991). Behavior disorders and the social context of regular class integration: A conceptual dilemma? In J. Lloyd, N. Singh, & A. Repp (Eds.), *The regular education initiative: Alternative perspectives on concepts, issues and models* (pp. 75–94). Champaign-Urbana, IL: Sycamore.

Walker, J.E., Shea, T.M., & Bauer, A.M. (2003). *Behavior management* (8th ed.). New York, NY: Prentice Hall.

Wall, T.A.E. (2003). The developmental skill-learning gap hypothesis: Implications for children with movement difficulties. *Adapted Physical Activity Quarterly, 21,* 197–218.

Wang, J.C., Liu, W.C., Chatzisarantis, N.L., & Lim, C.B. (2010). Influence of perceived motivational climate on achievement goals in physical education: A structural equation mixture modeling analysis. *Journal of Sport and Exercise Psychology, 32*(3), 324–338.

Wang, M.C., & Baker, E.T. (1986). Mainstreamed programs: Design features and effects. *Journal of Special Education, 19,* 503–521.

Wang, M.C., Reynolds, M.C., & Walberg, H.J. (1987). Rethinking special education. *Journal of Learning Disabilities, 20,* 290–293.

Wang, W.Y., & Ju, Y.H. (2002). Promoting balance and jumping skills in children with Down syndrome. *Perceptual and Motor Skills, 94*(2), 443–448.

Ward, E., DeSantis, C., Robbins, A., Kohler, B., & Jemal, A. (2014). Childhood and adolescent cancer statistics, 2014. *CA: A Cancer Journal for Clinicians, 64*(2), 83–103.

Ward, P., & Ayvazo, S. (2006). Class-wide peer tutoring in physical education: Assessing its effects with kindergarteners with autism. *Adapted Physical Activity Quarterly, 23,* 232–244.

Waterhouse, L. (2013). *Rethinking autism: Variation and complexity.* London, United Kingdom: Academic Press.

Watson, D., & Clocksin, B. (2013). *Using physical activity to teach personal and social responsibility through physical activity.* Champaign, IL: Human Kinetics.

Webb, D., & Hodge, S.R. (2003). Factors that influence career choice of African American students to enter the adapted physical education profession. *Physical Educator, 60*(3), 134–149.

Weber, J.D. (2000). *Children with Fragile X syndrome: A parents' guide.* Bethesda, MD: Woodbine House.

Webster, G.E. (1987). Influence of peer tutors upon academic learning time-physical education of mentally handicapped students. *Journal of Teaching in Physical Education, 6,* 393–403.

Wehman, P., & Schleien, S. (1981). *Leisure programs for handicapped persons: Adaptations, techniques, and curriculum.* Austin, TX: PRO-ED.

Wehmeyer, M. L., Abery, B.H., Mithaug, D.E., & Stancliffe, R.J. (2003). *Theory in self-determination: Foundations for educational practice.* Springfield, IL: Charles C. Thomas.

Wehrly, B. (1995). *Pathways to multicultural counseling competence: A developmental journey.* Pacific Grove, CA: Brooks/Cole Thomson Learning.

Wein, H., & Contie, V. (2013). *NIH news in health: Childhood cancer—Coping with the diagnosis.* Retrieved from http://newsinhealth.nih.gov/issue/Jun2013/Feature1

Weinberg, R.S., & Gould, D. (2011). *Foundations of sport exercise psychology* (5th ed.). Champaign, IL: Human Kinetics.

Wei, X., Yu, J.W., & Shaver, D. (2014). Longitudinal effects of ADHD in children with learning disabilities or emotional disturbances. *Exceptional Children, 80*(2), 205–219.

Weleber, R.G., Francis, P.J., Trzupek, K.M., & Beattie, C. (2013). *Gene reviews: Leber congenital amaurosis.* Retrieved from http://www.ncbi.nlm.nih.gov/books/NBK1298

Wessel, J.A., & Kelly, L. (1986). *Achievement-based curriculum development in physical education.* Philadelphia, PA: Lea & Febiger.

Wessinger, N.P. (1994). Celebrating our differences: Fostering ethnicity in homogeneous settings. *Journal of Physical Education, Recreation and Dance, 65*(9), 62–68.

West, J.F., Idol, L., & Cannon, G.S. (1989). *Collaboration in the schools: An in-service and pre-service curriculum for teachers, support staff, and administrators.* Austin, TX: PRO-ED.

Wheelchair and Ambulatory Sports, USA. (n.d.). *About us.* Retrieved from http://www.wasusa.org/aboutus.htm

Whyatt, C., & Craig, C.M. (2012). Motor skills in children aged 7–10 years, diagnosed with autism spectrum disorder. *Journal of Autism and Developmental Disorders, 42,* 1799–1809.

Wiegersma, P.H., & Van der Velde, A. (1983). Motor development of deaf children. *Journal of Child Psychology and Psychiatry, 24,* 103–111.

Wilhite, B., Mushett, C.A., Goldenberg, L., & Trader, B.R. (1997). Promoting inclusive sport and leisure participation: Evaluation of the paralympic day in the schools model. *Adapted Physical Activity Quarterly, 14*(2), 131–146.

Will, M.C. (1986). Educating children with learning problems: A shared responsibility. *Exceptional Children, 52,* 411–416.

Willcutt, E.G., Nigg, J.T., Pennington, B.F., Solanto, M.V., Rohde, L.A., Tannock, R.,. . . Lahey, B.B. (2012).

Meat-analysis of DSM-IV attention-deficit/hyperactivity disorder dimensions and subtypes. *Journal of Abnormal Psychology, 121*(4),991–1010.

Williams, L.J., Mai, C.T., Edmonds, L.D., Shaw, G.M., Kirby, R.S., Hobbs, A.,. . . Levitt, M. (2002). Prevalence of spina bifida and anencephaly during the transition to mandatory folic acid fortification in the United States. *Teratology, 66,* 33–39.

Williams, N.F. (1992). The physical education hall of shame. *Journal of Physical Education, Recreation & Dance, 63*(6), 57–60.

Williams, N.F. (1994). The physical education hall of shame: Part II. *Journal of Physical Education, Recreation & Dance, 65*(2), 17–20.

Williams, N.F. (1996). The physical education hall of shame: Part III: Inappropriate teaching practices. *Journal of Physical Education, Recreation & Dance, 67*(8), 45–48.

Willoughby, C., Polatajko, H., & Wilson, B.N. (1995). The self-esteem and motor performance of young learning disabled children. *Physical and Occupational Therapy in Pediatrics, 14*(3–4), 1–30.

Winnick, J.P. (2011). *Adapted physical education and sport* (5th ed.). Champaign, IL: Human Kinetics.

Winnick, J.P., & Short, F.X. (1986). Physical fitness of adolescents with auditory impairments. *Adapted Physical Activity Quarterly, 3,* 58–66.

Winnick, J.P., & Short, F.X. (1999). *The Brockport Physical Fitness Test.* Champaign, IL: Human Kinetics.

Wiskochil, B., Lieberman, L.J., Houston-Wilson, C., & Petersen, S. (2007). The effects of trained peer tutors on academic learning time-physical education on four children who are visually impaired or blind. *Journal of Visual Impairment & Blindness, 101,* 339–350.

Wolfensberger, W. (1972). *The principle of normalization in human services.* Toronto, Canada: National Institute on Mental Retardation.

Wolff, P.H., Michel, G.F., Ovrut, M., & Drake, C. (1990). Rate and timing precision of motor coordination in developmental dyslexia. *Developmental Psychology, 26*(3), 349–359.

Woodard, R.J., & Surburg, P. (1997). Fundamental gross motor skill performance by girls and boys with learning disabilities. *Perceptual and Motor Skills, 84*(3), 867–870. doi:10.2455/pms.1997.84.3.867

Woodard, R.J., & Surburg, P.R. (1999). Midline crossing behavior in children with learning disabilities. *Adapted Physical Activity Quarterly, 16,* 155–166.

Woodard, R.J., & Surburg, P. (2001). The performance of fundamental movement skills by elementary school children with learning disabilities. *Physical Educator, 58*(4), 198–205.

Woodruff, G., & McGonigel, M.J. (1988). Early intervention team approaches: The transdisciplinary model. In J.B. Jordan, J.J. Gallagher, P.L. Hutinger, & M.B. Karnes (Eds.), *Early childhood special education: Birth to three* (pp. 163–182). Reston, VA: Council for Exceptional Children.

World Heart Federation. (2014). *Types of heart disease observed in children and youth.* Retrieved from http://www.world-heart-federation.org/press/fact-sheets/cvd-in-children-and-youth

Wright, P.W.D., & Wright, P.D. (2004). *Children with disabilities under No Child Left Behind: Myths and realities.* Retrieved from http://www.wrightslaw.com/nclb/info/myths.realities.napas.htm

Wright, P.W.D., Wright, P.D., & Heath, S.W. (2004). *Wrightslaw: No child left behind.* Hartfield, VA: Harbor House Law Press.

Yan, J.H., & Thomas, J.R. (2002). Arm movement control: Differences between children with and without attention deficit/hyperactivity disorder. *Research Quarterly for Exercise and Sport, 73*(1), 10–18.

Yap, R.L., & Van der Leij, A. (1994). Testing the automatization deficit hypothesis of dyslexia via a dual-task paradigm. *Journal of Learning Disabilities, 27*(10), 660–665. doi:10.1177/00221949402701006

York, J., Vandercook, T., MacDonald, C., Heise-Neff, C., & Caughey, E. (1992). Feedback about integrating middle-school education students with severe disabilities in general education classes. *Exceptional Children, 58*(3), 244–258.

Young, S. (2014). *I'm not your inspiration, thank you very much: Transcript.* Retrieved from http://www.ted.com/talks/stella_young_i_m_not_your_inspiration_thank_you_very_much/transcript#t-91580

Zamora-Duran, G., & Artiles, A.J. (1997). Disproportionate representation: Current issues and future directions. In A.J. Artiles & G. Zamora-Duran (Eds.), *Reducing disproportionate representation of culturally diverse students in special and gifted education* (pp. 1–6). Reston, VA: Council for Exceptional Children.

Zhang, D., Katsiyannis, A., Ju, S., & Roberts, E. (2014). Minority representation in special education: 5-year trends. *Journal of Child & Family Studies, 23*(1), 118–127.

Zipursky, A., Poon, A., & Doyle, J. (1992). Leukemia in Down syndrome: A review. *Pediatric Hematology-Oncology, 9*(2), 139–149.

Zygmunt, L., Larson, M.S., & Tilson, G.P., Jr. (1994). Disability awareness training and social networking. In M.S. Moon (Ed.), *Making school and community recreation fun for everyone: Places and ways to integrate* (pp. 209–226). Baltimore, MD: Paul H. Brookes Publishing Co.

Index

References to tables, figures and notes are indicated with a *t*, *f*, and *n*, respectively.